WRITING
REFLECTIVE
ACTION

A READER

Duncan Carter
Portland State University

Sherrie Gradin
Ohio University

Longman

New York   San Francisco   Boston
London   Toronto   Sydney   Tokyo   Singapore   Madrid
Mexico City   Munich   Paris   Cape Town   Hong Kong   Montreal

brothers' memory

Wesley Charles Gradin
1953–1998

Editor-in-Chief: Joseph Terry
Acquisitions Editor: Lynn M. Huddon
Marketing Manager: Carlise Paulson
Supplements Editor: Donna Campion
Media Supplements Editor: Nancy Garcia
Production Manager: Denise Phillip
Project Coordination, Text Design, and Electronic Page Makeup:
      WestWords, Inc.
Cover Designer/Manager: John Callahan
Cover Photo: "Windows With Birds" by Valerie Spain, courtesy of The
      Stock Illustration Source, Inc.
Manufacturing Buyer: Al Dorsey
Printer and Binder: The Maple-Vail Book Manufacturing Group
Cover Printer: Lehigh Press

For permission to use copyrighted material, grateful acknowledgment is made to the copyright holders on pp. 554–555 , which are hereby made part of this copyright page.

Library of Congress Cataloging-in-Publication Data

Carter, Duncan A.
    Writing as reflective action : a reader/Duncan Carter, Sherrie Gradin.
      p.   cm.
    Includes index.
    ISBN 0-321-02673-X
    1. College readers. 2. Report writing—Problems, exercises, etc. 3. English language—Rhetoric—Problems, excercises, etc.   I. Gradin, Sherrie L.
II. Title.

PE1417.C318 2000
808'.0427—dc21

                                                                00-053476

Please visit our website at http://www.ablongman.com/carter

ISBN 0–321-02673-X
1 2 3 4 5 6 7 8 9 10—MA—03 02 01 00

Contents

2 Constructing Identity: The Self as Social Artifact / 149

3 Engaging Culture: The Reflexive Self / 261

4 Writing in the Community: Reflection, Reflexivity, and Action / 347

Meta-Sequences / 544

Preface to Teachers

The conceptual framework for *Writing as Reflective Action* took shape when we were both working together at Portland State University. Several aspects of our work at PSU, the kind of institution PSU has been in the process of becoming, and our hopes and dreams for our students formed a fulcrum for creating this text. Students at Portland State are often uneasy guests at the university, which is virtually an open admissions institution. They are often first-generation college students and many score low on SAT or ACT admissions tests. We did not want to create a text that assumed these students were not able to rise to the challenges of academic work. We wanted to give both the franchised and disenfranchised a curriculum that might support their entry into critical writing, critical reading, and critical thinking. Since many of our students are unsure how their own ideas, thoughts, concerns, and private voices might lead to a public voice and public action we wanted to create a text that placed the composition and rhetoric classroom in a milieu of action: the act of learning, rhetorical action, and civic action.

Our devotion to the community-based aspects of this book also has its roots in our work at Portland State. PSU is an urban institution trying hard to dissolve the barriers between itself and the community in which it resides. As many institutions now recognize, PSU has seen a need to work harder to make students' academic learning experiences more relevant to life experiences beyond the classroom. At the same time, the university has come to acknowledge its responsibility to the community and has therefore aggressively sought ways to engage with that comunity. The community has needs; the students need to be in the community—there's a certain symmetry here, a kind of parallelism we have worked hard to understand and to enact. More than anything else, *Writing as Reflective Action* grows out of this work.

Reflection and reflexivity are at the heart of this composition text. Thus, there is a definite shape and theoretical drive behind *Writing As Reflective Action*. However, we intend for this shape and drive to be flexible and supportive, not restrictive or confining. We have both taught writing and mentored others who teach writing long enough to realize that most of us reshape the texts we use to suit our own styles and goals, no matter how much we like the texts we have chosen.

What we have set out to do in *Writing As Reflective Action* is create a composition text that features integrated instruction in reading and writing, presents readings in cultural, intellectual, and social issues, and invites writers-in-training to engage in extended reflection and reflexivity, collaborative learning, and community-based learning and writing. Our text differs from others in that we combine the best of composition practice and theory with the possibility for community-based writing courses in ways not previously done. This seems the most promising way for students to become critical readers and thinkers as well as engaged writers of private, academic, and public discourse. You could say that our approach blends expressivist and social-epistemic rhetorics into a focus on academic discourse. We encourage students to explore the tension between private and public discourses so that they come to see in their own writing how self and role might be interdependent, interpenetrating, yin and yang. While we want students to develop facility with academic discourse, we do not expect them to do so as though academic discourse were severed from their lives. We are, therefore, especially interested in helping students to explore the intersection of the personal and the public, the private and the social, in their thinking, their writing, and their lives. We see the split between writing for, by, and about the self and analytical, synthetic, academic discourses as a false dichotomy. Yes, the self is a social construct; at the same time, even academic discourse is personal, expressive. Or at least it should be.

We have, then, constructed a text that is built on the students' sense of who they are and what they find important in the readings and topics we ask them to tackle. Crucial to the success of this text is a commitment to the informal writing found at the end of each reading and in the use of dialectical notebooks, reader-response journals, dialogue journals, and/or triple-entry incident journals. Such work is important for many reasons, but in part we hope the informal writing will trigger both reflection and reflexivity. We hope, too, that you make use of collaboration and group work as a way to create possibilities for reflexive moments for your students. The readings we ask you and your students to work with are interesting and rich, but they are thick and difficult as well. While we have a strong apparatus with questions and activities to help guide students through this reading, they will need equally strong direction from you as a model of an active and engaged reader. The formal writing assignments are meant to spark writing for public consumption. Some are more tied to personal views and experiences, some to more external, and some are clearly a blend. All, however, are intended to engage students in careful analytical, reflective, and reflexive writing that will eventually "go public."

We hope to achieve this in our writing prompts by offering both direction and a sort of general openness that gives students room to construct their own thoughts or theses. Some prompts, then, are more specific and others more general. We also assume that the more detailed work asked for at the end of readings (reflecting on reading, rhetorical strategies, and informal writing) will provide students with the material and the momentum to respond in a focused way to the fairly open questions of our end-of-chapter sequences and make them their own. We also fully expect that some teachers will want to "tweak" those prompts to send their students in particular directions. We have attempted to fashion writing prompts that might be used as is or with teacher modification.

We wanted to draw special attention to the sequencing set up in this text because it is at the heart of using *Writing As Reflective Action* successfully. We have constructed *Writing As Reflective Action* so that the assignments are sequenced in a variety of ways. The book overall moves students through a sequence of positions from reflection to social construction, to reflexivity, to writing in the community, and ending with end-of-text formal writing prompts ("meta sequences") relying on what students learned in that movement through these positions. Each chapter of the text also has a sequence. Students start with prewriting, engage in informal writing and large and small group discussions, keep some form of journal or dialectical notebook, and end with end-of-chapter sequences where students draw on all of this previous reading, writing, and talking to write a formal essay. Teachers need to remind students to return to all of this previous work—the informal writing, journals, discussion notes, and prewriting—for ideas for the formal essays. Another mini sequencing takes place within both the end-of-chapter and end-of-text sequences when we ask you to work in small discussion groups to generate ideas and to think critically in ways that lead toward the formal essay prompts. Hopefully, these many layers of sequencing will help students produce strong, critical, formal essays.

Writing As Reflective Action starts with a general introduction to students. We urge you to have them read this introduction carefully and to spend some time discussing it with them. Doing so will help unmask the curricular goals and objectives of the book; it will help you, and your students, understand what we mean by reflection, reflexivity, and action as they pertain to our vision of the writing course.

The remainder of *Writing As Reflective Action* is in four major chapters. Each builds upon previous chapters while also standing as a coherent unit on its own. (We leave ample room, of course, for individual instructors to reorder readings, assignments, and even chapters to fit their own needs). Each chapter begins with a set of prompts for reflective prewriting followed by a short chapter introduction to help contextualize the readings and assignments. Each reading is then introduced briefly in a manner intended to provide a context for that particular piece as well as to give students some sense of direction as they read. At the end of each reading students are asked to engage in informal writing, which includes examining content, rhetorical strategies, and issues raised by the reading; they are encouraged to engage in collaborative work and to respond to prompts for further thinking about the reading just completed. Each section ends with assignment sequences that invite collaborative discussion and require students to engage in a variety of formal writing tasks. At the end of *Writing As Reflective Action* we have constructed a number of "meta" assignment sequences that draw on readings from all parts of the book, suggesting various paths through the text as a whole. The shape of the text, then, is as follows:

CHAPTER 1 EXPLORING THE SELF: REFLECTION

This section introduces students to reflective practice and some of the tools that support it (e.g. dialogic and dialectic notebooks, etc.—modeled and discussed in some detail in the Introduction). Reading and writing assignments center on examining who we are, how we look at ourselves and our world, and why we hold the assumptions we do.

CHAPTER 2 CONSTRUCTING IDENTITY: THE SELF AS SOCIAL ARTIFACT

This section asks students to begin analyzing the ways in which their understandings of themselves are socially constructed, as well as the part they play in constructing their own "individualities."

CHAPTER 3 ENGAGING CULTURE: THE REFLEXIVE SELF

This section asks students to evaluate issues within our culture such as poverty, gender, race, education, individualism in a mass society, and the like, through the writings and methodologies of academics from a variety of fields. By this point students have reflected on their own identity and the social elements that are a part of it. This section encourages them to engage in reflexivity, to "step into" the identity of another in order to look back at their own identity and culture with new eyes. We ask students to try on the roles, the angles of vision, and the language(s) of academics from a variety of fields as ways of exploring and evaluating issues within our culture. While most selections show academic discourse at work, some—such as Tompkins'—also examine the tension academics often experience between (personal) self and (academic) role.

CHAPTER 4 WRITING IN THE COMMUNITY: REFLECTION, REFLEXIVITY, AND ACTION

Having learned the principal elements of self-awareness—the ability to reflect upon their own identity and its social dimensions, and the ability to use the unique perspectives of others as instruments of reflexivity—students are ready to "go public." That is, they are at this point positioned to enter the community in the most productive way and to profit from the experience. This section introduces students more fully to community-based learning possibilities and to the kinds of reflection and reflexivity especially pertinent to community work. It is the most challenging part of the text for students and teachers alike. In this section we offer two different kinds of possible community experiences as examples: the gathering and preserving of oral histories and work with AIDS projects. Each of these examples includes readings selected to stimulate reflective and analytical thinking around the communities with which students might involve themselves. These are examples that might be perfect for community-based work in your community. Chances are, however, that your community will have different local needs and contexts. Yet even if your projects differ in major ways, this section of the book remains valuable, exemplifying the kinds of reading, writing, reflection, and reflexivity that can (and should) be built into any community-based learning or community-service writing course. Should you find it necessary to design your own project, note that we provide a list of other possible kinds of projects together with suggestions about how to structure them.

As we see it, there are at least three ways you might want to work with Chapter 4: Writing in The Community: Reflection, Reflexivity, and Action. The readings and writing assignments in this chapter might be used in the traditional way, quite apart from the strains and logistical difficulties of community-based learning. Or this section might be treated as a part of a larger sequence moving from private to public discourses, as the entirety of *Writing As Reflective Action* lays it out. Or this section, with its emphasis on community-based learning, might become the primary focus for an entire course.

Before deciding how you wish to use this chapter, you must determine whether you have the time or inclination to integrate a community component into the course. Community-based writing and service learning add new dimensions and possibilities to the composition class. Engaging in such work, however, is not always easy or successful. Those of you who don't have a service learning director must make the connections with possible community partners on your own. While establishing such connections is usually rewarding, it is also time consuming. Sometimes the needs of a community partner do not square with the academic and disciplinary goals of the course. If these differences cannot be ironed out, the project should not go forward. In fact, service learning and community-based writing projects are sufficiently complex that instructors may want to focus an entire term (or two if they have a composition sequence) on Chapter 4 of *Writing As Reflective Action.*

In any case, this section is not something to spring on students in the last couple of weeks of the course. If, however, you use most or all of the rest of *Writing As Reflective Action,* much of the groundwork, both in terms of students having had contact with community members outside the classroom and in terms of the reflection, reflexivity, and analytical and critical thinking that students have participated in, will have been set for the section on community work. What we have done in *Writing As Reflective Action,* then, is to provide an overarching structure. We do make suggestions for ways in which you could move through the entire book: from constructing reflective and reflexive selves who can grapple with understanding personal ideologies and locate themselves in relation to experience and culture, to exploring selves as they construct and are constructed in culture and experience, to studying academic inquiry and discourses as they investigate issues related to understanding the self in society, and finally to selves in action in our communities. However, these structural features of the text allow individual instructors to put together their courses using either parts of the text, or the whole. Our experiences teaching from this text have been rich, challenging, and almost always successful in a variety of ways. We hope the same for you.

In addition, an Instructor's Manual and companion Web site are available as resources for teachers who adopt *Writing as Reflective Action.*

ACKNOWLEDGMENTS

In a project such as this there are always a great many people who deserve recognition and thanks. If we should unintentionally forget any of you who deserve such recognition here, please know that your support was welcomed and no doubt very helpful.

It is customary to thank the editors one works with, and in this case it is a pleasure and not just mere gesture to do so. Our first thank you, then, goes to Anne Smith, formerly rhetoric and composition editor at Longman Publishers, who got us off to a good start. Likewise, Lynn Huddon, English Acquisitions Editor, and the editor who took over the project, while managing to remain upbeat, decent, and humane, has offered a sharp and critical eye, has poked and prodded us along, and has offered all the right feedback at just the right times. Karen Helfrich and Chuck Schuster were both very helpful during the early stages of our project. Rebecca Gilpin has helped keep us organized. Nancy Garcia has provided momentum behind the companion website, and Project Manager Jennifer Maughan graciously saw us through the copy-editing, proofreading, and the like. A heartfelt thank you to the entire crew at Longman Publishers.

Our friends and colleagues in the writing program at Portland State University have been invaluable. Trista Cornelius and Tiffany Werth researched and wrote headnotes; Jacqueline Arante, our most practiced teacher of community-based writing at PSU, provided us information, ideas, and student examples. Carol Burnell, Susan Reese, and Greg Jacob offered advice and revisions on early drafts of the text.

Trista Cornelius, Barbara Gray, Tony White, Scott Kozuma, Heather Gaddy, Melissa Storms, Kelly Kinney, and Micah Robertson tested *Writing As Reflective Action* in both the freshman composition course and the advanced composition course. We are beholden to them for their ideas on what should change and what should stay the same, as well as for their reports on student reactions to the text. Some of them have provided us with journal examples from students in their courses grappling with the reading and ideas we set before them. We would like to thank our former graduate student Rich Rice, now at Ball State, for creating the web page to accompany this book. And a special thanks to the students who were so brave as to allow us to use their journal entries.

Finally, we must thank the many reviewers who read and commented on *Writing As Reflective Action* along the way. Moira Baker, Radford University; Lisa Bernhagen, Western Washington University; Brenda Bruggemann, Ohio State University; Matthew Cariello, Indiana University; Alice Gillam, University of Wisconsin-Milwaukee; Bernice Hausman, Virginia Polytechnic Institute & State University; T.R. Johnson, University of New Orleans; Anne Righton Malone, SUNY Potsdam; Roark Mulligan, Christopher Newport University; Libby Rankin, University of North Dakota; Robert Newman, SUNY at Buffalo; and Connie Rothwell, UNC Charlotte.

Duncan Carter
Sherrie Gradin

Introduction

Students coming to college for the first time often feel like they have just stepped into a new and different culture. They have. Kenneth Burke, noted rhetorician, suggests what it is like to find yourself in a new culture:

> Imagine that you enter a parlor. You come late. When you arrive, others have long preceded you, and they are engaged in a heated discussion, a discussion too heated for them to pause and tell you exactly what it is about. In fact, the discussion had already begun long before any of them got there, so that no one present is qualified to retrace for you all the steps that had gone before. You listen for a while, until you decide that you have caught the tenor of the argument; then you put in your oar. Someone answers; you answer him; another comes to your defense; another aligns himself against you, to either the embarrassment or gratification of your opponent, depending upon the quality of your ally's assistance. However, the discussion is interminable. The hour grows late, you must depart. And you depart, with the discussion still vigorously in progress.

(The Philosophy of Literary Form: Studies in Symbolic Action, 110–111)

Burke captures the feelings of the outsider, the person on the fringe of the conversation who doesn't (yet) understand what's going on, or how to participate. But notice that he also captures something of the process by which the outsider becomes insider, becomes part of the conversation without losing his or her own identity in the bargain.

1

This is precisely the process that interests us. We believe that to flourish in the academy, you must first learn to read, write, and think like a member of the academic community. So *Writing As Reflective Action* is a collection of essays designed to engage you in reflective and reflexive reading, writing, and critical thinking, practices vital to academia. Being able to function in academia is not the whole story, however, because there is a larger community within which you must also live and work—the world at large. It is our belief, given a world as complex, diverse, and sometimes difficult as ours, that students benefit from an education that helps them both to survive in the academy and to become thoughtful, caring, and productive members of society. To these ends, we invite you to engage in extended reflection and reflexivity, collaborative learning, informal writing and formal writing, writing for the academy, and writing in service to or in relationship with the community in which you live.

We recognize that when you come to college or the university, you bring your individual self, your personal history, your beliefs, your prior schooling, your regional or national origin, your rich cultural heritage. While we want to see you develop facility with academic discourses, we do not expect you to check your individual identity at the door on the way in, as you might a hat or coat. We are, therefore, especially interested in helping you explore the intersection of the personal and public, the private and social in your thinking, your reading, your writing, and your life.

KEY CONCEPTS

Let us try to define more clearly what we mean by terms such as *reflection*, *reflexivity*, and from the title of our textbook, *action*.

Reflection

We believe that reflection is central to learning and to taking thoughtful, compassionate, and appropriate action in the world. We mean by *reflection* the careful, ongoing consideration of a subject. Notice the metaphor in the word, reflection. Think of the subject of your reflection as the reflective surface—a kind of mirror—and yourself (complete with your experiences and your culture) as the light source. When you examine the subject in your own light, what do you see? And how do you see yourself in the reflection? To reflect on something you have read would be to focus your attention on it, to play around with it in your mind, perhaps to analyze it, perhaps to think about its significance or how it connects to other things you have read. To be self-reflective is to examine yourself, your ideas, your assumptions and so on. Reflection, especially self-reflection, is the grounding point for the work we ask you to do throughout this book. It is also the springboard for even more important work—that of reflexivity. Reflection, as important as it is, is a process that remains centered on the self to a degree. It casts you as an independent agent capable of careful consideration and examination separate from a wider encounter with other beings, assumptions, cultures, and the like. Once reflection becomes a habit of thought, it is easier to engage in its counterpart, reflexivity.

Reflexivity

Perhaps our colleague at Western Washington University, Donna Qualley, explains reflexivity best: In her book *Turns of Thought,* she shares a personal story that illustrates an act or moment of reflexivity:

> At the age of 22, I went to Australia to teach high school for fifteen months; I stayed nine years. I packed my suitcase with my suburban, midwestern values (tempered by a 1960's philosophy), and headed to the Land Down Under with a state university certified, guaranteed-to-work-anywhere-in-the-world, objective theory of education . . . . I had lived in Australia for five months, when one day I drove to the lumber yard in Moe to purchase some molding and kitchen faucets. It was just after New Year's. When I arrived, I found the place closed for the rest of the month. I then drove to the hardware store, which had plumbing supplies, but not the correct ones. The sales clerk said that he could order the taps, but they would not arrive until the first of February, since most of their suppliers were closed between Christmas and the end of January. I was stunned. I couldn't understand why these businesses didn't stagger their employees' vacations over the year. Didn't they realize that if they kept their business open, the company would make more money?
>
> The sales person seemed to read my thoughts. He looked at me and shrugged. "This isn't America, mate," he said, "we're not all bloody capitalists here". . . . It had never occurred to me that the work ethic that was so much a part of my own country was not a universally ingrained truth. Nor had it occurred to me how much I actually subscribed to it. But Australia had been (un)settled by convicts, not Puritans. Australians did not see work as a direct route to goodness.

> (*Turns of Thought,* 8–9)

Qualley's encounter with this different culture and its different assumptions led her to examine her own views and assumptions in ways she had not been able to do previously. She had an experience that was clearly reflexive as she defines it in *Turns of Thought*:

> Reflexivity is a response triggered by dialectical engagement with the other—an idea, theory, person, culture, text, or even an other part

of one's self . . . . By dialectical, I mean an engagement that is ongoing and recursive [meaning roughly *repeated, looping back on itself*] as opposed to a single, momentary encounter. In the process of trying to understand an other, our own beliefs and assumptions are disclosed, and these assumptions, themselves, can become objects of examination and critique.

(Turns of Thought, 11)

Reflexivity, then, involves trying on the perspective, the world view of an "other" for long enough to look back critically at ourselves, our ideas, our assumptions, our values. Careful attention to the places where two (or more) perspectives come into conflict may well lead to new understandings and to growth. Setting conflicting perspectives into opposition or discussion with each other is what we mean by "dialogic."

But we don't have to visit another country to engage in reflexivity. A willingness to cultivate habits of reflexivity means that we can put ourselves into a state of learning, inquiry, and transformation in many kinds of settings, even while watching a movie, for instance. Most people find *Dances With Wolves* an entertaining movie, but for those who have learned something about reflection and reflexivity it can become an occasion for learning. Watching *Dances With Wolves* can be a reflexive occasion on a couple of levels. One way is through the perspective of Kevin Costner's character. Costner goes west as a soldier, as a mercenary certain to make the Indians he encounters his mortal enemies. Through a combination of circumstances he is allowed a rare glimpse into the lives and daily existence of Native Americans. This intersecting of lives causes Costner's character to look back at his own life through the eyes of Indian culture. When he takes this look back, makes this reflexive move, some things that were once important to him become less so. For instance, he stops wearing his uniform and no longer feels compelled to see these people from another culture as enemies deserving of death. To a degree, he even begins to see those from his own culture as the enemy.

The audience is probably also engaging in reflexivity. Many of us watching the film identify with Costner's white male character and are thereby invited to see things through his eyes. When he has a reflexive encounter that transforms him, we as the audience can also be reflexive and transformed through our identification with him; we are asked to question our own lives and our own assumptions about past and present White and Native American cultures and their interactions. Like Costner's character, we are made to wonder whose side we are on, or whether "sides" are even appropriate as a way to think about the matter.

As Qualley suggests, it is in this encounter with an "other" that we can begin not just to reflect on, but examine, critique, and perhaps transform our thoughts and assumptions, to enter a state of openness or readiness for real learning and inquiry. Paradoxically, then, this use of another perspective or culture enables us to engage in independent thinking—even a kind of creativity—of our own, because reflexivity gives us enough distance from our own beliefs to imagine alternatives. It's as if we need others in order to be ourselves.

Learning to see yourself and your culture through the lens of another culture is perhaps the single most important intellectual move you will learn to make in college. At the heart of college life is intellectual debate. Intellectual debate *is* a dialectical engagement (by *dialectical* we mean the back-and-forth interplay of opposing ideas) in which differing assumptions, representations, ways of seeing, and ideas are pitted against each other. This kind of engagement leads to an understanding of opposing points of view with out losing your own, understanding the sources of your own point of view, understanding how the two differ, and ultimately a purposeful consideration of the choices available to you as you construct your own belief system. In this way it is possible to have a transformation of individuals as well as ideas and knowledge. So it's fair to say that reflexivity is the mental work that fuels intellectual debate.

Action

What do we mean by the term *action*? Just as reflection leads to reflexivity, we hope that reflexivity will lead to action. To take action generally means to do something, to make some movement, perhaps make a decision. What it isn't is inertia, stasis, or nonmovement. We mean for action to happen in at least a couple of different ways as you work with the reading, writing, and possible assignments we set forth in *Writing As Reflective Action*. First, we imagine something we might call rhetorical action. Although we often think of writing as sedentary, or inactive, writing is itself a form of action. Finding, ordering, and articulating ideas are activities that interrupt inertia, imposing order on the chaos that is our stream of consciousness: Clearly, this is a form of action. This is true even of the most mundane examples of writing, such as the daily "to do" list, or the grocery list. Whenever we write, we force those amorphous ideas swirling around in our heads to line up in an orderly way, subjects and predicates all in a row. Interestingly, it is this very capacity of writing to bring order out of chaos that probably accounts for its important role in more overtly social or political action. Think, for example, of the role of the labor contract, or the international peace treaty. Think of the role of the *Declaration of Independence*, or *Brown v. the Board of Education*, a role played out daily, albeit in a minor key, in the editorial pages and letters to the editor of your daily newspaper. Writing establishes the social order, disrupts it, transforms it.

We also intend action to mean going outside the physical walls of your school and into the community. That movement from school to community is itself one form of action. What happens once you get there is another. Community-based action can take any number of forms, which we will summarize under the general heading of applying what you know, of putting your knowledge to work for the good of the community. Not that we're talking about a form of missionary work here; instead, action in the community more closely resembles some intricate dance in which the partners take turns leading. It's reciprocal: You talk, but you also listen; you teach, but you also learn. Ultimately, we hope that the action you engage in involves conscious steps to make changes in some or all the communities with which you find yourself in contact. That is, through reflexive reading, writing, and thought, through writing projects that take you into the community, we hope that you will take action by engaging in writing that matters, both to you and to others.

BECOMING REFLECTIVE AND REFLEXIVE

To help develop habits of mind that support reflection, reflexivity, and eventually action, we have structured this text in such a way as to engage you in several forms of reflective and reflexive practice: prewriting, critical reading, dialectical notebook responses, reading-response journals, dialogue journal responses, triple-entry incident journals, and collaborative group work.

Prewriting

At the beginning of every chapter we offer possibilities for reflective prewriting. These are questions or prompts that ask you to begin the process of reflection that will carry on throughout each chapter. We call these writing prompts "prewriting" because we are interested in your getting down on paper the ideas you might have about a particular subject prior to doing further study or reading. Prewriting is one of the ways you can begin to create a habit of reflection. Doing this requires you to make explicit what you think about things. The next step, then, is to look at what you know and think and begin to ask questions. How did I know that? Why do I think this? Was it something I experienced? Did I learn this from a book?

Although these prewriting activities are meant to be informal (and perhaps even private if your instructor thinks they should be), our hope is that you will begin to think seriously about the ideas and themes to be presented in the chapter and your relationship to those themes and ideas. Prewriting, then, is informal writing meant to get you thinking through the act of writing rather than actually communicating finished and polished ideas to an audience.

Critical Reading

Many of the readings we have included are difficult and complex. They are hard for us, too. Some are likely to seem strange and foreign to you, making it tough to connect and understand on your first reading. Please do not get discouraged. We urge you not to be afraid of the difficult passages but rather to believe in yourself and in the fact that you do have ideas about what the author is trying to say. You will want to practice being an active reader by marking up the text, asking questions in the margin, and asking others about their understanding of the readings. Be patient and give yourself time to reread. If you keep at it, if you work hard to get inside the passage that is troubling, you will eventually find a thread you can pull, unraveling the meaning. The various kinds of informal journal writing that we suggest next are important tools for supporting your critical reading.

The Dialectical Notebook

During your reading of the essays your teacher might ask that you keep a dialectical notebook, or perhaps a reading-response journal, or a dialogue journal, or some combination of response and dialogue. The dialectical notebook is a tool for rethinking and reforming ideas. Simply divide your page into vertical halves. As you read you will keep a list of important quotations, ideas, words, themes, etc., together with page numbers, on the left-hand side of the page. At some later time, after you have finished the reading and had time to think about it, you'll revisit the notes you made on the left-hand side of the page, using the right-hand side of the page to make further comments. The comments you make here may extend thoughts you initially noted. Or, you might see something differently now from how you did originally and would want to note that. Perhaps you will want to place your earlier, briefer notes in a larger context after having finished your reading and thought about things more thoroughly. Or perhaps you will think of connections between your initial notes and ideas you have encountered elsewhere, whether in another essay or even another course. Notice that the format itself encourages reflective thought: the left-hand column may include summary and direct quotation, but the right-hand column will always be reflective. Figure 1 is an example of a dialectical notebook.

Figure 1

DIALECTICAL NOTEBOOK

Joanna Lunkiewicz

11/15/98

"At some deep emotional level, he has trapped himself, and doesn't know how, doesn't want to know how, is afraid to know how, to untrap himself (131)."

" . . . because there is no father to love him to stabilize his world, his human worth is forever up for grabs, definable by the highest bidder (132)."

"His fear of being weak is mainly fear of letting his tough image slip—the image of a man, a superhero, self-sufficient, unneedy, indifferent to sympathy or kindness, unaffected by others' claims on him (135)."

They quotes represent what a stable person requires . . . freedom . . . emotional freedom, love, and security. The first quote is a result of what Rambo does, all of the dehumanising kills (murders) he committed, trapped his emotions, because if a person does not surpress the fear, he will not kill.

The second quote describes why he is so insecure . . . he is always trying to please his "fathers," by doing exactly what they comand. And the 3rd is the sterotype that Rambo thinks is the true "man." All of the descriptions that make up a whole person are left out.

Reading-Response Journal

The reading-response journal is another good way to learn habits of reflection and reflexivity. The purpose of this type of journal is to help you process—and collect your thoughts about—what you read. Your teacher might have a particular place he or she would like you to write about the readings, say a spiral notebook or a bound journal, but almost any medium will do, including e-mail and specially designed web pages. For the reading-response journal we recommend that you write both during and upon completion of the reading selection you have been assigned. Writing during your reading encourages active reading. It slows you down, opens opportunities for you to reread a particularly complex passage; it forces you to think as you read, not just glide over the words. Writing after you

Figure 1 (Continued)

DIALECTICAL NOTEBOOK

12/03/98	
"I am very depressed. It always takes a while to sort out what's wrong, but it usually starts with some kind of perfectly irrational thought such as " I hate being a lawyer" (3).	These first three quotes are so very personal. She is using the same approach as bell hooks in "Killing Rage," using something personal in to intro and a little farther. William's is using contractions.
"I let my hair stream wildly and the eyes roll back in my head. (4). " I feel like a monkey" (4). "Conditions are bad, very bad, all over the world" (4).	Here she is making generalizations from the t.v. news.
"A concise, modular, yet totally engaging item on the 'MacNeil/Lehrer News Hour . . .'" (5).	Here she switches into a professional mode, using more academic words, no slang.
"My book will concern itself with the interplay of commerce and constitutional protections and will be organized around discussion of three basic jurisprudential forces: autonomy, community, & order." (6).	The conclusion of this article is that even this educated person . . . lawyer, has trouble with connecting info to all aspects of her life. And so, like Tompkins, wants to include all aspects of her life to understand where she is coming to understand it the way she does.

have completed your reading allows you to gather your thoughts about the essay or story. You can reflect on what you have read, ask questions, argue with the author if you'd like. You can see that when we ask for response, we have in mind something more than summary. While summarizing is a crucial first step in understanding a text, and therefore a skill your teacher might want you to work on, possibly even in the pages of your reading-response journal, we are ultimately more interested in your ability to analyze and write critically about what you have read. What do you think the author is trying to say? Do you agree? Why or why not? Does anything you have read in the article make you angry, upset, sad? Have your own experiences taught you anything about what the author is trying to say? Having read the article, do you see something differently from the way you saw it previously? These questions indicate the kinds of writing you would do in the reading-response journal. In other words, the writing you would do in this journal would call for you to engage with the reading in both reflective and reflexive ways. Figure 2 is a sample page from a response journal. Note that it does not make use of columns, as is the case with the dialogue journal.

Dialogue Journal

There are other ways to keep journals as well. Two of our favorites are the reading-response dialogue journal and the triple-entry incident journal. We recommend the triple-entry incident journal primarily for use with community service writing and community-based learning. The dialogue journal resembles a reading-response journal but differs in that it asks somebody else to respond to your response. That is, after you have responded to the reading on one-half of your page, somebody reads what you have written and responds to you in the pages of the journal—has a conversation in writing with you. Hence the name, "dialogue journal." This allows for a kind of "layered" conversation or dialogue among the texts you have read, you, and your dialogue partner, adding a social dimension to your thinking. Your dialogue partner could be your teacher or it could be another student in the class. Dialogue journals can use a format very much like that of the dialectical notebook, or they can use e-mail or bulletin board discussion on a class web page. Figure 3 presents an example of a reader-response dialogue journal.

Triple-Entry Incident Journal

The triple-entry incident journal requires that you make three entries at three different times. As we mentioned earlier, we like to have students work with the triple-entry incident journal during community-based learning, but it can be used in other ways as well—as another way to write about what you are reading, for example. The first entry you make in the journal is prior to your first encounter with a community partner (or an essay, or a chapter). This first entry is, in essence, a prewriting exercise in which you explore possibilities, expectations, preconceptions. The second entry immediately follows your first community experience (or first reading). Here you will describe what

Figure 2
RESPONSE JOURNAL

Ebony Mackey
Response Journal #1
April 4th, 1999

The first thing that comes to mind when I think of "On Being Self Forever" was what do I believe? What do I believe in? Is there an afterlife?

I read the material as best I could but I must admit it was rather confusing the writer often went on tangents to make a point. He often referenced early childhood stories to make clear or understandable his ideas and what he believes to be true of after-life, religion and self. It is hard to understand Updike's tone, is it sarcastic or serious? I was often offended to hear him speak so freely and opinionated of other religions. It is as if he almost wants you to contradict your religion. Especially when he speaks of Christ in the beginning of the essay and where we go when we die.

I guess that I could say that the article left me confused and I would like to further discuss it to get a better understanding of what point the author is trying to make. The essay seems to be full of contradictions. For example if the past is dead how can the person we are today still be a part of that past. He even goes so far as to contradict the various religious beliefs of others.

However several of his comments where interesting to think about and some of the thoughts he shared I could see being common thought of others. For example the statement on page 213, "Our waking thoughts tend to be absurd." That I think is the one thing in the essay that may get universal agreement. We all tend to think of silly things upon our rising. And what he said about dreams and how we basically trust ourselves to fall into that unknown. But I describe dreams as a chance to let yourself go crazy without anyone knowing.

happened, how you felt, what surprised you, what you learned, and how your preconceived ideas and images held up or were changed. The third entry is a reflective narrative of sorts and comes

Figure 3
READER-RESPONSE DIALOGUE JOURNAL

Tom Young

Robert Coles idea's about entitlement and the rich, was very intriguing. I had never really thought about putting the well-to-do into two different categories. One being the spoiled rich kid that most people identify with in regards to the leisure class. People who feel that they should be entitled to what every they want whether they have earned it or not. That just by wanting allows them the right to possess. This type of entitlement has caused strife between the "Social Classes" for hundreds of years. Wars have been fought any many people have died at the whim of the elite. This is a very harmful type of entitlement. Not just for the people in the lower classes that have to deal with them but also the so called entitled can struggle. They usually do not have the skills to deal with situations that their money or social status cannot control. Unless these rich stay under their umbrella of entitlement they would find the world a very difficult place to cope.

That's true but I believe that all levels of class structure believe in some kind of entitlement that they deserve. (Food Stamps, Welfare)

That is a sad but true statement. The elite are the puppeteers and we, the lower class, are the puppets.

I think that this is why they live so far away from the community they belong it.

Figure 3 (Continued)

READER-RESPONSE DIALOGUE JOURNAL

The type of entitlement is not a selfish, spoiled form. It is more of a inner self-confidence. That no matter what happens things will be okay. The example of the dad dieing showed this perfectly. The family did not sit at home and feel sorry for themselves. The girls could have been so self absorbed with the potenial loss of her father that she only focused on how her death effected her. And not how it was going to really screw up her dads life. This self-confidence has been instilled in this girl since she was young. It does show that she expects a lot from people around her but not as much as she expects from herself. This type of entitlement produces the leaders of the world.	That little girl had too much confidence for her age that she was never able to feel what real emotions are all about.

later in your experience with your community-based learning project after at least two or three encounters with the community participants, or, if your teacher prefers, at the end of the project. Or, if you are using your triple-entry incident journal in connection with your reading, this third entry might be an effort at reflection, synthesis, and/or speculations about the significance of what you have read, written at the end of a group of readings or even at the end of the course. For further discussion of the triple-entry incident journal and an example, see the Introduction to Chapter IV.

Obviously you won't be asked to keep all of these different journals and a dialectical notebook, at least not all at once. Your teacher might choose one for you, ask you to explore more than one of them, or perhaps you would be assigned different journals or the dialectical notebook for different reading and writing assignments. But whether you were to use one or all of them, consistent practice with these forms of writing will help you cultivate habits of reflection and reflexivity. Your thinking will develop, which should in turn lead to learning about writing and to writing well.

Collaborative Group Work

As you look through this book you will see that we ask you to do some group work, especially in response to the assignment sequences at the back of the book. Questions at the end of each reading under the headings "Reflecting on the Reading" and "Understanding Rhetorical Strategies" should probably also be considered in groups, though they may be done individually. We are asking you to collaborate on making meaning and on coming to grips with the readings. Sometimes we ask you to help each other prepare and hone your thinking for a particular writing assignment. We suggest that you work together in these ways because we believe that learning and knowledge are social. By working together you can pool what you know, ask each other questions, debate differing views, and help each other extend or complicate your thinking, and thus, ultimately, your writing—much as the two of us have done in writing this book. We see collaborative work of this kind as leading directly to reflexivity. By coming together you have set the stage for dialectical engagement. More than likely, at least some of the time, you will encounter different assumptions, ideas, and ways of seeing as you work with other students.

Some Rhetorical Concepts

Your instructor will probably want to introduce a number of rhetorical terms or concepts along the way to provide a vocabulary for you and the members of your group to use as you analyze and discuss the readings. Even so, we would like to introduce a few very basic concepts we believe you will find useful immediately.

Aristotle, a Greek teacher and rhetorician born in 384 BC, gave us many terms and ideas that we still use when we talk about rhetoric today. He taught us the importance of understanding our audience and how to persuade our audience through various appeals. Aristotle focused on three appeals, ethos (ethical), logos (logical), and pathos (emotional). While we oversimplify here, we could say that *ethos* relates to a person's character—whether or not the person is believable, an upstanding citizen, or a sincere person, for instance. We could say that *logos*, or logic, has to do with how a speaker or writer makes an argument or tells a story. Is the evidence sound? Does the text make logical sense in the ways information is presented or the ways in which the evidence is used? And finally, we could say that *pathos* appeals to our emotions. Good writers and speakers hit us in the gut or the heart. They move us—perhaps to anger, perhaps to sadness, perhaps to happiness.

Two more useful concepts are voice and tone. *Voice* is our sense of the person behind the words, though it is something we infer from the words on the page. *Tone* is closely related. Tone is our sense of the author's attitude toward the subject and/or the audience; it is the emotional coloring the author gives to, or through, the words. It, too, must be inferred.

THE WRITING ASSIGNMENTS

The writing we ask you to do in *Writing As Reflective Action* is varied, but these various kinds of writing interact with each other in some way. For example, the informal writing is a building block for more formal writing. Also, the personal writing you do can be, and sometimes is, an integral part of an academic or more "public" writing task. As we noted earlier, at the beginning of every chapter we ask you to engage in reflective prewriting. We call it *prewriting* because we are interested in getting you to write down your ideas, assumptions, and experiences prior to beginning the readings collected in the chapter. We call it *reflective* because it is here that we want to begin the practice of asking you to examine yourself, what you think, and why you think the way you do.

Working Through Drafts

We expect that almost all your formal papers will go through a drafting process that we call *revision*. We use the term *revision* rather than *rewriting* because we want to avoid the common belief that having to rewrite is a form of punishment, something you have to do because you didn't get it right the first time. Requesting that you revise papers several times is not about right or wrong. Rather, it is a way of working through ideas, of discovering ideas and ways of presenting them as you rethink and reimagine what it is you want to say, and why, and to whom. Writing is not a matter of transcribing ideas already fully formed in your head; it is about finding out new things, new twists about what you are writing. You might think of drafting as scaffolding. Earlier drafts are not the end point, the completed building project, but rather the scaffolding that enables you to build another, fuller, more complex form. When the work is done, the builder takes away the scaffolding and the finished product stands by itself as an interesting and complete architectural endeavor. Drafting works in similar ways.

It is far too easy to think of revision as a matter of crossing out a word here and there, as changing a bit of grammar or correcting a spelling error. We would call this sort of thing *editing* and not revision. The distinction is an important one. Editing is what you do when you are ready to submit something in polished form. It involves fixing the sentence-level errors revealed by careful proofreading. Revision, by contrast, is about rolling up your sleeves and diving headlong back into your text. It is about moving things around, finding more examples, changing your mind. It is a way of turning things inside out. It is about pushing your ideas further, making explicit what might now just be implicit, reaching an audience. It is "re-vision" or "re-seeing."

We recognize that it is not always easy to get started on this kind of revision. That is why we recommend that you enlist others to help, including your teacher and other students in your class. Teachers can be wonderful resources during your early drafts. They can ask questions, raise concerns, give you feedback on places in your essay that seem strong or weak. But your classmates can be helpful too. Peer response to drafts is something that we take very seriously. Your peers can be yet another set of thoughtful eyes; they too can ask questions, let you know what they don't understand, and let you know how an audience is responding to you.

Informal and Formal Writing

At the end of every reading we ask you to do both informal and formal writing. The informal writing is meant to be writing that sparks your thinking, writing that you use to discover something new about yourself, what you think, or what you have just read. It is writing that is meant not to be graded but to support your move toward reflective and reflexive reading, writing, and thinking. The formal writing, on the other hand, is meant to offer you the opportunity to formulate an idea and to work it fully through as an essay intended for a public audience. Your instructor will probably want to decide which writing prompts you would do as formal or informal assignments.

While the writing assignments in the sequences are meant to lead to formal writing targeted for a larger public audience, they also ask you to work in rich, and sometimes even mixed genres as deemed appropriate for exploring, explaining, critiquing, analyzing, and/or synthesizing personal ideologies. In all of them, however, we are asking you to emphasize reflection, reflexivity, and understanding yourself in relation to culture.

As you work through this text with your teacher and your class-mates, we ask you to engage in a journey of sorts, a journey toward reflective and reflexive reading, writing, and thinking. We want you to flourish in the academy but also in the world at large. And in a world as diverse and complex as ours, it is crucial that you have a public voice, that you be an active and caring member of a democratic culture. To that end, we hold up this goal: to bring your selves—personal and public, readerly and writerly—together to inquire, to learn, and to act.

Exploring the Self: Reflection

Chapter 1

Reflective Prewriting

1. Make a short list of moments in your life that stand out as conceptual turning points, moments when you remember having some kind of significant insight into an idea or belief you had held for a long time.

   Write about one of these moments using as much detail as you can muster, detail about where you were, what you were doing, what your thoughts were, and what provoked the insight. If you feel stuck, try starting by using the prompt, "I remember . . . ."

2. Think about the members of your family or others with whom you have (or have had) a close relationship, persons you think have influenced your attitudes and beliefs.

   Write about the attitudes and beliefs that have been shaped or influenced by at least one of these persons. Have these attitudes and beliefs been useful to you? Harmful in some way? Does (or has) the person who shaped these attitudes influence(d) you in other ways?

3. Think about your gender, race, and religion and the role they play in your life.

   Write about the ways in which your gender, race, or religion might have shaped your attitudes about yourself (or about other people), about what you find important, or about the kinds of issues or events on which you might take a firm stand.

INTRODUCTION

In Chapter 1 we ask you to begin the process of reflection by exploring your "self." Remember that reflection is central to learning to be reflexive, critical thinkers and writers. To be reflective means that you give careful and thoughtful consideration to any subject that you might be engaged with or studying. It requires an *extended* effort, pushing beyond the easy explanations with which we have grown comfortable to arrive at some new understanding. It also means going against the grain of habit in some other ways, since our culture tends to bombard us with stimulation while doing next to nothing to encourage reflection. Being reflective means slowing things down, taking your time—simply spending more time at it. Since we are asking you to be self-reflective in this chapter, it will require that you turn a penetrating eye inward, that you consider thoughtfully who you are, what you think, and why you think the way you do. The prewriting exercises you worked with at the very beginning of Chapter 1 were the first step in this process. Now we are asking you to delve further into reflection by carefully and critically reading the five essays, "On Being a Self Forever" by John Updike, "Entitlement" by Robert Coles, "Excerpts from My Life" by Annie Neeposh Iserhoff, "Boys Will Be Men," by Peter Middleton, and "Killing Rage" by bell hooks.

Each of these essays models reflection, creates a climate for reflection through its subject matter, or offers a methodology leading to reflection. Some essays do all three. As you read you need to think about what "self" means. It is a common word that we use on a daily basis. Yet we tend to use it without giving much thought to what the self really constitutes or what constitutes the self. As you read the essays, all of which address the idea of self in some way, you will begin to see that the idea of self is addressed through a range of possibilities—physical, familial, political, cultural, and so on. Pay attention to which aspect of the self, or which primary identifier (physical, political, etc.) the authors are most conscious of as they work with understanding themselves or forming theories about the self. Note, too, that each author conceives of the self differently, with the result that they are frequently in conflict with each other. What differences do you notice? Are these differences irreconcilable?

We'd like you to approach the essays as a sort of double personality, assuming both the reader's stance and the writer's stance simultaneously. As a reader you might concentrate on understanding definitions, on issues and ideas, on what each author is saying about the self. As you read like a writer you might pay attention to what the author is doing that you might do, that you might add to your own writerly repertoire. How does the author use images, tell stories, support his or her arguments? How does each choose to represent him or herself? What are the authors' notions of self and how do they each represent them? What methodology do they use to think and write about the self that you could borrow for your reflections on your self?

The questions and informal writing we ask you to engage with at the end of each reading are meant to help you become comfortable with both the readerly and writerly stance. They are also meant to help guide you toward the reflective exploration of self that is the focus of this chapter. Now is also the time for you to begin working with at least one of the other tools for reflection that we write about at some length in the general introduction—the dialectical notebook, reading-response journal, dialogue journal, or triple-entry incident journal. These are all exceptional tools for beginning your exploration of self.

JOHN UPDIKE

John Updike was born in 1932 and spent his early years in and around the small town of Shillington, Penn., which was later to be memorialized in many of his stories and novels. Shillington plays an important role in this essay, "On Being a Self Forever" (1989). During high school, Updike worked as a copy boy for the Reading *Eagle,* where some of his first stories were to be published. In the fall of 1950 he entered Harvard University on a tuition scholarship and began drawing and writing for the *Harvard Lampoon.* In the year of his graduation from Harvard, 1954, a poem and story of Updike's were accepted by *The New Yorker,* beginning his lifelong relationship with that magazine. After studying fine arts at Oxford for a year, he accepted a staff position at *The New Yorker.*

Eventually, Updike left *The New Yorker* to devote his time more fully to writing. Updike soon began to focus on writing novels though he continued, for the remainder of his career, to produce a copious number of stories, poems, essays, and criticism. He is probably best known for his Harry (Rabbit) Angstrom tetralogy, *Rabbit, Run; Rabbit Redux; Rabbit is Rich;* and *Rabbit at Rest.* Of these, the latter two both won the National Book Critics Circle Award and the Pulitzer Prize for fiction.

The essay included in this anthology, "On Being a Self Forever," is from Updike's book of memoirs titled *Self-Consciousness (1989).* In this essay he strives to be as conscious of his self as possible—or rather the whole series of selves that have evolved into the present one doing the writing. In the process of sifting through these selves, Updike meditates on human mortality and the idea of immortality (which is to say, how long the self persists). Near the beginning of the essay he writes: "In fact we do not try to picture the afterlife, nor is it ourselves in our nervous tics and optical flecks that we wish to perpetuate; it is the self as window on the world that we can't bear to think of shutting. . . . The yearning for an afterlife is the opposite of selfish: it is love and praise for the world that we are privileged, in this complex interval of light, to witness and experience."

But Updike, in his self-conscious scrutiny, is skeptical of statements that attempt to sum up or reach some kind of objective "truth." As he later says, "The pragmatic undercurrent in this exposition troubles me. I am selling short something or someone precious." Consequently, Updike's method is to alternate between abstract statements and personal anecdotes, not quite trusting either medium completely but achieving a unique balance between them that approximates, in real life, the seesaw between general thought and specific action.

As you read, pay particular attention to Updike's use of personal anecdotes. What is their function in this project of self-definition?

On Being a Self Forever

When I look up at a blank blue sky, or rest my gaze on a bright surface of snow, I become aware of a fixed pattern of optical imperfections—specks in my vitreous humor like frozen microbes—that float always, usually unnoticed, in the field of my seeing. These are part of my self. From the distant days when I wanted to be a graphic artist, I have an odd habit of tracing what I see with a mental finger or pen—outlining a shoe or foot, drawing diagonals across windowpanes, tracing a curtain pattern while my real finger slightly twitches. This, too, this idiotic tic, is my self. Throughout each and every day of my life, scraps of old songs come into my head—most persistently and irresistibly, the opening lines of a faded tune from my high-school days called "The Old Lamp Lighter":

> *He made the night a little brighter*
> *Wherever he would go,*
> *The old lamp lighter*
> *Of long, long ago.*

And also, at other times, this catchy couplet—

> *Your good-bye*
> *Left me with eyes that cry—*

5   not to mention

> *I'm bidin' my time;*
> *'Cause that's the kind-a guy I'm.*

These random bytes of recollection are part of my self, as is that ridiculous repetitive voice that, with its rehashed anxieties and blurred recollections, keeps me company during insomnia, and has an intelligence so feeble it sometimes forgets the Lord's Prayer.

When I sign my name, which I seem to do ever more often, to books and checks, I find it increasingly difficult to get past the "d"—something in the rhythm of the "Up" produces a forced rest, a freeze in the little motor muscles, at the top of the "d," so that the ink, if from a felt-tip pen, begins to bleed, and to make a blue star, and to leak through to the other side of the paper. This unprompted hesitation, in what should be a fluent practiced signature, I think of as my self—a flaw that reveals my true, deep self, like a rift in Antarctic ice showing a scary, skyey blue at the far bottom. And in the palm of my right hand, in the meaty part below the index finger, exists a small dark dot, visible below the translucent skin, a dot that is, I know, the graphite remains of a stab with a freshly sharpened pencil that I accidentally gave myself in junior high school one day, hurrying between classes in the hall, a moment among countless forgotten moments that has this ineradicable memorial. I still remember how it hurt, and slightly bled—a slow dark drop of blood, round as a drop of mercury. I think of it often. Our waking thoughts tend to be absurd. I think about whether or not my fingernails need cutting and why my shoelaces keep coming untied (obviously, because I didn't learn how to tie them properly in Miss Becker's kindergarten). Since adolescence, I have frequently noticed that, when I lift the first knuckle of the index finger of my left hand to my nose, I can detect a distant putridity, a faint bad smell that is always (somehow satisfyingly) there, no matter how often I wash my hands. Such embedded data compose my most intimate self—the bedrock, as it were, beneath my more or less acceptable social, sexual, profession performance. Do I really want it, this self, these scattered fingerprints on the air, to persist forever, to outlast the atomic universe?

Those who scoff at the Christian hope of an afterlife have on their side not only a mass of biological evidence knitting the self-conscious mind tight to the perishing body but a certain moral superiority as well: isn't it terribly, well, *selfish,* and grotesquely egocentric, to hope for more than our animal walk in the sun, from eager blind infancy through the productive and procreative years into a senescence that, by the laws of biological instinct as well as by the premeditated precepts of stoic virtue, will submit to eternal sleep gratefully? Where, indeed, in the vast spaces disclosed by modern astronomy, would our disembodied spirit go, and, once there, what would it do? The *New Yorker* cartoonist, to occasion a laugh, has merely to limn white-robed people on clouds, with harps—a popular image derived from a single Biblical verse, Revelation 14:2—and haloes thrown in for added risibility. The Bible in fact says very little about Heaven, aside from the extensive measurements in Ezekiel and the glimpses of the crystalline city with streets of gold in Revelation 21. The founders of the Christian faith were not unaware, even in their relatively naive cosmos, of potential posthumous absurdities; Jesus fended off the question of the Sadducees about the après-resurrection embarrassments of the often-married (Mark 12:18–27; Matthew 22:23–33; Luke 20:27–40), and Paul, as he expounds to his captors in Caesarea how Christ was the first of many to rise from the dead, is told by the Roman procurator that much learning has made him mad (Acts 26:23–24). Paul waveringly tends to construe resurrection metaphorically, as the spiritual renewal that righteousness in Christ brings, and to distinguish as if Platonically between the natural body and the spiritual body (1 Corinthians 15:44). He rejected, however, the Gnostic idea that the resurrection has already taken place (2 Timothy 2:18), and in 1 Corinthians 15:12–14 ringingly rebuffed doubters within the early Church: "How say some of you that there is no resurrection of the dead? But if there is no resurrection of the dead, then is Christ not risen; and if Christ be not risen, then is our preaching vain, and your faith is also vain." The church, in arriving at its orthodoxy, insisted no less firmly than modern materialism that the body *is* the person, and left us with a tenet, the resurrection of the dead, that has become unthinkable, though it remains part of the Apostles' Creed professed in chorus by millions every Sunday.

10   If we picture the afterlife at all, it is, heretically, as the escape of something impalpable—the essential "I"—from this corruptible flesh, occurring at the moment of death and not at "the last trump" as Paul stated and as hundreds of medieval sculptors tried to imagine on church tympani. The thought of this long wait within the tomb afflicts us with claustrophobia and the fear of becoming lost forever; where is our self during the long interval?[1] The winged heads on Puritan tombstones do not represent ascended angels but souls hovering in that abyss between death and resurrection. The idea that we sleep for centuries and centuries without a flicker of dream, while our bodies rot and turn to dust and the very stone marking our graves crumbles to nothing, is virtually as terrifying as annihilation. Every attempt to be specific about the afterlife, to conceive of it in even the most general detail, appalls us. Our medically clever era has achieved many practical resurrections, and the testimony of these returnees from the beyond, their reports of a radiant tunnel and a suffusing love, have a kitschy triviality, a funhouse air, that allows an atheistic novelist like Kurt Vonnegut to incorporate them good-humoredly into his novel *Galápagos*. Our brains are no longer conditioned for reverence and awe. We cannot imagine a Second Coming that would not be cut down to size by the televised evening news, or a Last Judgment not subject to pages of holier-than-Thou second-guessing in *The New York Review of Books*. Not only do we feel morally superior to the Biblical notions of atonement and damnation, but our sharpened sense of fact and image resists vague reassurance. Another good-humored clear thinker, George Bernard Shaw, at the age of ninety-two proposed that personal immortality would be an "unimaginable horror";[2] and we do find it

---

[1]"'Well, where is our soul, then, in this gap?'"—*Pigeon Feathers* (1960)

[2]In his preface to *Buoyant Billions*: of the Spiritualists, he says, "They believe in personal immortality as far as any mortal can believe in an unimaginable horror." Thirty-seven years earlier, prefacing *Misalliance* (1910), he struck much the same note: ". . . if some devil were to convince us that our dream of personal immortality is no dream but hard fact, such a shriek of despair would go up from the human race as no other conceivable horror could provoke. With all our perverse nonsense as to John Smith living for a thousand million eons and for ever after, we die voluntarily, knowing that it is time for us to be scrapped, to be remanufactured [here Shaw offers some cold comfort, Life-Force variety], to come back, as Wordsworth divined, trailing ever brightening clouds of glory. . . . After all, what man is capable of the insane self-conceit of believing that an eternity of himself would be tolerable even to himself?"

hard to picture any endlessly sustained condition or activity that would not become as much a torture as live entombment.

In fact we do not try to picture the afterlife, nor is it our selves in our nervous tics and optical flecks that we wish to perpetuate; it is the self as window on the world that we can't bear to think of shutting. My mind when I was a boy of ten or eleven sent up its silent screams at the thought of future aeons—at the thought of the cosmic party going on without me. The yearning for an afterlife is the opposite of selfish: it is love and praise for the world that we are privileged, in this complex interval of light, to witness and experience. Though some believers may think of the afterlife as a place of retribution, where lives of poverty, distress, and illness will be compensated for, and where renunciations will be rewarded—where the last shall be first, in other words, and those that hunger and thirst shall be filled—the basic desire, as Unamuno says in his *Tragic Sense of Life,* is not for some *other*world but for *this* world, for life more or less as we know it to go on forever: "The immortality that we crave is a phenomenal immortality—it is the continuation of this present life."

Life as we know it is inextricable from change: our bodily growth and decay, the daily news and weather, the resolution of old adventures and the possibility of beginning new ones. The Book of Common Prayer concedes this by speaking of our "going from strength to strength" in some unspecified progress beyond the grave, and a puritan religion like Buddhism, founded by an atheist and austere even to the exclusion of deliberate austerity, acquires in popular application a heaven of bustling, bejewelled complexity—the Land of Bliss, the Buddha Realm of Amitabha. Ridiculous, excessive, unreasonable, you say? No more, the response must be, than existence as it is, than the worlds that are, with trees and flowers, ocean and sky, stars and stones, animals and insects and men. Our self is thrust into a manifold reality that is thoroughly gratuitous, and the faith in an afterlife, however much our reason ridicules it, very modestly extends our faith that each moment of our consciousness will be followed by another—that a coherent matrix has been prepared for this precious self of ours. The guarantee that our self enjoys an intended relation to the outer world is most, if not all, of what we ask from religion. God is the self projected onto reality by our natural and necessary optimism.[3] He is the not-me personified.

All mysteries are subject to the modernist dissolution. God having been, in the general intellectual mind, thoroughly dissolved into psychology and anthropology, the self itself, that core "I" which we

---

[3]"'We are natural believers,' Emerson says in his essay on Montaigne. 'Belief consists in accepting the affirmations of the soul; unbelief, in denying them.' It was Emerson's revelation that God and the self are of the same substance."—"Emersonianism" (1983)

imagine to be so crystalline and absolute within us, can also be attacked and analyzed as a construct that human society bestows, in widening rings out from the mother who first holds and feeds and talks to us and begins to fill our void with her substance. *"Je est un autre,"* Rimbaud said a hundred years ago, and a best-selling contemporary novel's hero concludes that "Your *self* . . . is *other people,* all the people you're tied to, and it's only a thread," and a less well-selling novel, *Friday,* by Michel Tournier, taking Defoe's islanded hero Robinson as its hero, observes of the self:

> A first point that must be noted, in attempting to depict the *self* unrelated to others, is that it exists only intermittently and, when all is said, comparatively seldom. Its presence corresponds to a secondary and as it were reflexive mode of knowledge. What happens in the primary, direct mode? Well, the objects are all there, shining in the sun or buried in the shade, rough or smooth, light or heavy; they are known, tested, touched, even cooked, carved, folded, and so on; whereas I who do the knowing, the tasting, touching, and cooking, have no separate existence except when I perform the act of reflection which causes *me* to emerge—a thing which in fact rarely happens. In that primary state of knowledge my awareness of an object is the object itself, the thing known and perceived without any person knowing and perceiving it. We cannot use the image of the candle shedding its light upon objects. We must substitute another: that of objects shining unaided, with a light of their own. . . . Then suddenly there is a click. The subject breaks away from the object, divesting it of a part of its color and substance. There is a rift in the scheme of things, and a whole range of objects crumbles in becoming *me* . . . .

15   The frangibility and provisionality of the self is well within our modern competence to perceive. The modern science of psychology treats of the anomalies and discontinuities of self-awareness. The self of schizophrenics splits into voices they hear in their heads, friendly at first and then quarrelsome and strident. The child's ego-sense does not come at birth but slowly emerges from a confusion of its self with the mother's. We each chronically entrust our selves to the subconscious realm of sleep, of dreams where the self wanders among its own raw materials, in an unquestioning present tense, without those limits which give the waking world stability. To me, an astonishing thing about dreams is that we are not more astonished by them, and descend into them each night with so little fear and anticipation of their perils. In our dreams, without feeling a discontinuity, we become smaller or younger or even another person altogether, who leans up against our real self like a doleful contiguous bodyguard. And who can say in what sense self-consciousness resides within a cretin, a dog, an ant, a tree? Trees, it lately seems, communicate, and become anxious when the chain saw approaches. How much more distinctly individual are bees in a hive than the cells in our body, cells which apparently have appropriated organelles like mitochondria

from some earlier stage of individuation? Is not the self, as under-stood in the United States of the "me decade," a precarious and luxu-rious invention quite different from the constantly shared and submerged self of a primitive tribesman, or the compacted identity of those Roman soldiers who would shout out, "Decimate us!"?

When does the self dawn? The impressions we acquire before the age of three remain subconscious, though they flavor our lives forever. My own deepest sense of self has to do with Shillington, and (at a certain slant) the scent or breath of Christmas. I become ex-hilarated in Shillington, as if my self is being given a bath in its own essence. There—in the words of the Tournier quotation—objects shine unaided, with a light of their own. This light is less strong, now, around the white Shillington house in which I was raised than around those two bulky brick houses across from the new movie theatre, where the luncheonette and the post office once were, and where Ernie Rothermel performed his first dental operations upon my mouth, and at the back of one of which lived Carl Leh, our brave policeman, under some cloud of disgrace, and on the porch of an-other of which I used to wait for my father to get done counting ath-letic receipts in the living room of Fred Grimes. Fred was a cripple, like Shorty Wartluft—not a hunchback but with one leg in a brace, and an arduous, backbending way of walking, of poling himself along. I believe he was also, like Shorty, a staunch churchman, or perhaps his patiently suffering smile made me imagine so. At any rate he was a solid Shillington citizen whose living room served as the locus of this fond vision, in the short story "In Football Season":

> I would stride through the hushed streets, where the rustling leaves
> seemed torn scraps scattered in the wake of the game, and go to
> Mr. Lloyd Stephens' house [a transposition, since Walt and Boo
> Stephens' luncheonette had been two doors away]. There, looking in the
> little square window of his front storm door, I could see down a dark
> hall into the lit kitchen when Mr. Stephens and my father and Mr. Jesse
> Honneger [a fictional version of my cough-drop savior Al Richards]
> were counting money around a worn porcelain table. Stephens, a local
> contractor, was the school-board treasurer, and Honneger, who taught
> social science, the chairman of the high-school athletic department. They
> were still counting; the silver stacks slipped and glinted among their fin-
> gers and the gold of beer stood in cylinders beside their hairy wrists.
> Their sleeves were rolled up and smoke like a fourth presence, wings
> spread, hung over their heads.

This suggestion of a hovering angel should not distract us from the glinting center of the young voyeur's happy vision: the money, stacks of it, a glorious excess over the coins and worn bills in the Recipes box that sat on top of the icebox at 117 Philadelphia Avenue. It occurs to me now that these Lancaster Avenue houses, between the Borough Hall and the house and garage of our important relatives the Beckers, represented to my innocent mind city life—the central, power-laden Shillington transactions from which my own family, for all their originality and pretensions to quality, was excluded.

Not only are selves conditional but they die. Each day, we wake slightly altered, and the person we were yesterday is dead. So why, one could say, be afraid of death, when death comes all the time? It is even possible to dislike our old selves, these disposable ancestors of ours. For instance, my high-school self—skinny, scabby, giggly, gabby, frantic to be noticed, tormented enough to be a tormentor, relentlessly pushing his cartoons and posters and noisy jokes and pseudosophisticated poems upon the helpless high school—strikes me now as considerably obnoxious, though I owe him a lot: without his frantic ambition and insecurity I would not now be sitting on (as my present home was named by others) Haven Hill. And my Ipswich self, a delayed second edition of that high-school self, in a town much like Shillington in its blend of sweet and tough, only more spacious and historic and blessedly free of family ghosts, and my own relative position in the "gang" improved, enhanced by a touch of wealth and celebrity, a mini-Mailer in our small salt-water pond, a stag of sorts in our herd of housewife-does, flirtatious, malicious, greedy for my quota of life's pleasures, a distracted, mediocre father and worse husband—he seems another obnoxious showoff, rapacious and sneaky and, in the service of his own ego, remorseless. But, then, am I his superior in anything but caution and years, and how can I disown him without disowning also his useful works, on which I still receive royalties? And when I entertain in my mind these shaggy, red-faced, overexcited, abrasive fellows, I find myself tenderly taken with their diligence, their hopefulness, their ability in spite of all to map a broad strategy and stick with it. So perhaps one cannot, after all, not love them.

20   *The New Yorker* of the Shawn era (1951–87) was a club of sorts, from within which the large rest of literary America—the many other less distinguished and fastidious magazines, the coarsely striving book trade, the tawdry best-seller lists, the sharp-tongued quarterlies and partisan reviews—could be politely disdained. Our good self-opinion, which Shawn maintained with an intellectual confidence and Buddhistic serenity that transcended Ross's agitated perfectionism, made a useful shelter for me, a hard shell I didn't have to grow myself. While I can now almost glimpse something a bit too trusting in the serene sense of artistic well-being, of virtual invulnerability, that being published in *The New Yorker* gave me for over thirty years, the self who looked up into the empyrean of print from the dusty farm in Pennsylvania with its outhouse and coal-oil stove is not so remote from me that I can still think it anything less

than wonderful to have become a writer. The very selves that make me most cringe to remember—the self of 1945–48, the little unwilling 4-H member with his strawberry project, picking them for hours in the buggy June heat and peddling them to old family friends in Shillington, and the pathetic undersized catechumen newly enrolled at the Robeson Lutheran Evangelical Church, sucking his bad postwar teeth and painful theological doubts in a class of beefy country cousins: and the self of 1950–51, beset by homesickness and hemorrhoids in his first New England winter and showing up at the *Lampoon* tryouts in slightly wrong clothes (they had a word for it: "wonky") in blissful ignorance of the social dimension of the bastion he is trying to storm—are yet the bravest boys, exiles clinging to a vision, to a belief in print, in ink, in a sacred realm of publication that will redeem them.

And then there are the favorite, pet selves—the Faithful little habitué of the Shillington playground, in his shorts and sneakers, getting in line for game after game of roof ball, playing checkers and braiding gimp in the shade of the playground pavilion; the lonely psoriatic explorer of Caribbean islands, again in shorts and sneakers, wandering with his poor baked skin through the jostle of tourists and natives, savoring the tattered, fragrant, sleepy traces of the old West Indies, before the jets made it too easy to get to; and the copyboy, in his penny loafers and tucked-back shirtsleeves, for the Reading *Eagle*. During my eighteenth, nineteenth, and twentieth summers (in my twenty-first, I was married), I fetched coffee and doughnuts for the editorial room and carried copy to the linotype room, responding to the shout of "Boy!," joking with the chummier reporters, and admiring the dashing look of the copy itself, the triple-spaced sheets rubber-cemented together in long festoons emended with loops and slashes by the darkest of dark pencils. The factorylike clamor of the linotypes, and the whiff of hot lead, and the operators each with his green eyeshade under his private lamp like so many monks in conical cells of yellow light: these phenomena gratified me, as did the air of early-morning Reading when I made the eight-o'clock coffee run to a diner on Penn Street—the sidewalks damp in spots and the young women tapping to work in their heels and taut skirts, the broad downtown blocks bestirring themselves for another busy weekday, every store from Whitner's up to Pomeroy's occupied in those last years before shopping malls gutted the inner city.

My morning hours were the busiest; by the time I came back from the lunch run with sandwiches for the diners-in, the paper had been put to bed, and there was little to do but perch on a desk and gab until the first run of papers came off the press around two. My remaining duties included taking a paper to Mr. Hawley Quier, who owned both the *Eagle* and its morning counterpart, the Reading *Times;*

he had a harelip, and I had trouble understanding, at first, his pleasantries from on high. Sometimes (I seem to remember) one took the
paper to him at a little dive a half-block up Court Street, where he
sat at a round table playing cards of an afternoon. Small-city rich
have this engaging way of mingling, in shirtsleeves, with the common man. Reading was a friendly town; its mayors were friendly
with racketeers and its mill owners with their tenant farmers and its
sole newspaper magnate with a teen-aged copy boy. Like me, Mr.
Quier had his problems—not only the harelip but his unusual
French name; the radio station he owned called itself the Hawley
Broadcasting Company, rather than the Quier one. Once in a while,
after I had distributed papers through the editorial room, someone
would spot a typo bad enough to justify breaking the press run; then
the city editor would give me the scrawled slip I would carry—*run,
boy!*—down to the thunderous chamber where the presses themselves rotated their great curved plates and gray rivers of newsprint
flooded forth. But generally these afternoon hours were idle enough
for me to type, on a spare machine, poems on such topical subjects
as the Rosenbergs' execution, or light verse that Jerry Kobrin might
publish in his column, or a letter to my Radcliffe girlfriend. In my
sense of myself I tap-danced through this palace of print disguised
as the lowliest of employees, with my mother-ironed shirtsleeves
nicely folded back and my shirt pocket cockily squared by a pack of
cigarettes, of Kools in their minty, icy white and green or Philip
Morrises in their old-fashioned pack of homely tobacco brown.

It seems marvellous to me that once I smoked. Old photographs
in which I am holding a cigarette have in my eyes the black-and-
white glamour of stills from Hollywood films noirs. I smoked a
great deal, in fact, beginning at the age of fifteen (or could it have
been fourteen?) when, as part of my campaign to become more
"popular," I bought a pack in Reading, at the railroad station on
Seventh Street, and lit my first cigarette as I walked along past the
little banistered porches, beneath the buttonwood trees. At the initial puff, the sidewalk lifted as if to strike my forehead, but I fought
the dizziness and persevered. The beckoning world of magazines
(loaded with cigarette ads) demanded this, not to mention the world
of girls. With some determined tutorial work in Stephens'
Luncheonette, I learned how to inhale, to double-inhale, to French-
inhale, and (just barely) to blow smoke rings. At Harvard, I was up
to three packs a day, and my fingertips turned orange. In Oxford,
the little stiff cardboard packages of five or ten Churchman's were a
novelty, as was, at the back of the slideout part of the package, the
lined blank space entitled "Notes"—conjuring up an empire full of
Englishmen coolly taking notes, amid grapeshot and cavalry hoof-
beats, on their cigarette boxes. In New York, getting worried, I began

to experiment with holders, including that awkwardly long type which employs as a filter an entire other cigarette, replaced when it darkens through and through and drips with tar juice. By the time of the move to Ipswich, my self-glamorization in other respects had proceeded far enough that I almost felt able to do without cigarettes as a prop. Now I have long since, in deference to my emphysema, given up smoking, even the smoking of little cigars that, after I broke the cigarette habit, used to get me through the stress of composition. Also, I have given up salt and coffee in deference to high blood pressure and alcohol in deference to methotrexate. The big-bellied Lutheran God within looks on scoffingly. *"Hunde, wollt ihr ewig leben?"* Frederick the Great thundered at his battle-shy soldiers— "Dogs, would you live forever?"

So writing is my sole remaining vice. It is an addiction, an illusory release, a presumptuous taming of reality, a way of expressing lightly the unbearable. That we age and leave behind this litter of dead, unrecoverable selves is both unbearable and the commonest thing in the world—it happens to everybody. In the morning light one can write breezily, without the slightest acceleration of one's pulse, about what one cannot contemplate in the dark without turning in panic to God. In the dark one *truly* feels that immense sliding, that turning of the vast earth into darkness and eternal cold, taking with it all the furniture and scenery, and the bright distractions and warm touches, of our lives. Even the barest earthly facts are unbearably heavy, weighted as they are with our personal death. Writing, in making the world light—in codifying, distorting, prettifying, verbalizing it—approaches blasphemy.

25   "Consciousness is a disease," Unamuno says. Religion would relieve the symptoms. Religion construed, of course, broadly, not only in the form of the world's barbaric and even atrocious religious orthodoxies but in the form of any private system, be it adoration of Elvis Presley or hatred of nuclear weapons, be it a fetishism of politics or popular culture, that submerges in a transcendent concern the grimly finite facts of our individual human case. How remarkably fertile the religious imagination is, how fervid the appetite for significance; it sets gods to growing on every bush and rock. Astrology, UFOs, resurrections, mental metal-bending, visions in space, and voodoo flourish in the weekly tabloids we buy at the cash register along with our groceries. Falling in love—its mythologization of the beloved and everything that touches her or him—is an invented religion, and religious also is our persistence, against all the powerful post-Copernican, post-Darwinian evidence that we are insignificant accidents within a vast uncaused churning, in feeling that our life is a story, with a pattern and a moral and an inevitability—that, as Emerson said, "a thread runs through all things: all worlds are strung on it, as beads: and men,

and events, and life, come to us, only because of that thread." That our subjectivity, in other words, dominates, through secret channels, outer reality, and the universe has a personal structure.

How gorgeously strange the religions of others seem! The world's outstanding believers these days are the Moslems: what forms has God taken in their heads—what does Allah mean to them as they surge forward in their Iranian human waves or Palestinian suicide missions? What common image animates all these close-packed male bodies bowing in unison on some dusty equatorial *masjid?* It is not the Christian God—or gods, for out of Paraguayan Catholics, Vermont Congregationalists, Utah Mormons, and New Zealand Anglicans sprout as many gods as are carved on a Jain temple wall. The Jewish God, as best He can be glimpsed in the United States, wears yet a different face. He seems meatier, more unbuttoned than His Christian offspring; He does not excite the churchgoer's anxious either/or, that "Does He?" or "Doesn't He?" in regard to His existence, that angst-generating crux of faith. Christianity has somehow taken hold of religion at the wrong end of the stick—the inhuman, or wholly other, end. The Jewish attitude seems in comparison humorous and submissive: it's His choice, to exist or not. The Old Testament God seems brashly free, compared to the locked-in God of Aquinas or Anselm. What theologian was it who, asked for a proof of God's existence, answered, "The Jews"? As long as Jews exist, even as atheistic Marxists or Freudians, a chosen people exists, and in its existence indicates that of a Chooser. Meanwhile, the gods of the Australian aborigines are silenced as if by rotting telephone wires; the bedaubed and naked old men who know the rituals and the sacred places die away, leaving behind grandsons, in boots and bush hats, to whom all rocks are merely rocks. Picasso once chastised Matisse for designing and decorating a chapel. Both men were professed atheists. Matisse retorted, "Yes, I do pray; and you pray too, and you know it all too well: when everything goes badly, we throw ourselves into prayer. . . . And you do it; you too. It's no good saying no." All anger, a psychotherapist recently informed me, is anger at God. "God" is a word, however problematical, we do not have to look up in the dictionary. We seem to have its acquaintance from birth.

For many men, work is the effective religion, a ritual occupation and inflexible orientation which permits them to imagine that the problem of their personal death has been solved. Unamuno: "Work is the only practical consolation for having been born." My own chosen career—its dispersal and multiplication of the self through publication, its daily excretion of yet more words, the eventual reifying of these words into books—certainly is a practical consolation, a kind of bicycle which, if I were ever to stop pedalling, would dump me flat on my side. Religion enables us to ignore nothingness and get on with the jobs of life.

Perhaps there are two kinds of people: those for whom nothingness is no problem, and those for whom it is an insuperable problem, an outrageous cancellation rendering every other concern, from mismatching socks to nuclear holocaust, negligible. Tenacious of this terror, this adamant essence as crucial to us as our sexuality, we resist those kindly stoic consolers who assure us that we will outwear the fright, that we will grow numb and accepting and, as it were, religiously impotent. As Unamuno says, with the rhythms of a stubborn child, "I do not want to die—no; I neither want to die nor do I want to want to die; I want to live forever and ever and ever. I want this 'I' to live—this poor 'I' that I am and that I feel myself to be here and now."

The objections of material science and liberal ethics to this desperate wanting belong to the outer, sunlit world, of sense and the senses; our wanting and its soothing belong to the elusive dark world within. Emerson, in *Nature*, points out "the total disparity between the evidence of our own being, and the evidence of the world's being." Evidence of God's being lies with that of our own; it is on our side of the total disparity that God lives. In the light, we disown Him, embarrassedly; in the dark, He is our only guarantor, our only shield against death. The impalpable self cries out to Him and wonders if it detects an answer. Like the inner of the two bonded strips of metal in a thermostat, the self curls against Him and presses. The need for our "I" to have its "Thou," something other than ourselves yet sharing our subjectivity, something amplifying it indeed to the outer time of creation, survives all embarrassments, all silence, all refusals on either side. The sensation of silence cannot be helped: a loud and evident God would be a bully, an insecure tyrant, an all-crushing datum instead of, as He is, a bottomless encouragement to our faltering and frightened being. His answers come in the long run, as the large facts of our lives, strung on that thread running through all things. Religion includes, as its enemies say, fatalism, an acceptance and consecration of what is.

30   The thermostat image needs adjusting: God is a dark sphere enclosing the pinpoint of our selves, an adamant bubble enclosing us, protecting us, enabling us to let go, to ride the waves of what is.

Early in my adolescence, trapped within the airtight case for atheism, I made this logical formulation:

1.   If God does not exist, the world is a horror-show.
2.   The world is not a horror-show.
3.   Therefore, God exists.

The second premise, of course, is the weaker; newspapers and biology lessons daily suggest that it *is* a horror show, of landslides and plagues and massacres and falling airplanes and incessant carnivorousness. And of—we cannot but be especially conscious these days—venereal disease: what more fiendish proof of cosmic irresponsibility than a Nature which, having invented sex as a way to mix genes, then permits to arise, amid all its perfumed and hypnotic inducements to mate, a tireless tribe of spirochetes and viruses that torture and kill us for following orders? Yet this and all bad news merits reporting because our general expectation is for good: an instinctive vision of health and peace underlies our horror stories. Existence itself does not feel horrible; it feels like an ecstasy, rather, which we only have to be still to experience. Habit and accustomedness have painted over pure gold with a dull paint that can, however, be scratched away, to reveal the shining underbase. The world is good, our intuition is, confirming its Creator's appraisal as reported in the first chapter of Genesis.

During that same adolescence, I reluctantly perceived of the Christian religion I had been born into that almost no one believed it, believed it really—not its ministers, nor its pillars like my father and his father before him. Though signs of belief (churches, public prayers, mottos on coins) existed everywhere, when you moved toward Christianity it disappeared, as fog solidly opaque in the distance thins to transparency when you walk into it. I decided I nevertheless *would* believe. I found a few authors, a very few—Chesterton, Eliot, Unamuno, Kierkegaard, Karl Barth—who helped me believe. Under the shelter (like the wicker chairs on the side porch) that I improvised from their pages I have lived my life. I rarely read them now; my life is mostly lived. God is the God of the living, though His priests and executors, to keep order and to force the world into a convenient mould, will always want to make Him the God of the dead, the God who chastises life and forbids and says No. What I felt, in that basement Sunday school of Grace Lutheran Church in Shillington, was a clumsy attempt to extend a Yes, a blessing, and I accepted that blessing, offering in return only a nickel a week and my art, my poor little art.

35   Imitation is praise. Description expresses love. I early arrived at these self-justifying inklings. Having accepted that old Shillington blessing, I have felt free to describe life as accurately as I could, with especial attention to human erosions and betrayals. What small faith I have has given me what artistic courage I have. My theory was that God already knows everything and cannot be shocked. And only truth is useful. Only truth can be built upon. From a higher, inhuman point of view, only truth, however harsh, is holy. The fabricated truth

of poetry and fiction makes a shelter in which I feel safe, sheltered within interlaced plausibilities in the image of a real world for which I am not to blame. Such writing is in essence pure. Out of soiled and restless life, I have refined my books. They are trim, crisp, clean, especially in the moment when they arrive from the printer in a cardboard box, before the reviewers leave their smudges all over them, and I discover, like a tiny flower that insists on blooming in the expanse of a shining level salt flat, the first typographical error.

Yet fiction, like life, is a dirty business; discretion and good taste play small part in it. Hardly a story appears in print without offending or wounding some living model who sees himself or herself reflected all too accurately and yet not accurately enough—without that deepening, mollifying element of endless pardon we bring to our own self. Parents, wives, children—the nearer and dearer they are, the more mercilessly they are served up. So my art, like my religion, has a shabby side. These memoirs feel shabby. Truth should not be forced; it should simply manifest itself, like a woman who has in her privacy reflected and coolly decided to bestow herself upon a certain man. She will *dawn* upon that man. My writing here about my religion feels forced—done at the behest of others, of hypothetical "autobiography" readers. Done, I believe, in an attempt to comfort some younger reader as once I was comforted by Chesterton and Unamuno. A *worthy* attempt, which is not, in a larger sense, good: the attempt to work an altruistic good through print is generally a mistake, a miscarriage. I am in these paragraphs struggling to expose what should be—in decency, to conserve potency—*behind:* behind the façade, the human courtesies, my performance, my "act." But there seems, my having gone this unfortunately far, still this to say: one believes not merely to dismiss from one's life a degrading and immobilizing fear of death but to possess that Archimedean point outside the world from which to move the world. The world cannot provide its own measure and standards; these must come, strangely, from outside, or a sorry hedonism and brute opportunism result—a greedy panicked heart and substance abuse. The world punishes us for taking it too seriously as well as for not taking it seriously enough.

Wherever there is a self, it may be, whether on Earth or in the Andromeda Galaxy, the idea of God will arise. Religion, once the self has taken its hook, preaches selflessness. The self is the focus of anxiety; attention to others, self-forgetfulness, and living like the lilies are urged, to relieve the anxiety. Insomnia offers a paradigm: the mind cannot fall asleep as long as it watches itself. At the first observed lurch into nonsensical thought, we snap awake in eager anticipation, greedy to be asleep. Only when the mind moves unwatched and becomes absorbed in images that tug it as it were to one side does self-consciousness dissolve and sleep with its healing, brilliantly detailed fictions pour in upon the jittery spirit. Falling asleep is a study in trust. Likewise, religion tries to put us at ease in this world. Being human cannot be borne alone. We need other presences. We need soft night noises—a mother speaking downstairs, a grandfather rumbling in response, cars swishing past on Philadelphia Avenue and their headlights wheeling about the room. We need the little clicks and sighs of a sustaining otherness. We need the gods.

The pragmatic undercurrent in this exposition troubles me. I am selling short something or Someone precious. It is not enough, surely, to strive for faith because it makes us more effective and holds off terror until the—as Gibbon said—"bad fifteen minutes at the end." Pragmatic belief becomes cynical belief, a papering-over of the secret conviction that eventual annihilation will harmelssly resolve this strenuous unease of living.[4] Religion and nothingness, that is, are successive doses of anesthetic, the first temporary and imperfect, in throwaway wrappings of dogma and Christmas tinsel, the second permanent and perfect. An age of anxiety all too suitably takes God as a tranquillizer, just as feudal times took Him as Lord or King, leaving us a language of piety loaded with obsolete obeisances, and other eras took him as a magical incantation, or an insatiable repository of blood sacrifice and self-mutilation, or an imperturbable Watchmaker, or a surge of the Life Force. The self's echo and companion must be not only that. One believes not only to comfort one's self but for empirical and compositional reasons—the ornate proposed supernatural completes the picture and, like the ingredient that tops up and rounds out the recipe, gives reality its true flavor. Similarly, in art one has to add a little extra color, some overanimation, to bring the imitation up to the pitch, the bright roundedness, the repletion, of the actual model.

Of my own case, looked at coldly, it might be said that, having been given a Protestant, Lutheran, rather antinomian Christianity as part of my sociological make-up, I was too timid to discard it. My era was too ideologically feeble to wrest it from me, and Christianity gave me something to write about, and a semblance of a backbone, and a place to go Sunday mornings, when the post offices were closed.

---

[4]Can the sweetness of riddance extend to *everything?* Emerson wrote in his journals: "Old age brings along with its ugliness the comfort that you will soon be out of it—which ought to be a substantial relief to such discontented pendulums as we are. To be out of the war, out of debt, out of the drouth, out of the blues, out of the dentist's hands, out of the second thoughts, mortifications, and remorses that inflict such twinges and shooting pains—out of the next winter, and the high prices, and company below your ambition—surely these are soothing hints. And, harbinger of this, what an alleviator is sleep, which muzzles all these dogs for me every day?"

40   What I have written here strains to be true but nevertheless is not true *enough*. Truth is anecdotes, narrative, the snug opaque quotidian.

    Pennsylvania. There. Here. Staying in my mother's farmhouse. Yet again. I cannot count the times I have gone back over these years since 1950—by train from Harvard, by car from New York and New England, and now most commonly by airplane, often on the way back from somewhere else.
    My mother is old, she has not been well. This summer she fell in the kitchen, and the fall hurt her back and abdomen and has taken something out of her. She has taken to her bed, and says it is too painful to get up and walk around.
    I don't know quite what to do about her. "She lives *alone?*" people ask me, with round eyes and an implication of filial neglect. In this conservative region family members tend to stick close to one another. Four generations of Mennonites live all together on the neighboring farm. I am waiting for her to tell me what to do about her. I find that the older she becomes, the more my image of her is of someone young: the young mother in the Shillington back yard with the fireflies and flowering cherry trees, the tall laughing college girl posing with my father in his football sweater, and even the little girl raised on this farm with a batch of complaining and ailing old people. She taught herself from books to name the birds and flowers, setting out a little wildflower garden under a black birch tree that, grown thick and lopsided, is still there, though now only weeds grow beneath it—weeds and wild raspberries and a few scraggly Japanese lanterns brought from the Shillington yard forty years ago. When she was very small, my mother once settled herself in a basket of clean wash in imitation of a nesting robin, and was scolded by her mother for it. An only child like me, she made her paradise, her escape hatch, out of the nature around her, leaving no living thing on her father's farm unnamed, much as I, once, could identify all the cartoonists in *Collier's* upside down. Her diary, kept sporadically over the years, takes note of the weather and the songs of the birds, returning year after year, as they sound in the woods to the west, through whose branches the red sun sets. During these more than a dozen years since my father died, her voice over the telephone has always sounded young—quick and playful and interested in life, in the reality modulated by our "vocabulary," by our "gay-making" slant on the world. I am alarmed and depressed by what seems her withdrawal from the world—she stopped, after her fall, cooking, driving, watching television, writing, reading, and eating. All she manages to do is feed the dog and the cats and talk on the telephone

to her well-wishers and to the numerous charity fund-raisers who call up relentlessly from Reading, asking an annual renewal of her little widow's mite of ten or fifteen dollars. There is no end of giving.

Her will to live, anciently involved with mine, has been slowly reviving this autumn. Tonight she let herself be driven out to dinner with some friends from Lancaster. Now we have returned, adjusted the dog and the thermostat, and gone to bed. Our bedrooms have between them a wall and door so thin we can hear each other breathe. My wife wonders how five of us once managed in this little house, all sleeping in this same upstairs, and all I can say is that at the time, to the child I was, it seemed big enough. My parents and grandparents each had a room and I slept in a bed in a space that served also as a kind of hall at the head of the stairs. There were voices, true—coughs and sighs and snoring, bedsprings creaking and the sound of my father patting my mother and making a humorous woo-woo noise that signified affection; but when one is young space curls up tight inside the blankets and it is not so hard to fall asleep through the hole that opens at the bottom of one's brain.

45   Now, it is harder. I am old, though not as old as my mother. It was not easy for me to drive her back from the restaurant, through an unseasonable sleet storm, early in this November. The wipers struggled against the freezing rain, the headlights coming at us were smeared and magnified, and she had been fearful that I was going to hit a deer, because deer did now and then cross this dark highway. Without saying so, I found her repeated concern rather sentimental and hysterical, especially since the deer would be slaughtered in hunting season less than a month away. Now the sleet patters on the windows and makes a crinkling sound in the fireplace, as the individual pellets tumble through, into the room. It would be cozy if the bed were not so cold, unwarmed by a woman. My wife stays away, as a gift, she says, to my mother. The room has two windows, a low ceiling, this never-used fireplace, and wallpaper, patterned with rosettes and little pink roses, that hasn't changed since I can remember. Even the decorative changes are slow: an uncompleted oil painting I did of my first wife was retired to a drawer around the time of our divorce, and more recently a felt piece of local kitsch I always disliked has been taken down. It showed an Amishman standing erect with a hammer and a carpenter's square, above the slogan WHAT A MAN DOES, THAT HE IS. I believe it but didn't like reading it. My suitcase is spread open across two straight chairs, and a Harvard yearbook and an early Peter Arno cartoon anthology sit on a bedside table; these books never change, and in the table's drawer are pencils so old their erasers don't erase and even the graphite has gone waxy and refuses to write. Time moves slowly here but does

move, and is overtaking my mother. Which visit will be my last? We do not know, or speculate. I can hear her breathe, with the loudness that signifies sleep.

The drive home from the restaurant, the unseasonable sleet, and my entire life all rankle in me. I have come here from some Midwestern university where I read and talked into a microphone and was gracious to the local rich, the English faculty and college president, and the students with their clear skins and shining eyes and inviting innocence, like a blank surface one wishes to scribble obscenities on. I need these excursions, evidently: they reassure me that I don't stutter, or stutter too much. They leave me feeling dirty and disturbed, as though I have wasted this time away from my desk, posing as an author instead of being one, and it is hard to get back from the academic unreality and ponderous flattery into my own skin. These leftover feelings are complicated by the sensations of enchantment and claustrophobia that occupy me now in this little overfamiliar room, surrounded by musty memories and the whisper of sleet and the sounds of my mother and the dog sleeping. My light is on and I feel this as a discordant note in the countryside; Plowville, once so empty that not another houselight could be seen from our house, is being invaded by developments. The farms are being broken up into two-acre lots. The thousands of acres between here and Morgantown once owned by Bethlehem Steel, and kept as forest against the potential exploitation of their low-grade iron ore, have been sold to a Chester County developer who has visions of golf courses and amusement parks and incinerators that will turn all of Philadelphia's trash into smoke. A raw new development begins on the other side of my mother's meadow, which she has not been able to mow this fall, since her injuries prevent her from getting up on the tractor. I can see its lights through my window, whose sash rattles. By my bedside light I am reading a book for review: book-reviewing is another superfluous chore that I do, like the public readings, for the money and for the easy exposure of it, the showing-off, the quick certification from a world that I fear is not hearing me, is not *understanding* me, like Eddie Pritchard long ago. And tomorrow (or is it the next day?) I must drive to Trenton, to research the fifth chapter of this exposition of my self-consciousness.

I rub my face. My forehead, full of actinic damage from all those years of seeking the healing sun, hurts. My public, marketable self—the self put on display in interviews and slightly "off" caricatures in provincial book-review sections, the book-autographing, anxious-to-please me—feels like another skin and hurts also. I look over at my younger self on the wall: a photograph taken in Earl Snyder's studio on Penn Street when I was five, wearing a kind of sailor collar, the edges blurred away—"vignetted"—in old-fashioned studio style, an image cherished by my mother, nicely framed the work-manlike way they do things in Reading, and always hanging here, in this spot, for me to admire and remember: little Johnny, his tentatively smiling mouth, his dark and ardent and hopeful eyes. For a second he looks evil. He has got me into this.

In this room, with its cold clammy bed and cobwebbed corners and sandstone fireplace hearth, I have often on these visits had asthma, so that I slept only a few hours and woke with a pulse racing from repeated use of isoproterenol. But my asthma, like my stuttering, seems to be less a factor, as the actualities of aging overtake me, and the shadows lengthen around my walk in the sun. Earlier today, we had driven into Shillington, so my mother could visit her doctor. The doctor's office, as it happens, is next to the movie theatre where, seven years before, *Being There* had been playing while I waited for my lost luggage. Now the daughter whose failure adequately to tip the porter at Logan perhaps delayed the luggage is the mother of my two grandsons. Now the theatre, the last trace of Mr. Shverha's legacy of fantasy to this small town, is closed; to see a movie in Berks County now, one must go to a shopping mall. The marquee bears the unchanging advertisement GRACE FELLOW-SHIP; the building has become a church. Across Lancaster Avenue, the big orange brick duplex, with its aura of downtown power, that had held Stephens' Luncheonette and the post office and Carl Leh at the back are now Admixtures, Inc., and, next door to it, the taller, older, graver building where Fred Grimes had counted money and where Ernie Rothermel had first sat me in his chair have been joined by a new, unharmonious structure in what had always been a vacant lot or generous side yard. My mother's doctor's office is in another new building, on a site where, when I was a child, travelling fairs would set up their rides and stalls. One of the few times I ever sat in a saddle was on this land, at such a fair; I was small and seemed appallingly high up, on a huge, warm, smelly, rough-haired, nervous thing, though the animal was a mere pony, led by a boy not much older than I.

After the visit to the doctor, my mother and I had driven down Lancaster Avenue to the area of the Poorhouse Lane, now a shopping mall one of whose attractions was a medical center where she could have her blood drawn for some tests. Her young doctor seemed determined to keep her alive. As her arm, its dry skin extra loose from her weight loss since her fall, was pierced, she engaged in one of her flirtatious, slightly baffling exchanges with the nurse; how like, it now seemed, my father she was, spontaneously grappling with strangers, aggressively seeking contact in inappropriate places. In my embarrassment I wandered off and pondered the marvellous devices offered in this medical center for the use and easement of old age—canes and braces and pans and wheelchairs, and toilet seats thickened like a club-foot's shoe, and long canelike pincers to retrieve what can no longer be bent over for: a veritable armory as complex as a medieval knight's, our Grail now simply the indefinite prolongation of life.

50   And then in this medical center, astoundingly, a miracle of sorts had occurred. In came a living relic of my Shillington boyhood—Reverend Rhoads, who had been, with Reverend Kroninger, one of the two pillars of the local Protestant clergy, the pastor of the Reformed Church up New Holland Avenue, a frequent and orotund speaker at high-school assemblies and civic observances. He had been a short owlish man with wobbly jowls and a strong voice. Under the impact of old age his face had as it were exploded into separate elements—plump cheeks, button nose, mottled forehead, thick throat wattles—but his voice was still vibrant and his eyes alert behind their bifocals; and his wife in all these years that had flowed by since I had left Shillington had turned white-haired but remained handsome and even frisky, with good trim ankles and a dazzling broad smile. She told me she remembered watching my mother carry me up New Holland Avenue. Did she mean carrying me in her arms, or carrying me in her womb? I tried to picture my mother, a young woman walking about Shillington at the outset of the Depression, her husband still off with the phone company, the auto-mobiles in the street dark and boxy, the porches and brick house-fronts of Shillington much then as they are now, and New Holland Avenue then as now slanting up to the cemetery and the tree-lined lane that led to Cedar Top past the Dives Estate. In this remoteness of time I had been somehow present, and the Rhoadses, and my mother, and here we all still were, standing in a geriatric emporium where once there had been a cornfield you could see from the trolley car, part of the poor farm. Our bodies since that earlier conjunction had been considerably worked upon by time—mine enlarged and strengthened, theirs somewhat shrunken and enfeebled, but *here* was what we were, quite animated in our ten minutes of pleasantries.

        The Rhoadses' son, Bobby, had been two grades ahead of me in school and often stood with me in the Shillington playground roof-ball line. Indeed, a photograph of such a line exists. Bobby had in-herited his father's position as the town's Reformed minister, in a new church built on a street that hadn't existed until the 1950s. My having moved away, first eleven miles and then hundreds, made the Shillington of my boyhood seem more remote than it really was—a mere fraction of a lifetime away, a ship sinking so slowly that many survivors still had their heads above water. Karl Barth, another Reformed clergyman, responding in an interview late in his life to a question about the afterlife, said he imagined it as somehow *this life* in review, viewed in a new light. I had not been as comforted as I wanted to be. For is it not the *singularity* of life that terrifies us? Is not the decisive difference between comedy and tragedy that tragedy denies us another chance? Shakespeare over and over demonstrates life's singularity—the irrevocability of our decisions, hasty and even mad though they be. How solemn and huge and deeply pathetic our life does loom in its once-and-doneness, how inexorably linear, even though our rotating, revolving planet offers us the cycles of the day and of the year to suggest that existence is intrinsically cyclical, a playful spin, and that there will always be, tomorrow morning or the next, another chance.

I hear my mother turn and breathe in her bed. The sleet sprinkles in the fireplace and a mouse scrabbles behind the baseboard beneath the table and the picture of me as a pretty child. My mother knows this mouse; she has told me that in the darkest of her post-fall, bedridden days, he used to come into her bedroom and, standing right there on the floor beside the baseboard, would vigorously make noises, trying to tell her something. His attempt to offer advice amuses her in the telling and she does not yet have the heart, nor perhaps the muscular strength, to set a trap for him.

So here I lie in this damp old Pennsylvania farmhouse listening to an animated mouse. My first artistic love and inspiration was Mickey Mouse—his piping voice, his yellow shoes, his nimble skill on any sort of musical instrument, his patience with Goofy and his courage against Peg Leg Pete, and the way his face would come bursting into Mr. Shverha's movie theatre, radiating golden beams to the edges of the screen—and I have taken that jubilant commercial inspiration further than most of my fellow Shillingtonians would have predicted. But perhaps with an undue effort, with an attenuated result. My life behind me feels rickety. My sleeping mother and I seem to be out on a precarious, swaying limb. The house rustles and sighs. I feel up in the air, scared. In our chance encounter, the Rhoadses told me how much I resembled my mother, and I felt slightly offended, as though a dirty secret were being advertised. Standing there in the bright medical center I was aware of the little flecks of psoriasis at the edge of my mother's white hair, and in the wings of her nostrils, and of all the spots of actinic damage mottling her skin, which had once been as smooth and fair as the boy's in the picture. My mother was my future, as well as my past.

Now the dog heaves in its sleep, woofing at some dream-prey, its claws scratching on the soft old pine floorboards. Sleep will not come for me. The house is too noisy, the bed clammy as though I am already dead. I cannot escape myself. The sleet, the fear that we will hit a deer keep revolving in me. My brain buzzes with selfish, scared thoughts. We fall asleep in selflessness, when our thoughts turn self-forgetful. Masturbation and prayer both attempt this; I feel too old for either. I feel forsaken, lost. But when I am not looking, perhaps when I am thinking of the dog's dreams or of the old roof-ball line at the playground, sleep does come. I awake in light, feeling as if my soul has a slight sore throat, my membranes still chafed by the fear of earthly existence. I hear my mother and the dog talking downstairs. She is recovered enough now from her fall to get out of bed in the morning and go downstairs and make breakfast. She has turned on television, which rumbles with the barely suppressible urgency of a new day begun, in Philadelphia and nationally. The morning light gives the pale wallpaper a deep exciting sheen, a subtle luminosity from beneath the surface.

55   It has snowed during the night; through the window, as I rise to dress and shave, I see an inch or two of snow on the still-green lawn, and on the boughs of the pine tree holding the bird feeder. In this low-ceilinged room the light is antique, preserved from the Philadelphia Avenue house, my first tender winters in it, with their evergreen secret of Christmas. The light holds my first inklings of celebration, of reindeer tracks on the roof, of an embowering wide world arranged for my mystification and entertainment. It has the eggshell tint, the chilly thrilling taste, of my self.

For all the physical handicaps, neurotic symptoms, aberrant thought patterns, and characterological limitations touched upon in these pages, I think of myself, and believe that I "present" (as psychoanalysts say) to others, as an amiable, reasonable, interested, generally healthy, sexually normal, dependable, hopeful, fortunate human being. Which goes to show what a vexed thing even a fortunate human being is.

Surprisingly few clues are ever offered us as to what kind of people we are. Carleton Boyer said I had an excellent compositional sense. Ernie Rothermel said I had exceptionally large nerves, which gave a certain stylishness to my sufferings in his chair. Peggy Lutz once told me I had nice shoulders (maybe it was the only nice thing she could think to say). A woman seated behind me in the bleachers at a football game accidentally touched the hair on my head and exclaimed, "*Oh*—so soft!" At Harvard, playing the associational word game called "Botticelli," I was, unknown to me, the subject, and in asking for an identifying animal was told, by Manfred Karnovsky, who as a professor of biology would certainly have known, "A sloth—please don't misunderstand me—a nice, good-tempered sloth." The modifier "good-tempered" came up again when my second wife, in my startled hearing, told the producer of a TV show focused on me that I was the best-tempered person she had ever known. If I am good-tempered, it must be the daily venting of words that makes me so, because as a child I often felt irate and frantic, and have fought all my life sensations of being smothered and confined, misunderstood and put-upon.

We assume that only children are spoiled and pampered; but they also are made to share adult perspectives. Possibly the household that nurtured me was a distracted and needy one—in severe Depression-shock—which asked me to grow up too early; at some point I acquired an almost unnatural willingness to make allowances for other people, a kind of ready comprehension and forgiveness that amounts to disdain, a good temper won by an inner remove. If I'm nice and good, you'll leave me alone to read my comic books. Have I ever loved a human being as purely as I loved Mickey Mouse or, a bit later in latency, Captain Marvel and Plastic Man?

Even toward myself, as my own life's careful manager and promoter, I feel a touch of disdain. Precociously conscious of the precious, inexplicable burden of selfhood, I have steered my unique little craft carefully, at the same time doubting that carefulness is the most sublime virtue. He that gains his life shall lose it.

In this interim of gaining and losing, it clears the air to disbelieve in death and to believe that the world was created to be praised. But I inherited a skeptical temperament. My father believed in science ("Water is the great solvent") and my mother in nature. She looked and still looks to the plants and the animals for orientation, and I have absorbed the belief that when in doubt we should behave, if not like monkeys, like "savages"—that our instincts and appetites are better guides, for a healthy life, than the advice of other human beings. People are fun, but not quite serious or trustworthy in the way that nature is. We feel safe, huddled within human institutions—churches, banks, madrigal groups—but these concoctions melt away at the basic moments. The self's responsibility, then, is to achieve rapport if not rapture with the giant, cosmic other: to appreciate, let's say, the walk back from the mailbox.

Reflective Reading, Informal Writing

REFLECTING ON THE READING:

- Updike suggests that "the person we were yesterday is dead," but the title of his work is "On Being a Self Forever." In what ways does this appear to be a contradiction? In what ways does it appear to make sense?
- Updike talks about writers, famous people, people he knew as a kid growing up, and people he has met during his adult life. How do the

people he encounters shape the person Updike sees himself to be? How was his "self" affected by these encounters with others?

- Updike's essay moves freely back and forth in time; he talks both about his childhood and his adulthood. What episodes or memories from his childhood seem most important to his sense of who he is as a grown man? What definition of manhood does Updike seem to fashion for himself and how does it relate to the child he recalls?

- It should not be surprising that Updike's sense of himself as a writer should become a large part of this effort at self-definition. Find some of the passages in which he deals with writing. How do his ideas and attitudes about writing relate to his sense of his own identity?

UNDERSTANDING RHETORICAL STRATEGIES:

- On pages 24–25 Updike begins alluding to several passages from the Bible. Why do you think he does this? How does it relate to his discussion about the self or the "I"? Do you think these allusions to Biblical passages are good support or evidence for what he is trying to tell us? Why or why not?

- At certain moments in his essay Updike turns to personal stories to illustrate a point. How many different places in the essay does he do this? What specific points does Updike illustrate with each of these stories? Do these stories contribute to your interest or under-standing, or do they confuse the reader or detract from the essay in some other way? Why? What does he mean when he writes, on page 38, that "What I have written here strains to be true but nevertheless is not true *enough*. Truth is anecdotes, narrative, the snug opaque quotidian."

- Updike was trained in the visual arts. In the very first sentence of his essay, he writes about the specks in his own eyes that he sees when he looks at the sky. How does this image relate to the point or points he goes on to make in the remainder of the essay? Are there other places where he uses visual images to make important points? What does he gain (or lose) by using these images to convey meaning rather than simply "saying what he means" in a more direct fashion?

- What do you notice about the way this essay is organized? Does it march in a linear fashion to establish one overarching point, or the-sis? Or is it more fragmented, as if Updike were making several dis-tinct runs at the truth? How do you account for this organizational strategy? Does it work?

INFORMAL WRITING:

- Examine and explain, using an experience or experiences of your own, how yesterday's self is dead and yet how you remain a self forever. Or conversely, examine and explain how your experience or experiences contradict this assertion. How does your experience resemble what Updike shares with his readers? How does your experience differ?

- Describe some of the encounters or relationships with others you have had in your life. How have they affected who you are? How has your "self" been influenced by these encounters?
- What definition of manhood or womanhood would you fashion for yourself? What episodes in your life have helped to shape this definition?
- What does it feel like to write about yourself? Is writing about your life like writing "a story, with a pattern and a moral and an inevitability"? An "illusory release"? Is it, like insomnia, a matter of the mind watching itself? To put it another way, to what extent does writing about yourself truly *reveal*? Conceal or misrepresent?

ROBERT COLES

As a pediatrician, child psychiatrist, researcher, and writer Robert Coles utilizes his knowledge of the humanities and literature in his personal, professional, and scholarly life. He received his first degree from Harvard University in 1950 and then earned his M.D. from Columbia University in 1954. He currently works as a research psychiatrist, lecturer in general education, professor of psychiatry and medical humanities, and as a writer of a wide range of articles and books.

His series, *Children in Crisis*, won the Pulitzer Prize and established his reputation as an academic who wrote accessible, engaging, narrative prose that set him apart in a field known for jargon and scientific "objectivity." This series evolved from events Coles witnessed in the South during the first stages of integrating public schools in the early 1960s. The courage and bravery young black children showed in front of the crowds of hostile adults struck Coles profoundly, and he began working with children, listening to them, and narrating their experiences and stories in order to better understand their lives.

While at Harvard, Coles met the celebrated poet/physician, William Carlos Williams. His admiration for Williams led him to earn his medical degree and continue his work in both science and the humanities. Williams taught Coles how to listen to his patients and let them teach him about their ailments. Later, Coles worked in the Catholic Worker Hospitality House that Dorothy Day organized. Day became an important figure in Coles' personal, religious, and spiritual life.

Probably the most notable mentors Coles has learned from, however, are the children he observes and researches. These children taught him how to move away from the "uptight and austere" world of science and medicine and notions of what a doctor "ought" to be to the less confining world of children. Coles would sit in their midst and let the children teach him and give him a kind of language for understanding their world.

Currently, in his teaching, Coles uses literature as stories of "moral moments" conveyed through language. These stories make sense and meaning out of life for the reader and writer just as the stories of the doctor and patient do for each other. In this essay, from *Privileged Ones* (volume V of *Children in Crisis*, published in 1977), Coles defines "entitlement" and tells a variety of stories illustrating how children become aware of their entitlements—what they believe they are entitled to and what their future holds in store for them. Coles writes that children become increasingly conscious of what belongs to whom when they are two or three years old. As you read this essay, consider what you are entitled to and when this feeling of what belongs to whom began in your own life. How does it relate to or differ from the sense of entitlement of the children represented here?

Entitlement

The poor both are and are not alike. On the one hand they struggle against the same odds—hunger and malnutrition in the worst instances, or a marginal life that poses constant threats. Yet Eskimos do not regard their poverty in the same way that Appalachian yeomen do, or Chicanos in Texas or southern California. In the four volumes that have preceded this one[1] I have tried to show how the common social economic vulnerability of the poor does not make for a uniform pattern of child-rearing. Historical precedents, cultural experiences, religious convictions exert their influence on parents and children, make boys and girls differ in all sorts of respects, depending on where they live and who their parents are. The same holds for the well-to-do or the rich. It won't do to talk of *the* affluent ones in America (never mind the world!). It won't do to say that in our upper-middle-class suburbs, or among our wealthy, one observes clearcut, consistent psychological or cultural characteristics. Even in relatively homogeneous suburbs, there are substantial differences in home life, in values taught, hobbies encouraged, beliefs advocated or virtually instilled.

But there are indeed distinct groups among the well-off—equivalent in their way to the various kinds of poor people. It is the obligation of someone who wants to know how children make sense of their lives—agricultural migrancy, Indian reservation life in the Southwest, the upper-income life of large homes amid ample acreage in rich towns or in wealthy urban enclaves—to document as faithfully as possible the way the common heritage of money and power affects the assumptions of individual boys and girls. Each child, however, is also influenced by certain social, racial, cultural, or religious traditions, or thoroughly idiosyncratic ones—a given *family's* tastes, sentiments, ideals, say. The issue is "class"; but the issue is not only "class."

Many of the influences, even some of the more idiosyncratic ones, that distinguish some children from others are themselves subject to side influences—a "rebound effect," one rather prosperous Illinois Mormon called it. He was anxious for me to know (just as he could not forget) that there was only so much his faith could resist. He took pains, constantly, to tell his children that he was not like his father; that he was not like his brother either, who lives in Salt Lake City and works for a bank. To live near Chicago and be a

---

[1]Coles is referring to the first four volumes of the series, *Children of Crisis: A Study of Courage and Fear; Migrants, Sharecroppers, Mountaineers; The South Goes North,* and *Eskimos, Chicanos, Indians.*

doctor, to be a Mormon living in a highly secular upper-middle-class world, was to be an exile. He felt stronger in his faith, but also weaker; he felt like his neighbors in many ways, but unlike them in critically important preferences and articles of faith.

What binds together a Mormon banker in Utah with his brother, or other coreligionists in Illinois or Massachusetts? What distinguishes such people, one from the other? Old New Orleans upper-class families are not in certain respects like families who live in, say, Wellesley Hills, Massachusetts, or Haverford, Pennsylvania, or up the hills outside San Antonio. There *are* resemblances, based on class, occupation, religion, common experiences, expectations, ideas conveyed to children. And yet, again, there are distinctions, shades of feeling and thinking, emphases of one sort or another—even within those families and well-to-do neighborhoods.

5   I use the word "entitlement" to describe what, perhaps, all quite well-off American families transmit to their children—an important psychological common denominator, I believe: an emotional expression, really, of those familiar, class-bound prerogatives, money and power. The word was given to me, amid much soul-searching, by the rather rich parents of a child I began to talk with almost two decades ago, in 1959. I have watched those parents become grandparents, seen what they described as "the responsibilities of entitlement" get handed down to a new generation. When the father, a lawyer and stockbroker from a prominent and quietly influential family, referred to the "entitlement" his children were growing up with, he had in mind a social rather than a psychological phenomenon: the various juries or committees that select the Mardi Gras participants in New Orleans's annual parade and celebration. He knew that his daughter was "entitled" to be invited here, to attend a dance there, to feel part of a carefully limited and sometimes self-important social scene.

He wanted, however, to go beyond that social fact; he wanted his children to feel obligated by how fortunate they were, and would no doubt always be, all things being equal—or unequal! He talked about what he had received from his parents and what he would give to his children, "automatically, without any thought," and what they too would pass on. The father was careful to distinguish between the social entitlement and "something else," a "something else" he couldn't quite define but knew he had to try to evoke if he were to be psychologically candid: "Our children have a good life ahead of them; and I think they know it now. I think they did when they were three or four, too. It's *entitlement*, that's what I call it. My wife didn't know what I was talking about when I first used the word. She thought it had something to do with our ancestry! Maybe it does! I don't mean to be snide. I just think our children grow up taking a lot for granted, and it can be good that they do, and it can be bad. It's like anything else, it all depends. I mean, you can have spoiled brats for children, or you can have kids who want to share what they have. I don't mean give away all their money! I mean be responsible, and try to live up to their ideals, and not just sit around wondering which island in the Caribbean to visit this year, and where to go next summer to get away from the heat and humidity here in New Orleans."

At the time he said no more. It was 1960, and I was interested mainly in what his son and his daughter thought about black children—and about the violence then being inflicted on a few black children brave enough and stubborn enough to walk past the mobs into two elementary schools. But as months became years, I came back to that word "entitlement," especially because it was one I had heard years earlier, in Boston, when I was receiving my training in child psychiatry. "Narcissistic entitlement" was the phrase I had been taught to be familiar with, to use occasionally when speaking of a particular kind of "disturbed" child. The term could be used in place of more conventional, blunter ones that everyone else uses from time to time: a smug, self-satisfied child; or a child who thinks he (or she) owns the world, or will one day; or a self-centered child who expects a lot from just about everyone.

I recall a boy of eight I was treating in Boston, before I went South; my supervisor, a child psychoanalyst who had worked with a similar child for three years, and anticipated, alas, another year or two, at least, of thrice weekly office visits, told me that I was being naïvely hopeful, and a touch simpleminded, when I remarked upon the curiosity of the boy, his evident willingness to ask me questions about all sorts of persons, places, things—and so his capacity for engagement with the world around him. Yes, she pointed out, there was indeed a measure of that, but it was best that *we* ask questions about the nature of *his* questions. As we did, they all came back to him—to quite specific experiences he had gone through and wanted to talk about. And he had told me that, actually; he never asked a question out of intellectual interest—rather, in his words, "because I like to know what might happen next to me."

It is hard to describe the special fearfulness and sadness such a child struggles with. He was not the "ordinary" child; he was quite troubled. And I suppose the parents of such children (even if those mothers and fathers have other, relatively solid children, psychologically speaking) must be disqualified as "normal" or "average." They may be like anyone else on the street; may be rather knowing, psychiatrically—able to sense something "wrong" with a child's "behavior" and go do something about it by seeking out a doctor. But the analyst-supervisor I was myself "seeing" once a week was convinced that there was a "special narcissism," she called it, that a certain kind of parent offers a child: "Narcissism is something we all struggle with; but some people have more of it than others, and some children come from homes that have so much that all the money and possessions, all the rugs and furniture and toys and vacations and savings accounts and insurance policies come crashing on the child's head. There is a shift from narcissism to narcissistic entitlement."

10   I wasn't sure exactly what she meant, or how the "shift" she had mentioned did indeed take place. I know, because she is someone I still discuss psychoanalytic theory with, that she was not sure herself what the exact dimensions were of that childhood journey. But she knew even then, before there were "fields" like "social psychiatry" or "community psychiatry," that at some point a family's psychology and psychopathology engage with its social and economic life; and that when a migrant child or a ghetto child has to contend with narcissism, it will take on a certain flavor (narcissistic despair, for instance); whereas for a child who lives in a big house and whose parents have a lot and want to give a lot to their offspring, "narcissistic entitlement" may well be a possibility. The child withdraws not only into himself or herself but, by extension, into a certain world of objects, habits and rituals—the comfortable world of room, a home, a way of life. The child has much, but wants and expects more—only to feel no great gratitude, but a desire for yet more: an inheritance the world is expected to provide. One's parents will oblige, as intermediaries. And if underneath there lie apprehension and gloom and, not least, a strain of gnawing worthlessness, that is of no matter to many children whose "narcissistic entitlement" becomes what psychoanalytic theorists refer to as a "character trait," rather than a "symptom" that prompts a visit to a doctor. That is, the child is regarded by everyone, psychiatrists included, as "normal," as "all right," or different, but not all *that* different. One doesn't send every cocksure, greedy, self-centered child to a child psychiatrist.

In many other well-to-do homes I've visited, parents who have known in their bones what child psychiatrists think and wonder as they talk with their children. Will a certain child get too much—so much that he or she runs the danger of turning away from life, forsaking people for a life of passionate involvement with objects? Less ominously, might a mild tendency in that direction become especially evident when things get tough, psychologically, for one reason or another? Will the child be willing to reach for people, and get along with them, but always with certain limits on the involvement? Often when children are four, five, and six, parents who have felt able to offer them virtually anything begin to pull back, in concern if not outright horror. A son not only has become increasingly demanding or petulant; even when he is quiet he seems to be sitting on a throne of sorts—expecting things to happen, wondering with annoyance why they don't, reassuring himself that they will, or, if they haven't, shrugging his shoulders and waiting for the next event.

It was just such an impasse—not dramatic, but quite definite and worrisome—that prompted that New Orleans father to use the word "entitlement." He had himself been born to wealth, as will future generations of his family be, unless the American economic system changes drastically. But he was worried about what a lot of money can do to a person's "personality"; he uses that word as a layman, but he knows exactly what he has in mind. It isn't so much a matter of spoiling or indulging children; he is willing to let that happen, "within limits." But he knew precisely what those limits were: when the child begins to let his or her situation, the life that he or she lives, "go to the head." It is then that children begin "to act as if they have royal blood in them." And conservative though he is, for him each generation has to prove itself—not necessarily by finding new worlds to conquer or by becoming extraordinarily successful. He has wanted his children to show an interest in the world, to reach out and touch others, to develop their own initiatives, however circumscribed, undramatic, and conventional. It is those kinds of initiative he naturally finds appealing. He is rather satisfied with the life he was born to. He finds each day to be pleasant, interesting, and by his lights, quite useful. He has, however, worried at times that his children were taking *too* much for granted. When his young daughter, during a Mardi Gras season, kept *assuming* she would one day receive this honor and that honor—indeed, become a Mardi Gras queen—he realized that his notion of "entitlement" was not quite hers. *Noblesse oblige* requires a gesture toward others. Had a parent sensed the danger of what my supervisor referred to as a "shift" from "entitlement" to "narcissistic entitlement"?

He would not be the only parent to express such a concern to me in the course of my work. In homes where mothers and fathers profess no explicit reformist persuasions (to say the least!) they nevertheless worry about what happens to children who grow up surrounded by just about everything they want, virtually, on demand. And if much of the apprehension is conventional—that the child will become "spoiled"—there is an element of uneasiness that runs deeper. The parents may begin to regard spoiled behavior as but a symptom: "I don't mind if my children become a little spoiled. That's bound to happen. I worry that they will think that everything is coming to them; that they will grow up with the idea that if they're frustrated, or if they want something, then all they have to do is say a few words, and they'll have what they asked for. When they're like that, they've gone from spoiled to spoiled rotten—and beyond, to some state I don't even know how to describe."

When children are two and three they become increasingly conscious of what belongs to whom. They also become, usually, more and more willing and able to leave themselves behind, so to speak—reach out for objects as well as individuals. They develop their first friends, their first interests or regular and cherished activities. They learn too, most of them, a variety of restraints and frustrations. They must gain control of their bodies, manage without diapers, remember to empty their bladders before going to bed, and get up at night and do likewise in the bathroom rather than on the sheet and mattress. They must learn not to touch hot stoves; not to leave refrigerator doors open; not to spill things, break things, step on things; not to intrude on what belongs to others; not to confuse their prerogatives or possessions with the rights and property of parents, brothers and sisters, friends. At three and four, children from homes like those in new Orleans's Garden District have often started nursery school, have also started making visits to other homes or receiving visitors at their own homes. There are toys to share, games to play, a sandbox or a lawn or indeed a swimming pool or a paddock with its animals. All children have to struggle with themselves for the strength to offer as well as take, or to yield with tact and even a touch of gratitude what has been loaned rather than made an outright gift.

15   But for some children, a relative handful of the world's, such obligations and struggles are muted. Obviously it is possible for parents to have a lot of money yet avoid bringing up their children in such a way that they feel like members of a royal family. Yet even parents determined not to spoil their children often recognize what might be called the existential (as opposed to strictly psychological) aspects of their situation, and that of their children. A father may begin rather early on lecturing his children about the meaning of money; a mother may do her share by saying no, even when yes is so easy to say—but the child may well sense eventually what the parents know quite well: the difference between a voluntary posture and an utterly necessary one.

Such a child, by the age of five or six, has very definite notions of what is possible, even if not always permitted; possible because there is plenty of money that can be spent. That child, in conversation and without embarrassment or the kind of reticence and secretiveness that comes later, may reveal a substantial knowledge of economic affairs. A six-year-old girl in New Orleans knew that she would at twenty-one inherit a half a million dollars. She also knew that her father "only" gave her twenty-five cents as week—whereas some friends of hers received as much as a dollar. She was vexed;

she asked her parents why they were so "strict." One friend had even used the word "stingy" for the parents. The father, in a matter-of-fact way, pointed out to the daughter that she did, after all, get "anything she really wants." Why, then, the need for an extravagant allowance? The girl was won over, told her friends thereafter that it was no matter to her whether she even received an allowance; the important point was the future and what it had to offer. The friends then checked back with their parents, who were rather alarmed—that such young children were talking so freely and openly about family financial matters.

As a result the girl learned from her friends that she had disclosed what ought to be kept firmly under wraps. She decided on the basis of such declarations that her friends may well be "comfortable," but they are not as rich as her parents are or as she will one day be. They in turn explained to her that she had gone beyond the bounds of available evidence. The friends may simply have been told to keep quiet about their family's monetary status—a good idea, the girl was reminded by her parents. The girl agreed, but was not really prepared at the time to follow such advice. She had heard her parents talk with *their* parents about money matters and had been told that it is best that she, too, gradually understand what her financial situation is and will be. That being the case, she wondered out loud why it wasn't appropriate for her to share what she had learned about her future prospects with those she considered good friends. Her parents could only repeat their conviction that certain matters are quite definitely and properly kept within the confines of the family.

Such conversations between young children and their parents help consolidate in boys and girls a conviction of present and future affluence. It obviously never occurs to these children that they won't have food at some point in the near or distant future. Nor do they ever really lack for anything. There are differences in amount, and lectures and sermons may accompany parental acts of generosity. But admonitions don't modify the quite shrewd appraisal children make of what they are heir to, and don't at all diminish the sense of entitlement.

In an Appalachian mine-owner's home, for instance, a boy of seven made the following comment in 1963, after his father's mine had suffered an explosion, killing two men and injuring seriously nine others: "I heard my mother saying she felt sorry for the families of the miners. I feel sorry for them, too. I hope the men who got hurt get better. I'm sure they will. My father has called in doctors from Lexington. He wants the best doctors in all Kentucky for those miners. Daddy says it was the miners' fault; they get careless, and the next thing you know, there's an explosion. It's too bad. I guess there are a lot of kids who are praying hard for their fathers. I wish God was nice to everyone. He's been very good to us. My Daddy says it's been hard work, running the mine and another one he has. It's just as hard to run a mine as it is to go down and dig the coal! I'm glad my father is the owner, though. I wouldn't want him to get killed or hurt bad down there, way underground. Daddy has given us a good life. We have a lot of fun coming up, he says, in the next few years. We're going on some trips. Daddy deserves his vacations. He says he's happy because he can keep us happy, and he does. If we want something really bad, we go tell him or Mum, and they oblige us almost all the time. That's what Daddy always says—and he's glad to oblige my sister and me!"

20   The father is not *always* "glad to oblige"; he can be quite stern at times, but the children have learned that his lectures have only a limited applicability to their life. Yes, there are restraints; not every request for money or a present is granted forthwith. On the other hand, their life is sufficiently comfortable to belie the parents' insistence on caution, lest there be nothing left. In fact, the lectures only seem to reinforce in the children a certain materialistic preoccupation. Having been told to make do with what they already have in such abundance, the boy and girl (and their counterparts in the homes I have visited in other parts of the United States) retreat to their respective rooms, get out their possessions, and begin to use them as well as simply gaze at them. The boy can be quite pointed and expressive about what he has—and is doing with what he has—at such moments: "I have my soldiers, and my trucks, and the tanks and the helicopters. I get them lined up. I build a fort. I have the blocks and the logs, and I make the fort strong. I have my helicopter pad. I make sure the pad is protected by tanks and some men with machine guns. Some terrorists might come and try to attack, and destroy the pad and the helicopter. It's best to keep a few planes in the air, to scout. You have to keep your eyes open, or there will be a surprise attack. I surround the fort with men, and I have these bushes and trees, and I put men behind them. And I have some men on horses."

He stops and looks at what he has done. He is rather proud of himself. He has thought at times of working toward a military career, but he knows that he "most likely" will follow in his father's footsteps. There is a profitable coal company to run and his father has told him that, in the boy's words, "coal has a big future now because there's an energy problem." That observation prompts him to worry about his fort. Does *it* have enough energy or might there one day be a shortage? No, he is sure that his fort will be able to manage successfully. There is a large stack of wood set aside in the stockade.

As for the tanks, helicopters, airplanes, they will not lack fuel; there is an oil well nearby. And in the event that should give out, the boy is certain that oil can be flown in or, if necessary, a "secret pipeline" could be built, just in case some disaster should come upon the airfield landing pad.

His sister has on some occasions become provocative, even truculent. She has asked him, after watching him "declare war" on an unseen enemy, why he always wins. He has replied that the answer is quite simple; he has the best army. She will occasionally express her misgivings: there might be, just *might* be, an army that could overcome his army, with its nineteenth-century fort and twentieth-century military hardware. The boy replies with scorn that his sister is being far too literal-minded. Anyway, America has never lost a war, he knows for sure, and he is an American and does not intend to lose one either. Nor has his father, when brought into the argument later, been anything but encouraging. True, Vietnam was "a mess"; but the country was never "really determined" to win—and maybe never should have involved itself in such a struggle, waged in "distant jungles." The sister has by then lost all interest in her younger (by one year) brother's "game."

The boy is not obsessed with the war game, either. He has many other opportunities to play—other games or, more personally, friends to have over, to go visit. When he plays the war game with them, however, there is invariably a battle of wits, a stalemate. The boy and his friend are tireless in the resourcefulness they summon to their encounters. If necessary, they find themselves in possession of atomic bombs, supersonic planes, surprise tunnels, magical weapons of all kinds, secret supply bases, hidden contingents of men. Eventually, they each declare the other "a winner." The boy realizes: "I know there has to be a losing side. My sister is right. You can't win all the time. But she doesn't like to lose, either. She's always saying her guinea pig is the prettiest, and she says she can ride her bike faster than anyone. I hope I'll get a five-speed bike soon; as soon as I'm a little taller, I'll get one. Then you can really go zoom, zoom down the roads. They say that when I'm grown up, we'll be landing on the moon all the time and we'll be landing on the planets—Mars, for sure. This country will do it! Maybe I could be an astronaut for a while, and then come back and help Daddy in his business. He says he may buy a couple more mines, and by the time I'm out of college, there will be a lot to do. He says I should plan to be a lawyer, because it really helps you, if you have a business, to know how to go to court and protect yourself. The unions want to interfere a lot, and Daddy has to fight them. He has to give some ground, but he's the boss, and they can't push too hard or he'll close up his mines. Then they'd all be out of work! And Daddy could hire some other miners. There are a lot of people who would be glad to get a job!"

So it goes: an abundance of energy for his fort and air force base and an abundance of workers for his father's mines. Abundance is his destiny, he has every reason to believe. He may even land on the stars. Certainly he has traveled widely in this country. He associates the seasons with travel, among other events. In winter, for instance, there is a trip South, to one or another Caribbean island. Winters can be long and hard in Appalachia, and a respite is invigorating—and "healthy." The boy watches his father exercise, hears his mother talk about certain foods, and remarks upon something else that has to do with his future: he may well live to be over a century old. Why not?

25   His parents are not health faddists, or unusually self-preoccupied: given exercise, a careful diet, and medical progress, one will do (in the father's words) "right well." As an additional boost to the family's collective health, a sauna has been installed, and the children are entranced with it. They also are preoccupied with their two dogs, and their other animals—the guinea pigs, hamsters, rabbits, chickens. There is always someone in the house, a maid, a handyman. Still, it is sad to say good-bye. Now, if the family owned a plane, the animals could come along on those trips!

The boy doesn't really believe that his father ever will own a Lear jet; yet, at moments he can imagine himself wrong. And he can construct a fantasy: suddenly an announcement, most likely at breakfast, of a "surprise." It is a familiar sequence. The boy has come to associate breakfast with good news. What is ahead for the day? When does a certain vacation start? During one breakfast the father announced that he had a surprise. The children were all ears. So was their mother; she knew of no forthcoming surprise. The father paused, waited for a bit of suspense to build up, then made his announcement: a new car—a red MG, a fast car that takes curves well and seats only two, in which he would take his wife and children for rides, one at a time.

Yet the boy had apparently been hoping for another kind of surprise: "I woke up and it was very funny, I remember that I'd just had this dream. In it I was walking through the woods with Daddy, and all of a sudden there was an open field, and I looked, and I saw a hawk, and it was circling and circling. I like going hunting with Daddy, and I thought we were hunting. But when I looked at him, he didn't have his gun. Then he pointed at the hawk, and it was coming down. It landed ahead of us, and it was real strange—because the hawk turned into an airplane! I couldn't believe it. We went toward the plane, and Daddy said we could get a ride any time we wanted, because it was ours; he'd just bought it. That's when I woke up, I think. I even forgot about the dream until I looked at my fort and the airplanes, and then I remembered the dream, and once I remembered it, I didn't forget it again."

Dreams evoke a social as well as psychological reality. Dreams show what a child can hope for, unashamedly expect. It so happens that among rich children one day's apparently fatuous, excessive fantasy or dream can turn into the next day's actuality. Four years after that boy had dreamed that his father owned a plane, the father got one. The boom of the 1970s in the coal fields made his father even richer. The boy was of course eager to go on flying trips; eager also to learn to fly. The family owned a horse farm by then, near Lexington, Kentucky, and when the boy and girl were not flying, they were riding. The girl learned to jump well, the boy to ride quite fast. At thirteen he dreamed (by day) of becoming an astronaut or of becoming the manager of his father's horse farm or of going to the Air Force Academy and afterward becoming a "supersonic pilot."

He would never become a commercial pilot, however; and his reasons were interesting: "I've gone on a lot of commercial flights, and there are a lot of people on board, and the pilot has to be nice to everyone, and he makes all these announcements about the seat belts, and stuff like that. My dad's pilot was in the air force, and then he flew commercial. He was glad to get out, though. He says you have to be like a waiter; you have to answer complaints from the customers and apologize to them, just because the ride gets bumpy. It's best to work for yourself, or work for another person, if you trust him and like him. If you go commercial, like our pilot says, you're a servant. You can't really speak your mind. I'd like to fly, but I'm worried about going into the air force. Our pilot says it can be fun, or it can be murder, depending on your superior officer. If I got a bad one, I guess I'd just quit. They can't keep you in forever against your will."

30   He has only confidence about the future, no real sense of danger. At times he talks (at thirteen) as if he could simultaneously hold down several jobs. He would run the family horse farm. He would take part in any number of races and hunts. He would also fly his own plane. He would learn how to parachute; he might even become a professional parachutist. He met one at a fair, and found the man not only brave, but "real nice to talk to." In more restrained (realistic?) moments, he forgets the horse farm, forgets the airplanes or just plain air; he talks about law school—the place his father would like him to race to, land upon. When only an eighth-grade student he imagined himself, one day, owning an airplane, flying it back and

forth from law school (at the University of Kentucky) to his father's horse farm, some fifty miles away.

He has never had any patience for lines, for traffic jams, for crowded stores. Many of the children I have worked with are similarly disposed; they do not like large groups of people in public places—in fact, have been taught the distinct value not only of privacy but the quiet that goes with being relatively alone. Some of the children are afraid of those crowds, can't imagine how it would be possible to survive them. Of course, what is strange, unknown, or portrayed as unattractive, uncomfortable, or just to be avoided as a nuisance can for a given child become a source of curiosity, even an event to be experienced at all costs. An eight-year-old girl who lived well outside Boston, even beyond its suburbs, on a farm, wanted desperately to go to the city and see Santa Claus—not because she believed in him, but because she wanted to see "those crowds" she had in fact seen on television. She got her wish, was excited at first, then quite disappointed, and ultimately made rather uncomfortable. She didn't like being jostled, shoved, pushed, and ignored when she protested. She was only too glad when her mother suggested that they had gone through quite enough. Yes, they had, the daughter agreed. Soon they were in a cab, then on a commuter train. The latter was going to be the limit for the girl thereafter; if she would venture into the world, the train would be its microcosm. She would travel by train to Boston, then turn right around and travel back— unless, of course she were going to a restaurant or an art gallery or to her parents' club. In those places one is not overcome by people who shout, and step on the feet of others, and ignore any protests made.

A week after the girl had gone through her Boston "adventure" (as she had called the trip *before* she embarked upon it), each student in her third grade class was asked to draw a picture in some way connected to the Christmas season, and the girl obliged eagerly. She drew Santa Claus standing beside a pile of packages, presents for the many children who stood near him. They blended into one another—a mob scene. Watching them but removed from them was one child, bigger and on a higher level—suspended in space, it seemed, and partially surrounded by a thin but visible line. The girl wrote on the bottom of the drawing "I saw Santa Claus." She made it quite clear what she had intended to portray: "He was standing there, handing out these gifts. They were all the same, I think, and they were plastic squirt guns for the boys and little dolls for the girls. I felt sorry for the kids. I asked my mother why kids wanted to push each other, just to get that junk. My mother said a lot of people just don't know any better. I was going to force my way up to that Santa Claus and tell him to stop being so dumb! My mother said he was probably a drunk, trying to make a few dollars, so he could spend it in a bar nearby that evening! I don't want to be in a store like that again. We went up to a balcony and watched, and then we got out of the place and came home. I told my mother that I didn't care if I ever went to Boston again. I have two friends, and they've never been in Boston, and they don't want to go there, except to ride through on the way to the airport."

She sounds at that moment more aloof, condescending, and downright snobbish than she ordinarily is. She spends some of her time with two or three girls who live on nearby "estates." Those girls don't see each other regularly, and each of them is quite able to be alone—in fact, rather as anxious to be by themselves, do things by themselves, as to be with one another and find things to work on together. Sometimes a day or two goes by with no formal arrangement to play. They meet in school, and that seems to be enough. Each girl has obligations—a horse to groom, a stall to work on. They are quite "self-sufficient," a word they have heard used repeatedly by their parents. Even within one's own social circle there is no point in surrendering to excessive gregariousness!

The girls meet by accident (or unacknowledged design) on various riding trails. On such daily expeditions one learns to be very much alone with one's thoughts. In the beginning they have to do with riding; but eventually they embrace the weather, the landscape, and, almost always, the child's body: "I think of my leg muscles, my hold on the horse. It's funny how you can forget a lot of your muscles until you mount that horse. Once up there you notice your feet and your knees and your hips, and you watch your arms and hands, and you think of your head and back—how straight are you sitting. It's your whole body that's on your mind, like the teacher says. It's a little like that with skiing, and a lot like that with ballet lessons; but for me, riding is when I'm most in touch with my body! And I'm also in touch with the horse's body. We're sort of one!"

35   Once up on the horse, riding, she is (by her own description) in her "own world." She has heard her mother use that expression. The mother is not boasting, or dismissing others who live in other worlds. The mother is describing, as does the child, a state of progressive withdrawal from people and, selectively, the familiar routines or objects of the environment, in favor of a mixture of reverie and disciplined activity. And when the girl, for one reason or another, is unable to ride, she misses not only the sport, but the state of mind that goes with riding.

Her mother is more explicit about what happens; she tells her daughter, at times, that she wants to "leave everything" and go riding. She tells her daughter that when she is on the horse, cantering across the field or trotting down a trail, she has a "feeling" that is "better than being on a plane." She finds that she can put everyone and everything into "perspective." Nothing seems impossible, burdensome, difficult. There are no distractions, nuisances, petty or boring details to attend to. One is not only away from it all, but above it all. And one is closer to one's "self." The mother talks about the "self" and the child does too. "It is strange," the girl comments, "because you forget yourself riding or skiing, but you also remember yourself the way you don't when you're just sitting around watching television or reading or playing in your room."

With none of the other American children I have worked with have I heard such a continuous and strong emphasis put on the "self." In fact, other children rarely if ever think about themselves in the way children of well-to-do and rich parents do—with insistence, regularity, and, not least, out of a learned sense of obligation. These privileged ones are children who live in homes with many mirrors. They have mirrors in their rooms, large mirrors in adjoining bathrooms. When they were three or four they were taught to use them; taught to wash their faces, brush their teeth, comb their hair. Personal appearance matters and becomes a central objective for such children. A boy of eight expresses his rebelliousness by clinging to sloppy clothes, but leaves the house every day for school in a neat and well-fitted uniform. A good number of these children wear them—shirts or sweaters with a school's name and/or insignia on them. Even when the child relaxes, comes home, and changes into "old" clothes, there is an air of decisiveness about the act—and certainly, the issue is one of choice: to wear *this*, or *that*; to look a particular way, in keeping with a particular mood, time of day, event.

The issue also is that of the "self"—its display, its possibilities, its cultivation and development, even the repeated use of the word. A ten-year-old boy who lives in the outermost part of Westchester County made this very clear. I had originally met him because his parents, both lawyers, were active in the civil rights movement. His father, a patrician Yankee, very much endorsed the students who went South in the early 1960s and, nearer to home, worked on behalf of integrated schools up North. His own children, however, attended private schools—a source of anguish to both the father and the son, who do not lend themselves easily to a description that only emphasizes the hypocritical element in their lives.

The boy knew that he also *would* be (as opposed to wanted to be!) a lawyer. He was quick to perceive and acknowledge his situation, and as he did so he brought himself (his "self") right into the discussion: "I don't want to tell other kids what to do. I told my father I should be going to the public schools myself. Then I could say anything. Then I could ask why we don't have black kids with us in school. But you have to try to do what's best for your *own* life, even if you can't speak up for the black people. When I'm growing up, I'll be like my father; I'll help the black people all I can. It's this way: first you build *yourself* up. You learn all you can. Later, you can *give of yourself.* That's what Dad says: you can't help others until you've learned to help *yourself.* It's not that you're being selfish. People say you're selfish, if you're going to a private school and your parents have a lot of money. We had a maid here, and she wasn't right in the head. She lost her temper and told Dad that he's a phony, and he's out for *himself* and no one else, and the same goes for my sister and me. Then she quit. Daddy tried to get her to talk with us, but she wouldn't. She said that's all we ever do—talk, talk. I told Daddy she was contradicting herself; because she told me a few weeks ago that I'm always doing something, and I should sit down and talk with her. But I didn't know what to say to her! I think she got angry with me because I was putting on my skis for cross-country skiing, and she said I had too much, that was my problem. I asked her where the regular skis were, and she said she wouldn't tell me, even if she knew! It's too bad, what happened to her.

40   "I feel sorry for her, though. Like my sister said, it's no fun to be a maid! The poor woman doesn't look very good. She weighs too much. She's only forty, my mother thinks, but she looks as if she's sixty, and is sick. She could take better care of herself. She said my sister and I make big messes in the bathroom. But that's because we *use* the bathroom! And her breath—God, it's terrible. She isn't as clean as she should be. My mother wanted to get her some deodorant, but we were afraid she'd just blow up at us. But she did anyway. So it didn't make any difference! Like my Dad said, it's too bad about her; she didn't know how to take care of herself and now she's thrown away this job, and she told my mother last year that it was the best one she'd ever had, so she's her own worst enemy. I wonder what she'll think when she looks at herself in the mirror and tries to figure out what to do next."

He was no budding egotist. If anything, he was less self-centered, at ten, than many other children of his community or others like it. He was willing to think about, at least, others less fortunate than himself—the maid, and black people in general. True, he would often repeat uncritically his father's words, or a version of them. But he was trying to respond to his father's wishes and beliefs as well as his words. It was impossible for him, no matter how compassionate his nature, to conceive of life as others live it—the maid, and yes, millions of children his age, who don't look in the mirror very often and may not even own one; who don't worry about what is worn, and how one looks, and what is said and how one sounds, and what is done (in the bathroom) and how one smells.

Sometimes minor details of life tell more than larger attitudes spoken and duly recorded by outside observers. A boy's fingernails, for instance; or his sister's skin—in each instance, a reflection of much more. Here is the boy from Westchester County, at eleven, talking about the new pair of scissors he has received from his father: "I like them. I didn't want my mother to clip my fingernails any longer. I'd rather take care of myself! I'll be shaving soon. I look forward to that! I've watched my father a lot. He showed me how to use the scissors and end up with nails that aren't too short and aren't too long. There's a kid in my class, he lets his nails get longer and longer and there's a lot of dirt under them, and you wonder how long they'll get, and then all of a sudden, one day, you notice that they've been cut off. His parents have got a divorce, and they have a maid taking care of him and his kid brother, and she runs the house and there's no one supervising her. You have to tell the help what to do, because if you don't, they forget and they don't live up to your standards, and they're acting as if they were back in their own homes."

So it happens—a boy's developing sense of himself as against a collective, amorphous "them." It is a "sense" that has both sociological psychological dimensions to it. The former are perhaps more painful to spell out but also more readily apparent. The boy has learned that in the ghetto people live who don't use his parents' kind of judgment, and don't, either, have the same personal habits or concerns. The boy's sister has a similar kind of knowledge. At twelve she could be quite pointed: "We've had a couple of maids, and they don't know why I use my mother's Vaseline lotion on my arms and hands—and in winter on my face, too. They say I've got a wonderful complexion; but I don't think they know how to look real carefully at my skin—or their own either. Maybe they don't have the time. But I see them taking a 'break,' and what do they do? They go put on a prize show in the morning or a 'story' in the afternoon. I don't know how they can stand looking at that stuff! I've got a lot of chores. We're not spoiled here! I have to clean out the stalls and brush the horses carefully before we go riding. I have to pick up my room. My mother told me when I was real little, before I even was old enough to go to school, that she wasn't going to have me sitting and looking at television while the maid was straightening out my room. The same goes for outside the house; we have a gardener, but he's not allowed to come into the barn and help us with the animals.

"We had one maid, and she said we spent more time with the animals than she does with her children. I felt sad when she told me that. She has no understanding of what an animal needs. She was the one who was always telling me I was beautiful, and so I didn't need any lotion on my skin. I wanted to give her the lotion. She needs it. Her skin is in terrible shape. It's so dried and cracked. My mother says you can be poor and still know how to take care of yourself. It's not the money; it's the attitude you have toward yourself. If our maid stopped buying a lot of candy and potato chips, she could afford to get herself some skin lotion. And she wouldn't be so fat!"

45   A child has learned to distinguish between her own inclinations or preferences and those of another person—a whole category of people. This girl was, at the time, not quite an adolescent; for years, however, she had been prepared for that time, for adulthood as well—prepared by parents who not only wanted her to know how to use skin lotions, or choose "tasteful" lipstick, or shun anything but "natural" fingernail polish, or learn how to care for her hair and wash it, and pay attention to the scalp as well. Those parents wanted her to give an enormous amount of attention to *herself*—to her thoughts, which she has been taught are worthy of being spoken, and to her body, which is going to be, one day, "attractive." So she has been told by several maids—far too emphatically to suit the taste of her parents. They prefer a more understated, indirect approach. They remind the girl that she looks like her grandmother ("a handsome lady") or her aunt ("who was quite beautiful"). They let her know how graceful she is as a young dancing student, how agile and accomplished a rider she has become, how fast and accurate a game of tennis she has developed, even at her age. They smile at pictures of her smiling, applaud her once again when watching home movies. Her picture is on the mantle over the living room fireplace, on her father's desk, on her mother's desk, and is on her own desk, for that matter.

When she was six and seven she asked a lot of questions about herself. They were answered patiently, thoughtfully, and often with enthusiastic pride—a contrast indeed with many poor children, whose parents are tired, embittered, sad, or all too resigned to their fate, and hardly able to boast about the circumstances of life. The girl's questions occur to all children, rich or poor—are the banal inquiries we never quite stop asking ourselves: who am I, why am I here, whence do I come, and where am I going—the continuing preoccupations of philosophers, novelists, and painters. Children prefer the painters' approach. They sometimes don't pay much attention to the answers to their questions. After all too verbal family meals they retire to a desk or table, draw pictures meant to suggest what life is and will be about. When the girl mentioned above wonders who she is or has questions about her future, she picks up crayons and draws herself with care and affection—on a horse, in a garden, high up in a tower, surveying the countryside.

In doing so she draws upon her concrete, day-to-day experiences. She also uses those experiences in order to suggest something larger about her particular life. Especially noteworthy is the care she and others like her take with themselves as they draw. So often poor children treat themselves cursorily; they quickly sketch a rather un-flattering self-portrait. Sometimes they are unwilling to complete what they have begun—as if they are unsure of life itself. A migrant child once told me in a matter-of-fact way that he had no expectation of living beyond twenty. He was simply a child who knew the score. The children of doctors and lawyers and business executives have learned the score too. The girl mentioned above spends a half hour drawing herself, moves her eyes toward a mirror every once in a while to check on how she actually does look, and is eventually quite proud of what she has drawn. She also spends long periods of time looking at old photographs—of herself, her parents, her grand-parents. Such observations and bits of anecdotal family history have become consolidated in the girl's mind. She regards herself—though she has learned to be affectingly modest—as a rather attractive per-son. No wonder she once posed herself, in a picture, beside a giant sunflower. She was in no way overshadowed by the flower; if any-thing, it adorned her own luminous presence.

When that girl became ill with chicken pox the anguish of her mental state was noticeable and instructive. She wanted to scratch the many lesions on her face and arms but was told, of course, by her parents that she must not. She heeded their advice. In the beginning she did scratch one pustule midway on her upper right arm. Her mother become quite upset. Before the mother could say a word, the child spoke up, acknowledged her awareness of the future implica-tions of her deed. She had lost control, and she would suffer. Her de-scription of that talk and of her later, more successful, bout with the disease, has struck me as a classic of sorts: "I don't want to look ugly. If I had scratched my face, like I did my right arm, I'd look a mess for life. I knew that. But I had *such* a bad case! The doctor said it was one of the worst he'd seen in the last few years. He told me he had seen even worse than mine, and I was sort of disappointed. I figured that I'd like to go through the biggest challenge, and come out on top!

"After a day or two, I began to wonder if I'd be able to survive! I got very weepy. I began to wonder whether I'd done anything wrong—to deserve this punishment. I couldn't look myself in the mirror. I didn't want to wash at all. I felt so dirty and horrible look-ing. I asked my brother and my parents not to look at me! My brother tried to kid me out of my mood. He came in with his Polaroid camera and said he'd take a picture of me, and I could keep it, and when I was over the disease, I could just laugh! Instead I started crying, right in front of him. He apologized.

"The worst part of the chicken pox was the waiting and the try-ing to keep control. My mother sat with me, and my Dad did too, when he got home. On the worst day, he offered to stay with me and not go to his office. I said no, I'd be all right. But he decided to stay anyway. He just sat there and read to me. We watched some television—the news and a cooking class. We talked a little. Dad kept telling me I was great, and not to worry; he was sure I was going to have a wonderful life, because I've got everything going for me. I told him 'not the chicken pox,' when he said that. But he just laughed and told me that the chicken pox would soon be a bad memory, and I'd forget about it completely in a couple of months. I'm not sure I ever will, though. I have this scar on my arm, and I'll always have it. My mother says no one will notice; but *I* do! She got angry the other day. She said I was worrying too much. But I've seen her worry a lot too. If a dress doesn't fit her, she sends it right back. She's always either on a diet or coming off one, or getting ready to go on one again. We have scales in every bathroom, and one in her bedroom. I told her I don't need to weigh myself and my brother doesn't; but she wants us to get in the habit, so we'll know later when to start being careful about food. She tells the maid to give us cookies only when she's not around; she doesn't want to be tempted. And her hair—well that's 'a whole subject,' as my Daddy says. When he was with me that day, I asked him why Mom worries so much about her hair, and dyes it. Who cares if there's some gray in her hair! But Dad said that gray hair for Mom is like the chicken pox for me. I could see what he meant, but it's not exactly the same."

She did not for long insist upon the difference; she went along with her father's comparison. She did so not reluctantly, but with the detachment that goes with complete recovery—a feeling of remove from what was once painful. Her mother has always been regarded as a rather lovely woman; the girl was prepared to emphasize that fact in her mind, and associate her own present and future appearance with her mother's deserved reputation. The girl was also prepared to acknowledge quite candidly what a relatively severe case of a basically benign disease could do to her thoughts about herself: "I began to worry whether I really was as pretty as everyone had been saying. It was a mood; I'm over it now. I do have a few bad memories. Dad says they'll go. I hope so. I look at myself in the mirror and I'll suddenly be afraid that the chicken pox is coming back. I get scared. It's silly. I know I'm never going to get the chicken pox again!

"I wish I hadn't scratched that one place. It's such a small scar. But it gives me nightmares! I woke up the other night and my parents were in my room. I guess I'd been crying or shouting. In the morning my mother said I'd half-awakened, and I'd told them that a cat had been chasing me, and scratched me, and I was afraid there'd be a scar. I wonder a lot about the man I'll marry. Will he have brown hair or blond hair or black hair? My mother asked me if it makes any difference; I told her I like brown hair and green eyes, and I hope he'll be tall and thin. I wouldn't even want to go out once with a man who was overweight!"

This is no petty, superficial, half-witted, or empty-headed girl. She has gone to very good private schools—each of which has high academic standards and expectations. She can be serious, thoughtful, and idealistic—that is, worried about others less fortunate and hopeful that they somehow get to live better lives. As a child she can hardly be expected to come up with solutions for the world's various problems, but some of those problems do at times weigh upon her. Yet she can, all of a sudden, move from writing a composition about "world hunger" to discussing with her mother the virtues of various cosmetics or the appropriateness of certain dresses for one or another social occasion. She can also, rather disarmingly, stop thinking about "the troubles in America" her teacher has asked the class to write about, because her parakeet needs food or water, her two gerbils require new bedding, her alarm clock has to be set, her desk is cluttered and ought be straightened out, or her phone has rung. She has a room with its own demands and requirements, with a bureau mirror and one on the back of the door, a full-length mirror. Sometimes she gets tired of thinking of arithmetic problems and social problems, and spelling problems, of coming up with ideas meant to straighten out society.

The last word, incidentally, has two meanings for her. She started, at ten, dancing lessons. She was aware then that later on she would be going to parties, would become a debutante. Her mother plays down that word, debutante. Her mother is a New Englander who doesn't like "fuss," abhors elaborate, pretentious parties, the stuff of social climbing; but she also has a keen eye for who is acceptable to whom in her social circle, what name elicits deference, and whose "situation" is what mixture of "position" and "real wealth."

55   Those words are used discreetly, but they do not go unnoticed by a ten or eleven-year-old child. The girl asks questions about her family, its origins and "place" in the social and economic system. "Our minister tells us to think of others, but it's hard, because I've never seen the poor. I gave half of some money I saved for Christmas to the starving people of Africa. Daddy said he was real proud of me. He gave me the money I'd contributed. He says that when I grow up I should marry a man who is kind and worries about other people, not just himself; that's the type of man who makes a good husband. I agree. It's best to marry someone who's pretty much like yourself, though. Otherwise you might run into

trouble. He'll think one way, and you'll think another. There are a lot of divorces that take place. My parents have a lot of friends whose marriages aren't good. If you marry a person who thinks like you, and he has the same beliefs, then you have a better chance of staying married.

"When I leave this room and stay at a friend's, or when we go up skiing or down to our summer house, I get a funny feeling. I really miss my dolls and my bureau—the shells and dishes my parents have brought me when they have come back from trips. I have all kinds of shells, from all the Caribbean beaches. I have dishes and ashtrays from a lot of countries. I have posters; I love French posters. I hope I learn to speak French fluently. It's a beautiful language. It's strange, leaving your room and sleeping in a place that hasn't got much of anything that belongs to you, that's yours, that's *you*."

That last progression deserves respectful attention as a rather forceful, intelligent, and exact analysis of the complicated psychology of class-connected "narcissistic entitlement." She and others like her grow up surrounded by possessions, animate as well as inanimate. They have learned to live with them, to look after them, and to depend upon them for support. They have also learned to give of themselves to those "objects." When they leave for a winter or summer vacation they try to take some of their most treasured belongings with them, but often still experience a sense of emptiness or a feeling of being alone, isolated, bereft. Child psychiatrists use the expression "transitional object" to refer to a child's blanket or teddy bear or doll—taken to bed, carried around, held tight at the age of four, five, six.

Few children are unable to find those "transitional objects." I have seen the poorest of American children, living the most uprooted of lives, cling to a dirty old rag, a stick, a rock, the cheapest of plastic toys, often obtained secondhand, maybe from someone's trash barrel. Children of working-class parents or of so-called "middle-income" families seldom experience such sad desperation. On the other hand, many of those children share rooms with brothers and sisters and by no means assume that they are to be recipients of an apparently endless succession of gifts, vacations, pleasant surprises. In the homes of the rich, in contrast, the children almost invariably have their own rooms and the quantitative difference in their material acquisitions prompts a qualitative psychological difference: an enhanced expectation of what life has to offer, and with that, a strong inclination to build a sanctuary out of one's room and one's property. The girl is subtle but sharp and exact when she distinguishes between what belongs to her (a piece of property) and what has become hers—an existential psychological transformation. The next step is of course an ironic act of personal surrender: the object and the person merge somewhat—from "that's yours" to "that's *you*."

All children struggle when very young—starting at a little under a year, in fact—to distinguish between themselves and their parents. They begin to realize, at two and three, that it is *they* who exist—individuals who crawl and walk and make noises and talk. As they separate, to a degree, from their mothers, especially then, at two or three, they first know loneliness. Certainly, thereafter, for most children, there are reattachments to the mother, new attachments to other persons—and to things. But the child turns inward too upon occasion, makes an effort to find comfort and even pleasure in a newfound solitariness. Freud, at one point, referred to "the purified pleasure ego"—by which he meant a child's delight in the various excitements or satisfactions he or she can manage to find. I recall a four-year-old boy in one home I visited, not far from that of the girl quoted just above, who slid up and down a wonderfully solid, circular staircase, shouting me, me, me; he was in love with the dizzying speed, with the feeling of control and power he had—with himself.

Later on, at five and six, such a child becomes quite conscious of rights and wrongs, of what ought to be done to please parents and teachers, not to mention one's own developing conscience. Psychoanalysts describe the "idealized parent image"—the part of the child's mind that holds up examples, insists upon directions. The child absorbs from significant persons his or her notions of what matters and how he or she should in general be trying to live—and tries to go along. The "you" that the girl mentioned above at age ten—a summary, almost, of which belongings had become part of her "self"—was preceded by the earlier "you" comprehended at the age of six: "I'd like to do good in school, and learn to ski, and ride my bike fast, and get to make real tasty cookies with the maid, and then I'll be good, and people will say, she's doing everything she should be doing, and I'll say that to myself. When I'm finished brushing my teeth, they'll be clean, and my mother will soon be upstairs and check me out, and I'll say to myself: you're doing okay. And a few minutes later my mother says the same thing: 'You're doing okay!'"

That child has had ample opportunities—beyond using a toothbrush well—to prove herself, as well as find pleasure in competence. She has been taught tennis and swimming by coaches, cooking by a maid, riding by her mother. The girl has also learned how to draw and paint, play the piano, "do" ballet. She has gone abroad often, has mastered words, used her own passport. She has become acquainted with forms of etiquette, with new protocols. She knows when to defer, when to speak up. She knows how to recognize various songs, symphonies, operatic pieces. She knows how to walk the corridors of museums, recognize the work of certain artists. And

60

too, she has acquired some of the psychological judgment good hostesses have: who is like whom, who belongs near whom at the table, who will be a "disaster" with whom. She used that word sometimes, when eleven and twelve, and in so doing revealed more than a "prepubescent" affinity for a way of talking, or a superficial cleverness about people. In fact, she was indicating something significant about her sense of *herself.*

One such "disaster" was her mother's much younger cousin, and the girl knew why: "She's sloppy. She's always been sloppy. She speaks sloppy. She had a harelip, and that was what ruined her. The parents didn't take her to the right doctor, and the girl became shy, and she didn't' want to talk to anyone, and when she was a teenager she became even worse. She just stayed in her room a lot. Then she got religious, in a weird way. She was always praying. My mother says they should have sent her to a doctor. She decided to become a nun, I think. She wanted to convert and be a Catholic, and then be a nun. They talked her out of that. She came to life a little. She began to go out and meet people. Then she met this guy, and he was a music teacher, and he was poor, and they fell in love, and they wanted to get married. He was a disaster, my mother says. He could barely open his mouth, and he didn't know which fork to use, and he wore real funny clothes, and he had a bad complexion, and the worst case of dandruff my mother has ever seen. He just sat there, and it didn't even seem to bother him that he didn't talk. But my mother's cousin was a disaster, too. She was just an oddball, that's what. They got married, and my mother says they've been good for each other.

"They would be poor now, if it wasn't that my mother's aunt left them some money. I think they have enough to get by. We see them sometimes; they come to visit my grandmother. We have to keep a straight face. We can't laugh. That would be bad. You should feel sorry for people who aren't as fortunate as you are. If you don't, then you are rude and you don't have charity. If you're not nice to someone, you've lost. You sink down to the other person's level. That's what Daddy tells us, and he gets angry if we don't pay attention. He says we've got a responsibility to show good manners at all times. I'd never call someone a 'disaster' in front of him; at least while we're having supper. Sometimes he'll be having a drink, and then even he will call someone a fool or *no good*; that's *his* way of calling someone he knows and doesn't like a 'disaster.'"

In "Forms and Transformation of Narcissism" (*Journal of the American Psychoanalytic Association,* April, 1966), Heinz Kohut observes that the "form and content of the psychic representation of the idealized parent thus vary with the maturational stage of the child's cognitive apparatus." Then he adds, significantly, that the form and content "are also influenced by environmental factors that affect the choice of internalizations and their intensity." There may seem, at first glance, a considerable distance in substance if not tone between the child's reflections on her second cousin and a psycho-analyst's theoretical observations, addressed to this scholarly col-leagues. But the psychiatrist is trying to formulate what the child is living through and occasionally able to comment upon. Even as a migrant child or ghetto child learns to feel weak and vulnerable, a child of well-off parents learns to feel, in many respects, confident. There are idiosyncratic variations, of course. One can be rich and psychotic, for instance, and instill fear, apprehension, and a sense of worthlessness in one's children. Yet even among the disturbed young children of well-to-do parents there are concerns and expec-tations that contrast profoundly with the notions other children, from other backgrounds, possess about themselves. At a certain point in every child's life, as Dr. Kohut suggests, and as Freud re-peatedly pointed out, culture and class became matters of a child's fantasy life and affect the tone of his or her self regard. The girl who wants to look a certain way, speak a certain way, who anticipates a certain way of life, and who derives personal strength and compe-tence from the sense of herself she has learned to have, is a person whose "narcissism," whose "idealized parent image," has drawn upon many daily conversations and experiences, rewards and lessons.

65   At another point in his paper Dr. Kohut points out that our "ambitions and ideals" don't just appear out of nowhere. They have a psychological history, not to mention a social and economic back-ground. He refers to their "preconscious correlates" and locates them (structurally speaking) in the "narcissistic self," whose various "ego ideals" have, of course, been acquired over countless intimate encounters—the family involvements that set the stage for a child's view of what "life" is going to be like. Dr. Kohut points out that am-bitions do not always coincide with ideals. A child whose parents are poor or of working-class background may have heard a mother or father (or, rather often, a teacher) say that anyone can be President in this country, or rise to the top of a company, or become a doctor, a lawyer, a "success"—given "hard work." But the child has seen and heard much evidence to the contrary. The child has seen his or her parents curbed, scorned, exhausted, frustrated, em-bittered. The child has hears that "life" is no picnic, that wages don't keep up with prices, that the factory is laying off more and more people, including his or her father or mother. The child has heard, upon breaking a dish or a toy, upon failing to follow instructions, or falling short at school, that soon enough the difficulties and tensions of grown-up life will fall upon him or her. In contrast, privileged

children, far fewer in number, are destined for quite another fate. In his own manner, Dr. Kohut approaches their lives; speaking of their "ambitions and ideals," he observes that "they are at times hard to distinguish, not only because ambitions are often disguised as ideals but also because there are indeed lucky moments in our lives, or lucky periods in the lives of the very fortunate, in which ambitions and ideals coincide."

For those "lucky," a sense of entitlement develops—the merger of what they have learned would be "ideal" and what they have actually experienced, into an ongoing attitude toward the world. Let others feel diminished, impeded, burdened; or let them long for a different kind of life, knowing all too clearly by the age of six or seven the difference between a castle in Spain and a ranch house in Levittown, or a ghetto tenement, or a tenant farmer's shack. For privileged children, there is every reason to feel entitlement. But let us not forget that entitlement is perfectly compatible with doubts, misgivings, despair. A child can feel—being realistic—entitled to a certain kind of life and yet have other reasons to be confused or hurt. Even schizophrenics experience the distinctions that have to do with class and caste, race and place of residence. The girl whose words I called upon above had her own thoughts, one day, about these theoretical issues of mental life—after she had heard, at the age of twelve, that her father was sick and required surgery: "I hope he'll be all right. It's serious, my mother told me. I can tell it is; Daddy hasn't been smiling much. He's been worried. He's been talking a lot about his insurance, and he took my brother and me to the bank, and he told us we'll be going there for the rest of our lives, or calling them up and asking them to send us over some money. He says that is we're careful, our children will have the same amount of money we have. It's best to use the interest and not the capital. The bank knows how to keep your money invested in the best stocks.

"Daddy will be all right. He's strong. He has the best doctor in the country; he's the best surgeon. I met him, and he was very nice. He gave my brother and me a book he'd written, about the seashore and the clams and oysters and lobsters you find in the water and the sand. He owns a lot of land by the ocean, and he's a marine biologist, my father says, besides being a surgeon. And he's an artist, too. I wouldn't mind being a doctor myself, but I don't know if I'd want to operate on anyone. The surgeon offered to show my brother and me how he operates; we could watch him—but not when he works on Daddy. My brother says yes, but I said no. I'd rather not be there, if anything goes wrong; then, when Daddy is being operated on, I'd worry even more.

"We'll be all right. My mother says everything will turn out good. Daddy may not be home for a couple of weeks, but we can go and see him all the time. We can eat with him in his room. It'll be like going out to a restaurant. He'll have television and his own phone. We can talk with him any time we want. He says he'll get a lot of reading done. He'll have a nice view from his room, and he'll get all the rest he'll need. Then, when he gets home, we're going away. Daddy says we'll be in Barbados for two weeks. He's promised to take us out of school. We'll get all our homework, and we won't fall back at all. My mother says it may turn out to be a blessing in disguise that Daddy got sick; he'll get a lot of rest, and he'll be much stronger. I hope so."

She was not about to acknowledge, even to herself, how worried she sensed her mother to be. But she (and her mother) has resources that very much ameliorated an anxious period of waiting. The dreaded outcome of the father's illness, a malignancy, did not materialize. All the money in the world could not have converted cancerous cells into normal ones. But during those day that preceded surgery the girl and her brother felt more hope than dread, and had quite valid sources of support for that hope. And during the father's convalescence, instead of hearing their mother and father lamenting bills, expressing worries about the loss of a job, or complaining about the "conditions" in the hospital, their time of trouble became for everyone concerned an opportunity for pleasure, relaxation, new initiatives and accomplishments. The girl and her brother ended up becoming scuba divers in the warm Caribbean water; went on motorcycle rides such as they had never had before; began to realize more exactly than ever how well-off their parents are and they as children are. "It all came out for the best," the girl said, weeks after her father was pronounced able to return to his work as a business executive. In a sense the words are a slogan of sorts, constantly kept in mind by her and others: life works out "for the best," mostly—and one has a right to conclude that if one has had ample confirming evidence.

70   For some of these children, the privileged life presents a danger of what clinicians have referred to as "secondary narcissism"— the "narcissistic entitlement" I mentioned at the beginning of this section. However, on the evidence of the privileged children I have come to know, I would emphasize the possibility that a feeling of "entitlement" may develop in a child without the potentially treacherous development of an excessively narcissistic tone. When a feeling of "entitlement" becomes "narcissistic," it has departed from what James Agee called "human actuality." Suppose the girl whose father had taken ill began, for her own reasons, to imagine that her father's illness would be associated with some extraordinary development: a call to the theater or television as a

young actress; a medal of honor awarded by the school she attended; a party given her as an expression of her popularity. Suppose that girl, alternatively, expected the surgeon to cure her father, no matter *what* was discovered upon operating. Suppose that girl began crying constantly before her father entered the hospital; and did so petulantly, plaintively, as if less interested in her father's troubles than her own. At that point her narcissism would have taken its form from her private experiences, although the same child in other moments might lose her despairing self-centeredness. The point to emphasize is the mind's capacity to appreciate the reality of a certain kind of life. The mind can of course undercut a good thing, make a bad thing even worse, or make the best of it.

It is important that a privileged child's normal sense of "entitlement" be distinguished not only from pathological narcissism, but from the more common phenomenon known as being "spoiled." It is a matter of degree; "spoiled" children are self-centered all right, petulant and demanding—but not saddled with the grandiose illusions (or delusions) clinicians have in mind when using the phrase "narcissistic entitlement." The rich, the "well-to-do" are all too commonly charged with producing spoiled children. Yet one sees spoiled children everywhere, among the very poor as well as the inordinately rich. A child can be spoiled by a mother's attitude. What the child is "given" can be called excessive instinctual leeway or, in everyday words, however politicized in recent years, "permissive indulgence." I remember a migrant mother who knew precisely and uncannily what she was doing "wrong"—knew, indeed, to call it all "wrong." She told me one day that she had given birth to a particular child with more pain than usual and had been in lower spirits than ever before in her life during the first months of that child's life. When the baby began to notice the mother and the world, start crawling and separating himself from her, she felt a fierce desire within herself, expressed with unforgettable intensity, "to let that boy have anything he wants, anything he can lay his hands on." She was careful, for all her lack of education and her troubled spirits, to qualify herself. She moved quickly, immediately, from "anything he wants" to "anything he can lay his hands on." She knew that in the first or second year of life the child would have all he could do to reach and hold on to what he wanted.

But soon enough a child begins to see things that others have; on a rented, only half-working television set the migrant child saw a lot, and looked around the room and realized a lot. His was no blessed life! He continued, however, to want to take what little he could get. And of course children (or adults) can want things that are psychological in lieu of what is "material." They can become demanding, possessive, insistent, if allowed to be. They can compete with others for attention, push hard against others who try to assert themselves. They can make every effort to obtain center stage at all times. The migrant mother developed, deep within her hurt and sad self, a pride about her child and his stubborn, indulged, expropriative, loud-mouthed, and at times impossibly egotistical behavior.

He was the child who would shout and scream and swagger, shake his fists, really, at the wretched world he had been born to. No matter that such behavior, whether allowed or even encouraged, is hardly a guarantee of a future rise to success. On the contrary, a child of migrant parents who acts like that one is headed, quite likely, for future trouble. The mother knew that too. She knew that migrants are virtually peons; that they submit to endless demands and manipulations. Perhaps one of her children would be so "spoiled" that he would be utterly incapable of becoming a migrant or lasting as one for very long. She answered along those lines when her husband asked her why she doesn't spank the "spoiled one" as she does the other children.

He in turn mentioned the grim likelihood that the boy would not indeed last as a migrant. He would instead end up in jail—or soon dead. All right, better a last stand, the mother replied. But she knew that really there was no point to such a hope; it would never even come to that, because the boy would either learn to mind his manners, and submit to the only life he would most likely ever know, or go down not in defiant resistance but through the slow attrition of cheap wine and harmless side-of-the-road braggadoccio—the "maladjusted" migrant who works inefficiently, goes to the bars before and after work, dies in a car accident or drowns drunk in one of the hundreds of irrigation canals that crisscross the agricultural counties of Florida, where this particular family spent its winters.

75   The parallel with spoiled children of upper-income families is not so farfetched. In one of the first such families I came to know there was a girl who was described by both parents as "spoiled." At the time, I fear, I was ready to pronounce every child in New Orleans's Garden District spoiled.

Nevertheless, I soon began to realize that it wouldn't do to call one set of children spoiled, by virtue of their social and economic background—as against another set of children who were obviously less privileged. Though one meets among the poor any number of spoiled children, one also meets among the rich restrained, disciplined children; sometimes, even, boys and girls who have learned to be self-critical, even ascetic—anything but "spoiled" in the conventional sense of the word. True, one can find a touch and more of arrogance in those apparently Spartan boys and girls, who seem quite anxious to deny themselves all sorts of apparently accessible privileges. But one also finds in these children a consistent willingness to place serious and not always pleasant burdens on themselves. They often struck me, as I came to their homes fresh from visits with much poorer age-mates, as remarkably *less* spoiled: not so much whining or crying; few demands for candy or other sweets; even sometimes a relative indifference to toys, a disregard of television—so often demanded by the children I was seeing across the city, on the other side of the tracks.

Those children from prominent families appeared, even at the age of four or five, to put their energies in the service of "constructive" play or "useful" activities. They had begun to learn at two and three how important it was for them to do "right" as against "wrong"; to build rather than destroy; to concentrate their energies, devote them to particular tasks, which were to be finished rather than started and abandoned. They had, in some instances, even learned to take care of their own rooms—keep them neat, pick up after themselves, be conscious of what belongs where. Maids came to help, or lived with the family, but sometimes a particular boy or girl, as young as five or six, was a taskmaster to the maid rather than, certainly, a helpless or indulged child. And sometimes the maid herself became astonished by the example set by such children—and became their strong admirer.

A New Orleans black woman said to me in 1961: "I don't know how to figure out these rich, white kids. They're something! I used to think, before I took a job with this family, that the only difference between a rich kid and a poor kid is that the rich kid knows he has a lot of money and he grows up and he becomes spoiled rotten. That's what my mother told me; she took care of a white girl, and the girl was an only child, and her father owned a department store in McComb, Mississippi, and that girl thought she was God's special creature. My mother used to come home and tell us about the 'little princess'; but she turned out to be no good. She was so pampered she couldn't do a thing for herself. All she knew how to do was order people around. It's different with these two children here in New Orleans. I've never seen such a boy and such a girl. They think they're the best ones who ever lived—like that girl in McComb—but they don't behave like her. They're never asking me to do much of anything. They even ask if *they* can help *me!* They tell me they want to know how to do everything. The girl says she wants to learn how to run the washing machine and the dishwasher. She says she wants to learn all my secret recipes. She says she'd like to give the best parties in the Garden District when she grows up, and she'd like to be able to give them without anyone's help. She says I could serve the food, but she would like to make it. The boy says he's going to be a lawyer and a banker, so he wants know how much everything costs. He doesn't want to waste anything. He'll see me throw something away, and he wants to know why. I wish my own kids were like him!

"I wish my kids weren't so lazy; they don't care what's going on; they just want to play and play, and they waste a lot of food, and they break the toys I get them real fast. I even told my children I wish they could learn from these two children here. But these children here are special, and don't they know it! That's what being rich is: you know you're different from most people. These two kids are even more special, because they act as if they're going to be tops in everything, and they're pleased as can be with themselves, because there is nothing they can't do, and there's nothing they can't get, and there's nothing they can't win, and they're always showing off what they can do, and then before you can tell them how good they are, they're telling the same thing to themselves. It's confusing! They're not spoiled one bit, but oh, they have a high opinion of themselves!

80   "And I'll have to admit, there are times when I have the same high opinion of them! I'll look at them, and I'll say they could be dropped on an island in the middle of a big ocean, and they'd know what to do, and if they didn't have anyone around to be pleased with them, they'd be all right because they'd be pleased with themselves! And it wouldn't take them long to know where to go and what to do on that island, because they are just so sure of themselves and so full of themselves that they always have their chins up, and they're happy, and they know where they're going, and they know what's ahead—that everything will come out fine in the end. When you have that kind of spirit in you, then you'll always get out of any jam you're in, and you'll always end up on top, because that's where you started, and that's where you believe you're going to end up, and if it's in your mind that it is like that, and it *going* to be like that, and if you're willing to work hard, like these kids are, and if you're careful about everything, like they are, then you just *can't* lose, and don't these kids know it, I'll tell you!"

Actually the children she speaks of aren't as confident of themselves as she thinks, though she certainly has accurately conveyed their appearance. The kind of children she knows so well are extraordinarily privileged by virtue of background and money, are also intelligent and of attractive appearance; but those children have demons that occasionally urge them on, and their nature is not always easy to divine. Boys and girls may seem without anxiety or self-doubt at, say, eight or nine. Yet, there are moments of hesitation, if not apprehension. An eleven-year-old boy from a prominent and quite brilliant Massachusetts family (three generations of first-rate lawyers) told his teachers in an autobiographical composition about the vicissitudes of "entitlement": "I don't always do everything right. I'd like to be able to say I don't make any mistakes, but I do, and when I do, I feel bad. My father and mother say that if you train yourself, you can be right *almost* 100% of the time. Even they make mistakes, though. I like to be first in sports. I like to beat my brothers at skiing. But I don't always go down the slopes as fast as I could and I sometimes fall down. Last year I broke my leg. That was the first time I'd ever gone to a hospital and stayed there. It was my mother who reminded me that I'd been in the hospital for a week just after I was born! I'd forgotten! I was saying that I'd *never* been in a hospital overnight, and she corrected me.

"My great-grandfather is eighty-four, and he's in the best of health. It worries me that I have bad sinus trouble a lot of times after I get flu. I'd hate to be sick when I'm older. There's too much to do; it you get sick, you can't do much of anything, except stay home and rest. When I get a bad cold, I feel disappointed in myself. I don't think it's right to be easy on yourself. If you are, then you slip back, and you don't get a lot of the rewards in life. If you really work for the rewards, you'll get them."

His teachers have often given him that kind of platitude. In the fourth grade, for instance, his teacher had written on the blackboard (and kept it there for weeks): "Those who want something badly enough get it, provided they are willing to wait and work." The boy has been brought up to believe that it will be like that for him. He knows that others are not so lucky, but he hasn't really met those "others," and they don't cross his mind. What does occur to him sometimes is the need for constant exertion, lest he fail to "measure up." The expression is a family one, used repeatedly. No matter how difficult a task, no matter how frustrating it is for others, one "measures up" when one does it well. One "measures up" when one tries hard, succeeds. One measures up because one *must*. No allowance is made for any possible lack of ability or endowment. The assumption is that one has been "given a lot" (another family expression) and so a "return" is obligatory if justice is to be done. If one slackens or stumbles, one ought take oneself to task. The emphasis is on a quick and efficient moment of scrutiny followed by "a fast pickup," yet another admonitory injunction handed down.

Such counsel is not as callous or psychologically insensitive as it may sound—or even as it may have been *intended* to sound. The child who hears it gets briefly upset, but "a fast pickup" does indeed take place quite often. Again, it is a matter of feeling "entitled." A child who has been told repeatedly that all he or she needs to do is try hard does not feel inclined to allow himself or herself much skeptical self-examination. The point is to feel *entitled*—then act upon that feeling. The boy whose composition was just quoted from wrote again, apparently about his younger (aged five) brother: "I was watching my brother from my bedroom window. He was climbing up the fence we built for our corral. He got to the top, and then he just stood there and waved and shouted. No one was there. He was talking to himself. He was very happy. Then he would fall. He would be upset for a few seconds, but he would climb right back up again. Then he would be even happier! He was entitled to be happy. It is his fence, and he has learned to climb it, and stay up, and balance himself."

85   The little brother was indeed happy on top of the fence. He would talk to himself with obvious pleasure—tell nameless, invisible people that they are stupid and inadequate because, unlike him, they are unable to climb the fence and stay there and enjoy themselves. Yes, he was obviously talking to himself. He was also speaking to an earlier version of himself, to the boy of four who had wanted to climb that fence, wanted to get on top, and, just as important, stay there and enjoy the experience. Once he had succeeded, he enjoyed his new-found competence. He would practically never be curbed, humiliated, denied interesting or engaging occasions because of the "reality" of the world around him. Quite the contrary; there would be one inviting adventure after another over the months and years. One day, as a matter of fact, he ran across the field after he had shown himself able to climb a particular fence with ease—in search of a taller, slightly more precarious fence on the other side of the corral. And when that climb was "nothing" and the position of balance a giant bore, he predicted quite casually that he would never see a fence that he couldn't rather quickly master. His father did not want the boy to be completely unrealistic, however. To whistle in the dark, to assume that one can always triumph, is to be vulnerable—the weakness of the overconfident. One ought to have a great deal of drive and ambition, a conviction that the world will eventually be made to oblige—but only after a substantial effort.

It is absurd to say that all children whose parents make a certain amount money or work at certain occupations, or live in a certain neighborhood, possess at attitude of mind (and an attitude toward the world) that might be sensibly tucked into the generalization referred to here as "entitlement." More than once I have insisted that each individual has his or her unique way of pulling together the various elements of mental life. I have wanted, however, to suggest a common manner of response toward life among children of a certain class background. I realize that the particular word "entitlement" has complicated psychoanalytic implications or, for some, pejorative social or political implications, or indeed, for others, quite defensible and justifiable implications. For the children I have worked with, however, the word is simply a description of a certain actuality. There are both social and psychological dimensions to that actuality, and deep down these children know them rather well.

I have in mind especially the son of a powerful Florida grower. When the child was five he kept using the words "I'm entitled to." His parents were much annoyed. The father did not want his son using such a peremptory, self-important, demanding expression. He began interrupting the boy, telling him that he was not "entitled" to *anything,* that he must ask for what he wanted, and be grateful when he got it. The boy kept asking why, why. The father kept explaining— a litany of ought and musts. The boy in turn fell back upon his considerable intelligence and powers of observation. He reminded his father of his own words: "If you earn something, you are entitled to keep it." Had not the boy "earned" the right to make his various requests—by trying to be "good" or "quiet"? Had not the father told him on a number of occasions that he was "coming along nicely," that he was "making his parents proud"?

The boy spoke up for himself in fits and starts, but he got his message across, because his father eventually settled for an ironic statement: "A boy who stands up for himself like that boy has— well, he's entitled to say every once in a while, that he's *entitled* to something!" It must be rather obvious—it was to the grower, for all his lack of interest in the plight of the hundreds of impoverished migrants who worked his land so long and hard—that not every father can be grateful for his son's outspokenness, his young son's assumption that he was entitled to political freedom, social equality, economic privilege.

Reflective Reading, Informal Writing

REFLECTING ON THE READING:

- Define what Coles means by "entitlement." How does this definition resemble your own understanding of entitlement? How does it differ?
- Summarize Coles' major points or arguments in "Entitlement." What method or methods does he use to gather data for the evidence that supports his arguments? Does Coles seem to be objective, or do you think he has a particular bias when he interprets his data? What evidence leads you to your conclusion?
- Find at least one passage from Coles' text where you realized someone was misinterpreting another's life because of cultural blindness.

What is the nature of the cultural blindness you identified? What are the consequences for the person being misunderstood? The person doing the misunderstanding? Does anybody stand to lose something or otherwise be hurt by this misunderstanding? Does anybody stand to gain anything from this misunderstanding?

UNDERSTANDING RHETORICAL STRATEGIES:

- On page 49 Coles writes, "Each child . . . is also influenced by certain social, racial, cultural, or religious traditions, or thoroughly idiosyncratic ones—a given family's tastes, sentiments, ideals, say. This issue is 'class'; but the issue is not only 'class.'" What specific evidence does Coles use to show us that the issue is "class"? Does this evidence seem appropriate? Is it logical, helpful, problematic in any way? What specific evidence does Coles use to support his idea that the issue is "not only 'class'"?

- Like Updike, Coles is writing, at least in part, about the self and how selves come to be, to change, to stay static, etc., and like Updike, he uses a number of specific anecdotes to do so. Coles differs from Updike, however, in that he does not draw upon his own personal experience to illustrate his ideas about the self. Which approach do you like better? Why? Would it be appropriate for Coles to use his own life as support in this chapter from his book? Why or why not?

- Think for a moment about Coles' use of quotation marks to set single words apart from the rest of his text, as with the term, "class." The most common use of quotation marks, of course, is to indicate that we are quoting someone else's words. But they can also serve other functions. We use quotation marks (or italics) when we refer to a word as a word, as in "the term, 'class.'" We might also use them when we wish to indicate that "this is what other people call it, but I'm not so sure they have it right." We are distancing ourselves from a particular use of a word, re-opening the question of how that word is to be defined or understood. Find instances in Coles' essay where he puts single words (or concepts, like "narcissistic entitlement") into quotation marks. Why, in each case, does he do so? Does he find it difficult to accept other people's definitions? Is this the product of some kind of arrogance, or is he simply trying to be more precise? Is there a sense in which this whole essay is an attempt to sharpen definitions?

- Pay attention to how Coles organizes this chapter. Does he begin with generalities and then move to specific examples? Does he do the opposite? Does he move back and forth between generalities and specifics? Why do you think he chooses to organize this chapter the way he does? How does his organizational strategy relate to the point he is trying to make?

INFORMAL WRITING:

- List several things that you feel you are entitled to. Explain why you feel entitled to these things.
- Write a description of your family life applying Coles' arguments to yourself and the psychological and economic context of your childhood. To what things, rights, advantages did you come to feel "entitled," and where did this sense of entitlement come from?
- Write about and analyze an area of cultural blindness that you think you might have developed as a product of where and how you grew up. How has it harmed or limited you? How has it harmed or limited someone else?

ANNIE NEEPOSH ISERHOFF

Annie Neeposh Iserhoff's personal narrative, "Excerpts From My Life," comes from a collection of essays by 28 women graduates of McGill University. The anthology collects reflections by these alumnae about what it is like to be a woman in Canada in the 1990s. Part of the purpose of the collection, *Our Own Agendas* (1995), edited by Margaret Gillett and Ann Beer, is to bring women's personal and private experiences into the public realm to make their experiences part of contemporary culture's collective knowledge. The editors write that these narratives "speak vividly of the relation between the self and society, and are often written with great power." Only recently have memoirs and autobiographies by "everyday" people been accepted into the literary world; such personal texts were previously marginalized and only found their way into print if presented as didactic, perhaps teaching young girls lessons of virtue and Christianity, or if they were written by powerful leaders. The availability of such texts today shows how the lives of "everyday" people help construct our society and our history. Iserhoff's narrative follows a trail of memories that shaped the woman she is today, a Cree teacher at the Voyageur Memorial School in Mistassini. She labels the memory of separating from her mother at the age of eight as her most powerful memory. Returning home from the first summer after being away she recalls as her saddest memory.

Language plays a key role in Iserhoff's story—not only in her ability to render her life's turning points on paper for readers outside of her experience to empathize with—but in her forced conversion from her Cree heritage, an Algonquin dialect, to English. When taken from her mother to attend the Moose Factory school, Iserhoff is no longer allowed to speak in her "mother tongue." This connection between the family and language underlies her story, and perhaps continues to fuel her teaching and empathy for students' lives, culture, family, and experience. As you read Iserhoff's narrative, consider the editors' goal of bringing women's private or personal experiences into the public realm. Do you see tensions between the public and private realms in her story? Does her private story seem a story worth telling?

Excerpts from My Life

There are many things that come to mind as I recall my youth. There were the good times and the not so good times. Most people say that they can only recall the good memories. Why is it, then, that the not so good times seem to dominate my memory when I try and recall my youth? Why do I remember all the things that frightened me? All the circumstances that caused me to feel intimidated or insecure?

As in most native families, my parents had numerous children. There were twelve of us, six girls and six boys. I was the eighth child. My mother used to tell her family and close friends that she wanted to have a boy so much. She ended up having three girls before the first boy arrived and then she had two more girls before she had another boy. Then I came along. Probably my mother thought that she'd end up with mostly girls, but she was blessed with four more boys one after another, after my birth.

My father, Matthew, has always been a very overbearing figure in my life. We never had a close relationship, although I craved for his attention during my youth. Matthew was the authoritarian, and, although my mother had a fighting spirit, in the end she would succumb to his wishes.

The bits of memory I recall begin around the time my brother Joseph was born. I must have been two years old. I remember being weaned from my mother's breast. We were living in a tent that was shaped like a cross. On the arm to the left, that's where our family lived. On the next arm, which is the head, lived another family, then again another family lived right across from us. The fourth arm was the porch, which was to our right. There were three stoves, one for each family, which were situated around the middle of this complex. It felt very cosy when all the stoves were ablaze with fire. I'd be mesmerized when I saw the mouth of the stove where I could watch the fire as it snapped and crackled. On one of those days, I remember going over to sit on my mother's lap and pulling her blouse up to nurse. She pulled her blouse back down and looked at me and said, "I can't nurse you any more, you have a little baby brother, who needs to nurse more than you now. How about going to Mary? She volunteered to nurse you if you want." Mary was the neighbour. All I felt was dejection and it sure didn't feel right to go to another woman to nurse. From then on, I was weaned. It was hard to accept what had happened, not because I loved to nurse but because that was when I felt close to my mom. But, anyway, it was time to be independent.

5   Then I remember the times we travelled from the old camp to set up a new camp or in search of food, animals that is. I recall being laid down and wrapped in blankets and a tarpaulin and being strapped to a sled or a toboggan. There would be enough space for me to breathe and see the sky, the clouds, and the tops of both coniferous and deciduous forests when we were travelling by land. I remember feeling so helpless, so out of control, so claustrophobic. I wanted out. Finally, probably because of my fuss, someone decided to sit me up on the sled even though I was still tied down. That felt a lot better and I was able to observe what was happening all around me.

As in all societies, there were a lot of superstitions. It was hard not to be affected by them, and some stick with me because they were instilled in me when I was a child. It seemed that many of these beliefs were directed more towards the girls or women. This used to vex me or make me feel vile, although more than likely, I'd succumb to them.

The girls were not allowed to play with boys' toys and vice versa. The toys both the boys and the girls had were always made of wood, hide, canvas, or cloth depending on the toy. The girls were told, if they ever played with the boys' toys, that when they grew up they'd be dragging their breasts and that would be a horrendous burden. The boys were told that they in turn would lose their strength and would become very poor hunters if they played with the girls' toys. Another superstition was that if a girl or woman stepped over a boy's or man's legs, he would become an incompetent worker and hunter.

Our parents used to tell the boys to run out in the nude during the winter, hit their chests with their fists, and cry out, "Giiwedin, giiwedin," which means north wind, north wind. Then they'd come running back in within a few seconds. This was meant to bring on the wind so the men could have a better hunt. During one of these times, a girlfriend and I decided to beat the boys to it. We got undressed as fast as we could and ran out, beating our chests and yelling, "Giiwedin, giiwedin." As we ran out we heard our mothers and older sisters yelling, but it was too late, we were out there already. Did we get the lecture of our lives! Of course, we hadn't realized that only the boys could do something like that. It had looked like so much fun. We were told, "Now, we are going to have a real bad storm because of what you two did." Sure enough, there was a terrible storm, and the two of us felt we were the cause of it. However, afterward some of the older people thought it was very funny, and even to this day, one woman laughing reminds me of this incident.

One day our parents were talking about a place called Mistissini. They said we would be travelling there as soon as all the lakes and rivers were clear of ice. They talked about seeing all their friends.

10   My first experience upon arriving in Mistissini seemed like waking up from a dream. I had been sleeping at the bottom of the head of the canoe covered with some blankets and a tarpaulin to keep out the water. The humming of the motor had lulled me to sleep during most of the travel by water, which was a good three-quarters of the trip. Each time the motor would stop, I'd wake up, get up, and look around to see if we were there yet, but I'd end up

being disappointed. However, this time when the motor stopped, I got up to see a whole bunch of tents, and people swarming towards the bank where we were to beach. I couldn't believe my eyes. Who were these people? How come I hadn't seen them before? Had they lived here all the time? I couldn't wait to get off the canoe and venture to their tents.

Somehow, I don't have any recollection as to when I first saw the Hudson's Bay store. The only thing I can recall was it was different from the tents we lived in. Every part of the building was made out of wood, including the floor, and you could see outside through the glass (windows). That was the only thing I remember, that impressed me. Oh yes, and the Englishmen who worked there spoke the language I used to hear from the talking box (radio). Some had hair the colour of the sun during the day, others had hair that nearly matched the colour of the sky at sunset. Oh, and their skin was so white. I was a little leery of them because they looked different and they spoke in a language that I couldn't understand.

Summertime was when the nurses got flown in. Parents were told to bring their children to the nursing station for their annual check-up and immunization. My mother took us there one morning after giving us a bath in a washtub. She was saying that we must be clean and put on clean clothes before we saw the nurses. On this particular morning, my mother mentioned that she had seen worms in my stool. She described the worms. The interpreter translated the message to the nurses. The nurses had a little conference on the side.

The next thing I knew, my mother said I was going to be shipped to the hospital. On that day, there were at least half a dozen or more of us being shipped out, adults, teenagers, and children. As we boarded the plane, I heard my mother say to one teenager, named Caroline, "Take care of my daughter, don't let the French convert her to their church." It sounded like something terrible was going to happen if this happened to me.

The departure was a very traumatic experience. I cried until I was exhausted and probably fell asleep after a while.

15   There was a whole world out there. Everything we saw was new. It was beyond our comprehension. There were moving vehicles, of all sizes, big houses, huge buildings with many floors. Everything was so overwhelming. It felt as if I was being kidnapped to an alien land and that I would never see my family again. I voiced my terror, and the girl who was to look out for me assured me that I would be going home soon.

We seemed to be travelling forever, then one or two would be dropped at a certain town or hospital. By the time we got to our destination, there were only a few of us left. A nurse took me to the children's ward and it seemed like a long time before I ever saw a familiar face again.

There was one very frightening experience. A woman, whom I believed to be a nurse, was bathing me. She held my head under water until I struggled, swallowing some water while gasping for air. I cried and I'm sure she shut me up somehow for a while, because it happened more than once, before this stopped. She must have been caught because after a while this treatment finally ended. It was such a relief not to have to be bathed by this person again.

One morning, the nurses were fussing over me. Somehow, I knew they were planning to take me to the chapel. I recalled my mother's words to Caroline. I cried, asking for "Caroline, Caroline!" The nurses didn't know why I was so upset. So one of them went to fetch Caroline and she came. I was hysterical and told her what I was afraid of. She must have picked up some French because she was able to translate my fear. Caroline calmed me down and told me they weren't going to take me to their church after all. I don't know what other message Caroline told them, but I know I never did go to see the inside of the chapel.

Fall came and went, winter set in and I sensed panic setting in on me. Again, I carried on calling for Caroline. Finally they brought her to me and I told her I was terribly homesick and I wanted to go home. I said I'd been in the hospital long enough. It was time to go home. She told me it was too late, we were all stuck there for the winter. She reassured me that we would all eventually go home, the next summer. I must have cried for days. After many months, one bright sunny morning, Caroline came to see me and told me we were going home. It was the best news I'd ever heard and I felt so light and happy. Within a few days we got ready and as before we travelled by car first, then we took a plane which landed in Mistissini.

20   Fall came and it was thrilling to know that I would be going to the bush again. My father received his food voucher from Indian Affairs. He and my mother went to the Bay and got all the basic foods, such as flour, lard, sugar, baking powder, tea, coffee, powdered milk, currants, raisins, yeast, rice, oats, beans, and a few little surprises. Plus, he would buy on credit the essentials he needed to replace for hunting, fishing, and trapping. Most families had at least two or three canoes of various sizes to accommodate their different needs while hunting. These canoes were all very useful during the transportation from the village to one's hunting grounds. Everyone travelled by either paddling or using a two-and-a-half horsepower motor if they had enough money to spare to own one. Somehow, we were lucky enough to share our hunting grounds with someone

who owned a motor. Anyway, we travelled into the bush in style that autumn. There was a whole string of canoes as we left for another ten and a half months in the wilds.

One day, I overheard my dad say to my mom, "Let's make some firewater. We'll need raisins, beans and sugar." The first time, I was very curious and watched the process, not realizing that it was going to cause me terror when they consumed it. They said it would be ready a couple of weeks after it was made.

The day finally arrived when it was time to drink the home-brew. Needless to say, I wanted to try it. I was flatly refused and was told it was only for grown-ups. I asked why, and I was told that I'd get drunk. I didn't know what they meant and I managed to sneak a sip that was left at the bottom of a cup, just to taste it. It had a sweet, strong, pungent taste, yet it was pleasant enough. The grown-ups were laughing and seemed to be enjoying themselves.

However, as the evening wore on the adults seemed to get louder and louder. I realized they were arguing. The children were told to go to sleep. I guess I slept. Someone stepped on my feet and it woke me up. There was a lot of arguing now. Some of the adults were ready to punch each other. I couldn't believe that my parents sounded so hysterically loud and unreasonable. Children woke up crying. My heart was beating fast with fright. The adults seemed to have gone crazy. Suddenly, a fight broke out and I saw my parents involved in it. My young brothers and I started to cry. We were told to shut up while one of my older sisters took the youngest child and tried to calm him.

On later occasions, my older sisters and oldest brother were permitted to drink too and I felt like all hell broke loose. The early memories of the terrible drunken fights amongst my father, mother, sisters, brother, and other adults haunted me for a long time. We, the young ones, soon learned fast what it meant when our parents talked about making firewater. We learned to detest these events and hated the mention of such a drink.

25   On one such day, my older brother and I conspired to do something to stop these events. We decided to tip over all the pails containing the firewater. When we finally got our opportunity, we fulfilled our decision. Boy, when our parents found out, they were beyond reason. They quickly deduced who the culprits were. I can say now, if I had known then what judgment day meant, that's the term I would have used to describe my brother's and my predicament. With the use of a burning branch, we had one of the major tannings of our hides. It was terrifying to feel the extent of our parents' anger. This was the first of a few beatings that I recall vividly.

When I was six years old, the Indian agent came to the community to visit all the parents. He informed the parents that he was enlisting all the children of school age to go to school at Moose Factory. Moose Factory is in Ontario at the tip of James Bay. It is about 450 kilometres by air west of Mistissini, which is in central Quebec.

My family did a thorough cleaning in and around our tent. This was their way of showing respect for the Indian agent. It was almost like receiving royalty, and I never questioned it at the time. Finally, the agent arrived at our tent. There was a lot of apprehension and I felt it. After his greeting to my parents, he started to read off the names of their children, their birthdates and their ages. My heart was beating fast as he read my name. He asked, "Where is Annie?"

I had been hiding behind one of my sisters' skirt, hoping against hope that he didn't have my name. Who was I kidding? My sister pulled me out and around in front of her and replied, "Here she is!" The agent looked at me and said a few words which I didn't understand. Then one of my sisters, who had been in school for the last few years, translated his speech. He said I was old enough to go to school but that I would never make it because I was too skinny and too small for my age. For all that was worth, I was relieved to know I had more time to live with my parents.

Two summers later I wasn't so lucky when the Indian agent came to our tent. He stated, "Annie looks ready for school now." My mother spoke up and said, "I don't really want her to be sent away to school because I need to raise and prepare her to take care of us when we get old."

30   The agent responded that if they didn't let me go, he would have her family allowance revoked and their food vouchers for basics cancelled for the year. My father spoke to my mom and tried to convince her that I must go to school. My mother didn't relent at that time, but my dad told the Indian agent to put me on the new student list. My mom was very upset with my father.

They argued for days about my situation. Finally, my dad said, "I'm going fishing for a week or so. When I get back, I don't want to find Annie here." That was the end of the argument. My father had had enough and he was gone the following day without so much as a good-bye.

Someone from the village heard the plane as it headed towards our tiny settlement on the day the students were to fly out. A lot of the parents were very unhappy. Children were trying to hide because they hated the thought of leaving their parents for another ten and a half months. My brother Murray ran into the bush and tried to hide. He had been doing this time and time again.

He had told stories about the place. The terrible way they were treated both by the staff and their peers. The food, which made one puke. He used to refer to it as dog food. The many times he went to bed hungry. We all had heard horror stories of the place. Our parents felt helpless because they couldn't do anything about it.

This was to be the most powerful memory of my youth. I begged and pleaded with my mother not to let me go. She braided my hair. Then she asked one of my sisters to help get me dressed up and ready for the plane. All the while, I sensed her sadness as she was sitting there in the middle of the cabin floor. Meanwhile, my oldest brother, Philip and one of my sisters were still looking for Murray. Philip finally found him and dragged him back to our cabin. By this time, my mother started to sniffle and I knew she was crying. Murray saw my mom sitting there crying and he felt he was the cause of it. He cried out, "Don't cry mom, I'll go to school, just don't cry." I threw myself beside her and grabbed her waist crying. I held on tight for dear life. My sisters were told to unclench my hands from my mom's waist. They dragged me out of the cabin and dragged me all the way to the plane. I fought them for all I was worth. Someone lifted me up and pushed me into the plane and closed the door. I cried, and realized that nearly all the children were crying except maybe a few of the older boys.

35   We all tried to look out with our tear-streaked faces. I noticed that some of the parents were crying. The picture of my mom sitting in the middle of the floor crying kept appearing in my mind and I'd burst out crying again and again. The plane smelled strongly of gas and it was making most of us sick. Some children were stuffing themselves with sweets to console themselves. It was a devastating sight. The plane started. My head was aching as the plane took off and most of us started to cry all over again. Finally, one by one, pupils fell asleep from exhaustion.

I woke up with the smell of vomit and I couldn't go back to sleep. Children were getting sick all around me and I got sick too. We all must have longed for the plane to land.

This experience was new to most of the youngest children. Some like myself had been exposed to these types of surroundings before. I sensed the overwhelming effect it had on all of us, especially on the inexperienced.

We arrived and got into a snowmobile and were driven to the residence. Some youngster translated what we were expected to do. We were told to go to the shower room, undress and shower. A couple of the counsellors came into the showers and helped us wash. Afterward, we were all herded into the washroom. Everyone was given a delousing treatment which left our skulls burning. This treatment was very degrading.

The first month or so was the hardest month for all of us. There were nights we would be crying ourselves to sleep. Some nights the counsellor would hear us and threaten that if we kept it up we would be spanked. Many of us young ones got a good spanking because we got caught crying from loneliness. Finally we learned to muffle our cries.

40   Everything my brother and others said about the school became a reality. Most of the time we all hated the place. However, there were a few happy times when we forgot our homesickness. Times when we were involved in organized activities such as movies, picnics, walks, canteen, or Brownies.

We heard that some of the older girls tried to run away, but got caught. They got the strap when they got caught. We also saw the older ones get humiliated, until they finally fought back physically. This again would require another strapping.

We, the younger ones, were informed that we were not allowed to speak our mother tongue. It was hard to follow such a requirement, since we didn't know the second language. Many a time did we get a spanking for getting caught speaking in Cree. For a while, we, the first-year students, only spoke in one-syllable words, then short phrases in English.

Whenever we were out of sight or out of hearing from the counsellor we would speak in our native tongue. After a while, we learned to treat this requirement with a bit of play and humour. Some of us would compete to see who couldn't be caught speaking their language or who could pick up the English language fastest.

The first summer we went home is one of the saddest memories I have. The plane landed in our community. There were a lot of happy faces, both in the plane and on the dock where the parents and siblings were waiting for the airplane. Each of us was eagerly looking for familiar faces. My sister Helen had come to meet my brother and me. Her face shone with excitement as she came towards us, as I'm sure all our faces were shining. I was thrilled to be home again.

45   My father was at our tent and he greeted us with a handshake. I felt shy, a little weird and uncomfortable. Where was my mom? I thought, she probably went to the store to buy us some goodies and stopped to visit some of her friends along the way like she used to do. I waited for her to come home.

Helen prepared a meal for us and we all sat down to eat. Still, my mother hadn't come home. I was starting to get anxious, but finding excuses for why she wasn't home yet. After supper, I sat by the doorway, waiting and watching out for her to arrive any moment. Finally, my father said, "Annie, why are you sitting by the door? It's getting chilly. Get in and get your blankets ready, so you can go to sleep." I asked, "When is mama coming home?"

That's when they told us that my mother had been taken away to a hospital in Quebec City late last fall. I didn't ask any more questions. It hurt too much, but there were no tears that night. Somehow,

I felt a premonition that it was worse than I wanted to find out. As the summer wore on, and the years came and went, little by little I was told all about my mother's situation.

For a long time, my siblings and I all felt we were the cause of my mother's condition. Each of us had been carrying a guilt that was heavy in our hearts. Of course, we weren't aware that we all had this guilt until many years later, after each of us led separate lives.

For seven straight years my mother was in that hospital and was never home. After her seventh year she finally came home, but she only lasted a couple of weeks. This time, they sent her to the Roberval Institute. She was there for the next five years. They'd release her for a couple of weeks during the summer and then she would go back.

50　　Finally, after much negotiation, the family persuaded the Chibougamau hospital to keep her there. Now it wouldn't be so difficult and complicated to go and visit her. My mother has been kept there ever since. Once a year, she would be home for a few weeks and then would want to go back.

Today, it seems it would be impossible for her to come home at all. She is in a wheelchair and is now a wisp of a woman. Each of us, her children, find it almost impossible to be in her presence. It is unbearable to have seen her wither away all these years.

For the first five summers that I was home from school, I would beg my father not to let me go back to that horrid place. It was torture to have to go back there. During that time he never budged once.

In my fourth year, in midwinter, a group of us decided to run away from the residence to Rupert House, where we hoped to take a plane back to our community. The planning took about a month. One of us drew a map of the region, and mapped out where we would be going. There were a few students in the school who were from the Moose Factory community. We depended on their help and they gave us information on what we wanted to find out. Also we felt the native people in the region would help us. Some camps were placed on the map on the route we planned to take.

Towards the last couple of weeks we would store food, such as peanut butter and jam in plastic bags, apples, oranges, cookies. We were planning to ask a native family to provide us with bread and some sleeping bags. Of course, we were very naïve, but we didn't know it then. We felt we would succeed.

55　　The time arrived when we were planning to leave. It was during the evening, after the night watchman made his first rounds. We were to leave in two groups of about six. My group was the first to go. We sneaked downstairs to the playroom, where our lockers were, to get our coats. However, one of the girls accidentally slammed her locker door and we all were deathly quiet for a few seconds. We heard footsteps and we all got into our lockers hoping against hope that we wouldn't be caught. There was no such luck; someone had heard the noise and reported to another person who spread the word. Within minutes, one of the counsellors came into the playroom and started to open the lockers one at a time. One by one we finally all got out of the lockers.

We were told to wait in line. There were about five staff members. Four were female and one male. One stood in the playroom, one, the male, at the bottom of the steps, one at the top of the first set of steps, another at the top of the second set of steps, and our counsellor was waiting at the door of our dormitory. Every one of them had taken off one of their shoes or slippers, and the male counsellor had taken off his belt. We were all terrified of the male staff member because we all knew he would hurt us the most. As we arrived at each staff member we each got the spanking of our lives. Our bottoms must have been black and blue, for it hurt to sit down for days. All our privileges were taken away from us for at least a month.

Although I understood after a few years why we got punished, no one ever spoke to us about it. All we knew then was that we had done something that was bad in their eyes. However, we felt justified by our actions. All we wanted was to see and live with our parents.

There are a lot of horror stories that I can recall, during the time we spent in Moose Factory. We lost a lot of pride, self-confidence, and self-respect, and we developed an identity conflict. The separation of brothers and sisters drew families apart. We became like strangers to each other. We no longer knew or confided in each other. We all lived in some kind of shell. We only came partly out when we found someone who genuinely seemed to care. Even then we needed a lot of coaxing. Our bond had been broken.

In the fifth summer, we were informed that we were going to be sent to a new residential school in La Tuque. This time all the students who were still in elementary would be transferred to this new place. Everyone hoped it would be a better place for us, and the Indian agent assured us it would be.

60 Our parents were beginning to realize that we were developing different life attitudes and habits from theirs. They felt we were becoming a problem in the community. Many students in their early teens were starting to drink, especially the boys. The elders felt they were starting to lose control of their schoolchildren.

The students were being criticized that they didn't know how to work. The boys didn't know how to pitch a tent, how to set up nets, or how to hunt. The girls were being told that they couldn't handle a woman's work, such as getting boughs for the tent floor, washing clothes as fast as the bush women, chopping wood, or lugging pails of water. Soon we were referred to as the lazy school kids. These comments made us feel even worse about ourselves than before. It seemed that everyone was disappointed with us. We got the impression that we were failures. Some of the students were able to persuade their parents into letting them quit school. After a couple of years, it seemed that these adolescents had regained some of their self-esteem, whereas the schoolchildren were getting worse.

After a year in La Tuque, a lot of the students said that, for the first time, they actually enjoyed being in school. I was one who felt that way. Although we still got the most demeaning punishments when we were in trouble, it was a lot better than Moose Factory. The food was more edible. We could interact more with our male siblings and the activities were more coeducational with more variety. The seniors had more freedom and responsibilities. For the first time we actually filled out more and gained some weight. That summer when we came home, my father made a comment that I had grown up a lot and that I didn't look too skinny any more. It made me feel good to finally receive a positive comment from my dad, however small. By then, like all the schoolchildren, I needed and was starving for positive reinforcement, but words of praise came few and far between.

For the first time, in the summer when I was fourteen, I didn't ask if I could quit school. In fact, most of us were looking forward to going back. When my father returned, he made little hints on how much I was improving in doing the housework. Finally, he said, "You can quit school and go in the bush with us this winter."

It was my moment of triumph. I responded, "I asked you, year after year, if you would take me in and each time you refused me. Now it is too late. I like going to school now and I'm going back. You cannot hold me back. I want to finish school." My father looked at me with a weird smile and didn't say anything. He never made a comment, not then or afterwards. I went back to school that year.

65   In our third year in La Tuque, we were informed that about fifteen students, both boys and girls, would be placed in private homes. These students would be: senior group, promising pupils, and ones attending the La Tuque High School. The housemother (staff member in charge) read out the names and my name came up. It was an exciting time and we all looked forward to a new experience and a more homelike environment.

The French people I lived with were a very close-knit family. Mme Beland was sixty-two years old and separated from her husband. Her eldest daughter Micheline, about twenty-seven then, was confined to a wheelchair, and her youngest daughter, Pauline, who was fifteen, lived with her. There was another sister, Diane, who was about twenty-three, a nurse working in Montreal.

Without realizing it, this family was a great help to me both socially and psychologically. The healthy attitude I developed was all due to their way of life and what transpired between us. I realize how lucky I was to have been a part of their family. To this day, I still have a very close contact with Pauline, who is like a sister to me.

Pauline is a very special person. In her mind, she adopted me as her sister, as she told me later. The first year it was difficult for me to get used to Pauline. She tried hard to be a friend, but I wasn't very cooperative. I had a few hang-ups that I couldn't cope with and I felt she was interfering. As months went by, I got settled in. Pauline began to seem less of a nuisance. We had our fights and disagreements like any healthy siblings and we learned to forgive and forget.

Since then, Pauline has always been a big part of my life. She was and is my salvation. She has shared and been with me through happy and traumatic times in my life. Because of Pauline and her family I was able to put my life into perspective.

70
One summer, I invited Pauline to spend a few weeks with me at home. She accepted my invitation. This was a wonderful experience for all concerned. We spent a week in Mistissini. By this time, my father had stopped travelling. This was his second year running a sturgeon camp, within his hunting ground. Pauline and I flew in and she spent a couple of weeks in the bush. Many a time, Pauline retells the time she spent in the bush with my family.

To this day, I believe my life is intertwined with the Beland family's. My experience living with them prepared me for my present situation.

In my last high school year I went home at Christmas. On New Year's Eve my girlfriend and I, like every teenager, had a few drinks. We decided to go out and find a party. Of course, we headed straight to the place where there seemed to be a big drinking party. Someone was playing fiddle music and we heard people step dancing. When we entered, the place was very crowded. The floors were wet and slippery because of all the snow the people tracked in, combined with the drinks that had been spilled. We saw many friends there. They were all drinking with bottles in their hands. We were offered a sip, which we took. One of the boys, Matthew, had never drunk before. Matthew was receiving his education in the States. He was in his last year in a prep school and was also home for the holidays. He was an Iserhoff, one of the non-status people in our village. My girlfriend and I both found him very attractive.

Tonight Matthew looked like he must have had too much. He fell to the floor. My girlfriend and I helped him up, before someone toppled on him. We took Matthew outside so the cold fresh air could sober him up a bit and sat him up on a skidoo that was stationed there. We told him to stay there until he felt better. Matthew asked me to stay with him and I was happy to comply. However, I asked him why he drank. He said his friends offered him the alcohol and he wanted to try it. He said he didn't enjoy it because it was making him quite sick and he didn't plan to try it again. That was how our relationship started.

The year we were to graduate, a friend of mine and I didn't quite make it, but our counsellor had faith in us and told us we were bright and had a lot of potential. He did a bit of research and found out that Brandon University was training native students to become teachers. These students didn't necessarily graduate from high school and some were even mature students.

75   Of course, this came about so fast. I never thought I could ever be a teacher. It was a real shock to realize that this counsellor had such unattainable ambition laid out for us. My ambition had fallen along the lines of secretary, hairdresser, or interior decorator if I was lucky. In my wildest dreams, I wanted to be an actor, in plays or, if I had a chance, in films. My counsellor got the forms. I was planning to apply at Banff Fine Arts University, but I chickened out. I thought I'd die of loneliness if I went that far alone. So I never fulfilled that dream.

Meanwhile, the counsellor kept encouraging us to go for the training. Finally, we were brave enough to consent although we didn't feel all that confident. It turned out to be an experience which would be engrained in our lives forever, a time when harsh realities hit us full force on our faces. We had encountered prejudice many times before with our peers and some authoritarian figures, but it seemed subtle compared to what we experienced in Manitoba. It was like a brutal awakening and rape of our innocence.

People on the street were rude and called us names in public even if we were minding our own business in broad daylight. Violence erupted between the natives and non-natives at dusk. Someone always got hurt and it was usually a native. It was a very painful experience.

The professors and our student counsellor were not aware of what was happening to us. They tried to make us change our minds, once we decided we were going to go back to Quebec. We couldn't cope with the circumstances that were arising. The natives there had never known any other way of life, so they were coping better than we could. That is, if drinking is one way of coping. My friend and I left and only wondered what happened to the friends we made. J.J. Harper was one of the close friends we made there. He had always been very supportive, although we saw what racism was doing to him. It was a real shock to see his name in the front pages: shot by a policeman and later in the same night declared dead.

After I went back to Mistissini that year, I called the Indian Affairs and asked if I could apply to study at O'Sullivan College in Montreal for the full term. They gave their consent. So, I applied and I got accepted. However, fate had other plans for me, which were not visible right away.

80   In summer my father arrived from the bush. Then my mother came home from the hospital. For a little while everything seemed normal. The family was all together.

Finally, our differences arose. We had been scattered too long and our personalities had developed into the different lives we had experienced. Apparently, I had become very independent and I expected my younger brothers to be the same. However, they and my parents expected me to treat them in the traditional way, to serve the men. It was infuriating to be expected to do every little thing for them around the house. After a while I retaliated. It was a "no no" and I paid for it.

At the time, I felt like I was no good for anything or for anybody and I wanted to disappear. These types of words had been thrown enough into my face and I was beginning to believe that it was so. It seemed like everyone was venting their anger at me. Many hurting things were said and I knew my people felt justified, but their values were not mine any more. I was a lost cause as far as my grandmother and parents were concerned.

I gathered some stuff and ran out of the cabin. I didn't know where I would go. I felt like the world was against me so I didn't feel like seeing anyone. Finally, I headed for the houses referred to as student residences, which were supposed to be closed for the summer. I checked one door and it was unlocked. I went in and locked the door. I hid in there for two or three days but no one seemed to realize that I wasn't around. I cried and cried for hours at a time while I was in there, feeling like my whole world had crashed around me. I felt I didn't belong anywhere any more. Finally, I went back out. I hadn't eaten anything during that time and I realized I was hungry. However, I had made a decision. It was time to leave the community.

Most of the younger members of my family seemed to have disowned me as well as my grandmother, my parents, and my unmarried siblings that summer. I left the community as soon as I could and headed south to Montreal, hopefully to prepare for my future.

85   The following year, after a negative experience at O'Sullivan College, I ended up at McGill with other native students who were undergoing teacher training. We were being trained to be teacher aides within our prospective communities.

Most of us finished the year successfully. That summer, I worked at the Chibougamau hospital as an interpreter for the native people. My French was quite poor, so I had to make do with the little I knew and picked up a little more French while I was working.

Meanwhile, I, along with other native teacher trainees, had applied to be teacher aides. The interview took place that summer, in our community. A few days later, we found out we were hired, not as teacher aides, but as teachers. I was going to teach pre-k and kindergarten.

That summer was 1973. Matthew had asked me to marry him and I consented. Finally, the good times had come back.

Reflective Reading, Informal Writing

REFLECTING ON THE READING:

- Iserhoff describes several ways in which her cultural background as a Native Indian living in Canada clashed with other cultures. What are some of the "clashes" she experienced? What seem to be the specific causes of these clashes? Can you identify some of the differing cultural assumptions that produced them?
- What are the major experiences Iserhoff has while growing up that lead her to changes or to seeing the world differently? Do you find yourself surprised at Iserhoff's responses to any of these experiences? Why or why not? Choose a specific passage to illustrate your thinking.
- Iserhoff finds herself shifting from one culture to another, and in so doing she experiences both loss and gain. What does she seem to think she has lost and/or gained? Does your reading of her experience concur with, or differ from, her own? That is, looking just at her experience and ignoring, for the moment, her interpretations of that experience, do you think she has lost and/or gained things that she doesn't seem to see?

UNDERSTANDING RHETORICAL STRATEGIES:

- Reread Iserhoff's opening paragraph carefully. What do her questions lead you to believe her essay will be about? Does her essay fulfill the expectations set forth in this first paragraph? Do you like the fact that she used questions in this opening? Considering what follows, how else might she have started her essay?
- How would you describe Iserhoff's tone in this essay? Since, as a writer, Iserhoff can't fall back on "tone of voice" as speakers can, what language choices does she make that allow her to convey a sense of tone (sometimes described as the author's attitude toward

the subject under discussion and/or the author's attitude toward the reader). How does her tone differ from that of the other essays you have read? How does her tone relate to the content of her story? To her purpose in writing this piece?

- Choose a passage from Iserhoff's narrative that seems particularly striking to you. What makes this passage striking? What do you notice about the way she put this passage together? About her diction? Tone? How does this passage relate to the rest of the narrative?

- Updike's style could be described as luxurious, playful, even at points excessive. By contrast, Iserhoff's style is sparse, lean, understated. "We all lived in some kind of shell," she writes. How does her style help convince you that she *does* live in a shell? How does her use of understatement shape your view of her? Of her subject matter? Another way to ask this question: How does a writer communicate the absence of communication?

INFORMAL WRITING:

- Describe and explain ways in which your own cultural background might clash with Iserhoff's. For the moment, try to avoid thinking of one culture as "superior" to the other, focusing instead on how they are different. What purposes might these clashes serve? Is somebody hurt by these clashes? Do you or does anybody else gain something by these clashes of culture?

- Describe and explain what you learn about the world when you look at it through the lens provided by Iserhoff's experiences. Have you also had experiences that have changed how you view the world? In what respects were these experiences similar to Iserhoff's? Different?

- Write about times (or a time) when you have found yourself shifting cultures. Was this painful in any way? How might understanding Iserhoff's experiences in shifting cultures help you to rethink your own transition(s) between or among cultures?

BELL HOOKS

bell hooks belongs to the foremost rank of black intellectual figures in America. Growing up in the racially divided South, she attended the Crispus Attucks High School in Hopkinsville, Ky. Her education was furthered at Stanford University where she obtained a B.A. degree in English in 1973 and three years later at the University of Wisconsin in Madison where she earned an M.A. in the same subject. Her next important career step was to begin teaching English and ethnic studies at the University of Southern California in Los Angeles. In the early 1980s she continued to teach, broadening her range of subjects to include creative writing, African-American literature, and composition. While teaching at the University of California at Santa Cruz she also worked on her doctoral dissertation, on the writings of the African-American novelist Toni Morrison. She received her doctorate in 1983. In the late 1980s hooks moved east—first to teach African and Afro-American studies at Yale University, and then to teach women's studies and American literature at Oberlin College.

Meanwhile, hooks had published her first book, a chapbook of poetry called *And There We Wept* (1978), as well as her first full-length political work *Ain't I a Woman: Black Women and Feminism* (1981). This full-length book, which she had begun writing at the age of 19, challenged stereotypical attitudes about the place of black women in historic and contemporary times as well as their position in the feminist and black liberation movements. These ideas were expanded in her next work, *Talking Back: Thinking Feminist Thinking Black* (1989). hooks took a more personal approach and discussed her own experiences with racism in order to suggest to her readers practical ways of overcoming the psychological trauma of existence in a racist and sexist culture.

Two works from the early 1990s, *Yearning: Race, Gender, and Cultural Politics* and *Black Looks: Race and Representation*, have tackled the representation of African-Americans in popular culture. Another work, *Sisters of the Yam: Black Women and Self-Recovery*, was inspired by hooks' work with support groups for black women and her work as a monthly columnist for *Zeta* magazine. hooks has also sought, in *Teaching to Transgress: Education as the Practice of Freedom*, to show how the principles of the progressive Brazilian educator Paulo Freire can be used to help students develop their own "critical consciousness" by actively participating in their educational processes.

In 1994 hooks accepted the position of distinguished professor of English at the City College of New York, where she currently teaches. In that year she also won the Lila Wallace-Reader's Digest Writer's Award for $105,000. Her work can be seen regularly in such publications as *Callaloo, Emerge, Essence, The Utne Reader,* and *Catalyst.*

In "Killing Rage" (1995), the present essay, hooks describes the incidents of racism that occur in the course of an ordinary trip and seeks to analyze the fierce, overwhelming rage that is their result. This examination leads her back to the segregated South of her childhood where such rage had necessarily been suppressed out of the need to survive. But what is the ultimate outcome of such repression? Are short-term benefits really worth the sacrifice of long-term freedom? hooks argues that this outpouring of rage, rather than inevitably being wholly negative or merely a sign of powerlessness, can be used positively without physical violence. For hooks, this means political writing expressing how to seek and make change. Near the conclusion of the essay she writes: "At the end of the day, as I considered why it had been so full of racial incidents, of racist harassment, I thought that they served as harsh reminders compelling me to take a stand, speak out, choose whether I will be complicit or resist. All our silence in the face of racist assault are acts of complicity. What does our rage at injustice mean if it can be silenced, erased by individual material comfort?"

As you read this essay, notice how hooks makes connections between personal experiences and larger political realities.

Killing Rage: Militant Resistance

I am writing this essay sitting beside an anonymous white male that I long to murder. We have just been involved in an incident on an airplane where K, my friend and traveling companion, has been called to the front of the plane and publicly attacked by white female stewardesses who accuse her of trying to occupy a seat in first class that is not assigned to her. Although she had been assigned the seat, she was not given the appropriate boarding pass. When she tries to explain they ignore her. They keep explaining to her in loud voices as though she is a child, as though she is a foreigner who does not speak airline English, that she must take another seat. They do not want to know that the airline has made a mistake. They want only to ensure that the white male who has the appropriate boarding card will have a seat in first class. Realizing our powerlessness to alter the moment we take our seats. K moves to coach. And I take my seat next to the anonymous white man who quickly apologizes to K as she moves her bag from the seat he has comfortably settled in. I stare him down with rage, tell him that I do not want to hear his liberal apologies, his repeated insistence that "it was not his fault." I am shouting at him that it is not a question of blame, that the mistake was understandable, but the way K was treated was completely unacceptable, that it reflected both racism and sexism.

He let me know in no uncertain terms that he felt his apology was enough, that I should leave him be to sit back and enjoy his flight. In no uncertain terms I let him know that he had an opportunity to not be complicit with the racism and sexism that is so all-pervasive in this society (that he knew no white man would have been called on the loudspeaker to come to the front of the plane while another white male took his seat—a fact that he never disputed). Yelling at him I said, "It was not a question of your giving up the seat, it was an occasion for you to intervene in the harassment of a black woman and you chose your own comfort and tried to deflect away from your complicity in that choice by offering an insincere, face-saving apology."

From the moment K and I had hailed a cab on the New York City street that afternoon we were confronting racism. The cabbie wanted us to leave his taxi and take another; he did not want to drive to the airport. When I said that I would willingly leave but also report him, he agreed to take us. K suggested we just get another cab. We faced similar hostility when we stood in the first-class line at the airport. Ready with our coupon upgrades, we were greeted by two young white airline employees who continued their personal conversation and acted as though it were a great interruption to serve us. When I tried to explain that we had upgrade coupons, I was told by the white male that "he was not talking to me." It was not clear why they were so hostile. When I suggested to K that I never see white males receiving such treatment in the first-class line, the white female insisted that "race" had nothing to do with it, that she was just trying to serve us as quickly as possible. I noted that as a line of white men stood behind us they were indeed eager to complete our transaction even if it meant showing no courtesy. Even when I requested to speak with a supervisor, shutting down that inner voice which urged me not to make a fuss, not to complain and possibly make life more difficult for the other black folks who would have to seek service from these two, the white attendants discussed together whether they would honor that request. Finally, the white male called a supervisor. He listened, apologized, stood quietly by as the white female gave us the appropriate service. When she handed me the tickets, I took a cursory look at them to see if all was in order. Everything seemed fine. Yet she looked at me with a gleam of hatred in her eye that startled, it was so intense. After we reached our gate, I shared with K that I should look at the tickets again because I kept seeing that gleam of hatred. Indeed, they had not been done properly.

5   I went back to the counter and asked a helpful black skycap to find the supervisor. Even though he was black, I did not suggest that we had been the victims of racial harassment. I asked him instead if he could think of any reason why these two young white folks were so hostile.

Though I have always been concerned about class elitism and hesitate to make complaints about individuals who work long hours at often unrewarding jobs that require them to serve the public, I felt our complaint was justified. It was a case of racial harassment. And I was compelled to complain because I feel that the vast majority of black folks who are subjected daily to forms of racial harassment have accepted this as one of the social conditions of our life in white supremacist patriarchy that we cannot change. This acceptance is a form of complicity. I left the counter feeling better, not feeling that I had possibly made it worse for the black folks who might come after me, but that maybe these young white folks would have to rethink their behavior if enough folks complained.

We were reminded of this incident when we boarded the plane and a black woman passenger arrived to take her seat in coach, only the white man sitting there refused to move. He did not have the correct boarding pass; she did. Yet he was not called to the front. No one compelled him to move as was done a few minutes later with my friend K. The very embarrassed black woman passenger kept repeating in a soft voice, "I am willing to sit anywhere." She sat elsewhere.

It was these sequences of racialized incidents involving black women that intensified my rage against the white man sitting next to me. I felt a "killing rage." I wanted to stab him softly, to shoot him with the gun I wished I had in my purse. And as I watched his pain, I would say to him tenderly "racism hurts." With no outlet, my rage turned to overwhelming grief and I began to weep, covering my face with my hands. All around me everyone acted as though they could not see me, as though I were invisible, with one exception. The white man seated next to me watched suspiciously whenever I reached for my purse. As though I were the black nightmare that haunted his dreams, he seemed to be waiting for me to strike, to be the fulfillment of his racist imagination. I leaned towards him with my legal pad and made sure he saw the title written in bold print: "Killing Rage."

In the course on black women novelists that I have been teaching this semester at City University, we have focused again and again on the question of black rage. We began the semester reading Harriet Jacobs's autobiography, *Incidents in the Life of a Slave Girl*, asking ourselves "where is the rage?" In the graduate seminar I teach on Toni Morrison we pondered whether black folks and white folks can ever be subjects together if white people remain unable to hear black rage, if it is the sound of that rage which must always remain repressed, contained, trapped in the realm of the unspeakable. In Morrison's first novel, *The Bluest Eye*, her narrator says of the dehumanized colonized little black girl Pecola that there would be hope for her if only she could express her rage, telling readers "anger is better, there is a presence in anger." Perhaps then it is that "presence," the assertion of subjectivity colonizers do not want to see, that surfaces when the colonized express rage.

10   In these times most folks associate black rage with the *underclass*, with desperate and despairing black youth who in their hopelessness feel no need to silence unwanted passions. Those of us black folks who have "made it" have for the most part become skilled at repressing our rage. We do what Ann Petry's heroine tells us we must in that prophetic forties novel about black female rage *The Street*. It is Lutie Johnson who exposes the rage underneath the calm persona. She declares: "Everyday we are choking down that rage." In the nineties it is not just white folks who let black folks know they do not want to hear our rage, it is also the voices of cautious upperclass black academic gatekeepers who assure us that our rage has no place. Even though black psychiatrists William Grier and Price Cobbs could write an entire book called *Black Rage*, they used their Freudian standpoint to convince readers that rage was merely a sign of powerlessness. They named it pathological, explained it away. They did not urge the larger culture to see black rage as something other than sickness, to see it as a potentially healthy, potentially healing response to oppression and exploitation.

    In his most recent collection of essays, *Race Matters*, Cornel West includes the chapter "Malcolm X and Black Rage" where he makes rage synonymous with "great love for black people." West acknowledges that Malcolm X "articulated black rage in a manner unprecedented in American history," yet he does not link that rage to a passion for justice that may not emerge from the context of great love. By collapsing Malcolm's rage and his love, West attempts to explain that rage away, to temper it. Overall, contemporary re-assessments of Malcom X's political career tend to deflect away from "killing rage." Yet is seems that Malcolm X's passionate ethical commitment to justice served as the catalyst for his rage. That rage was not altered by shifts in his thinking about white folks, racial integration, etc. It is the clear defiant articulation of that rage that continues to set Malcolm X apart from contemporary black thinkers and leaders who feel that "rage" has no place in anti-racist struggle. These leaders are often more concerned about their dialogues with white folks. Their repression of rage (if and when they feel it) and their silencing of the rage of other black people are the sacrificial offering they make to gain the ear of white listeners. Indeed, black folks who do not feel rage at racial injustice because their own lives are comfortable may feel as fearful of black rage as their white counterparts. Today degrees and intensities of black rage seem to be overdetermined by the politics of location—by class privilege.

I grew up in the apartheid South. We learned when we were very little that black people could die from feeling rage and expressing it to the wrong white folks. We learned to choke down our rage. This process of repression was aided by the existence of our separate neighborhoods. In all black schools, churches, juke joints, etc., we granted ourselves the luxury of forgetfulness. Within the comfort of those black spaces we did not constantly think about white supremacy and its impact on our social status. We lived a large part of our lives not thinking about white folks. We lived in denial. And in living that way we were able to mute our rage. If black folks did strange, weird, or even brutally cruel acts now and then in our neighborhoods (cut someone to pieces over a card game, shoot somebody for looking at them the wrong way), we did not link this event to the myriad abuses and humiliations black folks suffered daily when we crossed the tracks and did what we had to do with and for whites to make a living. To express rage in that context was suicidal. Every black person knew it. Rage was reserved for life at home—for one another.

To perpetuate and maintain white supremacy, white folks have colonized black Americans, and a part of that colonizing process has been teaching us to repress our rage, to never make them the targets of any anger we feel about racism. Most black people internalize this message well. And though many of us were taught that the repression of our rage was necessary to stay alive in the days before racial integration, we now know that one can be exiled forever from the promise of economic well-being if that rage is not permanently silenced. Lecturing on race and racism all around this country, I am always amazed when I hear white folks speak about their fear of black people, of being the victims of black violence. They may never have spoken to a black person, and certainly never been hurt by a black person, but they are convinced that their response to blackness must first and foremost be fear and dread. They too live in denial. They claim to fear that black people will hurt them even though there is no evidence which suggests that black people routinely hurt white people in this or any other culture. Despite the fact that many reported crimes are committed by black offenders, this does not happen so frequently as to suggest that all white people must fear any black person.

Now, black people are routinely assaulted and harassed by white people in white supremacist culture. This violence is condoned by the state. It is necessary for the maintenance of racial difference. Indeed, if black people have not learned our place as second-class citizens through educational institutions, we learn it by the daily assaults perpetuated by white offenders on our bodies and beings that we feel but rarely publicly protest or name. Though we do not live in the same fierce conditions of racial apartheid that only recently ceased being our collective social reality, most black folks believe that if they do not conform to white-determined standards of acceptable behavior they will not survive. We live in a society where we hear about white folks killing black people to express their rage. We can identify specific incidents throughout our history in this country whether it be Emmett Till, Bensonhurst, Howard Beach, etc. We can identify rare incidents where individual black folks have randomly responded to their fear of white assault by killing. White rage is acceptable, can be both expressed and condoned, but black rage has no place and everyone knows it.

15   When I first left the apartheid South, to attend a predominantly white institution of higher education, I was not in touch with my rage. I had been raised to dream only of racial uplift, of a day when white and black would live together as one. I had been raised to turn the other cheek. However, the fresh air of white liberalism encountered when I went to the West Coast to attend college in the early seventies invited me to let go some of the terror and mistrust of white people that living in apartheid had bred in me. That terror keeps all rage at bay. I remember my first feelings of political rage against racism. They surfaced within me after I had read Fanon, Memmi, Freire. They came as I was reading Malcolm X's autobiography. As Cornel West suggests in his essay, I felt that Malcolm X dared black folks to claim our emotional subjectivity and that we could do this only by claiming our rage.

Like all profound repression, my rage unleashed made me afraid. It forced me to turn my back on forgetfulness, called me out of my denial. It changed my relationship with home—with the South—made it so I could not return there. Inwardly, I felt as though I were a marked woman. A black person unashamed of her rage, using it as a catalyst to develop critical consciousness, to come to full decolonized self-actualization, had no real place in the existing social structure. I felt like an exile. Friends and professors wondered what had come over me. They shared their fear that this new militancy might consume me. When I journeyed home to see my family I felt estranged from them. They were suspicious of the new me. The "good" southern white folks who had always given me a helping hand began to worry that college was ruining me. I seemed alone in understanding that I was undergoing a process of radical politicization and self-recovery.

Confronting my rage, witnessing the way it moved me to grow and change, I understood intimately that it had the potential not only to destroy but also to construct. Then and now I understand rage to be a necessary aspect of resistance struggle. Rage can act as a catalyst inspiring courageous action. By demanding that black people repress and annihilate our rage to assimilate, to reap the benefits of material privilege in white supremacist capitalist patriarchal culture, white folks urge us to remain complicit with their efforts to colonize, oppress, and exploit. Those of us black people who have the opportunity to further our economic status willingly surrender our rage. Many of us have no rage. As individual black people increase their class power, live in comfort, with money mediating the viciousness of racist assault, we can come to see both the society and white people differently. We experience the world as infinitely less hostile to blackness than it actually is. This shift happens particularly as we buy into liberal individualism and see our individual fate as black people in no way linked to the collective fate. It is that link that sustains full awareness of the daily impact of racism on black people, particularly its hostile and brutal assaults.

Black people who sustain that link often find that as we "move on up" our rage intensifies. During that time of my life when racial apartheid forbid possibilities of intimacy and closeness with whites, I was most able to forget about the pain of racism. The intimacy I share with white people now seldom intervenes in the racism and is the cultural setting that provokes rage. Close to white folks, I am forced to witness firsthand their willful ignorance about the impact of race and racism. The harsh absolutism of their denial. Their refusal to acknowledge accountability for racist conditions past and present. Those who doubt these perceptions can read a white male documenting their accuracy in Andrew Hacker's work *Two Nations: Black and White, Separate, Hostile, Unequal.* His work, like that of the many black scholars and thinkers whose ideas he draws upon, highlights the anti-black feelings white people cultivate and maintain in white supremacist capitalist patriarchy. Racial hatred is real. And it is humanizing to be able to resist it with militant rage.

Forgetfulness and denial enable masses of privileged black people to live the "good life" without ever coming to terms with black rage. Addictions of all sorts, cutting across class, enable black folks to forget, take the pain and rage away, replacing it with dangerous apathy and hard-heartedness. Addictions promote passive acceptance of victimization. In recent times conservative black thinkers have insisted that many black folks are wedded to a sense of victimization. That is only a partial truth. To tell the whole truth they would have to speak about the way mainstream white culture offers the mantle of victimization as a substitute for transformation of society. White folks promote black victimization, encourage passivity by rewarding those black folks who whine, grovel, beg, and obey. Perhaps this is what Toni Morrison's character Joe Trace is talking about when he shares in *Jazz* the knowledge his play-father Mr. Frank taught him, "the secret of kindness from white people—they had to pity a thing before they could like it." The presence of black victimization is welcomed. It comforts many whites precisely because it is the antithesis of activism. Internalization of victimization renders black folks powerless, unable to assert agency on our behalf. When we embrace victimization, we surrender our rage.

20   My rage intensifies because I am not a victim. It burns in my psyche with an intensity that creates clarity. It is a constructive healing rage. Vietnamese Buddhist monk Thich Nhat Hanh teaches that self-recovery is ultimately about learning to see clearly. The political process of decolonization is also a way for us to learn to see clearly. It is the way to freedom for both colonized and colonizer. The mutuality of a subject-to-subject encounter between those individuals who have decolonized their minds makes it possible for black rage to be heard, to be used constructively.

Currently, we are daily bombarded with mass media images of black rage, usually personified by angry young black males wreaking havoc upon the "innocent," that teach everyone in the culture to see this rage as useless, without meaning, destructive. This one-dimensional misrepresentation of the power of rage helps maintain the status quo. Censoring militant response to race and racism, it ensures that there will be no revolutionary effort to gather that rage and use it for constructive social change. Significantly, contemporary reinterpretations and critiques of Malcolm X seek to redefine him in a manner that strips him of rage as though this were his greatest flaw. Yet his "rage" for justice clearly pushed him towards greater and greater awareness. It pushed him to change. He is an example of how we can use rage to empower. It is tragic to see his image recouped to condone mindless anger and violence in black life.

As long as black rage continues to be represented as always and only evil and destructive, we lack a vision of militancy that is necessary for transformative revolutionary action. I did not kill the white man on the plane even though I remain awed by the intensity of that desire. I did listen to my rage, allow it to motivate me to take pen in hand and write in the heat of that moment. At the end of the day, as I considered why it had been so full of racial incidents, of racist harassment, I thought that they served as harsh reminders compelling me to take a stand, speak out, choose whether I will be complicit or resist. All our silences in the face of racist assault are acts of complicity. What does our rage at injustice mean if it can be silenced, erased by individual material comfort? If aware black folks gladly trade in their critical political consciousness for opportunistic personal advancement then there is no place for rage and no hope that we can ever live to see the end of white supremacy.

Rage can be consuming. It must be tempered by an engagement with a full range of emotional responses to black struggle for self-determination. In midlife, I see in myself that same rage at injustice which surfaced in me more than twenty years ago as I read the *Autobiography of Malcom X* and experienced the world around me anew. Many of my peers seem to feel no rage or believe it has no place. They see themselves as estranged from angry black youth. Sharing rage connects those of us who are older and more experienced with younger black and non-black folks who are seeking ways to be self-actualized, self-determined, who are eager to participate in anti-racist struggle. Renewed, organized black liberation struggle cannot happen if we remain unable to tap collective black rage. Progressive black activists must show how we take that rage and move it beyond fruitless scapegoating of any group, linking it instead to a passion for freedom and justice that illuminates, heals, and makes redemptive struggle possible.

Reflective Reading, Informal Writing

REFLECTING ON THE READING:

- bell hooks is writing about an anger that shakes her to the core, a "killing rage." What personal events does she tell us about that lead to this rage? What societal structures and events does she analyze for us?
- hooks suggests that racism is tied to social class and economics. Look for passages in her text where she seems to be making these arguments. What evidence does she use? Analyze and try restating her argument in your own words.
- hooks writes, "Confronting my rage, witnessing the way it moved me to grow and change, I understood intimately that it had the potential not only to destroy but also to construct." Read this sentence as a blueprint of hooks' essay itself and examine how her rage moves her to change and grow within the essay.

UNDERSTANDING RHETORICAL STRATEGIES:

- hooks doesn't kill anyone; in fact, it could be argued that while she certainly was angry at the time of the events she describes, she uses "anger" in her essay as a calculated means of moving us to action rather than as a serious call to violence. Consider the possibility that her "killing rage" is a rhetorical ploy. Is it meant to make us uncomfortable? If so, why? How does her anger influence the way we read this essay?

- Who do you think hooks intends her primary audience to be for this essay? Why do you think this? Point out specific passages or words that support your understanding of who her audience is intended to be.
- Many people would characterize hooks' writing as confrontational. Would you? Why or why not? Does her tone and the stories she tells seem appropriate for the subject matter?
- What does hooks accomplish by opening her essay with an extended anecdote? Does it matter that it is set on a plane, in the first-class section, no less? How do you respond to the very first sentence? How does this anecdote relate to the major themes of the essay as a whole?
- hooks draws liberally from the vocabularies of both psychology (repression, internalize, psyche, self-actualization, self-recovery) and politics (colonized, underclass, apartheid, transformative revolutionary action). Could a case be made that, in this essay, style *is* argument, that the whole point of this essay has to do with the collision of psychology and politics? With the idea that "the personal is the political," as the early feminists liked to point out?

Informal Writing:

- Describe a time when you were so angry that you might have described your feelings as a "killing rage." What events, personal and/or societal, led to these feelings? How does your "killing rage" and the reasons for it differ from hooks'? If you have never felt that much anger, explore the personal and societal reasons that you have never experienced a "killing rage."
- Examine closely your race and ethnicity and how you think they relate to your economic and social class. Examine your race and class through hooks' eyes. How do her arguments help you "re-see" your own race and class and how they might be related?
- We tend to think of anger as a negative, but hooks suggests something else. Can you think of an experience or instance in which anger helped you or somebody else change? Was this a positive change, as hooks imagines the result of her anger to be, or was it a negative change?

PETER MIDDLETON

The idea for Peter Middleton's book, *The Inward Gaze* (1992), came about after Middleton and his friend, John Colvin, put together an anthology of men's writing about changing masculinities. Middleton discovered the difficulty men had in writing about their gender and finding a language and tools for extensive analysis of their gender. His work is about "men's representations of their subjectivity and power as men." In this excerpt, he uses scenes from DC Comics' Batman and Superman because comics blend manhood and boyhood, negotiating between men and boys. Comics form a dialogue between men and boys, a form of dialogue that has few articulate outlets other than sports. The complex fantasies lend comics symbolic potential that even film lacks. Images and words within the frame are not hindered by reality and explore fantastical realms.

Middleton spent part of his childhood in Washington, D.C. and Maryland while his father worked with the British embassy. Here he became an avid reader of American comics not readily available in his home, the United Kingdom. In his thirties, he rediscovered American comics, and the visual style captivated him. He appreciated the way a single frame would have an "existential moment isolated in action and words simultaneously." Some readers felt the juxtaposing of comics and classic texts in his book was an offensive confusion of "high and low culture." He chose to use literary and cultural texts to begin this work on exploring men's consciousness of themselves as men because literary and cultural studies are concerned with subjectivity and with power relations as well as "one of the means by which our societies generate their knowledge of self, society, and the natural world." In the introduction to his book, Middleton states that his argument will be "that masculine subjectivities can only begin to be comprehensible if men rethink existing concepts of gender and identity in terms of the relations between society, reason and emotion." Subjectivity is the process of the self knowing itself; the self is somehow aware of its existence, and this awareness is called subjectivity. The term is used to express a very abstract level of mental activity that is different from terms like "consciousness" or "mind." Although Middleton's work is about men and masculinity, he writes with respect for the differences between "men, women, cultures and histories." He focuses on American and British men because these are the two cultures he knows the best, having lived in both.

Middleton's own writing process has been strongly influenced by Peter Elbow's work on writing. He believes in the importance of both freewriting and of separating the composing process from editing. The process is messy, and revision is very important. As a poet, Middleton tries to hear the sound of his words and the patterns of phrasing and syntax in his text. In prose, he attempts to create a pattern of sentences that has some suspense and resolution to it. Although the topic and content of this chapter prove difficult, Middleton's lyric prose and conversational style help pull the reader through the text. The engaging use of comics illustrates his argument. Superman, for instance, is a "heuristic device," a reminder of the connection between boyhood fantasy and modern masculinities. He is a figure of "cultural unconsciousness of masculinity" to which Middleton believes men's studies must turn with self-awareness in order to analyze and understand modern masculinity. As you read Middleton, think about other forms of popular culture that might be a reminder of the connection between boyhood and manhood.

Boys Will Be Men: Boys' Superhero Comics

INTROSPECTION AS METHOD

Where might we begin to find out about the formation of modern masculine subjectivities? We could being with the question: how does a boy become a man? This question is asked by most current theories of masculine subjectivity (and has recently been made the central issue by *Iron John: A Book about Men* (Bly 1990) and the renewed interest in initiation rituals it has encouraged). These theories assume that by concentrating on what divides boys from men we may be able to learn more about adult masculinities. One way of answering these questions would be to turn our gaze inward, those of us who are men, or to look to the confessions of men, if we are women, and rely on introspection and memory. Surely men's histories and experiences could provide plenty of material for such an enquiry? Or can they? I shall begin this enquiry by putting two of my own stories to the test to consider the problems of using introspection as a method for developing a theory and politics of masculine subjectivities. The first is a recollection of boyhood, the second an anecdote about fatherhood.

My own boyhood, from the age of 8 to 12, now seems to have been dominated by intense, obsessive and serious pleasures. Some, like stamp and coin collecting, seem fairly intelligible still. Others like reading comics and 'trainspotting' provided pleasures that seem to be peculiar to that part of my life. The joy of watching trains all day seems especially remote. With other boys I sat on the edge of a path at the top of a grassy bank above the Birmingham to Bristol railway line, and wrote down the numbers of the engines as they passed. Long waits were punctuated by the intense excitement of trying to see the often dirty numberplate of a fast train. At home I underlined the numbers I had collected, in a special reference book, the 'combined edition', which listed all the current steam and diesel engines on British Railways. The memory of those 'combines', as we nicknamed them, is still powerful. I can still feel that one of these volumes would be valuable to own even though the information in it is of absolutely no interest to me now.

Sometimes I and my friends caught a train to the nearby city of Gloucester, where we never left the platform. We took sandwiches and did a good day's work, watching the activities of the trains and engine sheds. At a station there was always the possibility of the greatest achievement of all, 'cabbing' an engine. Most railway workers ignored us or chased us away, but occasionally a friendly driver might let one or two of us climb up into the open cab of a steam locomotive waiting at the platform. How exposed the cab felt! We found it difficult to believe that all the coal needed for the journey was shovelled by one man into the boiler's incandescent mouth. That was real man's labour. The shared pleasure of trainspotting was intense. I always travelled with friends to nearby stations. The days on platforms and railway banks were spent talking and speculating about the trains. Trainspotting satisfied a desire for independence, because it could take place outdoors away from parents and teachers, and much of the time in places unsupervised by adults. Yet none of these reasons would have been sufficient in itself to make trainspotting the centre of my life for nearly three years. I think its great attraction lay in an unconscious fantasy of access to men's power, a fantasy made possible by the tangible power of the locomotives and their highly visible male drivers. Cabbing a locomotive was exciting because we were stepping into the mysterious place where men derived their power from real work. For a moment we were men too.

5   The best engines were those that had names: Corfe Castle, Leckampton Hall. Some Western Region engines had been given a name, written in an arch of brass letters on the side of the engine beside the boiler, that referred to country houses and castles in the west country. A geography of social power in the region thundered past us. I could not have put into words then why these engines so fascinated me. The intense feelings they aroused lay outside the logic of ordinary consciousness, just as the excitement of comics did. Now I can say that these engines seemed to embody the power of the places they were named after, but then the connection felt real and immediate. The engine was the estate. That was how I understood the nature of social power. The names conveyed a sense of the great British heritage, helped by glimpses of other rarer locomotives which didn't come along our line and could be seen only if we sent to faraway stations, engines named after kings, princesses, earls and so forth.

Steam engines have highly visible pistons and crankshafts. They are colourful, large, powerful but simple forms of machinery, visibly engaged in acts of speed and power. Their independent mobility makes them good symbols for animate power. This force is visually available in readily symbolized form and controlled by men. It would be a mistake immediately to call this power phallic, because such a label too readily converts itself into some kind of visual equation between engine and male sexuality, when it is men's social and political power, as well as the power of adult men's bodies as perceived by a boy, which the engine is made to represent. Power is usually understood as potential for the future, but in these engines we also saw the power of history. An entire recent history of men's achievements was figured by the locomotives, a history fuelled by the knowledge that many of these engines were much older than we were. They belonged, like the men who drove them, to the adult world, a specifically male adult world whose history they made tantalizingly visible and inaccessible. All we could do was watch it, excluded, and daydream about our eventual assumption of its power. Trainspotting was our way of negotiating with the world of manhood which lay all about us outside the home, so mysteriously powerful and remote. Trainspotting was a bricolage of accessible, visible elements of the adult men's world, out of which we could form rituals to provide the space for us to understand our current exclusion and eventual arrival in that world. Perhaps the dream of seeing all the locomotives on the railway, 'copping' every single number listed in our combined volumes of engine numbers, was a symbol of that achievement. At that point introspection fails me. I shall turn to another kind of introspection, less vulnerable to the vicissitudes of memory, a recent anecdote. Once you begin looking, moments exemplary of the relations between boys and men seem to occur everywhere.

One afternoon in early 1990, I took my two children to the playpark in a double buggy. I had wanted to go to the shops but my 2-year-old son insisted we go to the park first. Fortunately my 5-month-old daughter was fast asleep, and stayed asleep the whole time we were in the playground. She doesn't like to be left in an unmoving buggy too long if she's awake. When we arrived at the park I felt apprehensive and embarrassed. Six youths were sitting on the benches and equipment in the toddlers' section of the playpark. As I arrived at the gate they all fell silent and watched me from their perches. I looked back at them. Then without a word or any sign of acknowledgment they go up together and walked off to find somewhere else to sit. It was half term and they had no school to keep them busy. They seemed embarrassed to be found in a playground, but then so was I, despite my determination to spend time during the day with my children, embarrassed to be witnessed pushing a pram and cuddling a little boy.

My son began to ride one of the wooden motorcycles mounted on a large spring. Another older boy of about 8 ran up and began to ride the other one. I said something to him by way of hello and he quickly became chatty. He showed my son and me his tricks. He stood up on the wobbling platform; he made it weave from side to side. My son thought this was very funny. The boy then got off and told me he had made a sword out of a stick, using his penknife. Turning out his pocket to show it to me, he held out his other prize possessions as well. What caught my eye besides the knife in the little heap in his hand were a miniature gun and a plastic female figure with a tuft of hair, all of which seemed to belong on a chain of some kind. After proudly showing me the gun's workings, he told me about his secret den, and about his friend, who could be very 'naughty'. The friend cycled up, and the boy said, 'Do you want to play?' only to receive a daunting reply, a curt, suspicious, mannered 'What?'. These two certainly gave the impression that they wanted to avoid too much familiarity between themselves, at least in front of a man. They may have felt extra pressure to do this because only their behavior identified them as male. Both had long hair, and the other boy could have been a girl if not for his manner, which was self-consciously masculine and 'tough'. After some talk the boys went off together, having told me that they had to be home respectively at four and seven. These return times were apparently significant measures of their status, because the 'naughty' boy who didn't have to be back until seven was clearly one up on the other. The more independent you were the better.

The incident stuck in my mind because it seemed to sum up something about boys and men. The only boy who played there unselfconsciously was my 2-year-old son. The boys of 8 or so were willing to play but very selfconscious about it, and the teenage youths were there almost nostalgically, if it was a secure, familiar place where they could talk seriously about what was on their minds, even if they couldn't quite be seen to be enjoying the playground. And above all the boy's pocket contents fascinated me. They were so perfectly symbolic. A knife, a gun and a female fetish seemed to symbolize both what the boy wanted, and the violence to which this play version of manhood could be a prelude. The boy was fascinated in his turn by me, and what he seemed to want was some kind of approval of his symbols. Just before his friend appeared he tried to enlist my help searching something he had lost in the shrubbery nearby. He wouldn't say what. I was a little suspicious and refused. I think now that the help he wanted was symbolic approval by a man, something he had trouble finding. All of us males except my 2-year-old son felt awkward about seeming to enjoy the pleasures of play, especially in the presence of other males. Only a serious masculine purpose could legitimate it. Two themes emerge from this anecdote, which I shall pursue further. One is the way the fantasy of manhood seems to be created out of a bricolage of fragments from the masculine public world, and the other is the difficulties that males, especially males of different ages, have articulating their relations with one another.

10   This anecdotal illustration of one alleged feature of contemporary masculinities can, I believe, be substantiated by both empirical and theoretical methods. Yet problems arise even before the anecdote itself begins. The collective pronoun in the opening sentences of this chapter shifted uneasily from the collective readership of this text, to the entirety of those who are male and female, and back again, blurring distinctions of all kinds which might make any such larger 'us' a fantasy. Even the conventional collective pronoun for the readership and writer is obviously subject to some conflict, as the fourth and fifth sentences indicate. So the apparent ease of the appeal to experience hides a potentially manipulative levelling of differences. But there is worse. My story contains a fairly obvious subtext: 'I am able to be both an academic and a good parent, a father who can do what are traditionally a mother's tasks.' It would be much more difficult for a woman academic to tell this story because it would be received very differently, perhaps as 'women's talk', something at the opposite extreme from an intellectually respectable conclusion based on close scientific observation. My anecdote also has traces of confessional narrative that has been an element of a large part of the autobiographical writing on masculinity. This imposes on the story a subsequent, more informed, more worked-out viewpoint. Indeed the more self-critical the tone of such writing, paradoxically the more virtuous the narrator will appear. In feminist writing, confessional narratives commonly work in reverse because they show a progress towards the recognition that self-criticism was internalized oppression. Criticism within the narrative will be counterposed with an understanding critical of that criticism, and the process will have a complex and self-adjusting dialectic likely to be unavailable to a man writing such material. Moreover, existing models of women's writing lend themselves to adaptation for such purposes (think of the women violists on whom feminists can now draw). For men, the existing models of heroic acquisition of manhood are likely to appear part of the problem they are addressing.

Similar problems adhere to the use of childhood recollections. Such personal memories will be resonant for some readers, but they cannot claim representative status. This introspective analysis of my trainspotting memories leaves a lot assumed or unexplored. I have added the emotions and desires retrospectively to the presentation of my memories, in a form which then colludes closely with interpretation. A fuller account would be something more like prose fiction. Desires would be embedded in the narrative in such a way that they were not wholly dependent on my interpolated framework of interpretation. A more general difficulty will have occurred to anyone familiar with contemporary literary and cultural theory. Experience, it is argued, is never simply given to us, but comes structured by ideology and discourse. Class, race, history and gender itself are determinants whose effects are likely to the largely unconscious. Such experiential material as this needs to be interpreted within some other, wider framework which is then subject to analysis, but it is questionable whether the same author can both write autobiographically and present a self-analysis. That it can be done is clear. Freud provides a famous modern example, and an indication of the difficulty. We are not all such polymaths, and are unlikely to have or perhaps even to want to develop a complex system of thought such as psychoanalysis. This doesn't mean confessional writing is worthless. Far from it. Much of the impetus towards a better understanding of masculinity by men has come from just such confessional material. The courage and acuity of such writing are impressive, and will remain important. Alongside it we need to develop more articulate insight into the inner life of masculinity than the strictly autobiographical form makes possible. A better model is modern prose and poetry where the presentation of introspection about manhood, sexuality and modernity can call on the widest linguistic resources. Such work, which I will discuss later in this book, precludes, in all but exceptional cases, the kind of argumentative analysis central to my project here. Therefore the remainder of this book will largely eschew personal writing because it is not yet possible to produce such writing and have it mesh with theoretical analysis in the way feminism has demonstrated. One day it may be possible, when men's movements and self-awareness of gender amongst men have generated languages and occasions for such discussion. For now a man writer discussing the inner dimensions of masculinity faces a choice between theoretical analysis and autobiography. I shall occasionally make personal observations but I shall not try and ground my arguments in any more general personal narrative.

The other obvious place to look for an account of masculine subjectivities would be that dominant form of contemporary investigation in the social sciences, the interview. Ask men about themselves in questions which foreground their gender, and then analyse the record. Such work accounts for most of the remainder of what is currently available about masculine subjectivity. Interviewing men about themselves has become widespread. Collections of representative interviews by journalists, the massive narrativized sampling of questionnaires in Shere Hite's (1981) work, and the more cautious, empirical work of academic sociology, have given us a wealth of material. Almost all of this work necessarily relies on the subject representing himself in a speech which is not only conscious but to some extent self-aware of gender politics. Masculinity, however, as feminists have repeatedly demonstrated, is often unaware of its areas of blindness. Any method that relies on articulate speech in a dialogue, even with the anonymous questionnaire, will be limited in its access to the field of subjectivity. Analysis of unconscious features may circumvent this limitation, but much will remain untouched by such ready-made narratives of self-explanation. Less conscious, less articulated and less resolved areas of masculine subjectivities are likely to remain unexamined by the subject's verbalized self-analysis. For a wider investigation of masculine subjectivities we need to look at symbolic forms, at fantasies, inarticulate experience and the activities of what has been called the unconscious, but might be more precisely called an unconscious, in modern men.

Childhood is both a condition and a history. Their condition of childhood continues in our own and others' children, whose presence can help us recover and recapitulate our own historical childhood, but cannot entirely overcome its increasing remoteness. Our physical shape has changed, especially our size, and with it, our environment and its scale. We are now a part of the adult world, however far from its centers of power. All that remains of childhood are memories and compulsions which lie in the foundations of our being, out of sight and apparently beyond control. Indeed they are what control us according to many modern psychologies. Hume's dictum that reason is the slave of the passions has been slightly rewritten. Now in a postpsycholoanalytic age we believe that reason is the slave of childhood passions. Psychoanalytic study of these primary materials has made us aware of how such processes make us what we are, even when we cannot quite put this knowledge to work in our own specific histories. Infant desire and its reawakening in adolescent sexuality draw us back to the world of the under–5s and the over–12s. In between is a life which remains remote in a quite different way, seemingly not of interest to such theoretical representation. Between 5 and 12 is a spell of consciousness and dormant sexuality in which other pleasures dominated our lives, pleasures whose seriousness makes them now seem more remote than the stirrings of Oedipal desire. It is not that we cannot remember what we did then. My own memories of that period of my life seem exceptionally clear. Subjectively I felt more rational and intelligent than at any other time before or since. Those pleasures of later childhood are not repressed or forgotten but displace into another economy of desire whose lack of familiar teleologies of sexual behaviour can make it seem both attractive and irrelevant to adults for whom sexual priorities determine lives.

BOYS AND COMICS

15 Trainspotting is just one of many boyhood rituals whose significance is hard to assess because it leaves so few visible traces. Boys construct a symbolic universe and its ritual actions out of a chosen set of activities and objects, which have little to do with the adult socioeconomic purposes of rail transport, and, like some cargo cult, create an almost metaphysical negotiation with what is to them a seemingly transcendent power. Boys have many such rituals and they will always be changing, local and much of them invisible to the adult world. Some, like sport, produce more direct relations between men and boys, but they probably do so because sport itself is a game deliberately set aside from the productive processes of economics and daily life (this may be one reason why games have provided men philosophers with attractive paradigms for language and aesthetics). Boys are excluded from the activities which define men in the public and domestic sphere. At present there are few ways that boys can find a dignified and respected entry into the men's worlds of defining work. For me, and for most boys still, the only access lay through the media.

Film, television and comics provide armatures on which boys can wind all kinds of fantasy. Comics, relatively low-budget, highly targeted and visually simple, offer a useful means of anlysing the pre-emptive structures of fantasy which I am suggesting can be found in most boyhood rituals of entry into manhood. Martin Barker (1989) has pointed out that comics provide the analyst of popular culture and ideology with an easier point of reference than many other forms because comics are easily described and presented. For this discussion, the comic fantasies of masculinity and hypermasculinity have the advantage of being presented in a less censored form than in many other kinds of popular culture. The reality principle is also less evident. For this reason larger claims can be made for the comic's importance as a medium of fantasy. Without wishing to endorse Wiley Lee Umphlett's theory of nostalgia neurosis—'an undermining of self-actualization by compelling us to retreat into our private dream world' (Umphlett 1983: 17) which impairs people's ability to see their environment and past at all clearly—I think that his claim about the comic book is worth taking seriously:

Thus the comic book persists as both a psychological and sociological expression of the times that produce it, substantiating my interpretation of the medium as thriving on the nostalgia neurosis of our popular culture. The comic book, because of its obsession with the exploration and dramatization of fantasy, is capable of plumbing the depths of both our psychic wish fulfilments and dreads as no other medium can, with the possible exception of the movies.

(1983: 104)

Fantasy, however, cannot just be read off like a simple code. Its addressees and its hierarchy of structures, from individual panels to entire narratives, need to be considered.

20   The panels of sketchily drawn figures give desires a space for fantasies of manhood which can go beyond the machinery of masculinity to its fears, angers and imperatives in a private moment of imaginary privilege. Cartoon images are often highly expressive. Both speech and imagery can be so clear and well outlined that they become resonant in the way a short poem can. Terse, forceful expressions of desire and images of the human body at full stretch often have that ironic quality which pop artists isolated in the 1960s for their canvases. Said and shown with such self-certainty, these moments reveal their suppositions as an excess of assertion which becomes funny. Into that humour rushes an intellectual awareness that doesn't conceal the seriousness of the dilemmas they present, but can recognize and rethink it.

What follows is not a history of comics nor a study of representative cartoon strips, but an analysis of psychological structures within extracts chosen to demonstrate a thesis about men, boys and masculinities. Most of my examples and generalizations are drawn from the various genres of science fiction action comics, especially the American Marvel and DC comics, and the British comics *2000AD*, and *Eagle*. My choice of comics has some representative status, but I shall not try to demonstrate that. Instead I shall focus on developing a picture of masculinities which can then provide a route into the more theoretical chapters that follow. Comics are of limited value but the visibility of those limits makes them valuable for this discussion precisely because they are so visible. Their simplicities can illuminate the greater complexities to be found elsewhere.

Comics are commercially produced for profit by adults. Their appeal rests on several features. They offer powerful fantasies in a graphic mode which doesn't intrude too much disruptive reality either in the storyline or in the sketchy visual representation. The combination of visual and written material is both easy to read and, like other mixed media, more powerful than either would be on its own. Comics are also transgressive, in the way that pop music and films can be. Their content is not controlled or monitored in quite the way that most of the material accessible to children is. Fantasies of violence against other males and against property, which would be unacceptable in photographic realism, can be left uncensored. Unlike school books and 'good' literature for children, nothing is expected of these comic books. Printing techniques make it possible to produce comics cheaply, so children can buy them themselves, and therefore have some economic control over their pleasure. Above all, comics offer the inside story on the adult world. Hypermasculine action comics are offered to boys as the inside information on men's lives, information that they find hard to get from anywhere else. The marginal, slightly disreputable status of comics helps make them all the more attractive to their readers, who are likely to trust them more than something more official or more sanctioned.

One of the most revealing images of men I have ever seen appeared in *2000AD,* a futuristic action comic, which is popular with boys of all ages (*2000AD* 1987). This picture shows a battle-scarred man, the hero of the strip, with his allies, a robot and a fierce animal on a chain. The hero's enormous automatic rifle, enlarged by perspective to alarming size, rests on his hip and points out at the enemy and the reader. This mechanical phallus threatens the reader as if he were a potential enemy, as if just the reader's gaze were a threatening challenge. The man's monolithic, rock-like body is wrapped in bullets, guns and a chain. His granite face is expressionless except for bared teeth. An eyepatch and facial scars make him look angry, fearful and dangerous. The machinery of war has become a machine-man in the figure of the robot behind him. Its large robotic teeth, sightless eyes and enormous spiked barrel chest, bigger even than the large chest of the soldier in front of it, make it a parody of a man. The spanner strapped to its chest is a comic reminder that this is a machine, and can be controlled by whoever wields the tools. Perhaps there is even a parody of castration.

According to Aristotle (1948: 8), 'the man who is isolated . . . is no part of the polis, and must therefore be either a beast or a god.' The modern spectrum of masculine possibility has replaced gods with machines, but the cause of the limit cases is the same: isolation. Men who become self-sufficient cease to be men, as Batman appeared to be warning Superman in the story we read in the previous chapter. The picture of the ugly trio in *2000AD* offers an image of manhood pervasive in action comics. The man stands between the robot and the beast, caught between feeling like a wild animal completely mastered by his passions, and a robot incapable of feeling, totally under someone else's control. Both are degraded images of humanity. Between them is the man trying to restrain the fury of the beast, and overshadowed by the robot behind him. Robots and beasts are externalizations of inner experiences. In most of the stories they appear as the agents of destruction that must be destroyed or tamed (as our soldier has done). Robots and monsters are the extremes which manhood can easily attain, and which must be fought. The stories almost never present these threats as inner emotional or psychological struggles, but place them outside the protagonists, who can then use simple physical force to defeat the problem. This physical force is the gift and confirmation of manhood. Yet it entails a very destructive paradox. To save ourselves we have to go to war against embodiments of ourselves. Masculinity wars against itself.

25   This intestine war creates its own special verbal and visual codes in the comic strip as means of representing masculinities. Consider a typical issue of the revived *Eagle* of the 1980s, which employs a feature borrowed from its more violent American cousins (*Eagle* 1987). The comic is full of linguistic innovations. Bdam. Fwadooomf. Koff. Haaaaaaa. Eeeeek. Gnawwgh. Aaaowwgh. Wurrgghhh. Aaaaaaaaa. Graaaaach. Gaack. Yeaaaaaargh. Fzzzk. This sound poetry is of course the noise made by men in battle, by their cries and crashes. They are either neologisms uttered by the characters in extremes of stress, or the sound effects of violent action, both evidence of manhood's struggles. Why do the cartoon strips use such hard-to-pronounce neologisms, and what do they signify?

On the back page of the *Eagle* is that old favourite, Dan Dare. A rocket has kidnapped one of our heroes. Everyone looks stunned. Tremloc, a blue-skinned figure, not unlike the battered soldier who stood between the beast and the robot, aims another of these enormous rifles at the rocket ship. 'Relax lady! I'll soon bring that Treen snoop-bucket down to earth!', he cries. Dan Dare shouts back, 'No, you fool! Don't shoot!' In the next frame Dan Dare hits Tremloc, one of his own men, with his gun, to stop him shooting. 'You'll kill the boy!" he explains. We see Tremloc reeling from the blow, his mouth wide open, baring his teeth to show a bright red (bloody?) mouth. He utters one of these neologisms: 'Aaauulllgh!" Dan Dare and his team watch the rocket disappear as Tremloc crouches with his back to us, in suppliant posture, head bowed, and body obviously recovering from shock. One of the others says, 'It's moving off, Marshal! We've lost him!' Tremloc responds from his bowed position: 'And the Mekon has gained a prisoner! You may be a galactic marshal, Dare, but you'll always be an Earthie . . . .' In the final frame we see Tremloc from the front, head and neck raised assertively again, a red stain on his blue skull, saying, 'And that blasted soft heart of yours could foul up the whole mission! Just five minutes with the Mekon's torturers, and that kid is going to betray us all!' Tremloc is pointing a finger straight out of the frame at the reader, and presumably also at Dan Dare. We readers are accused of having feelings and, worse, showing them, and therefore being too soft like Dan Dare. We are in good company if we do have such feelings, but the narrative is warning us about their dangers. The casual treatment of Tremloc's injury sets the tone.

How is it that Tremloc not only accepts the blow which drew blood, but can speak of Dan Dare's 'softness' as the cause of this violence? Tremloc's cry, 'Aaauulllgh', is indicative of his pain at being hit, but why does he need this neologistic exclamation? Why could he not use a traditional interjection like 'ah' or 'ow'? The word he uses is effectively unpronounceable. No one would mistake it for English (or probably any other language). This word, like the words listed earlier, is not strictly a word at all. Such words make a sound but do not speak to us. This silence is made all the more poignant because the letters of each word are familiar, and insisted upon by their repetition, but instead of cohering into a word in the language that will form an utterance, even a one-word sentence, the letters never make it. The speaker remains inarticulate. Tremloc's pain remains unspoken. These words are not even phatic. They are moments of great emotion, great passion, which cannot speak. At these points the transition between cries and utterances has failed to occur.

Dan Dare is angry with Tremloc for preparing to shoot the rocket and thus endanger the young man who has been captured. Dan Dare is also probably scared and angry with his enemy, the Mekon. He is clearly very fond of the boy who has been kidnapped (boys don't often appear in boys' comics and when they do, appear to be a liability). All these feelings issue in the blow to Tremloc's head, not, as we might reasonably assume, in a command to stop trying to shoot down the escaping rocket. Tremloc is physically hurt by the blow, but he must also be grieved to be hurt so unexpectedly by the leader to whom he is loyal. This emotional hurt is buried under the inarticulate cry, 'Aaauulllgh', and so never allowed full expression. The emotional issues are not allowed to come into the open and be negotiated. Instead, his verbal response, once he has his breath back, is to use logic to argue with Dan Dare's strategy. Doing so, he translates his complex feelings of embarrassment, grief, shock, fear and anger into ideas which deliberately conflict with those of Dan Dare. What Tremloc cannot do is speak directly of what he feels about the incident, which is therefore left unresolved. The emotional mess will be left to clutter up their relationship.

These neologisms found everywhere in action comics are points where the languages of interaction have broken down. The strange stuttering repetition of letters hides emotional crises even as it indicates their inaccessible presence. What remains hidden is the complexity and relational nature of these feelings. All that can emerge is the meaningless cry, pre-linguistic and therefore impossible to have a dialogue with. Sometimes, when the sound effects of men's conflicts are written as neologisms across the space of their battle, it is the material environment which seems to cry out, in an even more dislocated repression of utterance. Cries and blows are the repeated climaxes of these plots, points beyond which the masculine narrative cannot go.

Anecdotal observation suggests that boys commonly use sound effects in their games, especially when they are fantasizing battle. The sounds are fun, clearly a release of energy, and never discussed. They often begin as attempts to mimic guns, engines and crashes, and then go beyond this to pure sound poetry. Is suspect they function similarly to the sound effects in comics, but I am not sure. Such sound play also seems to differentiate boys from girls.

30

In action comics for boys the characters the reader is invited to identify with are already adult men. Boys rarely appear. When they do appear the strip is usually 'comic' in the ordinary sense of the word. The action comics are aimed almost exclusively at males. Androgynous British comics like *Beano* and *Dandy* show adults outwitted by clever children who finally have to submit to adult control of the world and its laws. The big difference occurs in comics exclusively aimed at girls. These tend to show girls learning to live in a world controlled by powerful but understandable adults in which they are already beginning to participate. Where boys want to read about men, the publishers appear to believe that girls want to read about girls more than women (although there have been signs that this is changing with the appearance of comics like *She Hulk*). Girls are usually the heroines. We could infer from this that manhood is much more exclusive that womanhood. Perhaps women welcome girls into their world in a way the men don't welcome boys.

'Your Best Friend', a story in the British girls' comic *Nikki* (*Nikki* 1986), demonstrates how this works. Compared to almost anything in a boys' comic it is a complex narrative. It begins with two girls writing an agony aunt column for their school magazine in which they offer advice to a girl who has trouble looking after her two younger brothers while her mother is at work. One of the writers, Sally, has an older sister who is a teenage 'hooligan'. Most of the strip is taken up with the responsibilities of looking after children on behalf of parents. The tables are turned on Sally when her father insists that she needs a babysitter and makes her older sister do the babysitting. Sally's sister bring round her punk friends and they follow her school magazine advice and play at cooking with her. As the cake mix flies and the punks turn boisterous Sally shouts, 'Stop it, Alison! Stop it!' We leave Sally sitting alone, downcast, saying, 'Mum and Dad's evening will be ruined if they come home to this lot! I'll have to try to clear up. Life's just not fair! Other people can ask "Your Best Friend" [the agony aunt column] for advice, but there's no one who can help me!' The loneliness is seen to have causes and remedies, unlike the isolation of characters like Spider Man (whose alter ego Peter Parker is often alone) and Hulk, and derives from a reflection on the nature of authority. The givers of advice may themselves need it. There can be no absolute solutions to problems. This strip is more emphatic about a girl's responsibilities than some but it is only a matter of degree. We see Sally learning about child care, expecting to take care of the environment when other people have made a mess (Peter Parker appears to live in a permanent mess and rarely does anything about it), and learning to negotiate with adults. She is not excluded from the adult world depicted in the strip, but expected to have a (minor) place in it. Significantly it is her father who thinks she is still a child and resists letting her have more responsibility. Her mother already treats her like a little woman. As the story shows, that has its own burdens. There is conflict which cannot be easily resolved, certainly not by the kind of violent solutions which action comics propose. Conflict is contained in words, as it is in almost all girls' comics, where there is rarely anything more than a smack to contend with. The most violent moment in this story occurs when plates of food are thrown around the kitchen.

The *Nikki* story shows a girl learning a task that adult women carry out. It is educative about human relations, and suprisingly subtle about emotions like pride and arrogance. Sally is shown to have overvalued the power of her good advice. Such subtlety is nowhere to be seen in boys' comics. Men in comics are strong, and fight other men when they are angry. There is no place for boys who are less than men, and therefore no way to negotiate the transition into adult responses and their responsibilities. At the end of the *Nikki* story, our heroine Sally has to recognize the unfairness of the world she lives in. It will not always conform to her wishes and ideals. The story ends with a personal sense of injustice met with both irritation and intelligent acceptance. She will clear up and think of her parents' needs (even though her father neglected hers). In this resolution we can see the emergent shape of the self-denial feminists have exposed as the enforced character of a girl's development, as well as a lesson in the complexity of justice. Boys' comics hardly ever show such understanding of unjustice or the necessity to recognize that others' legitimate needs may conflict with one's own; they simply show anger against such needs, leading to violence. Dan Dare hits Tremloc; he doesn't try and understand Tremloc's feelings or points of view. This example from girls' comics suggests that the possibilities for showing the process of learning to become an adult, a woman, are likely to be greater than in boys' comics, although one example is only enough to hint at this.

BATMAN'S WAY OF SOLVING CONFLICT

Many action comics make justice a central mechanism in the plot. Crimes are committed by others and it is the duty of the superhero to bring them to justice. Their ability to become superheroes actually depends on this prior transgression of the law. Their powers spring into life when the rule of law breaks down. Then the criminals can be hunted down and brought to book. The story will end with the excitement of their capture, not their trial or punishment, because the law itself is never examined. Exciting fight scenes depend completely on the unexamined assumption that the injustice is external. Even when one of our superheroes does momentarily go off the rails it always turns out to be the result of mind control or some similar form of external cause. No growth in self-knowledge or acknowledgement of complicity in transgression is necessary to end it, only physical contention against its source. These superheroes can be said to gain their power from the law. The resultant equation of law and manhood means that the law is the sole reason for manhood, its only purpose. In itself it is nothing. There is no story in 'Dr Robert Bruce Banner, Thoroughly Obsessed with Himself' (*Hulk* 1981: 7). It takes the challenge of giants from another planet to rouse him from his introspection and become his Mr Hyde self, Hulk, before the narrative can really begin, and it never returns to the original troubling introspection. In the *Nikki* story justice emerges from within the thoughts and behaviour of the heroine and her immediate circle. In the superhero comics justice exists independently of the hero, although he draws the power of his manhood from it. One ideological consequence is that this law is much too readily identifiable with the actual laws of the United States (since most of these comics come from the US). In the 'Justice League of America' comics this becomes explicit. The superheroes are simply special federal agents operating from a base in science fiction.

35   Not all agents of the law are so pure. Batman's popularity must surely have been the result of his relative independence of the law as well as his absence of superpowers. Not that he is a criminal but he is not simply an agent of city hall. In many of the stories he is at odds with the official handling of an investigation, and in the way very

like a private eye. Batman also seems to have attracted the most explicit attempts to dramatize relations with boys, men and women. Robin is not just a teenage clone like Superboy or Supergirl. The Joker, who loves to pursue and torment Batman, is so camp it is almost redundant to say that he represents a homophobic portrait of gay culture. And Batman does get romantically entangled with women, perhaps because he is, strictly speaking, mortal. He may seem to fly, but there is always a grappling hook and some very tough climbing rope to help him on his way. The sense of his limits gives the stories much of their suspense, as is particularly evident in a story like 'The Joker's Five-way Revenge' (*Batman* 1990). In this story Batman is engaged in a battle of wits with a criminal who, like Moriarty in the Sherlock Holmes stories, reappears regularly to test the hero to his limits, knowing all his weaknesses. The Joker has escaped from the state hospital for the insane and is killing one by one all of his former gang members, because one of them betrayed him. The Joker delights in murder, and we see him kill one former colleague, Alby, with an exploding cigar, laughing as the man dies, saying, 'Rest in pieces, Alby' (ibid.: 171). We know that the Joker is dangerous because he has green hair, a mauve suit and a green shirt. He even wears lipstick. The Joker's face is very expressive, he smiles, laughs and uses his high cheekbones and narrow chin to great effect. No hero would have a face like that. Batman has a mask over his eyes to conceal any telltale expressiveness as well as his identity. His face is square, granite-jawed, and only expressive of anger when he bares his teeth or parts his lips.

Heroic men's faces in the hypermasculine comics are either expressionless, smooth undefined areas, or the teeth are bared in anger, and the ends of the lips droopy with sadness. The face is an important way of revealing emotion. We have very sensitive responses to the minutest changes of facial gesture, although we do not ordinarily translate what we see into a consciousness of these coded signs of character. These men in comics are giving little away. When they do show an emotion it is usually one that depends on bared teeth or a downturned mouth. Happiness, when it does make its rare appearance, is merely hinted at by showing the mouth in a slightly upturned crescent without any other facial signs at all. Sadness and anger are the most common emotions by far. Consider the face of the law. Judge Dredd, shown in profile, wears a mask that obscures any trace of the expressive part of his upper face (*2000AD* 1986). The deeply shadowed furrows of his cheek and chin describe a series of downward arcs. His lips are pursed together and fall a long way down at the ends in the classic image of sadness. His chin has a wonderful forward thrust, solid and stubbled, which counters this old terrain of suffering. This map of repressed pain is the face he wears when confronting a murderer at the end of the story (called with typical irony, 'Sob Story'). Part of the narrative tension of the comics derives from the strain of concealing emotion according to the codes of manhood at times when the pressure to let it out is very great. Facial gestures are not something an individual graphic artist has much liberty to invent. For readers to understand the expression, the facial pattern must be fairly close to codes they can understand and which find support in their culture. The art work cannot always rely on the additional support of the words in the bubbles to give them a clear interpretation. These comic-book faces are the male faces of a code that boys learn to recognize and then expect to see and emulate in their own lives.

The Joker may wear a suit to go to work, but no respectable hero would wear anything so concealing. Batman wears a cape that falls almost to the ground, but, like a flasher, wears only trunks underneath. His large muscular body strains and stretches as he fights the villains. Comic men are tall and square-shouldered. Only the foolish or the bad have bodies which don't conform to this stereotype. Roundedness or fatness or any sign of effeminacy are all clear indications of weakness. A code as rigid as phrenology is at work. Much the commonest form of the heroic male figure depends on an almost erotic exaggeration of the male physique, especially in the superhero comics. Wearing clothes that reveal as much of their bodies as possible, these muscular but sexless characters are displayed in every possible pose. The male body is on display (a display able to bypass the ego's censorship because, as one artist puts it, 'readers saw our pictures only out of the corners of their eyes' (Abbott 1986: 171)—a glance like that of the fetishist) and it is rippling with muscles apparently unconscious of their sexual potential.

These are the bodies of boyhood homoerotic desire. They have as much and as little sex as the boys who read them. They are ideal figures of what the male reader would like to be: strong, tall, handsome and awesomely powerful. Heavy shading on the drawings outlines their tense muscles. Many of them look like the men in photos of body builders. To achieve the muscle definition such photos require, the men in the pictures have to tense their muscles very hard. Hence the various odd poses taken up by body builders in competition. The muscle definition shown in the comics is the result not only of muscular power but also of tension. The high rounded calves, the long bulging thighs, the layers of finely detailed stomach muscle are the result of postures which embody extremes of tension. These are bodies ill at ease with themselves, either in the middle of some violent action or ready to perform one. Above all they are bodies to be looked at. A whole history could be written about the subtle changes in the idealization of the body. The earliest superhero comics show a Superman, for example, who is not especially impressive. Marvel went for much more muscular development until they reached an apogee of monstrous beefcake which the newer cartoonists, like those on *2000AD,* often seem to be caricaturing. Judge Dredd's epaulettes emphasize that his shoulder width owes more to tailoring than muscle.

The action-comic image of the male body is of one reduced to its basic motor functions. These bodies kick, punch, stretch, with the maximum use of the limbs and maximum occupancy of space (by contrast girls' comics allow a much greater range of human capacities to be made visible). The exaggerated emphasis on motor functions seem to lead naturally to superhuman attributes in many of the action-comic narratives. After reading a few of these comics you have to remind yourself that men can't fly, because such abilities are so commonly taken for granted. The artists fly with their heroes, surveying the world from the height of superior power and vision, yet the superheroes never fly just for pleasure, as the readers do. They are purposefully on their way to the scene of trouble, flying into action against the foe, and because they can fly they are freed from the ordinary bothersome constraints of travel and all the social obligations earthbound movement requires. Money, vehicles, timetables, tickets and inquisitive companions who don't understand why you are in your underwear can be avoided. Not surprisingly, when a story does explore the consequences of a superhero being brought to earth by a temporary cessation of superpowers yet still required to rush to the scene of the action, it is a woman, Supergirl, whom we see riding a bus across town (*Supergirl* 1973: 5). Thanks to the power to fly, the usual plot and its hero can concentrate on what really matters, the violent masculine action.

40
Batman has no superpowers but paradoxically he thereby becomes even more effectively the embodiment of complete manhood. In 'The Joker's Five-way Revenge' he wrestles a shark as well as several more human enemies. At first the Joker gets the better of him with a punch, and knocks him out with a well-aimed kick (the Joker would never be able to win with a manly punch). But then standing over him, the Joker relents, saying he wished to win after a 'cunning struggle', not as the result of 'mere luck' (*Batman* 1990: 175). He lets Batman go, later traps him in a tank with a shark, and then unluckily succumbs to a knockout punch from Batman after slipping on oily sand as he tries to make his getaway. For Batman, mere luck is good enough if he can get in his punch. The other common attribute of hypermasculinity is superhuman strength, a fantasy of masculine

bodily omnipotence. Batman may not be a 'man of steel' like the invincible Superman, but he is still one of the best fighters around, as his first opponent in the story, a former pugilist, acknowledges: 'The manly art of pugilism lost a champ when ya put on your mask, fella!' (ibid.: 169). All disputes are settled by the matching of physical force, along with any amount of legitimate weaponry which can be counted as an extension of one's own personal power. To see how marked this is we need to stand back, as we did with the Dan Dare strip, and ask ourselves how this conflict could have been settled by some other means. Fortunately most disputes in our own lives are resolved by discussion and negotiation, not violence. In these comics, language is seemly not available for conflict resolution; the best method is to smash your opponent. We might suspect therefore that the real motive for the violence is not the resolution of conflict at all, but the release of anger, because the fighting is apparently such a satisfactory means of emotional catharsis. The use of violence, especially by young males, would be a dangerous move in most real circumstances. According to Peter N. Stearns, American public perceptions of the acceptability of anger have changed over the past century and a half. From the late nineteenth century until the 1940s anger was recognized to have a limited place as a motive for political and commercial drive. But in the 1940s this waned, and advice for parents became less and less tolerant of male anger, especially male anger in the home. Similar changes occurred in the workplace (Stearns 1987: 87). Comics may have offered a fantasy fulfilment for the cathartic release of anger during such changes.

To make the fantasy work the hero with whom the reader can identify therefore needs the additional safeguard of superhuman strength in the face of such risks. Now we can really weigh in without hesitation and hit our enemy hard. For this reason the stories are usually coy about the degree of invulnerability of the superheroes. The heroes must have some vulnerability or there would be no satisfaction in the overcoming of danger because there would be no threat of hurt or death. Hence narrative moments of weakness abound (Superman is always bumping into Kryptonite) but our heroes rarely sustain a lasting injury from their fisticuffs.

Strength is crucial to the hero. Almost all the stories are tests of physical strength. Outwitting an opponent is fine as long as it is not a substitute for sheer physical power. The only options these comics recognize are physical attack and defence, a simplification which is part of that inarticulacy signalled by the neologistic cries. There is no language for such negotiations. The body has to carry all the force of expression, and is apparently only allowed to express anger. Yet these drawings of men flying into action in extremes of physical tension could represent men in extremes of physical passion. The male

body is used as a signifier of states of emotion which cannot otherwise be articulated. Strong taboos against men showing certain
kinds of affection for each other, and the widespread homophobia in
our society, make the depiction of men as objects of desire nearly impossible. The comics show what is possible for men. These heroes
can't keep their hands off one another, but when they touch their desire turns to blows.

The Batman/Joker stories come close to thematizing this homoeroticism. Batman is an isolated figure in the story. His isolation, his
withdrawn demeanor, his identification with the law, and the importance of physical combat for him, are related to his attraction to
and fear of other men. The Joker says, 'The caped crusader will locate me! He always does! However, I will be ready for him!' (*Batman*
1990: 170). He manages to make it sound like an obsession of
Batman's. The Joker takes pleasure in violence, just like the heroes,
but they always have to appear to be engaged in angry righteous execution of the law. He simply takes a sensual pleasure in violence,
and always signs it with a play on words. He repeatedly emphasizes
that he is mad, and happily so ('it's my most charming trait' (ibid.:
180)). The Joker has all the fun, all the jokes, because he has reneged
on manhood, but manhood can't keep its hands off him. The Joker is
a homophobic portrait of homosexuality as a feared part of the
hero's personality. If beasts and robots are the images of internal
and external control which need to be defeated, the Joker is an image
of homoeroticism run wild. The Joker represents the fear that manhood will come to love what it ought to be doing solely to maintain
the law, the killing of other men, and contains that fear by showing
that loving men too much will kill them.

THE HULK

45   An apparent exception to the celebration of justice occurs in the *Hulk*
series of comics. In most cases the superhero has an easy relation
with his own superpowers. Difficulties only arise in ordinary life
where his true identity must be kept secret, and he is not devoted
solely to the pursuit of lawbreakers, human or alien. Violence and
destruction are permissible during the active pursuit of justice because they are presented as necessary means for halting the violence
already initiated by the men and monsters who have threatened the
social order. The superhero takes pleasure in defeating the enemy,
and therefore indirectly in the violence he uses, but that pleasure is
not presented as a problem. The *Hulk* series makes the split between
ordinary man (boy) and superhero (manhood) its central theme,
showing that what this division symbolizes is not the easy partner-

ship represented by such images as Clark Kent's telephone booth transformations. Bruce Banner could never just pop into a phone booth as if to get in touch with his super alter ego. Hulk would tear it apart. The Hulk stories suggest how close the heroes are to terrorists. The destruction of the urban environment which became popular in comics and then moved into the action movie (in *Terminator* for example) has more in common with terrorism and counter-terrorism than fisticuffs and one-to-one combat. But following that up would take us away from the case of the Hulk.

Hulk began in May 1962, the creation of the brilliant team of Stan Lee and Jack Kirby at Marvel (Maurice Horn (1982: 429) describes Kirby as the 'most accomplished of all comic book creators' and he is widely credited for having helped sustain the development of comic books for several decades). Like the Superman series, the Hulk stories centre on an endlessly repeated origin myth, but whereas the Superman story is one of separation from the father, the Hulk story derives from the threat of nuclear destruction. Every issue of *The Hulk* retells the story. Dr Bruce Banner was about to test a deadly new weapon, a 'gamma bomb', when a young man, Rick Jones, strayed into the test area at the crucial moment. Banner managed to save his friend by pushing him clear as the bomb exploded but he was heavily irradiated himself. Now he has not just an alter ego but an alter body, Hulk. When Banner is in danger his body spontaneously undergoes a mysterious transformation. A large green man tears his way out of Banner's sober clothing and goes on what Banner himself describes as 'mindless murderous rampages'. Hulk actually began grey, but between a very early issue in 1962 when he was greened, and a temporary reversion to grey in the late 1980s, Hulk was synonymous with greenness. The temporary colour change also signaled a change to a more intelligent Hulk, one capable of fairly sophisticated dialogue. My guess is that one reason for the attempted colour change was the political validation of green as a very positive colour. Once supermarkets began selling green products, another colour might have seemed needed to signify elemental fury and opposition to human culture, but readers didn't think so and green returned. Unlike Bruce Banner, who represents the good sense of masculine reason, the *Hulk* comics are ambivalent about the rampages, and both condemn and condone this violence. One part of the series ('another untold episode of those early days when the Rampaging Hulk first made his gamma-powered presence known to a fearful and awestruck world' (*Hulk* 1978), even appeared in what was called *Rampage Monthly* as if in celebration of Hulk's behaviour.

Hulk's massive green body is that of a muscular green giant, an idiot, wild descendant of the virile, moral spirit of the landscape who tested Sir Gawain's knighthood in the medieval poem, *Gawain and the Green Knight*. For most of the series Hulk is childlike and simple-minded. All he understands is pain, his own or someone else's. Otherwise in his own words, 'Hulk wants to be alone' (*Hulk* 1978: 29) (he often refers to himself in the third person as if he had little self-awareness). Hulk is a body whose drives are all rages. Hulk fights and fights, saying 'anyone . . . anything . . . can be smashed' (ibid.: 28). Bruce Banner by contrast is an uncertain, gentle, bespectacled scientist. This division between the two sides of this male persona is frequently explained in the stories as a mind/body split.

The origin myth suggests a different meaning. Perhaps the division is integral not to a Cartesian subject but to a masculine subject. Hulk is the result of an accidental nuclear irradiation in the process of weapons testing. Nuclear threat is both embodied and contained (but only just) by Hulk. If he had not split into two personae Banner would presumably have died from the radiation. All the irrational fear, hatred and anger symbolized by the explosion of nuclear weapons is made visible as the image of an uncontrollable raging male. His greenness is an allusion to the force of nature, and also to the deadliness of perverted murderous science which turns the flesh a deathly green. This origin myth begins with the dilemma posed by nuclear weapons. They are the ultimate embodiment of the forces of justice and law, but their power, uncontrollability and excessive destructiveness hint at forces out of control in men's psyches as well as in nature. Has men's law produced a rampaging mutant?

Hulk is as strongly contrasted with his host body as could be. Other superheroes sometimes express a little concern about the relationship between the demands of their ordinary life (if they can manage to have one) and their omnipotent persona, but Hulk presents a big problem. He is too large, and lacks the taut graceful lines of other heroes. You could never bring him home to dinner. He is green. Worst of all in this world of exacting codes of justice and style, he doesn't comb his hair and wears unfashionably torn trousers. But perhaps we ought to think of Hulk as the host body (there is certainly more of him). Is Bruce Banner really the problem, and does Hulk find himself embarrassed by this paragon of reason, science and restraint? What does this division signify?

50 In one story Banner is about to marry (*Hulk* 1986). Each page splits the storyline between the wedding preparations and a parallel but not obviously related plotline, in which Hulk (who has an autonomous but connected existence at this point in their history) fights for his life against 'Hulk hunters'. Meanwhile Banner, his friend Rick Jones, and the bride-to-be, discuss the disappearance of her father. The contrast between the violence and apparent harmony of the two plotlines is made more evident in the strong contrast

between the maleness of the two alter egos. Banner's borderline masculinity is signaled by his prominent glasses, toothless mouth (Hulk bares his teeth at every opportunity) and short chin. As we read the story of Banner's wedding (there is not much story to Hulk's fight), the two sets of plotlines seem to have nothing in common, but their juxtaposition (like an Eisenstein montage) offers an implicit comment on both. The passionate violence of the green man becomes what cannot be spoken by the mild, friendly men in the other strip. Something is being left out of the emotional life of the husband-to-be. And something is left out of Hulk's story. Yet none of this is made explicit in the two narratives.

Such splitting is a common device in the comic books. The ordinary guy/superhero split is fundamental to many of them even before other less conscious narrative fissions take place. Alan Moore's virtuoso Superman story 'For the Man Who Has Everything' (1985), reprinted in the DC Comics anthology of best Superman stories (*Superman* 1987), also uses it. Superman has been attacked by a strange plant-like creature which attaches itself to his chest and induces paralysis and a hallucination of what the monster, Mongul, who has used it as a weapon, calls the victim's 'heart's desire' (ibid.: 282). Moore's Superman is shown dreaming of a planet Krypton that never blew up, a Krypton undergoing a slow breakdown of social order. Meanwhile the monster from outer space responsible for the attack on Superman is personally fighting Superman's friends, Batman, Robin and Wonder Woman, one by one. Mongul is shown engaged in violent combat, breaking up the floors and walls, hurtling back and forth as the battle rages. Batman frees Superman from the creature that induces hallucinations, only to fall prey to it himself. Superman meanwhile ignores Batman and concentrates on the real action, replacing Wonder Woman at the front, and carrying on the fight against Mongul. Finally Mongul is overcome, the dream-inducing creature is attached to him and he safely dreams the total destruction of the entire universe. The cleverness of the Alan Moore story lies in its projection of the internal structures of fantasy, and its suggestion that figures like Superman must be fundamentally unhappy to live as they do. The splitting of the narrative between battle with a monster and super-civilized life on Krypton can be read as a symbolic projection of the emotion generated by the dream, especially the father-son relations. In the dream world, Superman has a son, with whom he drives across the city, after a visit to his own father. The affection (and mild conflicts) between father and son are then projected into large-scale violent clashes between superheroes and Mongul. Splitting is repression, a moment when part of the psychic process goes underground and refuses consciousness. It is a counterpart to the neologistic cries which lie like buoys on the surface of what cannot be articulated and made visible between men.

The *Hulk* story about Banner's marriage is unusual for the degree of warmth that the two men show each other. In one frame Banner holds Rick at arm's length, hands on his shoulders, and they greet each other by looking affectionately into one another's eyes (*Hulk* 1986: 2). The next frame is double-size and shows a monstrously enraged Hulk, whose green body has been turned momentarily sallow by the glare of an explosion meant to kill him, roaring 'Rr-ahrr!' out of an irregular set of bared canines (this display of bad dental work reminds us how little care the excessively physical male takes of his physical needs). Banner's open affection for a man nearly destroys the Hulk. Such affection demands a high counterbalance of anger and fear. This schizophrenic narrative never addresses these emotional relations, but the ending, in which the friend is shot by the bride's father, indicates how dangerous it is for men to allow themselves to express love and friendship. The story shows us all the parts of the dilemma but offers no resolution to them. The best it can do is show us the whole picture, both sides of manhood, Hulk and Banner.

In the 1970s, comic-book heroes began to be much more reflective, in a style especially associated with the 'Amazing Spider Man' series, and its alter ego, Peter Parker. A series like 'Amazing Spider Man' or Hulk or Superman is drawn and written by many different artists and writers over the years, artists and writers who have a similar, possibly greater, freedom to that of the soap-opera script writer. There is a formula, a set of precedents and a history with which to maintain continuity, but the audience is tolerant and forgetful (2000*AD* in its monthly form recycles the weekly stories of about five years earlier, apparently assuming that there is a new set of readers ready for them), so innovation and transformation are always possible. Comic-book art is a reflexive, incremental form. Later stories can presuppose not only earlier stories but even earlier interpretations. The Peter David/Todd Macfarlane series of Hulk comics which appeared in the late 1980s made some of the issues I have discussed quite explicit. In one of their stories, Betty, who is pregnant, insists on staying with Bruce Banner until nightfall when he becomes the Hulk (*Hulk* 1988). Hulk and Betty have a long confrontation on a bleak snowy mountain peak, in which she insists, to Hulk's fury, that he and Banner are part of each other. 'I'm *not* Banner . . . never *was,* never *will* be' (ibid.: 27), shouts Hulk. But Betty fights back: 'You're *not* just anger and rage! You have Bruce's real *love* and *passion* locked in you too!' (ibid.: 29). Earlier she had described Bruce Banner as 'a man who considers emotions so *horrible* that he can only show them if it's through somebody . . . or something . . . else' (ellipses in original) (ibid.: 14). This exchange comes close to making explicit the very dynamic of the strip in such a way that its fantasy symbols might become redundant. A letter in the same issue goes even further:

> We've already established, since issue no. 312, for that matter, that Bruce Banner was a very emotionally disturbed child, and repressed all emotion. The Hulk, therefore, is a creature of emotion. We can go a step further and say this—the Hulk, because he is an alter-ego of Banner, can get away with nasty things that Banner cannot. The Hulk and Banner, then, are two separate people—they are the same person, but one acts out the will of the other. Hulk is the id, and Banner is the super-ego.
>
> (ibid.: 31)

55

These developments show how close to allegory this work can get. The comic book can sustain a considerable weight of self-interpretation. What the letter does, however, is to equate emotion with anger, and use the misleading parallel of the late Freudian model with a set-up in which the Hulk/Banner division depends on a lack of consciousness on both sides. As Banner puts it to Betty:

> 'It's not that I'm *afraid* to show emotions, Betty, just what can happen . . . if they get out of *control*. Don't you *understand*? For me, getting upset or angry has always gone hand-in-hand with violence. . . . First with my *father*, and then with the *Hulk*.'
>
> (ibid.: 14)

The clever panel art shows Banner's face cut off below the nose and above the eyes, hidden behind the reflective faces of his glasses. All we can see are those large sightless lenses where his eyes should be. The inward gaze turns all emotion backwards, because all it can see is anger and rage.

60   The Hulk comics show that the relations between the two forms of masculinity, boy and man, or wish and ideal, are not so easily justified as other narrative paradigms (Superman for example) tended to assume. Masculinity may not be justifiable, may even be redundant or, worse, destructive. A noticeable feature of Hulk's story is how little he wants—it is others who want things of him (as Hulk Hunters, lovers of Bruce Banner or tyrants who want to use his power for their own ends) and precipitate the plots. Hulk embodies an alarming if appealing redundancy in his very persona.

FROM BOYS TO MEN

It is men who write and draw these comics (recently a few women artists have begun to emerge—their presence is sure to make a difference). These are men's images, ideas and fantasies which are offered to boys, but they cannot be understood simply as the ideology of manhood imposed on young readers, as if this were a one-way process. The 'commercial production of symbolic violence' (Connell 1989: 198) is a negotiation between men and boys, which, however, it almost entirely absent from the storylines. One comic-book artist, Steve Englehart, comments in an interview:

> If I had to put a label on it, which I never really did when I was doing it, I think most of the readership of comics is young boys who are having to come to terms with growing into manhood.

> (Lanyi 1984: 143)

65   To the interviewer's interesting comment that perhaps 'it's a lack of fathering in the national soul that might be responsible for the invention of comics here and our continued world leadership in their production' (ibid.: 144), the artist seems to have no reply. His earlier disclaimer, 'I just write fantasy' (ibid.: 142), is all he can say.

The stories are about being, not becoming, a man. Superheroes may lead ordinary lives in disguise, but they can be transformed in a moment from boy to man, from failed man to real man. Peter Parker may be modest, self-effacing and easily dominated by his aunt, but the moment justice is threatened he can become a real man of power, Spiderman. There is no long, arduous process of learning the emotional, moral and intellectual requirements for manhood. That is the beauty of it: power is all you need. These action-comic stories are about the excitements of hypermasculinity, but they are substitutes for an apprenticeship to manhood. For boys, Superman and Spiderman are as much fantasy figures as they are for the men who produce them on behalf of men's culture, but these fantasies are not given the same role in the psychic economy of each side of the divide between men and boys. For a boy, the image of Superman is an image of what he dreams of becoming. The necessity of that dream lies in his present boyhood, but he dreams it as a possibility. It represents an actual future for him. This is why so many of the superhero comics overlay future and present (and sometimes past) in a bewildering fashion. Technologies from the future are shown as if they already existed. They signify the future projected for the child reading the comic, and the imperialist success of the contemporary masculine order at maintaining itself. For men this fantasy is a sign of failure. They have failed to become supermen, and the fantasy is therefore an imaginary resolution of the difficulties their failure to achieve this power of manhood appears to demand. Men are offering an image of power which conceals a loss, to boys who are encouraged to believe that this imagery of manhood is not just a fantasy; it is a symbol of their destiny, thus ensuring the continuing reproduction of that failure. The more powerful the muscles of the soaring hero, the greater the symbolic loss.

Yet these soaring fantasy compensations for the failure to achieve the ideal of manhood are what redeem these comics. The celebration of manhood in erotic physical display makes these comics one of the special areas of boys' culture. Where else can they see their desires so openly revealed, and the wonders of sheer physical maleness celebrated so fully? There is another plot at work too. Those desires show up as homoerotic celebration of men's power simply as men. That is why the muscles are much more important than reason. The desire evoked by these comic pinups has to be paid for with violent blows and the fiction of justice. Each blow is a caress. The anger at themselves that such erotic excitement provokes then flies from scene to scene always ready for the next confrontation, in the confident knowledge that there will always be more enemy males longing to provide tests of manhood. Manhood will never become redundant. This is borne out by comments by the artists. Jack Kirby describes comic-book heroism in very positive terms: 'male heroism, to my mind, is the prelude to romantic love' (Lanyi 1983: 28). Frank Miller is even more emphatic:

> As a reader, I *love* to fall in love with characters, to get to know them, to see what they go through. I love to see heroics. And I love to see extravagant, wonderful things done by characters that are fascinating. I'm not at all attracted to doing comics with a specific intent to persuade people on political issues. Emotion is what I write about. I'm not trying to tell people how to vote or how to live.
>
> (1990: 31)

70   Jack Kirby's defense of comics—against the charge that they 'maim young sensibilities' by replacing attentiveness to quieter inner thought with headlong inner excitement—is to say that 'we're creatures of emotion' (Lanyi 1983: 28). These two artists, who between them are responsible for much of the look and feel of modern comics, testify to the importance of identification and emotion in the comic book. Falling in love with the superheroes is both a form of extreme identification and homoerotic fantasy. To say that 'we are creatures of emotion' is to say that men are dominated by emotion, made beasts by it. Only heroism can redeem such emotional thralldom.

Boys of course read comics for many reasons. I have emphasized two, both based on a lack. One is a desire to be powerful enough to act out one's anger and satisfy it. The other is a wish to know about the man's world. Many social critics have pointed out the absence of men in the lives of children but the full force of that absence on boys' conceptualization of their relation to men is not always recognized. Men's absence at work (or the substitutes which even the most unemployed men usually find) means that the defining activities of manhood are largely invisible, even as the scope and power of this masculine world are everywhere evident. The material world of man-made things is evidence enough. Meanwhile the small space of domestic life is the scene for at least some of a woman's defining activities as the culture represents them. Whatever her other work outside the home, her domestic work is seen by children as a central part of her adulthood because our societies assume that too. That is not so for men. Their defining activities take place elsewhere. Yet this elsewhere is vast and pervasive. Technology, factories, traffic, offices, all the apparatus of the human universe, seem to testify to the power of this world from which boys are excluded by their own sex, the same sex that is supposed to have created it. Men's work is a mystery, and mysteries create awe and longing (as many religious leaders have known). Comics are part of a culture which aims to satisfy that longing by translating manhood's awe-inspiring processes into images a boy can understand, images of hand-to-hand combat, guns, machines and the capture of criminals.

Men don't want boys in their world, so they give them a surrogate one because their admission into the world of manhood would force unacceptable changes. Men would have to care for the boys and this would mean sharing power with women and children, and transforming those laws which call comic manhood into being. For men, manhood must remain a separated condition, not one of emergence and dependency. Boys can be given by comics and other forms of this culture (such as television and cinema) fantasies of what manhood most desires: unlimited strength, unrestricted movement and unbounded space. Men exclude boys from their world, but give them comic-book adventure fantasies in which they are allowed to identify with manhood's adventures in return for something. What is it that boys have to trade with in this settlement? Their money certainly, and the child market is profitable, but something else is involved too. Boys trade their belief. In return for admission to the picture palace of men's exploits, they provide the credence which makes it possible. For this is the inner secret of manhood's relation to boyhood. This masculinity of pure motor drives fuelled by anger is sustained by the longing felt by boys excluded from acceptance as proper males by their elders. Manhood is a long-running fiction which men construct out of boyhood's worship generated by boyhood's exclusion—of idealized masculinities—just as the old gods needed worshippers to offer up their faith. But there never was such a manhood to be excluded from. What boys were excluded from was the loving care of adult males. Boys wanted it and needed to be reminded that real men hit one another. Every caress should be a blow. If such real men are a hit with boys it is because of the complex negotiation that goes on between boys and men over the fantasies of manhood.

The comic-book fantasies of masculinity are a symptom of the social structures of desire and emotion produced by the general absence of continuity between men and children. For boys this means not so much an absence of initiation rituals as an absence of everyday involvement largely formalized in the separation of work and the domestic sphere, and the sanctioned absence of men from most of the extended responsibilities of all care of children from infants to teenagers. Individual men resist these pressures but the separation of spheres continues. The action comics train boys in a code of manhood that is, however unfortunately, a necessary part of the social order as far as most men are concerned, and at times that even makes visible to boys some of its more obvious contradictions. Nevertheless, action comics for boys are certainly damaging because they offer false solutions to the difficulties of growing up which both sexes face. There are better ways to negotiate relations with other men than annihilating them and hoping that one's own invulnerability will triumph.

Reflective Reading, Informal Writing

REFLECTING ON THE READING:

- In the introduction to the book from which this selection comes, Middleton asks the questions "What happens when men reflect on their gender? What does a 'real man' see when he looks inward?" How would you answer these questions and why?
- Middleton argues that "Above all, comics offer the inside story of the adult world. Hypermasculine action comics are offered to boys as the inside information on men's lives, information they find hard to get from anywhere else." Did you read action comics like Superman, Batman and Robin, Spiderman, the Green Hornet or the Silver Surfer? If you did, why did you read them? What did you learn from them about men's lives? Can you think of any women action heroes? Are they different in some fundamental way from the male action heroes?
- Also in his introduction, Middleton says "Women writers know there are men writers, and black writers know there are white men writers but we white men writers . . . often don't see our own condition. Reflexivity works imperfectly for men because they don't see what they are seeing when they see themselves." Why wouldn't white men see themselves when they gaze inward? Does it make more sense that white men would see themselves more clearly by analyzing comic books than by looking inward and reflecting on their own experience, as Middleton seems to argue? Why or why not?

UNDERSTANDING RHETORICAL STRATEGIES:

- Middleton's essay is written for an academic audience. Traditionally, "academic essays" are thought to be objective and about something other than the author him- or herself. Yet, Middleton begins by telling two personal stories. What purpose does telling these stories serve? How do they set up or further his argument? Do they detract from the essay as a whole or make it better? Why or why not?
- The section in which Middleton tells his personal stories is entitled "Introspection and Method." This suggests that looking inward and then telling stories is a legitimate rhetorical strategy. Why, then, does he write that "the remainder of this book will largely eschew personal writing because it is not yet possible to produce such writing and have it mesh with theoretical analysis in the way feminism has demonstrated . . . For now a man writer discussing the inner dimensions of masculinity faces a choice between theoretical analysis and autobiography"? Does this seem contradictory? What rhetorical purpose do you think it serves for him to say that combining personal writing with academic methodology is good (and okay for feminism), but then to say he won't do any more personal writing?
- This essay "reads" particular aspects of our culture, manhood and comic books, for instance. Manhood, in fact, is "read" and understood through comic books. Identify Middleton's strategies for doing this. How does he go about analyzing these comic books? How does he define terms such as manhood? What does he use for evidence and how does he present that evidence?

INFORMAL WRITING:

- Identify, if you can, a favorite comic book or cartoon character. Write about why you are attracted to this character. Also write about what you think it says about you that you like this character.
- Middleton argues that publishers believe girls want to read about girls more than they want to read about women, and that their heroes are girls and not women. From this he infers that manhood is much more exclusive than womanhood, perhaps because "women welcome girls into their world in a way that men don't welcome boys" (125). Middleton is speculating here. Reread this passage in the text and then do some speculating of your own, writing out as many ideas as you can for why men appear in boys' comic books and girls in girls' comic books.
- Middleton writes that boys' comics don't illustrate understanding of injustice or any need or desire to recognize that others' needs are legitimate and may conflict with one's own. Rather, "they simply show anger against such needs, leading to violence." In small groups, think back to comic books or cartoons you are familiar with (bring some to

class if you'd like). Do those that seem to be specifically for boys fit Middleton's description? Give specific examples. Are those that seem to be specifically for girls about caretaking and other tasks that adult women involve themselves in? Again, give specific examples. Together, based on your discussions about what an analysis of comics might tell us, write a thesis about comics and gender. Also write out what you think are the best examples supporting your thesis.

Chapter Assignment Sequences

Sequence One: Rhetorical Moves

"On Being a Self Forever"
"Killing Rage"
"Boys Will Be Men"

SMALL GROUP DISCUSSION:

1.   Return to pages 14–15 of the Introduction and read again the passage on rhetorical strategies and ethos, logos, and pathos. Examine how the authors of these essays establish their "ethos." That is, how do they convince us they are sincere? How do we know they are experts or even believable? What do they do to earn the right to make the kinds of claims they make? To make us trust them?

2.   Discuss the voice and tone of these essays. How might such considerations as purpose, audience, and method be tied to each author's choice of voice and tone? How important is voice and tone in helping us to understand each author's argument?

WRITING:

1.   Write either a personal essay or an essay that includes a personal story or anecdote. Once you have completed that essay, write another essay in which you analyze the first essay for your own "rhetorical moves." Consider such things as: What is your purpose? Who do you imagine your audience to be? How have you constructed your ethos? What can you say about your voice and tone? Why did you choose the personal story you did and what does it reveal about you? And finally, what do all these "rhetorical moves" have to do with who you believe yourself to be and how you want others to understand who you are?

2.   Write an essay in which you compare what you see as the intended purposes and audiences of these three essays. In what ways do these rhetorical concerns differ for the authors? In what ways are they similar?

3.   The authors in these three essays write about the self in one way or another. How does each of these writers create his or her "self"? Why do you think they chose to construct themselves in this way? What purpose does it serve? How do you react to these selves?

Sequence Two: Cultural Blindness

"Entitlement"

"Killing Rage"

"Boys Will Be Men: Boys' Superhero Comics"

"Excerpts from My Life"

SMALL GROUP DISCUSSION:

1. Locate and discuss passages from each of these essays that you believe either reveal cultural blindness at work or intentionally raise cultural blindness as an issue.

2. Form a working definition of cultural blindness based on your ideas and the ideas you uncover in the passage you looked at in the first activity.

WRITING:

1. Write an essay in which you define cultural blindness (make sure to include examples to help your reader understand your concept of cultural blindness). Examine your own life through this definition of cultural blindness. Consider such questions as how and when you might have been (or are) culturally blind and how this might affect your life and your understanding of others. When has others' cultural blindness affected your life?

2. Define entitlement and cultural blindness and discuss how they are related. Focusing on one of the essays listed, discuss the connection between the two concepts and how they relate within the essay you have chosen.

Sequence Three: Stories

"On Being a Self Forever"

"Excerpts from My Life"

"Killing Rage"

"Boys Will Be Men: Boys' Superhero Comics"

SMALL GROUP DISCUSSION:

1. All four of these essays rely, to one degree or another, on personal anecdotes or stories. Selecting one story from each of the essays, determine the function performed by each story within the context of the essay in which it occurs. How does each story relate to the purpose of

the essay in which it appears? Is the location of the story within the essay important? What differences do you see among the authors in the use to which their stories are put?

2. In question 1 you concerned yourselves with *why* the authors told personal stories. Now, look at *how*. Perhaps turning to the same stories you worked with before, what differences do you see in the ways these stories are told? How do they compare with respect to setting? Depth of characterization? Amount of sensory detail? Length? Tone? Pace? Can you account for these differences in terms of the different rhetorical purposes of the essays in which they appear?

WRITING:

1. Write an essay in which you illustrate a point using personal stories of your own. This will be a stronger essay if you work with points of significant realization or change in your life. If you are a risk taker, work with experiences or parts of your life that you do not yet fully understand.

2. Writers extract stories from their own lives for rhetorical purposes. On another plane altogether, there is a sense in which we are all inclined to think of as our lives as stories. That is, our acquaintance with storytelling, which began in childhood, has provided us with patterns we habitually use to think about our own lives. Updike, for example, speaks of the feeling "that our life is a story, with a pattern and a moral and an inevitability." And while narrative patterns may give us ways to make sense of our lives, there are also many ways in which our lives are not like stories. We may come to wonder whether our own lives have an organization, a climax, a point, even a hero or heroine. Write about your own life, playing with this idea. Into what story line does your life fit? Cinderella? Rags to riches? The tragic hero? The rebel/outcast/loner society does not understand? A love story? Write both about how this story line fits your life and about how it misrepresents or oversimplifies.

Sequence Four: The Self as Academic

"Entitlement"
"Boys Will Be Men: Boys' Superhero Comics"
"Killing Rage"

SMALL GROUP DISCUSSION:

1. Robert Coles, Peter Middleton, and bell hooks are all academics. That is, all are university-based and all teach, do research, and publish within a particular academic discipline. Would you call their essays academic? What makes them so? Is it a particular type of diction or voice? A particular kind of question they are trying to resolve? A particular type of evidence they use, or interpretation they do? The fact that they have

footnotes and/or bibliographies? See if you can agree on a definition of academic writing.

2. Assuming, for a moment, that all three of these essays are academic essays, how are they different? How do you account for their differences? To what extent are differences among their disciplinary orientations involved? Looking again at the differences, what discipline would you say each author represents?

WRITING:

1. Define "academic voice." Establish your definition using examples from any or all of these three essays. Where does this voice come from? What is its function, or purpose?

2. Write an essay in which you examine whether any one of these three authors conforms to academic expectations to one degree or another. Then consider whether the writer also writes from a position of self-expression. Does the author you have selected distance himself/herself from his/her own academic discipline? In other words, do you find sections of the essay in question where there seems a tension or conflict between (personal) self and (academic) role?

3. Write what you would consider to be an academic essay about at least two of these selections. Attach a cover letter to your essay that explains, specifically and in some detail, what makes your essay an academic essay as opposed to, say, a personal essay or a journalistic essay.

Constructing Identity: The Self As Social Artifact

Chapter 2

Reflective Prewriting

1. Make a short list of the kinds of reading you like to do now or have done in the past (e.g., adventure stories, romances, comic books, histories, biographies, etc.).

    Write about one or two of these types of reading, or "genres," explaining why you like them and what they have meant to you. Have they helped you see the world in particular ways? Have they changed how you think about your personal circumstances in life?

2. Think about the most important relationships among and for people (e.g., brother/sister, brother/brother, person/dog, mother/son, father/daughter, husband/wife, etc.).

    Write about one of these relationships and why you think it is so important. What role does this relationship play in your life? In the culture at large? What do you see as the positive and negative aspects of this relationship?

3. Think about what you know about popular culture—music, film, art, etc.

    Write about how you think popular culture relates to you. Does it help shape your ideas about what is important? About what is right and wrong? Is there one film or song that has had a particularly strong impact on you—for example, on how you view yourself or your world?

4. Think about your gender, race, and religion and the roles they play in your life.

Write about the ways in which your gender, race, or religion might have shaped your attitudes about yourself (or about other people), about what you find important, or about the kinds of issues or events on which you might take a firm stand.

Write about times when the stereotypical expectations that accompany your gender, race, or religion have seemed to you somehow not to "fit" your own inner realities, when you felt like a square peg being forced into a round hole.

INTRODUCTION

artifact (n.) An object produced or shaped by human workmanship.
—*American Heritage Dictionary*

While we are accustomed to thinking of the "self" as the core of our being, the seat of our individuality, the essence of what we are as individual persons, it is also useful to think of the self as partially—if not wholly—a social artifact. By "social artifact" we mean something produced or shaped socially, by others, our traditions, our institutions.

There's a sense in which we are on dangerous turf here. After all, Americans have a heavy investment in rugged individualism, in a view of ourselves as autonomous, independent beings with unique personalities who live alone, act alone, think alone. We are the country that gave the world the *Bill of Rights,* the most impressive statement of individual rights and freedoms ever written. Our lore is chock full of the stories of rugged individuals who "did it my way," from Daniel Boone and Davy Crockett to Henry David Thoreau, Amelia Earhart, John Wayne, and Rambo. Horatio Alger's popular fiction of the nineteenth century gave shape to the "rags to riches" myth, already fairly well established in the popular imagination: As an American, regardless of your origins, you can become whatever you want to be and do whatever you want to do, so long as you are willing to work hard to achieve it. Why, we've had presidents who were born in log cabins. So pervasive is the belief that any individual can make his or her way to the top through individual effort that it has come to be known as "the American Dream."

Unquestionably, our belief that individuals can invent or reinvent themselves has historically served as a powerful incentive. It's what attracts immigrants from all over the world. It's what gives hope to the young, the poor, the marginalized. It could even be said to be the driving force behind the successes of capitalism. It may well have been what motivated you to attend college.

Yet individualism also has a dark side. It discourages (or ignores) interdependence, collaboration, and community-mindedness. And the belief that individuals are wholly responsible for their own fate leads fairly directly to some form of "blaming the victim." That is, if we can be anything we want to be, then the poor, the disenfranchised, the marginalized, the imprisoned, and even the sick must be that way because they chose to be that way. They got what was coming to them.

We hold tenaciously to our faith in our own individuality despite considerable evidence to the contrary. Every day we enact scenes in plays we didn't write, performing roles we did not invent. Every day, each of us inhabits one or more roles that are socially constructed, handed down to us by our families, our traditions, our laws, our institutions. We are taught how to be a son or daughter, husband or wife, teacher or student, auto mechanic or accountant, historian or mathematician, man or woman. These are not roles that we, as individuals, have invented. They are social artifacts. One branch of social psychologists believes that we are nothing more than a composite of the different roles we play, that there is no "self" playing those roles in the sense that an actor might play Hamlet. The moderates, while agreeing that much of what we do can be accounted for in terms of socially imposed roles, still hold that it is appropriate to think of a "self" that is more or less consciously playing those roles, emphasizing one role over another, resolving conflicts among the multiple roles we all play, even re-defining certain roles from the inside. Both factions, however, would agree that much of what we are as individuals is determined by others. So would such post-modern theorists, cultural critics, and rhetoricians as Lyotard, Foucault, or Bakhtin. In this sense, then, the self is a social artifact.

Where does this leave us? It leaves us with a paradox. On the one hand, we have our traditional belief in the self as a free agent (itself a socially constructed belief), and on the other the idea that the self is a social construct, a loose collection of socially defined roles. How does the tension between these two ideas play out in the lives of real people? How do we learn these roles? How do we sort out what parts of our own identity is really *us*, as opposed to the parts that were taught to us by parents, schools, or the songs, movies, and stories we ingest? How do we get free of limiting, straitjacket roles and become ourselves? Or is this even the right question? Are there ways in which these roles make our lives easier by reducing the number of problems we have to worry about on a given day?

The reflective prewriting exercises at the beginning of this chapter are designed to help you begin an exploration of these and related questions, to help you reflect on some ways in which others have had a hand in shaping your identity, and whether these influences have been positive or otherwise. Now we ask you to reflect further by carefully considering the five essays that follow: Gloria Steinem's "Ruth's Song (Because She Could Not Sing It)," Doug Robinson's "The Hurt, Betrayed Son," an excerpt from Victor Villanueva's *Bootstraps*, Adrienne Rich's "The Domestication of Motherhood," and Paula Rust's "Sexual Identity and Bisexual Identities: The Struggle for Self-Description in a Changing Sexual Landscape."

While each of these essays presents a rich exploration of the self as social artifact, with all the complications that idea introduces, none of them is likely to yield to a single, quick reading. We invite you to work on them in all the same ways you learned to work on texts in the Introduction and Chapter 1. The discussion questions and informal writing at the end of each essay are aids to reflection, and of course we also encourage you to continue keeping a journal or notebook, using one of the journal types described in the Introduction. In a paradox that befits this chapter, we encourage you to reinvent the traditional role of "student" by using these reflective tools to fulfill your own intellectual needs as you come to define them—rather than simply following the agenda set for you by your instructors.

GLORIA STEINEM

Gloria Steinem, one of the best-known feminists of our time, was born in Toledo, Ohio, in 1934. She has described the three seminal events of her life as her departure from Toledo to attend college and escape small-town life, her travels in India (which allowed her to see that the Ghandi-inspired peace movement was still in existence), and her gradual discovery of feminism—a discovery not fully realized until she was working as a journalist in 1969, pre-*Roe* v. *Wade* days, and covered a demonstration in favor of women's right to abortion. This led to her understanding of the sexual caste system as political rather than natural, and thus potentially subject to positive change. Steinem further realized that, because it was difficult to publish feminist articles at that time, the most direct way for her to make a personal impact was to develop public-speaking skills—a terrifying process for her at the age of 35.

Her books include a study of Marilyn Monroe, *Marilyn: Norma Jean* (1986), which is an international best-seller translated into 15 languages, *Revolution from Within: A Book of Self-Esteem* (1992), and her most recent work, a collection of six major essays, *Moving Beyond Words* (1994). In 1968 Steinem helped found *New York Magazine* and then worked as a political columnist until 1972 when she cofounded *Ms. Magazine,* a feminist monthly for which she is currently a consulting editor. She has also written for numerous other magazines, newspapers, and anthologies as well as for radio and television.

Today she is president of Voters for Choice, an independent bipartisan political action committee that promotes candidates who support reproductive rights for women, and founding president of the Ms. Foundation for Women, a national fund organized to aid grassroots projects benefiting females of all ages and races. *Parenting Magazine* selected her for its 1995 lifetime achievement award for her work promoting self-esteem among adolescent girls.

"Ruth's Song (Because She Could Not Sing It)" (1983), is a personal narrative that also functions as a prose elegy for Steinem's mother, Ruth, who suffered from a nervous breakdown. "Happy or unhappy, families are all mysterious," begins Steinem's bittersweet story that investigates the disturbing and mysterious question: How does a bright, vital, adventurous young woman become a depressed housewife scared to be left alone? In order to examine the significant factors in this traumatic transformation, Steinem searches her own past for clues and is able to see her mother more clearly and fairly now than she could as a young girl struggling against the hopelessness and helplessness of her mother's situation. Which of the clues presented by Steinem do you see as the most important to understanding Ruth's life and her imminent breakdown?

Ruth's Song (Because She Could Not Sing It)

Happy or unhappy, families are all mysterious. We have only to imagine how differently we would be described—and will be, after our deaths—by each of the family members who believe they know us. The only question is, Why are some mysteries more important than others?

The fate of my Uncle Ed was a mystery of importance in our family. We lavished years of speculation on his transformation from a brilliant young electrical engineer to the town handyman. What could have changed this elegant, Lincolnesque student voted "Best Dressed" by his classmates to the gaunt, unshaven man I remember? Why did he leave a young son and first wife of the "proper" class and religion, marry a much less educated woman of the "wrong" religion, and raise a second family in a house near an abandoned airstrip; a house whose walls were patched with metal signs to stop the wind? Why did he never talk about his transformation?

For years, I assumed that some secret and dramatic events of a year he spent in Alaska had made the difference. Then I discovered that the trip had come after his change and probably been made because of it. Strangers he worked for as a much-loved handyman talked about him as one more tragedy of the Depression, and it was true that Uncle Ed's father, my paternal grandfather, had lost his money in the stockmarket Crash and died of (depending on who was telling the story) pneumonia or a broken heart. But the Crash of 1929 also had come long after Uncle Ed's transformation. Another theory was that he was afflicted with a mental problem that lasted most of his life, yet he was supremely competent at his work, led an independent life, and asked for help from no one.

Perhaps he had fallen under the spell of a radical professor in the early days of the century, the height of this country's romance with socialism and anarchism. That was the theory of another uncle on my mother's side. I do remember that no matter how much Uncle Ed needed money, he would charge no more for his work than materials plus 10 percent, and I never saw him in anything other than ancient boots and overalls held up with strategic safety pins. Was he really trying to replace socialism-in-one-country with socialism-in-one-man? If so, why did my grandmother, a woman who herself had run for the school board in coalition with anarchists and socialists, mistrust his judgment so much that she left his share of her estate in trust, even though he was over fifty when she died? And why did Uncle Ed seem uninterested in all other political words and acts?

Was it true instead that, as another relative insisted, Uncle Ed had chosen poverty to disprove the myths of Jews and money?

5   Years after my uncle's death, I asked a son in his second family if he had the key to this family mystery. No, he said. He had never known his father any other way. For that cousin, there had been no question. For the rest of us, there was to be no answer.

For many years I also never imagined my mother any way other than the person she had become before I was born. She was just a fact of life when I was growing up; someone to be worried about and cared for; an invalid who lay in bed with eyes closed and lips moving in occasional response to voices only she could hear; a woman to whom I brought an endless stream of toast and coffee, bologna sandwiches and dime pies, in a child's version of what meals should be. She was a loving, intelligent, terrorized woman who tried hard to clean our littered house whenever she emerged from her private world, but who could rarely be counted on to finish one task. In many ways, our roles were reversed: I was the mother and she was the child. Yet that didn't help her, for she still worried about me with all the intensity of a frightened mother, plus the special fears of her own world full of threats and hostile voices.

Even then I suppose I must have known that, years before she was thirty-five and I was born, she had been a spirited adventurous young woman who struggled out of a working-class family and into college, who found work she loved and continued to do, even after she was married and my older sister was there to be cared for. Certainly, our immediate family and nearby relatives, of whom I was by far the youngest, must have remembered her life as a whole and functioning person. She was thirty before she gave up her own career to help my father run the Michigan summer resort that was the most practical of his many dreams, and she worked hard there as everything from bookkeeper to bar manager. The family must have watched this energetic, fun-loving, book-loving woman turn into someone who was afraid to be alone, who could not hang on to reality long enough to hold a job, and who could rarely concentrate enough to read a book.

Yet I don't remember any family speculation about the mystery of my mother's transformation. To the kind ones and those who liked her, this new Ruth was simply a sad event, perhaps a mental case, a family problem to be accepted and cared for until some natural process made her better. To the less kind or those who had resented her earlier independence, she was a willful failure, someone who lived in a filthy house, a woman who simply would not pull herself together.

Unlike the case of my Uncle Ed, exterior events were never suggested as reason enough for her problems. Giving up her own career was never cited as her personal parallel of the Depression. (Nor was there discussion of the Depression itself, though my mother, like millions of others, had made potato soup and cut up blankets to make my sister's winter clothes.) Her fears of dependence and poverty were no match for my uncle's possible political beliefs. The real influence of newspaper editors who had praised her reporting was not taken as seriously as the possible influence of one radical professor.

10   Even the explanation of mental illness seemed to contain more personal fault when applied to my mother. She had suffered her first "nervous breakdown," as she and everyone else called it, before I was born and when my sister was about five. It followed years of trying to take care of a baby, be the wife of a kind but financially irresponsible man with showbusiness dreams, and still keep her much-loved job as reporter and newspaper editor. After many months in a sanatorium, she was pronounced recovered. That is, she was able to take care of my sister again, to move away from the city and the job she loved, and to work with my father at the isolated rural lake in Michigan he was trying to transform into a resort worthy of the big dance bands of the 1930s.

But she was never again completely without the spells of depression, anxiety, and visions into some other world that eventually were to turn her into the nonperson I remember. And she was never again without a bottle of dark, acrid-smelling liquid she called "Doc Howard's medicine": a solution of chloral hydrate that I later learned was the main ingredient of "Mickey Finns" or "knockout drops," and that probably made my mother and her doctor the pioneers of modern tranquilizers. Though friends and relatives saw this medicine as one more evidence of weakness and indulgence, to me it always seemed an embarrassing but necessary evil. It slurred her speech and slowed her coordination, making our neighbors and my school friends believe she was a drunk. But without it, she would not sleep for days, even a week at a time, and her feverish eyes began to see only that private world in which wars and hostile voices threatened the people she loved.

Because my parents had divorced and my sister was working in a faraway city, my mother and I were alone together then, living off the meager fixed income that my mother got from leasing her share of the remaining land in Michigan. I remember a long Thanksgiving weekend spent hanging on to her with one hand and holding my eighth-grade assignment of *Tale of Two Cities* in the other, because the war outside our house was so real to my mother that she had plunged her hand through a window, badly cutting her arm in an effort to help us escape. Only when she finally agreed to swallow the medicine could she sleep, and only then could I end the terrible calm that comes with crisis and admit to myself how afraid I had been.

No wonder that no relative in my memory challenged the doctor who prescribed this medicine, asked if some of her suffering and hallucinating might be due to overdose or withdrawal, or even consulted another doctor about its use. It was our relief as well as hers.

But why was she never returned even to that first sanatorium? Or to help that might come from other doctors? It's hard to say. Partly, it was her own fear of returning. Partly, it was too little money, and a family's not-unusual assumption that mental illness is an inevitable part of someone's personality. Or perhaps other family members had feared something like my experience when, one hot and desperate summer between the sixth and seventh grade, I finally persuaded her to let me take her to the only doctor from those sanatorium days whom she remembered without fear.

15   Yes, this brusque old man told me after talking to my abstracted, timid mother for twenty minutes: she definitely belongs in a state hospital. I should put her there right away. But even at that age, *Life* magazine and newspaper exposés had told me what horrors went on inside those hospitals. Assuming there to be no other alternative, I took her home and never tried again.

In retrospect, perhaps the biggest reason my mother was cared for but not helped for twenty years was the simplest: her functioning was not that necessary to the world. Like women alcoholics who drink in their kitchens while costly programs are constructed for executives who drink, or like the homemakers subdued with tranquilizers while male patients get therapy and personal attention instead, my mother was not an important worker. She was not even the caretaker of a very young child, as she had been when she was hospitalized the first time. My father had patiently brought home the groceries and kept our odd household going until I was eight or so and my sister went away to college. Two years later when wartime gas rationing closed his summer resort and he had to travel to buy and sell in summer as well as winter, he said: How can I travel and take care of your mother? How can I make a living? He was right. It was impossible to do both. I did not blame him for leaving once I was old enough to be the bringer of meals and answerer of my mother's questions. ("Has your sister been killed in a car crash?" "Are there German soldiers outside?") I replaced my father, my mother was left with one more way of maintaining a sad status quo, and the world went on undisturbed.

That's why our lives, my mother's from forty-six to fifty-three, and my own from ten to seventeen, were spent alone together. There was one sane winter in a house we rented to be near my sister's college in Massachusetts, then one bad summer spent house-sitting in suburbia while my mother hallucinated and my sister struggled to hold down a summer job in New York. But the rest of those years were lived in Toledo where both my mother and father had been born, and on whose city newspapers an earlier Ruth had worked.

First we moved into a basement apartment in a good neighborhood. In those rooms behind a furnace, I made one last stab at being a child. By pretending to be much sicker with a cold than I really was, I hoped my mother would suddenly turn into a sane and cheerful woman bringing me chicken soup à la Hollywood. Of course, she could not. It only made her feel worse that she could not. I stopped pretending.

But for most of those years, we lived in the upstairs of the house my mother had grown up in and her parents left her—a deteriorating farm house engulfed by the city, with poor but newer houses stacked against it and a major highway a few feet from its sagging front porch. For a while, we could rent the two downstairs apartments to a newlywed factory worker and a local butcher's family. Then the health department condemned our ancient furnace for the final time, sealing it so tight that even my resourceful Uncle Ed couldn't produce illegal heat.

20   In that house, I remember:

. . . lying in the bed my mother and I shared for warmth, listening on the early morning radio to the royal wedding of Princess Elizabeth and Prince Philip being broadcast live, while we tried to ignore and thus protect each other from the unmistakable sounds of the factory worker downstairs beating up and locking out his pregnant wife.

. . . hanging paper drapes I had bought in the dime store; stacking books and papers in the shape of two armchairs and covering them with blankets; evolving my own dishwashing system (I waited until all the dishes were dirty, then put them in the bathtub); and listening to my mother's high praise for these housekeeping efforts to bring order from chaos, though in retrospect I think they probably depressed her further.

. . . coming back from one of the Eagles' Club shows where I and other veterans of a local tap-dancing school made ten dollars a night for two shows, and finding my mother waiting with a flashlight and no coat in the dark cold of the bus stop, worried about my safety walking home.

. . . in a good period, when my mother's native adventurousness came through, answering a classified ad together for an amateur acting troupe that performed Biblical dramas in churches, and doing several very corny performances of *Noah's Ark* while my proud mother shook metal sheets backstage to make thunder.

25   . . . on a hot summer night, being bitten by one of the rats that shared our house and its back alley. It was a terrifying night that turned into a touching one when my mother, summoning courage from some unknown reservoir of love, became a calm, comforting parent who took me to a hospital emergency room despite her terror at leaving home.

... coming home from a local library with the three books a week into which I regularly escaped, and discovering that for once there was no need to escape. My mother was calmly planting hollyhocks in the vacant lot next door.

But there were also times when she woke in the early winter dark, too frightened and disoriented to remember that I was at my usual after-school job, and so called the police to find me. Humiliated in front of my friends by sirens and policemen, I would yell at her—and she would bow her head in fear and say "I'm sorry, I'm sorry, I'm sorry," just as she had done so often when my otherwise-kindhearted father had yelled at her in frustration. Perhaps the worst thing about suffering is that it finally hardens the hearts of those around it.

And there were many, many times when I badgered her until her shaking hands had written a small check to cash at the corner grocery and I could leave her alone while I escaped to the comfort of well-heated dime stores that smelled of fresh doughnuts, or to air-conditioned Saturday-afternoon movies that were windows on a very different world.

But my ultimate protection was this: I was just passing through, a guest in the house; perhaps this wasn't my mother at all. Though I knew very well that I was her daughter, I sometimes imagined that I had been adopted and that my real parents would find me, a fantasy I've since discovered is common. (If children wrote more and grownups less, being adopted might be seen not only as a fear but also as a hope.) Certainly, I didn't mourn the wasted life of this woman who was scarcely older than I am now. I worried only about the times when she got worse.

30   Pity takes distance and a certainty of surviving. It was only after our house was bought for demolition by the church next door, and after my sister had performed the miracle of persuading my father to give me a carefree time before college by taking my mother with him to California for a year, that I could afford to think about the sadness of her life. Suddenly, I was far away in Washington, living with my sister and sharing a house with several of her friends. While I finished high school and discovered to my surprise that my classmates felt sorry for me because my mother *wasn't* there, I also realized that my sister, at least in her early childhood, had known a very different person who lived inside our mother, an earlier Ruth.

She was a woman I met for the first time in a mental hospital near Baltimore, a humane place with gardens and trees where I visited her each weekend of the summer after my first year away in college. Fortunately, my sister hadn't been able to work and be our mother's caretaker, too. After my father's year was up, my sister had carefully researched hospitals and found the courage to break the family chain.

At first, this Ruth was the same abstracted, frightened woman I had lived with all those years, though now all the sadder for being approached through long hospital corridors and many locked doors. But gradually she began to talk about her past life, memories that doctors there must have been awakening. I began to meet a Ruth I had never known.

. . . A tall, spirited, auburn-haired high-school girl who loved basketball and reading; who tried to drive her uncle's Stanley Steamer when it was the first car in the neighborhood; who had a gift for gardening and who sometimes, in defiance of convention, wore her father's overalls; a girl with the courage to go to dances even though her church told her that music itself was sinful, and whose sense of adventure almost made up for feeling gawky and unpretty next to her daintier, dark-haired sister.

. . . A very little girl, just learning to walk, discovering the body places where touching was pleasurable, and being punished by her mother who slapped her hard across the kitchen floor.

35
. . . A daughter of a handsome railroad-engineer and a schoolteacher who felt she had married "beneath her"; the mother who took her two daughters on Christmas trips to faraway New York on an engineer's free railroad pass and showed them the restaurants and theaters they should aspire to—even though they could only stand outside them in the snow.

. . . A good student at Oberlin College, whose freethinking traditions she loved, where friends nicknamed her "Billy"; a student with a talent for both mathematics and poetry, who was not above putting an invisible film of Karo syrup on all the john seats in her dormitory the night of a big prom; a daughter who had to return to Toledo, live with her family, and go to a local university when her ambitious mother—who had scrimped and saved, ghostwritten a minister's sermons, and made her daughters' clothes in order to get them to college at all—ran out of money. At home, this Ruth became a part-time bookkeeper in a lingerie shop for the very rich, commuting to classes and listening to her mother's harsh lectures on the security of becoming a teacher; but also a young woman who was still rebellious enough to fall in love with my father, the editor of her university newspaper, a funny and charming young man who was a terrible student, had no intention of graduating, put on all the campus dances, and was unacceptably Jewish.

I knew from family lore that my mother had married my father twice: once secretly; after he invited her to become the literary editor of his campus newspaper, and once a year later in a public ceremony, which some members of both families refused to attend as the "mixed marriage" of its day.

And I knew that my mother had gone on to earn a teaching certificate. She had used it to scare away truant officers during the winters when, after my father closed the summer resort for the season, we lived in a house trailer and worked our way to Florida or California and back by buying and selling antiques.

But only during those increasingly adventurous weekend outings from the hospital—going shopping, to lunch, to the movies—did I realize that she had taught college calculus for a year in deference to her mother's insistence that she have teaching "to fall back on." And only then did I realize she had fallen in love with newspapers along with my father. After graduating from the university paper, she wrote a gossip column for a local tabloid, under the name "Duncan MacKenzie," since women weren't supposed to do such things, and soon had earned a job as society reporter on one of Toledo's two big dailies. By the time my sister was four or so, she had worked her way up to the coveted position of Sunday editor.

40   It was a strange experience to look into those brown eyes I had seen so often and realize suddenly how much they were like my own. For the first time, I realized that she might really be my mother.

I began to think about the many pressures that might have led up to that first nervous breakdown: leaving my sister who she loved very much with a grandmother whose values my mother didn't share; trying to hold on to a job she loved but was being asked to leave by her husband; wanting very much to go with a woman friend to pursue their own dreams in New York; falling in love with a co-worker at the newspaper who frightened her by being more sexually attractive, more supportive of her work than my father, and perhaps the man she should have married; and finally, nearly bleeding to death with a miscarriage because her own mother had little faith in doctors and refused to get help.

Did those months in the sanatorium brainwash her in some Freudian or very traditional way into making what were, for her, probably the wrong choices? I don't know. It almost doesn't matter. Without extraordinary support to the contrary, she was already convinced that divorce was unthinkable. A husband could not be left for another man, and certainly not for a reason as selfish as a career. A daughter could not be deprived of her father and certainly not be uprooted and taken off to an uncertain future in New York. A bride was supposed to be virginal (not "shop-worn," as my euphemistic mother would have said), and if your husband turned out to be kind, but innocent of the possibility of a woman's pleasure, then just be thankful for kindness.

Of course, other women have torn themselves away from work and love and still survived. But a story my mother told me years later has always symbolized for me the formidable forces arrayed against her.

It was early spring, nothing was open yet. There was nobody for miles around. We had stayed at the lake that winter, so I was alone a lot while your father took the car and traveled around on business. You were a baby. Your sister was in school, and there was no phone. The last straw was that the radio broke. Suddenly it seemed like forever since I'd been able to talk with anyone—or even hear the sound of another voice.

45   I bundled you up, took the dog, and walked out to the Brooklyn road. I thought I'd walk the four or five miles to the grocery store, talk to some people, and find somebody to drive me back. I was walking along with Fritzie running up ahead in the empty road—when suddenly a car came out of nowhere and down the hill. It hit Fritzie head on and threw him over to the side of the road. I yelled and screamed at the driver, but he never slowed down. He never looked at us. He never even turned his head.

Poor Fritzie was all broken and bleeding, but he was still alive. I carried him and sat down in the middle of the road, with his head cradled in my arms. I was going to *make* the next car stop and help.

But no car ever came. I sat there for hours, I don't know how long, with you in my lap and holding Fritzie, who was whimpering and looking up at me for help. It was dark by the time he finally died. I pulled him over to the side of the road and walked back home with you and washed the blood out of my clothes.

I don't know what it was about that one day—it was like a breaking point. When your father came home, I said: "From now on, I'm going with you. I won't bother you. I'll just sit in the car. But I can't bear to be alone again."

I think she told me that story to show she had tried to save herself, or perhaps she wanted to exorcise a painful memory by saying it out loud. But hearing it made me understand what could have turned her into the woman I remember: a solitary figure sitting in the car, perspiring through the summer, bundled up in winter, waiting for my father to come out of this or that antique shop, grateful just not to be alone. I was there, too, because I was too young to be left at home, and I loved helping my father wrap and unwrap the newspaper around the china and small objects he had bought at auctions and was selling to dealers. It made me feel necessary and grown-up. But sometimes it was hours before we came back to the car again and to my mother who was always patiently, silently waiting.

50   At the hospital and later when Ruth told me stories of her past, I used to say, "But why didn't you leave? Why didn't you take the job? Why didn't you marry the other man?" She would always insist it didn't matter, she was lucky to have my sister and me. If I pressed hard enough, she would add, "if I'd left you never would have been born."

I always thought but never had the courage to say: *But you might have been born instead.*

I'd like to tell you that this story had a happy ending. The best I can do is one that is happier than its beginning.

After many months in that Baltimore hospital, my mother lived on her own in a small apartment for two years while I was in college and my sister married and lived nearby. When she felt the old terrors coming back, she returned to the hospital at her own request. She was approaching sixty by the time she emerged from there and from a Quaker farm that served as a halfway house, but she confounded her psychiatrists' predictions that she would be able to live outside for shorter and shorter periods. In fact, she never returned. She lived more than another twenty years, and for six of them, she was well enough to stay in a rooming house that provided both privacy and company. Even after my sister and her husband moved to a larger house and generously made two rooms into an apartment for her, she continued to have some independent life and many friends. She worked part-time as a "salesgirl" in a china shop; went away with me on yearly vacations and took one trip to Europe with relatives; went to women's club meetings; found a multiracial church that she loved; took meditation courses; and enjoyed many books. She still could not bear to see a sad movie, to stay alone with any of her six grandchildren while they were babies, to live without many tranquilizers, or to talk about those bad years in Toledo. The old terrors were still in the back of her mind, and each day was a fight to keep them down.

It was the length of her illness that had made doctors pessimistic. In fact, they could not identify any serious mental problem and diagnosed her only as having "an anxiety neurosis": low self-esteem, a fear of being dependent, a terror of being alone, a constant worry about money. She also had spells of what now would be called agoraphobia, a problem almost entirely confined to dependent women: fear of going outside the house, and incapacitating anxiety attacks in unfamiliar or public places.

55 Would you say, I asked one of her doctors, that her spirit had been broken? "I guess that's as good a diagnosis as any," he said. "And it's hard to mend anything that's been broken for twenty years."

But once out of the hospital for good, she continued to show flashes of the different woman inside; one with a wry kind of humor, a sense of adventure, and a love of learning. Books on math, physics, and mysticism occupied a lot of her time. ("Religion," she used to say firmly, "begins in the laboratory.") When she visited me in New York during her sixties and seventies, she always told taxi drivers that she was eighty years old ("so they will tell me how young I look"), and convinced theater ticket sellers that she was deaf long before she really was ("so they'll give us seats in the front row"). She made friends easily, with the vulnerability and charm of a person who feels entirely dependent on the approval of others. After one of her visits, every shopkeeper within blocks of my apartment would say, "Oh yes, I know your mother!" At home, she complained that people her own age were too old and stodgy for her. Many of her friends were far younger than she. It was as if she were making up for her own lost years.

She was also overly appreciative of any presents given to her—and that made giving them irresistible. I loved to send her clothes, jewelry, exotic soaps, and additions to her collection of tarot cards. She loved receiving them, though we both knew they would end up stored in boxes and drawers. She carried on a correspondence in German with our European relatives, and exchanges with many other friends, all written in her painfully slow, shaky handwriting. She also loved giving gifts. Even as she worried about money and figured out how to save pennies, she would buy or make carefully chosen presents for grandchildren and friends.

Part of the price she paid for this much health was forgetting. A single reminder of those bad years in Toledo was enough to plunge her into days of depression. There were times when this fact created loneliness for me, too. Only two of us had lived most of my childhood. Now, only one of us remembered. But there were also times in later years, when, no matter how much I pled with reporters *not* to interview our friends and neighbors in Toledo, *not* to say that my mother had been hospitalized, they published things that hurt her very much and sent her into a downhill slide.

On the other hand, she was also her mother's daughter, a person with a certain amount of social pride and pretension, and some of her objections had less to do with depression than false pride. She complained bitterly about one report that we had lived in a house trailer. She finally asked angrily: "Couldn't they at least say 'vacation mobile home'?" Divorce was still a shame to her. She might cheerfully tell friends, "I don't know *why* Gloria says her father and I were divorced—we never were." I think she justified this to herself with the idea that they had gone through two marriage ceremonies, one in secret and one in public, but been divorced only once. In fact, they were definitely divorced, and my father had briefly married someone else.

60 She was very proud of my being a published writer, and we generally shared the same values. After her death, I found a mother-daughter morals quiz I once had written for a women's magazine. In her unmistakably shaky writing, she had recorded her own answers, her entirely accurate imagination of what my answers would be, and a score that concluded our differences were less than those "normal for women separated by twenty-odd years." Nonetheless, she was quite capable of putting a made-up name on her name tag when going to a conservative women's club where she feared our shared identity would bring controversy or even just questions. When I finally got up the nerve to tell her I was signing a 1972 petition of women who publicly said we had had abortions and were demanding the repeal of laws that made them illegal and dangerous, her only reply was sharp and aimed to hurt back. "Every starlet says she's had an abortion," she said. "It's just a way of getting publicity." I knew she agreed that abor-

tion should be a legal choice, but I also knew she would never forgive me for embarrassing her in public.

In fact, her anger and a fairly imaginative ability to wound with words increased in her last years when she was most dependent, most focused on herself, and most likely to need the total attention of others. When my sister made a courageous decision to go to law school at the age of fifty, leaving my mother in a house that not only had many loving teenage grandchildren in it but a kindly older woman as a paid companion besides, my mother reduced her to frequent tears by insisting that this was a family with no love in it, no home-cooked food in the refrigerator; not a real family at all. Since arguments about home cooking wouldn't work on me, my punishment was creative and different. She was going to call up *The New York Times,* she said, and tell them that this was what feminism did: it left old sick women all alone.

Some of this bitterness brought on by failing faculties was eventually solved by a nursing home near my sister's house where my mother not only got the twenty-four-hour help her weakening body demanded, but the attention of affectionate nurses besides. She charmed them, they loved her, and she could still get out for an occasional family wedding. If I ever had any doubts about the debt we owe to nurses, those last months laid them to rest.

When my mother died just before her eighty-second birthday in a hospital room where my sister and I were alternating the hours in which her heart wound slowly down to its last sounds, we were alone together for a few hours while my sister slept. My mother seemed bewildered by her surroundings and the tubes that invaded her body, but her consciousness cleared long enough for her to say: "I want to go home. Please take me home." Lying to her one last time, I said I would. "Okay, honey," she said. "I trust you." Those were her last understandable words.

The nurses let my sister and me stay in the room long after there was no more breath. She had asked us to do that. One of her many fears came from a story she had been told as a child about a man whose coma was mistaken for death. She also had made out a living will requesting that no extraordinary measures be used to keep her alive, and that her ashes be sprinkled in the same stream as my father's.

65 Her memorial service was in the Episcopalian church that she loved because it fed the poor, let the homeless sleep in its pews, had members of almost every race, and had been sued by the Episcopalian hierarchy for having a woman priest. Most of all, she loved the affection with which its members had welcomed her, visited her at home, and driven her to services. I think she would have liked the Quaker-style informality with which people rose to tell their memories of her. I know she would have loved the presence of many friends. It was to

this church that she had donated some of her remaining Michigan property in the hope that it could be used as a multiracial camp, thus getting even with those people in the tiny nearby town who had snubbed my father for being Jewish.

I think she also would have been pleased with her obituary. It emphasized her brief career as one of the early women journalists and asked for donations to Oberlin's scholarship fund so others could go to this college she loved so much but had to leave.

I know I will spend the next years figuring out what her life has left in me.

I realize that I've always been more touched by old people than by children. It's the talent and hopes locked up in a failing body that gets to me; a poignant contrast that reminds me of my mother, even when she was strong.

I've always been drawn to any story of a mother and a daughter on their own in the world. I saw *A Taste of Honey* several times as both a play and a film, and never stopped feeling it. Even *Gypsy* I saw over and over again, sneaking in backstage for the musical and going to the movies as well. I told myself that I was learning the tap-dance routines, but actually my eyes were full of tears.

70   I once fell in love with a man only because we both belonged to that large and secret club of children who had "crazy mothers." We traded stories of the shameful houses to which we could never invite our friends. Before he was born, his mother had gone to jail for her pacifist convictions. Then she married the politically ambitious young lawyer who had defended her, stayed home and raised many sons. I fell out of love when he confessed that he wished I wouldn't smoke or swear, and he hoped I wouldn't go on working. His mother's plight had taught him self-pity—nothing else.

I'm no longer obsessed, as I was for many years, with the fear that I would end up in a house like that one in Toledo. Now, I'm obsessed instead with the things I could have done for my mother while she was alive, or the things I should have said.

I still don't understand why so many, many years passed before I saw my mother as a person and before I understood that many of the forces in her life are patterns women share. Like a lot of daughters, I suppose I couldn't afford to admit that what had happened to my mother was not all personal or accidental, and therefore could happen to me.

One mystery has finally cleared. I could never understand why my mother hadn't been helped by Pauline, her mother-in-law; a woman she seemed to love more than her own mother. This paternal grandmother had died when I was five, before my mother's real problems began but long after that "nervous breakdown," and I knew

Pauline was once a suffragist who addressed Congress, marched for the vote, and was the first women member of a school board in Ohio. She must have been a courageous and independent woman, yet I could find no evidence in my mother's reminiscences that Pauline had encouraged or helped my mother toward a life of her own.

I finally realized that my grandmother never changed the politics of her own life, either. She was a feminist who kept a neat house for a husband and four antifeminist sons, a vegetarian among five male meat eaters, and a woman who felt so strongly about the dangers of alcohol that she used only paste vanilla; yet she served both meat and wine to the men of the house and made sure their lives and comforts were continued undisturbed. After the vote was won, Pauline seems to have stopped all feminist activity. My mother greatly admired the fact that her mother-in-law kept a spotless house and prepared a week's meals at a time. Whatever her own internal torments, Pauline was to my mother a woman who seemed able to "do it all." "Whither thou goest, I shall go," my mother used to say to her much-loved mother-in-law, quoting the Ruth of the Bible. In the end, her mother-in-law may have added to my mother's burdens of guilt.

75　　　Perhaps like many later suffragists, my grandmother was a public feminist and a private isolationist. That may have been heroic in itself, the most she could be expected to do, but the vote and a legal right to work were not the only kind of help my mother needed.

The world still missed a unique person named Ruth. Though she longed to live in New York and in Europe, she became a woman who was afraid to take a bus across town. Though she drove the first Stanley Steamer, she married a man who never let her drive.

I can only guess what she might have become. The clues are in moments of spirit or humor.

After all the years of fear, she still came to Oberlin with me when I was giving a speech there. She remembered everything about its history as the first college to admit blacks and the first to admit women, and responded to students with the dignity of a professor, the accuracy of a journalist, and a charm that was all her own.

When she could still make trips to Washington's wealth of libraries, she became an expert genealogist, delighting especially in finding the rogues and rebels in our family tree.

80　　　Just before I was born, when she had cooked one more enormous meal for all the members of some famous dance band at my father's resort and they failed to clean their plates, she had taken a shotgun down from the kitchen wall and held it over their frightened heads until they had finished the last crumb of strawberry shortcake. Only then did she tell them the gun wasn't loaded. It was a story she told with great satisfaction.

Though sex was a subject she couldn't discuss directly, she had a great appreciation of sensuous men. When a friend I brought home tried to talk to her about cooking, she was furious. ("He came out in the kitchen and talked to me about *stew!*") But she forgave him when we went swimming. She whispered, "He has wonderful legs!"

On her seventy-fifth birthday, she played softball with her grandsons on the beach, and took pride in hitting home runs into the ocean.

Even in the last year of her life, when my sister took her to visit a neighbor's new and luxurious house, she looked at the vertical stripes of a very abstract painting in the hallway and said, tartly, "Is that the price code?"

She worried terribly about being socially accepted herself, but she never withheld her own approval for the wrong reasons. Poverty or style or lack of education couldn't stand between her and a new friend. Though she lived in a mostly white society and worried if I went out with a man of the "wrong" race, just as she had once married a man of the "wrong" religion, she always accepted each person as an individual.

85   "Is he *very* dark?" she once asked worriedly about a friend. But when she met this very dark person, she only said afterward, "What a kind and nice man!"

My father was the Jewish half of the family, yet it was my mother who taught me to have pride in that tradition. It was she who encouraged me to listen to a radio play about a concentration camp when I was little. "You should know that this can happen," she said. Yet she did it just enough to teach, never enough to frighten.

It was she who introduced me to books and a respect for them, to poetry that she knew by heart, and to the idea that you could never criticize someone unless you "walked miles in their shoes."

It was she who sold that Toledo house, the only home she had, with the determination that the money be used to start me in college. She gave both her daughters the encouragement to leave home for four years of independence that she herself had never had.

After her death, my sister and I found a journal she had kept of her one cherished and belated trip to Europe. It was a trip she had described very little when she came home: she always deplored people who talked boringly about their personal travels and showed slides. Nonetheless, she had written a descriptive essay called "Grandma Goes to Europe." She still must have thought of herself as a writer. Yet she showed this long journal to no one.

90   I miss her, but perhaps no more in death than I did in life. Dying seems less sad then having lived too little. But at least we're now asking questions about all the Ruths and all our family mysteries.

If her song inspires that, I think she would be the first to say: It was worth the singing.

Reflective Reading, Informal Writing

REFLECTING ON THE READING:

- "Unlike the case of my Uncle Ed, exterior events were never suggested as a reason for [Ruth's] problems," writes Steinem. How were Uncle Ed's problems accounted for, and how did those explanations differ from the accounts given of Ruth? Why the difference?
- As is the case with most children, Steinem's view of her mother changes as Steinem herself grows up. What steps or stages can you identify in the process of Steinem's changing perspective? You will probably find the progression considerably more complex than just "then" and "now." How is Steinem's feminism related to these changes in the way she understands her mother?
- What evidence can you find that the disintegration of Ruth's personality occurred because she was a woman? How does her life compare with those of the other women mentioned in this essay— her mother, for example, or her mother-in-law, or Gloria herself?

UNDERSTANDING RHETORICAL STRATEGIES:

- If this is to be an essay about Ruth, why does it start with five paragraphs about Uncle Ed? Why not get to the point?
- On pages 158-160 Steinem recites lists of items, each of which begins with the punctuation normally used to indicate ellipsis, or omission (. . .), as if to suggest that what follows is incomplete, a fragment rather than a complete idea. Taken together, these lists of related fragments create a kind of collage as opposed to the linear type of argument we are accustomed to seeing, with its complete sentences and its careful transitions. Why, in each case, a "collage" rather than a traditional argument? What is Steinem trying to accomplish by using these lists, and why choose this means to accomplish that purpose?
- Do a reverse outline of this essay to determine how it is organized. Notice that paragraphs are themselves grouped together into larger units, indicated by additional white space between sections. How is the organization of the essay related to Steinem's purpose in writing?
- What does Steinem mean by "song"?
- At one point Steinem writes, "Like women alcoholics who drink in their kitchens while costly programs are constructed for executives who drink . . . my mother was not an important worker." This is an essay that is very sharply focused on a single woman, and yet it is also about all women, or at least many. As in the sentence quoted, Steinem is clearly suggesting that what happened to Ruth—both its causes and its effects—represents a fairly common pattern in our

culture. This is a private story with public implications. Reread the essay, this time looking for the stylistic features that allow Steinem to indicate that this is not merely a story about Ruth.

INFORMAL WRITING:

* Imagine two Ruths: "an earlier Ruth" and the Ruth Gloria Steinem knew, the Ruth shaped by social forces more or less beyond her control. Based on what Gloria Steinem tells us, what were some of those forces that shaped the second Ruth? What indications do we have that the earlier Ruth was never completely extinguished by these forces?
* Mark Twain once wrote that "When I was a boy of fourteen, my father was so ignorant I could hardly stand to have the old man around. But when I got to be twenty-one, I was astonished at how much the old man had learned in seven years." Describe the changes you have gone through over the years in your view of someone important to you—a parent, a teacher, a role model, a close friend. While the person you are writing about may, in fact, have changed during this period, to what extent were the changes in your understanding of that person actually a function of changes in you?
* Write about what limits you think society imposed on women of Ruth's day that are or are not present today. One place to look: What limits are imposed on her daughter, Gloria? Then again, how representative is Gloria Steinem?
* There are probably thousands of women whose "song" has never been heard either because—like Ruth—they could not sing it, or because no one ever asked, and they themselves had (or have) been conditioned to think that it wasn't very important anyway. Together with your classmates, set out to collect the stories of women you know of various ages, and as best you can of various (including no) occupations, ranging from the traditional conservative to the feminist. You will probably want to work together to identify and refine some standard interview questions that you can all begin with, but think of these questions as attempts to answer the previous question. What are the obstacles to personal growth and development women encounter, or have encountered, in their lives? How do they become aware of these obstacles—or do they even think of them that way? What are their strategies for surmounting these roadblocks? Identify any trends or patterns you might notice. Write about what you think is most interesting, most painful, or most joyful from what the people you interviewed told you. Use pseudonyms to protect your subjects' anonymity, and assure them in advance that you will be doing so.

DOUG ROBINSON

As an undergraduate in the early 1970s, Doug Robinson was drawn to women's studies when the women's movement was just beginning to earn respect as an academic field and serious political movement. Women's studies offered Robinson a way to understand both men and women, starting with his own parents and himself. This interest in women's studies continued through his early 30s when he shifted his focus to men's studies. This led him to his book, *No Less a Man* (1994). Robinson uses the term "masculist" as an adjective for the men's movement that is allied with the women's movement and gender liberation.

After living in Finland for 14 years, Robinson returned to the United States to teach at Ole Miss (University of Mississippi) and currently teaches at the University of Iowa. He will soon be living in Spain as a Fulbright scholar teaching translation studies at the University of Vic near Barcelona. Since his undergraduate years, Robinson has loved to write. His dissertation in American culture and literature was completed at the University of Washington in 1983 and published two years later. He has directed his writing at topics that have a deep and personal resonance for him—topics that will change him and potentially change his readers. He believes writing is heuristic, allowing the writer to discover new possibilities while writing. Although many writers start with awkward drafts, through continued writing and revision, they gradually build a sense of what they want to say and how best to convey their ideas.

As the keynote speaker at a psychology conference, Robinson read a one-and-a-half page monologue originating from an 18-page monologue written by Sylvester Stallone for the first Rambo movie. Robinson sees this monologue as a key text in men's studies. Before he finished reading at the conference, he was surprised to discover that he was crying in front of the large audience. He was more surprised, and later pleased, to find that half the audience was crying as well. This happened three additional times when he read the monologue to other audiences.

The movie *Rambo* has become an emblem of blind, unthinking machismo and the myth of the macho man who does not feel or think—a killing machine. According to Robinson, Rambo represents the tension for men in a patriarchal society between outward hardness and inward softness. Doug Robinson suggests renting the first Rambo movie, *First Blood*, after reading this chapter. Many viewers, especially feminist viewers, have found the Rambo movies anything but positive experiences and models for males. Does Robinson's reading of *Rambo* seem convincing to you?

The Hurt, Betrayed Son

The open, friendly face Stallone wears in the opening frames of the movie tells us that his closed face now is only a reaction to bad news, specifically a defensive reaction, a pretend indifference that says: I don't care that my friend died. Please don't let me care. The thing is, and this is a sign of Stallone's much-maligned artistry as an actor, we *know* he's pretending. We know he cares. Stallone is often criticized for being an expressionless actor; but while it is true that the emotional range his face can express is fairly narrow, he works that narrow range with a highly charged subtlety. The macho mask that Rambo puts on when he learns his buddy is dead and wears for most of the rest of the movie is shot through with a characteristic Stallone sadness, a mournfulness, an emotional sensitivity that in some sense will save him from the death Morrell envisaged for him. In Stallone's face a battle is being waged between conditioned masculine control and an overwhelming impulse to give in, let go, release pent-up emotion. His violence throughout the movie will be an ongoing attempt to maintain control that will culminate in a redemptive failure": in the end he will lose control, break down, cry, need consolation.

The novel Rambo is different—on the edge, boiling with resentment, spoiling for a fight:

> Rambo knew there was going to be trouble, though. Big trouble, if somebody didn't watch out. The car he was trying to thumb a ride with nearly ran him over when it left the pump. The station attendant crammed a charge slip and a book of trade stamps into his pocket and grinned at the tire marks on the hot tar close to Rambo's feet. Then the police car pulled out of traffic toward him and he recognized the start of the pattern again and stiffened. "No, by God. Not this time. This time I won't be pushed." (11)

Morrell's Rambo has only been home from Vietnam six months, and has already been run out of 15 towns. With long, greasy hair and a thick greasy beard, he looks like a hippie, maybe, as Morrell himself says, but even more like a bum, a drifter. Sheriff Will Teasle is protecting his decent middle-class town's "aesthetic" sense—their unease with dirt, their cleanliness obsession, whose personal expression (a rigid dress code) and political expression (law and order) converge in Teasle's determination to "clean him up," bathe, barber, and shave him. The relaxation of middle-class dress codes in the ten intervening years, combined with the movie producers' desire to make Rambo a sympathetic victim, together make Stallone look much less offensive: with his rumpled hair and fashionable stubble, he looks like anybody else in the eighties, at least anybody who would be walking around in rural Washington State. (He couldn't pass for a Wall Street stock broker, or even a Seattle lawyer. He might pass as a small-town lawyer in the Cascades.) This has the effect of making Teasle's determination to railroad him out of town unconvincing: what could the sheriff possibly have against him?

The actual confrontation between Teasle and Rambo here in the beginning, Teasle's attempt to get Rambo out of town and Rambo's stubborn attempt to come back in, is roughly the same in the novel and the movie, the major difference being that in the novel we know what Rambo is thinking:

> His clothes were filmed yellow with dust, his long hair and beard were matted dirty, and all the people driving by took a look at him, and nobody stopped. So why don't you clean up your act? he thought. Shave and get a haircut. Fix up your clothes. You'd get more rides that way. *Because. A razor's just one more thing to slow you down, and haircuts waste money you can spend on food, and where would you shave anyhow; you can't sleep in the woods and come out looking like some kind of prince.* Then why walk around like this, sleeping in the woods? And with that, his mind moved in a circle and he was back to the war. Think about something else, he told himself. Why not turn around and go? Why come back to this town? It's nothing special. *Because. I have a right to decide for myself whether I'll stay in it or not. I won't have somebody decide that for me.*
>
> But this cop is friendlier than the rest were. More reasonable. Why bug him. Do what he says.
>
> *Just because somebody smiles when he hands me a bag of shit, that doesn't mean I have to take it. I don't give a damn how friendly he is. It's what he does that matters.*
>
> But you do look a little rough, as if you might cause trouble. He has a point.
>
> *So do I. In fifteen goddamn towns this has happened to me. This is the last. I won't be fucking shoved anymore.*
>
> Why not explain that to him, clean yourself up a bit? Or do you want this trouble that's coming? You're hungry for some action, is that it? So you can show him your stuff?
>
> *I don't have to explain myself to him or anybody else. After what I've been through, I have a right without explanation.*
>
> At least tell him about your medal, what it cost you.
>
> Too late to stop his mind from completing the circle. Once again he returned to the war. (21–22)

The problem with the circle he wants to avoid completing is that it is vicious. Thoughts of the war make him think of what "they" (the symbolic fathers who ran the war) *made* him do, the horrors he was trained to perpetrate and withstand; and so he turns to civilian life to take his mind off the war. But thoughts of civilian life make him think of what "they" (the symbolic fathers who run the towns he travels through) *won't let* him do, the humiliations he is forced to suffer; and so he turns back to the war. It is a vicious circle of paternal oppression: the fathers get him coming and going.

Note, though, in that internal dialogue, that some voice inside Rambo keeps offering an out, an escape from the vicious circle, or at least a consciousness that is not trapped in the vicious circle, an outside voice (like Susan Silverman's for Spenser) that tries to force him to work through his emotional fixations: "Then why walk around like this, sleeping in the woods?" The only answer Rambo can think of to this is the war, which he doesn't want to think about; like Scarlett O'Hara, therefore, he tells himself to think of something else. He thinks he is trying to repress the circular logic in which he is trapped; but all he is really successfully repressing is the possibility of escape. At some deep emotional level, he has trapped himself, and doesn't know how, doesn't *want* to know how, is afraid to know how, to untrap himself.

I don't mean to say that he is clinically paranoid—that he is, say, only imagining the hostility civilians, especially their law enforcement officers, feel toward him. That hostility is there. But he is, as his inner voice of self-conscious admonition knows, also provoking it, precisely by not shaving, not taking baths, not cutting his hair, not fixing up his clothes. Not getting a job and a wife and a ranch-style house and two-point-one kids. Sleeping in the woods is a defiant act that is *designed* to stir up civilians' hostility toward him.

The problem is, the military used him in the war as a tool to do terrible things, dehumanizing things: he was appreciated, esteemed, "loved" by his military "fathers" only insofar as he was useful to them, only insofar as he was skillful at doing their dirty work for them. This is bad enough: like everybody else, he wants to be appreciated for who he is, loved as himself, not as a killer, not as a tool. As he says explicitly at the end of *Rambo: First Blood Part II*, when Trautman urges him not to hate his country, he wants "*once* for our country to love us as much as we love it."

But however dehumanizing this "instrumentalization" by the Special Forces was, at least he could feel it was marginally worthwhile: he was good at it, he served his country, and received recognition for it, the highest recognition of all, the Congressional Medal of Honor. When he returned to civilian life he got no recognition at all. He was just a nothing kid. Overnight he went from feeling used to feeling abandoned, and the transition made him feel betrayed.

20   This is a familiar feeling in Morrell novels, and it will recur in the second Rambo film when Murdock, the government heavy played by Charles Napier (who looks remarkably like Brian Dennehy as Will Teasle), gives the order to abort the mission and leave Rambo to die.[1]

---

[1] Visually, the scene is striking: the helicopter circles nervously overhead, first trying to land, then receiving the order to abort and playing out conflicting responses to the order (Trautman orders the pilot to land anyway but is countermanded by Murdock's man in the back of the chopper, who pulls a gun on Trautman and warns him not to be a hero); 30 or 40 feet below, at the vortex of its tight circles, stands an obedient and suppliant Rambo, looking about six inches tall, the good little boy who did what he heard his daddy tell him to do and now wants to be rewarded with love,

The feeling has something to do with the insecurity of a boy in a "fatherless" world: because there is no father to love him, and by loving him to stabilize his world, his human worth is forever up or grabs, definable by the highest bidder. Bidding for the little boy's human worth (self-esteem) is conducted in the currency of kindness, affection, appreciation, respect, recognition; but the very use of these emotional expressions as a currency empties them out into sheer abstract markers, like dollar bills, which can be taken away as easily as they are given. The fatherless boy feels absurdly grateful for any attention at all from a father-figure, and devotes himself body and soul to the man who seems to love him; but the very intensity of his gratitude and devotion reveals its source in insecurity, in the fear of abandonment. That precarious balance between devotion and anxiety makes even the smallest sign of conniving or calculation on the father-figure's part a mortal offense, and sets the avalanche of feeling used, abandoned, and betrayed into motion.

And all that needs to be added to this analysis is the observation that, under conditions of patriarchy, which imposes and enforces the myth of the absent father, it is not just literally fatherless boys like David Morrell who suffer from this insecurity; it is all of us. Boys who grow up with fathers who are physically present but emotionally absent themselves become fathers who are afraid to be emotionally present for their own children, and the patriarchal cycle continues.

Morrell develops the used-abandoned-betrayed dynamic most explicitly in *The Brotherhood of the Rose,* where Saul and Chris discover that their foster-father Eliot never loved them:

> "He made us. Yes." Chris pursed his lips in anger. "And these other men as well [Eliot has "adopted" a total of eighteen boys in nine different orphanages and brought them up to be intelligence agents]. He programmed us to be absolutely dedicated to him."
>
> "Never to question anything. Like the Paradigm job," Saul said. "I never dreamed of asking him why he wanted it done. If he ordered something, that was good enough."
>
> "We were so naive he must have been tempted to laugh. When we snuck from school that night and the gang beat us up . . ." Chris glared. "I only now realized. Something about them always bothered me. They looked too neat. Their leather jackets were new. They drove an expensive car." He shivered. "They must have been operatives. He sent them to work us over, to make us angry so we'd grab the chance to learn [self-defense] at the *dojo.* God knows how many other ways he manipulated us."

25

---

or at least with rescue. He holds an exhausted POW at his side; Vietnamese soldiers are advancing on him, firing on him with Kalashnikovs. The camera angles make us first identify with the father on high, fleshed forth in the metal body of the helicopter thirty feet up and the three men torn by internal conflicts over the treacherously cold voice in their ears; then with Rambo down on the ground, as the chopper pulls away and the Vietnamese troops close in on him.

"Those Baby Ruth candy bars. He gave me one in Denver when he set me up to be killed."

"The same when he asked me to hunt for you," Chris added. "We're Pavlov's dogs. Those candy bars are the symbol of his relationship with us. He used them to make us love him. It was easy. No one else showed us kindness. An old man giving candy to kids."

The rain drummed harder on the roof.

"And now we find out everything he said was wrong. A trick. A lie," Saul said. "He never loved us. He used us."

30   "Not only us," Chris seethed. "These other men must have felt he loved them too. He lied to everyone. We were all just part of a group. I could almost forgive his lies—the things he made me do!—if I thought we were special to him. But we're not." He listened to the storm, his words like thunder. "And for that, I'll see him die." (202–03)

"I could almost forgive his lies—the things he made me do!—if I thought we were special to him." Rambo too was made to feel special, by his Green Beret instructor Captain Trautman, and is betrayed by him, eventually killed by him, later in the novel. But Morrell has not yet developed his finely honed sense of being used, abandoned, and betrayed in *First Blood*. Rambo reacts, and tries futilely to figure out why he's reacting as he does. At some point in the novel, fairly early on, he stops trying to understand—just acts. Acts as he was programmed to act: kills as many of the enemy as possible. For the Rambo of Morrell's *First Blood* there is no escape from programming, no escape from Pavlovian killing, as the heroes of the Brotherhood series start to hope, and as Rambo himself, brought back to life in the movies and in Morrell's novelizations of the sequels, begins to hope. Chris Kilmoonie, Drew MacLane, and Rambo III all retire to monasteries to find peace, to work through the programmed need to kill with professional coldness, to work down past the coldness to the deepseated needs for paternal love and approval and fears of paternal abandonment and betrayal that drive them. None of them finds peace, probably because their creator hasn't found peace and doesn't know what it feels like—although he claims Rambo does at the end of *Rambo III*. It is the dubious peace that comes from conforming yourself to your programming, doing what you were programmed to want to do:

Yes. It was clear now. He finally did what Trautman had wanted.
He accepted his destiny.
The thought surprised him.
35   Destiny?
But what exactly *was* it?
The answer came at once. God had fated him to be a warrior. As long as innocent people were brutalized, he had a meaning. He served a purpose.
To protect. To suffer so that others would not.
He smiled as he stared toward the draw into Pakistan, toward the future and, God willing, salvation. (242)

40   His destiny is to be the Incredible Hulk, a superhero in rags.[2] The thing is, this is somebody else's destiny *for* him, Trautman's, and beyond Trautman patriarchy's. Men shall protect. Men shall suffer so that others will not. Salvation and peace of mind lie in accepting that programmed patriarchal imperative.

But if this appears to be the "goal" of the Rambo series, Morrell's *First Blood* exploration of the circumambient path to that goal leaves room for another kind of hope, another kind of peace, another kind of salvation. Like Chris in *The Brotherhood of the Rose* and Drew in *The Fraternity of the Stone*, in *Rambo III* Rambo brings monastic discipline to bear on his unruly self: a *con*formative ending, an attempt to conform to social norms. But back in *First Blood* Rambo's self-control fails in ways that are destructive but also potentially *trans*formative. Just before he breaks in the police station, Morrell gives us a glimpse of the defensiveness of Rambo's intense need to keep himself in check:

> He was determined to keep control. There would be just the next five minutes and the continual touch of the scissors, and then it would be over, he would be all right.
> He started toward the chair, his feet slick in the water, and behind him Shingleton said, "Good God, where did you get all the scars on your back?"
> "In the war." That was a weakness. He should not have answered.
45 > "Oh sure. Sure you did. In which army?"
> Rambo almost killed him right there. (52)

His fear of being weak is mainly a fear of letting his tough image slip—the image of a man, a superhero, self-sufficient, unneedy, indifferent to sympathy or kindness, unaffected by others' claims on him. To admit that he had been wounded in the war is first of all to try to impress these men, to brag about being tough in an area they will admire; but it is also, more profoundly, a play for their sympathy. Look what I suffered in Vietnam. Look how badly I've been treated. Don't be mad at me; understand me. Love me. Care for me. Pamper me, cuddle me, make me feel safe again. In other words,

---

[2] A more recent image-parallel to Stallone than Davy Crockett, as he walks down the road behind the opening credits, is in fact Bill Bixby as David Banner in the TV series *The Incredible Hulk*—and that hero's radiation-caused transformation into a raging green-skinned monster—who is, finally, *nice*, a good guy, is entirely congruent with the *First Blood* movie image of Rambo. Significantly enough, Spenser identifies with the Incredible Hulk in *Valediction* (74), when he has been abandoned by Susan. It is an attractive image for the macho loner: the "nothing kid" who, when pushed hard enough by external circumstances, when pushed to the edge of his tolerance, is suddenly transformed into a violent monster whose violent powers have been *conditioned* by society (radiation, Special Forces training) but are *channeled* by the macho hero into a force for good. The movie Rambo doesn't actually get a chance to do much good in this first episode, of course (and it is largely an ideological question whether what he does in the second and third episodes is good); but he is so clearly a *good person*, a nice guy in a bad situation, that our hearts go out to him.

make me feel like a baby being loved by his mommy. But infancy is the time of total vulnerability, total defenselessness, and that makes it frightening. Rambo, like most of us programmed for traditional masculinity, feels compelled to defend against defenselessness, to muster a defensive strength against weakness.

But he can't. By *Rambo III,* he can—he has internalized the self-discipline of four different religious traditions in support of his defenses, and it seems to be working—which makes that novel, and the movie it exfoliates, much less interesting to me than *First Blood.* Here in the first installment of the myth his needs and fears are stronger than his defenses, and he moves toward what he knows with a terrible certainty is trouble. Trouble is what follows from losing self-control. And my guess is that he senses the trouble will not only be with the police. Losing self-control means psychological trouble too, the incursion of all the frightening monsters from the locked chambers deep down inside:

> What the hell did you expect? he told himself. You asked for this, didn't you? You wouldn't back off.
>
> Damn right I wouldn't. And I still won't. Just because I'll be locked up, doesn't mean I'm finished. I'll fight this as far as it goes. By the time he's ready to let me out, he'll be fucking glad to get rid of me.
>
> Sure you'll fight. Sure. What a laugh. Take a look at yourself. Already you're shaking. Already you know what this place reminds you of. Two days in that cramped cell and you'll be pissing down your pantlegs.
>
> "You've got to understand I can't stay in there." He would not stop himself. "The wet. I can't stand being closed in where it's wet." The hole, he was thinking, his scalp alive. The bamboo grate over the top. Water seeping through the dirt, the walls crumbling, the inches of slimy muck he had to try sleeping on.
>
> Tell him, for God's sake.
>
> Screw, you mean beg him. (39)

50

55   The reason torture and murder are so powerfully traumatizing and dehumanizing is that, whether you inflict them or suffer them, you are brought face to face with your own deepest and most terrifying impulses: the subliminal desire to escalate self-hatred into self-torture and suicide, or to escalate anger at a recalcitrant outside world into total destruction. Being locked up in the "hole" in Vietnam meant, in the economy of Rambo's psyche, being locked into the hole of his own worst nightmares. All the desires "decent" citizens successfully repress are now reality, a horrifying, mind-numbing reality that doesn't seem possible. How can a nightmare be as real as a ride in a car or a conversation with a cashier at the grocery store? How can I deal with what I fear most on that level? Once those monsters are let loose, there is no putting them back. They must either be frozen, stunned, shunted off to some holding tank of the imagination, by strict discipline—the road Morrell's most sym-

pathetic heroes tend to take—or they must be befriended, transformed into acquaintances, familiars, and so rendered harmless.[3]
The latter is the path to health; but it leads through a cathartic release of the monsters that is potentially very dangerous indeed: it is,
in fact, the path that Rambo takes in *First Blood*. In the novel, the
dangers inherent in the path are realized, and Rambo self-destructs.
In the movie, Rambo manages to veer just this side of self-destruc-
tion, and (perhaps) is saved.

In any case, here is the prison block in Teasle's police station,
Rambo feels forced into too oppressive a proximity to his own nightmares, his terrible memories of torture in Vietnam: the wet floor, the
hostile male bodies crowding around him, the razor brought too
close to his throat. Sensitized by his Vietnam experience to the fluid-

---

[3] One of the contemporary American popular writers who knows this best is Stephen
King—not only in his horror fiction but in his wonderful critical book on horror, *Danse
Macabre*. I was, in fact, sorely tempted to include a discussion of King's novels in this
book, but, for reasons of economy, in the end didn't. Next time. But I can't forebear
pointing out here that, in the King novel I take to be his most explicitly emancipatory,
Firestarter, he creates a Rambo-like character called John Rainbird, who uses a carefully
tailored story about a POW experience in Vietnam to gain the sympathy of the novel's
eight-year-old heroine, Charlie McGee. King is on record as a major fan of Morrell's—
he once taught a writing course based around *First Blood* and one other novel, saying
that if apprentice writers could learn how to build and maintain suspense like Morrell,
they'd be set for life—and it seems clear to me that in the "Blackout" chapter of *Firestarter* he is specifically (though maybe only unconsciously?) alluding to *First Blood*.
Rainbird sounds like Rambo, of course; and both are Vietnam vets who were highly
trained in warfare. Rainbird has made the transition back to civilian life by becoming a
hit man for a clandestine government agency called the Shop—very much like the heroes of Morrell's "Brotherhood" series. Still, though he does well in espionage, better
than any of his employers, to the point of absolute contempt for them, he shares with
Rambo a mystical fascination with dying, and is ultimately satisfied when Charlie kills
him with her fire—he loves her, admires her, and her fire is a kind of psionic enactment
of female sexuality, fiery passion—just as Rambo is satisfied by his violent death at
Trautman's hands. Two odd similarities: both Rambo and Rainbird are named John,
but Rambo didn't get a first name until 1982, when the movie was released, and
Firestarter was published in 1980; and both Rambo and Rainbird are half-Indian, but
Morrell didn't give Rambo Indian blood until the novelization of *Rambo: First Blood Part II*,
in 1985. Could King have seen the Sackheim-Kozoll script before writing *Firestarter*, and
could Morrell have borrowed Rambo's Indian blood from King's novel—or were both
mere coincidences? Or were both writers tapping into a collective myth?
  Note that, despite the moral differences between the two heroes—Rambo is driven, a
man doing his best in a bad situation, while Rainbird is devious, evil, a man in the service of paternal repression—both represent for their creators deadends to a certain programmed form of masculinity who therefore *must* die and be superseded by a new
generation with a new potential for emancipation. The new "generation" in Rambo's
case may well be Stallone's Rambo ten years later; in King's novel the new generation is
more obvious: it is little Charlie McGee, the pyrokinetic girl who transforms the evil accident that programs her genetically into liberating empowerment.
  It's also worth noting that King, like Morrell, cannot remember his father: Don King
left his wife and children when little Stevie was two. (He discusses his fatherlessness in
chapter four of *Danse Macabre*, "An Annoying Autobiographical Pause." I recommend
Danse Macabre, by the way, as an absolutely delightful romp through not only horror but
popular culture, based on much the same premise about repression and release as
Fiedler's *What Was Literature?* but with a good deal less vestigial elitism.)

ity of nightmare in the world and in his head, he loses the ability to impose rational, logical distinctions on the world, and the prison block, the hole in Vietnam, and the nightmares in his head all fuse in one mystical moment of total terror, and he explodes with violence. He kills Galt—by slicing open his belly, not, as in the movie, by hurling a rock at the helicopter from which Galt is trying to shoot him—and the manhunt is on.

The movie Rambo is pursued by the same nightmares as the novel Rambo, and reacts to Teasle's pushing in much the same way, exploding with violence and escaping the prison block into the woods. But Stallone has made important changes in the character. He is, for one thing, no longer so intensely driven as his predecessor in print. Self-control seems to come easier to him, and yet he is also closer to his fears, less fearfully shut off from them. Since we don't know what Rambo is thinking on the screen, this is a feeling I at least get from Stallone, from the body signals Stallone conveys with his acting—which is, as I say, Stallone's many detractors to the contrary—extremely subtle. Stallone draws powerfully on his own personal access to failure and weakness and vulnerability and need, his own ability to slip back and forth across the patriarchal barrier between defensive hardness and terrified softness.

Much of this is Stallone's ability to access the conflicted, angry, lost, frustrated and defensively self-destructive feeling of his childhood. Born in the charity ward of New York Hospital in 1946, Stallone spent the first five or six years of his life (neglected by his American mother Jacqueline, terrorized by his Sicilian father Frank) on the streets of Hell's Kitchen, an ugly nothing kid; and, even after his parents were divorced and his mother was remarried to a wealthy pizza manufacturer, Sly clung to his street-urchin ways, his working class mannerisms. (He still sounds working-class, despite his later private education in Leysin, Switzerland.[4]) This is self-destructive behavior in an upper-middle-class family, as Spenser discovered in his dealings with the Orchards back in *The Godwulf Manuscript*; it does, however, yield some tiny measure of embattled integrity, even of self-definition, in and through the very fury it arouses in your parents. And some of that hurt but pathetically (and hopelessly) defiant little boy plays across Stallone's nerve-damaged slab of a face still today, whenever he plays the part of a man thwarted by the superior force of patriarchal fathers (Teasle in *First Blood*, Murdock in *Rambo: First Blood Part II*, his father-in-law in *Over the Top*). Even when he is acting his toughest, when he is portraying a character defensively given to macho blankness, there is an overwhelming sense

---

[4] There is no full-scale biography of Stallone; I take this biographical information from St. Pierre's brief pictorial life.

of the little boy inside crying "Please don't do this to me! Don't hate me! Don't torment me! Please love me!"[5]

My guess is, in fact, that the critics' hostile reaction to Stallone is at least partly itself a defense. The vulnerability of a macho man is embarrassing to almost everybody, and Stallone reeks of both machismo and vulnerability. Thanks largely to Stallone, Rambo has become a byword for personally focused but professionally unfeeling American imperialism, SS tactics—torture and murder and destruction. Stallone himself is attacked as Mr. Expressionless. But one wonders. There is an intensity to these attacks that cannot be explained away as mere ideological repugnance, mere liberalism, mere middle-class distaste for violence. Could it be that male critics insecure about their own masculinity (and female critics insecure about their fathers' masculinity) react subliminally to that element of emotional frailty that is always just under Stallone's macho surface, and are so afraid of what they feel that they must escalate the attack on the safest, most predictable, most easily explainable part of Stallone's act? Certainly it is easier emotionally to criticize Stallone for being too tough than for not being tough enough. Machismo is too heavily under attack anyway, these days, for a critic to hold it up uncritically as an ideal; to admit that Stallone feels not too strong but too weak, not too impregnable but too vulnerable, would be to admit one's own fears of being weak and vulnerable, and that would be frightening.

---

[5] I should note that Jerry Goldsmith's music contributes enormously to the sense I get of Rambo's emotional vulnerability. Stallone doesn't do it all—although it's also possible that Stallone's acting encourages me to feel the impact of Goldsmith's music as emotionally congruent. (It is also possible that I'm projecting my own feelings of vulnerability onto Stallone's acting and Goldsmith's music.) I want to draw particular attention to a recurring running bass line played by synthesized cellos, which first begins when Rambo turns back toward town in blatant defiance of Teasle's orders; then starts up again (after some fright chords while Rambo is breaking free of his captors) when he escapes the police station and jumps on the motorcycle; again when Teasle and Orval Kellerman and the deputies and Orval's dogs are chasing Rambo in the dark; again when the National Guard chase him into the mine; and finally, at half-tempo, when Rambo is plunging through the mine in search of a back way out. The base line is modified throughout the movie, sometimes running in straight (hopeful) 4/4 time, sometimes stumbling into a tortuous 10/8 or 14/8 time; sometimes modulating up a half-tone from the basic C-B♭-sus chord progression.

It sounds to me like the beating of a heart under stress, fibrillating perhaps—the heartbeat of fear, excited fear, the fear that follows great adventure, but it is not a heady excitement, a glorified, manly adventure, certainly not something Rambo enjoys or wants to be involved in. Significantly, again, this melodic theme is reworked (often counterpointed with the similarly transformed "It's a Long Road" theme) in *Rambo: First Blood Part II* to signify precisely the heroic adventure that the earlier movie avoided.

Andrew Laszlo's photography, too, plays its part in the first movie's expression: his blending of stark colors with black shadows, the dark green of the Canadian evergreens and the misty gray of dusk; the orange of Rambo's body illuminated by the torch in the mine and the blackness around him, the cold blue of his body against the blackness as he drops his torch and climbs up the ladder out of the mine.

60   Because the movie Rambo is less eager for action than the novel Rambo, shifts had to be made in the other two main characters as well, Teasle and Trautman. Teasle had to become more of a caricature, more of a cut-out figure (color me Oppressor)—more, in other words, of the heavy father. In order to be the sympathetic underdog, Rambo cannot push Teasle; Teasle must push him, out of some inexplicable inner rage. When Rambo walks back into town, he must do so not because he is looking for a fight, but because he is hungry (in the novel, Rambo makes it into town, gets a hamburger and eats it, and *then* is escorted out of town, for the second time, by Teasle). The novel Rambo has no external excuse for his stubbornness; his only excuse is that he has been pushed around one too many times. In the movie Teasle, not Rambo, feels like the man who has been pushed one too many times:

> Rambo: Why are you pushing me?
> Teasle: What did you say?
> Rambo: I said, why are you pushing me? I haven't done anything to you.
> Teasle: First of all, I ask the questions around here, you understand? Secondly, we don't want guys like you in this town. Drifters. First thing you know we got a whole *bunch* of guys like you in this town. That's why. Besides, you wouldn't like it here. This is a quiet little town. In fact you might say it's boring. But that's the way we like it. And I get paid to keep it that way.

65   This kind of print rendition of the exchange between Stallone and Brian Dennehy doesn't do justice to the movie's visual dynamic. Stallone is calm in his vulnerability, if that makes sense: so comfortable in his vulnerability that he doesn't have to play the rebellious son. Dennehy is the insecure, driven one. When Stallone asks why he's pushing, Dennehy gives us the scared authoritarian father, his lip and cheek muscles twitching nervously, his eyes shifting as he struggles to keep himself firmly under control, the anger rising but being carefully transformed into authoritarian rhetoric. He comes up with a two-point list of reasons why he is pushing: the first is insecure, the uneasy claim made by a father unsure of his authority. The gist is: you shut up and let me talk, which translates as, you scare me, your defiance is profoundly threatening to me, so if you don't shut up and behave yourself and do exactly what I say, I don't know what I'm going to do. By the second point he has got himself more under control; and as he works out the details of why the town doesn't like drifters, he gradually relaxes into his benevolent sheriff's role, joking humorlessly about how he is paid to keep the town boring.

       This is, in fact, the father seen from the outside: the father as inscrutable tyrant, irrationally rational in his determination to use any and every means to keep the unruly son in line. This is the novel Teasle too, up to a point. But, perhaps surprisingly, given Morrell's declared

intention to make the novel an allegory in which Rambo would symbolize the disaffected and Teasle the establishment, he also makes
Teasle sympathetic. Some readers, he tells us in the *Playboy* article,
even thought Teasle was the hero of the novel. As the story progresses
the Oedipal battle increasingly becomes, in fact, a kind of brother-bat-
tle, a battle between two rough equals who begin to intuit the other's
position, to know, in some extrasensory way, where the other is and
what he is doing and thinking and feeling. Morrell makes Teasle a
Korean war hero, winner of the Distinguished Service Cross; and,
though fat and out of shape and out of practice, by the end of the novel
he has virtually become Rambo's military peer. The movie people
make Teasle a fat, blustering, insecure, incompetent bully who survives the novel only because Rambo really doesn't want to hurt anybody, and takes every chance he gets to spare lives and even feelings.
The movie Rambo is the victimized son who could kill the father but
doesn't want to; the novel Rambo is the conflict-locked son who wants
to kill the father and does, but only when he is next to death himself.

Morrell also goes inside Teasle's head, and gives us the inner torment of an insecure man whose father was killed in a hunting accident
(here, in Teasle, even more than in Rambo, is Morrell's fictional version
of his own fatherless childhood) and was raised by a foster-father
whose expertise in hunting matters always made him feel inadequate.
In the movie Orval Kellerman (John McLiam) is just some old fart with
a bunch of trained Dobermans who gets shot in the leg by Rambo; in
the novel he is Teasle's foster-father and Oedipal foil:

> "The dogs," Teasle called. "Did you bring the dogs?"
> "Sure, but I don't see the use of sending that deputy to help rush
> them into the van," Orval answered at the top, slowing. "Look at that
> sun. It'll be dark in an hour."
> "Don't you think I know it."
> "I believe you do," Orval said. "I didn't mean to try and tell you any-
> thing."
> Teasle wished he had kept quiet. He could not afford to let it start
> again. This was too important. Orval was always treating him like he
> was still thirteen, telling him everything to do and how to do it, just as he
> had when Teasle lived with him as a boy. Teasle would be cleaning a
> gun or preparing a special cartridge load, and right away Orval would
> step in, giving his advice, taking over, and Teasle hated it, told him to
> butt out, that he could do things himself, often argued with him. He un-
> derstood why he did not like advice: there were teachers he sometimes
> met who could not stop lecturing once they were out of class, and he was
> a little like them, so used to giving orders that he could not accept some-
> one telling him what to do. He did not always refuse advice. If it was
> good, he often took it. But he could not let that be a habit; to do his job
> properly he had to rely on himself alone. If Orval had only on occasion
> tried to tell him what to do, he would not have minded. But not every
> time they were together. And now they had almost started at each other
> again, and Teasle was going to have to keep himself quiet. Orval was the

70

one man he needed right now, and Orval was just stubborn enough to take his dogs back home if they got into another argument.

Teasle did his best to smile. "Hey, Orval, that's just me sounding miserable again. Don't pay attention. I'm glad to see you." He reached to shake hands with him. It had been Orval who taught him how to shake hands when he was a boy. Long and firm, Orval had said. Make your handshake as good as your word. Long and firm. Now, as their hands met, Teasle felt his throat constrict. In spite of everything, he loved this old man, and he could not adjust to the new wrinkles in his face, the white hair at the sides of his head that had become thinner and wispy like spider strands.

Their handshake was awkward. Teasle had deliberately not seen Orval in three months, ever since he had walked yelling out of Orval's house because a simple remark he had made had turned into a long argument over which way to strap on a holster, pointed forward or back. Soon after, he had been embarrassed about leaving the house like that, and he was embarrassed now, trying to act natural and look Orval straight in the face, doing a poor job of it. "Orval—about last time—I'm sorry. I mean it. Thanks for coming so quick when I need you."

75   Orval just grinned; he was beautiful. "Didn't I tell you never to talk to a man when you're shaking hands with him? Look him straight in the eyes. Don't jabber at him. I still think a holster should be pointed backward." He winked at the other men. His voice was low and resonant. "What about this kid?" Where's he gone to?" (64–66)

Teasle is as quick to react to the slightest hint that Orval doesn't love him for *himself* as Rambo is to the slightest hint that he is being denied his rights as an American citizen. Both men, like Spenser parking in front of hydrants, are insecure about their "integrity," their masculine autonomy, their power and ability and space to "rely on themselves alone," and invariably overreact in any situation in which they feel that their "freedom"—the freedom to exert their will unhampered—is being curtailed. (Will Teasle's name is itself a complex miring of "autonomous" masculine will in childhood teasing and tousling, and in the anxious cunning that we proverbially associate with weasels.) Rambo and Teasle are not only made *for* each other, in some sense they are made *by* each other: they occupy the mutually activating father and son roles in the vicious patriarchal circle of emotional withdrawal and the repressed demand for love, the circle that leads to feeling used, abandoned, and betrayed.

Trautman too, in both the novel and the movie, plays his part in this patriarchal drama: he is a kind of father-figure to both Rambo and Teasle, and invokes variations on the same feelings of uneasy respect and resentment in both men. Teasle's resentment is the strongest: he is the local sheriff and is jealous of his jurisdiction, both when Dave Kern the state cop comes in to take over and when Trautman the Green Beret comes in to help out. In the novel, however, Teasle's insecurity around Trautman is muted, and linked specifically to his ambivalent feelings about Orval Kellerman:

"You've pointed out enough faults. Can't you offer something positive?"

He said it stronger than he intended, so that when Trautman answered "Yes," there was something new, resentment, hidden in that even voice: "I have a few details to settle on yet. I don't know how you run your police department, but I like to be sure before I go ahead on something."

80   Teasle nodded his co-operation and immediately tried to ease off. "Sorry. I guess it's me who sounds wrong now. Don't pay attention. I'm just not happy unless I get miserable once in a while."

Again it came, that strange intense doubling of past and present: two nights ago when Orval had said "It'll be dark in an hour," and he himself had snapped "Don't you think I know it" and then had apologized to Orval in almost the same words he had just said to Trautman.

Maybe it was the pills. (173)

The pills are, of course, a convenient scapegoat: always better, for a traditionally programmed man, to blame uncontrollable behavior on something chemical or mechanical than something emotional. In any case, the novel Teasle is half-aware of his father-problems and backs off. (It is enough, maybe, for us to know his twisted inner feelings. Morrell doesn't have to hit us over the head with Teasle's insecurity, the way the movie does.) When this same scene is transposed to the movie, Trautman is assigned more or less the same lines, but Teasle's response is escalated to a paroxysm of insecure bullying; and the same relationship recurs throughout the rest of the movie, Trautman the calm, condescendingly conciliatory father who rests secure in his superior knowledge and skill, Teasle the touchy, anxious, resentful son. This is perhaps nowhere clearer than in the woods in front of the mine entrance, where everybody thinks the National Guard have just killed Rambo with a rocket:

85   Teasle: Buried in a hole by weekend warriors. I thought he was the best you ever trained.

Trautman: However he ended up, there was a time when he was very special.

Teasle: Special my ass. He was just another drifter who broke the law.

Trautman: Vagrancy, wasn't it? That's going to look real good on his gravestone at Arlington: "Here lies John Rambo, winner of the Congressional Medal of Honor, survivor of countless incursions beyond enemy lines, killed for vagrancy in Jerkwater, USA."

Teasle: Aw, don't give me any of that crap, Trautman. Do you think Rambo was the only guy who had a tough time in Vietnam? He killed a police officer, for Christ's sake!

Trautman: You're goddamned lucky he didn't kill all of you.

90   Again, Teasle's insecurity is mainly conveyed by Dennehy's body language: his restless stamping about in the woods like a wounded bull around Richard Crenna, who does Trautman as serene matador; his anxious mouth, his need to thrust his jaw in Trautman's face to make a point. Trautman is shown gazing speculatively at the

smoking ground over the mine, guessing correctly that Rambo is still alive, and this has the effect (especially on a second viewing) of rendering Trautman even more superior, distant, and autocratic: he can afford to let little-boy Teasle rant and rave, because he possesses paternal knowledge that he is not imparting. The conversation continues in a bar back in town, where Trautman is having a drink surrounded by a carnival atmosphere of laughter and lights (Christmas, maybe? Morrell's novel is set in October) and Teasle comes up to apologize.

> Teasle: Aw, I dunno, I just feel—
> Trautman: Like you were cheated out of your chance?
> Teasle: I wanted to kill that kid. I wanted to kill him so bad I could taste it.
> Trautman: That doesn't sit well with that badge . . . It can get confusing sometimes. In Vietnam you can bet that Rambo and I got pretty confused. We had orders: When in doubt, kill. What the hell, you're a civilian. I mean, you can go home to your wife and your house and your little flower garden. You're under no pressure to figure all this out.
> Teasle: Yeah, what about you, Colonel, what did you figure out from all of this, huh? I mean, what would you have done with him, if he came in? Would you have put your arms around him, given him a big, sloppy kiss, or would you have blown his brains out?
> Trautman: I couldn't answer that until I met him face to face.

95

Here Trautman remains the cold, aloof, authoritarian and somewhat patronizing father—jabbing at Teasle about going home to his wife and house and "little flower garden," but also trying, like an uneasy father trying hard not to antagonize a difficult son, to put Teasle at his ease by admitting his own confusion in Vietnam. But the last couple lines of that exchange begin to point ahead to a significant shift in Trautman's role: the choice between giving Rambo a kiss and blowing his brains out is in one sense a choice between the movie's ending, where Rambo survives to cry in Trautman's arms, and the novel's ending, where Trautman does blow Rambo's brains out with a shotgun. In another and deeper sense, however, what Teasle is giving Trautman is a choice between being a traditional mother and a traditional father. A mother would have put her arms around Rambo and kissed him: that is the loving role we assign, almost exclusively, to women in our society. A father would blow his brains out.

The implications are initially horrifying: that is what being a father is. That is what being a man is. Being hard, unforgiving, unloving and ready to blow your son's brains out if he doesn't knuckle down to your law. But the horror depends on our willingness to knuckle down to another "law," the felt compulsion of patriarchal programming. Paternally aloof as he is through most of the movie, Trautman here fights that programming by remaining flexible, willing to read the situation in its complexity rather than blindly applying a fixed principle; and in the end he shifts even further out of the traditional father-role by "mothering" Rambo, showing him love and kindness, throwing up a magic shield of protective warmth, as it were (telling the police to hold their fire), which gives Rambo the security he needs to release the fears he has been carrying around inside him for seven years.

This shift is anticipated in the movie in Trautman's relationship with Rambo early on. In the novel Trautman is a captain who had trained the men who trained Rambo; when he contacts Rambo over the radio of the police car he steals, Rambo remembers his voice over the loudspeakers at Special Forces training camp, cold, metallic, distant, disembodied:

100   "Rambo."
The voice startled him, coming from the car radio.
"Rambo. Listen to me. I know you can hear me."
The voice was familiar, years off. He could not place it.
"Listen to me." Each word smooth, sonorous. "My name is Sam Trautman. I was director of the school that trained you."
105   Yes. Of course. Never in sight. The persistent voice over the camp's loudspeaker. Any hour. Day after day. More running, fewer meals, less sleep. The voice that never failed to signal hardship. So that was it. Teasle had brought in Trautman to help. That explained some of the tactics the searchers had been using. The bastard. Turning on his own kind.
"Rambo, I want you to stop and surrender before they kill you."
Sure, you bastard.
"Listen to me. I know this is hard to understand, but I'm helping them because I don't want you killed. They've already begun to mobilize another force ahead of you, and there'll be another force after that, and they'll wear you down until there's nothing left of you. If I thought there was the slightest chance of your beating them, I'd gladly tell you to keep on the move. But I know you can't get away. Believe me. I know it. Please. While you still can, give up and get out of this alive. There's nothing you can do."
Watch me. (227–28)

110   Used, abandoned, betrayed. Morrell will have Eliot say almost exactly the same thing as Trautman to Chris and Saul in *The Brotherhood of the Rose*—you can't get away, give yourself up—and will let them prove him half wrong: Eliot kills Chris, Saul kills Eliot. Trautman is completely right in *First Blood*: Rambo can't get away. But that still doesn't change Rambo's feeling of betrayal, his anger at Trautman for "turning on his own kind." That feeling is, in fact, only exacerbated by the disembodied coldness by which Rambo knows Trautman: like Morrell's own father, absent in body and present only in his impoverished mother's stories about him, Trautman was present for Rambo only in "the voice that never failed to signal hardship."

In the movie Trautman is promoted to a colonel, but also made Rambo's personal instructor and team leader, a man who fought alongside him in Vietnam. Despite his higher rank, in the movie he is closer to Rambo when the action starts—a mate, a trusted buddy, not just an impersonal voice. In a modification of the novel's car radio conversation scene added to the Sackheim-Kozoll script by Larry Gross, Trautman contacts Rambo in the mine by radio and gets Rambo to break radio silence (thus allowing the police to get a fix on his position) by invoking military hierarchy. He pretends to be with Rambo back in Vietnam, calls him by his code name, calls off the roll of Baker-team. There is a warmth to their conversation that clearly anticipates the ending: when Trautman says "Look, John, we can't have you running around out there killing friendly civilians," for example, and Rambo replies laconically, and famously, "There are no friendly civilians," one senses that Trautman and Rambo agree on this. There is a shared body of experience between them. But Trautman's next line rings false: "Well, I'm your friend, Johnny." Trautman is trying too hard to be the paternal pal. There is a lot of this falseness in Crenna's voice as he talks to Rambo, saying "Let me come in and fly you the hell out of there," and Rambo quite rightly says "I can't do that, sir." Trautman does seem to be a kind of stable authority figure for Rambo, someone he can trust, someone he can tattle on the cops to ("They drew first blood, not me"). But he is specifically a distant authority figure, an absent father ("I tried to get in touch with you," Rambo says, "but the guys at Bragg never knew how to find you") who can't resist adding his own little reproach:

> Rambo: There wouldn't have been any trouble if it hadn't been for that king-shit cop. I just wanted to get something to eat, but he kept pushing.
> Trautman: Well, you did some pushing of your own, Johnny.

Did he? Maybe he did. Trautman is, of course, in a delicate position: by virtue of his friendship and war experience with Rambo, and their joint contempt for incompetent civilians, he is largely on Rambo's side (he says he has come to protect the cops from him), but he is also constrained to help the police find him and bring him in. Making contact with Rambo over the radio that Rambo stole off Galt's dead body is a way of reestablishing their friendship, of stroking away the effect of absence; but it is also a ruse to give the police a chance to find out where he is. Trautman would like, one gathers, to fly in and take Rambo out; but since he has no authority to make that kind of decision (as Teasle points out, Rambo is a civilian now, and a criminal in his jurisdiction), offering to do so must be understood by both Teasle and Rambo as just another ruse. If for both Teasle and Rambo Trautman feels like an authoritarian father, he probably thinks of himself as a sympathetic mediator, an uncle, maybe, or a much-older brother, caught awkwardly *between* father and son. It is not until the ending that Trautman meets Rambo face to face, without

Teasle consciously present (when Rambo and Trautman meet in the police station, Rambo has just shot Teasle through the ceiling and he, Teasle, is lying unconscious on the floor), and is able to work through the father-son conflicts to an empathetic, egalitarian embrace.

Works Cited

1. Morrell, David. *The Brotherhood of the Rose.* 1984. New York: Fawcett Crest/Ballantine, 1985.

2. Morrell, David. *First Blood.* 1972. New York: Fawcett Crest/Ballantine, 1988.

3. Morrell, David. *Rambo: First Blood Part II.* 1985. New York: Berkley/Jove, 1988.

4. Morrell, David, *Rambo III.* New York: Berkley/Jove, 1988.

Reflective Reading, Informal Writing

REFLECTING ON THE READING:

- Robinson speaks of Rambo's "programming." Is there a sense in which men in our culture are "programmed"? Programmed to do (or think, or be) what? How is this programming accomplished? In other words, think about both the content and the form of that programming.
- What are the connotations of the word "programmed" here? How does this term differ from others we might use for this phenomenon, like "trained," or "conditioned," or "steered," or "raised," or even "nurtured"? In your experience, which best describes the process by which men come to learn what it means to be men?
- In the quotation from the novel, *Rambo*, on page 174, there are two distinct voices playing in Rambo's head. How would you characterize the difference between these two voices? Where do these voices come from?

UNDERSTANDING RHETORICAL STRATEGIES:

- As Robinson sees it, *Rambo* (both as a novel and as a film) deals with more than one set of father-son relationships. In addition to the Teasle/Rambo relationship, there is the relationship between Teasle and his father, and that between Trautman and Rambo, and even that between Trautman and Teasle. Why does Morrell include multiple father-son relationships? Are they related, or do they somehow serve to comment on each other?
- Drawing either from Robinson's essay or from your own familiarity with both the novel and film versions of *Rambo*, what do you see as the essential differences between the two versions? How do you account for the difference? Which version do you prefer, and why?

• A paradox of academic writing is that we are expected to produce original ideas while leaning heavily on the ideas and the words of others. Our use of other writers can range from casual references to long, block quotations. Because he relies fairly heavily on quotation, Robinson provides an opportunity for us to see how this process works. Study each quotation in context. What is its function? How does it relate to his argument? What does it add to his essay? How does Robinson maintain a sense of control over the essay? Does he introduce quotations? Does he analyze the passages he quotes? Does he do so before or after quoting? How would the essay be different without the quotations?

INFORMAL WRITING:

• Robinson writes that Rambo is trapped in a "circular logic," and that in some sense he has "trapped himself." What is that circular logic, and how could Rambo be said to have trapped himself? How might he "untrap himself"? Are there other men in the story who are caught up in that same logic, and yet are capable of untrapping themselves?

• When Robinson speaks of Rambo as waging a battle between "conditioned masculine control and an overwhelming impulse to give in, let go, release pent-up emotion," or as a victim of the "circular logic" of a "patriarchal drama," do you see him merely as describing one especially twisted war veteran, or do you see him as describing men in general? Write about any man you know fairly well—other than a sibling, parent, or spouse. To what extent do the patterns Robinson writes about apply to this man of your acquaintance? How do you account for the similarities? The differences?

• Instead of assuming that you already know how men define themselves, and instead of taking Robinson's word for it, conduct some field work. Together with your classmates, set out to collect the stories of men of various ages, of various (including no) occupations, ranging from the macho conservative to the (whatever the other extreme is). Be sure to include some veterans in your sample, whether of Vietnam or the Persian Gulf. You will probably want to work together to identify and refine some standard interview questions that you can all begin with, but think of these questions as attempts to answer the previous question. How do they define manhood? How did they learn that definition? What are the advantages and disadvantages of being a man? Have they ever thought that having to fit some particular definition of manhood has limited them in some ways? Write about what patterns or trends you see. Identify what your interviews taught you the most about manhood. Use pseudonyms to protect your subjects' anonymity, and assure them in advance that you will be doing so.

VICTOR VILLANUEVA

Victor Villanueva's book, *Bootstraps: From an American Academic of Color* (1993), from which the present selection is excerpted, blends the personal with the scholarly. The mix of genres and voices has been well received and rewarded. Villanueva's book received two national awards, one from the National Council of Teachers of English and another from the Conference on English Education. He also won the Martin Luther King, Jr. Distinguished Service Award for Faculty and earned tenure partly because of the strength of the book. Such positive response shows a growing awareness of and acceptance of the blend of personal and scholarly, private and public, and the scholar's lived experience in relation to his or her critical inquiry.

Villanueva didn't make it into the college prep school in Brooklyn, but was assigned to a vocational school. When his family moved to California, they learned that the California system didn't recognize the vocational schools. Villanueva would have to start over. He stopped going to high school and worked instead. He enlisted in the army and earned his GED in Vietnam. After being in the army for seven years, he attended community college, transferred to the University of Washington in 1977, and earned his Ph.D. in 1986. He had his first full-time, tenure-track academic post in 1985 before he completed his Ph.D. Villanueva now teaches at Washington State University.

Three distinct voices woven throughout Villanueva's text represent the variety of experiences he has lived and the "selves" he has come to represent. The first-person voice presents the autobiography, the details of Villanueva's life. The third-person narration lends an air of distance and analysis. The third voice is a "kind-of non-person," the academic voice commenting on the theoretical consideration prompted by the narrative. This layering of voice illustrates the complexity of the self and reveals how our identity and our experience shape our perceptions and beliefs. Perhaps even the most abstract and esoteric theoretical language begins with the personal experience of the writer; Villanueva makes this transparent and allows us to see the different origins of thought and theory working together.

Villanueva believes that all writing is personal. That no matter what the genre, tone, language, or purpose, writing comes from "one's set of personal experiences." He adds that personal experience includes experience with books. What you learn and what you experience are not separate sets of knowledge but work together as this chapter reveals. As you read, pay special attention to how Villanueva brings his personal experience to bear on the arguments he wants to make.

An American of Color

A party, a bloody knife hanging from a hanging arm, eye level, Mom and Dad by the hand, running. Maybe three years old. Brooklyn. The picture remains, forty years later.

Seated behind a pegboard desk in the middle of a furnitureless living room, 41 Bartlett Street, Williamsburg, Brooklyn, Mrs. Ashell nearby, Dad walking in with a roll of linoleum. Why this memory? Maybe a three-year-old's sense of affluence: a step up from the storefront flat.

Walking from Bartlett to John Lee's hand laundry, alone. Maybe aged four. From Bartlett to somewhere near the Myrtle Avenue el. Shortest person on street corners. The only one waiting for lights to turn green. No memory of anyone asking where his Mommy is.

Just last week, 1992, Flagstaff, Arizona. A little three- or four-year-old child is wandering around the supermarket. A concerned woman bends over: "Did you lose your Mommy?" The same week, the same store, a little three- or four-year-old American Indian child is wandering, bawling loudly. People stop and stare. No one asks.

5   Sometime around six, the television. All kinds of kids, some of them strangers, congregate in the living room on Sunday evening for Walt Disney. The rest of the week, there are the Uncles who emcee cartoon shows, and there is Buffalo Bob, Lucy, Ralph Cramden. It was nice to see someone who lived like we did, maybe a little worse: loudmouth Ralph and his "one a dese days, Alice." He talked like the Micks, the Patties, the policemen. Some part of me has always been thankful that Ricky Ricardo was Cuban, even if he did sound portorican, what with his exaggerated accent, his complacency at the jibes on his accent. I stopped watching when Lucy and Ricky moved from the block to the 'burbs. I didn't need Ricky. I had Zorro. On Wednesday nights I could stay up past bedtime to watch Zorro. He was my special hero. On TV, he alone gave the Latino dignity for me. The Cisco Kid and Pancho were too foreign—another time, another place, another Spanish. Pancho was sillier than Ricky. But there was something Latino and not Mexican about Zorro, Don Diego, Don Alejandro—something old-world, Spaniard. Mami called my grandfather Don Basilio. Mami, especially, liked to claim Spain. I don't think I understood the colonial picture being presented in Zorro, just knew that the Latino could have a dashing, good-looking Robin Hood too.

Time and place and television didn't quite come together in the child's mind. I thought Beaver lived in another time, closer to the present than the Lone Ranger, even closer than Sky King, but not the present, not the 1950s I knew. It hadn't occurred to me that there would be Beavers in other places, neighbors on a global scale. The Cleavers, Sky King and Penny, the Lone Ranger and Tonto (Mami: *"Mira, tonto!"* when I would do something dumb; "Wake up, dummy," same thing). Not one of those TV folks fit my idea of contemporary Americans.

Before we got the neighborhood TV, before lessons on Liberty Statues and melting pots in school, the Americans I knew were the older folks who cared for me: portoricans from the family, Enchi's mom, *la comai,* portorican for *comadre,* godmother; and from as far back as I can remember, there was the old Jewish woman and the old Chinese man.

It wasn't a *barrio,* really, Williamsburg, Brooklyn, where I grew up before we moved up to Bed-Stuy. There was no one overriding ghetto culture, "ghetto" in the formal sense, an ethnic way-station to assimilation. We were portoricans, mostly, but not all alike: some of us *nuyorcinos,* natives to New York, Spanglish speakers: *"Dame la cuada"*; "Give me the quarter"; some of us from great cities on "the Island," like San Juan and Rio Piedras, pronouncing my name *"Vi-lya-neuva"*; some of us *jibaros,* country folk, with their strange Spanish: "Bi-ja-nueba." We were browns. We were black, the African Americans of the block, almost exclusively, it seemed, pouring out of one house on Bartlett Street, my street, the block. And we were many other colors, the world's poor. There was a *barrio* in Manhattan, Spanish Harlem, where *mi Tia Fela* lived, where there were more PRs hanging out on front stoops, and fewer broes, fewer of *los negros* who were not portorican, where there were more Cochifrito signs. So, it wasn't a *barrio,* but Bartlett Street and Williamsburg district were the block.

The block had many hues and many sounds, mainly black and brown hues and sounds, but others as well, yellows and olives, and variations on white. Except for the Whites I would meet later, except for the middle class (having met the truly wealthy where my *abuela* lived as a resident cook for a Central Park family), I grew up among the poor, some passing through, some permanent residents.

10   Mrs. Ashell was never not an old woman: wrinkled face with wire-rimmed glasses, white hair in a topknot, print housedresses that buttoned up the front, nun's shoes. She lived next door, the next apartment. Yet her home was older. Always dark. It even smelled of old. Milk bottles on the fire escape, an ice box, not a refrigerator. Mrs. Ashell would speak of the old country, of being a greenhorn, when Sol was a doughboy, the change in the neighborhood when the *schwartzes* moved in, her Sonny wanting to put her away (probably to a retirement community, Sonny, the successful lawyer). From

Mrs. Ashell came the smell of potato pancakes, latkes, an offering on Sunday mornings, knishes on occasion, matzah balls and chicken fat (pronounced something like *fiat*) when I was sick, with a *gesundheit* or a "Bless you" but not "God bless you." From her I knew of *yalmalkes* and *sheitelah*. And I was *bubbela*, sometimes *bubby*.

Mrs. Ashell. She had likely lived in that third-floor apartment next to ours longer than my folks had been alive. And I knew that, what with the icebox and all. She was America, but she was not as American as my family and me. Mom and Dad would talk of life *en la isla. La isla* was part of America. The old country was not.

A tale from "the Island."

Story has it that my mother had been sold into servitude to a wealthy Chicago family. She had been shipped to Chicago to save her from my father, it I remember rightly. Dad, fresh out of the army, followed her there, and together they fled to New York. That was in 1947. I was born a year later. Their telling was not political; it was romantic. There was no "Can you imagine!?" My guess was that it was easily imaginable on the Island. I get the sense that they even felt they had committed a wrong in not having abided by the contract that had conscripted my mother. Their telling is of a love story. And it is. A forty-four year marriage, as I write this, no trial separations.

So it was that I remember thinking that Mom was so American that she could be bought and sold; Dad so American that he could come and go. Mrs. Ashell had to have papers, a stay at Ellis Island, no talk of having gone back to the Jewish ghetto of London. She was foreign. I was American.

15   John Lee owned a Chinese hand laundry. I would go to his place during lunch or after school. I think of John Lee whenever I see Edward G. Robinson in *Key Largo*. Few parallels in the personalities, likely. But there was something in the way John Lee and Edward G. Robinson wore their fifties, broad, pleated pants, the waist high over round bellies, so high that their torsos seemed short, still shorter by broad ties; something in the way each held a cigar. Just that John Lee had the eyes of an Asian, but then, so did Edward G. Robinson. Stereotypes can be a bother.

Maybe age eight, I asked John Lee (who was never John or Mr. Lee) his age. "Sickty-fye Chinee; sickty-foe Amelican." Thick black hair, endless energy, laughing loudly when he would take me on amusement park rides in Coney Island: he didn't seem sixty-four or sixty-five to me. Mami explained that the Chinese counted life from inception. No conflict. That was their way, and it made sense. We had our way, and it made sense too.

That there are different worldviews, different notions of what constitutes reality, was always a given. That this is a heavy philosophical concern among academics today, even a radical rhetorical concern, only shows the limits of experience within a stratified society. Freire writes about "experts on Marx" who have never had a cup of coffee in a worker's home. How much can they know, really?

John Lee had a wife in Kowloon. He had supported her for years, thirty-five years or thereabouts. John Lee owned a high-rise apartment building in Kowloon, too. I have no idea what his wife looked like. There was a framed picture of his apartment building in the "almost-a-back room" of his laundry though.

The almost-a-back room was the social center. It was where we went when the laundry was closed. The kitchen was there, a table and chairs, a vinyl couch, the bathroom. The front room held a narrow entrance for customers, a counter with chicken wire to the ceiling, a small two-foot by two-foot opening with a little door where tickets and money and bundles of clothes wrapped in butcher paper would pass. I'd help wrap, sometimes count out change. On the other side of the counter were two large ironing tables, maybe six-feet square, with heavy irons, small tubs where the irons would be dipped before hitting a shirt, steam spewing out; beside the irons, copper bottles with what looked like kazoos attached for blowing mist over stubborn wrinkles, a tabletop steam roller, where starched collars and cuffs got pressed, a picture on the wall of Chiang Kai-Shek in full military regalia. Between the front and the back, "walls" of painted wood sheets on studs and a curtain, making four walls that surrounded a bed and a dresser. It always smelled of incense in that little area, the bed's room, not much larger than the bed. I would sleep there when I was still young enough to require naps.

20 The "real back room" held a coal-burning potbelly stove in the middle, four large tubs and a large washboard in one corner, a couple of saw horses that I would ride, wires strung from the ceiling. Laundry was washed there, then hung to dry from ceiling wires. John Lee's hand laundry smelled of clean and of steam and of Niagara starch in boiling water. Sometimes there would be a loud hiss, and the smell of soy sauce and soybeans and vegetables would pour in from the almost-a-back room. Sometimes a fried egg sandwich for my lunch. Sometimes egg foo yung, when fish-head soup was the specialty for Mom and Dad. Store fronts and store-front apartments, a laundry, a business, Chinese food unlike Chinatown's. This was part of my world, part of America—yet foreign, foreign to most Americans, I'd guess.

In the almost-a-back room: the picture of John Lee's apartment building back in China and a picture of John Lee himself, suit and tie, speaking into a microphone. John Lee was a big shot in the

Chinese community (which was larger than Chinatown). Other Chinese launderers seemed to seek his advice. John Lee was a merchant, with a "China-side wife," his own high rise, able to dispense silver dollars on my birthdays and on Christmases and Easters. He was the affluent among the poor. It was a sign of affluence that when John Lee would take us out to a Chinese restaurant, waiters would seat us in the back room among the silk-suited Chinese men and fur-collared Chinese women; a sign of affluence that waiters would bow often, that they would actually write down our order. Mom and Dad could claim none of that.

Mami on the assembly line at Standard Toycraft. Forty dollars a week—a dollar an hour. Dad, a machinist's assistant, then shop steward for a time, as well as working downstairs at Jimmy Vriniotis's deli in the evenings, short order at a greasy spoon. John Lee had more than we. But John Lee was an immigrant. He could never look American (thoughts of a child). He had an accent. So did Mom and Dad, but John Lee's was foreign. He'd say "fly lice" or "loose poke" instead of "fried rice" and "roast pork." He'd call me "Bobby," despite my lessons on calling me "Papi."

There is a point here that I'll get to in detail below. It is that we behave as if the minority problem is the immigrant problem. Two generations of learning the language and the ways of America, and all will be better, we hear. But two generations come and go and all that happens is that the minority's native tongue is gone. The African American lost his native tongue two hundred years ago. More on this too. For now, look to how far the analogy has been drawn. After sociolinguists posited a "language interference" to explain a transitional period in a foreign-language learner's acquisition of a new language, linguists and compositionists posited a dialect interference among Black English speakers (see Hartwell). Learn the language and all will be better, they suggested, a promise to African Americans as well as non-English speakers (e.g., Farrell). Two generations and blacks will melt? We need to look more broadly, historically, to the differences between minorities and immigrants, so as to break from the not helpful analogy between the two in the classroom and in our theorizing.

School.

25

All Saints, the Catholic school around the corner from Bartlett, across the street from PS 168, the public school. All Saints charges a dollar a month for tuition (three a month in the seventh and eighth grades). It is my school from kindergarten till eighth-grade graduation. There I am filled with Catholicism, "Ave Maria," and with

"Jingle Bells," maxims from Poor Richard, laws from Newton, the Beaver's neighbors—Dick and Jane, the parts of speech, times tables. There I play in the melting pot.

Or maybe it was a stewpot. A stew, not the easy mixes of the saladbowl metaphor, the static coexistence of the mosaic metaphor. The stew metaphor maintains the violence of the melting-pot metaphor while suggesting that some of the ingredients do not lose all of their original identity, though altered, taking in the juices from the other ingredients of the pot, adding to the juices; all of us this one thing, Americans, and all of us some things else; for some of us, never complete integration and never complete integrity. With the stewpot comes the sense that not all the ingredients are equally important, that the stew needs the beef of a Yankee pot roast cut more than fatback or red beans and *sofrito*.

As I saw it, prestige belonged to the Wattses, Andrew and Stephen. There were nuns and priests in their family. They lived in one of the brownstones, around the corner, not of the block. The kids on the block didn't look like the Wattses, didn't talk like them. I don't recall ever thinking they were better, in the sense of superior—they just had it better. And I don't recall ever thinking about what "having it better" meant; I just knew that they did.

There was something special about Jarapolk Cigash and his family too. But theirs was different from the Wattses. The Wattses were connected to All Saints, somehow, to culture, though that word—culture—only occurs to me now. Jarapolk, "Yacko," Jerry, was one of my two best friends (superlatives have no meaning for children). The Cigashes lived in the neighborhood, but there was something special about their apartment: a piano that his sister played; a stand for sheet music alongside a violin case. Jerry practiced the violin. His parents would speak of their escape from the Ukraine, explain what it meant to be a satellite country. They had accents, thick accents, but there was an air about them. They were educated, in that special sense in which *educated* is sometimes used. It was clear to me even then that Brooklyn would only be a stopover for the Cigashes. It was not their home nor would it be. That wasn't clear about the Villanuevas.

I had the sense that there was something different about Charles Bermudez. He was kind of pale, allergic to milk. There was something strange about the way Charles's father held his cigarettes: palm up, the cigarette pinched between thumb and middle finger, like a movie oldworld aristocrat or a monocle-wearing fascist general. Yet I didn't see prestige in the Bermudezes, really, just difference. Now as I look back, I wonder if the Bermudezes were Latin Americans on the run. Back then, I just assumed they were portoricans. Portoricans could not be foreign, like the foreignness of the very American Wattses or the foreignness of the Eastern European Cigashes.

30   Marie Engells, the German girl, was another stopover. We were in school together from kindergarten through the eighth grade, yet I never knew her. Some of that was due to childish gender discrimination, no doubt, though Rose Marie, Peanuts, the Italian girl, was always a special friend, not boyfriend-girlfriend, not one of the boys, and not so as I feared being seen as a sissy, just a special friend. We'd buy each other knishes or soft, salted pretzels from the pushcart after school. But there was something about Marie Engells: an awfully erect back, the hint of a smile constantly on her lips. Maybe all this was in my imagination, but she seemed aloof to me. Marie Engells was the girl valedictorian at eighth-grade graduation. Jarapolk Cigash was the boy. They were immigrants. And something was theirs that wasn't mine. Yet I was American and so were my parents and the generation before them, full citizens since 1919.

Some fell into a grey area between the immigrants and those like me, the spics or the blacks. I knew Peanuts wasn't like us, but she wasn't like Marie Engells or Jarapolk Cigash either. And I was less sure about Frankie Thompson, the Irish kid who introduced me to my first cigarette in one of the neighborhood abandoned lots where we jumped burning Christmas trees every year. I was less sure about Paul Caesar, "the Polack." I was less sure about their advantage despite the same school, the same neighborhood.

They would have been "new immigrants," not as easily assimilable, the bad-element immigrants that prompted the latent footnote to the Statue of Liberty: "in limited numbers." In terms of ethnicity, the Cigashes should have been "new immigrants" too, but pianos and violins suggested maybe these new immigrants came from higher in the class system. Class comes into the academic's thoughts. The child only knew that Peanuts and Frankie Thompson and Paul Caesar were not in the same league as Jerry or Marie Engells, the Wattses, maybe even Charles Bermudez. And it didn't have anything to do with brains. Yet I still believed they had something over Lana Walker and Irving Roach and me.

Irving Roach was the only African American kid I knew who didn't live on the same street I did. The African American kids went to PS 168. "You know we ain't Catholic," I was told once when Hambone said he wished he could read like I did, when I asked why his folks didn't send him to All Saints. Irving Roach didn't live on the block, but was of the block. I had a life on the block—with Butch, the black bully (stereotypes sometimes have bases in fact—Black Butch the Badass Bully, Darnell the Dude, Lazy Leroy, Hambone with the thick glasses and bookish ways), Papo, the PR bully, Mike and Steven Figueroa and Enchi and Hershey. And I had a life at All Saints. And only Juan Torres, Johnny, my best friend from kindergarten till my family moved to California, and Irving Roach crossed over. And Irving Roach was kind, would bring his baby sister with him when he came to visit. And we would talk school things. He was smart. But I don't recall imagining him "making it."

Lana Walker might. She was as aloof as Marie Engells, as smart, too, I thought. And Lana Walker was beautiful, black and slender (but not skinny) and tall. I was short and chubby and all too insecure to do more than talk with her in passing in the nine years we were in school together. At eighth grade graduation Marie Engells would win the math award I really wanted. Lana Walker would get some special recognition, though I no longer remember what. I would get the spelling and the penmanship awards: the Merriam-Webster spelling bee champ that year. Jerry and Marie Engells went to the Catholic college-prep high school. Lana Walker made the alternate list. I never saw Irving Roach again. Juan Torres ended up in the vo-tech school in his area. I went to Alexander Hamilton Vocational-Technical High School.

35   So what had happened? I was an "A" student, third or fourth in the class, able with language, Saturdays spent on special classes in preparation for the entrance exam to the college prep high school. Why hadn't I made it? Mom says the Bishop's Fund, but that seems inconsistent with a dollar tuition. Cultural bias in standardized tests is the more obvious answer.

I think of cultural bias in two ways. The first is a linguistic and rhetorical bias. It has to do with the test-makers' assumption that words have fixed meanings that are not arbitrary. The psychologist Lev Vygotsky, literary critic Mikhail Bakhtin, the philosopher Jacques Derrida, the archeologist and social critic Michel Foucault, as well as the Sophists of fifth-century B.C. Greece, and a score of others, call this into question, seeing language tied to time and place and culture and even ideology. So do kids who are bilingual and bidialiectical. Sociolinguist Fernando Peñalosa sees the code switcher, the bidialectal speaker, as "the skillful speaker [who] uses his knowledge of how language choices are interpreted in his community to structure the interaction so as to maximize outcomes favorable to himself" (quoted in Gilyard 31). In plain English: the code-switcher is a rhetorical power player. He knows language isn't fixed, has a relativistic perception of language, knows that words take on hues of meaning when colored by cognates; and for the bilingual there are words seeming the same in both languages, derived from the same sources, but nevertheless having undergone change through time and place. A relativistic notion of language is bound to be a problem for the standardized-test taker. A solution: English Only. One of the many problems with the solution: better writers have a heightened metalinguistic awareness, an awareness of language's multiplicity (Hartwell). So do the bidialectal and the bilingual. English Only could destroy the very metalinguistic awareness that could make for a better writer. Doomed if we teach to the test: doomed to lose the power of having a greater metalinguistic awareness. Doomed if we don't: doomed to be denied access.

The second way I think of cultural bias in standardized tests has to do with the differences between the minority and the immigrant. The immigrant seeks to take on the culture of the majority. And the majority, giving certain preconditions, not the least of which is displaying the language and dialect of the majority, accepts the immigrant. The minority, even when accepting the culture of the majority, is never wholly accepted. There is always a distance.

The minority looked at the immigrants like John Lee and Mrs. Ashell, who had been on the continental United States far longer than his parents, who had some economic advantages (Mrs. Ashell through her Sonny, at least), and still felt they were less American than he. The minority looked at his immigrant school friends, second generation, maybe, and believed that theirs was the advantage.

More recent.

40   A discussion concerning a minority issue takes place at a national conference. It starts to get heated. One person tells of his sympathy. He says, "After all, we're all minorities in a sense." And in a sense he is right. In a sense. Relatively few these days can claim direct lineage to the majority culture of England. But he misses essential differences between immigrants and minorities.

A writing group in a graduate composition course. Martha Lopez's and Paul Reyes's group-work gets loud, drowning out the rest. Martha: black eyes, thick black hair, an accent to her voice. Paul: pale skinned, green eyed, red haired, no accent. Martha argues that her writing suffers from having learned English through grammar instruction, rather than through real conversation and writing practice. Paul argues that even after learning the language there is still the problem of thinking like white folks. He'd *be* white to anyone's eyes. He's drawing on contrastive rhetoric, the notion that different cultures display different rhetorical patterns in their discourse (more of which later). Yet there is more going on than Paul's contrastive rhetoric contention. Martha is arguing the case for assimilation through learning the language of the majority. Paul is arguing that learning the language isn't all there is. Both are Latinos, Spanish speakers. But Martha is Colombian; Paul is Puerto Rican. Martha, the immigrant. Paul, the minority. Martha believes in the possibilities for complete, structural assimilation; Paul is more cautious.

I think of those who try to calm others by saying that it takes two generations for ghetto dwellers to move on. This has been the pattern for immigrants. But what then do we do with the African American or the Latino, especially the Mexican-American, on American soil, in American society, far longer than two generations? What happens to them—to *us*—those of us who are of color, those of us normally labelled "minority"? The answer, I believe, comes in looking more closely at how one becomes assimilated.

Three factors affect the possibilities for complete structural assimilation:

45
1. The historical mode of entry into the dominant society;
2. The number and distribution of those attempting to take part in the overall society; and
3. The racial and cultural characteristics of those seeking equity with the majority.

I condense a list drawn by political scientist Mario Barrera. And even these three are interrelated. But let me continue with the convenience of the separation. To begin, if the mode of entry of the new group is voluntary, the new group does not carry the baggage of having become part of American through bloodshed. The bloodshed of the Civil War was the price paid for the admission of all African Americans as freed citizens ("all" because there were free blacks, as well as slaves, prior). Bloodshed marked the relationship to American Indians. There was the blood let at the Mexican War of 1846; at the Spanish-American War, the war which led to the acquisition of Puerto Rico. If the mode of entry is voluntary, the general attitude is that the new folks will attain full citizenship in time because they would most wish to do so (though we know that first-generation folks, especially refugees from war-torn countries, often hold dreams of returning).

If the mode of entry is voluntary, then the numbers entering would not be great enough to cause a threat to the majority. Should race become a factor, the numbers can be legally controlled.

The Chinese were granted only limited access from 1882, explaining John Lee's China-side wife. Limited access also explains attitudes toward Southeast Asian refugees, Koreans, Filipinos (Asian and Polynesian and, often, Spanish-surnamed, and from a former colony).

50
Among Europeans, the "New Immigrants" were not welcomed with open arms. Liberty's torch of freedom burned low. In 1907, President Theodore Roosevelt appointed an immigration commission to study what was being perceived as an immigration problem.

By 1911 the commission issued a forty-two volume report. Its findings were that "new immigrants," Eastern and Southern Europeans, were inherently inferior to old immigrants. The commission cited anthropologist Madison Grant:

> The new immigration contained a large and increasing number of the weak, the broken, and the mentally crippled of all races drawn from the lowest stratum of the Mediterranean basin and the Balkans, together with hordes of the wretched, submerged populations of the Polish ghettoes. Our jails, insane asylums, and almshouses are filled with human flotsam and the whole tone of American life, social, moral, and political, has been lowered and vulgarized by them. (quoted in Estrada et al. 115)

By 1924 there were legal restrictions against the admission of ruddy-skinned Eastern European and Mediterranean new immigrants to the United States.

And so the numbers remain relatively small, the small numbers initially locating in ethnic pockets surrounded by the dominant group, ghettos, with smaller numbers moving out, for the most part, only after having achieved cultural assimilation. That is, if race weren't a factor. Chinatowns remain all through the country. There are fewer Little Italies, I think.

His first professional job, Kansas City. His co-workers, college professors, the middle class, mainly white, say he and his family have moved into the Italian neighborhood. And the old housing projects of the neighborhood do bear a faded wooden imitation of an Italian flag. There is an Italian deli, and the local warehouse supermarket bears an Italian name. But there are no Italians. The neighborhood belongs to the white working class with southern-like twangs to their speech, not Italians but folks claiming rural Arkansas, mainly.

55   When entry is by conquest, the numbers in the conquered land tend to be greater than the numbers of the conquerors, like the residents of Mexico or New Spain, or like those of Puerto Rico. The restricted landmass of Puerto Rico, a small island, pretty much assured that the numbers could not be turned around in the way the numbers were turned around in parts of conquered Mexico. Since the people are conquered in their own lands, they remain rooted to the land's history and culture.

New Mexico: denied statehood until Anglos outnumber the Hispanics (Conklin and Lourie 67).

Arizona: statehood denied, several times, because of the territory's Mexican "mongrel racial character."

From 1891, the Court of Private Claims overturns one land grant after another, until almost all Mexican landowners in New Mexico, Arizona, California, and Texas are displaced (Utah and Colorado never having had large numbers of Mexican landowners).

1928. Congressional hearings on Western Hemisphere Immigration. There is a concerted attempt at preventing the Mexican migrants from working farms, railroads, and mines, of damming the first wave of Mexican immigration which had begun in 1910 (and which would end in 1930). One speaker before the hearings describes Mexicans:

60   Their minds run to nothing higher than animal functions—eat, sleep, and sexual debauchery. In every huddle of Mexican shacks one meets the same idleness, hordes of hungry dogs, and filthy children with faces plastered with flies, disease, lice, human filth, stench, promiscuous fornication, bastardly, lounging, apathetic peons and lazy squaws, beans and dried fruit, liquor, general squalor, and envy and hatred of the gringo. These people sleep by day and prowl by night like coyotes, stealing anything they can get their hands on, no matter how useless to them it may be. Nothing left outside is safe unless padlocked or chained down. Yet there are Americans clamoring for more of these human swine to be brought over from Mexico. (quoted in Estrada et al. 116)

The description lumps the Mexicans with the American Indians ("lazy squaws"), another conquered people. Yet the bad-mouthing does not stop the solicitation of Mexican stoop laborers as long as there is profit in having them—and does not distinguish the Mexican from the Mexican American.

When the Great Depression hits, Mexicans and Mexican Americans who apply for relief are directed to "Mexican Bureaus." The Bureaus' job turns out to be *ex*patriation sold as *re*patriation. Mexicans are herded into cattle cars and railroaded to a home that for many has never been theirs. In 1933, a Los Angeles eyewitness to the expatriation process gives voice to the usual rationale:

The repatriation programme is regarded locally as a piece of consummate statecraft. The average per family cost of executing it is $71.14, including food and transportation. It cost one Los Angeles County $77,249.29 to repatriate one shipment of 6,024. It would have cost $424,933.70 to provide this number with such charitable assistance as they would have been entitled to had they remained—a savings of $347,468.40. (quoted in Estrada et al. 118)

From 1929 to 1934, the number of repatriated Mexicans exceeds 400,000. Approximately half are native to the United States—expatriated. The conquered (minorities) and the voluntary (immigrants) had gotten mixed.

65   Nor is the confusion of conquered and voluntary out of the ordinary. Others with the same racial and cultural attributes as the conquered, including language, enter voluntarily and follow the pattern of the voluntary immigrant. Puerto Ricans solicited to work in New York and Chicago and Colorado get mixed with other

Spanish West Indians and with Central Americans who voluntarily immigrate to the mainland. The same story for the Mexicans of the Southwest, shipped to Pennsylvania and to the Midwest to work mines and stockyards, for Mexicans of the West solicited to work the farms of California and Washington. All get mixed with the Mexican immigrant. And to the extent that structural assimilation is possible for the immigrant, those of the historically conquered who get confused for the Mexican join in the advantage sometimes. But this isn't the rule. More often, the voluntary share in the fate of the historically conquered.

Southeast Asian refugees suffer the historical fate of the Chinese excluded, the fate of the Japanese interred. Cuban refugees suffer the fate of the Puerto Rican and Mexican American. Haitians are black West Indians—a double whammy. I overgeneralize, I know, but I believe the distinction holds generally.

The voluntary of the same or similar cultural and racial attributes as the conquered share in the fate of the conquered. The depression-era expatriation of Mexican Americans with Mexicans was not an isolated instance. The post-Korean War economic recession saw "Operation Wetback" with 3.8 million Mexican expelled (Murguía 72). The series of economic recessions which began in the 1970s has seen a resurgence of "green card" checks. The rationale behind repatriation and expatriation involves the too great numbers, and underlying the rationale is the attitude of conquerors over the conquered. The result tends to exclusion rather than assimilation.

Race is the final factor affecting assimilation. The crackdowns on Mexicans in the 30s, the 50s, and the present have immigration authorities checking documents of those who "look Mexican" (Murguía 72). The closer the features of a minority correlate to the general features of the majority, the greater the chances for assimilation (and so the Jewish or East Indian or something-looking—but not Puerto Rican-looking—gets his Ph.D. and gets to write this book).

Tato Laviera, a Puerto Rican poet, describes the problem of race, culture, and language:

70

> *i want to go back to puerto rico*
> *but i wonder if my kink could live*
> *in ponce, mayaguez and carolina*
>
> *tengo las venas aculturadas*
> *escribo in spanglish*
> *abraham in español*
> *abraham in english*
> *tato in spanish*
> *"taro" in english*
> *tonto in both languages* (quoted in Flores et al. 214)

Acculturated veins (*"las venas aculturadas"*), yet not American and no longer quite Puerto Rican, linguistically a fool in both English and Spanish ("tonto in both languages"). The minority lives in a netherworld. Not quite American. No home to return to.

While the immigrant tends to become American in two generations, two generations only manages to erode the possibility for migration, for the Puerto Rican's return to the Island, or the Mexican American's (assuming the Mexican American's heritage is not from Mexico's ceded land, Texas and the like, but from present-day Mexico) return to Mexico.

Puerto Rico is not my home. It's my parents'. Some of its cultural ways are mine. Some of its language. But I'm more Brooklyn than anything else. The Nuyorcino, often racially closer to the African American than to the majority, takes on much of African-American culture.

Tato again:

75

> a blackness in spanish
> a blackness in english
> mixture-met on jam sessions in central park,
> there were no differences in
> the sounds merging inside.

And even when external attributes are not black or mulatto, the merging remains. I no longer speak with a blackness, not without the affected quality of white folks trying to sound black, but it resounds more of "home" within me nevertheless.

The new Teaching Assistant was videotaped. He saw and heard the sounds of a New York Jewish intellectual. He was shocked. Something had happened to the sounds of the Brooklyn boy. Yet he knew his portorican blackness remained within.

Nor am I alone in this. There remains Paul Reyes, the green-eyed, red-haired Puerto Rican who referred to "white folks." There remains the empirical—Paul and I are racially white. So Paul Reyes is a graduate student of English in Northern Arizona—and I am one of his English professors. And together we watch the more blatant instances of racism directed at the American Indians where we live: the conquered, their numbers great in Northern Arizona, near America's largest Indian reservation. And the local Navajos tend to be more racially distinct than Paul is or than I am. We have had chances not afforded other Puerto Ricans because we are racially closer to the majority, because we are not part of Northern Arizona's local memory and lore of conquest, because our numbers are so very few in the mountain city. And yet we know we are not assimilated. We are still "Hispanics," a word which says "other-American."

The immigrant enters; the minority is entered upon. Race and culture, sheer numbers and concentration, how one comes to be American: these are the factors that tell of the degree of melt in the pot. The difference between the immigrant and the minority amounts to the difference between immigration and colonization.

80 No other theory holds up as well as colonial theory—not theories on biological deficiency nor cultural deficiency nor racial inequality. Biological deficiency theories no longer gather large followings. Few today would listen to the likes of the nineteenth-century Harvard naturalist, Louis Agassiz, who claimed that the brain of the Negro adult "never gets beyond that observable in the Caucasian in boyhood" (quoted in Franklin 3). Still, Arthur Jensen could argue the case that African Americans are genetically inferior to Whites in 1969 in the *Harvard Educational Review* and again in 1973 in the popular press— *Psychology Today.* And R. J. Herrnstein could provide the same argument in a 1971 *Atlantic Monthly* (see Labov "Academic Ignorance" 59). Thomas Farrell's counter to biological deficiency theories would not be much better. In his version of cultural deficit theory, African Americans suffer a cognitive disadvantage because they reside in an oral culture. His counter would look at relativistic notions of what constitutes cognitive development—different ways of thinking for different social contexts: Scribner and Cole on the social determinants of cognitive functions, Shirley Brice Heath on the unlikelihood of an exclusively oral culture among African Americans, other counters. Biological and cultural deficit theories are not tenable.

Racial inequality theories, on the other hand, do have a kind of merit. They make sense to me. I think, in particular, of John Ogbu's assertion that there are different kinds of minorities, with some minorities suffering a castelike status. For Ogbu there are three different kinds of minorities in America: the castelike, the autonomous, and the immigrant minority. The immigrant minority is clear. Even if she maintains her ethnicity—like, say, Italians often do—the qualities ascribed to her ethnicity are not such that she would be necessarily excluded from the mainstream. The autonomous are those who are subject to ethnic or religious distinctiveness yet manage to accommodate the mainstream, even if not assimilate. Ogbu cites American Jews and Mormons as instances of autonomous minorities. The castelike are those who are regarded primarily on the basis of some particular birth ascription, in this country, race or a particular ethnicity, like Latinos. A while back the media focused less on Jesse Jackson's platform than on his race. Jackson, a castelike minority, was the black candidate. But Dukakis got the more usual coverage. Dukakis was not the second-generation Greek immigrant candidate, except when he himself asserted it. There can be no denying that some minorities cannot transcend their race or ethnicity, even when vying for the presidency of the United States or a seat on the Supreme Court.

For all their worth, however, racial inequality theories have a historical shortcoming. The ideology of racial difference, for instance, is relatively new historically, traceable to the eighteenth century (Barrera 197). African Americans were savages; American Indians, noble savages—culturally inferior, not necessarily biologically. The cultural inferiority (or religious inferiority) of some races determined their suitability for slavehood or other forms of oppression. Racial inequality theory does not explain, for example, why East Indians are considered black by the British but not by Americans. The most suggestive answer: India was a British colony, not an American colony. The American East Indian is more often just another foreigner, another immigrant. Race alone is not the distinctive factor. Race and a history of subservience to those who remain dominant makes for the castelike minority.

Colonial theory refines the concept of the castelike minority by looking to the common feature in the castelike's histories—colonization or colonization's explicitly commodified form, slavery. The autonomous minority holds no memory of colonization in this country. There is no national memory of long-term subjugation of the autonomous minority or the immigrant, as there is of the Puerto Rican, the Mexican, the American Indian, the African American, the Asian (mainly by way of the Pacific Islands, colonies once). Looking to colonization makes a distinction not contained in race alone.

And we can look at present-day colonialism. Political scientists today speak of neo-colonialism, when the colonial power, the metropole, exercises economic control over a colony, saving on having to provide resident military and political forces, using the military only as a final resort. Think of Panama. Think of the Philippine Islands, the former colony granted independence by the United States, but with the United States still managing to mess with Marcos and with Aquino. Then think of the numbers of American minorities who do not enjoy equal status with their peers, even when managing to move within the class system, the many who must remain dependent on financing from the State, the great numbers—an overwhelming majority—of minorities who people the prisons, not because of a pathology but because of money, political prisoners in an economic sense, as then Ambassador to the United Nations, Andrew Young, and then head of "Operation Push," Jesse Jackson, pointed out back in 1978 (Stavrianos 25). There is a kind of neo-colonialism at play right here in the United States.

85   Minorities remain a colonized people. Sociologist Gail Omvedt sees colonialism as "the economic, political and cultural domination of one cultural-ethnic group by another" (quoted in Barrera 193). And Gonzales Cazanova goes a step further, writing in terms of the "domination and exploitation among culturally heterogeneous, distinct groups," thereby accounting for a colonialism even when the colonized live and work among the colonizers (quoted in Barrera 194). Casanova is referring to internal colonialism. Colonial theory—internal colonialism—gives a historical precedent and gives a contemporary explanation for how minorities remain castelike, even when racially white, even when white and an expert, a practicing Ph.D. in the language of the dominant.

Mami believed in the traditional idea of language and assimilation. She and Dad had had English instruction in their schooling in Puerto Rico. It was required, an old-fashioned colonialism. Mami had gone as far as the third year of high school; Dad started high school under the GI Bill but switched to a trade school; still, there was the English of the army, though like most Puerto Ricans, his service was mainly on the Island, segregated forces, with the English coming mainly from the officers who were, more often than not, not Puerto Rican. There hasn't been a Villanueva yet who has completed high school (including the one with the Ph.D. and his twenty-one-year-old, GED-toting son).

Mami tells of her and Dad listening to radio shows in English and trying to read the American newspapers, tells of speaking to their Papi in both Spanish and English from the start. He remembers their insistence that he speak in English, that he teach it to them.

Sister Rhea Marie, his kindergarten teacher, visits his home. She is short, thin, plain, a little gap to her front teeth. She wears the traditional Dominican nun's habit: white starch circumscribing her face, seeming severe, as if it would cut off circulation to her face, topped by a black veil, long white apron in front, long rosary beads marking the contrast. For a many-generationed Catholic home, her apparel tells of authority. Her face tells of kindness.

She visits to speak with his Mami and Dad. And she tells them they should speak to Papi in English because "Victor speaks with an accent." But a simple bit of logic has gotten by the good sister: *they* speak with an accent and the accent is passed on with the English. Victor (always "Victor" before Authority) spoke with an accent *because* they spoke in English. There was no verbal deprivation at play, just a process that takes time, "interlanguage," to use a sociolinguistic term.

90   It took TV for Papi to discover the ways of white language. Watching TV, he discovered that the dessert-that-there's-always-room-for and the rainbow color weren't pronounced the same. It

would be a while longer before he stopped pronouncing the *e* when pronouncing certain words—like a fenc*e*d jard.

Then in college he's told to pronounce the *e* when reading Shakespeare, Donne, Marvell, and the like—wing*e*d steed. And he discovers that the British prestige dialect, the Received Pronunciation, prefers a trilled *r*: the r*r*ain in Spain. He discovers this after having worked at removing the trill from the word *three* back in gr-rade thrree. His English was better than Sister Rhea Marie knew.

Bedtimes, before my mom started working swing and Dad started moonlighting, was reading time. Stories came from *Classics Illustrated*, a kind of comic book. The *Morte d'Arthur*, stories of King Arthur's court, stuck with me, the illustrations leaping to memory a quarter-century later, when reading Mallory in college. Comic books would be my reading supplement to the end of my teen years, a one-a-day within longer readings. And the readings would include Homer and Shelley and Sir Arthur Conan Doyle. Reading and TV and Saturday matinees filled my time more than anything else. And by the time eighth-grade graduation rolled around, I was a spelling-bee champ. And when the school-sponsored reading stopped, reading didn't. And the accent disappeared, and Spanish no longer came easily, sometimes going through French or through Latin in my head, the languages of my profession, searching for the Spanish with which to speak to my family. Assimilation.

And the immigrant went to college prep. And the minority didn't.

Reflective Reading, Informal Writing

REFLECTING ON THE READING:

- In the early pages of this chapter from his book, Villanueva, through the eyes of his childhood self, makes a clear distinction between Americans from the "old country" and Americans from the "island." Why do you think this distinction was important to Victor the child? How might it relate to a sense of alienation or, conversely, inclusion?
- Why, according to Villanueva, is it so important to look at the differences between minorities and immigrants? What are those differences? What do his ideas around minorities and immigrants have to do with understanding how individual selves are socially and culturally shaped?

- Toward the end of his essay Villanueva writes: "The immigrant enters; the minority is entered upon. Race and culture, sheer numbers and concentration, how one comes to be American: these are the factors that tell of the degree of melt in the pot. The difference between the immigrant and the minority amount to the difference between immigration and colonization" (p. 206). This is a difficult passage and a crucial one for understanding how Villanueva sees the minority American defined and created within the larger American culture. Carefully reread this passage. What do you think he means when he suggests that the minority is "entered upon" as opposed to "entering"? How does this distinction relate to the statement at the end of this passage regarding colonization? If the concept of colonization changes our idea of the melting pot, how does that, in turn, change our understanding of the definition of "American"?

UNDERSTANDING RHETORICAL STRATEGIES:

- Villanueva's argument rests on the reader's understanding what he means by certain words: immigrant, minority, American, assimilation, colonization. Try to find the places in the text where he defines these terms. How does he go about these definitions (e.g., through the work of other scholars, examples, stories, statistics, etc.)? Why do you think he chooses to define these words in the ways he does? What do they add to the overall "flavor" of the essay?
- Villanueva has constructed a rich but difficult argument about the minority in America. Summarize what you believe his argument to be in three or four sentences. Once you have his argument summarized, look for two or three key passages that support his arguments. How do these passages strike you as a reader? Are they strong support for the argument you have summarized? Why or why not?
- Villanueva's essay is a mixture of "straight" academic explanation and a collage of personal stories. Why do you think he chooses to make his argument in this way? Is it disruptive in any way? What purpose do the stories serve? The more academic explanation? What might this strategy for putting together the argument have to do with the content of his argument?

INFORMAL WRITING:

- Villanueva seems to suggest that the common metaphor of the melting pot is not such a good one. Neither is the metaphor of the stew pot since the Yankee pot roast is more important in that stew than the red beans. Write down your own metaphors for describing a diverse America. Point out what works well about your metaphors and also what might be a problem according to you, and perhaps, Villanueva.

- Write a letter to Professor Villanueva responding to his essay. Tell him what you like about it and what you don't like, and why. Let him know where you are confused and where you clearly understand him. Tell him which are your favorite stories. Argue with him if you find yourself disagreeing with part or all of his essay. Ask him any questions you might have.
- Think back through your own memories of childhood and young adulthood. Write a brief collage of your own. Use your memories as the stories or vignettes. Read back over your collage noticing connections or similar themes and ideas about your identity. Identify one theme or idea that you find and add or delete stories to create a kind of clustering of stories around that theme.

ADRIENNE RICH

Adrienne Rich's poetry captured national attention when she graduated from Radcliffe College and won the Yale Series of Younger Poets prize in 1951 for her collection of poetry, *A Change of World*. Although the title talks about change, Rich's poetry in this collection was applauded for its objective stance, nonpersonal account (restraint of the self that obscures voice according to W.H. Auden), and detached, gender-neutral voice. Poets and critics praised Rich for being a woman poet able to write like a man. This collection of poetry and critique now stands as the first step in a lifelong process of transformation for Rich as documented in her poetry and essays.

Rich has moved from a woman-poet praised for her careful adherence to tradition to a feminist scholar both criticized and admired for her political poetry and essays. This life pattern of change is reflected in her writing process where revision becomes more than an editing process, but an opportunity to re-see and rethink an idea or perspective: "I tear up answers/I once gave . . . " Rich defines the art of re-vision as looking back, seeing something with "fresh eyes" and "entering an old text from a new critical direction." Her transformation attests to the power of writing. Writing is not a neutral medium but has the ability to shape society, to name, rename, and re-see ourselves, our history, and our culture.

Of Woman Born (1976), the book from which this excerpt was taken, was criticized for being too full of rage, for indulging in stereotypes, and for using the "oppressor's tactics." This excerpt offers a historical perspective, a cultural history, from a unique point of view. Rich follows the transformation of a goddess-worshiping species to a god-centered species. In spite of controversy surrounding much of Rich's work, she defines the purpose of poetry as "The drive/to connect. The dream of a common language." As you read "The Domestication of Motherhood," look for places where you might see Rich also striving for the drive to connect as she suggests she does with her poetry.

The Domestication of Motherhood

. . . there is a Persian myth of the creation of the World which precedes the biblical one. In that myth a woman creates the world, and she creates it by the act of natural creativity that is hers and which cannot be duplicated by men. She gives birth to a great number of sons. The sons, greatly puzzled by this act which they cannot duplicate, become frightened. They think, "Who can tell us, that if she can *give* life, she cannot also *take* life." And so, because of their fear of this mysterious ability of woman, and of its reversible possibility, they kill her.

—Frieda Fromm-Reichman,
"On the Denial of Woman's Sexual Pleasure."

Frederick Engels identified father-right and the end of the matrilineal clan with the beginnings of private ownership and slavery. He saw women as forced into marriage and prostitution through economic dependency, and predicted that sexual emancipation would come with the abolition of private property and the end of male economic supremacy. For Engels (as for succeeding generations of Marxists) the oppression of women has, simply, an economic cause, and an economic solution. He actually discourages our trying to speculate on *how* the transition to sexual equality would come about:

> What we can now conjecture about the way in which sexual relations will be ordered after the impending overthrow of capitalist production is mainly of a negative character, limited for the most part to what will disappear. But what will there be new? That will be answered when a new generation has grown up: a generation of men who never in their lives have known what it is to buy a woman's surrender with money or any other social instrument of power, a generation of women who have never known what it is to give themselves to a man from any other considerations than real love, or to refuse to give themselves to their lover from fear of the economic consequences. When these people are in the world, they will care precious little what anybody today thinks they ought to do; they will make their own practice and their corresponding public opinion about the practice of each individual—and there will be the end of it.[1]

This is an excellent illustration of what Karen Horney means when she says that "it is in the interest of men to obscure [the fact that there is a struggle between the sexes]; and the emphasis they place on their ideologies has caused women, also, to adopt these theories." In her delicately worded essay, "The Distrust Between the Sexes," Horney speaks of the resentment and anxiety harbored by all men toward women—even, she says, by "men who consciously have a very positive relationship with women and hold them in high esteem as human beings."[2]* Materialist analysis and masculine bias allow Engels to assume that an economic solution will cleanse false consciousness, create a new concept of gender, purge the future of the pathologies of the past. But he fails to understand that it is the mother-son and mother-daughter relationship, as much as, perhaps more than, that between man the buyer and woman the bought,

---

*Erich Neumann goes much further. In an essay called "Psychological Stages of Feminine Development" (translated by Rebecca Jacobson and revised for *Spring* by Hildegarde Nagel and Jane Pratt), he discusses the myth of feminine evil and the use of woman as scapegoat "which . . . means that the feminine is 'recognized' as evil by the patriarchally stamped cultures, the Judeo-Christian, Mohammedan and Hindu. Therefore, it is suppressed, enslaved, and outwardly eliminated from life, or else—which is what happens in witch trials—persecuted and done to death as the carrier of evil. *Only the fact that man cannot exist without woman has prevented the extirpation . . . of this group of 'evil' humans upon whom the dangerousness of the unconscious has been projected.*" (Emphasis mine.) This raises the question of how extrauterine reproduction and cloning techniques could be applied toward a gynocidal future, if they remain under male control.

which creates the sexual politics of male supremacism. Even under the pressures of a growing, worldwide, women's consciousness, the overwhelming bias of socialist and revolutionary movements is male, and reflects a wish to have a social revolution which would leave male leadership and control essentially untouched.* Eli Zaretsky has at least attempted to respond to the challenge directed by radical feminism at socialism, acknowledging that in the Bolshevik Revolution,

5
>Revolution through economic development left intact a major part of women's oppression. The psychosocial heritage of male supremacy was scarcely challenged by the entry of women into industry; while the strengthening of the family encouraged a resurgence of traditional patriarchal ideals, such as the exaltation of motherhood . . .

and that Marxism has assumed the traditional division of labor within the family along with heterosexuality as a "natural" condition.[3] But the effort to marry psychoanalysis and Marxism—two creations of the nineteenth-century masculine intellect—seems unavailing, since we find that it is "the family" which is seen as the problem, rather than the attitudes—acknowledged and hidden—held toward women by men. A woman is for a man both more and less than a person: she is something terribly necessary and unnecessarily terrible. She is not simply "more than an exploited worker";[4] she is not simply the "other"; she is first of all the Mother who has to be possessed, reduced, controlled, lest she swallow him back into her dark caves, or stare him into stone.

Rationalizations of patriarchy which deny this fact exist, of course, outside the Left. In a little book on kinship systems, the anthropologist Robin Fox describes, in several bland sentences, the "basic female function." After acknowledging that the essential human bond, the foundation of all social bonds, is that between mother and child, he goes on to explain how the longer extrauterine gestation required by the upright, bipedal human has resulted in woman's necessary preoccupation with bearing and nurturing for long periods, "probably getting pregnant again while doing so." This necessitated, according to Fox, a system whereby the mothers, thus incapacitated, had to be "protected." Where Engels sees male dominance as evolving from the possession of private property, Fox sees it as naturally evolving from this "protective" role: "it was the men who hunted the game, fought the enemies, and *made the decisions*." (Emphasis mine.)[5] Apart from the question of how far decisions must be made by a protective group, we have already seen that, in fact, decision-making—in whatever sense that concept would have had meaning in elementary society—was

---

*Horney notes that to confess dread of women is far more threatening to masculine self-regard than to acknowledge dread of a man. Since the notion of class assumes that women are merely subsumed under either the dominant males of the ruling class, or the oppressed males of the working class, it has perhaps been only natural that class analysis, male-created, has taken precedence over a sexual analysis.

probably originally inseparable from the maternal role. Fox creates a somewhat Victorian image of the early male (and, incidentally of himself), implying that "protection" rather than power and force, is at issue—a familiar rhetoric. If, however, we are to assume that from woman's original child-nurturing function flowed a "natural" division of all labor, generally accepted as natural by women and men, how do we account for the fact that laws, legends, and prohibitions relating to women have, from the early patriarchal myths (e.g., Eve) through the medieval witch-massacres and the gynocide of female infants down to the modern rape laws, mother-in-law jokes, and sadistic pornography of our time, been hostile and defensive, rather than "protective"?

One of the themes of post-Freudian psychology is that man's contributions to culture are his way of compensating for the lack of the one, elemental, creative power of motherhood. Bruno Bettelheim has analyzed male initiation rituals as outgrowths of deep male envy of this female power.[6] Horney suggests that, despite male dominance in every other sphere, a residual envy and resentment has remained which has expressed itself in phallocentric thinking (including such concepts as "penis envy"), in the devaluation (I would call it *reduction*) of motherhood, and in a generally misogynist civilization.*

She finds that besides the very ancient resentment of women's power to create new life, there is fear of her apparent power to affect the male genitals. Woman as elemental force, and as sexual temptress and consumer of his sexual energies, thus becomes, for man, a figure

---

*Misogyny is not a projection of women who resent men. That it exists, and has been validated by patriarchal culture at all times, is clearly documented. There are a number of recent works—all by men—on this subject, most of them quite interestingly misogynist in their leanings and conclusions. R. E. L. Masters and Eduard Lea, in an anthology called *The Anti-Sex* (1964), assert at regular intervals that "true misogyny is an unwarranted generalization" and suggest that despite the evidence to the contrary they have accumulated, misogyny is really an aberrant strain in human culture. At the same time they admit that misogyny is "cultural and ideological" rather than individual. Both Masters and Lea, and Wolfgang Lederer (*The Fear of Women* [1968]) deny in the dedications of their books that they are misogynists. Lederer accumulates vast research on male fear of the female, but his conclusion is that it is justified because women's drive to reproduce ("Some women are excessively—one is tempted to say, pathologically—fertile") is a genuine threat to civilization. What man really fears is not woman, but an overcrowded planet on which she is determined to go on breeding. A similar case of denial is found in the classical scholar H. D. F. Kitto, who, after amassing evidence of the repression of Athenian women, writes: "What is wrong is the picture it gives of the Athenian man. The Athenian had his faults, but pre-eminent among his qualities were lively intelligence, humanity and curiosity. To say that he habitually treated one-half of his own race with indifference, even contempt, does not, to my mind, make sense" (*The Greeks* [Baltimore: Penguin, 1960], p. 222).

H. R. Hays, who nowhere in his book presents credentials of gynophilia, has written the least misogynist treatment of the subject. His *The Dangerous Sex* (New York: Putnam, 1964) is an attempt "to make men aware of the shameful burden of fantasy and rationalization which they have been trailing down the ages . . . By using this symbolic magic he has either imprisoned [woman], made her an outcast, or treated her as a scapegoat" (p. 295). Hays's book is unhysterical and straightforward and should be basic reading for men who want to think seriously about sexual politics.

generating anxiety: "Woman is a mysterious being who communicates with spirits and thus has magic powers that she can use to hurt the male. He must therefore protect himself against her powers by keeping her subjugated." (It is possible that the more "rational" and antisubjective the male, the greater his unconscious servitude to these magical ideas.) "Motherliness" is split off from both sexual attractiveness (the temptress) and "motherhood" (the powerful Goddess) and is acceptable in its "nurturing, selfless, self-sacrificing" form: thus, in the fourteenth century, the Virgin Mary could be worshipped while living women were brutalized and burnt as witches.

2

Joseph Campbell, tracing the universality of the Great Goddess or Great Mother image from prehistory onward, asserts that "there can be no doubt that in the very earliest ages of human history the magical force and wonder of the female was no less a marvel than the universe itself; and this gave to woman a prodigious power, which it has been one of the chief concerns of the masculine part of the population to break, control and employ to its own ends."[7] He associates the glorification of hunting over agriculture, and the disappearance of female figurines at the end of the Aurignacian period (c. 30,000 B.C.), with the rise of this male self-assertion against the elemental power of woman. Female figurines were, he finds, "the first objects of worship by the species Homo sapiens. But there is a shift in the magic, ritual and imagery of Homo sapiens from the vagina to the phallus, and from an essentially plant-oriented to a purely animal-oriented mythology."

10   G. Rachel Levy offers a convincing and beautifully concrete recreation of Neolithic consciousness. She bases her conclusions, which are never dogmatic, on her actual explorations of Aurignacian caves, on a great variety of artifacts and wall-tracings, on the architecture of post-Neolithic cultures, and on studies of the prehistoric movements of wild herds and the distribution of wild grasses throughout Eastern and Western Europe. She suggests that a unified life-giving principle—the female principle embodied in the caves themselves and the goddess-cult figurines found within them—informed the existence of the hunting peoples. The beginnings of animal domestication and grazing, the development of agriculture, led, she feels, to the first consciousness of "movement in time"—i.e., the seasons' cycles, the rotation of the stars, the gestation, birth, and death of animals and crops. This earliest sense of "movement in time" generated a sense of numerical relation, balance, cyclic symmetry which in turn made possible such advances as the development of pottery.[8] But one essential by-product of this "mental revolution" was a growing consciousness of *duality*—a way of perceiving which, carried to its extreme and bifurcated, was later to become fundamental to patriarchal consciousness.

To acknowledge a cyclic change of aspects (that birth is followed by death, death by reincarnation; that tides ebb and flow, winter alternates with summer, the full moon with the dark of the moon) is to acknowledge that process and continuity embrace both positive and negative events—although, as parts of a process, events are less likely to become stamped as purely "positive" or "negative." Prepatriarchal consciousness, according to Levy, begins with an elemental unity which is sensed as female; and proceeds to an awareness of dynamics still presided over by a female presence: "In the growing consciousness of duality, the Mother retained her former abiding and fundamental status as the earth into which men return and out of which all birth emanates . . . no cult of a male divinity is discoverable in Neolithic archaeology. . . . Female potency [was] the great subject of Aurignacian sculpture."[9]

Even death was part of a movement in time, part of the cycle leading to reincarnation and rebirth. A "dark" or "negative" aspect of the Great Mother was thus already present from the beginning, inseparable from her benign, life-giving aspect. And, like death, violence, bloodshed, destructive power, were always there, the potentially "evil" half of the Mother's profile, which, once completely split off, would become separately personified as the fanged blood-goddess Kali, the killer-mother Medea, the lewd and malign witch, the "castrating" wife or mother. (As I was writing this, one of my sons showed me the cover of the current *National Geographic*—the photograph of a Peruvian Indian rowing a pure white llama to the annual ceremony on Titicaca Island where it would be sacrificed to the Earth Mother in exchange for a good harvest. This ceremony is performed by sorceresses and the llama's blood sprinkled onto "Pacha Mama" [Mother Earth].[10] Thus the bringing of life—i.e., food—is associated, as in ancient times, with bloodshed and killing, and both are associated with the Great Mother. Such customs, if rare today, were once legion.)

Women's blood is different from the blood of men or animals. It is associated not only with the "curse" and mysteries of the menstrual taboo, but with the *mana* of defloration, the transformation mystery of birth, and with fertility itself. There is thus a complex fusion of associations derived from the several aspects of the female, which might be visualized as a cluster.

As Joseph Campbell acknowledges: "the natural mysteries of childbirth and menstruation are as directly convincing as death itself, and remain to this day what they must also have been in the beginning, primary sources of a religious awe."[11]

15   In the recurrent hero myth, the male infant grows up into the son/lover, who later undergoes *violence* (murder or castration) at his mother's hands. The myth of killing the dragon (another violence/blood myth) recounts the test by which the young man tries to surmount his dread of the Terrible Mother—his elemental fear of

women. According to Mycenean myth, Apollo had to battle a female dragon before he could enter Delphi, which became his shrine.[12]

The Neolithic triangle or the *yoni*—female genital symbols anciently inscribed at the entrance to a sacred area—became, in this struggle against female power, fanged Kali, or Medusa's face with its snarl of snaky hair. The beneficient "Cow Goddess beyond the grave" who "suckled the souls of the newly dead" is transformed into the pregnant monster, "hippopotamus and crocodile, lioness and woman in one."[13]

Neumann sees an *adult* male ego as one which is able to enter into a creative connection with the Great Mother—presumably both in her dark and her benign aspects, since full adulthood requires eventually entering into some creative relationship with death itself. It is the adolescent ego that is still so uncertain of itself that it perceives the female as threatening; as "the unconscious and the non-ego . . . darkness, nothingness, the void, the bottomless pit." Of course the issue here is not one of a chronological phase ending at, say, twenty, or even of a more primitive stage of human consciousness, but of an aspect of male sexuality, which in a great many, probably a majority of men, continues into middle life and beyond. In fact, patriarchy is by nature always trying to "kill the dragon," in its negation of women; and the fully adult woman in patriarchal society may still often find only an adolescent son/lover, who wants her for his emotional sustenance even while somewhere within him he fears castration and death at her hands. This fear is the real dragon that has to be destroyed.

3

Woman has always known herself both as daughter and as potential mother, while in his dissociation from the process of conception man first experiences himself as son, and only much later as father. When he began to assert his paternity and to make certain claims to power over women and children on that basis, we begin to see emerging the process through which he compensated for—one could say, took revenge for—this previous condition as son-of-the-mother.

Patriarchal monotheism did not simply change the sex of the divine presence; it stripped the universe of female divinity, and permitted woman to be sanctified, as if by an unholy irony, only and exclusively as mother (without the extended *mana* that she possessed prepatriarchally)—or as the daughter of a divine father. She becomes the property of the husband-father, and must come to him *virgo intacta*, not as "second-hand goods"; or she must be ritually deflorated. If he is to know "his" children, he must have control over their reproduction, which means he must possess their mother exclusively. The question of "legitimacy" probably goes deeper than even the desire to hand on one's possessions to one's own bloodline;

it cuts back to the male need to say: "I, too, have the power of procreation—these are *my* seed, *my* own begotten children, *my* proof of elemental power." In addition, of course, the children are the future receivers of the patrimony; by their prayers and sacrifices, they will ensure the father's spirit a safe passage after death; but they are also present assets, able bodies to work fields, fish, hunt, fight against hostile tribes. A wife's "barrenness" (until very recently it was the woman who was declared "barren" rather than the husband infertile) was a curse because she was, finally, the means of reproduction. A man needed children to enhance his position in the world, and especially, a man needed sons. The command of Yahweh: "Be fruitful and multiply,"* is an entirely patriarchal one; he is not invoking the Great Mother but bidding his sons beget still more sons. Thus, Engels is correct in his famous statement that in the patriarchal family the husband is the bourgeois and the wife and children the proletariat. But each is something more to each, something which both cements and can outlast economic bondage.

20   In the Middle East to this day, God is believed to strike a woman barren as punishment for some impiety (the woman is assumed to be the sinner, not her husband) and the production of daughters is a disaster, not simply for the mother, but for the daughters. The Hebrew scholar Raphael Patai says that "we know from historical documents relating to the Arab world from pre-historic times down to the 19th century that often a father decided to put to death a daughter either immediately upon her birth or at a later date. The usual method of putting a newborn daughter to death was to bury her in the sands of the desert." He quotes from the Koran the words of a father who asks himself, of his newborn daughter: "Shall he keep it in contempt, or bury it in the dust?"[14] The earlier background of female primacy I have described needs to be held in mind against the violence of this question—along with the fact that the Yahwists savagely repressed the cults of Astarte (originally Tanit, Asherah, or Ishtar) and denounced all worship of the Goddess as "an abomination."[15]

The Mother Goddess is gradually devalued and rejected; the human woman finds her scope and dignity increasingly reduced. Patriarchal man impregnates "his" wife and expects her to deliver "his" child; her elemental power is perceived more and more as a service she renders, a function she performs. In the *Eumenides* of Aeschylus, the Erinyes, representing mother-right, claim vengeance on Orestes for the crime of matricide. But Apollo declares that Orestes's murder of his mother was a just act because it avenged the death of his father Agamemnon; and he continues:

---

*That imperative in Genesis is of course preceded by the myth of Adam, in which woman's procreative power is denied and *she* is taken out of the man's body. When Adam and Eve are cursed, Eve is told that "in sorrow [she] will bring forth children."

> The mother is no parent of that which is called her child, but only nurse of the newplanted seed that grows. The parent is he who mounts.

Athena, also a representative of father-right, denies having had any mother; she sprang from her father Zeus's brain and she acts like a true token woman, loyal only to "the man" as she does not hesitate to announce.[16] And the medieval church held that a minuscule, fully formed *homunculus*, complete with soul, was deposited by the male in the female body, which simply acted as incubator.[17]*

The image of the divine family also changes. The Goddess, whether in Sumer, Minos, Mycenae, Phrygia, Knossos, or Syria, had often been represented with a young god, her son, servant, or consort, but always subsidiary to her. E. O. James perceives these young male images as the first sign of recognition of the male's part in fertilization. But for a long time the young god remained more son than husband, more consort than equal. Mellaart finds the role of the son of the goddess "strictly subordinate to hers"; of a male figure found in one of the Çatal Hüyük shrines, he says: "Presumably he represents an aspect of hunting, which alone was responsible for the presence of an independent male deity in the neolithic of Çatal Hüyük."[18] But in his earliest appearance he is a vegetation god, who must die and be reborn for the vegetative cycle to continue. In a sense, he is thus still annexed to the Mother of grains, fruits, and growing things. Later, the virgin-mother with her youthful childmate is replaced by a father, his wife, and his children. In contrast to the "Divine Triad" of Mycenae cited by Leonard Palmer, which consists of two queens and a king, we find such images as the Egyptian Amarnan family, consisting of a father, his son, and his small grandson.[19] The mother is no longer virgin, "she-unto-herself"; she is "unto-the-husband," his unequal consort or his possession and subordinate, to be reckoned up with his cattle.*

25   Devaluations of the Goddess are legion. Patai describes the struggle of Jewish patriarchal monotheism with the goddess-cults, of which the golden calf was one remnant (the horned bull or cow having been sacred to the Goddess throughout the world.)* He tells of women weaving "houses"—possibly garments—for Asherah in the temple at

---

*Margaret Mead notes that it has always been more difficult to obscure the woman's role in procreation than the man's—yet she gives contemporary examples—the Rossel Islanders, the Montenegrins—of cultures in which the mother's role is held to be purely passive or is denied outright (*Male and Female* [New York: Morrow, 1975], p. 59–60).

*In Judaism there is no divine family. Christianity's Holy Family—really the human family of Jesus—is distinct from the Trinity, or three-part Godhead of Father, Son, and Holy Spirit. Daly notes the ambiguity surrounding the Holy Spirit, which is invested with stereotypically "feminine" qualities but referred to by a masculine pronoun and supposed to have impregnated the Virgin Mary. As for the human family of Jesus, his words spoken to the Virgin Mary in the Gospels are suggestive: "Woman, what have I to do with thee?" The Virgin is, of course, *virgo intacta*, not *virgo* in the sense associated with the cult of Artemis.

Jerusalem, and the baking of cakes for Astarte or Anath. Some remnant of female presence—heavily laden with what Jung would call anima-projection—survived in the concept of the Shekhina, "the loving, rejoicing, motherly, suffering, mourning and in general emotion-charged aspect of deity" (with what implications for centuries of Jewish mothers?). A female deity also reemerged in the Kabbalistic renascence of the thirteenth century, under the name Matronit, who, according to Patai is a distinct and often independent presence, but who seems to have left few ripples in the mainstream of Judaism.[20] The pig, declared an unclean animal in the Koran and the Old Testament, was a reiterative figure in goddess-religion; the sow was sacred in Crete, sometimes appeared as an embodiment of Isis, was sacrificed at the feast of Aphrodite, and was a symbol of the Eleusinian cult of Demeter. "Wherever the eating of pork is forbidden and the pig is held to be unclean, we can be sure of its originally sacred character."[21]

Jane Harrison describes the descent (in every sense) of the Hellenic figure of Pandora from the Cretan Earth-Mother, her conversion from the All-Giver to merely a beautiful girl dowered with gifts by all the Olympians and then sent as a temptress to man. Pandora's famous "box" which when opened released every kind of grief and trouble among men, was originally a *pithos* or *jar* in which the Earth-Mother stored all the goods of wine, grain, and fruits. Jane Harrison was struck by the "ugly and malicious theological animus" in Hesiod's telling of this tale: "he is all for the *Father* and the Father will have no great Earth-Goddess in his man-made Olympus."[22]

Slater sees the entire Olympian mythology as saturated with fear of the mature, maternal woman; the much-admired goddess, Athena, is born from her father Zeus's brain, is virginal, childless, and, as has been seen, affirms her loyalty to the male. Hera is a jealous, competitive consort, and destructive mothers like Gaea, Rhea, Medea, and Clytemnestra abound. He theorizes that this fear of the maternal woman derived from the sexual politics of fifth-century Greece, where women were ill-educated, were sold into marriage, and had no role except as producers of children, the sexual interest of men was homoerotic, and for intellectual friendships a man sought out hetaeras (usually foreign-born women) or other men. He assumes the mother to have been filled with resentment and envy of her sons, and, in her own frustration, excessively controlling of her male children in their earliest years. Her feelings would have been

---

*In his *Ancient Judaism*, Max Weber hints at the rejection of "chthonic and vegetative" cults by the Hebrews; he is, of course, talking about cults of the Mother-Goddess. Another example of the method Daly has named "The Great Silence."

experienced by her sons as a potentially destructive hostility which is later embodied in mythology and classical drama.[23]*

4

Sun-worship, which always postdates worship of a lunar diety (whether feminine or masculine) is another feature of patriarchal thought. The ancients saw the moon not as a reflector of solar light, but as independently glowing in the darkness of night; the sun was the inhabitant, rather than the source of daylight.

It is extraordinary to see concretely, as in Egyptian art of the Amarna period, the coming-into-dominance of the sun. Although a solar deity had long been central in Egyptian religion, there was still a strong goddess-cult embodied in the figures of Isis, Hathor, Nut, Nepthys. The fourteenth-century B.C. pharaoh Akhenaton revolutionized Egyptian cosmology in setting up the Aten, or sun-disk, as the sole embodiment of a new religion. In his capital, the seat of the Aten at Tell-el-Amarna, he encouraged an art which over and over, in the sun-disk with its spreading rays, asserts the message of a monotheistic, heliocentric and patriarchal universe.

30   When we think of Amarnan art we tend to think of the famous portrait bust of Nefertite. But her popularity in our times should not make us exaggerate her importance in her own. Amarnan art, in fact, reiterates images of women and of the family which do not seem very different from contemporary stereotypes. In these incised or carven images, Akhenaton is already both patriarchal and deity (Incarnation of the Aten). With him is his queen, Nefertite, of extraordinary bearing and elegance, who comes far closer to contemporary ideals of feminine, aristocratic beauty than do most pre-patriarchal female images. But she is unmistakenly second; a consort, even a royal deity, depicted with dignity and pride, but essentially a token woman. In one *stele*, the royal family (Akhenaton, Nefertite, and three of their daughters) are represented in an informal, even intimate family scene showing a good deal of physical affection. But above them the Aten holds forth its rays, and *it* is the real center and keystone of the composition.

---

*Slater is another writer who comes close to a denunciation of patriarchy yet gets deflected. His thesis is that maternal overinvolvement with the son, deriving from the inferior and reduced status of women, results—in America as in fifth-century Greece—in a narcissistic male consciousness, given to "proving" itself through war, often through meaningless achievement and acquisitiveness, and through competition. He does not, like some writers, leave the problem at the mother's door; he is refreshingly aware that her relationship to her son occurs in a social context, the *reductio-ad-matrem* which gives no other opportunity for action, makes motherhood the definition of womanhood, and child-care (in the middle classes) a full-time, exclusively female occupation. Though many of Slater's observations are useful, his failure to connect the psychic pattern with the patriarchal context leaves his insights regrettably incomplete.

In establishing the worship of the Aten, Akhenaton not only ordered the destruction of many images of the earlier gods, and removed their names from monuments, but prohibited the plural form of the word "god." A reference in Cyril Aldred to the fact that "the words for 'mother' and 'truth' were cleansed of their old associations" is tantalizing, since the hieroglyph for "house" or "town" also symbolizes "mother," emphasizing the principle of collective as well as individual nurture.[24]

In the *Eumenides* of Aeschylus, Apollo, the Hellenic sun-god, becomes the spokesman for father-right, upheld by Athena, the goddess who denies her mother. Apollo is god of poetry and the lyre, twin brother of an independent sister, associated with light, with trees, with the art of healing. Jane Harrison notes that Apollo is derived from the god Paean, of the land where the styptic peony grows, and that this herb, which could stanch blood, was held in reverence throughout the East. But Artemis, his sister, is likewise associated with healing herbs, in her diminished state as goddess. Apollo's relationship to trees is interesting: The nymph Daphne, to escape rape by him, had herself turned into a laurel tree. This tree Apollo made his personal symbol; and it was with a laurel branch in his hand that he came to take over the oracular shrine of the earth-goddess, Themis, at Delphi[25]—killing, as we have seen, a female dragon on the way.

Thus Apollo assimilated a number of attractive aspects of the Great Mother—even to being paired with the moon. The Mother of Trees, of healing herbs and the preservation of life, becomes a male god; the lunar goddess becomes his sister. Slater calls him "the personification of anti-matriarchy, the epitome of the sky-god, a crusader against Earth-deities. He is all sunlight, Olympian, manifest, rational."[26] Now this of course is an extreme case of patriarchal "splitting"—in Jane Harrison's words, Greek orthodoxy would allow "no deed or dream of darkness" about Apollo. All was to be lucidity, radiant masculinity. Harding suggests that the worship of the moon embodies respect for the wisdom of instinct and natural law, and that sun-worship has to do with the idea of control of natural forces.[27] Indeed, Apollo is personified as driving the steeds of the sun. The "Apollonian" rational control of nature, as opposed to the instinctual excesses of the cult of Dionysus, the power of consciousness as opposed to the unconscious, the celebration of father-right over mother-right, come together in this mythology.

Why the sun should have come to embody a split consciousness, while the worship of the moon allowed for coexistent opposites, a holistic process, is an interesting question. The fact that the moon is itself continually changing, and is visible in so many forms, while the sun presents itself in one, single, unvarying form, may account for the kinds of human perceptions which would be powerfully drawn to one or the other. At all events, with the advent of solar religion, the Great

Mother, in her manifold persons and expressions, begins to suffer reduction; parts of her are split off, some undergo a gender change, and henceforth woman herself will be living on patriarchal terms, under the laws of male divinities and in the light of male judgments.

5

35   There are really two modes in which man has related to woman-as-mother: the practical and the magical. He has, at one time, been utterly dependent on her. Predominately, in all cultures, it is from women that both women and men have learned about caresses, about affectionate play, about the comfort of a need satisfied—and also about the anxiety and wretchedness of a need deferred.

    Briffault was convinced that maternal sentiment far predated the mating instinct; the first love being the love of mother and child. He perceived tender feelings as a secondary female sexual characteristic, derived in the course of female evolution from the biological nature of the female organism. It was the desire for that tenderness, which the male experienced from his mother, that originally induced him to modify his own sexual instinct in accordance with the mating, or stabilizing, impulse of woman.[28] According to Margaret Mead,

> The relationship in the male between his innate sexual impulses and reproduction seems to be a learned response . . . Male sexuality seems originally focussed to no goal beyond immediate discharge; it is society that provides the male with a desire for children, for patterned interpersonal relationships that order, control, and elaborate his original impulses.[29]

    Thus in prepatriarchal life the male child early perceived that the female power of procreation was charged with *mana*. The sacred, the potent, the creative were symbolized as female. When not absorbed in fending for existence, or ritually acknowledging the (female) powers ruling life and death, prepatriarchal man must have felt something of an outsider. As Mead remarks: "His equipment for love [sex] is manifest to the very small boy—but what is it to be a father? This is something that goes on outside one's own body, in the body of another."[30] The anthropologist Leo Frobenius gives us the words of an Abyssinian woman commenting on the richness and complexity of a woman's biological endowment as contrasted with a man's: "His life and body are always the same . . . . He knows nothing."[31]

    Patriarchal man created—out of a mixture of sexual and affective frustration, blind need, physical force, ignorance, and intelligence split from its emotional grounding, a system which turned against woman her own organic nature, the source of her awe and her original powers. In a sense, female evolution was mutilated, and we have no way now of imagining what its development hitherto might have been; we can only try, at last, to take it into female hands.

40   The mother-child relationship is the essential human relationship. In the creation of the patriarchal family, violence is done to this fundamental human unit. It is not simply that woman in her full meaning and capacity is domesticated and confined within strictly defined limits. Even safely caged in a single aspect of her being—the maternal—she remains an object of mistrust, suspicion, misogyny in both overt and insidious forms. And the female generative organs, the matrix of human life, have become a prime target of patriarchal technology.

Notes

1. Frederick Engels, *The Origin of Family, Private Property and the State* (New York: International Publishers, 1971), p. 73.

2. Karen Horney, *Feminine Psychology* (New York: Norton, 1967), pp. 106–18.

3. Eli Zaretsky, *Capitalism, the Family, and Personal Life.* Originally published in *Socialist Revolution*, January–June 1973, pp. 78, 72–73. (Available as a paperback from Harper and Row, N. Y., 1975.)

4. H. R. Hays, *The Dangerous Sex* (New York: Pocket Books, 1972), p. 270; first published 1964.

5. Robin Fox, *Kinship and Marriage* (Baltimore: Penguin, 1967), pp. 27–33.

6. Bruno Bettelheim, *Symbolic Wounds: Puberty Rites and the Envious Male* (New York: Collins, 1968); first published 1954.

7. Joseph Campbell, *The Masks of God: Primitive Mythology* (New York: Viking, 1972), pp. 315ff.; first published in 1959.

8. G. Rachel Levy, *Religious Conceptions of the Stone Age* (New York: Harper Torchbooks, 1963), pp. 83–85.

9. *Ibid.*, pp. 27, 86–87, 100.

10. *National Geographic*, Vol. 144, No. 6 (December 1973).

11. Campbell, *op. cit.*, p. 372.

12. Leonard Palmer, *Mycenaeans and Minoans: Agaean Prehistory in the Light of the Linear B Tablets* (New York: Knopf, 1965), p. 347.

13. Levy, *op. cit.*, p. 120; Erich Neumann, *The Great Mother* (Princton, N. J.: Princeton University Press, 1972), p. 153.

14. Raphael Patai, *Sex and Family in the Bible and the Middle East* (New York: Doubleday, 1959), p. 135.

15. Raphael Patai, *The Hebrew Goddess* (New York: Kiev, 1967), pp. 52, 97–98.

16. *Aeschylus, Oresteia*, trans. Richmond Lattimore (Chicago: University of Chicago Press, 1953), pp. 158, 161.

17. B. Ehrenreich and D. English, *Witches, Midwives and Nurses: A History of Women Healers* (Old Westbury, N. Y.: Feminist Press, 1973), pp. 8–9

18. E. O. James, *The Cult of the Mother Goddess* (New York: Praegar, 1959), pp. 47, 138; James Mellaart, *Çatal Hüyük: A Neolithic Town in Anatolia* (New York: McGraw-Hill, 1967), plate 84.

19. Palmer, *op. cit.*, p. 192; Cyril Alred, *Akenaten and Nefertite* (New York: Viking, 1973), p. 181.

20. Patai, *The Hebrew Goddess*, pp. 26–27, 52, 97–98.

21. Erich Neumann, *The Origins and History of Consciousness* (Princeton, N. J.: Princeton University Press, 1971), p. 86.

22. Jane Harrison, *Mythology* (New York: Harcourt Brace, 1963), pp. 44ff.

23. Phillip Slater, *The Glory of Hera* (Boston: Beacon, 1968).

24. Aldred, *op. cit.*, pp. 11-12: Lewis Mumford, *The City in History* (New York: Harcourt Brace and World, 1961), p. 13.

25. Jane Harrisson, *op cit.*, pp. 94–95.

26. Slater, *op. cit.*, pp. 137–41.

27. M. Esther Harding, *Women's Mysteries* (New York: C. G. Jung Foundation, 1971), p. 31.

28. Robert Briffault, *The Mothers* (New York: Johnson Reprint, 1969), I: pp. 131–41.

29. Margaret Mead, *Male and Female: A Study of the Sexes in A Changing World* (New York: Morrow, 1975), p. 229; first published 1949.

30. *Ibid.*, p. 82.

31. Campbell, *op cit.*, p. 451.

Reflective Reading, Informal Writing

REFLECTING ON THE READING:

- The title of Rich's essay is "The Domestication of Motherhood." What does she mean by this? In what ways has motherhood been domesticated? And, according to Rich, what is the result of this domestication?
- It is fairly easy to think of motherhood as a state of nature, a biological function. Rich, however, suggests that motherhood has also been "constructed" in certain ways. In fact, she opens her essay with a lengthy discussion of Marxist thought on the oppression of women. She then goes on to argue that while Engels was partially correct in arguing that ownership of property and slavery is behind misogyny, he obscures or ignores other theories and histories. What are those theories and histories that Rich goes on to illuminate for us?
- Rich ends the essay with the following passage: "It is not simply that woman in her full meaning and capacity is domesticated and confined within strictly defined limits. Even safely caged in a single aspect of their being—the maternal—she remains an object of mistrust, suspicion, misogyny in both overt and insidious forms. And the female generative organs, the matrix of human life, have become a prime target of patriarchal technology." By "safely caged" Rich does not mean that motherhood makes women safe. In fact, she is suggesting the exact opposite. What keeps women "safely caged" in the maternal and why? And what does Rich mean when she suggests

that woman's relationship to motherhood, her "generative organs, have become a prime target of patriarchal technology"?

UNDERSTANDING RHETORICAL STRATEGIES:

- In part, Rich's argument is an historical argument. How does she use history to make her point? Does she choose from more than one history? What do you notice about what she selects from history to use as her evidence? Do you find yourself convinced by her history or histories? Why or why not?
- As readers, if we are not diligent, we can miss a great deal of information that Rich has marked with an asterisk and placed at the bottom of the page. Was this disruptive to you as a reader? Did you even read these passages? How important did this information seem to her essay? Why might she have chosen to put this information at the bottom of the page rather than in the text?
- Unlike some essayists, Rich includes a great number of other sources to support her arguments. What kinds of sources does she cite? Why do you think she includes these sources? How might her use of these sources relate to her rhetorical ethos (that is, her persona, or the way she is perceived by readers)? Her purpose? Her audience?

INFORMAL WRITING:

- Think about how motherhood is currently constructed in mass media and popular culture. Write about how you see motherhood depicted in one of the following: movies, music, television, magazines, newspapers.
- Rich uses Marxism, religion, psychology, and anthropology to support her arguments. Write about which of these seem to yield the most information about motherhood and why you think that to be the case.
- Having read Rich's essay, consider whether you now think differently about the role of motherhood in our culture. Write about what has changed in your thinking, and why. Or conversely, write about why Rich has failed to make you reconsider your perception of motherhood.

PAULA RUST

Paula Rust began her education at Oberlin as a physics major. After 18 months, she changed to sociology and anthropology. She then earned her Ph.D. from the University of Michigan, Ann Arbor. Her dissertation grew out of her experience trying to understand and explain her own sexuality. After coming out at age 18, Rust was fascinated by how the whole world looked different to her. She noticed things she had taken for granted before, such as marriage—legal for heterosexual couples but not for same-sex couples. Rust developed a new level of awareness about social rules and began to see culture as something larger than the sum of all the individuals in it.

When she began her research in the late 1970s and early 1980s, lesbian-feminism, sado-masochism, and bisexuality were controversial topics talked about infrequently, and even then handled delicately. Rust noticed parallels between the dynamics of the lesbian community and the dominant community, but these dynamics played out differently in a minority group within the context of oppression.

Although research about such a controversial subject was considered career suicide by some, Rust was persistent enough to pursue her personal interests. Just as she finished her dissertation, bisexual and queer politics became popular academic topics, creating a space for her research about sexuality. Rust researches and writes about topics that are personally relevant and personally interesting. She believes that personalizing writing does not make it less valuable. She describes the prevailing devaluation of the personal as a distinctly white European convention. In some other cultures, including a personal element in writing is seen as a testament to the scholar's commitment, making the work more valuable. According to Rust, every writer's work is personal. All writers see their work (and their world) through their own eyes. The majority, however, has the luxury of ignoring that fact. In addition to writing about personally important topics, it is also important to learn as much as possible about different kinds of people. The only way to talk or write to different kinds of people, to communicate with cultures different from our own, is to know something about them.

In 1992, Rust did some research for a study about coming out and began questioning the common view of coming out as a linear process, which culminated in this 1996 article. She currently believes that we are always evolving and that there may not be one goal, one point we are trying to reach. Instead, life is a long process of maintaining an identity or sense of self, and as resources change, the ways we do things change. Resources for knowing ourselves include language, the words we have readily available to describe ourselves, and the existence of communities that we can attach our identities to and go to for support. As we define ourselves, we create new language, redefine old terms, and create new spaces for a diverse and changing population.

Sexual Identity and Bisexual Identities: The Struggle for Self-Description in a Changing Sexual Landscape

As we look back over our lives, we construct them as stories. A story has a conclusion, and the story line leads inexorably to the conclusion; events and details that are irrelevant to the conclusion are irrelevant to the story and distract the listener from the "real" story. When we construct our life stories, we tend to forget the irrelevant details of our pasts. We identify the relevant experiences and interpret them as the building blocks that made us into the people we are today, and we understand our past changes as the twists and turns in the road we took to reach our current selves. Even if we recognize that we have not yet completed our personal journeys and that we will continue to rewrite our stories until we reach the final draft at death, we still perceive our pasts as the paths by which we arrived at our present selves. Most of us who identify our present selves as gay, lesbian, or bisexual have constructed "coming out stories" that explain —to ourselves and to others— how we arrived at our sexual self-definitions.

Social scientists in the 1970s, seeking to redress the scientific sins that had been committed against lesbian and gay people in the past, sought to understand the lives of lesbian and gay people as they (we) understood their (our) own lives. Taking the cue from their lesbian and gay subjects, many sociologists and psychologists set out to study the process of coming out, i.e., the process of lesbian or gay identity formation. Researchers soon discovered "milestone events," or life events that lesbian and gay people had identified as relevant to their development and incorporated into their coming out stories. Typical milestone events were the first experience of a feeling of sexual attraction for someone of the same sex, the first sexual experience with someone of the same sex, the first labeling of one's self as homosexual, the first public expression of one's homosexual identity to significant others, the symbolic switch from a homosexual to a lesbian or gay identity as one's self-acceptance increased and, eventually, the integration of one's private and public identities as one came out of the closet.

Based on these observations, scientists elaborated developmental models of coming out that construct it as a linear process of self-discovery in which a false, socially imposed heterosexual identity is replaced with a lesbian or gay identity that accurately reflects the essence of the individual. These models rarely account for bisexual identity as an authentic identity; when they acknowledge bisexual identity at all, they usually cast it as a phase one might pass through on the way to adopting a lesbian or gay identity.[1] Researchers operating within these linear developmental models of coming out asked respondents for the ages at which they experienced each milestone, and then, reporting the average ages, described coming out as an ordered sequence of events. From this research, we learned that lesbians first experience sexual attraction to other women at an average age of twelve or thirteen, but do not become aware of these sexual feelings until late adolescence. They begin suspecting that they are lesbian at an average age of eighteen, but do not adopt lesbian identities until their early twenties. We learned that gay men experience these events at younger ages and in more rapid sequence than lesbians, and—from the few studies that treated bisexual identity as authentic—we learned that bisexuals come out later and more slowly than gays and lesbians.[2] Based on these findings, researchers began theorizing about why men come out more quickly than women and why bisexuals come out more slowly than the monosexuals.

The portrait of sexual identity formation that is painted by these average ages is not only grossly simplified but factually inaccurate. Based on research with lesbian-identified and bisexual-identified women,[3] I have shown that average ages conceal a great deal of variation in the coming out process, both among and between lesbian and bisexual women.[4] In contrast to the linear portrait painted by average ages, lesbian and bisexual women experience each milestone at a wide range of ages; many women do not experience all of the so-called milestone events; women who do experience these events experience them in various orders; and some women experience some events repeatedly.

5   Moreover, I discovered that the "finding" that bisexual women come out more slowly than lesbians is an artifact of the statistical methods used in studies based on linear models of coming out. When I calculated average ages for the over 400 women in my first study, the results confirmed earlier findings that bisexual women come out at later ages and more slowly than lesbian women. Bisexual women first felt attracted to women at an average age of 18.1, compared to 15.4 for lesbian women. Bisexual women first questioned their heterosexual identity 1.9 years later, at an average age of 20.0 years, whereas lesbians first questioned their heterosexual identity 1.6 years later, at an average age of 17.0. But a closer look at the data revealed that lesbian women were twice as likely as bisexual women to have questioned their heterosexual identity before they felt attracted to women (28% vs. 14%), probably because some women were encouraged by lesbian feminist arguments about the political nature of lesbianism to identify themselves as lesbian even in the absence of sexual feelings toward women. Among women who questioned their heterosexual identities only after feeling attracted to other women, bisexual women

actually did so sooner—not later—than lesbian women. In other words, the original finding that bisexual women come out more slowly than lesbian women was an artifact resulting from a failure to recognize variations in the coming out process as equally authentic patterns, rather than as deviations from an underlying linear course.

I also discovered that bisexual women had changed sexual identities more frequently in the past than lesbian women, often alternating repeatedly between lesbian and bisexual identities. Under linear development models, this finding would be taken as an indication of the instability of bisexual identity and the sociopsychological immaturity of bisexual-identified individuals.[5] Under more sophisticated, but still linear, social interactionist understandings of the creation of identity, this finding would be taken as evidence of the difficulty of constructing a bisexual identity in a social world that offers only two authenticated categories, heterosexual and homosexual.[6] But I also discovered that, at any given moment, a bisexual woman was as likely to be satisfied with her current sexual identity as a lesbian was with hers. This finding disproves the hypothesis that bisexual women are engaged in a constant struggle to establish a satisfactory sexual identity and suggests instead that bisexual women find different sexual identities satisfactory at different times and under different circumstances. Bisexual women's frequent identity changes do not indicate a state of searching immaturity, but a mature state of mutability.

Previous researchers have attempted to modify the linear model of coming out by introducing feedback loops, alternate routes, and contingencies.[7] Although these modifications produce models with ample room for deviation, they do not effectively describe the formation of sexual identity. They are unable to account for the findings that bisexual women incorporate their same-sex feelings into sexual identities more quickly than lesbians and that bisexual women are as satisfied with their sexual indentities as lesbians are. This inability highlights the need to develop a new model of the identity formation process.

To accommodate the empirical reality of identity change processes, linear developmental models of coming out must be abandoned in favor of a social constructionist view of identity as a description of the location of the self in relation to other individuals, groups, and institutions. The individuals, groups, and institutions to which we relate are landmarks on a sexual landscape that is itself socially constructed. From this perspective, identity change would be understood as a process of modifying one's self-description in response to changes in either the location of the self or the socially constructed landscape on which one is located. Identity change would be a necessary outcome of one's efforts to maintain an accurate self-description, not an indication that one has not yet achieved an accurate self-description. "Coming out" would not be a process of essential discovery leading to a mature and stable identity, but merely one story constructed around one of the myriad identity changes we all go through as mature adults attempting to maintain accurate self-descriptions in a changing social environment. Research on the so-called "coming out process" would be reconceptualized as research on the social contexts of identity changes that take place throughout life, and the goal of this research would be to discover the types of contextual changes that motivate individual identity change.

In the spring of 1993, I began a second study guided by the concept of sexual identity as a description of the self in relation to other individuals, groups, and institutions.[8] The overall goal of the study is to document the development of bisexual identity, community, and politics in the United States, the United Kingdom, and other, primarily English-speaking countries. A specific goal of the study is to explore the types of contextual changes that lead individuals to change their sexual identities, with an eye toward understanding why currently bisexual-identified individuals tend to have changed their sexual identities frequently in the past. The study includes people of all gender and sexual identities, including transsexuals and transgenderists.

10

Participants in the study were asked several questions about their current and past sexual identities, the first of which was "When you think about your sexual orientation today, what term do you use most often to describe yourself?" This question was followed by response choices ranging from lesbian, gay, straight, and bisexual to polysexual, polyfidelitous, queer, and pansensual and gave respondents the option of writing in other identities or indicating that they preferred not to label themselves or did not know what their orientations were. Respondents who chose or wrote in one or more sexual identities were asked "What does your sexual identity mean to you?" They were also asked to "[t]hink back to the most recent time when you began to think of yourself as _____," "to identify the experience, event, or circumstance [that] caused you to decide or realize that this was the term you should use to describe yourself at that time," and to "[d]escribe how this term came to have this meaning for you."

Respondents' answers to these questions provide insights into the social contexts within which their current sexual identities are anchored and in which their identity changes occurred. In particular, they reveal six general types of change that can lead to individual identity change. The first is change in an individual's location on the sexual landscape co[9] inhabits. As individuals' locations shift, so do their relationships to landmarks in the sexual landscape, and they must change their identities to maintain accurate descriptions of these relationships. Second, the landscape itself might alter as the landmarks in it move, change, or fade, and as new landmarks appear. Third, even in the absence of changes in individuals' own locations or in the landscape itself, the language available to individuals to describe their locations might be evolving. As old terms disappear or alter in meaning and new terms develop, individuals find that their sexual identities no longer describe their locations accurately, and they must search the language for new ways to identify themselves. Fourth, the sexual landscape is constructed differently in different social contexts, and a variety of languages for self-description are therefore available: individuals who move from one context to another during the course of their daily lives often use different identities in different contexts. Fifth, if we recognize that people sometimes, intentionally or unintentionally, describe themselves inaccurately to others and to themselves, we find that individuals' sexual identities can change as they become more or less honest about their locations on the sexual landscape. Finally, some individuals change their sexual identities, not in response to changes in their location, landscape, language, social context, or level of honesty, but instead to cause changes in their location, landscape, or language. Within each of these broad categories of change, there are many specific types of change that can lead to identity redefinition, as mature individuals attempt to maintain descriptions of their locations on the sexual landscape. The men, women, and transgendered individuals who participated in my current research provided numerous examples of these various types of sexual identity change.

CHANGES IN ONE'S LOCATION ON THE SEXUAL LANDSCAPE

The most common type of change reported by individuals is change in their own locations on the sexual landscape. Change is relative, and can only be defined in relation to objects other than the self; these objects might be other individuals, social groups, or social and political institutions. Many respondents recalled that they changed their sexual identities when they developed new relationships with particular people, usually romantic or sexual relationships with people whose genders were different from the genders of the people with whom they had expected to become intimately involved. For example, a White American[10] woman who used to identify herself as a Lesbian[11] explained why she began to identify herself as Bisexual:

> About two years ago, I had been in a sexual relationship with a wonderful woman for one year, and I was identifying as lesbian at the time. I found myself attracted to a man who was interested in me. I had a sense of being at a crossroads: lesbian or "something else." She wanted a monogamous relationship and . . . I didn't want that conservatism. We broke up and I began a sexual relationship with the man.[12]

Her previous Lesbian identity represented her sexual relationship with a woman. It also represented her lack of a relationship with a man, as evidenced by the fact that it had to change when she began to feel attracted to a man. The conflict between her Lesbian identity and her attraction to a man created, for her, a crossroads, i.e., the moment of change. When this attraction led to a sexual relationship with the man, she adopted a Bisexual identity that apparently represents both her (ex-)relationship to a woman and her current relationship to a man. The new identity represents her new location on the sexual landscape, a location that is described in relation to two other individuals, a woman and a man.

15   Sometimes the new relationship is not an actual sexual or physical one but merely a feeling of attraction toward another person, as was the case with an Irish woman who identified herself as Bisexual when she "[r]ealiz[ed] I was experiencing a sexual fantasy about a female friend." Or the relationships represented by an identity might be potential relationships. For example, a White man explained that he began identifying as a Gay Bisexual when he "recognized the reality of my past (and potential future) relationships."

For some respondents, a single relationship with an individual—whether actual, desired, or potential—is not enough to motivate a complete identity change. These respondents' identities represent their relationships to entire social groups, and they do not change their sexual identities until their relationships with individuals lead them to perceive changes in their relationships to entire social groups. For example, a Jewish Lesbian said that she fell in love with "a woman," but it was not until she realized she "was sexually attracted to women" that she "suddenly saw the possibility and even inevitability of a different (i.e., lesbian) erotic self-definition". In other words, noting that the individual with whom she had developed a relationship belonged to the social group "women," she generalized her feelings to the entire social group by "realizing" that she could potentially be attracted to any member of that group. She then adopted a Lesbian identity to represent her new relationship to this social group. Another woman explained that she did not begin to call herself Bi until her relationship to an individual man led to the realization that she was attracted to men as a social group. She wrote,

> I had been involved with a man for about two years, during which time I identified as "a lesbian who happens to be seeing a man until something else comes along." After a while I realized that I was really deeply committed to my other-sex relationship. . . . Also I became aware that I was starting to feel more generalized attraction to men other than just my lover. So "bi" seemed more accurate.

Many respondents said that their current identities represent a connection to social or political institutions. For example, one American man said that his Gay identity means "not only being attracted to members of the same sex . . . but also identification with an oppressed minority with a distinct identity and culture." Similarly, a White/Native American woman explained that she began calling herself a Lesbian after she became involved with a woman because "I was so immersed in lesbian culture after that, and felt so at home, it felt silly not to call myself a lesbian." In other words, her relationship with a woman led to her involvement in lesbian culture, and her Lesbian identity represents this relationship to lesbian social institutions as much as it represents her relationship to an individual woman.

Despite the fact that many respondents' sexual identities represent their relationships to social or political institutions, very few reported that they had changed their identities in response to changes in their relationships to social and political institutions. This finding suggests that relationships to social and political institutions usually develop after identity change. Identities that are originally adopted because of relationships to individuals or social groups can lead one to develop relationships with social and political institutions, and the identity subsequently comes to represent these institutional relationships as well.

20   Lesbian-identified, gay-identified, and heterosexual-identified respondents often described their identities as representing a single relationship to either an individual, a group, or an institution, whereas bisexual-identified respondents usually said that their identities represent multiple relationships to various individuals, social groups, and institutions. The larger number of relationships needed to anchor bisexual identity is a function of two facts. First, landmarks in the mainstream Euro-American sexual landscape are gendered. For example, individuals are recognized as either female or male, woman or man. Social groups include "men," "women," and "lesbians," and institutions include "gay male society," "legally recognized marriage," and "the feminist movement." Second, Euro-American sexual categories are defined in reference to gender; heterosexuality is defined in terms of relationships between persons of different gender, and homosexuality is defined in terms of relationships between persons of same gender. Thus, on the gendered sexual landscape, a minimum of one landmark is necessary to anchor a monosexual identity such as lesbian, gay, or heterosexual. But in this system of dichotomous sexuality based on dichotomous gender, bisexuality can only be understood as a hybrid combination of heterosexuality and homosexuality. Thus, to maintain a *bi*sexual self-description on the gendered landscape, one needs to locate oneself with respect to both female and male, or lesbian/gay and heterosexual, landmarks.

For example, a bisexual identity might represent relationships to two individuals of different genders, as it does to the White man who explained that he adopted his Bisexual identity because he "dated a man and woman at the same time." Or, it might represent relationships to two social groups, men and women, as it does to the Asian-American/Caucasian individual who wrote, "I realized I have always loved men. . . . At the same time I did not cease to love or feel attracted to women, so I discovered I was bisexual." Many bisexuals' identities represent an attraction to one gender as a social group and an actual physical or emotional relationship with a particular individual of the other gender. As one man explained, the incident that led him to adopt a Bisexual identity was "My first same-sex experience, but I realized I was still attracted to women." Although the particular landmarks varied, most bisexual-identified respondents were able to support their bisexual identities only by maintaining relationships to multiple landmarks of both genders.

CHANGES IN THE SEXUAL LANDSCAPE

Whether or not an individual changes co's location on the sexual landscape, the sexual landscape itself might change, creating new opportunities for self-description while transforming or eliminating existing possibilities. The types of landscape change reported by respondents included the appearance of previously invisible landmarks on the sexual landscape and historical changes in the sexual landscape.

Newly visible landmarks might consist of a single individual. For example, one Heterosexual-identified, Bisexual American woman wrote that she "had to sharpen up my own fuzzy feeling about my own bisexuality" when her daughter came out to her as bisexual. The appearance of a bisexual person in her life forced her to consider her relationship to this person, and in the process, to clarify her thoughts about her own sexuality. Conversely, the disappearance of an individual can eliminate the need for an identity that represents one's relationship to that individual, as it did for this Australian woman:

> I really craved to be a "lesbian" or "bisexual"—but somehow I couldn't take this label unless I had sexual encounters with women. . . . My period of confusion and questioning my heterosexuality passed away [when] the woman I was attracted to left—so I told myself I was hetero. again.

25 Historical changes, such as the development of social and political movements, create new social groups and institutions and modify or destroy others. As these historical forces transform the sexual landscape, individuals whose identities located them on the old landscape find that they have to relate themselves to their new environment. For example, in the very early days of the second wave of the (predominantly white) feminist movement, lesbianism was labeled a "lavender herring," and feminist lesbians were encouraged to demonstrate their commitment to the feminist movement by remaining in the closet.[13] But the reconstruction of the relationship between lesbianism and feminism in the early 1970s resulted in the

creation of the category of the "political lesbian" and led many women to adopt lesbian identities as an expression of commitment to the newly reconstituted feminist movement.[14] One respondent wrote that in 1977 she adopted her Lesbian identity because "Thru feminist politics I began to understand that my primary emotional/energetic commitment was with women." Several years earlier, a lesbian identity would not have served to express her feminist "emotional/energetic commitment" to women.

More recently, the development of a small but growing bisexual culture and social structure has created new social and political landmarks with which individuals can anchor bisexual identities. For example, an American woman mentioned that she had realized that she was bisexual since 1976, but that she only adopted a Bisexual identity "in the last five years since there was a movement." Another woman said that she "had previously identified as a Lesbian," but she "became aware of the Bi option" because "there was a growing, visible Bi community." As the number of bisexual social and political institutions continues to increase, more and more people will identify themselves as bisexual, abandoning the identities that they had considered satisfactory only a few years earlier—identities that became unsatisfactory because the landmarks to which they referred changed and new landmarks arose.

Individuals often experience changes in their personal social contexts. It is only later, when individuals look back over their lives and the lives of others, that they will see the changes they experienced as part of more global, historical contexts that had similar effects on other people. Therefore, few respondents referred to the effect of history on their sexual identities, but this lack of reference to historical change was complemented by an abundance of references to changes in respondents' individual social contexts. These alterations in social context were usually significant because they brought with them changes in the language available for self-description.

CHANGES IN THE LANGUAGE AVAILABLE FOR SELF-DESCRIPTION

The distinction between changes in the sexual landscape—whether historical or personal—and changes in language is largely theoretical; in practice, they are usually interdependent and virtually indistinguishable. The relevant distinction between different constructions of the sexual landscape is in the language available for self-description, and the relevant distinctions between various languages are the different landmarks and the different relationships to these landmarks that are created by each language, i.e., in the various ways that they construct the sexual landscape.

Some people intentionally put themselves in new social contexts in the hope of finding a new language for self-description. For example, a White American woman said that she went to Coming Out Day in 1990 because she was unsure about her sexuality, but by the time she left, she was a Dyke. Several respondents mentioned that they had read the book *Bi Any Other name: Bisexual People Speak Out,* and that this book had helped them develop bisexual identities. A Latino-American man explained that he was able to come out as Bisexual after he joined a therapy group in which a bisexual identity was available.

30   I joined a bisexual men's therapy group (while still with my female partner). I had always heard the term but never really claimed it until I joined this group. I think I knew that that's what I was but when you're living in a straight environment, you don't talk about it.

Other people, through no conscious intent of their own, find themselves in social contexts where they become involved in new relationships or encounter new identities, and then discover that they can use these identities to describe themselves. For example, a Native American/Caucasian man reexamined his own "repressed bisexuality" when he observed culturally approved intimacy among men while working in the Middle East. A Caucasian man became a "punk" while serving time in a U.S. Jail; he explained that he "got used to it and they treated me well so I got emotionally involved with them and dependent on them for security. There was no other term for that role." An Indian woman living in the U.S. was introduced to the Kinsey scale during a seminar on religion and sexuality. She learned that everyone "existed somewhere on this continuum" and scored herself right in the middle. Reflecting on the experience, she stated: "From that moment on, I have though of myself continuously as someone who is what I would call today 'bisexual.'" An English man explained that he "never really 'began' to think of myself as bisexual, any more than I guess most straights begin to think of themselves as straight." He had begun to use the word "bisexual" after seeing it appear more and more frequently on electronic mail postings.

Because the terms "lesbian" and "gay" are now nearly household words, they are available as self-descriptors even outside lesbian and gay social contexts. In contrast, the concept of an authentic bisexual identity is still limited to particular social contexts, and most bisexual-identified respondents reported that they had adopted their current sexual identities only after encountering the term "bisexual" for the first time when they joined a bisexual support group, therapy group, or political group. Before they encountered the concept of bisexuality, the only terms that were available to them were synonyms for heterosexual and homosexual. Most had chosen one of these two available identities based on their conceptions of the types of relationships that could be represented by each. For example, one man called himself heterosexual, although he had a male sexual partner, because he preferred his wife as a sexual partner. For him, a heterosexual identity was an accurate description of his location on the sexual landscape because it did not deny his relationship to his male lover; it merely indicated that his relationship to his female lover was stronger. When his male partner introduced him to the term "bisexual," he discovered that bisexual identity could also describe his location by representing both of his relationships, and he changed his identity accordingly.

Some individuals discover an identity only to find that they are barred from participating in the context where the identity is available. Lesbian male-to-female transsexuals, for example, are sometimes rejected by lesbian feminists. One lesbian transsexual explained why she calls herself a "Lesbian-identified Bisexual":

35
> I have always been attracted to and loved women only. I thought I was a straight man. Now I'm a woman but still love women and not men at all. Yet lesbians all reject me as one of them because I'm genetically male. Bisexual women, however, fully accept me.

Excluded from lesbian contexts, she adopted an identity that was available in a bisexual context where she was accepted.

Similarly, queer people of color often find themselves excluded from, tokenized by, or ignored within predominantly Euro-American LesBiGay communities, where positive lesbian, gay, and bisexual identities exist. At the same time, they fear exclusion from their racial or ethnic communities of origin, where positive racial and ethnic identities exist. Few have access to social contexts in which the landscape contains the landmarks necessary to anchor both their sexual identities and their racial or ethnic identities simultaneously.

Language also changes when familiar terms take on new meanings or change in meaning. Many respondents reported that they had been familiar with the term "bisexual" for some time but had understood it as a temporary phase that one passed through when coming out as lesbian or gay or as an identity used by those who wish to deny their homosexuality. Once they encountered the term as a reference to a stable set of relationships involving both female and male landmarks, they became comfortable describing themselves as bisexual. For example, one woman encountered a new meaning for "bisexual" when she began associating with a new group of people.

> [I] went to a bisexual convention. Though I'd known that I liked women and I like men, meeting a group of people who had chosen this as a viable identity—not just a resting place between gay and straight—gave me a word to use with myself and a sense of legitimacy.

In contrast, another woman felt that the meaning of the word had changed over time, eventually enabling her to adopt it as an identity:

40
> For a long time, I was afraid to say I was bisexual, because it was largely regarded as a term for a lesbian who didn't want to "fess up"

and I knew women who were like this and who used the term this way. I've only started calling myself "bisexual" in the last five years because the term seems to have lost the "closeted lesbian" connotation.

Other respondents began identifying themselves as bisexual when they discovered that the term could represent relationships to social and political institutions as well as relationships to individuals. This is a particularly common pattern among previously lesbian-identified Euro-American women, whose lesbian identities represented relationships to lesbian communities and lesbian politics more than relationships to individual women and who were loath to give up their lesbian identities for bisexual identities until they felt that a bisexual identity could connect them to a community and a movement. An American woman who had always "known" that she was bi was unable to identify herself as bisexual until she met Lani Ka'ahumanu, a well-known bisexual activist in the U.S. She said that "hearing [Lani] talk about bisexuality as a 'valid' identity and movement" made it possible for her to "choose this identity wholeheartedly."

For some individuals, a change in the meaning of a term allowed them to maintain an identity that might otherwise have had to change or forced them to change an identity that they might otherwise have been able to keep. An Anglo-American man explained that his concept of "gay" had recently broadened; previously, if he had had a heterosexual encounter, he would have given up his gay identity, but now he says, "If I were to have an occasional heterosexual encounter, I'd still call myself gay, not bisexual." Conversely, a woman who used to identify herself "solely as a Lesbian" was "distressed at the trend of women who used the word Lesbian to be femme, hetero-appearing career women with closet politics." Because of this trend, she no longer feels that the word "lesbian" adequately describes herself; she now calls herself a Dyke, among other things, and is "still sad over the loss of the label Lesbian."

CHANGES IN SOCIAL CONTEXT

The fact that different relationships and languages for self-description are available in different social contexts means that individuals who live their lives in multiple social contexts—which most people do, particularly those who identify as sexual minorities and/or as member of racial or ethnic minorities—have to describe themselves differently in different social contexts. The act of moving from one context to another entails a change in sexual identity simply to maintain an accurate description of one's location on the sexual landscape. At the very least, an individual might have to use different terms to describe coself in a heterosexual context than co uses in a sexual minority context and different terms in a Euro-American cultural context than in other racial and ethnic contexts.

For example, a Jewish American man explained that he often describes himself as "queer" in gay circles because "it expresses my political identity," but that he "generally uses[s] 'bi' in straight circles, since 'queer' is generally considered pejorative." In heterosexual contexts, the term "queer" does not accurately convey his sexual location because the political institution to which it refers—a radical sexual movement—is largely unknown. In contrast to Euro-American sexual culture, which emphasizes the genders of one's sexual partners, the Chicano cultures described by Joseph Carrier incorporate the Mexican cultural emphasis on the role one plays in the sex act over the gender of one's partner.[15] Thus, for Chicanos, the development of a gay identity requires a measure of assimilation to Euro-American culture, and this identity is only viable in contexts in which Euro-American concepts of sexuality operate. A Chicano, therefore, would have to describe his sexuality differently depending on the particular ethnic context he is in.

45   Even within LesBiGay Trans communities, there are contextual variations that necessitate identity changes as one moves from one part of a community to another. Some women identify themselves as bisexual only among other bisexuals and avoid identifying themselves as bisexual among lesbians, because a positive bisexual identity is often not available in lesbian contexts. Among lesbians, they might identify themselves as "lesbians," or they might call themselves "queer," because they feel that this is the most accurate identity available in that context. An Asian-American woman explained that she calls herself "bi" proudly—but only in certain contexts, because in other contexts her bi identity would be misunderstood and, hence, not accurately describe her location on the sexual landscape:

> [I]n a college environment, there are a few "fakes"—bi women who really do embody lots of bad bi stereotypes. In order not to be lumped in with them, I avoid that term here. However, when I go somewhere more Bi-aware . . . more aware of the diversity of us Bi women, I proudly use the term. . . . I think context is very important.

CHANGES IN THE ACCURACY OF SELF-DESCRIPTION

Individuals do not always describe their locations accurately, and identity changes occur as individuals become more accurate or more honest about describing their locations on the sexual landscape. There are many reasons that individuals might intentionally misrepresent their locations, but the most common reason is a belief that other people would disapprove of their true location. Lesbians and gay men often misrepresent their sexual locations when in heterosexual contexts, and bisexual women often misrepresent their location when in lesbian contexts. For example, a White American woman reported that she thinks of herself as a "bi dyke," but until recently, she called herself "queer" because she was afraid "bi dyke" would offend lesbians. She explained that "queer" was a word that she could "use among gay men and lesbians without them knowing I'm bisexual." Unlike the Asian-American woman quoted above, this White woman avoided identifying herself as bisexual in gay and lesbian contexts, not because she thought the term would be misunderstood and hence not accurately represent her, but because she wanted to mislead gay men and lesbians who would disapprove of her true bisexual identity. She also reported that she "just recently felt justified in calling [her]self a 'bi dyke'" among lesbians. In other words, she recently changed the identity she uses in lesbian contexts; this change represented, not a change in her location on the sexual landscape, but a change in her honesty about that location.

Although the politics surrounding bisexual identities are not as intense in gay male communities as they are in lesbian communities, men are also sometimes reluctant to identify themselves as bisexual rather than gay. A Latino man reported that he had known he was bisexual since childhood, but for eleven years he dated women secretly and called himself gay, because he didn't want to lose his friends in the gay community.

It is common for individuals to feel that their previous sexual identities were the result of their own lack of honesty with themselves, even if they did not experience these identities as dishonest at the time. Because "coming out" is traditionally conceptualized as a developmental process of discovering and coming to terms with one's essential sexuality, many people perceive their changes in identity as processes of becoming honest with themselves about their sexuality. For example, a Caucasian man wrote, "I began to question my sexuality and finally admitted that I was in denial about my feelings towards men." Whether the identity changes that these individuals experienced were the result of growing self-honesty, or whether they were the result of actual changes in their relationships or in the languages available to describe their relationships, which in hindsight they interpreted in terms of honesty, is a question that involves a discussion of essential existence that is outside the scope of this article.

THE EFFECT OF CHANGES IN IDENTITY ON THE SEXUAL LANDSCAPE: IDENTITY CHANGE AS A VOLITIONAL ACT

50   So far, I have been discussing various types of contextual changes that can lead to changes in an individual's sexual identity. But individuals do not merely observe the sexual landscape and passively adopt available terms to describe their locations on this landscape. Individuals also influence the landscape, both unintentionally and intentionally. First of all, the very act of locating oneself on the

landscape can alter it. At the very least, describing one's location on the landscape transforms one into a landmark to which other people can relate, such as the daughter, cited previously, who transformed herself on her mother's sexual landscape by identifying herself as bisexual.

Second, individuals who move from one context to another carry with them the memories of each context they have inhabited. Although the landmarks they need to maintain a particular sexual identity might not be readily available in another context, they can import them. In practice, this involves educating people about the existence of the types of people, groups, and institutions with which one has relationships. Coming out to one's parents by introducing them to one's lover is an example of this: the parents become aware of the lover as an individual with which their daughter or son has a relationship. The very act of using an identity term in a context in which it did not previously exist both creates the opportunity to construct for others the landmarks to which it refers and offers the term as a possibility for others in that context.

Third, some people intentionally use their identities to cause changes in particular social contexts. For example, one White American woman explained that she is "working toward the eradication of heterosexism," which she feels "is in part based on the essentialism that says there are relevant, universal differences between men and women." Therefore, in gay and lesbian circles she distinguishes herself by identifying as Bisexual, whereas in straight circles she is content to use the term "queer" and let people assume she is a lesbian. In each context, her identity is chosen for political purposes as a challenge to the identity assumptions usually made by people in that context.

Fourth, some individuals create new identity terms because they find the available ones unsatisfactory. A number of respondents who invented identity terms for themselves later discovered that others had invented the same terms. For example, a woman who calls herself a Bi-dyke said, "I think I made it up for myself (as did many others) out of necessity." Some reported having difficulty using their invented identities to describe themselves to others who are unfamiliar with the identity, so they endeavor to educate others about the meaning of their sexual identities. Through this educational process, they create the language and landmarks necessary to support their newly created identities.

Fifth, individuals who cannot find a context in which a satisfactory identity is available to them sometimes create a context for themselves. Many bisexual support groups have been established by women who found lesbian contexts unsupportive of a bisexual identity. Within these new contexts, a bisexual identity can grow and change in relative freedom from the constraints that are present in established social contexts.

55   Finally, many individuals are not satisfied with the gendered landmarks that are available for the anchoring of sexual identity, so they create new non-gendered landmarks, such as the non-gendered person or the non-gendered social group. Because there are, as of yet, no widely available terms for the description of relationships not tied to such landmarks, some of these individuals refuse to adopt a sexual identity at all. But doing so means spending considerable energy explaining one's location on the sexual landscape to others, as this Euro-American woman explained:

> [F]or most of those years I rarely used the term "bisexual." Instead I'd say "I have no sexual preference," or I gave a long-winded explanation about loving the person, not the gender.

Other individuals adapt existing identities, usually "queer" or "bisexual," to the purpose of representing their relationships to non-gendered landmarks. For example, a transgenderist who was unable to describe herself at all in traditional gendered language, discovered that "queer" surmounted her linguistic problems:

> About a year after I accepted my gender identity it was clear that the words "gay," "lesbian," and many others didn't quite work. And I knew I was not a "classic transsexual" since I was reasonably sure I did not want surgery. After getting involved with Queer Nation, the term "Queer transgenderist" seemed to be just right, and still does.

Similarly, an Asian/Pacific Islander woman explained that she calls herself Queer "because it is an inclusive term. . . . I feel that queer is a term broad enough to encompass my range of ideas and actions." A bisexual identity, on the other hand, is often adopted by people who initially use it to describe relationships to both male- and female-gendered landmarks and then find that bisexual identity is flexible enough to withstand the changes that occur when they begin to think in terms of non-gendered landmarks. For example, a Caucasian man explained that his Bi identity "used to mean I would live and date women and have an occasional affair with a man." Over the past fifteen years, however, he has realized that he is "attracted to people—not their sexual identity" and no longer cares whether his partners are male or female. He has kept his Bi identity and now uses it to refer to his attraction to people regardless of their gender.

BISEXUAL IDENTITY AS THE KEY TO UNDERSTANDING SEXUAL IDENTITY

60   Sexual identity has traditionally been conceptualized as a static description of an individual's sexual essence. From this point of view, alterations in an individual's sexual identity are considered evidence of immaturity, and only one type of identity change—a devel-

opmental process called "coming out"—is validated. Coming out is conceptualized as a process in which individuals become increasingly honest, both with themselves and with others, about the true nature of their essential sexualities.

This conceptualization of sexual identity and sexual identity change is no longer adequate. Sexual identify is more usefully understood as a representation of one's location on the sexual landscape, a location that is described in terms of one's relationships to other people, groups, and institutions on that landscape. From this perspective, identity change that occurs as a result of increasing honesty is only one type among many. Identity changes also occur as mature individuals attempt to accurately describe their locations on the sexual landscape. Sexual identity is thus not a static representation of essential being but a dynamic description of the self in relation to others.

This reconceptualization of sexual identity and sexual identity change calls for a shift in the focus of scientific research. Traditional thinking about sexual identity as a reflection of sexual essence suggests that we should study people who have completed the coming out process, because they are mature individuals whose sexual identities are stable and accurate representations of their essential sexuality. Social scientists working from this perspective studied the process of "coming out" as a topic of interest in its own right, because lesbian and gay people identified it as an important experience in their lives, not because of the light these scientists believed it would shed on the nature of sexual identity. If, however, sexual identity is reconceptualized as a dynamic description of sexual location on a changing sexual landscape, then the key to understanding sexual identity lies in understanding sexual identity change, not sexual identity stability. To understand what sexual identity represents, we have to study the circumstances under which it changes.

But change is relative and can only be perceived in relation to objects other than the self. Therefore, it is the existence of landmarks that makes movement visible; change in an individual's location can be perceived only when that change alters the individual's relationships to defined landmarks. If an individual moves without changing co's relationships to defined landmarks, co's movement will not be perceived as a change, and it will not necessitate a change in self-description.

Herein lies the critical theoretical importance of bisexual identity. Because our sexual landscape is gendered, people who relate to landmarks of only one gender rarely find it necessary to change their sexual identities: a single monosexual identity is often sufficient to carry them through changes in their relationships with individuals, groups, and institutions. The gendered sexual landscape facilitates stable monosexual identities. However, people who relate

to landmarks of both genders sometimes find that they have to alter their identities frequently as their relationships change.
Traditionally, these identity changes have been interpreted as evidence that bisexual people are more "unstable" than lesbian or gay
people or, euphemistically, that they are more "flexible" than either
lesbians and gays or heterosexuals. But frequent identity changes do
not indicate that people who relate to landmarks of both genders
traverse more sexual space than monosexual people do, only that in
the course of their movement they are more likely to alter their relationships to the gendered landmarks defined by a culture that fa-
vors monosexual identity. Because they change their relationships
to the landmarks on the sexual landscape more often, they are the
key to understanding that landscape. Consistently monosexual-
identified people provide little insight into the texture of the gendered landscape on which they locate themselves, because their
movements are not detectable on that landscape and not reflected in
their identities, whereas individuals whose relationships to gendered landmarks change provide clues to the locations of those
landmarks and to the nature of gender itself. The moment of change
reveals the boundaries of gender because the moment of change
marks the crossing of those boundaries.

65   This is not to say that monosexual-identified people necessarily relate to landmarks of only one gender. On the contrary, monosexual-identified people often relate to landmarks of both genders,
but their relationships to landmarks of one or the other gender are
subsumed, rather than represented, by their monosexual identities. Recall, for example, the man mentioned above who identified
himself as heterosexual because he prefers his wife over his male
lover; his heterosexual identity subsumes, but does not represent,
his relationship to his male lover. Or, consider the fact that substantial research shows that many lesbian-identified women have
had heterosexual relationships, a reality which is well known
among lesbians themselves.[16] Sometimes lesbians dismiss these relationships as the result of socialization or social pressure, thereby
negating any implications that these relationships might otherwise
have for perceived essence, and therefore identity. Other times,
lesbians acknowledge these relationships as authentic but subsume
them under lesbian identity, as in a "lesbian who has sex with men."
The fact that monosexual identities subsume relationships with both
genders defines bisexual identities—defined here as identities that
represent relationships with both genders—out of existence.
          If the monosexual construction of the sexual landscape sum-
marily denied the possibility of relating to landmarks of both genders, then the task of creating bisexual identity would be the
relatively simple one of demonstrating that such a possibility existed

and then proposing a language capable of describing these relationships. But the fact that monosexual constructions subsume relationships with both genders presents bisexuals—defined here as people who wish to create bisexual identities—with the more difficult task of reconstructing the sexual landscape. Individuals who wish to develop a language capable of representing relationships to landmarks of both genders have the formidable task of, not merely creating new relationships or demonstrating the existence of previously unnamed relationships, but also reconstructing/relabeling patterns of relationships that have heretofore been constructed as monosexual.

Another approach to the problem of creating bisexual identities is to construct nongendered landmarks and then develop a language capable of representing relationships to them, an approach used by some respondents in the current study. Certain kinds of landmarks, such as social and political institutions, can be created anew. But new types of people can be created only by reconstructing existing people and categories of people. Here again, the creation of a bisexual identity implies a reconstruction of the sexual landscape, this time by reconstructing/relabeling the landmarks on it.

The construction of a bisexual identity, whether via the creation of a language capable of representing relationships to landmarks of both genders or via the creation of non-gendered landmarks, is threatening to the monosexual identity. The reconstruction of relationships to landmarks of both genders implies the destruction of the language that provides people with monosexual identities. The reconstruction of gendered landmarks as nongendered landmarks implies the destruction of the gendered landmarks to which monosexual-identified people relate and with which they anchor their monosexual identities. In other words, bisexual identities are threatening to monosexual identities because they threaten to undermine the bases of monosexual identities. There is, therefore, great resistance on the part of some monosexual-identified people to the construction of bisexual identities. This resistance is born of the fear of existential annihilation, the same existential annihilation that bisexuals experience on the gendered monosexual landscape.

Because bisexual identity is a threat to monosexual identity, bisexuality is often characterized as a challenge to gendered categories and to dualistic thinking in general.[17] Jo Eadie has characterized it as a threat from within, arguing that the bisexuality which threatens lesbians and gay men is really their own bisexuality, with its attendant implication that lesbians and gays are not so clearly different from heterosexuals after all.[18] Bisexuality has also been described as a threat from without—the "double agent" who is dangerous because of co's link to the enemy "camp."[19] Both of these perspectives take dualistic thinking as a given and set up bisexuality as a threat to this thinking by assuming that bisexuality either does not or should not fit into dualistic categories. But, if sexual identity is viewed as representation of one's relationships to landmarks, then sexual identity is a mature state of dynamic self-description. This conception of sexual identity does not lend itself to the formation of categories, including the monosexual categories that allegedly compose the dualistic thinking against which bisexuality is presented as a challenge. Of course, people can build categories and communities based on sexual identity, and categories and communities have been built on monosexual identities. But the dynamic nature of identity is ill-suited for the formation of these categories and communities, which is why they need constant defense. Therefore, the challenge to monosexual identity is posed, not by bisexuality per se, but by the different understanding of sexual identity that an exploration of bisexual identities in a gendered world can facilitate. Monosexual identities are challenged by the dynamic nature of sexual identity; they are unstable and require constant defense and repair even without the threat of a bisexual identity. Bisexuality merely provides a convenient vehicle for identifying the weaknesses that are already inherent in the effort to create stable categories and communities based on dynamic self-descriptions.

70   Any attempt to create stable bisexual identities or bisexual communities will eventually encounter the same problems that lesbian and gay identities and communities now face. As David Bell points out, despite the theoretical attractiveness and exciting revolutionary potential of conceptualizing bisexuality as something that exists outside fixed categories, individuals seeking a "home" attempt to create positively defined bisexual identities and communities.[20] Indeed, success within current modes of political discourse might necessitate the creation of a bisexual "ethnicity."[21] Creating a bisexual "home" or "ethnicity" is difficult, and during the formative stage these difficulties are easily attributed to the adverse conditions afforded by the current gendered, monosexual construction of sexual identity. But, if some people eventually succeed in convincing themselves that they have managed to give a specific and definable form to bisexual identity and bisexual community, they will discover that bisexual identity and community, like their monosexual counterparts, need constant defense. At that point, in accordance with the principles of dialectic change, a new antagonist will arise, and the defenders of bisexual identities and communities will be able to attribute their difficulties to the new antagonist, who will be constructed as a threat. But the new antagonist will no more be the real threat to bisexual identities and communities than a bisexual identity is the real threat to monosexual identities and communities. The

real threat to all identity-based communities is the dynamic nature of identity itself; the appearance of a new antagonist will merely be the symptom of the tension inherent in attempting to build stable identities and communities on dynamic self-descriptions. The revolutionary potential of a bisexual identity is the potential to expose the dynamic nature of sexuality, and it has this potential only insofar as the current landscape is predominantly monosexual and gendered. If we succeed in reconstructing the sexual landscape to support a bisexual identity, we will have destroyed its revolutionary potential. We will have, in effect, created a new aristocracy and postponed the revolutionalization of sexual identity until the arrival of the next antagonist.

Fortunately, bisexual political ideology is not yet moving toward the solidification of a definition of bisexuality. On the contrary, the current tendency is to resist efforts to agree on a definition.[22] If we continue on this path and refuse to follow in the footsteps of lesbian and gay movements toward the creation of a bisexual ethnicity, then we will preserve the revolutionary potential of bisexuality.

Notes

Acknowledgments: This research was supported in part by a grant from the Horace H. Rackham School of Graduate Studies of the University of Michigan in Ann Arbor, by research funding from Hamilton College in Clinton, New York, and by a grant from the Society for the Psychological Study of Social Issues. I am grateful to Jackie Vargas, Ana Morel, Sandy Siemoens, and Michael Peluse for their help in tabulating the data. I am solely responsible for the content of this paper.

1. For example, Beata F. Chapman and JoAnn C. Brannock, "Proposed Model of Lesbian Identity Development: An Empirical Examination," *Journal of Homosexuality* 14, nos. 3/4 (1987): 69–80.

2. Alan P. Bell, Martin S. Weinberg, and Sue Kiefer Hammersmith, *Sexual Preference: Its Development in Men and Women* (Bloomington: Indiana University Press, 1981); Pat Califia, "Lesbian Sexuality," *Journal of Homosexuality* 4, no. 3 (Spring 1979): 255–66; Denise M. Cronin, "Coming Out among Lesbians," in *Sexual Deviance and Sexual Deviants*, ed. Erich Goode and Richard R. Troiden (New York: Morrow, 1974), 268–77; Karla Jay and Allen Young, eds., *The Gay Report: Lesbians and Gay Men Speak Out about Sexual Experiences and Lifestyles* (New York: Simon and Schuster, 1979); Harold D. Kooden, Stephen F. Morin, Dorothy I. Riddle, Martin Rogers, Barbara E. Sang, and Fred Strassburger, *Removing the Stigma: Final Report of the Board of Social and Ethical Responsibility for Psychology's Task Force on the Status of Lesbian and Gay Male Psychologists* (Washington, DC: American Psychological Association, 1979); Gary J. McDonald, "Individual Differences in the Coming Out Process for Gay Men: Implications for Theoretical Models." *Journal of Homosexuality* 8, no. 1 (Fall 1982): 47–60; Carmen de Monteflores and Stephen J. Schultz, "Coming Out: Similarities and Differences for Lesbians and Gay Men," *Journal of Social Issues* 34, no. 3 (1978): 59–72; Dorothy Riddle and Stephen Morin, "Removing the Stigma: Data from Institutions," *APA Monitor* (November 1977): 16–28; Siegrid Shäfer, "Sexual and Social Problems of Lesbians," *Journal of Sex Research* 12, no. 1 (February 1976): 50–69; Richard R. Troiden, *Gay and Lesbian Identity: A Sociological Analysis* (Dix Hills, NY: General Hall, 1988).

3. Henceforth, I will use the terms "bisexual" and "lesbian" to refer to women who were, respectively, self-identified as bisexual and as lesbian at the time of this earlier study.

4. Paula C. Rust, "'Coming Out' in the Age of Social Constructionism: Sexual Identity Formation among Lesbian and Bisexual Women," *Gender and Society* 7, no. 1 (March 1993): 50–77.

5. For example, Chapman and Brannock, "Proposed Model of Lesbian Identity Development."

6. For example, Philip Blumstein and Pepper Schwartz, "Intimate Relationships and the Creation of Sexuality," in *Homosexuality/Heterosexuality: Concepts of Sexual Orientation,* ed. David P. McWhirter, Stephanie A. Sanders, and June M. Reinisch (New York: Oxford University Press, 1990), 307–20; and Kenneth Plummer, *Sexual Stigma: An Interactionist Account* (London: Routledge and Kegan Paul, 1975).

7. For example, Vivienne C. Cass, "Homosexual Identity Formation: A Theoretical Model," *Journal of Homosexuality* 4, no. 3 (Spring 1979): 219–35; Vivienne C. Cass, "The Implications of Homosexual Identity Formation for the Kinsey Model and Scale of Sexual Preference," in *Homosexuality/Heterosexuality,* 239–66; Eli Coleman, "Development Stages of the Coming Out Process," *Journal of Homosexuality* 7, nos. 2/3 (Winter 1981/Spring 1982): 31–34: McDonald, "Individual Differences in the Coming Out Process for Gay Men."

8. I am collecting data via an anonymous self-administered questionnaire containing a postage-paid return envelope inside the U.S. or postal coupons outside the U.S. The cover of the questionnaire tells potential respondents that

> You can fill out this questionnaire if you are bisexual or if you call yourself bisexual, if you are coming out or questioning your sexuality, if you prefer not to label your sexual orientation, if you used to identify as bisexual, if you are lesbian or gay but have felt attracted to or had a sexual or romantic relationship with someone of the other sex at any time in your life, or if you are heterosexual but have felt attracted to or had a sexual or romantic relationship with someone of your own sex at any time in your life.

The cover of the questionnaire encouraged non-eligible individuals to give the questionnaire to an eligible friend. Respondents are, therefore, self-selected. The questionnaire is being distributed through bisexual and bisexual-inclusive social and political organizations: community centers and counseling services for gay, lesbian, and bisexual people and people exploring their sexuality; institutions dedicated to sexuality education and information dissemination; advertisements in bisexual newsletters and alternative community newspapers, fliers in alternative bookstores; conferences on topic related to sexuality and/or gender; electronic main networks; and friendship networks. More detailed information about the methodology will be forthcoming in later publications.

Distribution began in the U.S. in April 1993 and in the United Kingdom in September 1993. To date, questionnaires have been completed and returned by over 450 individuals in the U.S., 46 in the United Kingdom, and 22 in Australia and New Zealand. Men and women are equally represented in all countries, except the U.S., where women constitute 63% of the sample. Slightly under 4% of respondent are transgendered, including postoperative male-to-female transsexuals, non-transsexual transgenderists, and cross-dressers. The age distribution is broader among respondents in the U.S. than the U.K. The ages of U.S. respondents range from eighteen to eighty-two, with 39% in their twenties, 30% in their thirties, 19% in their forties, and 10% fifty years or older. The oldest respondent from the U.K. is fifty-nine years old, and 67% of respondents from the U.K. are in their twenties. The incomes of respondents in both countries follow normal distribution curves. In the U.S., the median income is in the range $20–29,999 with 18% earning less than $10,000 and 21% earning $50,000 or more. In the U.K., the mean income is £14,000, with 20% earning under £5,000 and 20% earning over £25,000. Eleven percent of respondents from the U.S. are people of color, including African-Americans, Asian Americans, Indigenous Peoples, and Latinas/os.

9. "Co" is a generic pronoun that refers to a person who might be female, male, or intersexed, and woman, man, or transgendered. It is used in some alternative communities in the United States whose members believe that gendered language, including the use of the masculine pronoun "he" as a generic pronoun, reinforces gender hierarchies. I use it here because it seems particularly appropriate in a paper that discusses the difficulties that gendered language poses for bisexual-identified people. "Co" is less disruptive to the appearance of written language than slashed formations like "s/he" and "his/hers" and avoids the problems of numerical agreement that arise when "they" is used as a generic pronoun for referring to a single individual.

   I invite the reader to use this chapter as an exercise in non-gendered language. Observe your emotional reactions to the non-gendered pronoun "co," and notice how it changes your understanding of the written word. Later in this paper, I discuss the importation of non-gendered concepts from one social context to another; the paper itself is an example of this process.

10. The terms used to describe respondents' racial and ethnic identities are the terms used by respondents themselves when they were asked, "What is your race and/or ethnicity?" Throughout this chapter, capitalization of identity terms indicates that these are the terms used by respondents themselves. Some respondents belong to small racial or ethnic groups with only a few representatives in this study, more general terms are used to describe their racial/ethnic identity in order to protect their anonymity. For example, respondents descended from indigenous tribes of North America are referred to collectively as Native Americans.

   This is an international study, and respondents are occasionally described in terms of their citizenship or country of residence as well as their racial or ethnic identities. For example, "Irish" indicates that a respondent resides in Ireland. "English" indicates that a respondent resides in England. "Australian" indicates that a respondent resides in Australia, and "American" indicates that a respondent resides in the U.S. This usage of "American" to describe residents of the U.S. is consistent with usage by citizens of other North, Central, and South American countries, who refer to citizens of the U.S. as "Americans" or "Americanos/as," and is not intended to imply that citizens of these other American countries are not also Americans in the continental, rather than the national, sense of the term.

11. Terms representing particular individuals' sexual identities are capitalized. However, when these terms are used to refer to sexual identities in general rather than to the identities of specific individuals, or when they are used as identity descriptors, even if in reference to particular individuals, they are not capitalized. In respondent quotes, respondents' choices regarding capitalization are retained.

12. Quotes from respondents have been edited for space. Identifying personal details have been omitted, and obvious spelling errors have been corrected.

13. Toby Marotta attributed "lavender herring" to Susan Brownmiller, who referred to lesbians as "a lavender herring, perhaps, but surely no clear and present danger." See Toby Marotta, *The Politics of Homosexuality* (Boston: Houghton Mifflin, 1981), 236; and Susan Brownmiller, "Sisterhood Is Powerful," *New York Times Magazine* (15 March 1970): 140.

14. Paula C. Rust, *Bisexuality and the Challenge to Lesbian Politics: Sex, Loyalty, and Revolution* (New York: New York University Press, 1995).

15. Joseph M. Carrier, "'Sex-Role Preference' as an Explanatory Variable in Homosexual Behavior," *Archives of Sexual Behavior* 6, no. 1 (January 1977): 55–63; Joseph M. Carrier, "Miguel: Sexual Life History of a Gay Mexican American," in *Gay Culture in America: Essays from the Field,* ed. Gilbert Herdt (Boston: Beacon Press, 1992), 202–24: J. R. Magaña and J. M. Carrier, "Mexican and Mexican American Male Sexual Behavior and Spread of AIDS in California," *Journal of Sex Research* 28, no. 3(August 1991): 425–41.

16. See Paula C. Rust, "The Politics of Sexual Identity: Sexual Attraction and Behavior among Lesbian and Bisexual Women," *Social Problems* 39, no. 4 (November 1992): 366–86 for data on heterosexual behavior among lesbians who participated in my earlier study of lesbian-identified and bisexual-identified women. Evidence of the prevalence of heterosexual behavior among lesbian-identified women is also provided by Chapman and Brannock, "Proposed Model of Lesbian Identity Development"; Jack H. Hedblom, "Dimensions of Lesbian Sexual Experience," *Archives of Sexual Behavior* 2, no. 4 (December 1973): 329–41: and Marcel T. Saghir and Eli Robins, *Male and Female Homosexuality: A Comprehensive Investigation* (Baltimore, MD: Williams and Wilkins, 1973).

17. Bisexuality has been described as or presumed to be a threat to dualistic or dichotomous thinking, particularly about gender, by numerous authors. Some examples not elsewhere cited in this chapter are Marilyn J. Freimuth and Gail A. Hornstein, "A Critical Examination of the Concept of Gender," *Sex Roles* 8, no. 5 (May 1982): 515–32; Richard J. Hoffman, "Vices, Gods, and Virtues: Cosmology as a Mediating Factor in Attitudes toward Male Homosexuality," *Journal of Homosexuality* 9, nos. 2/3 (Winter 1983/Spring 1984): 27–44; Abraham D. Lavender and Lauren C. Bressler. "Nondualists as Deviants: Female Bisexuals Compared to Female Heterosexuals-Homosexuals," *Deviant Behavior: An Interdisciplinary Journal* 2, no. 2 (January–March 1981): 155–65: Amanda Udis-Kessler, "Present Tense: Biphobia as a Crisis of Meaning," in *Bi Any Other Name: Bisexual People Speak Out,* ed. Loraine Hutchins and Lani Ka'ahumanu (Boston, MA: Alyson, 1991), 350–58; and the essays by Ruth Gibian, "Refusing Certainty: Toward a Bisexuality of Wholeness," Kathleen Bennett, "Feminist Bisexuality: A Both/And Option for an Either/Or World," and Karin Baker, "Bisexual Feminist Politics: Because Bisexuality Is Not Enough, "in *Closer to Home: Bisexuality and Feminism,* ed. Elizabeth Reba Weise (Seattle, WA: Seal Press, 1992).

18. Jo Eadie, "Activating Bisexuality: Towards a Bi/Sexual Politics," in *Activating Theory: Lesbian, Gay, Bisexual Politics,* ed. Joseph Bristow and Angelia R. Wilson (London: Lawrence and Wishart, 1993), 139–70.

19. Clare Hemmings, "Resituating the Bisexual Body: From Identity to Difference," in *Activating Theory,* 118–38.

20. David Bell, "The Trouble with Bisexualtiy," paper presented at the IBG, Nottingham, U.K., 1994.

21. Paula C. Rust, "Who Are We and Where Do We Go from Here? Conceptualizing Bisexuality," in *Closer to Home,* 281–310.

The term bisexual "ethnicity" refers to the notion of bisexuality as a group identity analogous to racial or ethnic group identities. It involves, for example, the concepts of group heritage and group pride. The concept of sexual ethnicity is drawn from Steven Epstein, "Gay Politics, Ethnic Identity: The Limits of Social Constructionism," *Socialist Review* 93, no. 4 (1987): 9–53, and Richard K. Herrell, "The Symbolic Strategies of Chicago's Gay and Lesbian Pride Day Parade," in *Gay Culture in America,* 225–52. Epstein and Herrell argue that the gay and lesbian movement, which is modeled after earlier racial and ethnic movements, is based on the notion of gayness as an ethnicity.

22. Rust, *Bisexuality and the Challenge to Lesbian Politics.*

Bibliography

Baker, Karin. "Bisexual Feminist Politics: Because Bisexuality Is Not Enough." *Closer to Home: Bisexuality and Feminism.* Ed. Elizabeth Reba Weise. Seattle, WA: Seal Press, 1992. 255–67.

Bell, Alan P., Martin S. Weinberg, and Sue Keifer Hammersmith. *Sexual Preference: Its Development in Men and Women.* Bloomington: Indiana University Press, 1981.

Bell, David. "The Trouble with Bisexuality." Paper presented at the IBG, Nottingham, U.K., 1994.

Bennett, Kathleen, "Feminist Bisexuality: A Both/And Option for an Either/Or World." *Closer to Home: Bisexuality and Feminism.* Ed. Elizabeth Reba Weise. Seattle, WA: Seal Press, 1992. 205–31.

Blumstein, Philip, and Pepper Schwartz, "Intimate Relationships and the Creation of Sexuality." *Homosexuality/ Heterosexuality: concepts of Sexual Orientation.* Ed. David P. McWhirter, Stephanie A. Sanders, and June M. Reinisch. New York: Oxford University Press, 1990. 307–20.

Califia, Pat. "Lesbian Sexuality." *Journal of Homosexuality* 4, no. 3 (Spring 1979): 255–66.

Carrier, Joseph M. "'Sex-role Preference' as an Explanatory Variable in Homosexual Behavior." *Archives of Sexual Behavior* 6, no. 1(January 1977): 53–65.

———. "Miguel: Sexual Life History of a Gay Mexican American." *Gay Culture in America: Essays from the Field.* Ed. Gilbert Herdt. Boston: Beacon Press, 1992. 202–24.

Cass, Vivienne C. "Homosexual Identity Formation: A Theoretical Model." *Journal of Homosexuality* 4, no. 3 (Spring 1979): 219–35.

———. "The Implications of Homosexual Identity Formation for the Kinsey Model and Scale of Sexual Preference." *Homosexuality/Heterosexuality: Concepts of Sexual Orientation.* Ed. David P. McWhirter, Stephanie A. Sanders, and June M. Reinisch New York: Oxford University Press, 1990. 230–66.

Chapman, Beata E., and JoAnn C. Brannock. "Proposed Model of Lesbian Identity Development: An Empirical Examination," *Journal of Homosexuality* 14, nos. 3/4 (1987): 69–80.

Coleman, Eli. "Developmental Stages of the Coming Out Process." *Journal of Homosexuality* 7, nos. 2/3 (Winter 1981/Spring 1982): 31–43.

Cronin, Denise M. "Coming Out among Lesbians." *Sexual Deviance and Sexual Deviants.* Ed. Erich Goode and Richard R. Troiden. New York: William Morrow, 1974. 268–77.

de Monteflores, Carmen, and Stephen J. Schultz. "Coming Out: Similarities and Differences for Lesbians and Gay Men." *Journal of Social Issues* 34, no. 3 (1978): 59–72.

Eadie, Jo. "Activating Bisexuality: Towards a Bi/Sexual Politics." *Activating Theory: Lesbian, Gay, Bisexual Politics.* Ed. Joseph Bristow and Angelia R. Wilson. London: Lawrence and Wishart, 1993. 139–70.

Epstein, Steven. "Gay Politics, Ethnic Identity: The Limits of Social Constructionism." *Socialist Review* 93, no. 4 (1987): 9–53.

Freimuth, Marilyn J., and Gail A. Hornstein. "A Critical Examination of the Concept of Gender." *Sex Roles* 8, no. 5 (May 1982): 515–32.

Gibian, Ruth. "Refusing Certainty: Toward a Bisexuality of Wholeness." *Closer to Home: Bisexuality and Feminism.* Ed. Elizabeth Reba Weise. Seattle, WA: Seal Press, 1992. 3–16.

Hedblom. Jack H. "Dimensions of Lesbian Sexual Experience." *Archives of Sexual Behavior* 2, no. 4 (December 1973): 329–41.

Hemmings, Clare. "Resituating the Bisexual Body: From Identity to Difference." *Activating Theory: Lesbian, Gay, Bisexual Politics.* Ed. Joseph Bristow and Angelia R. Wilson. London" Lawrence and Wishart, 1993. 118–38.

Herrell, Richard K. "The Symbolic Strategies of Chicago's Gay and Lesbian Pride Day Parade." *Gay Culture in America: Essays from the Field.* Ed. Gilbert Herdt. Boston: Beacon Press, 1992. 225–52.

Hoffman, Richard J. "Vices, Gods, and Virtues: Cosmology as a Mediating Factor in Attitudes toward Male Homosexuality." *Journal of Homosexuality* 9, nos. 2/3 (Winter 1983/Spring 1984): 27–44.

Hutchins, Loraine, and Lani Kaahumanu, ed. *Bi Any Other Name: Bisexual People Speak Out.* Boston, MA: Alyson, 1991.

Jay, Karla, and Allen Young, eds. *The Gay Report: Lesbians and Gay Men Speak Out about Sexual Experiences and Lifestyles.* New York: Simon and Schuster, 1979.

Kooden, Harold D., Stephen F. Morin, Dorothy I. Riddle, Martin Rogers, Barbara E. Sang, and Fred Strassburger. *Removing the Stigma: Final Report of the Board of Social and Ethical Responsibility for Psychology's Task Force on the Status of Lesbian and Gay Male Psychologists.* Washington, DC: American Psychological Association, 1979.

Lavender, Abraham D., and Lauren C. Bressler. "Nondualists as Deviants: Female Bisexuals Compared to Female Heterosexuals/Homosexuals." *Deviant Behavior: An Interdisciplinary Journal* 2, no. 2 (January–March 1981): 155–65.

Magaña, J. R., and J. M. Carrier. "Mexican and Mexican American Male Sexual Behavior and Spread of AIDS in California." *Journal of Sex Research* 28, no. 3 (August 1991): 425–41.

Marotta, Toby. *The Politics of Homosexuality.* Boston: Houghton Mifflin, 1981.

McDonald, Gary J. "Individual Differences in the Coming Out Process for Gay Men: Implications for Theoretical Models." *Journal of Homosexuality* 8, no. 1 (Fall 1982): 47–60.

Plummer, Kenneth. *Sexual Stigma: An Interactionist Account.* London: Routledge and Kegan Paul, 1975

Riddle, Dorothy and Stephen Morin. "Removing the Stigma: Data from Institutions." *APA Monitor* (November 1977): 16–28.

Rust, Paula C. "The Politics of Sexual Identity: Sexual Attraction and Behavior among Lesbian and Bisexual Women." *Social Problems* 39, no. 4 (November 1992):366–86.

———. "Who Are We and Where Do We Go from Here? Conceptualizing Bisexuality." *Closer to Home: Bisexuality and Feminism.* Ed. Elizabeth Reba Weise. Seattle, WA: Seal Press, 1992. 281–310.

———. "'Coming Out' in the Age of Social Constructionism: Sexual Identity Formation among Lesbian and Bisexual Women." *Gender and Society* 7, no. 1 (March 1993): 50–77.

————. *Bisexuality and the Challenge to Lesbian Politics: Sex, Loyalty, and Revolution.* New York: New York University Press, 1995.

Saghir, Marcel T., and Eli Robins. *Male and Female Homosexuality: A Comprehensive Investigation.* Baltimore, MD: Williams and Wilkins, 1973.

Shäfer, Siegrid. "Sexual and Social Problems of Lesbians." *Journal of Sex Research* 12, no. 1 (February 1976): 50–69.

Troiden, Richard R. *Gay and Lesbian Identity: A Sociological Analysis.* Dix Hills, NY: General Hall, 1988.

Udis-Kessler, Amanda. "Present Tense: Biphobia as a Crisis of Meaning." *Bi Any Other Name: Bisexual People Speak Out.* Ed. Loraine Hutchins and Lani Kaahumanu. Boston, MA: Alyson, 1991. 350–58.

Reflective Reading, Informal Writing

REFLECTING ON THE READING:

- Rust uses the term "sexual landscape" both in her title and as part of her argument. What does she mean by this term? Is it something more or different from sexual identity? What part does Rust's notion of sexual landscape play in her argument that identity is socially constructed? What, in this context, does "socially constructed" mean?
- Rust offers a list of possible sexual identities including lesbian, gay, straight, bisexual, polysexual, queer, and pansensual. She writes that "sexual identity is . . . not a static representation of essential being but a dynamic description of the self in relation to others." What do you think she means by this? What is sexual identity if it is not a static thing? How is it a description of the self in relation to others?
- Rust argues that "the construction of a bisexual identity, whether via the creation of a language capable of representing relationship to landmarks of both genders or via the creation of non-gendered relationships, is threatening to monosexual identities." If bisexual identities are in fact threatening, what does this suggest about the way our culture tends to define or "construct" sexual identity? Why would a monosexual identity be threatened by bisexual identity?

UNDERSTANDING RHETORICAL STRATEGIES:

- Rust's article is the most typically academic of the essays in Chapter 2. What do you notice about tone, style, and voice in this article? In what ways does it seem strikingly different from the other essays? In what ways similar?

- How does Rust inform her readers of the methodology she used to gather data? Does she tell you enough? Too much? Should she have introduced this information in some other way? Why or why not?
- Rust uses the word "co" throughout the essay. She explains the word in a footnote. Does her choice to use "co" bother you as a reader? Why or why not? Do you think it fulfills the rhetorical purpose she wants it to?
- The complex relationship between thought and language continues to perplex scholars and researchers. Relying on common sense, most of us would probably say that the idea comes first, then we look for the words to say it. But when Rust writes of "changes in the language available for self-description," she seems to be suggesting that we cannot arrive at a new sense of our identity until we have the language with which to describe it. Or, words first, then the idea. What evidence does she produce in support of this counter-intuitive notion? Do you find her evidence persuasive?

INFORMAL WRITING:

- Write in response to the idea that sexual identity can change, and is in fact socially constructed. Do you agree with Rust? Why or why not?
- Write about what you think sexual identity means in contemporary culture. How important is sexual identity in the overall understanding of who people are? In what contexts does sexual identity seem to matter or become important?
- Examine and analyze your personal response to this reading. What are your assumptions about sexual identity? Where do you think you got or learned these assumptions?

Chapter Assignment Sequences

Sequence One: American Dreams

"Ruth's Song (Because She Could Not Sing It)"
"The Hurt, Betrayed Son"
"An American of Color"
"The Domestication of Motherhood"

SMALL GROUP DISCUSSION:

1. We often speak of the "American Dream" as if there were only one. How would you describe the mythical "American Dream"? How do the dreams of Ruth Steinem, Gloria Steinem, Rambo, and Victor Villanueva compare to this archetype? How do you account for the discrepancy between their dreams and the American Dream?

2. Using the essays listed here as a starting point, how do such issues as gender and race affect one's pursuit of the American Dream, and the likelihood that one will achieve it?

WRITING:

1. Drawing upon the essays listed, write an essay in which you define the "American Dream," then describe some of the obstacles to achieving it. How, in your opinion, might some of these obstacles be either surmounted or removed?

2. Focusing on Ruth Steinem, Rambo, or Victor Villanueva, treat your subject as a case study of the kinds of obstacles—be they psychological, social, political, or economic—individuals face on their way to fulfilling their version of the American Dream. How did your subject get sidetracked or, as may be the case, succeed? Was it primarily a matter of individual character and will, or of socially constructed realities?

3. For many, the American Dream is primarily a dream of prosperity. And yet according to Engels, as quoted by Adrienne Rich, our capitalistic economy, the very means by which we obtain our wealth, is itself the main force behind the subjugation of women.

   Write an essay in which you argue that our nation's political or economic system does or does not make it more difficult for certain groups, such as women or people of color, to achieve the American Dream.

Sequence Two: Self vs. Role

"Ruth's Song (Because She Could Not Sing It)"
"The Hurt, Betrayed Son"
"An American of Color"

SMALL GROUP DISCUSSION:

1.   Together, make a list of all the socially constructed roles you find yourself playing in the course of a week. These may include, for example, son, daughter, husband, wife, brother, sister, student, employee, American, heterosexual male, African-American, and so on. Assuming we all play more than one role, can you think of occasions of role conflict—when two or more of the roles you ordinarily play came into conflict?

2.   Have you ever been in a situation where the role you were expected to play felt like a straitjacket, limiting your expression of the person you believe yourself to be? What, if anything, did you do about it?

3.   To look at the matter from the opposite angle, can you think of situations in which having a clearly defined role to fall back on was an advantage, saving you time, or trouble, or both?

WRITING:

1.   Often we feel as if the socially constructed roles we are called upon to play don't fit the people we are within. Select any one of the essays listed and write an essay describing both the nature of the socially imposed role involved and the personal reality (or realities) in conflict with it. Finally, how does the individual in question resolve (or fail to resolve) the conflict? Can you imagine alternative forms of resolution?

2.   Why do we have to have socially defined roles, anyway? What good are they? Why can't we just "be ourselves"? Write an essay in which you attempt to answer these questions, drawing evidence from the story of Ruth Steinem, Rambo, or Victor Villanueva (or any combination of the three).

3.   Since we aren't born with instruction booklets, these socially constructed roles we've been discussing must be something we learn. Thinking about one of the roles you play (gender or race, for example), how much of it is biological, or genetic, and how much of it is learned? As for the part that is learned, how did you "learn your lines"? From what social influences, from which people, did you learn the role? Compare your learning process with that of Ruth Steinem, or Rambo, or Victor Villanueva. Would you say you have been "programmed," as Doug Robinson says of Rambo, or have you been left with a good deal of freedom to reinvent the role, should you wish to do so?

Sequence Three: The Process of Social Construction

"An American of Color"
"Sexual Identity and Bisexual Identities"
"The Domestication of Motherhood"

SMALL GROUP DISCUSSION:

1. Is the sentence "Columbus discovered America in 1492" an historical fact, or a socially constructed statement? Examining each of the words in the sentence (and even the date) in turn, do you find any that are false, debatable, or only partially true? Alternatively, if there is a sense in which this statement is true, true for whom? Whose world view is left out of this sentence?

2. In Sequence Two we considered the process by which individuals learn their roles. Now we would like you to turn your attention to the process(es) by which society creates them—that is, the process of social construction. Reflecting on all five of the essays in this chapter, make a list of the people, the traditions, and the institutions that seem to be behind this process. Can you think of additional influencing forces?

3. Think of one type of role you ordinarily play (gender, racial, etc.). Describe that role as fully as you can. What parts of it are biological or genetic, what parts socially defined? Thinking about the parts that are social, speculate about where that particular role definition came from. What people, traditions, institutions, and other social practices reinforce that particular role definition? Why?

WRITING:

1. Of course, the true origins of many of our social practices remain shrouded in history, and so with much of the process of social construction. And history itself is, after all, generally written by the winners, as one commentator put it. One good way to get at this process, however, is to ask "Who profits by this arrangement?" Write an essay in which you consider one of the roles you play in your everyday life (gender, racial, occupational, etc.), and describe that role as fully as you can. Then ask the question, "Who profits by defining this particular role in this particular way"? Once you have arrived at a "who," go on to consider the "how." Draw upon Villanueva, Rust, or Rich, using their methods as appropriate.

2. Villanueva, Rich, and Rust each embody different views of the process of social construction and different ways of illustrating this process in action. Write an essay comparing any two of these figures with respect to the way they imagine the process of social construction, and the kind of evidence they present in support of their views. Which view do you find more effective, and for what purpose?

3. Often when we think of social construction, we think of the influence of individual role models, or a particular type of television ad, or some

other singular event. But Adrienne Rich attributes current gender role definitions to large-scale institutions such as capitalism, psychoanalysis, and even religion. Write an essay in which you consider the impact of a major social institution (for example religion, law, education, American history) in shaping a role you play.

Engaging Culture: The Reflexive Self

Reflective Prewriting

1. Write about your current understanding of the distinction between reflection and reflexivity. As you think back over the school year (or years) has there been anything in your studies—something you've read, written, heard, watched, or researched—that has triggered a reflective or reflexive moment, change, or action for you? If so, can you describe it? If not, why do you think your schooling has not generated either reflection or reflexivity?

2. How would you describe or define private writing and public writing? Are they alike in any way? Is one more important to you than the other? Why or why not? Is one more appropriate for school than the other? Why or why not? Is personal writing the same thing as private writing? Is social writing the same as public writing?

3. Write about what expectations you have when you know you are going to be reading or writing an academic essay. What rules do you think a writer writing an academic essay should follow? Why, and where did you learn this? Do you think there is something that might be the opposite of an academic essay? If so, what would you call that kind of writing? What does academic writing have to do with the world at large? Who benefits from academic writing?

INTRODUCTION

In Chapter 1, "Exploring the Self: Reflection," you read a number of essays of self-reflection and were encouraged to engage in similar reflection yourself. We asked you to turn a penetrating eye inward, consider thoughtfully who you are, what you think, and why you think the way you do. We think it is important to reflect on your own identity, your *self*, before contemplating the impact society has on you, and before setting out to act in the world. "Know thyself," read the ancient inscription at the Delphic oracle. Yet we are not encouraging you to think of yourself as an isolated, autonomous entity, somehow beyond the reach of social influences, as some kind of loner, hermit, or rugged individualist.

All of us probably like to think of ourselves this way from time to time, but before long we run smack into the reality that a sizeable chunk of our identity is, in fact, social in origin. Chapter 2, "Self As Social Artifact," explores this notion. For much of our lives we enact roles shaped by others before us—"the student," "the wife or husband," "the parent," "the professional"—but it is not always clear whether we should see this fact as a positive or negative element in our lives. The roles imposed on us can seem as limiting as straitjackets, as was the case with Ruth Steinem, or with Rambo. Yet the roles we inherit can be changed from within. We can reinvent them, reaccentuate them, or recombine them in new ways; emphasize one role (or set of roles) over another. There are ways in which socially constructed roles actually help us, or enable us to get on with our lives. Imagine a potential parent, teacher, or lawyer having to create the role from scratch—especially in a crisis. In these as in other cases, traditionally defined roles serve as guidelines, as models to emulate (or to depart from, as the need arises). Roles are an important part of how we learn. In short, we can let role definitions limit our freedom, or we can use them to our advantage, to fulfill our own needs.

In other words, the fact that we find ourselves inextricably enmeshed in a social context can be positive, if only we know how to go about it. This is where reflexivity comes in. In the Introduction we cited Donna Qualley's definition of reflexivity:

> A response triggered by dialectical engagement with the other—an idea, theory, person, culture, text, or even an other part of one's self. . . . By dialectical, I mean an engagement that is ongoing and recursive as opposed to a single, momentary encounter. In the process of trying to understand an other, our own beliefs and assumptions are disclosed, and these assumptions, themselves, can become objects of examination and critique.

(Turns of Thought, 11)

Reflexivity, then, involves using another's point of view to learn something new about your own. It is not a mechanical thing; rather, it requires considerable imagination and empathy to climb into another's skin and view the world through his or her eyes. It is a disciplined effort to "de-center," to move beyond the center of your own ego to reach a new vantage point, or perspective, from which to look. As such, reflexivity is a powerful aid to independent thought because it can give you some distance from your own deeply held ideas, values, and assumptions.

Everyone engages in something very close to reflexivity at one time or another. When you find yourself in a tight situation and catch yourself asking, "What would Mom do in this situation," or "How would my coach deal with this," you are getting close, especially if you are referring not to a single quotation or slogan but to a whole set of beliefs. But reflexivity, as we understand it, involves a more sustained effort. Academic thinking and writing rely on it, which is why most of the selections in this chapter are by academic writers: Jane Tompkins, "Me and My Shadow"; Clifford Geertz, "'From the Native's Point of View': On the Nature of Anthropological Understanding"; Gloria Anzaldua, "Tlilli, Tlapalli: The Path of the Red and Black Ink"; James William Gibson, "Paintball as Combat Sport"; and Patricia J. Williams, "The Brass Ring and the Deep Blue Sea."

As you read these selections, look for reflexivity at work. To understand reflexivity is to understand a central fact of academic writing. Academic writers might "read" political developments in Chile through the lens provided by Marx, the novels of D. H. Lawrence as Freud might read them, or the intellectual development of a group of children from the perspective of Piaget. How do the authors of the following essays use reflexivity? How might you use it in your own writing? Continue working in your journal. Particularly if you are keeping a dialectical notebook, consider using it to practice reflexivity. For example, respond to a series of entries as if you were Jane Tompkins or Clifford Geertz.

Relying as heavily as it does on empathy, reflexivity provides a bridge to Chapter 4, "Acting in the Community." To work successfully in the community requires a strenuous effort to imagine the world from the point of view of those you are working with. Such work demands a combination of empathy, understanding, and self-awareness–all linked, and promoted, by reflexivity.

JANE TOMPKINS

Jane Tompkins began her academic career by earning her bachelor's degree at Bryn Mawr College in 1961, her master's degree from Yale one year later, and her Ph.D. from Yale in 1966. Tompkins' swift entry into the academic world and the process of her intellectual and professional transformation has been preserved in her published writing since the beginning of her career. By 1992, Tompkins' work, *West of Everything: The Inner Life of Westerns,* was nominated for the Pulitzer Prize for nonfiction. Most recently, her work, *A Life in School,* has raised some controversy over what writing can be labeled "academic" or "scholarly" and whether personal writing can dwell within this realm. This work focuses on the emotional dimensions of teaching and has been labeled as a memoir (personal writing) while also dealing with a history of authoritarian teaching patterns that Tompkins experienced both as a teacher and as a student. Her "memoir" calls for a reform of such teaching and suggests that colleges need to focus on the whole human being, not just the intellect. The following essay, "Me and My Shadow" (1987) builds the framework for her current work. In this essay, she practices her private voice in public for the first time.

Tompkins insists on finding and using language to talk about the self within academe, focusing on the self and the imagination as well as the intellect. As colleges and universities grow more closely aligned with the corporate world and students look to higher education as the door to a secure career, Tompkins addresses the role of the self and the inner lives of students in pursuit of their professions. She believes that in order to produce the knowledge and skills students need to enter "lucrative professions," higher education cuts students off from both their inner selves and the world around them. Students may be prepared to attain a professional degree, but will not be developed as whole human beings. Such wholeness requires self-examination. According to Tompkins, higher education must provide an "opportunity for people to look at themselves and to understand who they are and where they are in their lives." This is "absolutely essential," because without it, "education is, if not worthless, only partial."

For herself as well as for her students, writing provides a way into understanding the self. Tompkins said in an interview about her writing and her commitment to a writing group, "people grow through their writing. Where they're going in their lives and their writing are not two separate things." Serving as an example of her own pedagogy and critical theory, Tompkins began experimenting with her own personal voice within academic writing as seen in the following essay. As is evident here, she shows how personal writing permits "fragmentation, permitting lots of different selves, or different aspects of the self." She looks at other academic voices and honestly assesses which ones matter to her, and in mattering to her personally, which voices convey and create meaning and knowledge. Through the process of her inquiry, she reveals and justifies the value of the personal as academic, the personal voice as legitimate scholarship, and the personally relevant as relevant scholarship. As you read "Me and My Shadow," think about the places in school where you have or have not been allowed to use your personal "voice" and experiences.

Me and My Shadow

I wrote this essay in answer to Ellen Messer-Davidow's 'The philosophical bases of feminist literary criticisms,' which appeared in the Fall 1987 issue of *New Literary History* along with several replies, including a shorter version of this one. As if it weren't distraction enough that my essay depends on someone else's, I want, before you've even read it, to defend it from an accusation. Believing that my reply, which turns its back on theory, constituted a return to the 'rhetoric of presence,' to an 'earlier, naive, untheoretical feminism,' someone, whom I'll call the unfriendly reader, complained that I was making the 'old patriarchal gesture of representation' whose effect had been to marginalize women, thus 'reinforcing the very stereotypes women and minorities have fought so hard to overcome.' I want to reply to this objection because I think it is mistaken and because it reproduces exactly the way I used to feel about feminist criticism when it first appeared in the late 1960s.

I wanted nothing to do with it. It was embarrassing to see women, with whom one was necessarily identified, insisting in print on the differences between men's and women's experience, focusing obsessively on women authors, women characters, women's issues. How pathetic, I thought, to have to call attention to yourself in that way. And in such bad taste. It was the worst kind of special pleading, an admission of weakness so blatant it made me ashamed. What I felt then, and what I think my unfriendly reader feels now, is a version of what women who are new to feminism often feel: that if we don't call attention to ourselves *as* women, but just shut up about it and do our work, no one will notice the difference and everything will be OK.

Women who adopt this line are, understandably, afraid. Afraid of being confused with the weaker sex, the sex that goes around whining and talking about itself in an unseemly way, that can't or won't do what the big boys do ('tough it out') and so won't ever be allowed to play in the big boys' games. I am sympathetic with this position. Not long ago, as organizer of an MLA session entitled 'Professional politics: women and the institution,' I urged a large roomful of women to 'get theory' because I thought that doing theory would admit us to the big leagues and enable us at the same time to argue a feminist case in the most unimpeachable terms—those that men had supplied. I busily took my own advice, which was good as far as it went. But I now see that there has been a price for this, at least there has been for me; it is the subject of my reply to Ellen. I now tend to think that theory itself, at least as it is usually practiced, may be one of the patriarchal gestures women *and* men ought to avoid.

There are two voices inside me answering, answering to, Ellen's essay. One is the voice of a critic who wants to correct a mistake in the essay's view of epistemology. The other is the voice of a person who wants to write about her feelings (I have wanted to do this for a long time but have felt too embarrassed). This person feels it is wrong to criticize the essay philosophically, and even beside the point: because a critique of the kind the critic has in mind only insulates academic discourse further from the issues that make feminism matter. That make *her* matter. The critic, meanwhile, believes such feelings, and the attitudes that inform them, are soft-minded, self-indulgent, and unprofessional.

5   These beings exist separately but not apart. One writes for professional journals, the other in diaries, late at night. One uses words like 'context' and 'intelligibility,' likes to win arguments, see her name in print, and give graduate students hardheaded advice. The other has hardly ever been heard from. She had a short story published once in a university literary magazine, but her works exist chiefly in notebooks and manila folders labelled 'Journal' and 'Private.' This person talks on the telephone a lot to her friends, has seen psychiatrists, likes cappuccino, worries about the state of her soul. Her father is ill right now, and one of her friends recently committed suicide.

The dichotomy drawn here is false—and not false. I mean in reality there's no split. It's the same person who feels and who discourses about epistemology. The problem is that you can't talk about your private life in the course of doing your professional work. You have to pretend that epistemology, or whatever you're writing about, has nothing to do with your life, that it's more exalted, more important, because it (supposedly) *transcends* the merely personal. Well, I'm tired of the conventions that keep discussions of epistemology, or James Joyce, segregated from meditations on what is happening outside my window or inside my heart. The public–private dichotomy, which is to say, the public–private *hierarchy*, is a founding condition of female oppression. I say to hell with it. The reason I feel embarrassed at my own attempts to speak personally in a professional context is that I have been conditioned to feel that way. That's all there is to it.

I think people are scared to talk about themselves, that they haven't got the guts to do it. I think readers want to know about each other. Sometimes, when a writer introduces some personal bit of story into an essay, I can hardly contain my pleasure. I love writers who write about their own experience. I feel I'm being nourished by them, that I'm being allowed to enter into a personal relationship with them. That I can match my own experience up with theirs, feel cousin to them, and say, yes, that's how it is.

> When he casts his leaves forth upon the wind [said Hawthorne], the author addresses, not the many who will fling aside his volume, or never take it up, but the few who will understand him. . . . As if the printed book, thrown at large on the wide world, were certain to find out the divided segment of the writer's own nature, and complete his circle of existence by bringing him into communion with it. . . . And so as thoughts are frozen and utterance, benumbed unless the speaker stand in some true relation with this audience—it may be pardonable to imagine that a friend, a kind and apprehensive, though not the closest friend, is listening to our talk. (Nathaniel Hawthorne, 'The Custom-House,' *The Scarlet Letter*, pp. 5–6)

Hawthorne's sensitivity to the relationship that writing implies is rare in academic prose, even when the subject would seem to make awareness of the reader inevitable. Alison Jaggar gave a lecture recently that crystallized the problem. Western epistemology, she argued, is shaped by the belief that emotion should be excluded from the process of attaining knowledge. Because women in our culture are not simply encouraged but *required* to be the bearers of emotion, which men are culturally conditioned to repress, an epistemology which excludes emotions from the process of attaining knowledge radically undercuts women's epistemic authority. The idea that the conventions defining legitimate sources of knowledge overlapped with the conventions defining appropriate gender behavior (male) came to me as a blinding insight. I saw that I had been socialized from birth to feel and act in ways that automatically excluded me from participating in the culture's most valued activities. No wonder I felt so uncomfortable in the postures academic prose forced me to assume; it was like wearing men's jeans.

10   Ellen Messer-Davidow's essay participates—as Jaggar's lecture and my précis of it did—in the conventions of Western rationalism. It adopts the impersonal, technical vocabulary of the epistemic ideology it seeks to dislocate. The political problem posed by my need to reply to the essay is this: to adhere to the conventions is to uphold a male standard of rationality that militates against women's being recognized as culturally legitimate sources of knowledge. To break with the convention is to risk not being heard at all.

This is how I would reply to Ellen's essay if I were to do it in the professionally sanctioned way.

The essay provides feminist critics with an overarching framework for thinking about what they do, both in relation to mainstream criticism and in relation to feminist work in other fields. It allows the reader to see women's studies as a whole, furnishing useful categories for organizing a confusing and miscellaneous array of materials. It also provides excellent summaries of a wide variety of books and essays that readers might not otherwise encounter. The enterprise is carried out without pointed attacks on other theorists, without creating a cumbersome new vocabulary, without exhibitionistic displays of intellect or esoteric learning. Its practical aim—to define a field within which debate can take place—is fulfilled by *New Literary History*'s decision to publish it, and to do so in a format which includes replies.

(Very nice, Jane. You sound so reasonable and generous. But, as anybody can tell, that is just the obligatory pat on the back before the stab in the entrails.)

The difficulty with the essay from a philosophical, as opposed to a practical, point of view is that the theory it offers as a basis for future work stems from a confused notion of what an epistemology is. The author says: 'An epistemology . . . consists of assumptions that knowers make about the entities and processes in a domain of study, the relations that obtain among them, and the proper methods for investigating them' (p. 87). I want to quarrel with this definition. Epistemology, strictly speaking, is a *theory* about the origins and nature of knowledge. As such, it is a set of ideas explicitly held and consciously elaborated, and thus belongs to the practice of a sub-category of philosophy called epistemology. The fact that there is a branch of philosophy given over to the study of what knowledge is and how it is acquired is important, because it means that such theories are generated not in relation to this or that 'domain of study' but in relation to one another: that is, within the context of already existing epistemological theories. They are rarely based upon a study of the practices of investigators within a particular field.

15 An epistemology does not consist of 'assumptions that knowers make' in a particular field; it is a theory about how knowledge is acquired which makes sense, chiefly, in relation to other such theories. What Messer-Davidow offers as the 'epistemology' of traditional literary critics is not *their* epistemology, if in fact they have one, but her description of what she assumes their assumptions are, a description which may or may not be correct. Moreover, if literary critics should indeed elaborate a theory of how they got their beliefs, that theory would have no privileged position in relation to their actual assumptions. It would simply be another theory. This distinction—

between actual assumptions and an observer's description of them (even when one is observing one's own practice)—is crucial because it points to an all-important fact about the relation of epistemology to what really gets done in a given domain of study, namely this: that epistemology, a theory about how one gets one's knowledge, in no way determines the particular knowledge that one has.

This fact is important because Messer-Davidow assumes that if we change our epistemology, our practice as critics will change, too. Specifically, she wants us to give up the subject–object theory, in which 'knowledge is an abstract representation of objective existence,' for a theory which says that what counts as knowledge is a function of situation and perspective. She believes that it follows from this latter theory that knowledge will become more equitable, more self-aware, and more humane.

I disagree. Knowing that my knowledge is perspectival, language-based, culturally constructed, or what have you, does not change in the slightest the things I believe to be true. All that it changes is what I think about how we get knowledge. The insight that my ideas are all products of the situation I occupy in the world applies to all of my ideas equally (including the idea that knowledge is culturally based); and to all of everybody else's ideas as well. So where does this get us? Right back to where we were before, mainly. I still believe what I believe and, if you differ with me, think that you are wrong. If I want to change your mind I still have to persuade you that I am right by using evidence, reasons, chains of inference, citations of authority, analogies, illustrations, and so on. Believing that what I believe comes from my being in a particular cultural framework does not change my relation to my beliefs. I still believe them just as much as if I thought they came from God, or the laws of nature, or my autonomous self.

Here endeth the epistle.

But while I think Ellen is wrong in thinking that a change of epistemology can mean a change in the kinds of things we think, I am in sympathy with the ends she has in view. This sympathy prompts me to say that my professionally correct reply is not on target. Because the target, the goal, rather, is not to be fighting over these questions, trying to beat the other person down. (What the goal is, it is harder to say.) Intellectual debate, if it were in the right spirit, would be wonderful. But I don't know how to be in the right spirit, exactly, can't make points without sounding rather superior and smug. Most of all, I don't know how to enter the debate without leaving everything else behind—the birds outside my window, my grief over Janice, just myself as a person sitting here in stockinged feet, a little bit chilly because the windows are open, and thinking about going to the bathroom. But not going yet.

20   I find that when I try to write in my 'other' voice, I am immediately critical of it. It wobbles, vacillates back and forth, is neither this nor that. The voice in which I write about epistemology is familiar, I know how it ought to sound. This voice, though, I hardly know. I don't even know if it has anything to say. But if I never write in it, it never will. So I have to try. (That is why, you see, this doesn't sound too good. It isn't a practiced performance, it hasn't got a surface. I'm asking you to bear with me while I try, hoping that this, what I write, will express something you yourself have felt or will help you find a part of yourself that you would like to express).

The thing I want to say is that I've been hiding a part of myself for a long time. I've known it was there but I couldn't listen because there was no place for this person in literary criticism. The criticism I would like to write would always take off from personal experience. Would always be in some way a chronicle of my hours and days. Would speak in a voice which can talk about everything, would reach out to a reader like me and touch me where I want to be touched. Susan Griffin's voice in 'The way of all ideology.' I want to speak in what Ursula LeGuin, at the Bryn Mawr College commencement in 1986, called the 'mother tongue.' This is LeGuin speaking:

> The dialect of the father tongue that you and I learned best in college . . . only lectures. . . . Many believe this dialect—the expository and particularly scientific discourse—is the *highest* form of language, the true language, of which all other uses of words are primitive vestiges. . . . And it is indeed a High Language . . . Newton's *Principia* was written in it in Latin . . . and Kant wrote German in it, and Marx, Darwin, Freud, Boas, Foucault, all the great scientists and social thinkers wrote it. It is the language of thought that seeks objectivity.
>
> . . . The essential gesture of the father tongue is not reasoning, but distancing—making a gap, a space, between the subject or self and the object or other. . . . Everywhere now everybody speaks [this] language in laboratories and government buildings and headquarters and offices of business. . . . The father tongue is spoken from above. It goes one way. No answer is expected, or heard.
>
> . . . The mother tongue, spoken or written, expects an answer. It is conversation, a word the root of which means 'turning together.' The mother tongue is language not as mere communication, but as relation, relationship. It connects . . . Its power is not in dividing but in binding. . . . We all know it by heart. John have you got your umbrella I think it's going to rain. Can you come play with me? If I told you once I told you a hundred times. . . . O what am I going to do? . . . Pass the soy sauce please. Oh, shit . . . You look like what the cat dragged in. (pp. 3–4)

25   Much of what I'm saying elaborates or circles around these quotes from LeGuin. I find that having released myself from the duty to say things I'm not interested in, in a language I resist, I feel free to entertain other people's voices. Quoting them becomes a pleasure of appreciation rather than the obligatory giving of credit, because

when I write in a voice that is not struggling to be heard through the screen of a forced language, I no longer feel that it is not I who am speaking, and so, there is more room for what others have said.

One sentence in Ellen's essay stuck out for me the first time I read it and the second and the third: 'In time we can build a synchronous account of our subject matters as we glissade among them and turn upon ourselves.' (p. 79)

What attracted me to the sentence was the 'glissade.' Fluidity, flexibility, versatility, mobility. Moving from one thing to another without embarrassment. It is a tenet of feminist rhetoric that the person is political, but who in the academy acts on this where language is concerned? We all speak the father tongue, which is impersonal, while decrying the fathers' ideas. All of what I have written so far is in a kind of watered-down expository prose. Not much imagery. No description of concrete things. Only that one word, 'glissade.'

> *Like black swallows swooping and gliding*
> *in a flurry of entangled loops and curves* . . .

Two lines of a poem I memorized in high school are what the word 'glissade' called to mind. Turning upon ourselves. Turning, weaving, bending, unbending, moving in loops and curves.

30   I don't believe we can ever turn upon ourselves in the sense Ellen intends. You can't get behind the thing that casts the shadow. *You* cast the shadow. As soon as you turn, the shadow falls in another place. Is still your shadow. You have not got 'behind' yourself. That is why self-consciousness is not the way to make ourselves better than we are.

Just me and my shadow, walkin' down the avenue.

It is a beautiful day here in North Carolina. The first day that is both cool and sunny all summer. After a terrible summer, first drought, then heat-wave, then torrential rain, trees down, flooding. Now, finally, beautiful weather. A tree outside my window just brushed by red, with one fully red leaf. (This is what I want you to see. A person sitting in stockinged feet looking out of her window—a floor to ceiling rectangle filled with green, with one red leaf. The season poised, sunny and chill, ready to rush down the incline into autumn. But perfect, and still. Not going yet.)

My response to this essay is not a response to something Ellen Messer-Davidow has written; it is a response to something within myself. As I reread the opening pages I feel myself being squeezed into a straitjacket; I wriggle, I will not go in. As I read the list 'subject matters, methods of reasoning, and epistemology,' the words will not go down. They belong to a debate whose susurrus hardly reaches my ears.

The liberation Ellen promises from the straitjacket of a subject–object epistemology is one I experienced some time ago. Mine didn't take the form she outlines, but it was close enough. I discovered, or thought I discovered, that the post-structuralist way of understanding language and knowledge enabled me to say what I wanted about the world. It enabled me to do this because it pointed out that the world I knew was a construct of ways of thinking about it, and as such, had no privileged claim on the truth. Truth in fact would always be just such a construction, and so, one could offer another, competing, description and so help to change the world that was.

35   The catch was that anything I might say or imagine was itself the product of an already existing discourse. Not something 'I' had made up but a way of constructing things I had absorbed from the intellectual surround. Post-structuralism's proposition about the constructed nature of things held good, but that did not mean that the world could be changed by an act of will. For, as we are looking at this or that phenomenon and re-seeing it, re-thinking it, the rest of the world, that part from which we do the seeing, it still there, in place, real, irrefragable as a whole, and making visible what we see, though changed by it, too.

This little lecture pretends to something I no longer want to claim. The pretense is in the tone and level of the language, not in what it says about poststructuralism. The claim being made by the language is analogous to what Barthes calls the 'reality effect' of historical writing, whose real message is not that this or that happened but that reality exists. So the claim of this language I've been using (and am using right now) lies in its implicit deification of the speaker. Let's call it the 'authority effect.' I cannot describe the pretense except to talk about what it ignores: the human frailty of the speaker, his body, his emotions, his history; the moment of intercourse with the reader—acknowledgment of the other person's presence, feelings, needs. This 'authoritative' language speaks as though the other person weren't there. Or perhaps more accurately, it doesn't bother to imagine who, as Hawthorne said, is listening to our talk.

How can we speak personally to one another and yet not be self-centered? How can we be part of the great world and yet remain loyal to ourselves?

It seems to me that I am trying to write out of my experience without acknowledging any discontinuity between this and the subject matter of the profession I work in. And at the same time find that I no longer want to write about that subject matter, as it appears in Ellen's essay. I am, on the one hand, demanding a connection between literary theory and my own life, and asserting, on the other, that there is no connection.

But here is a connection. I learned what epistemology I know from my husband. I think of it as more his game than mine. It's a game I enjoy playing but which I no longer need or want to play. I want to declare my independence of it, of him. (Part of what is going on here has to do with a need I have to make sure I'm not being absorbed in someone else's personality.) What I am breaking away from is both my conformity to the conventions of a male professional practice and my intellectual dependence on my husband. How can I talk about such things in public? How can I *not*.

40   Looking for something to read this morning, I took three books down from my literary theory shelf, in order to prove a point. The first book was Félix Guattari's *Molecular Revolution*. I find it difficult to read, and therefore have read very little of it, but according to a student who is a disciple of Deleuze and Guattari, 'molecular revolution' has to do with getting away from ideology and enacting revolution within daily life. It is specific, not programmed—that is, it does not have a 'method,' nor 'steps,' and it is neither psychoanalytic nor marxist, although its discourse seems shaped by those discourses, antithetically. From this kind of revolution, said I to myself, disingenuously, one would expect some recognition of the personal. A revolution that started with daily life would have to begin, or at least would have sometimes to reside, at home. So I open at a section entitled 'Towards a new vocabulary,' looking for something in the mother tongue, and this is what I find:

> The distinction I am proposing between machine and structure is based solely on the way we use the words; we may consider that we are merely dealing with a 'written device' of the kind one has to invent for dealing with a mathematical problem, or with an axiom that may have to be reconsidered at a particular stage of development, or again with the kind of machine we shall be talking about here.
>   I want therefore to make it clear that I am putting into parentheses the fact that, in reality, a machine is inseparable from its structural articulations and conversely, that each contingent structure is dominated (and this is what I want to demonstrate) by a system of machines, or at the very least by one logic machine. (p. 111)

At this point, I start to skip, reading only the first sentence of each paragraph.

45   'We may say of structure that it positions its elements . . . .'
           'The agent of action, whose definition here does not extend beyond this principle of reciprocal determination . . . .'
           'The machine, on the other hand remains essentially remote . . . .'
           'The history of technology is dated . . . .'
           'Yesterday's machine, today's and tomorrow's, are not related in their structural determinations . . . .'

I find this language incredibly alienating. In fact, the paragraph after the one I stopped at begins: 'The individual's relation to the machine has been described by sociologists following Friedmann as one of fundamental alienation.' I will return to this essay some day and read it. I sense that it will have something interesting to say. But the effort is too great now. What strikes me now is the incredibly distancing effect of this language. It is totally abstract and impersonal. Though the author uses the first person ('The distinction I am proposing,' 'I want therefore to make it clear'), it quickly became clear to me that he had no interest whatsoever in the personal, or in concrete situations as I understand them—a specific person, at a specific machine, somewhere in time and space, with something on his/her mind, real noises, smells, aches and pains. He has no interest in his own experience of machines, or in explaining why he is writing about them, what they mean to him personally. I take down the next book: *Poetry and Repression* by Harold Bloom.

50   This book should contain some reference to the self, to the author's self, to ourselves, to how people feel, to how the author feels, since its subject is psychological: repression. I open the book at page 1 and read:

> Jacques Derrida asks a central question in his essay on 'Freud and the Scene of Writing': 'What is a text, and what must the psyche be if it can be represented by a text?' My narrow concern with poetry prompts the contrary question: 'What is a psyche, and what must a text be if it can be represented by a psyche?' Both Derrida's question and my own require exploration of three terms: 'psyche,' 'text,' 'represented.'
>   'Psyche is ultimately from the Indo-European root. (p. 1)

—and I stop reading.

The subject of poetry and repression will involve the asking and answering of questions about 'a text'—a generalized, non-particular object that has been the subject of endless discussion for the past twenty years,—and about an equally disembodied 'psyche' in relation to the thing called 'a text'—not, to my mind, or rather in view of my desires, a very promising relation in which to consider it. Answering these questions, moreover, will 'require' (on whose part, I wonder?) the 'exploration' of 'three terms.' Before we get to the things themselves—psyches, texts—we shall have to spend a lot of time looking at them *as words*. With the beginning of the next paragraph, we get down to the etymology of 'psyche.' With my agenda, I get off the bus here.

But first I look through the book. Bloom is arguing against canonical readings (of some very canonical poems) and for readings that are not exactly personal, but in which the drama of a self is constantly being played out on a cosmic stage—lots of references to God, kingdom, Paradise, the fall, the eternal—a biblical stage on which, apparently, only men are players (God, Freud, Christ, Nietzsche, and the poets). It is a drama that, although I can see how gripping Bloom can make it, will pall for me because it isn't *my* drama.

55   Book number three, Michel Foucault's *History of Sexuality*, is more promising. Section One is entitled "We 'other Victorians.'" So Foucault is acknowledging his and our implication in the object of the study. This book will in some way be about 'ourselves,' which is what I want. It begins:

> For a long time, the story goes, we supported a Victorian regime, and we continue to be dominated by it even today. Thus the image of the imperial prude is emblazoned on our restrained, mute, and hypocritical sexuality. (p. 3)

Who, exactly are 'we'? Foucault is simply using the convention in which the author establishes common ground with his reader by using the first person plural—a presumptuous, though usually successful, move. Presumptuous because it presumes that we are really like him, and successful because, especially when an author is famous, and even when he isn't, 'our' instinct (I criticize the practice and engage in it too) is to want to cooperate, to be included in the circle and the author is drawing so cosily around 'us.' It is chummy, this 'we.' It feels good, for a little while, until it starts to feel coercive, until 'we' are subscribing to things that 'I' don't believe.

There is no specific reference to the author's self, no attempt to specify himself. It continues:

> At the beginning of the seventeenth century ...

60   I know now where we are going. We are going to history. 'At the beginning of the seventeenth century a certain frankness was still common, it would seem.' Generalizations about the past, though pleasantly qualified ('a certain frankness.' 'it would seem'), are nevertheless disappointingly magisterial. Things continue in a generalizing vein—'It was a time of direct gestures, shameless discourse, and open transgressions.' It's not so much that I don't believe him as that I am uncomfortable with the level or the mode of discourse. It is everything that, I thought, Foucault was trying to get away from, in *The Archaeology of Knowledge*. The primacy of the subject as the point of view from which history could be written, the bland assumption of authority, the taking over of time, of substance, of event, the imperialism of description from a unified perspective. Even though the subject matter interests me—sex, hypocrisy, whether or not our view of Victorianism and of ourselves in relation to it is correct—I am not eager to read on. The point of view is discouraging. It will march along giving orders, barking out commands. I'm not willing to go along for the march, not even on Foucault's say so (I am, or have been, an extravagant admirer of his).

So I turn to 'my' books. To the women's section of my shelves. I take down, unerringly, an anthology called *The Powers of Desire* edited by Christine Stansell, Ann Snitow, and Sharon Thompson. I turn, almost as unerringly, to an essay by Jessica Benjamin entitled, 'Master and slave: the fantasy of erotic domination,' and begin to read:

> This essay is concerned with the violence of erotic domination. It is about the strange union of rationality and violence that is made in the secret heart of our culture and sometimes enacted in the body. This union has inspired some of the holiest imagery of religious transcendence and now comes to light at the porno newsstands, where women are regularly depicted in the bonds of love. But the slave of love is not always a woman, not always a heterosexual; the fantasy of erotic domination permeates all sexual imagery in our culture. (p. 281)

I am completely hooked, I am going to read this essay from beginning to end and proceed to do so. It gets better, much better, as it goes along. In fact, it gets so good, I find myself putting it down and straying from it because the subject is *so* close to home, and therefore so threatening, that I need relief from it, little breathers, before I can go on. I underline vigorously and often. Think of people I should give it to read (my husband, this colleague, that colleague).

But wait a minute. There is no personal reference here. The author deals, like Foucault, in generalities. In even bigger ones than his: hers aren't limited to the seventeenth century or the Victorian era. She generalizes about religion, rationality, violence. Why am I not turned off by this as I was in Foucault's case? Why don't I reject this as a grand drama in the style of Bloom? Why don't I bridle at the abstractions as I did when reading Guattari? Well?

65   The answer is, I see the abstractions as concrete and the issues as personal. They are already personal for me without being personal*ized* because they concern things I've been thinking about for some time, struggling with, trying to figure out for myself. I don't need the author to identify her own involvement, I don't need her to concretize, because these things are already personal and concrete for me. The erotic is already eroticized.

Probably, when Guattari picks up an article whose first sentence has the words 'machine,' 'structure,' and 'determination,' he cathects it immediately. Great stuff. Juicy, terrific. The same would go for Bloom on encountering multiple references to Nietzsche, representation, God the father, and the Sublime. But isn't erotic domination, as a subject, surer to arouse strong feeling than systems of machines or the psyche that can be represented as a text? Clearly, the answer depends on the readership. The people at the convenience store where I stop to get gas and buy milk would find all these passages equally baffling. Though they *might* have uneasy stirrings when they read Jessica Benjamin. 'Erotic domination,' especially when coupled with 'porno newsstands,' does call some feelings into play almost no matter who you are in this culture.

But I will concede the point. What is personal is completely a function of what is perceived as personal. And what is perceived as personal by men, or rather, what is gripping, significant, 'juicy,' is different from what is felt to be that way by women. For what we are really talking about is not the personal as such, what we are talking about is what is important, answers one's needs, strikes one as immediately *interesting*. For women, the personal is such a category.

In literary criticism, we have moved from the New Criticism, which was anti-personal and declared the personal off-limits at every turn—the intentional fallacy, the affective fallacy—to structuralism, which does away with the self altogether—at least as something unique and important to consider—to deconstruction, which subsumes everything in language and makes the self non-selfconsistent, ungraspable, a floating signifier, and finally to new historicism which re-institutes the discourse of the object—'In the seventeenth century'—with occasional side glances at how the author's 'situatedness' affects his writing.

The female subject *par excellence,* which is her self and her experiences, has once more been elided by literary criticism.

70   The question is, why did this happen? One might have imagined a different outcome. The 1960s paved the way for a new personalism in literary discourse by opening literary discussion up to politics, to psychology, to the 'reader,' to the effects of style. What happened to deflect criticism into the impersonal labyrinths of 'language,' 'discourse,' 'system,' 'network,' and now, with Guattari, 'machine'?

I met Ellen Messer-Davidow last summer at the School of Criticism and Theory where she was the undoubted leader of the women who were there. She organized them, led them (I might as well say us, since, although I was on the faculty as a visiting lecturer, she led me, too). At the end of the summer we put on a symposium, a kind of teach-in on feminist criticism and theory, of which none was being offered that summer. I thought it really worked. Some people, eager to advertise their intellectual superiority, murmured disappointment at the 'level' of discussion (code for, 'my mind is finer and more rigorous than yours'). One person who spoke out at the closing session said he felt bulldozed: a more honest and useful response. The point is that Ellen's leadership affected the experience of everyone at the School that summer. What she offered was not an intellectual performance calculated to draw attention to the quality of her mind, but a sustained effort of practical courage that changed the situation we were in. I think that the kind of thing Ellen did should be included in our concept of criticism: analysis that is not an end in itself but pressure brought to bear on a situation.

Now it's time to talk about something that's central to everything I've been saying so far, although it doesn't *show*, as we used to say about the slips we used to wear. If I had to bet on it, I would say that Ellen Messer-Davidow was motivated last summer, and probably in her essay, by anger (forgive me, Ellen, if I am wrong) anger at her, our, exclusion from what was being studied at the School, our exclusion from the discourse of 'Western man.' I interpret her behavior this way because anger is what fuels my engagement with feminist issues; an absolute fury that has never even been tapped, relatively speaking. It's time to talk about his now, because it's so central, at least for me. I hate men for the way they treat women, and pretending that women aren't there is one of the ways I hate most.

Last night I saw a movie called *Gunfight at the OK Corral*, starring Burt Lancaster and Kirk Douglas. The movie is patently about the love-relationship between the characters these men play—Wyatt Earp and Doc Holliday. The women in the movie are merely pawns that serve in various ways to reflect the characters of the men, and to advance the story of their relationship to one another. There is a particularly humiliating part, played by Jo Van Fleet, the part of Doc Holliday's mistress—Kate Fisher—whom he treats abominably (everybody in the movie acknowledges this, it's not just me saying so). This woman is degraded over and over again. She is a whore, she is a drunkard, she is a clinging woman, she betrays the life of Wyatt Earp in order to get Doc Holladay back, she is *no longer young* (perhaps this is her chief sin). And her words are always in vain, they are chaff, less than nothing, another sign of her degradation.

Now Doc Holladay is a similarly degraded character. He used to be a dentist and is now a gambler, who lives to get other people's money away from them; he is a drunk, and he abuses the woman who loves him. But his weaknesses, in the perspective of the movie, are glamorous. He is irresistible, charming, seductive, handsome, witty, commanding; it's no wonder Wyatt Earp falls for him, who wouldn't? The degradation doesn't stick to Kirk Douglas; it is all absorbed by his female counterpart, the 'slut,' Jo Van Fleet. We are embarrassed every time she appears on the screen, because every time, she is humiliated further.

75   What enrages me is the way women are used as extensions of men, mirrors of men, devices for showing men off, devices for helping men get what they want. They are never there in their own right, or rarely. The world of the Western contains no women.

Sometimes I think *the world* contains no women.

Why am I so angry?

My anger is partly the result of having been an only child who caved in to authority very early on. As a result I've built up a huge storehouse of hatred and resentment against people in authority over me (mostly male). Hatred and resentment and attraction.

Why should poor men be made the object of this old pent-up anger? (Old anger is the best anger, the meanest, the truest, the most intense. Old anger is pure because it's been dislocated from its source for so long, has had the chance to ferment, to feed on itself for so many years, so that it is nothing but anger. All cause, all relation to the outside world, long since sloughed off, withered away. The rage I feel inside me now is the distillation of forty-six years. It has had a long time to simmer, to harden, to become adamantine, a black slab that glows in the dark.)

80   Are all feminists fueled by such rage? Is the molten lava of millenia of hatred boiling below the surface of every essay, every book, every syllabus, every newsletter, every little magazine? I imagine that I can open the front of my stomach like a door, reach in, and pluck from memory the rooted sorrow, pull it out, root and branch. But where, or rather, who, would I be then? I am attached to this rage. It is a source of identity for me. It is a motivator, an explainer, a justifier, a no-need-to-say-more greeter at the door. If I were to eradicate this anger somehow, what would I do? Volunteer work all day long?

A therapist once suggested to me that I blamed on sexism a lot of stuff that really had to do with my own childhood. Her view was basically the one articulated in Alice Miller's *The Drama of the Gifted Child*, in which the good child has been made to develop a false self by parents who cathect the child narcissistically. My therapist meant that if I worked out some of my problems—as she understood them, on a psychological level—my feminist rage would subside.

Maybe it would, but that wouldn't touch the issue of female oppression. Here is what Miller says about this:

> Political action can be fed by the unconscious anger of children who have been . . . misused, imprisoned, exploited, cramped, and drilled. . . . If, however, disillusionment and the resultant mourning can be lived through . . . , then social and political disengagement do not usually follow, but the patient's actions are freed from the compulsion to repeat. (p. 101)

According to Miller's theory, the critical voice inside me, the voice I noticed butting in, belittling, doubting, being wise, is 'the contemptuous introject.' The introjection of authorities who manipulated me, without necessarily meaning to. I think that if you can come to terms with your 'contemptuous introjects,' learn to forgive and understand them, your anger will go away. But if you're not angry, can you still act? Will you still care enough to write the letters, make the phone calls, attend the meetings? You need to find another center within yourself from which to act. A center of outgoing, outflowing, giving feelings. Love instead of anger. I'm embarrassed to say words like this because I've been taught they are mushy and sentimental and smack of cheap popular psychology. I've been taught to look down on people who read M. Scott Peck and Leo Buscaglia and Harold Kushner, because they're people who haven't very much education, and because they're mostly women. Or if not women, then people who take responsibility for learning how to deal with their feelings, who take responsibility for marriages that are going bad, for children who are in trouble, for friends who need help, for themselves. The disdain for popular psychology and for words like 'love' and 'giving' is part of the police action that academic intellectuals wage ceaselessly against feeling, against women, against what is personal. The ridiculing of the 'touchy-feely,' of the 'Mickey Mouse,' of the sentimental (often associated with teaching that takes students' concerns into account), belongs to the tradition Alison Jaggar rightly characterized as founding knowledge in the denial of emotion. It is looking down on women, with whom feelings are associated, and on the activities with which women are identified: mother, nurse, teacher, social worker, volunteer.

85   So for a while I can't talk about epistemology. I can't deal with the philosophical bases of feminist literary criticisms. I can't strap myself psychically into an apparatus that will produce the right gestures when I begin to move. I have to deal with the trashing of emotion, and with my anger against it.

This one time I've taken off the straitjacket, and it feels so good.

Notes

Parts of this essay are reprinted from *New Literary History* 19 (Autumn 1987), by kind permission.

Works Cited

Benjamin, Jessica 1983. 'Master and slave: the fantasy of erotic domination,' in *The Powers of Desire: The Politics of Sexuality*, ed. Ann Snitow, Christine Stansell, and Sharon Thompson. New York: Monthly Review Press: 280–9.

Bloom, Harold 1976. *Poetry and Repression: Revision from Blake to Stevens.* New Haven, Conn.: Yale University Press.

Foucault, Michel 1980. *The History of Sexuality, Volume I: An Introduction.* Trans. Robert Hurley. New York: Vintage Books. Copyright 1978 by Random House, Inc. [Originally published in French as *La Volonté de Savoir.* Paris: Editions Gaillimard, 1976.]

Griffin, Susan 1982. 'The way of all ideology,' in *Made from the Earth: an Anthology of Writings.* New York: Harper and Row: 161–82.

Guattari, Félix 1984. *Molecular Revolution: Psychiatry and Politics.* Trans. Rosemary Sheed, intro. David Cooper. New York: Penguin Books. [First published as *Psychanalyse et transversalité* (1972), and *La Révolution moléculaire* (1977).]

Hawthorne, Nathaniel 1960–1. *The Scarlet Letter and Other Tales of the Puritans*, Ed. with an intro. and notes by Harry Levin. Boston, Mass.: Houghton Mifflin Co.

LeGuin, Ursula 1986. 'The mother tongue,' *Bryn Mawr Alumnae Bulletin* (Summer): 3–4.

Miller, Alice 1983. *The Drama of the Gifted Child*. New York: Basic Books.

Reflective Reading, Informal Writing

REFLECTING ON THE READING:

- Tompkins refers to the "two voices inside me" as she responds to an essay by Ellen Messer-Davidow. How do the two voices differ? Where do they come from? How does this idea of the two voices relate to the central idea of the essay?

- Although Tompkins is reacting against developments in literary criticism, in particular, she is also reacting more generally to the conventions of academic discourse and the conventions related to the process of attaining knowledge (epistemology), which that discourse embodies. What's wrong with academia's definition of what counts as knowledge? With its characteristic ways of conveying or expressing that knowledge? Assuming you agree with Tompkins that these are problems, what can be done to correct them?

- Review Donna Qualley's definition of "reflexivity," quoted in the Introduction to Chapter 3. Can what Jane Tompkins is doing here be seen as a "dialectical engagement with . . . an other part of one's self"? What does Qualley say about the impact of reflexivity on one's original beliefs? Do we see some such result in Tompkins?

- Does the rage Tompkins speaks of toward the end of her essay compare with the "killing rage" of bell hooks (Chapter 2)? Where does this rage come from, and what does she use it to accomplish?

UNDERSTANDING RHETORICAL STRATEGIES:

- Do you find that Tompkins' "two voices" are stylistically different? Describe the stylistic features of each voice, and locate passages exemplifying each.

- Work through the essay, finding the points at which Tompkins switches from one voice to another. Do these transitions correspond with shifts in the ideas being developed? A related question: How does Tompkins decide when to refer to her colleague as "Ellen," and when as "Messer-Davidow"?

- Tompkins examines passages from Guattari, Bloom, Foucault, and Stansell. Why does she object to three of them and approve of the fourth? To what extent are stylistic features involved in her response?

INFORMAL WRITING:

- "The public–private dichotomy, which is to say, the public-private *hierarchy*, is a founding condition of female oppression. I say to hell with it." Write an essay about this dichotomy and Tompkins' attitude toward it. Does her essay attack this dichotomy or enact it? Or both?
- Find an example of academic discourse—say, a scholarly journal article—and analyze it. Does it demonstrate the features of academic writing that Tompkins objects to? Or does it include features she would approve? Is it an example of the "mother tongue" or the "father tongue"? Write about the sample you are working with, writing from what you imagine Tompkins' point of view would be.
- At one point Tompkins writes, "You can't get behind the thing that casts the shadow. *You* cast the shadow. As soon as you turn, the shadow falls in another place. It is still your shadow. You have not got "beyond" yourself. That is why self-consciousness is not the way to make ourselves better than we are." Later she states that "As we are looking at this or that phenomenon and re-seeing it, re-thinking it, the rest of the world, that part from which we do the seeing, is still there . . . ." And elsewhere: "Believing that what I believe comes from being in a particular cultural framework does not change my relation to my beliefs. I still believe them . . . ." Explain how these quotations are related. What do they suggest about the possibilities for reflexivity? What do they have to do with the main point of the essay? The title?

GLORIA ANZALDUA

Gloria Anzaldua grew up on a ranch named Jesus Maria of the Valley of South Texas. Her father died when she was 15, and Anzaldua and her family worked in the fields of south Texas to earn a living. Anzaldua labored in the fields until she earned her bachelor's degree from Pan American University in 1969. She later completed her master's degree in English and education at the University of Texas, Austin in 1972.

As a child, Anzaldua first caught a glimpse of other worlds and other ways of being from books. She learned about lives and cultures outside of her own Chicano culture in south Texas. As a writer, she aspires to provide the same honest glimpse into her world and her culture for her readers. Such honesty and in-depth study of her own life have not come without sacrifice. Anzaldua and her family have clashed over her Chicana-feminist-lesbian politics and her use of personal history in her writing. Her readers, however, appreciate her accessible language and personal, open writing style.

What her readers appreciate, Anzaldua labels "low theory." In academia, "high theory" is the norm. Anzaldua believes "high theory" requires writers to be objective and distanced, and use abstract, esoteric language. A theorist must set aside her own ideas and depend on a canon of accepted literature and theory. "High theory" does not depend on personal stories for evidence. Anzaldua's writing, however, mixes personal stories and genres like poetry and narrative to theorize her life experience and culture, and, as in this excerpt from her book, *Borderlands: La Frontera* (1987), she mixes Spanish and English. The theories, facts, philosophy, and debates presented in Anzaldua's writing pertain directly to her own life, to her personal history, and therefore, to our lived experience as well.

Gloria Anzaldua states, "I am my language"; ethnic identity and linguistic identity are the same. Our language, the words we use, reflect our culture and our experiences. By rendering her experiences honestly and powerfully, Anzaldua helps readers reflect upon their own experiences, cultures, and beliefs and come to a better understanding of themselves. As she says, by changing herself, she changes the world. Much of what Anzaldua says about her work, about personal experience and writing, seems similar to what Victor Villanueva has also said about his writing. Would you make the same arguments for your own writing?

Tlilli, Tlapalli: The Path of the Red and Black Ink

"Out of poverty, poetry;
out of suffering, song."
—A Mexican saying

When I was seven, eight, nine, fifteen, sixteen years old, I would read in bed with a flashlight under the covers, hiding my self-imposed insomnia from my mother. I preferred the world of the imagination to the death of sleep. My sister, Hilda, who slept in the same bed with me, would threaten to tell my mother unless I told her a story.

I was familiar with *cuentos*—my grandmother told stories like the one about her getting on top of the roof while down below rabid coyotes were ravaging the place and wanting to get at her. My father told stories about a phantom giant dog that appeared out of nowhere and sped along the side of the pickup no matter how fast he was driving.

Nudge a Mexican and she or he will break out with a story. So, huddling under the covers, I made up stories for my sister night after night. After a while she wanted two stories per night. I learned to give her installments, building up the suspense with convoluted complications until the story climaxed several nights later. It must have been then that I decided to put stories on paper. It must have been then that working with images and writing became connected to night.

INVOKING ART

5   In the ethno-poetics and performance of the shaman, my people, the Indians, did not split the artistic from the functional, the sacred from the secular, art from everyday life. The religious, social and aesthetic purposes of art were all intertwined. Before the Conquest, poets gathered to play music, dance, sing and read poetry in open-air places around the *Xochicuahuitl, el Arbol Florido,* Tree-in-Flower. (The *Coaxihuitl* or morning glory is called the snake plant and its seeds, known as *ololiuhqui,* are hallucinogenic.[1]) The ability of story (prose and poetry) to transform the storyteller and listener into something or someone else is shamanistic. The writer, as shape-changer, is a *nahual,* a shaman.

In looking at this book that I'm almost finished writing, I see a mosaic pattern (Aztec-like) emerging, a weaving pattern, thin here, thick there. I see a preoccupation with the deep structure, the under-lying structure, with the gesso underpainting that is red earth, black earth. I can see the deep structure, the scaffolding. If I can get the bone structure right, then putting flesh on it proceeds without too many hitches. The problem is that the bones often do not exist prior to the flesh, but are shaped after a vague and broad shadow of its form is discerned or uncovered during beginning, middle and final stages of the writing. Numerous overlays of paint, rough surfaces, smooth surfaces make me realize I am preoccupied with texture as well. Too, I see the barely contained color threatening to spill over the boundaries of the object it represents and into other "objects" and over the borders of the frame. I see a hybridization of metaphor, different species of ideas popping up here, popping up there, full of variations and seeming contradictions, though I believe in an or- dered, structured universe where all phenomena are interrelated and imbued with spirit. This almost finished product seems an as- semblage, a montage, a beaded work with several leitmotifs and with a central core, now appearing, now disappearing in a crazy dance. The whole thing has had a mind of its own, escaping me and insisting on putting together the pieces of its own puzzle with mini- mal direction from my will. It is a rebellious, willful entity, a preco- cious girl-child forced to grow up too quickly, rough, unyielding, with pieces of feather sticking out here and there, fur, twigs, clay. My child, but not for much longer. This female being is angry, sad, joyful, is *Coatlicue*, dove, horse, serpent, cactus. Though it is a flawed thing—a clumsy, complex, groping blind thing—for me it is alive, infused with spirit. I talk to it; it talks to me.

I make my offerings of incense and cracked corn, light my can- dle. In my head I sometimes will say a prayer—an affirmation and a voicing of intent. Then I run water, wash the dishes or my under- things, take a bath, or mop the kitchen floor. This "induction" period sometimes takes a few minutes, sometimes hours. But always I go against a resistance. Something in me does not want to do this writ- ing. Yet once I'm immersed in it, I can go fifteen to seventeen hours in one sitting and I don't want to leave it.

My "stories" are acts encapsulated in time, "enacted" every time they are spoken aloud or read silently. I like to think of them as performances and not as inert and "dead" objects (as the aesthetics of Western culture think of art works). Instead, the work has an identity; it is a "who" or a "what" and contains the presences of per- sons, that is, incarnations of gods or ancestors or natural and cosmic powers. The work manifests the same needs as a person, it needs to be "fed," *la tengo que bañar y vestir.*

When invoked in rite, the object/event is "present;" that is, "en- acted," it is both a physical thing and the power that infuses it. It is metaphysical in that it "spins its energies between gods and hu- mans" and its task is to move the gods. This type of work dedicates itself to managing the universe and its energies. I'm not sure what it is when it is at rest (not in performance). It may or may not be a "work" then. A mask may only have the power of presence during a ritual dance and the rest of the time it may merely be a "thing." Some works exist forever invoked, always in performance. I'm thinking of totem poles, cave paintings. Invoked art is communal and speaks of everyday life. It is dedicated to the validation of humans; that is, it makes people hopeful, happy, secure, and it can have negative effects as well, which propel one towards a search for validation.[2]

10   The aesthetic of virtuosity, art typical of Western European cultures, attempts to manage the energies of its own internal system such as conflicts, harmonies, resolutions and balances. It bears the presences of qualities and internal meanings. It is dedicated to the validation of itself. Its task is to move humans by means of achieving mastery in content, technique, feeling. Western art is always whole and always "in power." It is individual (not communal). It is "psychological" in that it spins its energies between itself and its witness.[3]

Western cultures behave differently toward works of art than do tribal cultures. The "sacrifices" Western cultures make are in housing their art works in the best structures designed by the best architects; and in servicing them with insurance, guards to protect them, conservators to maintain them, specialists to "view" them. Tribal cultures keep art works in honored and sacred places in the home and elsewhere. They attend them by making sacrifices of blood (goat or chicken), libations of wine. They bathe, feed, and clothe them. The works are treated not just as objects, but also as persons. The "witness" is a participant in the enactment of the work in a ritual, and not a member of the privileged classes.[4]

Ethnocentrism is the tyranny of Western aesthetics. An Indian mask in an American museum is transposed into an alien aesthetic system where what is missing is the presence of power invoked through performance ritual. It has become a conquered thing, a dead "thing" separated from nature and, therefore, its power.

Modern Western painters have "borrowed," copied, or otherwise extrapolated the art of tribal cultures and called it cubism, surrealism, symbolism. The music, the beat of the drum, the Blacks' jive talk. All taken over. Whites, along with a good number of our own people, have cut themselves off from their spiritual roots, and they take our spiritual art objects in an unconscious attempt to get them back. If they're going to do it, I'd like them to be aware of what they are doing and to go about doing it the right way. Let's all stop importing Greek myths and the Western Cartesian split point of view and root ourselves in the mythological soil and soul of this continent. White America has only attended to the body of the earth in order to exploit it, never to succor it or to be nurtured in it. Instead of surreptitiously ripping off the vital energy of people of color and putting it to commercial use, whites could allow themselves to share and exchange and learn from us in a respectful way. By taking up *curanderismo,* Santeria, shamanism, Taoism, Zen and otherwise delving into the spiritual life and ceremonies of multi-colored people, Anglos would perhaps lose the white sterility they have in their kitchens, bathrooms, hospitals, mortuaries and missile bases. Though in the conscious mind, black and dark may be associated with death, evil and destruction, in the subconscious mind and in our dreams, white is associated with disease, death and hopelessness. Let us hope that the left hand, that of darkness, of femaleness, or "primitiveness," can divert the indifferent, right-handed, "rational" suicidal drive that, unchecked, could blow us into acid rain in a fraction of a millisecond.

NI CUICANI: I, THE SINGER

For the ancient Aztecs, *tlilli, tlapalli, la tinta negra y roja de sus códices* (the black and red ink painted on codices) were the colors symbolizing *escritura y sabiduría* (writing and wisdom).[5] They believed that through metaphor and symbol, by means of poetry and truth, communication with the Divine could be attained, and *topan* (that which is above—the gods and spirit world) could be bridged with *mictlán* (that which is below—the underworld and the region of the dead).

15

> *Poet: she pours water from the mouth of the pump, lowers the handle then lifts it, lowers, lifts. Her hands begin to feel the pull from the entrails, the live animal resisting. A sigh rises up from the depths, the handle becomes a wild thing in her hands, the cold sweet water gushes out, splashing her face, the shock of nightlight filling the bucket.*

An image is a bridge between evoked emotion and conscious knowledge; words are the cables that hold up the bridge. Images are more direct, more immediate than words, and closer to the unconscious. Picture language precedes thinking in words; the metaphorical mind precedes analytical consciousness.

THE SHAMANIC STATE

When I create stories in my head, that is, allow the voices and scenes to be projected in the inner screen of my mind, I "trance." I used to think I was going crazy or that I was having hallucinations. But now

I realize it is my job, my calling, to traffic in images. Some of these film-like narratives I write down; most are lost, forgotten. When I don't write the images down for several days or weeks or months, I get physically ill. Because writing invokes images from my unconscious, and because some of the images are residues of trauma which I then have to reconstruct, I sometimes get sick when I *do* write. I can't stomach it, become nauseous, or burn with fever, worsen. But, in reconstructing the traumas behind the images, I make "sense" of them, and once they have "meaning" they are changed, transformed. It is then that writing heals me, brings me great joy.

To facilitate the "movies" with soundtracks, I need to be alone, or in a sensory-deprived state. I plug up my ears with wax, put on my black cloth eye-shades, lie horizontal and unmoving, in a state between sleeping and waking, mind and body locked into my fantasy. I am held prisoner by it. My body is experiencing events. In the beginning it is like being in a movie theater, as pure spectator. Gradually I become so engrossed with the activities, the conversations, that I become a participant in the drama. I have to struggle to "disengage" or escape from my "animated story," I have to get some sleep so I can write tomorrow. Yet I am gripped by a story which won't let me go. Outside the frame, I am film director, screenwriter, camera operator. Inside the frame, I am the actors—male and female—I am desert sand, mountain, I am dog, mosquito. I can sustain a four- to six-hour "movie." Once I am up, I can sustain several "shorts" of anywhere between five and thirty minutes. Usually these "narratives" are the offspring of stories and acted out in my head during periods of sensory deprivation.

My "awakened dreams" are about shifts. Thought shifts, reality shifts, gender shifts: one person metamorphoses into another in a world where people fly through the air, heal from mortal wounds. I am playing with my Self, I am playing with the world's soul, I am the dialogue between my Self and *el espíritu del mundo*. I change myself, I change the world.

20   Sometimes I put the imagination to a more rare use. I choose words, images, and body sensations and animate them to impress them on my consciousness, thereby making changes in my belief system and reprogramming my consciousness. This involves looking my inner demons in the face, then deciding which I want in my psyche. Those I don't want, I starve; I feed them no words, no images, no feelings. I spend no time with them, share not my home with them. Neglected, they leave. This is harder to do than to merely generate "stories." I can only sustain this activity for a few minutes.

I write the myths in me, the myths I am, the myths I want to become. The word, the image and the feeling have a palatable energy, a kind of power. *Con imagenes domo mi miedo, cruzo los abismos que tengo por dentro. Con palabras me hago piedra, pájaro, puente de serpientes arrastrando a ras del suelo todo lo que soy, todo lo que algún día seré.*

> *Los que están mirando (leyendo),*
> *los que cuentan (or refieren lo que leen).*
> *Los que vuelven ruidosamente las hojas de*
> *los códices.*
> *Los que tienen en su poder*
> *la tinta negra y roja (la sabiduría)*
> *y lo pintado,*
> *ellos nos llevan, nos guían,*
> *nos dicen el camino.*[6]

WRITING IS A SENSUOUS ACT

Tallo mi cuerpo como si estuviera lavando un trapo. Toco las saltadas venas de mis manos, mis chichis adormecidas como pájaras a la anochecer. Estoy encorbada sobre la cama. Las imagenes aleteán alrededor de mi cama como murciélagos, la sábana como que tuviese alas. El ruido de los trenes subterráneos en mi sentido como conchas. Parece que las paredes del cuarto se me arriman cada vez más cerquita.

Picking out images from my soul's eye, fishing for the right words to recreate images. Words are blades of grass pushing past the obstacles, sprouting on the page; the spirit of the words moving in the body is as concrete as flesh and as palpable; the hunger to create is as substantial as fingers and hand.

25   I look at my fingers, see plumes growing there. From the fingers, my feathers, black and red ink drops across the page. *Escribo con la tinta de mi sangre.* I write in red. Ink. Intimately knowing the smooth touch of paper, its speechlessness before I spill myself on the insides of trees. Daily, I battle the silence and the red. Daily, I take my throat in my hands and squeeze until the cries pour out, my larynx and soul sore from the constant struggle.

SOMETHING TO DO WITH THE DARK

> *Quien canta, sus males espanta.*
>   *—un dicho*

The toad comes out of its hiding place inside the lobes of my brain. It's going to happen again. The ghost of the toad that betrayed me—I hold it in my hand. The toad is sipping the strength from my veins, it is sucking my pale heart. I am a dried serpent skin, wind scuttling me across the hard ground, pieces of me scattered over the countryside. And there in the dark I meet the crippled spider crawling in the gutter, the day-old newspaper fluttering in the dirty rain water.

> *Musa bruja, venga. Cubrese con una sábana y espante mis demonios que a rempujones y a cachetadas me roban la pluma me rompen el sueño. Musa, ¡misericordia!*
>
> *Òigame, musa bruja. ¿Porqué huye usté en mi cara? Su grito me desarrolla de mi caracola, me sacude el alma. Vieja, quítese de aquí con sus alas de navaja. Ya no me despedaze mi cara. Vaya con sus pinche uñas que me desgarran de los ojos hasta los talones. Váyese a la tiznada. Que no me coman, le digo. Que no me coman sus nueve dedos caníbales.*

30

> *Hija negra de la noche, carnala, ¿Porqué me sacas las tripas, porqué cardas mis entrañas? Este hilvanando palabras con tripas me está matando. Jija de la noche ¡vete a la chingada!*

Writing produces anxiety. Looking inside myself and my experience, looking at my conflicts, engenders anxiety in me. Being a writer feels very much like being a Chicana, or being queer—a lot of squirming, coming up against all sorts of walls. Or its opposite: nothing defined or definite, a boundless, floating state of limbo where I kick my heels, brood, percolate, hibernate and wait for something to happen.

Living in a state of psychic unrest, in a Borderland, is what makes poets write and artists create. It is like a cactus needle embedded in the flesh. It worries itself deeper and deeper, and I keep aggravating it by poking at it. When it begins to fester I have to do something to put an end to the aggravation and to figure out why I have it. I get deep down into the place where it's rooted in my skin and pluck away at it, playing it like a musical instrument—the fingers pressing, making the pain worse before it can get better. Then out it comes. No more discomfort, no more ambivalence. Until another needle pierces the skin. That's what writing is for me, an endless cycle of making it worse, making it better, but always making meaning out of the experience, whatever it may be.

> *My flowers shall not cease to live;*
> *my songs shall never end:*
> *I, a singer, intone them;*
> *they become scattered, they are spread about.*
> —*Cantares mexicanos*

To write, to be a writer, I have to trust and believe in myself as a speaker, as a voice for the images. I have to believe that I can communicate with images and words and that I can do it well. A lack of belief in my creative self is a lack of belief in my total self and vice versa—I cannot separate my writing from any part of my life. It is all one.

35   When I write it feels like I'm carving bone. It feels like I'm creating my own face, my own heart—a Nahuatl concept. My soul makes itself through the creative act. It is constantly remaking and giving birth to itself through my body. It is this learning to live with *la Coatlicue* that transforms living in the Borderlands from a nightmare into a numinous experience. It is always a path/state to something else.

IN *XÓCHITL* IN *CUÍCATL*[7]

She writes while other people sleep. Something is trying to come out. She fights the words, pushes them down, down, a woman with morning sickness in the middle of the night. How much easier it would be to carry a baby for nine months and then expel it permanently. These continuous multiple pregnancies are going to kill her. She is the battlefield for the pitched fight between the inner image and the words trying to recreate it. *La musa bruja* has no manners. Doesn't she know, nights are for sleeping?

She is getting too close to the mouth of the abyss. She is teetering on the edge, trying to balance while she makes up her mind whether to jump in or to find a safer way down. That's why she makes herself sick—to postpone having to jump blindfolded into the abyss of her own being and there in the depths confront her face, the face underneath the mask.

To be a mouth—the cost is too high—her whole life enslaved to that devouring mouth. *Todo pasaba por esa boca, el viento, el fuego, los mares y la Tierra.* Her body, a crossroads, a fragile bridge, cannot support the tons of cargo passing through it. She wants to install 'stop' and 'go' signal lights, instigate a curfew, police Poetry. But something wants to come out.

Blocks (*Coatlicue* states) are related to my cultural identity. The painful periods of confusion that I suffer from are symptomatic of a larger creative process: cultural shifts. The stress of living with cultural ambiguity both compels me to write and blocks me. It isn't until I'm almost at the end of the blocked state that I remember and recognize it for what it is. As soon as this happens, the piercing light of awareness melts the block and I accept the deep and the darkness and I hear one of my voices saying, "I am tired of fighting. I surrender. I give up, let go, let the walls fall. On this night of the hearing of faults, *Tlazolteotl, diosa de la cara negra,* let fall the cockroaches that live in my hair, the rats that nestle in my skull. Gouge out my lame eyes, rout my demon from its nocturnal cave. Set torch to the tiger that stalks me. Loosen the dead faces gnawing my cheekbones. I am tired of resisting. I surrender. I give up, let go, let the walls fall."

40   And in descending to the depths I realize that down is up, and I rise up from and into the deep. And once again I recognize that the internal tension of oppositions can propel (if it doesn't tear apart) the mestiza writer out of the *metate* where she is being ground with corn and water, eject her out as *nahual,* an agent of transformation, able to modify and shape primordial energy and therefore able to change herself and others into turkey, coyote, tree, or human.

I sit here before my computer, *Amiguita,* my altar on top of the monitor with the *Virgen de Coatlalopeuh* candle and copal incense burning. My companion, a wooden serpent staff with feathers, is to my right while I ponder the ways metaphor and symbol concretize the spirit and etherealize the body. The Writing is my whole life, it is my obsession. This vampire which is my talent does not suffer other suitors.[8] Daily I court it, offer my neck to its teeth. This is the sacrifice that the act of creation requires, a blood sacrifice. For only through the body, through the pulling of flesh, can the human soul be transformed. And for images, words, stories to have this transformative power, they must arise from the human body—flesh and bone—and from the Earth's body—stone, sky, liquid, soil. This work, these images, piercing tongue or ear lobes with cactus needle, are my offerings, are my Aztecan blood sacrifices.

Notes

1. R. Gordon Wasson, The Wondrous Mushroom: Mycolatry in Mesoamerica (New York, NY: McGraw-Hill Book Company, 1980), 59,103.

2. Robert Plant Armstrong, *The Powers of Presence: Consciousness, Myth, and Affecting Presence* (Philadelphia, PA: University of Pennsylvania Press, 1981), 11, 20.

3. Armstrong, 10.

4. Armstrong, 4.

5. Miguel Leon-Portilla, *Los Antiguos Mexicanos: A través de sus crónicas y cantares* (México, D.F.: Fondo de Cultura Económica, 1961), 19, 22.

6. Leon-Portilla, 125.

7. In *Xóchitl* in *Cuícatl* is Nahuatl for flower and song, *flor y canto.*

8. *Nietzsche,* in *The Will to Power,* says that the artist lives under a curse of being vampirized by his talent.

Reflective Reading, Informal Writing

REFLECTING ON THE READING:

- For those of us trained as western readers, we may find Anzaldua's essay hard to follow at first. If it is hard for you to follow, make a list of what specifically makes it difficult. Reread the essay keeping in mind the items on your list. Was it easier to read and understand after you were aware of specific things that made it hard for you the first time? Why or why not?

- We might say that Anzaldua's piece is both a work of art and a work about art. Choose two passages from the reading, one that seems to be making an argument about art (specifically writing?) and one that seems to be art. What is she arguing in the first passage? (Is she saying something specific about what art is, how we should respond to art, how art is made, etc.?) How would you interpret the passage that you think is an example of art? What does this passage tell us? Do you see her art mirroring her artistic theories in any way?

- On page 286 Anzaldua argues that western cultures "behave differently toward works of art than do tribal cultures . . . tribal cultures keep art works in honored and sacred places in the home and elsewhere." Western cultures, on the other hand, put their art works "in the best structures designed by the best architects; and [services] them with insurance, guards to protect them, conservators to maintain them, specialists to mount and display them, and the educated and upper classes to 'view' them." What do you think this says about the different cultures? Does the way we "keep" art have anything to do with belief systems? With economic systems? With religious systems? If so, why so? If not, why not?

UNDERSTANDING RHETORICAL STRATEGIES:

- While this entire piece seems to be about writing, Anzaldua breaks it into subsections that don't always seem to follow logically one from the other, nor do they always seem to be about writing in the beginning. How would you say this essay is structured? Why do you think she chooses to go about it this way?

- Briefly summarize each of the sections. What specific "threads" or ideas do you see in each? Does having done this summary change your mind about how you just finished characterizing the structure of the essay? Why or why not?

- Anzaldua moves between Spanish and English. Do you find this disruptive? Do you think she means it to be? If she doesn't, why does she do it? If she does, what is she trying to accomplish with this disruption? Why do you think she uses more Spanish toward the end of the essay than in the beginning?

INFORMAL WRITING:

- Reread the sections "*Ni cuicani:* I, the Singer" and "The Shamanic State." Write about what you think Anzaldua is saying about the relationship between the inner and the outer world, the self and world, the private and public as they relate to her writing. Write also about how these things relate to your writing.
- Anzaldua suggests that western cultures are not tribal cultures. Write about what you think makes a culture tribal or nontribal. Does your understanding of tribal culture seem to match Anzaldua's?
- Based on your work with the previous question, locate a place or function where you think western culture might come close to displaying tribal culture traits. Write about why you think you might see tribal culture traits and what you would expect to see if you went to that place or function. If possible, visit or attend the place you are thinking of. Take careful notes about what you see or don't see in terms of tribal culture (take notes only if your notetaking is not disruptive in any way). Did you learn anything from this experience? Did it change you in any way?

JAMES WILLIAM GIBSON

While researching his first book, *The Perfect War* (1986), James Gibson read letters, journals, and memoirs written by ordinary soldiers from the Vietnam War. Nearly every one of them reminisced about John Wayne movies and the romance of war. Soldiers saw war as a ritual transition from boyhood to manhood. However, the violence, confusion, and political complexity of the Vietnam War left soldiers resentful of America's romantic warrior image. Partially as a result of this disillusionment, war movies and westerns fell out of popularity from about 1965 to the mid–1970s.

Many Americans thought that America lost the Vietnam War because the government wouldn't let soldiers fight. Men began to think that they must fight individually to restore America's pre-Vietnam glory. Gibson calls this paramilitary culture, when men try to be warriors outside of the military and police units. America celebrates war and the warrior and believes the nation wins wars because we morally deserve to win. Losing Vietnam created a crisis in national self-image. Gibson points to this shift in perspective as the resurrection of war fantasy culture beginning with Rambo and paintball. Rambo became a cultural hero who individually stood for traditional American values of self-reliance, bravery, and determination.

As part of his research for *Warrior Dreams* (1994), from which this chapter is taken, Gibson attended combat pistol training school and played paintball. The escalation of paintball from a game of tag to a game of sophisticated weaponry, costume, and strategy fascinated Gibson. Paintball started as the National Survival Game invented in 1981 by a screenwriter and a veteran of an Army Long Range Reconnaissance Patrol in Vietnam. This game initially involved collecting as many flags as possible while using the least amount of ammunition. With the influence of movies like *Rambo* and the glorification of the warrior, major paintball parks, magazines, and catalogues selling clothes and weapons carried the game to a more realistic and war-like level.

Paintball, at the time of Gibson's research, was almost exclusively a male sport. In American culture, the warrior is the only "certified" male, and a pretend warrior with pretend guns is still more of a man than without. Playing with killing, rather than engaging in actual war, became the new ritualized rite of passage from boy to man. Warrior fantasies and paramilitary culture suggest an attempt of the individual man to reaffirm America's pre-Vietnam national identity. As you read Gibson's essay, think about what role war and acting the warrior play (or have played) in the lives of men you have known.

Paintball As Combat Sport

In ancient societies, religious festivals were vitally important occasions during which people left their ordinary lives behind them and "lived" the myths of their society. They did not just celebrate the memory of the gods, but instead saw themselves as voyagers into a sacred realm. In modern America, religious festivals have lost much of their magical aura. But other ritual spectacles have arisen in their place. In 1955 Walt Disney opened Disneyland in Anaheim, California, and the modern theme park was born. Disneyland was created by the same set of designers who worked on Disney's films. Each "village"—such as "Frontierland," "Mainstreet USA," and "Tomorrowland"—was built like a three-quarters-scale movie set to give the place a more intimate feel. Visitors entered a "Magic Kingdom," a space where all of Disney's mythological universes came to life. "I don't want the public to see the world they live in while they are in the park," Disney said. "I want them to feel they are in another world."[1] Decades later, it was a principle the entrepreneurs of paramilitary culture took seriously.

Big Navy had served aboard an aircraft carrier in the early 1980s, a member of a squadron that flew helicopters in search of enemy submarines. He was a good six-two, and he carried a lean, mean 220 pounds on his hardened frame. In his massive steel-like hands he carried a big gun to match, a real smooth piece equipped with extended 16" barrel, a 12" noise suppressor, state of the art "red dot" optic scope, and folding metal stock. The CO_2 tank powering this baby rode high on the back of his bulging shoulders in its own special olive-drab nylon harness, while the black neoprene high-pressure hose connecting the tank to the gun looped under his armpit. Black Cordura nylon and elastic bandoliers crisscrossed his chest, holding 100–150 rounds of ammo. The bandoliers perfectly matched the tiger stripes on his camouflage fatigues, Big Navy's third outfit of the day. An olive-drab bandanna, pulled tight against his forehead and wrapped over his hair with the corners tied in back, completed his fashion ensemble. He definitely knew what he was about, and what was going down. His assignment was to lead a group of men deep into enemy-held territory, capture their flag, and return to home base. Along the way they would face their opponents, each armed with heavy-duty guns firing gelatin capsules filled with bright red, yellow, green, or blue paint. Big Navy and his men would have to "kill" as many of these bad guys as possible to win victory; they would also have to protect their own flag against enemy attacks.

All in all, the mission didn't look good. In front of him in the dusty parking lot stood his men, a motley assortment of ragtag pickup players. Cowboy's headgear, a genuine U.S. military Kevlar helmet, was an eye-catcher. He'd been badly hurt in a motorcycle accident not long before, and thought the $300 for the helmet well worth the price to protect himself. A complete set of U.S. military web gear—equipment belt, ammo pouches, canteen, and suspenders—wrapped around his waist and over his shoulders. He carried a big gun, too and said that he liked full-scale firefights, no matter what the odds; they didn't call him Cowboy for nothing. Burnt-orange goggles obscured his eyes; a Darth Vader-type *Star Wars* mask hid the rest of his face.

Next to him was a former professional football player with seven years of experience on the Minnesota Vikings. It was his very first game, and he wore brand-new camouflage fatigues that fit skin tight (not exactly the military concept). Although he was the largest man on the field that day, far bigger than Big Navy, the ex-pro was nervous. He'd been forced to retire from football because of a leg injury. "There's still a lot of nerve damage down there," the big man said anxiously to his friend. His buddy nodded in sympathy. He, like Cowboy, had been the victim of a motorcycle accident. Sometime before his accident, he had bought walkie-talkie radios with earplugs and mikes mounted on headsets similar to the kind worn by police SWAT teams and counterterrorist units. He brought them along today for the fight ahead.

5   The youngest members of Big Navy's squad of ten were two highschool kids from a San Diego military academy. Although they normally were allowed to fire M14 rifles, Colt .45 automatics, and the new Beretta 9mm's at least twice a month at school, recently the academy had rented out its entire arsenal to a movie production company. They needed to keep their shooting reflexes honed if they were going to make it to Annapolis and then move on to F–14 fighter-pilot training. One said he was aiming for Top Gun, the Navy's elite air-to-air combat instruction school at Miramar Naval Air Station near San Diego. Of course they'd seen the movie. Big Navy tried to discourage them. There weren't enough port calls and "things happen out there the Navy doesn't tell you about," he warned, referring to murders and thefts and accidents aboard ship. But the kids didn't want to listen, and besides, it was time.

With his squad collected, Big Navy led his men across the parking lot, past the gunmetal-blue Jaguar V–12 sedan with the "Whoever Dies with the Most Toys Wins" bumper sticker, on toward the gate. Overhead a Los Angeles County Sheriff's Department Bell Jetranger helicopter just cleared the tops of the Conquest playing field's palm trees as it approached the landing zone next door at the

Malibu substation. As the thump-thump-thump of the rotors faded away, Big Navy fired his gun through the chronograph, checking to make sure it was shooting just under 300 feet per second, the field limit. He finally turned and faced his team, pulled his full-length plastic face mask down, and gave the battle cry, "Okay, boys, it's time to rock and roll."

When they passed beneath the old wooden beams that arched over the gateway, the men found themselves in what looked like a ghost town, something out of the American West. And sure enough, some thirty to thirty-five yards down the dusty street lined by Old West style buildings that made up this former movie set, the enemy stood, spread out and waiting. They were a Latino team from the San Fernando Valley, just north of Los Angeles. Their leader, owner of a machine shop that made parts for air-to-air missiles, had bought team shoulder patches for all his employees who wanted in on the game: the three corners of the inverted triangle were labeled Judge, Jury, Executioner, while the middle in full caps stood the unit name—VIGILANTE.

Each player wore full camouflage, and each held an advanced "constant-air" gun with extended barrel and silencer like those used by their Anglo and black opponents. All of them carried a long 16" brush (used to clear gun barrels) in camouflage sheaths that hung from their waists. It gave them a special Central American jungle-fighter look, as if they were packing machetes and had just hacked their way through the underbrush into town for a rendezvous with destiny.

David, the man who ran Conquest, explained the rules for today's battle. He pointed to a line of banana trees that marked one of the boundaries; it wasn't legal to sneak past it. He described where each team's flag was, so that no one would be confused about where the key action was going to take place. He made sure every man was wearing a red or yellow strip of cloth on his arm and explained that a man who was hit was supposed to wave this cloth over his head as he marched off the field to keep from getting shot again. Any man seen with his eye goggles off would be instantly disqualified. Two referees were supervising the players to enforce these rules. Everybody looked bored; most had heard this story scores of times before and even the new guys knew what to expect. Besides, it was a hot, dry August afternoon, a time when the Pacific breeze couldn't make it past the beach a half-mile away. At last David gave the countdown—3–2–1— and blew his whistle. An instant later twenty or more shots filled the air as players ran for cover, firing from the hip. The fight was on.

10   David couldn't afford to stay and watch. New players were driving up all the time. He got from 20 to 120 customers on each weekend day, and each paid $20 to get in, and another $20 to $35 to rent one of the modern guns with the big air tanks. Everybody needed ex-

tra tubes of paintballs, and that ran a couple of bucks for a tube of ten. He still kept a finger in his old office supply business, but he liked doing this a lot more. It was ironic, David chuckled. His mother had always been against his playing war as a kid. "Now I make my living playing war," he said to me. He was especially busy this Saturday because on Sunday he was playing with his own "expert" team. With so much to do, he couldn't talk much more. "You know," David added, "the *A-Team* used to film here all the time. Really."

By now the battle of the Vigilantes versus Big Navy's walk-on players had been going on nearly half an hour. Casualties had been taken on both sides. The first victims waited at the gate to minister to their more recently fallen teammates, using a garden hose to wash the bright yellow or red or blue or green water-color splotches off their uniforms. No one seemed to take getting hit personally; no angry words were spoken. In fact, no one said anything at all to the other side that afternoon.

Off the battlefield, each group partied by themselves. The men popped open cans of beer—Corona, Coors, and an occasional Bud. They lit up Marlboros and sucked in that first heavy drag of smoke. Girlfriends woke up from tanning naps taken on lounge chairs in the back of spotlessly clean four-wheel-drive pickups. Some listened dutifully to war stories, while others just wanted to know when they were leaving. But the men were all willing to hear another teammate's war story of a good shot or a shot missed, and of course how they came to get hit; in exchange they told their own. Some blamed their woes on their guns, first cursing them, then taking them apart for cleaning. After reassembling the guns, the men twisted knobs and valves, test fired the guns, and then cursed some more to start the cycle again.

As the last shots were being fired between Big Navy, his team's last holdout, and the surviving (and victorious) Latino machinists, two fresh groups got ready for their battle. One new guy had just stumbled upon paintball the day before, having found *Action Pursuit Games* on the newsstand next to his magazine of choice, the *Hollywood Reporter*. The Conquest advertisements showed a handful of male players being held prisoner at gunpoint by long-legged, big-bosomed women wearing shorts and tight-fitting camouflage tank tops. "Another typical day at Conquest" read the caption.[2] So he came looking for some action. When a teammate tied a red ribbon to his arm he quipped, "Does this mean we're Communists? Do we have to read Marx?"[3]

The development of mock-combat war games in the United States a few short years after the Vietnam War is not in itself surprising. One scholar of games and sports, Brian Sutton-Smith, argues that historically what he calls "games of strategy" are developed as "models of problems in adaptation. They exist to simulate some adaptive problem that the group is having . . . Players are not hunting real tigers, or taking a chance with angry gods or trying to outwit diabolical adversaries. The dangers that go with these excitements in real life are largely curtailed and can therefore be studied within manageable levels of anxiety."[4] As suggested by its original name, the National Survival Game, paintball in effect transformed the cultural and political crisis of defeat in Vietnam into a game that combined elements of both combat and play.

15   What is surprising, though, is how quickly the emphasis in paintball shifted from play to combat. This was not the intention of those who founded the National Survival Game in the New Hampshire woods in 1981. They were inspired by a more archaic vision of the lone hunter-woodsman sneaking through the forests, killing an opponent only when absolutely necessary to capture the flag. The game was to be a test of cunning and stealth. As Lionel Atwill writes in *The New Official Survival Game Manual*, published in 1987: "There will be no machine guns on Game fields. No tanks. No helicopters. And the Game will always be played in the spirit in which it was conceived. In a spirit of fun and play. There will be no Viet Cong villages, no mock mutilations. No bogus wars."[5] But all these things would come to pass.

According to Mike Jasperson, publisher and editor of *Front Line*, the first paintball magazine, it was the coming of the New War movies in the mid–1980s that both helped the sport gain popularity and moved it in a paramilitary direction. In his words, "What they have done, more that saying war is good, they're saying that it is okay to wear camouflage, okay to play war." Paintball offered men the opportunity to participate in a film-fantasy world rather than just watch it. "You drive a forklift eight hours a day," says Jasperson. "You work a cash register eight hours a day or whatever; you watch television and here's *Magnum P. I.* and he's running around with his gun and here's Don Johnson running around with his gun on *Miami Vice*."[6] Compared to the stultifying routines of work and family responsibilities, the lives of these warriors were exciting and glamorous. Paintball provided a way for average men— and the game was played mainly by men—to get in on the action. Some players even watched action-adventure films the night before a game as a way to get "psyched up" and shouted lines from movies as they played.

The popularity of these movies and television shows was in turn noticed by new entrepreneurs who were opening new playing fields. Denis Bulowski, the Los Angeles policeman who built the famous Sat Cong Village with its bamboo compound flying a Vietnamese National Liberation Front flag, and the Nicaragua playing field with its facsimile of a downed cargo plane used for resupplying the contras, said that before he constructed his mock battlefields the idea of playing war "was already in people's minds. People see it in the movies. They think 'I wish I was out there doing that kind of stuff.'"[7] Paintball offered "better toys" to play with, and attractive theme parks like the Vietnam and Nicaragua playing fields to enrich the fantasy. That movies such as *Platoon* were in part filmed at Sat Cong Village added to the magic aura of the place.

Similarly, the manager of War Zone in Fountain Valley, California, said that although the game first hit California in 1983–1984, playing areas did not change from plain old marked fields to full-scale warrior theme parks until the fall of 1985, after *Rambo: First Blood, Part 2* and some of the other New War movies appeared. War Zone was the first playing field to develop mock tanks, hire helicopters, and provide teams with walkie-talkies and special "Heavy Fire Machine Guns" with 800-shot capability.[8] Not surprisingly, the bases on War Zone's playing fields were named after recent movies—the Hanoi Hilton, for example, and the Temple of Doom, and the Rambo Hotel.

At the same time that the fields become transformed, blue jeans and old shirts stopped being acceptable clothing. Increasingly, full camouflage outfits were perceived by all players, even novices, as a fashion necessity, not just better for hiding in the brush. Mike Jasperson described the transition as one that "makes the fantasy a little more complete. You know, now it's gone from imaginary to visual."[9] Indeed, magazine articles such as Frank Hughes's "Picking Your Paintball Persona" began to appear regularly to help players interpret the outfits worn by others and thus choose the ensemble best for them. The foremost fashion rule, writes Hughes, is to "keep in mind that while everyone knows 'dressing up' is one of paintball's enduring charms, it is considered bad form to admit it. Your clothes must have a rough utilitarian look to them (like you stopped to play paintball on your way to Nicaragua), and must never seem to be a costume."[10] Said another way, the "good" player always stays in character; he does his best to help himself and others maintain their "joint engrossment," as sociologist Erving Goffman calls it, in a fantasy world.[11]

20   On the other hand, the new player should avoid purchasing the cheapest, most readily accessible kind of camouflage clothing, the standard-issue U.S. Military BDUs [Battle Dress Utilities] in the common "woodland" camouflage pattern. Although such clothing can give newcomers a comfortable "anonymous look" for a while, they will be seen by others as "players who lack confidence." Instead the ideal fashion statement is that of the "Special Forces" soldier. According to Hughes, "this is more of a concept than a

specific outfit. The basic idea is to look military, but not regular military. You're a specialist, a dangerous individual . . . With the right patches and equipment, you'll leave them guessing as to whether or not you really were a SEAL."[12] As this paramilitary ideal spread, mixing and matching pieces of very expensive, exotic surplus outfits from Rhodesia, South Africa, and the Soviet Union became popular.

With the body now enclosed in full military camouflage, all that remained visible of the old self was the face. Although the advent of full-length plastic face masks was in some ways a "functional" improvement—paintballs sting painfully when they hit sensitive skin—more is at issue. In an effort to discourage aiming for the head, the overwhelming majority of field owners in the mid- and late-1980s declared that "head shots" did not count as legitimate hits. Still the masks became a regular accessory. As players hand painted fierce animal faces on them, and companies began marketing pre-painted masks of wolves' heads or savage "wild men," the archaic elements of this ostensibly functional accessory became clear.

Anthropologist J. C. Crocker writes that the "ornamented body" is a mode of "communicating at once to society and to the self a specific identity." Ceremonial masks in particular have potentially transformative powers: "By donning a mask one becomes what otherwise one could never be. Men into women, old into young, human into animal, mortals in to gods, dead into living (and vice versa)."[13] In paintball, masks facilitate a particular transformation: they help the civilian with no military experience "conjure up the spirit" and change into an imaginary warrior.[14]

Many players and paintball businessmen speak of the appeal of these costumes. One store manager alluded to the "military mystique" of "dressing up in cammies." His assistant manager put it plainly: "You dress bad to be bad."[15] But there are limits, as Mike Jasperson insists: "You know, the timid people are still timid on the field. The rest of the people—for example, salesmen—are aggressive. The underlying personality, well, I don't know if that changes. I don't think it does."[16]

Whether or not real personality changes occur through donning military fatigues, paintball certainly provides men the opportunity to gain the *appearance* of warrior power through playing dress-up. Ironically, then, an image of manhood is obtained by violating the social norms according to which playing with clothes is an exclusively feminine activity that real men disdain. As Brian Sutton-Smith says in his *Toys as Culture,* much of the appeal of games and sports comes from their openness and fluidity; games permit us "to express our desires and our contradictions in ways that are not possible within the conventional boundaries of society."[17]

25   The last material component of paintball to become radically militarized in the mid- and late–1980s was the basic paintball gun. The founders of the National Survival Game had from the beginning expressed some ambivalence concerning the role of the gun in the sport. An early page of Lionel Atwill's *New, Official Survival Game Manual* refers to it as a "long-range paintbrush" that is a gun "only in the semantic sense."[18] Later on, though, Atwill says this: "That the gun looks like *a gun* adds great weight to the Game. The gun is a tool that mimics a weapon. In its mimicry it becomes symbolic, and that symbolism, with its element of real or imagined fear, heightens the fantasy of the Game. The gun makes the Game work on several levels."[19]

    In the beginning, the physical limitations of the first paintball pistols gave some credence to the assertion that these were simply long-range paintbrushes. Built by the Daisy Manufacturing Company for a firm called Nel-Spot, these "guns" were initially intended for use by farmers and ranchers to mark trees and animals with watercolor paint contained in gelatin capsules. Powered by a small 12-gram CO_2 cartridge, the Nel-Spot had an accurate range of fifty feet and a maximum range of seventy-five feet. Each CO_2 cartridge could propel only twenty or so paintballs, and the last few shots didn't have much velocity. The pistol's magazine only held around ten paintballs, and loading a paintball from the magazine into the firing chamber required several slow hand movements. Changing CO_2 cartridges also took time. Although these features were perfectly adequate given its intended farm use, from a warrior's perspective the Nel-Spot wasn't much of a statement.

    For several years the National Survival Game founders wanted to keep the weaponry relatively low-tech. In late 1985 NSG, Inc., the corporation which developed and franchised the Game, introduced its own official paintball pistol, the Splatmaster. Made complete from plastic, the gun was relatively cheap (about $100 list price when first introduced). Easy to clean and maintain, the Splatmaster had a bit more range, held a few more paintballs, and was somewhat faster to operated than its predecessor. It was merely an improvement, though, and not a generational advance.

    Meanwhile, back in Southern California, things were headed in a very different direction. Beginning in 1985, more and more paintball devotees became entrepreneurs. One group persuaded Benjamin-Sheridan, a manufacturer of BB and pellet air guns, to begin production of paintball pistols and *rifles*. Several brand-new companies entered the gun market as well. Scores of men went into business as "airsmiths," specializing in customized modifications of Nel-Spots and other paintball guns. Stock-issue gun barrels were replaced by smoother, more carefully machined and polished substitutes to increase accuracy and range. Shotgun-like "pump" actions were added to radically increase the speed of loading a paintball from the magazine into the firing chamber, and the whole feeding mechanism was changed to make it faster and more reliable. Long pipes were welded onto the gun magazines, giving them at least a 20-shot capacity, easily replenished with a 10-shot tube. A modestly coordinated shooter could now fire well over a shot per second.

But he couldn't keep firing very long. The old 12-gram CO_2 canisters remained a real bottleneck in the whole paint-pumping process. They couldn't power much more than 20 shots, and changing the cartridges still took a long time, especially when the shooter was suffering from the debilitating stress of an on-going firefight. Then, one day in November 1985, the game's most eminent airsmith, 46-year-old Lou Grubbs (or "Gramps" as he's known in the trade) finally ran out of air one time too many. "This is bullshit," Gramps declared. He'd been raised in a machine shop and had spent seventeen years teaching industrial arts and loved "to tinker and play and design stuff."

30   And so he went to work. At first he tried connecting three standard 12-gram CO_2 cartridges in a "tray system," a gambit that didn't quite work. Then he found some steel tanks similar to, but smaller than, those used by scuba divers; these smaller tanks held five pounds of compressed carbon dioxide. The system had potential, but it was a heavy load on a man's back and, in action, the hose connecting the tank to the gun often got caught in the underbrush. Next he tried a smaller canister containing a pound and a half of air that could be carried on the chest in an equipment vest. Finally, in March 1986, Gramps mounted his first 10-ounce canisters directly onto the paint gun; ten ounces of CO_2 was enough to shoot over 400 rounds at full power. The "constant-air" gun was born.

During the spring of 1986 the newly modified constant-air guns started showing up at all the major Southern California playing fields. That summer Gramps's home field, War Zone, announced that it would hold the world's largest paintball fight. Its two major playing fields would be combined to create a 350-acre battleground for a contest involving five hundred warriors from teams all across the region. On Saturday morning, August 23, the epic struggle began; by dusk the constant-air guns had proved their mettle. In November, War Zone scheduled Big Game II. This time twelve hundred gunners showed up, and two-thirds packed the big customized constant-air paint-pushers.[20] As word spread, the industry changed forever.

Delivering more firepower became the primary goal of air-gun technology. "Your Search for Better Close-Combat Equipment Stops and Ends Here!!!" is how Para-Ordnance Mfg. introduced its full-automatic paintball submachine gun, a literal copy of the famous

Ingram MAC–10, the drug-dealer favorite.[21] The model 85 paint gun
fired 1,100 rounds per minute, just like its real gun inspiration. A
Tippman Pneumatics ad showed a player facing three adversaries.
"Never Be Outgunned Again!" read the caption, and clearly this guy
wasn't: his SMG–60 fired 600 rounds per minute and had "an authentic blow-back bolt system that duplicates the timing and feel of
a real submachine gun."[22] By 1989 even NSG, Inc. was forced to develop and market its own semiautomatic constant-air guns. Retail
list prices for these advanced weapons ranged from $250 to $450.
Extended barrels, noise suppressors, high-capacity magazines, and
scopes could easily add another few hundred dollars to the price.

Just as the weapons and accessories increasingly resembled
their military equivalents, so the advertisements mimicked more
and more directly the layouts and copy of ads in paramilitary magazines. In 1990 Brass Eagle introduced its Barracuda Semi-Automatic
DMR Series with an ad showing an armed man in camouflage face
paint wading waist deep in a swamp and carrying a coiled rap-
pelling rope—a direct knockoff of Heckler and Koch's familiar pro-
motions for their assault rifles on the back cover of *Soldier of
Fortune*.[23] Adventure Game Supplies, Inc., in turn touted its new
Landshark air gun by demonstrating its accuracy out at Sat Cong
Village; the target was a standard B–2 human silhouette, the same
one regularly used by gun writers testing combat weapons.[24]

A related advertising ploy was to link a paintball product as
closely as possible to real military and police units. The "Products
for Players" column in *Action Pursuit Games* proudly announced that
T. G. Faust, Inc., a "respected manufacturer of body armor," many
of whose "clients are government agencies," had now entered the
paintball market with the "M–68 Tactical Vest" capable of holding
36 tubes (360 rounds).[25] Pursuit Marketing, Inc. claimed that more of
its "Rough. Rugged. Reliable" line of air guns were used "by law enforcement and military for training than any other paintball gun."[26]
When Corliss Delay, Inc. introduced its paintball *land mine,* the
"Playmore P.D.S. Tripwire Activated Paintmine," it was clearly alluding to the U.S. military's "claymore" mine of Vietnam fame.[27]

35   Even leaving aside the paint grenades and land mines, paintball
firepower dramatically escalated in the late 1980s. Whereas players
armed with the original Nel-Spots might fire 20 rounds in a one-
hour game, gunmen equipped with constant-air powered pumps
and semiautomatics often fired over 100 rounds (and sometimes
much more). The advanced guns also had a longer range of accuracy, upwards of 100 feet, and a maximum range well beyond that.

With so much paint flying around, the nature of the game was
bound to change. In the beginning, the National Survival Game
founders prided themselves on their woodsman-like abilities to hide

and stalk silently. Indeed, in the opening game of June 1981 the victor was a professional forester named Ritchie White. Lionel Atwill, who also competed on that historic day, remembers that no one ever saw Ritchie, and he never fired a shot. "He crept through the woods from station to station, gathering flags as easily as a schoolgirl gathers flowers."[28]

But the high levels of firepower strongly favored a very different kind of tactical approach—the small-unit infantry practice known as "fire and maneuver." In fire and maneuver, one group of soldiers begins shooting either at a suspected enemy position or directly at enemy soldiers. Their objective is to make the enemy soldiers duck behind cover to protect themselves. While the enemy is thus blinded, part of the first unit them runs to a second position closer to the enemy. This second group then opens fire to cover the advance of the first group, who "leap-frog" past them to a third position. In this way an attacking force moves swiftly into a tactically favorable position.

Colonel Michael Duncan Wyle, vice president of Marine Corps University in Quantico, Virginia, was particularly impressed by the way paintball combat confirmed the military's own findings on how best to conduct fire and maneuver. Viewing the carnage generated during firefights at the Marine's Combat City training ground at Quantico in 1990, Colonel Wyle said: "One thing that I found particularly accurate was the fact that you need to get suppressive fire against the other guy in order to move . . . If you try it any other way, you get shot."[29] A second demonstration game was scheduled for viewing by the Marine Corps top brass; everyone was to be issued full-automatic paint guns and paint grenades. Colonel Wyle had been persuaded to host the exercise by a young private from California who, "despite his rigorous training schedule," had "continued to play the game he loved so well."[30]

Successful execution of fire and maneuver and the other infantry tactics described in game manuals and magazines required relatively high levels of social organization. Although paintball had always been a group-oriented sport that attracted teams of friends or coworkers, the militarization of the sport meant that disciplined units with a coherent leadership structure—from team captain down to lower fireteam leaders—had greater success than informal groups or makeshift collections of random individuals. Some teams became famous for both their ability on the field and their military aura. One motion-picture company even hired the famous Bushmasters to perform as soldiers in an action-adventure film—they showed up on the set with their own "cammies, weapons and a high degree of professionalism." The Bushmasters did so well that the producer promised he would "work with them again anytime and recommend them highly to any motion picture producer."[31]

All of these developments—the guns and especially the vast differences between novices and well-established teams—caused much worry and debate among paintballers. Many expressed concern that the constant-air guns had taken the basic woodsman skills out of the sport, leaving it to those who had the big money required to buy the advanced weapons. They also worried that first-time players were being slaughtered and so would never return. And indeed, industry analysts admit that turnover is something of a problem.

Playing-field operators developed some solutions to these problems. They began to schedule their playing fields for different kinds of games and different levels of ability. "Novices" were given their own games to be played with stock guns; constant-air gunmen got their own shootouts against similarly equipped foes; and "purists" who used sophisticated "tournament" style guns got their more sporting contests as well.

Still, despite this segmentation and stratification of the market, the overall direction throughout the 1980s was toward militarization and mock-combat, not woodsmanship. By 1986, there were over forty paramilitary playing fields in Southern California alone. A review of the sport in 1988 listed over a thousand playing fields throughout the country—from the green hills of upstate New York to the swamps of Louisiana to the indoor "urban warfare" ranges of Michigan. By that time well over two million highly armed men in camouflage and face masks had fought at least once in these mock wars and one million of them continued to play at least four times a year.[32] Even the National Survival Game had come around. Beginning in 1987, Worldwide Library, publishers of *Mack Bolan: The Executioner* and many other spin-off commando groups sagas, became the official sponsor for the annual National Survival Game tournaments and awarded the "coveted Mack Bolan Trophy."[33]

The rise of paintball, however, cannot be explained merely by the invention of better toys or bigger and badder playgrounds. Its appeal was much more basic: some men, especially young men, wanted to get as close to combat as possible. Denis Bulowski, owner of Sat Cong Village, said, "There's such a thing as actual combat, and this is about as close as you can get to the real thing."[34] This, as one player put it, was "the dark side of the game."[35]

Perhaps it was this "dark side" that made paintball unattractive to most Vietnam veterans. Mike Jasperson thought that at most 10% of the California paintball players were military veterans, while in Illinois and Florida the percentage went up to perhaps 20%. Other estimates were much lower. Russell Maynard of *Action Pursuit*

Games claimed that Vietnam veterans "wouldn't touch it with a ten-foot pole."[36] Out at Sat Cong Village one regular referee concluded that "maybe 5% of the players had seen action."[37] The owner of a large wholesale and retail store commented, "There's a lot of Vietnam veterans who come in here with their sons. They have no interest in putting on cammies and going out there."[38] Paintball businessmen thought that most combat veterans avoided the game because it threatened to bring back bad memories.

45   Indeed, most players of the game lacked any real combat experience; according to a Sat Cong employee, they were "people who wanted to be in a war; people who didn't get a chance."[39] Paintball was primarily played by men in their mid-twenties to their forties (playing fields do no allow players under sixteen). Most were white, except in California where Latinos and Asian-Americans also made very strong showings. Few black people ever played. No one knew why exactly, but one store salesman speculated that bad press coverage played a role, creating an impression among blacks that paintballers were "a bunch of Ku Klux Klan."[40] Nor was it a game for the very poor, as it required a significant outlay of cash. Beyond that, though, as one War Zone referee proudly explained, "all sorts of job types show up, blue collar and white collar. Everything from doctors, lawyers, down to the ditch digger. The field is an equalizer."[41]

The following November, *Esquire* published a sequel, William Broyles, Jr.'s essay "Why Men Love War." Broyles, like Buckley, emphasized the serene self-confidence that comes from having faced the enemy; he waxed lyrical about the brotherhood of war. "The enduring emotion of war," Broyles gushed, "when everything else has faded, is comradeship. A comrade in war is a man you can trust with anything, because you trust him with your life."[43] Like the New War movies and novels, articles such as these helped resurrect the warrior ideal for men.

Thus the two most commonly shared characteristics of players were that they were male, and that they had not fought in Vietnam. In the early 1980s, several books and magazine articles asserted that those American men who had missed the Vietnam War, either because of age or because they deliberately avoided the draft, were failures as men. Christopher Buckley published "Viet Guilt: Were the real prisoners of war the young Americans who never left home?" in *Esquire's* September 1983 issue. Buckley (who did not go to Vietnam) stressed how the war had *confirmed* the veterans as men. They had the security of knowing "*I have been weighed on the scales and have not been found wanting,*" whereas, poor Buckley confessed, "my sense at this point is that I will always feel the lack of it and will try to compensate for it, sometimes in good, other times in ludicrous, ways."[42]

These lessons were not lost on paintball publicists. Lionel Atwill begins one chapter of his 1987 manual with an epigram from Dr. Samuel Johnson: "Every man thinks meanly of himself for not having been a soldier."[44] Curiously enough, Christopher Buckley had quoted the same line in his 1983 essay. For those who felt cheated out of a war, paintball could serve as a test of manhood. Atwill writes: "A player might extrapolate Game performance to other stressful situations. Thus how you react in a Game may be an excellent clue to your behavior in the rest of your life."[45] Indeed, one corporation sponsored games during a corporate retreat and hired a psychologist to rate players on their aggressiveness.[46]

Atwill also promoted paintball as a means of creating comradeship. The NSG founders, he says, are men who "enjoy camaraderie," and the game as a whole is "so infused with a sense of honor, camaraderie, and fun that few players can walk away from it without feeling uplifted."[47] The idea that paintball encourages close friendships showed up again and again in players' accounts of the experience. One player told of how during his regular team meetings the goal was "for everyone to be tight with each other, both on and off the field."[48] Grubbs "Gramps" went further, declaring that when he played at War Zone, he didn't worry about watching his grandchildren because "I've got 500 baby-sitters who will watch them."[49] Paintball, then, provided him a new, extended family.

50   Courage and comradeship are honorable values. But they cannot be separated from the essential truth of the game. At its core, paintball simulates killing. The fundamental sequence of play involves hunting other men, aiming a gun at them, pulling the trigger, and making the kill. That this sequence so closely resembles part of what is involved in real killing undoubtedly contributes to the high that many players experience. As the manager of Paint Pistol Express said: "I get an adrenaline rush out of this sport that I've never received from any other sport."[50] Military men speak of the "combat high." Time is experienced as moving very slowly—a few seconds can seem like minutes, minutes like hours. In focusing on the hunt and kill, sensory perceptions change. For example, peripheral vision usually disappears, leaving only a narrow "tunnel" straight down the barrel to the target. Players get so pumped up that oftentimes they don't even feel the sting when they themselves are hit—the pain and welts come later.

Moreover, despite its advertised good, clean fun, paintball in effect reproduces the notion that the only true men are those who have been tried in battle and become warriors, and that the highest form of friendship is the brotherhood of war. The simulated killings at the core of the game provide this magic touch of transcendence. A group of friends who play paintball are not just friends anymore, but "veterans." And at the end of a match, a player has not simply played a good game, but has proved his character under the stress of "combat."

At the same time, paintball puts men into contradictory relationships with basic social rules. On the one hand, the game allows men the fantasy of being soldiers legally and morally licensed to kill. On the other, since players are not really soldiers or police, the actions of aiming and firing a weapon at another person constitute a major *transgression* of law and morality. Only children can legitimately pretend to shoot other people during their play (legitimately, because children are not expected to know what real violence and death mean). Thus, paintball offers men the opportunity to act against the adult world in two ways: first, by approximating real violence, and second, by essentially playing a child's game.

Over and over the thrill of paintball is described by players in terms of returning to childhood. "Once you're on the field, you're five years old again," says paintball entrepreneur Russell Maynard.[51] One player exclaimed after his first game, "I can't remember having more fun. God! It's like being a kid again. The adrenaline rush alone—I mean, pretending I was in a war. When would I ever get a chance at that?"[52] Out at War Zone, Gramps said, "Cowboys and Indians have been popular for ages. This is being seven years old again and playing cowboys and Indians. I'm a toy maker. These are big kids' toys. That's what they are."[53]

Just like the New War movies and novels, then, paintball provides males a ritual transition to warrior adulthood through regression to childhood. All the posturing to create the aura of "badness"—the frightening face masks and elaborate military gear, the vicious-sounding team names and the various battle cries, the casual references to body counts, and the "toy" guns with a rate of fire found in real military weapons—all these elements are shouts of defiance against an imaginary frowning adult.

55 On fields full of children in camouflage equipped with rapid-fire big kids' toys and lots of ammunition, the line between play and violence gets awfully thin. The role of adult is passed on to completely different people—the referees. A referee *freezes* the game when he calls out "Paint check. Nobody shoot. Nobody move." If a player has indeed been splattered, the referee cries, "Man's hit! Do not shoot him again!"[54] "We are the order out here," said a Sat Cong Village referee. "Without the referee this would not be a game."[55] In stopping paintball's violent momentum for everyone on the field, the referee temporarily breaks the "combat high" experienced by players.

After players are hit and officially declared out they walk off the field and wait for the rest of their teammates at a staging area. As

they leave the war zone, new players confront paintball's fundamental lesson. Everyone told a similar story, but Gramps was the
most eloquent:

> You find out very quickly that it's easy to die and as a result of
> that, you're just damn glad it isn't for real. They'd be putting you in a
> body bag. People realize that real fast. You ain't gonna get volunteers
> out of here for Nicaragua or anywhere else.
>
> This is one of the biggest anti-war movements in existence. To be
> against war in a parade is one thing, but it takes a change of thinking
> and heart. In this country most guys are raised with a semi-macho im-
> age, the John Wayne, the Rambo. We glorify war, all that. War, as any
> good general will tell you, is absolutely insanity at its most vulgar.
> Being raised with that macho, pro-war image in our mind is what
> must be overcome. This game destroys the image I'm invincible when
> the first paintball hits.[56]

The problem is not that Gramps and his fellow enthusiasts are
lying or even that they are providing rationalizations for violence.
On the contrary, it is undeniably true that being hit by a fast-moving
gelatin capsule in two or three out of every four games played (common averages) offers a crucial insight into the perils of real combat.
But their testimonies are only a partial truth. As in *Casca: The Eternal
Mercenary,* the paintball player dies only to walk off the battleground
and be reborn a warrior half an hour later. Surviving players in regular games never even see the "corpses" of their fallen comrades.
Instead, just as in the old war movies when the camera quickly cuts
away from the fallen soldier with the red dot on his chest, casualties
simply disappear from view. When Colonel Wyle ordered the
"dead" paintball soldiers to lie where they had fallen for five minutes
so that he could see the casualty pattern, author and player Jason
Rein sheepishly acknowledged, "I must admit that it was a highly
unusual sight to see individual 'bodies' (and in some cases, clusters)
as I made my way off the field."[57] Both the New War mythology and
the game obscure the fundamental reality that war creates death.

60   Indeed, what paintball does best of all is to fragment experience
and thus allow men to embrace contradictory thoughts and feelings.
The rapid changes from battle to game to battle create unusual opportunities for the self to "float," suspended from ordinary identity.
Men can play John Wayne or Sylvester Stallone when they posture
with their guns and make successful kills, and simultaneously reflect all fantasy warriors while nursing a stinging welt on the arm or
leg. At one moment the game can be seen as a test of true grit.
Minutes later a player can simply see himself as having become a
kid again for an afternoon, with presumably no implications for his
adult life.

In this shifting back and forth, the world blurs. Reality can be undone and reconfigured again and again. Even if the United States has problems winning military victories abroad, the Wolverines, Marauders, and Vigilantes can fight on indefinitely, with every man a hero and every hero a comrade for life. In this way good wars replace the bad one of the recent past. Yet it's all done, as Atwill says, tongue in cheek.[58] This is, after all, only a game.

Notes

1. Quoted from *Architectural Design,* September–October 1982, 10.
2. Advertisement for Conquest playing field, *Action Pursuit Games,* June 1988, 74.
3. All quotations from personal interviews at Conquest playing field, Malibu, Calif., August 12, 1988.
4. Brian Sutton-Smith, *Toys as Culture* (New York: Gardner, 1986), 64.
5. Lionel Atwill, *The New, Official Survival Game Manual* (New London, N.H.: The National Survival Game, Inc., 1987), 155.
6. Interview with Mike Jasperson, publisher and editor of *Front Line* magazine, Huntington Beach, Calif., May 16, 1987.
7. Interview with Denis Bulowski, Sat Cong Village paintball field, Corona, Calif., July 22, 1987.
8. Advertisement for War Zone playing field, *Front Line* magazine, February 1987, 31.
9. Interview with Mike Jasperson, publisher and editor of *Front Line* magazine, Huntington Beach, Calif., May 21, 1987.
10. Frank Hughes, "Picking Your Paintball Persona," *Action Pursuit Games,* April 1988, 27.
11. Gary Alan Fine, *Shared Fantasy* (Chicago: University of Chicago Press, 1983), 3, 182.
12. Hughes, "Picking your Paintball Persona," 27, 72.
13. J. C. Crocker, "Ceremonial Masks," in *Celebration: Studies in Festivity and Ritual,* ed. Victor Turner (Washington, D.C.: Smithsonian Institution, 1982), 80.
14. The concept that individuals "conjure up the spirit" and so change their subjectivity comes from Jack Katz, *Seductions of Crime: Moral and Sensual Attractions of Doing Evil* (New York: Basic Books, 1988), 7.
15. Interviews with two managers working at Adventure Game Supply, Bellflower, Calif., August 10, 1988.
16. Interview with Mike Jasperson, publisher and editor of *Front Line* magazine, Huntington Beach, Calif., May 21, 1987.
17. Sutton-Smith, *Toys as Culture,* 252.
18. Atwill, *Survival Game Manual,* 11.
19. Ibid., 31.
20. Interviews with Lou Grubbs, War Zone playing field, Fountain Valley, Calif., August 1, 1987. Grubbs's account of how he invented constant air appears to be universally accepted. I've never heard a story that contradicted or even slightly differed from his history.
21. Advertisement by Par-Ordnance Manufacturing, Inc., "Your Search for Better Close-Combat Equipment Stops and Ends Here!!!," *Front Line* magazine, December 1986, 36.
22. Advertisement by Tippman Pneumatics, Inc., "Never Be Outgunned Again!," *Action Pursuit Games,* January 1988, inside back cover.

23. Advertisement by Brass Eagle Paint Ball Air Guns, "Barracuda Semi-Automatic DMR Series," *Action Pursuit Games,* November 1990, 32.

24. Advertisement by Adventure Game Supplies, Inc., "Test," *Paintball Sports International,* November 1990, inside back cover.

25. "Products for Players," *Action Pursuit Games,* April 1988, 14.

26. Advertisement by Pursuit Marketing, Inc., "The New PMI-3 Semi-Automatic," *Action Pursuit Games,* November 1990, inside front cover.

27. Advertisement by Corliss Delay Inc., *Paintball International Sports,* November 1990, 85.

28. Atwill, *Survival Game Manual,* 27.

29. Jason Rein, "Paintball Meets the Marines," *Action Pursuit Games,* November 1990, 63–64.

30. Ibid., 62.

31. *"Front Line* Mail Call," *Front Line* magazine, February 1987, 2.

32. Interview with Russell Maynard, publisher and editor of *Action Pursuit Games,* Burbank, Calif., August 17, 1988.

33. Atwill, *Survival Game Manual,* 155.

34. Interview with Denis Bulowski, Sat Cong Village, Corona, Calif., July 22, 1987

35. Interview with one of the employees at Adventure Game Supply, Bellflower, Calif., August 10, 1988.

36. Interview with Russell Maynard, publisher and editor of *Action Pursuit Games,* Burbank, Calif., August 17, 1988.

37. Interview with Ken S., Sat Cong Village, Corona, Calif., July 22, 1987.

38. Interview with the owner of The Annihilator, a wholesale paintball company, Diamondbar, Calif., August 16, 1988.

39. Interviews with Denis Bulowski and one of his employees, Sat Cong Village, Corona, Calif., July 22, 1987.

40. Interview with an employee, Adventure Game Supply, Bellflower, Calif., August 10, 1988.

41. Interview with a paramedic and part-time referee, War Zone, Fountain Valley, Calif., August 1, 1987.

42. Christopher Buckley, "Viet Guilt: Were the Real Prisoners of War the Young Americans Who Never Left Home?" *Esquire,* September 1983, 72.

43. Ibid., 58.

44. Atwill, *Survival Game Manual,* 15.

45. Ibid., 153.

46. Ibid., 152.

47. Ibid., 23 and 153.

48. Interview with one of the Vigilantes, Malibu, Calif., August 12, 1988.

49. Interview with Lou Grubbs, War Zone, Fountain Valley, Calif., August 1, 1987.

50. Interview with the manager of Paint Pistol Express, Anaheim, Calif., August 15, 1988.

51. Ibid.

52. Rick Soll, "War Game: Adults Play Cowboys, Indians," *Los Angeles Times,* November 18, 1983, A1, 8.

53. Interview with Lou Grubbs, War Zone, Fountain Valley, Calif., August 1, 1987.

54. Referee, War Zone, Fountain Valley, Calif., August 1, 1987.

55. Interview with referee, Sat Cong Village, Corona, Calif., July 22, 1987.

56. Interview with Lou Grubbs, War Zone, Fountain Valley, Calif., August 1, 1987.

57. Jason Rein, "Tell It to the Marines," *Paintball Sports,* November 1990, 66.

58. Atwill, *Survival Game Manual,* 17.

Reflective Reading, Informal Writing

REFLECTING ON THE READING:

- Gibson's work is what we would call a cultural study—a study of a cultural artifact, event, or phenomenon. Based on what Gibson does in this piece, what do you think the goal or purpose of this kind of cultural analysis might be?
- Gibson's essay is not "personal" in the same ways that Tompkins', Anzaldua's, or Williams' essays seem "personal." Do you think this difference means Gibson (and Gibson's work) is not reflexive in some way? Why or why not? Point out at least one passage that proves your point, a passage showing either reflexivity or a clear lack of reflexivity.
- Gibson quotes one paintball aficionado (Gramps) as saying paintball is an antiwar movement. What is Gramps' evidence for this understanding of paintball? Do you think Gibson agrees with Gramps? Do you accept Gramps' argument? Why or why not?

UNDERSTANDING RHETORICAL STRATEGIES:

- While Gibson does not tell a narrative in which he appears to be an active character, he nonetheless tells a story that seems full of his presence. How does he accomplish this? You might want to consider tone, voice, point of view, and methodology.
- Gibson's essay is obviously an academic one and is meant to be a very public piece of writing. Look for specific clues in the text that might indicate it is more personal than might appear at first glance.
- From where and how does Gibson gather his evidence? How many different kinds of evidence can you identify? Does this evidence seem appropriate for Gibson's argument? Where does the method (or methods) for gathering this evidence seem reflective or reflexive for the author? For us as readers? For the persons Gibson observes or interviews?

INFORMAL WRITING:

- Is a violent video game really violent? Is it just a game? Is a movie like *Rambo* just a movie? Write about why you think each is or is not just a game or just a movie. Do you think Gibson would agree or disagree with you?
- Identify something you think would lend itself to a cultural study or critique. Observe and take notes. Briefly interview at least one person who is involved or touched in some way by the cultural item you've chosen. How does this artifact or phenomenon seem to work or engage in society?

PATRICIA J. WILLIAMS

After completing her education at Wellesley College and Harvard Law School, Patricia J. Williams worked as a consumer advocate and Deputy City Attorney for the City of Los Angeles and as a staff attorney for the Western Center on Law and Poverty. In her academic career she has been a faculty member of the University of Wisconsin School of Law, Harvard University's Women's Studies Program, and the City University of New York Law School at Queen's College. She has also received fellowships from the Center for Advanced Study in the Behavioral Sciences at Stanford University, the Humanities Research Institute of the University of California at Irvine, and the School of Criticism and Theory at Dartmouth College.

Williams' work has appeared in such publications as *USA Today, Harvard Law Review, Tikkun, The New York Times Book Review, The Nation, Ms. Magazine,* and the *Village Voice.* The *Voice Literary Supplement* included her book, *The Alchemy of Race and Rights,* in its list of the 25 best books of 1991; it was described by *Ms. Magazine's* twentieth anniversary edition as one of the "feminist classics of the last twenty years."

Currently, Williams teaches law at Columbia University School of Law and serves on the boards of the Society of American Law Teachers, the NOW Legal Defense and Education Fund, and the Center for Constitutional Rights.

In "The Ring and the Deep Blue Sea" from *The Alchemy of Race and Rights* (1991), Williams presents her case for the significance of the "subject position" in legal situations. She writes, "That life is complicated is a fact of great analytic importance. Law too often seeks to avoid this truth by making up its own breed of narrower, simpler, but hypnotically powerful rhetorical truths. Acknowledging, challenging, playing with these as rhetorical gestures is, it seems to me, necessary for any conception of justice. Such acknowledgment complicates the supposed purity of gender, race, voice, boundary; it allows us to acknowledge the utility of such categorizations for certain purposes and the necessity of their breakdown on other occasions." The idea of play is important to Williams because it allows her to show, instead of merely explain, her thesis. Consequently, she refers to an historical law case, describes herself writing in her home, takes a surreal sweep through the TV channels, records a presumably imaginary conversation with her sister, relates anecdotes from the law office and the classroom, and tells a story about dogs on the sidewalk. Williams' method pushes the reader to fill, from a necessarily subjective perspective, the "gaps" in her essay's varied writing style and, in the process, proves her point about the importance of subject positioning. As you read "The Brass Ring and the Deep Blue Sea," see if you can define for yourself what Williams means by the importance of subject positioning.

The Brass Ring and the Deep Blue Sea: (some parables about learning to think like a lawyer)

Since subject position is everything in my analysis of the law, you deserve to know that it's a bad morning. I am very depressed. It always takes a while to sort out what's wrong, but it usually starts with some kind of perfectly irrational thought such as: I *hate* being a lawyer. This particular morning I'm sitting up in bed reading about redhibitory vices. A redhibitory vice is a defect in merchandise which, if existing at the time of purchase, gives rise to a claim allowing the buyer to return the thing and get back part or all of the purchase price. The case I'm reading is an 1835 decision from Louisiana, involving the rehibitory vice of craziness:

> The plaintiff alleged that he purchased of the defendant a slave named Kate, for which he paid $500, and in two or three days after it was discovered the slave was crazy, and run away, and that the vices were known to the defendant . . .
>
> It was contended [by the seller] that Kate was not crazy but only stupid, and stupidity is not madness; but on the contrary, an apparent defect, against which the defendant did not warrant . . .
>
> The code has declared that a sale may be avoided on account of any vice or defect, which renders the thing either absolutely useless, or its use so inconvenient and imperfect, that it must be supposed the buyer would not have purchased with a knowledge of the vice. We are satisfied that the slave in question was wholly, and perhaps worse than, useless.

5   As I said, this is the sort of morning when I hate being a lawyer, a teacher, and just about everything else in my life. It's all I can do to feed the cats. I let my hair stream wildly and the eyes roll back in my head.

So you should know that this is one of those mornings when I refuse to compose myself properly; you should know you are dealing with someone who is writing this in an old terry bathrobe with a little fringe of blue and white tassels dangling from the hem, trying to decide if she is stupid or crazy.

Whenever I'm in a mood like this, it helps to get it out on paper, so I sit down to write even when I'm afraid I may produce a death-poem. Sometimes I can just write fast from the heart until I'm healed. Sometimes I look at my computer keyboard and I am paralyzed, inadequate—all those letters of the alphabet, full of random signification. I feel like a monkey. Those mornings, and this is one, I need a little extra push to get me started, and if I turn on the television, almost any story will do. I switch channels through a sea of news programs with the coopting, carnivorous eagerness of catharsis.

Conditions are bad, very bad, all over the world. The newscasters tell me that everyone is afraid of black men these days, even black women. Black people are being jailed in huge numbers, and the infant-mortality rate is staggering. Courts have authorized the custody removal of children at birth from mothers who are drug-addicted. Drugs bring pleasure to the biological catastrophe of having been born in the fearsome, loathsome packaging of an "other" body. Editorials talk about the efficiency of apartheid. Bigger better prisons. Spy satellites. Personnel carriers in Harlem. Door-to-door searches. State-sanctioned castration. Some neutral market thing devouring the resources of the earth at a terminally reckless rate. The Ku Klux Klan and the Aryan Brotherhood are the major unions among prison guards. Eastern Europe wants more freedom in the form of telephone-answering machines and video cassettes. AIDS spreads and spreads and spreads, among black and brown communities in particular. Subsistence farmers and indigenous people are dying all over the world, their ways and knowledge devoured and lost forever. According to the most authoritative scientists, the greenhouse effect is supposed to raise the temperature of the earth by two or three degrees over the next millennium. The winter of 1989 was five, ten, sometimes fifteen degrees above normal, all over the earth. It is the spring of 1990, and we are all worried about the summer to come.

I don't know how to find something to write about in the panic of this deadly world. There is more in the news than even my depression can consume.

10   Then I see it. A concise, modular, yet totally engaging item on the "MacNeil/Lehrer News Hour": Harvard Law School cannot find one black woman on the entire planet who is good enough to teach there, because we're all too stupid. (Well, that's not precisely what was said. It was more like they couldn't find anyone smart enough. To be fair, what Associate Dean Louis Kaplow actually said was that Harvard would have to "lower its standards," which of course Harvard simply cannot do.)

So now you know: it is this news item, as I sit propped up in bed with my laptop computer balanced on my knees, clad in my robe with the torn fringe of terry bluebells, that finally pushes me over the edge and into the deep rabbit hole of this book.

When I dust myself off, I am sitting with my sister at my parents' kitchen table. Grown now, she and I are at home for Christmas. We chat, catching up on each other's lives. My sister tells me how her house is haunted by rabbits. I tell her how I'm trying to write a book on law and liberation.

"The previous owner had hundreds of them," she says. "You can hear them dancing in the dining room after midnight."

"It will be a book about the jurisprudence of rights," I respond. "I will attempt to apply so-called critical thought to legal studies. I believe that critical theory has valuable insights to contribute to debates about the ethics of law and the meaning of rights; yet many of those insights have been buried in relatively arcane vocabulary and abstraction. My book will concern itself with the interplay of commerce and constitutional protections and will be organized around discussion of three basic jurisprudential forces: autonomy, community, and order. My chapters will address such issues as surrogate motherhood and ownership; neighborhood and homelessness; racially motivated violence and disownedness. I will try to write, moreover, in a way that bridges the traditional gap between theory and praxis. It is not my goal merely to simplify; I hope that the result will be a text that is multilayered—that encompasses the straightforwardness of real life *and* reveals complexity of meaning."

15   "But what's the book *about*?" my sister asks, thumping her leg against the chair impatiently.

"Howard Beach, polar bears, and food stamps," I snap back. "I am interested in the way in which legal language flattens and confines in absolutes the complexity of meaning inherent in any given problem; I am trying to challenge the usual limits of commercial discourse by using an intentionally double-voiced and relational, rather than a traditionally legal black-letter, vocabulary. For example, I am a commercial lawyer as well as a teacher of contract and property law. I am also black and female, a status that one of my former employers described as being 'at oxymoronic odds' with that of commercial lawyer. While I certainly took issue with that particular characterization, it is true that my attempts to write in my own voice have placed me in the center of a snarl of social tensions and crossed boundaries. On the one hand, my writing has been staked out as the exclusive interdisciplinary property of constitutional law, contract, African-American history, feminist jurisprudence, political science, and rhetoric. At the same time, my work has been described as a "sophisticated frontal assault' on laissez-faire's most sacred sanctums, as 'new-age performance art,' and as 'anecdotal individualism.' In other words, to speak as black, female, *and* commercial lawyer has rendered me simultaneously universal, trendy, and marginal. I think, moreover, that there is a paradigm at work, in the persistent perceptions of me as inherent contradiction: a paradigm of larger social perceptions that divide public from private, black from white, dispossessed from legitimate. This realization, while externally personal, inevitably informs my writing on a professional level."

"What's so new," asks my sister, losing interest rapidly, "about a schizophrenic black lady pouring her heart out about food stamps and polar bears?"

I lean closer to her. "Floating signifiers," I whisper.

I continue: "Legal writing presumes a methodology that is highly stylized, precedential, and based on deductive reasoning. Most scholarship in law is rather like the 'old math': static, stable, formal—rationalism walled against chaos. My writing is an intentional departure from that. I use a model of inductive empiricism, borrowed from—and parodying—systems analysis, in order to enliven thought about complex social problems. I want to look at legal issues within a framework inscribed not just within the four corners of a document—be it contract or the Constitution—but by the disciplines of psychology, sociology, history, criticism, and philosophy. The advantage of this approach is that it highlights factors that would otherwise go unremarked. For example, *stare decisis* (the judicial practice of deciding cases in a manner limited by prior court decisions in factually analogous situations), rather than remaining a silent, unquestioned 'given,' may be analyzed as a filter to certain types of systemic input. Another advantage is that this sort of analytic technique can serve to describe a community of context for those social actors whose traditional legal status has been the isolation of oxymoron, of oddity, of outsider. I am trying to create a genre of legal writing to fill the gaps of traditional legal scholarship. I would like to write in a way that reveals the intersubjectivity of legal constructions, that forces the reader both to participate in the construction of meaning and to be conscious about that process. Thus, in attempting to fill the gaps in the discourse of commercial exchange, I hope that the gaps in my own writing will be self-consciously filled by the reader, as an act of forced mirroring of meaning-invention. To this end, I exploit all sorts of literary devices, including parody, parable, and poetry."

20 ". . . as in polar bears?" my sister asks eagerly, alert now, ears pricked, nose quivering, hair bristling.

"My, what big teeth you have!" I exclaim, just before the darkness closes over me.

It is my deep belief that theoretical legal understanding and social transformation need not be oxymoronic. I want this book to occupy the gaps between those ends that the sensation of oxymoron marks. What I hope will be filled in is connection; connection between my psyche and the readers', between lived experience and social perception, and between an encompassing historicity and a jurisprudence of generosity.

"Theoretical legal understanding" is characterized, in Anglo-American jurisprudence, by at least three features of thought and rhetoric:

1. The hypostatization of exclusive categories and definitional po-larities, the drawing of bright lines and clear taxonomies that purport to make life simpler in the face of life's complication: rights/needs, moral/immoral, public/private, white/black.

25

2. The existence of transcendent, acontextual, universal legal truths or pure procedures. For example, some conservative theorists might insist that the tort of fraud has always existed and that it is part of a universal system of right and wrong. A friend of mine demanded of a professor who made just such an assertion: "Do you mean to say that when the first white settlers landed on Fiji, they found tortfeasors waiting to be discovered?" Yes, in a manner of speaking, was the profes-sor's response. This habit of universalizing legal taxonomies is very much like a cartoon I once saw, in which a group of prehistoric fish swam glumly underwater, carrying baseball bats tucked beneath their fins, waiting to evolve, looking longingly toward dry land, where a baseball was lying in wait on the shore. The more serious side of this essentialized world view is a worrisome tendency to disparage anything that is nontranscendent (temporal, historical), or contextual (socially constructed), or nonuniversal (specific) as "emo-tional," "literary," "personal," or just Not True.

3. The existence of objective, "unmediated" voices by which those transcendent, universal truths find their expression. Judges, lawyers, logicians, and practitioners of empirical methodologies are obvious examples, but the supposed exis-tence of such voices is also given power in romanticized notions of "real people" having "real" experiences—not be-cause real people have experienced what they really experi-enced, but because their experiences are somehow *made* legitimate—either because they are viewed as empirically le-gitimate (directly corroborated by consensus, by a community of outsiders) or, more frequently, because those experiences are corroborated by hidden or unspoken models of legiti-macy. The Noble Savage as well as the Great White Father, the Good-Hearted Masses, the Real American, the Rational Consumer, and the Arm's-Length Transactor are all versions of this Idealized Other whose gaze provides us either with in-ternalized censure or externalized approval; internalized paralysis or externalized legitimacy; internalized false con-sciousness or externalized claims of exaggerated authenticity.

The degree to which these three features of legal thought are a force in laws ranging from contracts to crimes, from property to civil liberties, will be a theme throughout the rest of this book. For the moment, however, a smaller example might serve to illustrate the interpretive dynamic of what I am speaking.

A man with whom I used to work once told me that I made too much of my race. "After all," he said, "I don't even think of you as black." Yet sometime later, when another black woman became engaged in an ultimately unsuccessful tenure battle, he confided to me that he wished the school could find more blacks like me. I felt myself slip in and out of a shadow, as I became nonblack for purposes of inclusion and black for purposes of exclusion; I felt the boundaries of my very body manipulated, casually inscribed by definitional demarcations that did not refer to me.

The paradox of my being black yet nonblack visited me again when, back to back, the same (white) man and then a (black) woman wondered aloud if I "really identified as black." When the white man said this, I was acutely aware that the choice of identifying as black (as opposed to white?) was hardly mine; that as long as I am identified as black by the majority of others, my own identifying as black will almost surely follow as a simple fact of human interdependency. When the black woman told me the very same thing, I took it to heart as a signpost of self-denial; as possible evidence within myself of that brand of social distress and alienation to which blacks and oppressed people are so peculiarly subject; and as a call for unity in a society that too often helps us turn against ourselves.

30   I heard the same words from each, and it made no difference to me. I heard the same words from each, but differently: one characterized me as more of something I am not, white; the other called for me to be more conscious of something I am, black. I heard the same-different words addressed to me, a perceived white-male-socialized black woman, as a challenge to mutually exclusive categorization, as an overlapping of black and female and right and male and private and wrong and white and public, and so on and so forth.

That life is complicated is a fact of great analytic importance. Law too often seeks to avoid this truth by making up its own breed of narrower, simpler, but hypnotically powerful rhetorical truths. Acknowledging, challenging, playing with these *as* rhetorical gestures is, it seems to me, necessary for any conception of justice. Such acknowledgment complicates the supposed purity of gender, race, voice, boundary; it allows us to acknowledge the utility of such categorizations for certain purposes and the necessity of their breakdown on other occasions. It complicates definitions in its shift, in its expansion and contraction according to circumstance, in its room for the possibility of creatively mated taxonomies and their wildly unpredictable offspring.

I think, though, that one of the most important results of reconceptualizing from "objective truth" to rhetorical event will be a more nuanced sense of legal and social responsibility. This will be so because much of what is spoken in so-called objective, unmediated voices is in fact mired in hidden subjectives and unexamined claims that make property of others beyond the self, all the while denying such connections. I remember A., a colleague, once stating that he didn't like a book he had just read because he had another friend who was a literary critic and he *imagined* that this critical friend would say a host of negative things about the book. A. disclaimed his own subjectivity, displacing it onto a larger-than-life literary critic; he created an authority who was imaginary but whose rhetorical objectivity was as smooth and convincing as the slice of a knife. In psychobabble, this is known as "not taking responsibility." In racial contexts, it is related to the familiar offensiveness of people who will say, "Our maid is black and *she* says that blacks want . . ."; such statements both universalize the lone black voice and disguise, enhance, and "objectify" the authority of the individual white speaker. As a legal tool, however, it is an extremely common device by which not just subject positioning is obscured, but by which agency and responsibility are hopelessly befuddled.

The propagated mask of the imagined literary critic, the language club of hyperauthenticity, the myth of a purely objective perspective, the godlike image of generalized, legitimating others—these are too often reified in law as "impersonal" rules and "neutral" principles, presumed to be inanimate, unemotional, unbiased, unmanipulated, and higher than ourselves. Laws like masks, frozen against the vicissitudes of life; rights as solid as rocks; principles like baseballs waiting on dry land for us to crawl up out of the mud and claim them.

This semester I have been teaching a course entitled Women and Notions of Property. I have been focusing on the semantic power and property of individualistic gendered perspectives, gender in this instance having less to do with the biology of male and female than with the semiotics of power relations, of dominance and submission, of assertion and deference, of big and little; as well as on gender issues specifically based in biology, such as reproductive rights and the complicated ability of women in particular to live freely in the territory of their own bodies. An example of the stories we discuss is the following, used to illustrate the rhetoric of power relations whose examinations, I tell my students, is at the heart of the course.

35   Walking down Fifth Avenue in New York not long ago, I came up behind a couple and their young son. The child, about four or five years old, had evidently been complaining about big dogs. The mother was saying, "But why are you afraid of big dogs?" "Because they're big," he responded with eminent good sense. "But what's

the difference between a big dog and a little dog?" the father persisted. "They're *big*," said the child. "But there's really no difference," said the mother, pointing to a large slathering wolfhound
with narrow eyes and the calculated amble of a gangster, and then
to a bedribboned Pekinese the size of a roller skate, who was flounc-
ing along just ahead of us all, in that little fox-trotty step that keep
Pekinese from ever being taken seriously. "See?" said the father. "If
you look really close you'll see there's no difference at all. They're all
just dogs."

And I thought: Talk about your iron-clad canon. Talk about a
static, unyielding, totally uncompromising point of reference.
These people must be lawyers. Where else do people learn so well
the idiocies of High Objectivity? How else do people learn to capit-
ulate so uncritically to a norm that refuses to allow for difference?
How else do grown-ups sink so deeply into the authoritarianism of
their own world view that they can universalize their relative big-
ness so completely that they obliterate the subject positioning of
their child's relative smallness? (To say nothing of the position of
the slathering wolfhound, from whose own narrow perspective I
dare say the little boy must have looked exactly like a lamb chop.)

I used this story in my class because I think it illustrates a paradigm of thought by which children are taught not to see what
they see; by which blacks are reassured that there is no real inequality in the world, just their own bad dreams; and by which
women are taught not to experience what they experience, in deference to men's ways of knowing. The story also illustrates the
possibility of a collective perspective or social positioning that
would give rise to a claim for the legal interests of groups. In a historical moment when individual rights have become the basis for
any remedy, too often group interests are defeated by, for example, finding the one four-year-old who has wrestled whole packs
of wolfhounds fearlessly to the ground; using that individual experience to attack the validity of there ever being any generaliz-
able four-year-old fear of wolf-hounds; and then recasting the
general group experience as a fragmented series of specific, isolated events rather than a pervasive social phenomenon ("You
have every right to think that that wolfhound has the ability to
bite off your head, but that's just your point of view").

My students, most of whom signed up expecting to experience
that crisp, refreshing, clear-headed sensation that "thinking like a
lawyer" purportedly endows, are confused by this and all the stories
I tell them in my class on Women and Notions of Property. They are
confused enough by the idea of property alone, overwhelmed by the
thought of dogs and women as academic subjects, and paralyzed by
the idea that property might have a gender and that gender might
be a matter of words.

But I haven't been able to straighten things out for them because I'm confused too. I have arrived at a point where everything I have ever learned is running around and around in my head; and little bits of law and pieces of everyday life fly out of my mouth in weird combinations. Who cam blame the students for being confused? On the other hand, everyday life is a confusing bit of business. And so my students plot my disintegration, in the shadowy shelter of ivy-covered archways and the margins of their notebooks . . . .

Reflective Reading, Informal Writing

REFLECTING ON THE READING:

- Williams opens with a legal decision from Louisiana that was written in 1835. How does this case relate to the larger concerns of her essay?
- Williams expresses concern for "the way in which legal language flattens and confines in absolutes the complexity of meaning inherent in any given problem." What does this mean? How would this concern apply, for example, to the Louisiana case with which she opens to the essay? To the exchange between a boy and his parents about the distinction between big and small dogs? To the legal principle of *stare decisis*?
- Like Jane Tompkins, Williams employs more than one voice. It is probably fair to say, however, that instead of two voices, Williams uses multiple voices. Identify as many different voices as you can. At one point, describing the nature of "theoretical legal understanding," Williams describes one of its key features as "The existence of objective, 'unmediated' voices by which . . . transcendent, universal truths find their expression." Why does Williams find this feature of legal thought and rhetoric problematic? How does her own use of multiple voices help to make her case against it?
- Paraphrase Williams' list of three key features of legal thought and rhetoric. In what respect do these features seem based on deductive reasoning, or lend themselves to being used deductively? In what ways does her own writing, which she characterizes as "inductive empiricism," differ? What would this list look like if Williams rewrote it to describe her own thought and rhetoric?

UNDERSTANDING RHETORICAL STRATEGIES:

- Why does Williams begin this essay by telling us about her "bad morning"? What is a "subject position," and why should we, as readers, care?

- Williams asserts that, in addition to her other departures from the conventions of traditional legal scholarship, she will make use of literary devices. What literary devices does she use, and why?
- As serious as the issues Williams discusses are, she nonetheless manages at points to communicate a sense of play, even a sense of humor. Identify one or more such places in her essay, and discuss their role. How are they related to the point(s) she is making?

INFORMAL WRITING:

- In what sense does this essay illustrate the concept of reflexivity in action? Is it relevant that Williams intends to bring to bear on her analysis of legal thought and rhetoric the disciplines of psychology, sociology, history, criticism, and philosophy?
- "Much of what is spoken in so-called objective, unmediated voices," Williams writes, "is in fact mired in hidden subjectivities and unexamined claims that make property of others beyond the self, all the while denying such connections." What does she mean here? Can you provide examples of "objective, unmediated voices" and show how they work? Is there a sense in which the use of these voices in this way amounts to the very *opposite* of reflexivity?
- Agree or disagree: "Neutral" legal thought and rhetoric further the oppression of minorities, women, and other marginalized groups. Explain.

CLIFFORD GEERTZ

Clifford Geertz is an anthropologist most known for his books on Bali, Java, and Morocco and for redefining the role and the experience of the anthropologist. As discussed in this excerpt from *Local Knowledge* (1983), the anthropologist interprets a culture through his or her own particular lens. Geertz labels this "reflexivity," the recognition that the observer inevitably becomes part of the observation. Rather than believing he is an invisible presence without impact on the scene he observes, Geertz considered the complications of his own presence within a culture and the culture's influence on him.

Geertz began his education as an English major and then switched to philosophy where a professor suggested he pursue graduate studies in anthropology. His diverse range of disciplines, from history and psychology to literary criticism, work to support and broaden his ideas. Geertz attended Antioch College and Harvard University. He earned his Ph.D. in 1956 and developed what he defines as "interpretive anthropology": looking at a culture's rituals, myths, and art for a sense of what daily life is like. Rather than removing the art from the context or considering the art as secondary to the people, Geertz looks at such signs of culture as a part of the lived experience. He defines culture as a system of ideas and symbols. The anthropologist's role is to decode the meaning of a culture's symbols and consider the particular as well as the universal—what is common to many people and cultures.

In addition to his admirable skill as a researcher and writer, Geertz brings an open attitude and sense of adventure to his work. For example, he first visited Morocco because a colleague at a conference in Cambridge suggested it. He flew to Morocco, rented a car and drove through almost all of the country, and decided immediately to do research there. He tells an interviewer, "Such things are kind of impulsive. One always tries in retrospect to make them look as if they were rational, deliberated decisions, but they really weren't." Do you see moments of impulsiveness anywhere in this essay?

"From the Native's Point of View": On the Nature of Anthropological Understanding

I

Several years ago a minor scandal erupted in anthropology: one of its ancestral figures told the truth in a public place. As befits an ancestor, he did it posthumously, and through his widow's decision rather than his own, with the result that a number of the sort of right-thinking types who are with us always immediately rose to cry that she, an in-marrier anyway, had betrayed clan secrets, profaned an idol, and let down the side. What will the children think, to say nothing of the layman? But the disturbance was not much lessened by such ceremonial wringing of the hands; the damn thing was, after all, already printed. In much the same fashion as James Watson's *The Double Helix* exposed the way in which biophysics in fact gets done, Bronislaw Malinowski's *A Diary in the Strict Sense of the Term* rendered established accounts of how anthropologists work fairly well implausible. The myth of the chameleon fieldworker, perfectly self-tuned to his exotic surroundings, a walking miracle of empathy, tact, patience, and cosmopolitanism, was demolished by the man who had perhaps done most to create it.

The squabble that arose around the publication of the *Diary* concentrated, naturally, on inessentials and missed, as was only to be expected, the point. Most of the shock seems to have arisen from the mere discovery that Malinowski was not, to put it delicately, an unmitigated nice guy. He had rude things to say about the natives he was living with, and rude words to say it in. He spent a great deal of his time wishing he were elsewhere. And he projected an image of a man about as little complaisant as the world has seen. (He also projected an image of a man consecrated to a strange vocation to the point of self-immolation, but that was less noted.) The discussion was made to come down to Malinowski's moral character or lack of it, and the genuinely profound question his book raised was ignored; namely, if it is not, as we had been taught to believe, through some sort of extraordinary sensibility, an almost preternatural capacity to think, feel, and perceive like a native (a word, I should hurry to say, I use here "in the strict sense of the term"), how is anthropological knowledge of the way natives think, feel, and perceive possible? The issue the *Diary* presents, with a force perhaps only a working ethnographer can fully appreciate, is not moral. (The moral idealization of fieldworkers in a mere sentimentality in the first place, when it is not self-congratulation or a guild pretense.) The issue is epistemological. If we are going to cling—as, in my opinion, we must—to the injunction to see things from the native's point of view, where are we when we can no longer claim some unique form of psychological closeness, a sort of transcultural identification, with our subjects? What happens to *verstehen* when *einfühlen* disappears?

As a matter of fact, this general problem has been exercising methodological discussion in anthropology for the last ten or fifteen years; Marlinowski's voice from the grave merely dramatizes it as a human dilemma over and above a professional one. The formulations have been various: "inside" versus "outside," or "first person" versus "third person" descriptions; "phenomenological" versus "objectivist," or "cognitive" versus "behavioral" theories; or, perhaps most commonly "emic" versus "etic" analyses, this last deriving from the distinction in linguistics between phonemics and phonetics, phonemics classifying sounds according to their internal function in language, phonetics classifying them according to their acoustic properties as such. But perhaps the simplest and most directly appreciable way to put the matter is in terms of a distinction formulated, for his own purposes, by the psychoanalyst Heinz Kohut, between what he calls "experience-near" and "experience-distant" concepts.

An experience-near concept is, roughly, one that someone—a patient, a subject, in our case an informant—might himself naturally and effortlessly use to define what he or his fellows see, feel, think, imagine, and so on, and which he would readily understand when similarly applied by others. An experience-distant concept is one that specialists of one sort or another—an analyst, an experimenter, an ethnographer, even a priest or an ideologist—employ to forward their scientific, philosophical, or practical aims. "Love" is an experience-near concept, "object cathexis" is an experience-distant one. "Social stratification" and perhaps for most peoples in the world even "religion" (and certainly "religious system") are experience-distant; "caste" and "nirvana" are experience-near, at least for Hindus and Buddhists.

5   Clearly, the matter is one of degree, not polar opposition—"fear" is experience-nearer than "phobia," and "phobia" experience-nearer than "ego dyssyntonic." And the difference is not, at least so far as anthropology is concerned (the matter is otherwise in poetry and physics), a normative one, in the sense that one sort of concept is to be preferred as such over the other. Confinement to experience-near concepts leaves an ethnographer awash in immediacies, as well as entangled in vernacular. Confinement to experience-distant ones leaves him stranded in abstractions and smothered in jargon. The real question, and the one Malinowski raised by demonstrating that, in the case of "natives," you don't have to be one to know one, is what roles the two sorts of concepts play in anthropological analysis. Or, more exactly, how, in each case, ought one to deploy them so as to produce an interpretation of the way a people lives which is neither imprisoned within their mental horizons, an ethnography of witchcraft as written by a witch, nor systematically deaf to the distinctive tonalities of their existence, an ethnography of witchcraft as written by a geometer.

Putting the matter this way—in terms of how anthropological analysis is to be conducted and its results framed, rather than what psychic constitution anthropologists need to have—reduces the mystery of what "seeing things from the native's point of view" means. But it does not make it any easier, nor does it lessen the demand for perceptiveness on the part of the fieldworker. To grasp concepts that, for another people, are experience-near, and to do so well enough to place them in illuminating connection with experience-distant concepts theorists have fashioned to capture the general features of social life, is clearly a task at least as delicate, if a bit less magical, as putting oneself into someone else's skin. The trick is not to get yourself into some inner correspondence of spirit with your informants. Preferring, like the rest of us, to call their souls their own, they are not going to be altogether keen about such effort anyhow. The trick is to figure out what the devil they think they are up to.

In one sense, of course, no one knows this better than they do themselves; hence the passion to swim in the stream of their experience, and the illusion afterward that one somehow has. But in another sense, that simple truism is simply not true. People use experience-near concepts spontaneously, unself-consciously, as it were colloquially; they do not, except fleetingly and on occasion, recognize that there are any "concepts" involved at all. That is what experience-near means—that ideas and the realities they inform are naturally and indissolubly bound up together. What else could you call a hippopotamus? Of course the gods are powerful, why else would we fear them? The ethnographer does not, and, in my opinion, largely cannot, perceive what his informants perceive. What he perceives, and that uncertainly enough, is what they perceive "with"—or "by means of," or "through" . . . or whatever the word should be. In the country of the blind, who are not as unobservant as they look, the one-eyed is not king, he is spectator.

Now, to make all this a bit more concrete, I want to turn for a moment to my own work, which, whatever its other faults, has at least the virtue of being mine—in discussions of this sort a distinct advantage. In all three of the societies I have studied intensively, Javanese, Balinese, and Moroccan, I have been concerned, among other things, with attempting to determine how the people who live there define themselves as persons, what goes into the idea they have (but, as I say, only half-realize they have) of what a self, Javanese, Balinese, or Moroccan style, is. And in each case, I have tried to get at this most intimate of notions not by imagining myself someone else, a rice peasant or a tribal sheikh, and then seeing what I thought, but by searching out and analyzing the symbolic forms—words, images, institutions, behaviors—in terms of which, in each place, people actually represented themselves to themselves and to one another.

The concept of person is, in fact, an excellent vehicle by means of which to examine this whole question of how to go about poking into another people's turn of mind. In the first place, some sort of concept of this kind, one feels reasonably safe in saying, exists in recognizable form among all social groups. The notions of what persons are may be, from our point of view, sometimes more than a little odd. They may be conceived to dart about nervously at night shaped like fire-flies. Essential elements of their psyches, like hatred, may be thought to be lodged in granular black bodies within their livers, discoverable upon autopsy. They may share their fates with *doppelgänger* beasts, so that when the beast sickens or dies they sicken or die too. But at least some conception of what a human individual is, as opposed to a rock, an animal, a rainstorm, or a god, is, so far as I can see, universal. Yet, at the same time as these offhand examples suggest, the actual conceptions involved vary from one group to the next, and often quite sharply. The Western conception of the person as a bounded, unique, more or less integrated motivational and cognitive universe, a dynamic center of awareness, emotion, judgment, and action orga-nized into a distinctive whole and set contrastively both against other such wholes and against its social and natural background, is, how-ever incorrigible it may seem to us, a rather peculiar idea within the context of the world's cultures. Rather than attempting to place the experience of others within the framework of such a conception, which is what the extolled "empathy" in fact usually comes down to, understanding them demands setting that conception aside and see-ing their experiences within the framework of their own idea of what selfhood is. And Java, Bali, and Morocco, at least, that idea differs markedly not only from our own but, no less dramatically and no less instructively, from one to the other.

II

10   In Java, where I worked in the fifties, I studied a small, shabby in-land county-seat sort of place; two shadeless streets of whitewashed wooden shops and offices, and even less substantial bamboo shacks crammed in helter-skelter behind them, the whole surrounded by a great half-circle of densely packed rice-bowl villages. Land was short, jobs were scarce, politics was unstable, health was poor, prices were rising, and life was altogether far from promising, a kind of ag-itated stagnancy in which, as I once put it, thinking of the curious mixture of borrowed fragments of modernity and exhausted relics of tradition that characterized the place, the future seemed about as remote as the past. Yet in the midst of this depressing scene there was an absolutely astonishing intellectual vitality, a philosophical passion really, and a popular one besides, to track the riddles of ex-istence right down to the ground. Destitute peasants would discuss questions of freedom of the will, illiterate tradesmen discoursed on

the properties of God, common laborers had theories about the relations between reason and passion, the nature of time, or the reliability of the senses. And, perhaps most importantly, the problem of the self—its nature, function, and mode of operation—was pursued with the sort of reflective intensity one could find among ourselves in only the most recherché settings indeed.

The central ideas in terms of which this reflection proceeded, and which thus defined its boundaries and the Javanese sense of what a person is, were arranged into two sets of contrasts, at base religious, one between "inside" and "outside," and one between "refined" and "vulgar." These glosses are, of course, crude and imprecise; determining exactly what the terms involved signified, sorting out their shades of meaning, was what all the discussion was about. But together they formed a distinctive conception of the self which, far from being merely theoretical, was the one in terms of which Javanese in fact perceived one another and, of course, themselves.

The "inside"/"outside" words, *batin* and *lair* (terms borrowed, as a matter of fact, from the Sufi tradition of Muslim mysticism, but locally reworked) refer on the one hand to the felt realm of human experience and on the other to the observed realm of human behavior. These have, one hastens, to say, nothing to do with "soul" and "body" in our sense, for which there are in fact quite other words with quite other implications. *Batin,* the "inside" word, does not refer to a separate seat of encapsulated spirituality detached or detachable from the body, or indeed to a bounded unit at all, but to the emotional life of human beings taken generally. It consists of the fuzzy, shifting flow of subjective feeling perceived directly in all its phenomenological immediacy but considered to be, at its roots at least, identical across all individuals, whose individuality it thus effaces. And similarly, *lair,* the "outside" word, has nothing to do with the body as an object, even an experienced object. Rather, it refers to that part of human life which, in our culture, strict behaviorists limit themselves to studying—external actions, movements, postures, speech—again conceived as in its essence invariant from one individual to the next. These two sets of phenomena—inward feelings and outward actions—are then regarded not as functions of one another but as independent realms of being to be put in proper order independently.

It is in connection with this "proper ordering" that the contrast between *alus,* the word meaning "pure," "refined," "polished," "exquisite," "ethereal," "subtle," "civilized," "smooth," and *kasar,* the word meaning "impolite," "rough," "uncivilized," "coarse," "insensitive," "vulgar," comes into play. The goal is to be *alus* in both the separated realms of the self. In the inner realm this is to be achieved through religious discipline, much but not all of it mystical. In the outer realm, it is to be achieved through etiquette, the rules of which here are not only extraordinarily elaborate but have something of the force of law. Through meditation the civilized man thins out his emotional life to a kind of constant hum; through etiquette, he both shields that life from external disruptions and regularizes his outer behavior in such a way that it appears to others as a predictable, undisturbing, elegant, and rather vacant set of choreographed motions and settled forms of speech.

There is much more to all this, because it connects up to both an ontology and an aesthetic. But so far as our problem is concerned, the result is a bifurcate conception of the self, half ungestured feeling and half unfelt gesture. An inner world of stilled emotion and an outer world of shaped behavior confront one another as sharply distinguished realms unto themselves, any particular person being out the momentary locus, so to speak, of that confrontation, a passing expression of their permanent existence, their permanent separation, and their permanent need to be kept in their own order. Only when you have seen, as I have, a young man whose wife—a woman he had in fact raised from childhood and who had been the center of his life—has suddenly and inexplicably died, greeting everyone with a set smile and formal apologies for his wife's absence and trying, by mystical techniques, to flatten out, as he himself put it, the hills and valleys of his emotion into an even, level plain ("That is what you have to do,": he said to me, "be smooth inside and out") can you come, in the face of our notions of the intrinsic honesty of deep feeling and the moral importance of personal sincerity, to take the possibility of such a conception of selfhood seriously and appreciate, however inaccessible it is to you, its own sort of force.

III

15   Bali, where I worked both in another small provincial town, though one rather less drifting and dispirited, and, later, in an upland village of highly skilled musical instruments makers, is of course in many ways similar to Java, with which it shared a common culture to the fifteenth century. But at a deeper level, having continued Hindu while Java was, nominally at least, Islamized, it is quite different. The intricate, obsessive ritual life—Hindu, Buddhist, and Polynesian in about equal proportions—whose development was more or less cut off in Java, leaving its Indic spirit to turn reflective and phenomenological, even quietistic, in the way I have just described, flourished in Bali to reach levels of scale and flamboyance that have startled the world and made the Balinese a much more dramaturgical people with a self to match. What is philosophy in Java is theater in Bali.

As a result, there is in Bali a persistent and systematic attempt to stylize all aspects of personal expression to the point where anything idiosyncratic, anything characteristic of the individual merely because he is who he is physically, psychologically, or biographically, is muted in favor of his assigned place in the continuing and, so it is thought, never-changing pageant that is Balinese life. It is dramatis personae, not actors, that endure; indeed, it is dramatis personae, not actors, that in the proper sense really exist. Physically men come and go, mere incidents in a happenstance history, of no genuine importance even to themselves. But the masks they wear, the stage they occupy, the parts they play, and, most important, the spectacle they mount remain, and comprise not the façade but the substance of things, not least the self. Shakespeare's old-trouper view of the vanity of action in the face of mortality—all the world's a stage and we but poor players, content to strut our hour, and so on—makes no sense here. There is no make-believe; of course players perish, but the play does not, and it is the latter, the performed rather that the performer, that really matters.

Again, all this is realized not in terms of some general mood the anthropologist in his spiritual versatility somehow captures, but through a set of readily observable symbolic forms: an elaborate repertoire of designations and titles. The Balinese have at least a half-dozen major sorts of labels, ascriptive, fixed, and absolute, which one person can apply to another (or, of course, to himself) to place him among his fellows. There are birth-order markers, kinship terms, caste titles, sex indicators, teknonyms, and so on and so forth, each of which consists not of a mere collection of useful tags but a distinct and bounded, internally very complex, terminological system. When one applies one of these designations or titles (or, as is more common, several at once) to someone, one therefore defines him as a determinate point in a fixed pattern, as the temporary occupant of a particular, quite untemporary, cultural locus. To identify someone, yourself or somebody else, in Bali is thus to locate him within the familiar cast of characters— "king," "grandmother," "third-born," "Brahman"—of which the social drama is, like some stock company roadshow piece—*Charley's Aunt* or *Springtime for Henry*—inevitably composed.

The drama is of course not farce, and especially not transvestite farce, though there are such elements in it. It is an enactment of hierarchy, a theater of status. But that, though critical, is unpursuable here. The immediate point is that, in both their structure and their mode of operation, the terminological systems conduce to a view of the human person as an appropriate representative of a generic type, not a unique creature with a private fate. To see how they do this, how they tend to obscure the mere materialities—biological, psychological, historical—of individual existence in favor of standardized status qualities would involve an extended analysis. But perhaps a single example, the simplest further simplified, will suffice to suggest the pattern.

All Balinese receive what might be called birth-order names. There are four of these, "first-born," "second-born," "third-born," "fourth-born," after which they recycle, so that the fifth-born child is called again "first-born," the sixth "second-born," and so on. Further, these names are bestowed independently of the fates of the children. Dead children, even stillborn ones, count, so that in fact, in this still high-birthrate, high-mortality society, the names do not really tell you anything very reliable about the birth-order relations of concrete individuals. Within a set of living siblings, someone called "first-born": may actually be first, fifth, or ninth-born, or, if somebody is missing, almost anything in between, and someone called "second-born" may in fact be older. The birth-order naming system does not identify individuals as individuals, not is it intended to; what it does is to suggest that, for all procreating couples, births form a circular succession of "firsts," "seconds," "thirds," and "fourths," an endless four-stage replication of an imperishable form. Physically men appear and disappear as the ephemerae they are, but socially the acting figures remain eternally the same as new "firsts," "seconds," and so on emerge from the timeless world of the gods to replace those who, dying, dissolve once more into it. All the designation and title systems, so I would argue, function in the same way: they represent the most time-saturated aspects of the human condition as but ingredients in an eternal, footlight present.

20   Nor is this sense the Balinese have of always being on stage a vague and ineffable one either. It is, in fact, exactly summed up in what is surely one of their experience-nearest concepts: *lek*. *Lek* had been variously translated or mistranslated ("shame" is the most common attempt); but what it really means is close to what we call stage fright. Stage fright consists, of course, in the fear that, for want of skill or self-control, or perhaps by mere accident, an aesthetic illusion will not be maintained, that the actor will show through his part. Aesthetic distance collapses, the audience (and the actor) lose sight of Hamlet and gain it, uncomfortably for all concerned, of bumbling John Smith painfully miscast as the Prince of Denmark. In Bali, the case is the same: what is feared is that the public performance to which one's cultural location commits one will be botched and that the personality—as we would call it but the Balinese, of course, not believing in such a thing, would not—of the individual will break through to dissolve his standardized public identity. When this occurs, as it sometimes does, the immediacy of the moment is felt with excruciating intensity and men become suddenly and unwillingly

creatural, locked in mutual embarrassment, as though they had happened upon each other's nakedness. It is the fear of faux pas, rendered only that much more probable by the extraordinary ritualization of daily life, that keeps social intercourse on its deliberately narrowed rails and protects the dramatistical sense of self against the disruptive threat implicit in the immediacy and spontaneity even the most passionate cermoniousness cannot fully eradicate from face-to-face encounters.

IV

Morocco, Middle Eastern and dry rather than East Asian and wet, extrovert, fluid, activist, masculine, informal to a fault, a Wild West sort of place without the barrooms and the cattle drives, is another kettle of selves altogether. My work there, which began in the mid-sixties, has been centered around a moderately large town or small city in the foothills of the Middle Atlas, about twenty miles south of Fez. It's an old place, probably founded in the tenth century, conceivably even earlier. It has the walls, the gates, the narrow minarets rising to prayer-call platforms of a classical Muslim town, and, from a distance anyway, it is a rather pretty place, an irregular oval of blinding white set in the deep-sea-green of an olive grove oasis, the mountains, bronze and stony here, slanting up immediately behind it. Close up, it is less prepossessing, though more exciting: a labyrinth of passages and alleyways, three quarters of them blind, pressed in by wall-like buildings and curbside shops and filled with a simply astounding variety of very emphatic human beings. Arabs, Berbers, and Jews; tailors, herdsmen, and soldiers; people out of offices, people out of markets, people out of tribes; rich, superrich, poor, superpoor; locals, immigrants, mimic Frenchmen, unbending medievalists, and somewhere, according to the official government census for 1960, an unemployed Jewish airplane pilot—the town houses one of the finest collections of rugged individuals I, at least, have ever come up against. Next to Sefrou (the name of the place), Manhattan seems almost monotonous.

Yet no society consists of anonymous eccentrics bouncing off one another like billiard balls, and Moroccans, too, have symbolic means by which to be sort people out from one another and form an idea of what it is to be a person. The main such means—not the only one, but I think the most important and the one I want to talk about particularly here—is a peculiar linguistic form called in Arabic the *nisba*. The word derives from the trilateral root, *n-s-b*, for "ascription," "attribution," "imputation," "relationship," "affinity," "correlation," "connection," "kinship." *Nsīb* means "in-law"; *nsab* means "to attribute or impute to"; *munāsaba* means "a relation," "an analogy," "a correspondence";

mansūb means "belonging to," "pertaining to"; and so on to at least a dozen derivatives, from *nassāb* ("genealogist") to *nīsbīya* ("[physical] relativity").

Nisba itself, then, refers to a combination morphological, grammatical, and semantic process that consists in transforming a noun into what we would call a relative adjective but what for Arabs is just another sort of noun by adding î (f., iya): *Sefrū*/Sefrou—*Sefrūwī*/native son of Sefrou; *Sūs*/region of southwestern Morocco—*Sūsī*/man coming from that region; *Beni Yazga*/a tribe near Sefrou—*Yazgī*/a member of that tribe; *Yahūd*/the Jews as a people, Jewry—*Yahūdī*/a Jew; *Adlun*/surname of a prominent Sefrou family—*Adlūnī*/a member of that family. Nor is the procedure confined to this more or less straightforward "ethnicizing" use, but is employed in a wide range of domains to attribute relational properties to persons. For example, occupation (*hrār*/silk—*hrārī*/silk merchant); religious sect (*Darqāwā*/a mystical brotherhood—*Darqāwī*/an adept of that brotherhood or spiritual status), (*Ali*/The Prophet's son-in-law—*Alawī*/descendant of the Prophet's son-in-law, and thus of the Prophet).

Now, as once formed, nisbas tend to be incorporated into personal names—Umar Al-Buhadiwi/Umar of the Buhadu Tribe; Muhammed Al-Sussi/Muhammed from the Sus Region—this sort of adjectival attributive classification is quite publicly stamped onto an individual's identity. I was unable to find a single case where an individual was generally known, or known about, but his or her nisba was not. Indeed, Sefrouis are far more likely to be ignorant of how well-off a man is, how long he has been around, what his personal character is, or where exactly he lives, than they are of what his nisba is—Sussi or Sefroui, Buhadiwi or Adluni, Harari or Darqawi. (Of women to whom he is not related that is very likely to be all that he knows—or, more exactly, is permitted to know.) The selves that bump and jostle each other in the alleys of Sefrou gain their definition from associative relations they are imputed to have with the society that surrounds them. They are contextualized persons.

25   But the situation is even more radical than this; nisbas render men relative to their contexts, but as contexts themselves are relative, so too are nisbas, and the whole thing rises, so to speak, to the second power: relativism squared. Thus, at one level, everyone in Sefrou has the same nisba, or at least the potential of it—namely, Sefroui. However, within Sefrou such a nisba, precisely because it does not discriminate, will never be heard as part of an individual designation. It is only outside of Sefrou that the relationship to that particular context becomes identifying. Inside it, he is an Adluni, Alawi, Meghrawi, Ngadi, or whatever. And similarly within these categories: there are, for example, twelve different nisbas (Shakibis, Zuinis, and so forth) by means of which, among themselves, Sefrou Alawis distinguish one another.

The whole matter is far from regular: what level or sort of nisba is used and seems relevant and appropriate (to the users, that is) depends heavily on the situation. A man I knew who lived in Sefrou and worked in Fez but came from the Beni Yazgha tribe settled nearby—and from the Hima lineage of the Taghut subfraction of the Wulad Ben Ydir fraction within it—was known as a Sefroui to his work fellows in Fez, a Yazghi to all of us non-Yazghis in Sefrou, an Ydiri to other Beni Yazghas around, except for those who were themselves of the Wulad Ben Ydir fraction, who called him a Taghuti. As for the few other Taghutis, they called him a Himiwi. That is as far as things went here, but not as far as they can go, in either direction. Should, by chance, our friend journey to Egypt, he would become a Maghrebi, the nisba formed from the Arabic word for North Africa. The social contextualization of persons is pervasive and, in its curiously unmethodical way, systematic. Men do not float as bounded psychic entities, detached from their backgrounds and singularly named. As individualistic, even willful, as the Moroccans in fact are, their identity is an attribute they borrow from their setting.

Now as with the Javanese inside/outside, smooth/rough phenomenological sort of reality dividing, and the absolutizing Balinese title systems, the nisba way of looking at persons—as though they were outlines waiting to be filled in—is not an isolated custom, but part of a total pattern of social life. This pattern is, like the others, difficult to characterize succinctly, but surely one of its outstanding features is a promiscuous tumbling in public settings of varieties of men kept carefully segregated in private ones—all-out cosmopolitanism in the streets, strict communalism (of which the famous secluded woman is only the most striking index) in the home. This is, indeed, the so-called mosaic system of social organization so often held to be characteristic of the Middle East generally: differently shaped and colored chips jammed in irregularly together to generate an intricate overall design within which their individual distinctiveness remains nonetheless intact. Nothing if not diverse, Moroccan society does not cope with its diversity by sealing it into castes, isolating it into tribes, dividing it into ethnic groups, or covering it over with some common-denominator concept of nationality, though, fitfully, all have now and then been tried. It copes with it by distinguishing, with elaborate precision, the contexts—marriage, worship, and to an extent diet, law, and education—within which men are separated by their dissimilitudes, and those—work, friendship, politics, trade—where, however warily and however conditionally, they are connected by them.

To such a social pattern, a concept of selfhood which marks public identity contextually and relativistically, but yet does so in terms—tribal, territorial, linguistic, religious, familial—that grow out of the more private and settled arenas of life and have a deep and permanent resonance there, would seem particularly appropriate. Indeed, the social pattern would seem virtually to create this concept of selfhood, for it produces a situation where people interact with one another in terms of categories whose meaning is almost purely positional, location in the general mosaic, leaving the substantive content of the categories, what they mean subjectively as experienced forms of life, aside as something properly concealed in apartments, temples, and tents. Nisba discriminations can be more specific or less, indicate location within the mosaic roughly or finely, and they can be adapted to almost any changes in circumstance. But they cannot carry with them more than the most sketchy, outline implications concerning what men so named as a rule are like. Calling a man a Sefroui is like calling him a San Franciscan: it classifies him, but it does not type him; it places him without portraying him.

It is the nisba system's capacity to do this—to create a framework within which persons can be identified in terms of supposedly immanent characteristics (speech, blood, faith, provenance, and the rest)—and yet to minimize the impact of those characteristics in determining the practical relations among such persons in markets, shops, bureaus, fields, cafés, baths, and roadways that makes it so central to the Moroccan idea of the self. Nisba-type categorization leads, paradoxically, to a hyperindividualism in public relationships, because by providing only a vacant sketch, and that shifting, of who the actors are—Yazghis, Adlunis, Buhadiwis, or whatever—it leaves the rest, that is, almost everything, to be filled in by the process of interaction itself. What makes the mosaic work is the confidence that one can be as totally pragmatic, adaptive, opportunistic, and generally ad hoc in one's relations with others—a fox among foxes, a crocodile among crocodiles—as one wants without any risk of losing one's sense of who one is. Selfhood is never in danger because, outside the immediacies of procreation and prayer, only its coordinates are asserted.

V

30   Now, without trying to tie up the dozens of loose ends I have not only left dangling in these rather breathless accounts of the senses of selfhood of nearly ninety million people but have doubtless frazzled even more, let us return to the question of what all this can tell us, or could if it were done adequately, about "the native's point of view" in Java, Bali, and Morocco. Are we, in describing symbol uses, describing perceptions, sentiments, outlooks, experiences? And in what sense? What do we claim when we claim that we un-

derstand the semiotic means by which, in this case, persons are defined to one another? That we know words or that we know minds?

In answering this question, it is necessary, I think, first to notice the characteristic intellectual movement, the inward conceptual rhythm, in each of these analyses, and indeed in all similar analyses, including those of Malinowski—namely, a continuous dialectical tacking between the most local of local detail and the most global structure in such a way as to bring them into simultaneous view. In seeking to uncover the Javanese, Balinese, or Moroccan sense of self, one oscillates restlessly between the sort of exotic minutiae (lexical antitheses, categorical schemes, morphophonemic transformations) that make even the best ethnographies a trial to read and the sort of sweeping characterizations ("quietism," "dramatism," "contextualism") that make all but the most pedestrian of them somewhat implausible. Hopping back and forth between the whole conceived through the parts that actualize it and the parts conceived through the whole that motivates them, we seek to turn them, by a sort of intellectual perpetual motion, into explications of one another.

All this is, of course, but the now familiar trajectory of what Dilthey called the hermeneutic circle, and my argument here is merely that it is as central to ethnographic interpretation, and thus to the penetration of other people's modes of thought, as it is to literary, historical, philological, psychoanalytic, or biblical interpretation, or for that matter to the informal annotation of everyday experience we call common sense. In order to follow a baseball game one must understand what a bat, a hit, an inning, a left fielder, a squeeze play, a hanging curve, and a tightened infield are, and what the game in which these "things" are elements is all about. When an *explication de texte* critic like Leo Spitzer attempts to interpret Keats's "Ode on a Grecian Urn," he does so by repetitively asking himself the alternating question "What is the whole poem about?" and "What exactly has Keats seen (or chosen to show us) depicted on the urn he is describing?," emerging at the end of an advancing spiral of general observations and specific remarks with a reading of the poem as an assertion of the triumph of the aesthetic mode of perception over the historical. In the same way, when a meanings-and-symbols ethnographer like myself attempts to find out what some pack of natives conceive a person to be, he moves back and forth between asking himself, "What is the general form of their life?" and "What exactly are the vehicles in which that form is embodied?," emerging in the end of a similar sort of spiral with the notion that they see the self as a composite, a persona, or a point in a pattern. You can no more know what *lek* is if you do not know what Balinese dramatism is than you can know what a catcher's mitt is if you do not know what baseball is. And you can no more know what mosaic social organization is if you do not know what a nisba is than you can know what Keat's Platonism is if you are unable to grasp, to use Spitzer's own formulation, the "intellectual thread of thought" captured in such fragment phrases as "Attic shape," "silent form," "bride of quietness," "cold pastoral," "silence and slow time," "peaceful citadel," of "ditties of no tone."

In short, accounts of other peoples' subjectivities can be built up without recourse to pretensions to more-than-normal capacities for ego effacement and fellow feeling. Normal capacities in these respects are, of course, essential, as is their cultivation, if we expect people to tolerate our intrusions into their lives at all and accept us as persons worth talking to. I am certainly not arguing for insensitivity here, and hope I have not demonstrated it. But whatever accurate or half-accurate sense one gets of what one's informants are, as the phrase goes, really like does not come from the experience of that acceptance as such, which is part of one's own biography, not of theirs. It comes from the ability to construe their modes of expression, what I would call their symbol systems, which such an acceptance allows one to work toward developing. Understanding the form and pressure of, to use the dangerous word one more time, natives' inner lives is more like grasping a proverb, catching an allusion, seeing a joke—or, as I have suggested, reading a poem—than it is like achieving communion.

Reflective Reading, Informal Writing

REFLECTING ON THE READING:

• What does the discipline of anthropology have to do with reflexivity? (You may wish to review the definition of "reflexivity" in the Introduction to Chapter 3.) Donna Qualley writes that "In the process of trying to understand an other, our own beliefs and assumptions are disclosed, and . . . can become objects of examination and critique." Does anything like this happen in Geertz's essay? That is, does his examination of other cultures provide an occasion for thinking anew about our own? In our Introduction we make the claim that reflexivity requires empathy. Would Geertz agree?

• Geertz cites Heinz Kohut's distinction between "experience-near" and "experience-distant" concepts. He makes the claim that "People use experience-near concepts spontaneously, un-self-consciously, as it were colloquially; they do not, except fleetingly and on occasion, recognize that there are any 'concepts' involved at all." What is the significance of this distinction to anthropologists? To us? How do we as individuals ever become aware of our own "experience-near" concepts? For example, what has to happen before you can form a concept of your own home town?

- In his conclusion Geertz speaks of "the characteristic intellectual movement" of his analyses (if not of anthropology in general) as "a continuous dialectical tacking between the most local of local detail and the most global of global structure in such a way as to bring them into simultaneous view." Is this "oscillation," this "hopping back and forth" at all related to Kohut's distinction, as just noted? Locate one instance of this movement in any of Geertz's three analyses and explain how it works.

UNDERSTANDING RHETORICAL STRATEGIES:

- What is the point of the opening anecdote about Malinowski? How would you characterize the point of view from which this anecdote is told? The tone? How does adopting this tone and point of view position Geertz himself, as teller of the tale?

- In section III of his essay, Geertz refers frequently to Western drama: from Shakespeare's view that "all the world's a stage," to a road-show production of *Charley's Aunt* or *Springtime for Henry*, to a flawed performance of *Hamlet*. Geertz uses analogy in the time-honored manner, to explain something unfamiliar to his readers in terms of something familiar. But why drama? And why in reference to the Balinese, but not the Javanese or the Moroccans? How, in particular, does each of these dramatic references work?

- If the characteristic intellectual movement of anthropology, at least as Geertz understands it, is this oscillation between local detail and global structure, wouldn't this commit him to a rhetorical strategy that would reflect this same movement? That is, a movement back and forth between the most concrete of details and the most abstract of generalizations, each supporting and explaining the other? Find what you would consider a particularly effective example of this strategy in Geertz's text.

- Aware that his own attempt to explain this "oscillation" is itself highly abstract, Geertz moves instinctively to the concrete to explain himself, drawing analogies between the process of understanding a culture with the process of understanding a baseball game, or making sense of a poem. Explain how these analogies work to clarify or explain Geertz's view of how anthropologists work.

INFORMAL WRITING:

- What does Geertz mean when he says that "Understanding the form and pressure of . . . natives' inner lives is more like grasping a proverb, catching an allusion, seeing a joke—or, as I have suggested, reading a poem—than it is like achieving communion." What popular view of anthropology is Geertz arguing against, and what does he offer in its place? How does this argument relate to the concept of reflexivity?

- Think of a time when you entered a strange (to you) culture. This could be a time when you traveled or studied abroad, or it could be a time when you moved to a new city, joined a new club or team, or entered college. What can you recall of the process you went through to make sense of this new culture? Was your own conception of yourself affected by the process?

- Thinking about one of the three cultures Geertz describes, how does that culture's concept of what it means to be a person differ from our own (Geertz attempts to summarize "the Western conception of a person" on p. 330)? Does learning about a different conception of personhood lead you think differently about your own idea of what it means to be a person?

Chapter Assignment Sequences

Sequence One: Versions of Reflexivity

"Me and My Shadow"
"Paintball as Combat Sport"
"The Brass Ring and the Deep Blue Sea"
"From the Native's Point of View"

SMALL GROUP DISCUSSION:

1. Rank the essays by Tompkins, Williams, Gibson, and Geertz from least reflexive to most reflexive. Make sure you come to at least a working agreement about the definition of reflection and reflexivity. Also make sure you make an argument for your rankings.

2. Discuss whether or not you think there might be different kinds or versions of reflexivity. Try to identify at least two or more versions of reflexivity from your readings of these four essays.

WRITING:

1. Write an essay in which you argue for or against different kinds or versions of reflexivity in these essays. Let your rankings and discussions from your group work support your writing of this essay. Also, make sure that readers have a clear understanding of how you are interpreting the term "reflexivity."

2. Would you assume personal writing or academic writing is more reflexive in nature? Why? Write an essay in which you explore the relationship of your personal self and your academic self to moments of reflexivity. Things you might think about to help you frame your exploration: Of the essays you read in Chapter 3, are the more "personal" essays more or less reflexive than the more "academic" essays? Does an academic essay have to have some personal connection to or for the writer before there can be either reflection or reflexivity? Would you consider any of these essays sustained moments of reflexivity?

Sequence Two: Stories and Reflexivity

"Me and My Shadow"
"From the Native's Point of View"
"Paintball as Combat Sport"
"The Brass Ring and the Deep Blue Sea"

SMALL GROUP DISCUSSION:

1. At the end of Chapter 1 (Sequence Three), you were asked to consider a series of questions about storytelling, some of which are relevant here. All four of these essays also rely, to one degree or another, on anecdotes or stories, some of which are personal. Selecting one story from each of the essays, determine the function performed by each story within the context of the essay in which it occurs. How does the story relate to the purpose of the essay in which it appears? Is the location of the story within the essay important? What differences do you see among the authors in the use to which their stories are put?

2. In the previous question you considered *why* the authors told personal stories. Now, look at *how*. Looking again at the stories listed above, what differences do you see in the ways these stories are told? How do they compare with respect to setting? Depth of characterization? Amount of sensory detail? Length? Tone? Pace? Can you account for these differences in terms of the different rhetorical purposes of the essay in which they appear?

3. Now, a new twist: To what extent are the stories here used for reflexive purposes, whether to promote reflexivity in the author, or the reader, or both? A good place to start: Does the story parallel the author's (or the reader's) experience in some significant way? Or does it offer a sharp contrast to that experience?

WRITING:

1. Often we identify with characters we discover in literature, imagining ourselves like them in some important ways and perhaps wondering whether we would have made the same decisions, given similar circumstances. In doing so, we have engaged with these stories reflexively. Intuiting the power of stories to promote reflexivity, teachers, preachers, coaches, and parents routinely tell us stories they hope we will "take to heart," and as a result be somehow changed. So with the authors in this chapter. Select three stories, each from a different essay, and compare them with respect to the way they are used to promote reflexivity in the reader.

2. Just as families regularly tell stories embodying complex messages about the family's values (or violations of them), so do academics. Tompkins, Geertz, and Williams all tell stories that comment on the basic values or methodologies of their respective disciplines. Write about these stories as examples of reflexivity at the disciplinary level, as opposed to the personal level. Are the two always that distinct?

Sequence Three: Automatically "Othered"

"Me and My Shadow"
"Tlilli, Tlapalli/The Path of the Red and Black Ink"
"The Brass Ring and the Deep Blue Sea"

SMALL GROUP DISCUSSION:

1. All three of these essays are written by women. All three are also deliberately fragmented and nonlinear. Do you see any connection between being marginalized and writing nonlinear prose?

2. Tompkins struggles against academic thinking and writing, Anzaldua against Western conceptions of art, Williams against the Western legal tradition. What do their "targets" have in common? What does the nature of their resistance have in common? What do they seem to be *for*?

3. Do you find evidence that each of these authors is conscious of working from a "minority" position in some respect? In what respects does this minority position shape her point of view, her thesis?

WRITING:

1. If reflexivity is a "response triggered by dialectical engagement with the other—an idea, theory, person, culture, text, or even an other part of one's self" (Qualley), what happens to reflexivity when one is already defined as an "other" by mainstream culture? Tompkins, Anzaldua, and Williams, as women and/or members of minority groups, are already in some sense outside of, or marginalized by, mainstream culture. Does this mean they can't engage in reflexivity? Or does this mean they are somehow already automatically positioned to bring a reflexive point of view to bear on mainstream culture? What does mainstream culture stand to gain from such a point of view?

2. Each of these authors is conscious of being pulled in two (or more) directions simultaneously: divided between the values and intellectual categories of mainstream culture (of which she is a part), on the one hand, and on the other the values and intellectual categories that accompany her status as an "other." Working with any two of these authors, describe the nature of the sense of division they experience. Do they see any prospects for bridging or healing this sense of division? How so?

Sequence Four: Private or Public, Mother Tongue or Father Tongue

"Me and My Shadow"
"Tlilli, Tlapalli,/ The Path of the Red and Black Ink"
"The Brass Ring and the Deep Blue Sea"
"From the Native's Point of View"

SMALL GROUP DISCUSSION:

1. Discuss your current ideas about, and definitions of, public and private writing. Have your ideas changed since reading the essays in this chapter? Of the essays by Tompkins, Anzaldua, Geertz, and Williams, which would you characterize as mostly private writing? As mostly public? Find at least one passage from each essay that supports your placing it in either the private or public category.

2. We generally think of academic writing as objective, distanced, and without the personal or emotions present. Tompkins, however, calls this idea into question—including the definition of personal. In "Me and My Shadow," she writes of being "completely hooked" by an essay by writer Jessica Benjamin that is as abstract and theoretical as Foucault's writing. Yet, she is not "turned off" by this writing because, she says, "it is personal without being personalized." What does she mean by this? Using Tompkins' framework, would Tompkins' own essay be personal or personalized? How about Geertz's? Williams'?

WRITING:

1. Write a critique of one or more of these four essays in which you intentionally blur the boundaries between public and private. Weave into your critique things that matter to you, your feelings and emotions around the essay or essays, personal stories, and so on.

2. In "Me and My Shadow," Tompkins quotes Ursula Le Guinn's speech at a Bryn Mawr college commencement (p. 270). Return to that passage and read it carefully. Write an analytical essay in which you examine Tompkins', Anzaldua's, Williams', and Geertz's essays for examples of "mother tongue" and "father tongue." Be sure to comment on how these examples work rhetorically and how they serve the writer in making his or her points and arguments. If you'd like, you could also critique the notion of mother tongue and father tongue as Le Guinn defines it and Tompkins makes use of it.

Writing in the Community: Reflection, Reflexivity, and Action

Reflective Prewriting

1. Write about the connections and/or lack of connections you see between your college work and other areas of your life and community.

2. Define "community" as best you can. What specific attributes or characteristics must be present in order for a community to exist? How many different communities would you consider yourself a part of? What communities would you say you are definitely not a part of?

3. What are your thoughts on entering a community (a community perhaps foreign to you) and on the possibilities for reflection, reflexivity, and learning that might come with such a move? What fears do you have? What excites you about entering a new community?

4. What are you thinking and feeling about either witing for a community or finding your writing topics from within your interaction with a community?

INTRODUCTION

As we see it, there are at least four ways your instructor might want you to work with Chapter 4: Writing in the Community: Reflexivity, Reflection and Action. The reading and writing assignments in this chapter might be used in the way previous sections of this book have been. That is, as layers of reading and writing leading toward reflection and reflexivity. Or this section might be treated as a part of a larger sequence moving from private to public discourses, as the entirety of *Writing As Reflective Action* lays it out. Or the projects outlined in this section might serve as models for other types of community-based projects, projects better suited both to your interests and your local context, as we suggest in Section C of Chapter 4, "Other Projects." Or this section, with its emphasis on community-based learning, might become the primary focus for your entire course. This latter choice gives Chapter 4 its name. Your teacher will, of course, have thought these options through carefully before deciding how you will engage with this part of the work.

This section of *Writing As Reflective Action* is probably the most challenging and difficult part of the text, and potentially the most interesting. Our goal here is for your personal, public, and academic selves, your private and public writing, your school and nonschool writing, your work with reflection and reflexivity to come together, or collide, in ways that are both a learning experience for you and useful in some way for the community that your teacher asks you to enter, either literally and physically or through the readings provided. Hopefully, having been engaged with the principal elements of self-awareness—the ability to reflect upon your own identity and its social dimensions, and the ability to use the unique perspectives of others as instruments of reflexivity—you are ready to "go public." That is, you are at this point positioned to enter the community in the most productive way (not as some cartoon version of a missionary, but as someone with something to learn from others) and to profit from the experience.

We'll be frank. While community-based writing and service learning add new dimensions and possibilities to the composition class, engaging in such work is not always easy or successful, though it is almost always rewarding. Instructors, especially those without a service learning director or support staff at their campus, must make the connections with possible community partners themselves. While establishing such connections is usually rewarding, it is also time consuming. Sometimes the needs of a community partner do not square with the academic and disciplinary goals of the course, or of you and your instructor. Other difficulties arise as well. Colleges and universities operate in modes of time and space that distinguish them sharply from most other communities. The temporality of the academy—terms, semesters, and time slots—can put stress on the relationship between students and the community they are entering. Most community-based writing projects place complex demands on students that regular writing classes simply don't, in part because community partners usually don't need student involvement in one-hour time increments three times a week, but rather on a schedule that is very different from the ways school demands that you divide up your time.

Another difficulty is negotiating—and understanding—your role. Are you essentially a student who happens to be in a community setting? Or are you more like a volunteer engaged in community service? The answer is probably neither, but both. The graphic below represents the spectrum of service learning; community-based learning projects generally position you somewhere in the middle of this spectrum:

community service   practicum/internship
(pure service)   (pure learning)

———————————— service learning ————————————

citizenship   structural change

charity   preprofessional
philanthropy   training

(Edward Zlotkowski, Bentley College,
Service Learning Workshop, May, 1999)

The point is that the best service learning projects are generally not 100% service or 100% learning, but a combination of the two.

When working with a community partner you will need to listen carefully and actively, contributing your knowledge where and when appropriate. If your community partner asks you to perform certain writing tasks, you will need to take the time to learn what that writing is supposed to accomplish. What should it look like? What is its purpose? For what audience is it intended? Depending on the needs of your community partner, your writing tasks can vary from letter writing to report writing, to observational notes, to no writing at all. But at the heart of your writing in this section, no matter what other writing you may be involved with, is your own reflective and reflexive writing about your experiences. We believe it is crucial that you be very actively engaged with journal writing of some kind. As we mentioned in our Introduction to *Writing As Reflective Action*, we believe that the triple-entry incident journal is best suited for the work on which you are about to embark.

The *triple-entry incident journal* requires that you make three entries at three different times. The first entry you make prior to your first encounter with a community partner. This first entry is, in essence, a prewriting exercise in which you explore possibilities, expectations, and preconceptions: Am I eager or reluctant to enter into this project? What do I expect will happen during this meeting? What preconceived ideas or images do I have about the other participants in this experience? What will I do if . . . ? The second entry immediately follows your first community experience. Here you will describe what happened, how you felt, what surprised you, what you learned, and how your preconceived ideas and images held up or were changed. The third entry is a reflective narrative of sorts and comes later in your experience with your community-based learning project after at least two or three encounters with the community participants, or, if your teacher prefers, at the end of the project. In this entry you explore such questions as: Did the experience meet my expectations? What complicating factors did I bring from my life or studies to this experience? Did I face logistical difficulties? Were there conflicts in values? Did this experience change me in any way? Figure 4.1 is an example of a triple-entry incident journal in response to the second meeting a student had with the Cascade AIDS Project.

Figure 4.1
***

TRIPLE-ENTRY INCIDENT JOURNAL

PART I

Prior to visiting the HIV daycare center in Northeast Portland, just 2 or 3 miles from my house on Martin Luther King Jr. Boulevard, I tried to remove all biases or experiences with people living with HIV from my mind. I had volunteered for a week service project in Boston, Massachusetts at the Foundation for Children with Aids back in 1994 as a incoming freshman at Boston University. The children and administrators of that institution made an indelible impression in my mind. Randice Roucher was the program director, she gave me a better understanding of how these children were born with a malady, but entitled a shot at life, and deserved not special attention, but equal treatment as any other child. I remember a frail speckled black

Figure 4.1 (Continued)

TRIPLE-ENTRY INCIDENT JOURNAL

boy Richard, who was cheery, attentive, and called me "nappy head."
I remember not wanting to go back because I was too afraid of
watching kids like Richard pass on, or loose there life struggling
against AIDS. I remember how I felt so angry, and sad for those
children and I soon found out they did not need my pity, but just my
company. A friend and older playmate was the most important
thing they needed, someone to help them live more happily for the
few days I was there. The experience showed me that the children
were perseverant human beings who did not quite understand their
condition at three, or four years old, to willfully endured it with
strong spirits. I remember my prejudgments before arriving to the
Foundation just blocks from the Orange line in the ghettoes near
Dorchester in Boston. I was apprehensive, on guard and an arrogant
and naïve eighteen-year old at the time.

My experiences with working with children with HIV or anyone
with HIV for that matter was nil. My motives for volunteering were
ulterior at the time, I wanted any excuse to get out of my parent's
house, arrive early to my first University in an urban environment.
Despite my reasons for being there, I suddenly emotionally
latched onto these children. I finger painted, cavorted the play
grounds with them, hung upside down from the jungle gym, and
sang songs with these developmentally disabled and infected
children. I was apprehensive, and ignorantly afraid of catching
something, it in there urine, or blood if it spilled on me, but I
quickly checked that fear with reason. I could not help but like
them, but pity them, or feel more important than them since I had
lived slightly longer and was born with, what I considered at the
time a death sentence. Four and half years later, and many
millions more people are born or infected with the virus, and
perhaps some of those children are not still alive. I try not to pity,
or have feelings or superiority to any virus carriers. I do not want
to feel like what I was doing was charity for selfish reasons. I try
to see people living with HIV, as equals, as humans, as souls who
are undeniably entitled the same rights and privileges as I or any

(Continued)

Figure 4.1 (Continued)
TRIPLE-ENTRY INCIDENT JOURNAL

American is entitled. but non the less living, existing, prospering, and perhaps spiritually gaining from an illness, not terminally ill and removed from any sort of providence or chance for a normal life. So my one-week stint with the organization in Boston did reshape my view of children with Aids, there parents practitioners of unsafe sex, and intravenuous drug users. I believe that no one is a victim, but a volunteer, these children born with a virus, are not more special, or disabled, cognitively they are not developed as much, however they are loving being non the less, fearless and more resilient than the average jaded cynical adult. I was trying to understand and confront my prejudices, as Jim Cole writes about, when working with HIV positive individuals, as I had tried to do years before, but never really did.

Although I tried not to have any judgment prior to investigation or experiencing for myself what the day care center was like, I spoke with an individual who works there every Wednesday and Friday. She gave me her opinions, and offered her experiences, and I remembered listening to the journals of others in class, so I had a vague inkling what to expect, and inadvertently did anticipate, or judge the situation before entering it. I realized I needed to be as objective, respectful, and considerate of the clients and personal before riding my bike there on a sunny afternoon.

PART II

The First Day of Volunteering Wednesday March 2, 1999
Prior to going to the day care center I had tried to readjust my attitudes and divorce myself of pity, empathy, or any sort of patronizing behavior or treatment towards these adults. I tried to conceptualize my hours of volunteering, as service work, not charity, or volunteering for my own selfish reasons. I did not go into this task with an unconscious motive to redeem any feelings of guilt or shame I once had, but to give of myself freely and not to pass judgment. I was intrigued, and thought about the writings of the other service worker students. I did not want to create any drama in my writings, or try

Figure 4.1 (Continued)

TRIPLE-ENTRY INCIDENT JOURNAL

to make my experience a sniveling sentimental literary memoir on paper. I anticipated the center to look a certain way, and that these "clients" to be ill, sullen, or perhaps bed ridden, despite my conscious efforts bit on these patients, which I later came to find out were clients, professionals, and one, in fact, was a service worker too.

I arrived at the daycare center at 10:30 after quickly pedaling my bike there, I headed straight for Gabrielle's office, and asked what I should do first. She pointed to a card board box full of clothes and told me to sort them out on the table, and do the same with the miscellaneous groceries bags of what I considered hand me downs, or recycled clothes. As I sorted, people started to mill in, and check out the nice clothing selection I laid out on the tables. I met the first client, who I thought must work here, since he was rather healthy looking, muscular and alert, he defiantly did not look like someone with HIV, as I had seen in movies, or read about in articles, or books, even highly accurate ones such as And The Band Played ON . . . By Randy Shilts, He had a brooding frame, with broad shoulders, large legs, and calves like rocks he looked like a bouncer or linebacker looked at him and said "Howzit goin?" and he swiftly replied "Wus' Up." It was only after he sifted through clothes I lay out and grabbed a pair of Nike High Top sneakers; it quickly entered my mind that he was a patient, or a client, as I should think of them as. This first impression wrecked any expectation or anticipation I had about what people would look like. I got a second look just to size him up, and he must have weighed at least 180 pounds, and looked like he use to lift weights. Already my expectations, were wrong and I had relied on stereotypes of all gay men that weighed ninety pounds, and were going to make sexual innuendoes towards me. As I got a second look at him, I did not think he even looked gay, and I caught myself thinking in stereotypes, or getting stuck in assumptions once again. The second individual was another black man, who said he actually recognized me, or had seen me around, I thought was this someone a member of another anonymous

(Continued)

Figure 4.1 (Continued)
TRIPLE-ENTRY INCIDENT JOURNAL

organization I am affiliated with? It could very well be, and we may have that common goal of living drug free. Yet another realization, that I may have much in common with these people I was to work with for the morning. Suddenly, Za ZA, a flamboyant, tied dyed clad portly man appeared cheery and somewhat flaming I thought to myself, now this guy was definitely gay and I assumed he must have contracted the disease by unsafe sex with another man, then I did it again, I told myself, I made an uninformed judgment, or assumption based on my intuition or stereotype, had I not learned like my high school coach always told me, "Assumption is the mother of all fuck-ups?" Apparently not. I from then on, was to be as open minded and receptive to everyone I met, and not to make assessments based on my fist impression. I muddled around the clothing a bit longer, and then played a game of pool of with one of the clients. He seemed, happy go lucky, and excited to be sporting the South Park cartoon character tee he had found in donation pile, I liked the shirt myself. He one the first game, by me scratching the eightball, and his eyes lit up with excitement and he jumped up and down like a hyperactive six year old on sugar binge of snickers bars, skittles, and thirst buster 64 ounce sized jolt cola. I laughed and was not peeved by my careless loss as I usually am. I one the next game, ran the table, and went on to sink the eight in the following game. I walked up to Za Za before long and started a conversation with him. He was quite a character, passionate about his piano playing, and a witty guy. I accidentally called him Zha Zha like that rich bitch, and he looked at me like I had called him asshole, and I suddenly blurted "Za Za, T committed a faux paus, now it is time for me to insert my foot in mouth, he laughed it off, and said I was not the first to do it. I was looking at his tyed dyed Grateful Dead T-shirt, rainbow colored dangling earrings, and tie dyed Birkenstocks and thought to myself this has to be the fist hippie queen I have ever met, and suddenly I corrected myself from thinking in such terms, although he was the self-proclaimed princess, or fruit of the jungle, his other comments about his openly flashy homosexual leanings made me laugh too.

Figure 4.1 (Continued)
TRIPLE-ENTRY INCIDENT JOURNAL

This was a person with a sense of humor, and a radical personality, and an artist to boot, I have always been drawn to such types. He asked me if I went to certain parties, and making references to the marijuana subculture, and imploring if I partook in it.

I casually replied no, but I know what sort of events or scene he was speaking of was all about. My overall impression of the first day was that of surprise, something that I did not really expect, and I did not in anyway feel pity to this clients, but hope and wished the best life for them possible.

PART III

Reflecting on that the day afterward and the following day, I put things in a more holistic perspective. What made me some different from the clients at the center, and how could I learn from them? The time I spent there made me see that people afflicted, or living with a fatal disease has the choose to be selfless and of service themselves. For instance, Doug an HIV positive client at the center chooses to spend much of his free time at Project Quest located directly behind my house on N.E. Martin Luther King Jr. Boulevard in Portland. Doug manages to work out several hours, and mentioned to me that he has a membership at several athletic clubs in Portland and physically and spiritually fit in spite of the fatal prognosis and stigma attached to AIDS. I spoke with several other clients at the center and some of them seem to still live a hazardous life, but they seem to do so from a different frame of mind. Or maybe I am just seeing them differently. While I wonder at how they can maintain this life I think I understand a little too ....

Whatever the work you end up doing, whatever writing comes about from your relationship with the community you read about and/or work directly with, it is likely to be both difficult and immensely rewarding. Other students have had the following to say about their experiences with community-based writing projects:

> At Beach [an elementary school], I felt a growing sense of responsibility to this community. I have been so busy with motherhood, career, and school, while trying to keep my head above water financially, that I had not considered the possibility of participating in community service. After having done so for 10 weeks, I have found that every aspect of my life has been affected by the experience. It has opened my eyes to new ideas in many different areas: at home, at work, in volunteer work, in teaching my son to read and write, and in the importance of one-on-one contact in learning. I will apply what I have learned in other aspects of my life long after this class has ended.
>
> Lynn Laroche

> Is it possible that one experience can change your entire outlook on life? I believe that it can. By giving to my community in a community-based writing class, I learned more about myself than a textbook in a classroom could ever teach me. This term has taught me a lot about patience and having to look "within," a term often used by Robert Coles.
>
> Yvonne Earnshaw

> In this class, we dealt with the issue of audience in a real-world way. From my work I learned that writing is not just about sitting down and turning out a paper that fits the exact specifications of some professor who already knows everything you have to say. At times, it was hard to discern whether the class grew out of the projects that the community needed, or whether those projects grew out of the class. However, I am sure that neither could have been as effective without the other. . . . Also, I now have an excellent grasp of what it means to be a service learner: being shown the real world uses of your education as you learn.
>
> Chris Smith

Ultimately, our goal in Chapter 4 is to bring reflexivity, writing, and action firmly together. We would like to see your experience of school, your experience of learning, and your experience of this writing course become more than just a personal or academic exercise. Robert Coles, an educator and leader in community-based and service learning courses (and the author of the piece on entitlement in Chapter 1), shares a reflection from his college days that illustrates how such work might change you and lead you to reflexivity and action.

ROBERT COLES

Community Service Work

When I was a college student I did "volunteer work," as we then called it. I tutored some boys and girls who were having trouble with reading, writing, arithmetic. I left one part of Cambridge, Massachusetts, for another—often on foot, so that I could enjoy what my father had taught me to call a "good hike." When I came back to "school," certain scenes I had witnessed and certain statements I had heard would stay with me—come to mind now and then as I pursued various courses, lived a certain late adolescent life.

Often, when I went home to visit my parents, they inquired after my extracurricular teaching life. My mother was inclined to be religiously sentimental: it was good that I was helping out some youngsters in trouble. For her the sin of pride was around any corner; hence, our need to escape that constant pull of egoism—to work with others on behalf of their lives, with our own, for a change, taking a back seat. My father, a probing scientist, commonly took a different tack and asked me many times the same question, "What did you learn?"

I was never quite sure how to answer my father, and often I had no need to do so. My mother was quick to reply, emphasizing her notion of the education such tutoring can afford a college student: "the lesson of humility," a favorite phrase of hers. If any amplification was necessary, she could be forthcoming with another well-worn piety: "There but for the grace of God . . ."

My father's question often came back to haunt me, no matter my mother's hasty, biblical interventions. What **did** I learn? What was **I supposed** to learn? I was, after all, the teacher, not the student. Anyway, these were elementary school children, and there was nothing new in the ground I was covering with them every week. But I had listened to my father too often, on long walks through various cities, to let the matter rest there. He was born and grew up in Yorkshire, England, and was a great walker, a great observer as he kept his legs moving fast. He was also an admirer of George Orwell long before *Animal Farm* and *1984* were published—the early Orwell who wrote *Down and Out in London and Paris*, *The Road to Wigan Pier*, and *Homage to Catalonia*; the Orwell, that is, who explored relentlessly the world around him and described carefully yet with dramatic intensity the nature of that world.

5   My father had introduced me to those books before I went to college, and they returned to me as I did volunteer work—a scene, some words, or more generally, Orwell's social and moral inquiry as both are conveyed in his several narrative efforts. I was beginning to realize that Orwell was a "big brother" for me in a manner far at variance to the already widespread meaning of that phrase. He was helping me make sense of a continuing experience I was having—sharing his wisdom with me, giving me pause, prompting in me scrutiny not only of others (the children I met, and occasionally their parents) but my own mind as it came up with its various opinions, conclusions, attitudes.

Later, at college, I would read the poetry and prose of William Carlos Williams—his long poem *Paterson,* his Stecher trilogy, *White Mule, In the Money, The Buildup.* Williams tried hard to evoke the rhythms of working class life in America—the struggle of ordinary people to make their way in the world, to find a satisfactory manner of living, of regarding themselves. He knew how hard it is for people like himself (well-educated, well-to-do) to make contact in any substantial way with others, who work in factories or stores or on farms, or indeed, who do not work at all or are lucky to be intermittently employed.

When he emphasized his search for an American "language," Williams was getting at the fractured nature of our nation's life—the divisions by race, class, region, culture which keep so many of us unaware of one another, unable to comprehend one another. Often as I went to do my tutoring, and heard words I never before knew—or heard words used in new and arresting ways—and as I learned about the memories and hopes and habits and interests of people in a neighborhood rather unlike the one where I lived, I thought of Williams's poems and stories and realized how much he owed to the humble people of northern, industrial New Jersey. As he once put it to me, years after I graduated from college, "Those house calls [to attend his patients] are giving me an education. Every day I learn something new—a sight, a phrase—and I'm made to stop and think about my world, the world I've left behind." He was reminding both of us that the "education" he had in mind was no one-way affair.

I fear it took some of us doing our volunteer work a good deal of time to learn the lesson Williams was putting to word. At my worst, I must admit, a sense of *noblesse oblige* was at work—a conviction that I would share certain (intellectual) riches with "them." Only when I went with Williams on some of his house calls—observed him paying close heed to various men, women, and children—did I begin to realize how much his mind grew in response to the everyday experiences he was having.

Now, many days later, I find myself a teacher at a university, offering courses for undergraduates and for students in professional schools (law, medicine, business, education). I work with many young people who are anxious to do community service of one kind or another—teach in urban schools, offer medical or legal assistance to needy families. At times I stand in awe of some of those youths— their determination, their decency, their good-heartedness, their savvy. I also notice in many of them a need for discussion and re- flection: a time to stop and consider what they would like to be do- ing, what they are doing, what they are having difficulty doing. A college senior put the matter to me this way one afternoon: "I started this work [volunteer work in a school near a large urban low-rent housing project] as something apart from my courses, my life here as a student. I wanted to be of use to someone other than myself— and in a really honest moment, I'd probably add that I was also be- ing selfish: It would beef up my brag sheet when I apply to a graduate school. But hell, I'd been doing this kind of [volunteer] work since high school—a part of our church's activities, so I shouldn't be too cynical about my motives! But the last thing I ex- pected was that I'd come back here [to his dormitory] and want to read books to help me figure out what's happening [in the neighbor- hood where he does volunteer work]. I've designed my own private course—and it helps; I can anticipate certain troubles, because I've learned from the reading I do, and I get less discouraged, because I've seen a bigger view, courtesy of those writers."

10   He said much more, but the gist of his remarks made me realize that there are social scientists and novelists and poets and essayists who have offered that student so very much—their knowledge, their experience, their sense of what matters, and not least, their companionship—as fellow human beings whose concerns are simi- lar to those of the youths now sweating things out in various student volunteer programs. Put differently, those writers (of filmmakers or photographers) are teachers, and their subject matter is an impor- tant one for many of our country's students, engaged as they are in acts of public service.

Our institutions of higher learning might certainly take heed— not only encourage students to do such service, but help them stop and mull over what they have heard and seen by means of books to be read, discussions to be had. This is the very purpose, after all, of colleges and universities—to help one generation after another grow intellectually and morally through study and the self-scrutiny such study can sometimes prompt.

———————

We conclude this book with two possible community experiences as examples: gathering and preserving oral histories and work with an AIDS project. Each of these examples includes readings selected to stimulate reflective, reflexive, and analytical thought and writing. The sample experiences we provide might ultimately lead to community service writing such as gathering and writing the stories of elderly persons or assembling the history of one's own college or university. The possibilities for oral history projects are endless. Other writing projects might include writing grants for AIDS support services, collecting and writing the stories of workers and clients in AIDS hospices, working with AIDS victims to complete reading and writing needs they might have, and so on. Or the types of projects we represent here may suggest still others more suited to your local context, as we indicate in Section C of this chapter.

Whatever project you find yourself involved in, we urge you to become consciously reflexive within your experiences, being open to transformation and to taking action.

SAMPLE PROJECT A: ORAL HISTORY

Traditional history is sometimes derided for its "kings and battles" or "great man" approach to history. There is some truth to these labels, just as there is to the old phrase that "history is written by the winners." Until this century, at least, history has generally constructed a version of the past that would meet the approval of those in power, with the predictable effect that the stories of their rivals, and of the common man and woman, have been lost. Some modern historians have attempted to rectify the resulting imbalance. For example, Howard Zinn's *People's History of the United States* tells American history from the perspective of the disenfranchised: the slaves, the indentured servants, the immigrants, the poor. A similar impulse has, since World War II, given rise to the collection of oral histories.

Oral history, at its simplest, consists of the life stories of ordinary folk, as told to an interviewer and recorded (often these recordings are also transcribed, though sometimes not). Typically oral histories are done of people whose stories would be unlikely to make the news, or who for one reason or another would be unlikely to write their own autobiographies. This is why so many of the oral histories that have been published are interviews with the aged rather than the young, members of racial or ethnic minorities rather than the mainstream, housewives rather than career women, foot soldiers rather than generals, and factory workers rather than managers. There are, of course, exceptions–oral histories of generals, politicians, political activists, and the like. In his collections of oral histories, Studs Terkel likes to include interviewees from a wide range of social strata. But often the lives of prominent figures are already well documented, and in any case their oral histories can tell us little about what it was like for ordinary people to live in–or live through–a particular period, event, or occupation in a particular geographical, social, political, and economic context. Oral histories not only capture the texture and detail of the lives of real people, but also their voices, their phrasing, and something of their ways of viewing the world.

The readings in this section of Chapter 4 are meant to give you an idea of the potential of oral history. The first three selections are actual oral histories. "Working the Land," from Studs Terkel's *Working*, includes two shorter interviews representing different perspectives on farm life. Wallace Terry's "Private First Class Reginald 'Malik' Edwards, Phoenix, Louisiana" is the story of a young Marine's service during the early years of the Vietnam War. And "Violet De Cristoforo—Tule Lake," from a collection edited by John Tateishi, is an account of life in one of the detention camps established for Japanese-Americans during World War II.

These selections suggest the range of possibilities for oral history. The Terkel interviews focus on particular occupations, though they might also be said to be about particular ways of life. By contrast, the others are about living through some historical event, the war in Vietnam and the internment of Japanese-Americans, respectively. A glance through entries under "oral history" in your library's catalog will suggest alternative focuses: on community, or place (from the history of Madison, Wis., to homesteading Colorado); on events (from the Depression and World War II to the "Long Walk" of the Navajo); on institutions (from NASA to factories and universities); on political movements (from anarchy to the Civil Rights Movement); on the history of ethnic groups in various settings; on music subcultures; on sports; and finally, of course, on biography. Family histories are also often assembled using these methods. Given the particular strengths and the flexibility of the oral history as a research tool, you can see why oral history has become a staple of biographers, historians, folklorists, ethnographers, psychologists, and sociologists.

Your instructor may ask your class to collaborate on some such community-based oral history project, such as assembling an oral history of your college or university, your community, or some subculture or institution within it. Your particular focus will depend on your resources, interests, and local context. The final selection in this section, "Varieties of Oral History Projects:

Community Studies," by Valerie Yow, is a scholarly discussion of such a project.

It may be that the specific design of the course you are in does not permit you or your class to conduct oral history interviews as part of the course's work. Instead, your instructor may want you to read, reflect, write, and collaborate as with previous parts of this text. Even so, we think these selections will repay your close attention, providing an introduction to a valuable tool for writers, a sense of the problems (and rewards) of interviewing real people, and perhaps a new way of thinking about history.

STUDS TERKEL

Currently regarded as a remarkable oral historian, Studs Terkel also worked as a radio broadcaster with his own talk show, as the host of a jazz radio show, and as a member of the Federal Writers' Project during the Depression. Born Louis Terkel, he adopted the name Studs in the mid–1930s from the name of a gangster he played in radio soap operas, Studs Lonigan. After being blacklisted as a communist because of his membership in a left-wing theater group and the resulting cancellation of Terkel's talk show, Andre Schiffrin, an editor at Pantheon Books, suggested the idea for *Working* (1974), from which this selection is taken.

Terkel traveled around the nation interviewing the "average" worker and taping oral histories for his book. He recorded approximately 10 times as much information as used in the book. Comparing it to gold mining, he explains that he processed that much material to find the "gold," then the chosen information was refined and "minted." The lives he captured on his tape recorder change the face of American history. Terkel told a reporter that most of our history comes from official documents, the memoirs of kings and ministers, and those with a privileged education. He explains that "no one ever bothered to ask the common soldier how he felt about the Battle of Hastings . . . but then the tape recorder came along, and changed everything."

In the introduction to *Working*, Terkel connects the nature of work with violence—to the spirit as well as the body—and describes the pattern of work "scars" being brought home to the "supper table and the TV set" that affect the "soul of our society." He lists the computer, nuclear energy, and the "sudden, simultaneous influences flashed upon everybody's TV screen" as causes of increased risk to people's lives. Possibilities of another way of living, a more privileged way of living known previously by only an elite few are easily recognized today because of the influence of TV and the "machine" (computer) that has accelerated society's pace.

Although researched and written more than two decades ago, the stories Terkel recorded remain true today and continue to affect our understanding of ourselves. *Working* was even adapted as a musical and produced on Broadway in 1978. According to Terkel, *Working* "celebrates the non-celebrated." As you read Terkel, look for the mark of the "remarkable oral historian," as he has become known. Are there places in his text where you are startled, surprised, or delighted?

Working the Land

*A*n autumn evening in a southern Indiana farmhouse. The city, Evansville, industrial and distending, is hardly fifteen miles away— and coming on fast.

It's a modern, well-appointed house. A grandfather's clock, tick-tocking, is the one memento of a "country" past. His father and his grandfather worked this land. "My father was born on the same spot this house is sittin'. And I was born here. We tore the old house down."

His wife, who has a job in the city, and their fourteen-year-old daughter live with him. His older child, a son, is elsewhere. Though he has a few head of beef cattle, soy beans and corn are his source of income. He describes himself as "a poor farmer."

I farm about five-hundred acres. I own in the neighborhood of two-hundred. The rest of it I sharecrop. I give the owners two-fifths and I keep three-fifths. They're absentee. One would be a doctor. And a bricklayer. One would be a contractor widow. (Glances toward his wife) What would you call Roger? An aeronautical engineer. I guess all of 'em have inherited from their parents. They hold it for an investment. If I owned a lot of farm land myself, if I had that much money, I don't think I'd be farming it. I'd let somebody else worry with it.

5   For a farmer, the return of your investment is so small now that it isn't really worthwhile. A younger person cannot start farming unless they have help from the father or somebody. 'Cause you have to be almost able to retire a rich man to start out. The only way the farmers are making it today is the ones in business keep getting bigger, to kinda offset the acreage, the margin income. I don't know what's gonna happen in the future. I'm afraid it's gonna get rough in time to come.

Your cities are moving out, taking the farm land. If you want to stay in the farming business, it best not to be too close to the city. But if you're thinking of disposing of your farm in a few years, why then it's an advantage, 'cause it'll be worth a lot more.

I don't see how I'll keep the thing goin'. As I get older and want to slow down . . . Well, that's one way of looking as it, retirement. It's either gritting it out or selling. It seems nowadays a lot of 'em do retire and rent it out to a neighbor or somebody. The end of the day, the older you get, the tireder you get.

City people, they think you're well off. When they drive by, I hear a lot of comments, 'cause most of my friends are city people. They drive by and see a big tractor and things settin' down. They envy me, but they don't know what's behind all that.

Farming, it's such a gamble. The weather and the prices and everything that goes with it. You don't have too many good days. It scares when you see how many working days you actually have. You have so many days to get the crop planted and the same in the fall to harvest it. They have this all figured down to the weather and it's just a few days. You try to beat the weather. It tenses you up. Whether we needed rain or we didn't need rain, it affects you in different ways. I have seen a time when you're glad to hear the thunder and lightning. Then again, I've wished I didn't hear it. (Laughs.)

10   *Mrs. Walker interjects: "In his busy season, every morning when we get up the radio goes on right away so we can get the weather report. About ten to six every morning. We just eagerly listen to this report. In the summer when he isn't too busy or like in the winter, we never pay too much attention to it. Otherwise, we watch it close."*

Weather will make ya or break ya. The crops have to have enough moisture. If they don't have enough, they hurt, If you have too much, it hurts. You take it like you git. There's nothing you can do about it. You just don't think too much about it. My wife says it doesn't bother me too much. Of course, you still worry . . .

I don't believe farmers have as much ulcers as business people 'cause their life isn't quite as fast. But I'll say there will be more as times goes on. 'Cause farming is changing more. It's more a business now. It's getting to be a big business. It's not the labor any more, it's the management end of it.

Your day doesn't end. A farmer can't do like, say a doctor—go out of town for the weekend. He has to stay with it. That's jut one of the things you have to learn to live with. I'd say a majority of the time a farmer, when he comes in at night and goes to bed, he's tired enough he's not gonna have trouble sleepin'. Of course, he'll get wore down.

He touches a weary cadence as he recounts a twelve-plus-hour workday in the fall: up at six (an earlier rising in the spring, four thirty-five) . . . "haul my grain to the elevator in town, which takes about an hour and a half . . . combine about three or four loads a day . . . there's headlights on the combine, so if I start a load, I'll finish it even though it's after dark . . . that'll run from fifteen hundred to two thousand bushel . . . five hundred bushels a truckload . . . first thing next morning, I'll take the load to town. . . ."

15   *In the winter he "loafs," helping his wife with her housework, preparing the machinery for spring, planning the fertilizer program, and "a lot of book work," getting all the records up to date for "tax time."*

We'll soon be storing the fall harvest. Machinery and a lot of equipment and everything ready to go when the crops mature. That's the big problem: machinery. Combine, you're speaking of twenty thousand dollars. And the eight-row planter for the spring, that's expensive. It's such a large investment for what small return you really get out of it. You won't use it but a month or two out of the year.

My father-in-law helps me an awful lot in the spring and a little in the fall. He drives the tractor for me. My daughter, she drives a tractor when school is out. When I was home there on the farm, there was five children, three boys, and we were on an eighty-acre farm. It took all of us, my father and three boys. You can see the difference machinery plays in it.

The number of farmers are getting less every day and just seems like it's getting worse every year. The younger ones aren't taking over. The majority of the people originated from the farm years ago. But it's been so long ago that the young ones now don't realize anything about the farm. What goes with it or anything like that. The gamble that the farmer takes.

The city people, when they go to the grocery store and the price of meat is raised, they jump up and down. They don't realize what all is behind that. They're thinking of their own self. They don't want to put up that extra money—which I don't blame them either. The same way when I go to buy a piece of equipment. I go jump up and down.

20   Break the dollar down for food and the farmer's down at the bottom of the list. He's got the most invested of all but he's the smallest percentage-wise out of the food dollar. The processors, it seems like that's the big end of it. The ladies like to buy this ready-prepared and frozen and all that, and that costs 'em.

And chemicals in farming, it's getting to be quite expensive. It seems as though we can't farm without it. They're tryin' to outlaw a lot of 'em, but I don't know. From my end of it, I'd hate to be without 'em. Seems as though if we didn't have chemicals, we wouldn't have crops. It seems like the bugs and the weeds would just about take care of 'em if we didn't have the chemicals. But I don't know . . . on the other end, either . . . whether it's good for our country or not.

What do you call these—organic farming? They have a lot of good points, but I never did see a large organic farm. They're just more or less small operators. I don't think you can do it on a large scale enough to be feeding a nation. You can see many small organic farms. They used to call 'em truck farmers. They had routes to town and deliver produce and like that. He more or less retailed his product to individual homes. He just couldn't get big enough, just like everybody else.

They're using airplanes more all the time. We had our corn sprayed this year by a plane—for blight. You hire a plane, he furnishes the material, and he does it for so much an acre. We had it sprayed twice—with fungicide.

When you get a good crop, that's more or less your reward. If you weren't proud of your work, you wouldn't have no place on the farm. 'Cause you don't work by the hour. And you put in a lot of hours, I tell ya. You wouldn't stay out here till dark and after if you were punchin' a clock. If you didn't like your work and have pride in it, you wouldn't do that.

You're driving a tractor all day long, you don't talk to anyone. You think over a lot of things in your mind, good and bad. You're thinking of a new piece of equipment or renting more land or buying or how your gonna get through the day. I can spend all day in the field by myself and I've never been lonesome. Sometimes I think it's nice to get out by yourself.

The grass is greener on the other side of the fence, they say. When I got out of high school I worked one summer in a factory in Evansville. I didn't like it. I've always been glad I worked that one summer. I know what it is to work in a factory for a little while. The money part of it's good, but the atmosphere, confined. The air and everything like that. I wasn't used to a smelly factory. They have a certain odor, you don't have it out in the field.

I might say I've been real lucky in farming. My wife has helped me an awful lot. She's worked ever since we've been married. My girl, she likes it and loves to get out on the tractor. Our boy really worked. He liked the farm and worked from the time he was old enough until he left. He graduated from Purdue last spring. From observing him from the time he grew up, I would say he'd make a good farmer. He's in Georgia now. He's in management training. He realized he could make more money in some other position than he can in farming. I hope he isn't putting money ahead of what he really wants to do. He says he likes what he's doin', so . . .

It seems like if they once get out and go to college, there' very few of 'em do come back. They realize that as far as the future and the money could be made from farming, it just wasn't there. So that was one thing that turned his mind away from it. Of course, he can always change, I'm hoping . . .

I do believe farmers are going to have to band together a little bit more than they have in the past. Whether it'll be through a cooperative or a union, I can't say. The trouble is they're too much individual for the rest of the country nowadays. You're bucking against the organized country, it seems like. And the farmers aren't organized, it seems like.

30   The big complaint you hear is that when you take your product to the market, you take what they give you. And when you go buy on the other end, you pay what they say. So you're at their mercy on both ends, more or less.

I don't like to—farmers really don't want to, deep in their hearts—but when it gets to a certain point, there's no alternative. 'Cause when a person gets desperate or is about to lose his farm, he'll do about anything he wouldn't do otherwise.

I hate to look at it that way, if the farmer is part of an organization, that would take all the—I wouldn't say enjoyment, no—but it'd be just like any other business. When you all had to sell at a certain time and all that went with it. But I believe it is going to come to that.

POSTSCRIPT: *"The family farm has never been stronger than it is now, and it has never been better serviced by the Department of Agriculture."—Earl L. Butz, Secretary of Agriculture, in the keynote speech at the 51st National 4-H Congress (Chicago Sun-Times, November 27, 1972).*

ROBERTO ACUNA

I walked out of the fields two years ago. I saw the need to change the California feudal system, to change the lives of farm workers, to make these huge corporations feel they're not above anybody. I am thirty-four years old and I try to organize for the United Farm Workers of America.

35   *His hands are calloused and each of his thumbnails is singularly cut. "If you're picking lettuce, the thumbnails fall off 'cause they're banged on the box. Your hands get swollen. You can't slow down because the foreman sees you're so many boxes behind and you'd better get on. But people would help each other. If you're feeling bad that day, somebody who's feeling pretty good would help. Any people that are suffering have to stick together, whether they like it or not, whether they be black, brown, or pink."*

According to Mom, I was born on a cotton sack out in the fields, 'cause she had no money to go to the hospital. When I was a child, we used to migrate from California to Arizona and back and forth. The things I saw shaped my life. I remember when we used to go out and pick carrots and onions, the whole family. We tried to scratch a livin' out of the ground. I saw my parents cry out in despair, even though we had the whole family working. At the time, they were paying sixty-two and a half cents an hour. The average income must have been fifteen hundred dollars, maybe two thousand.*

This was supplemented by child labor. During those years, the growers used to have a Pick-Your-Harvest Week. They would get all the migrant kids out of school and have 'em out there pickin' the crops at peak harvest time. A child was off that week and when he went back to school, he got a little gold star. They would make it seem like something civic to do.

We'd pick everything: lettuce, carrots, onions, cucumbers, cauliflower, broccoli, tomatoes—all the salads you could make out of vegetables, we picked 'em. Citrus fruits, watermelons—you name it. We'd be in Salinas about four months. From there we'd go down into the Imperial Valley. From there we'd go to picking citrus. It was like a cycle. We'd follow the seasons.

After my dad died, my mom would come home and she'd go into her tent and I would go into ours. We'd roughhouse and everything and then we'd go into the tent where Mom was sleeping and I'd see her crying. When I asked her why she was crying she never gave me an answer. All she said was things would get better. She retired a beaten old lady with a lot of dignity. That day she thought would be better never came for her.

40   *"One time, my mom was in bad need of money, so she got a part-time evening job in a restaurant. I'd be helping her. All the growers would come in and they'd be laughing, making nasty remarks, and make passes at her. I used to go out there and kick 'em and my mom told me to leave 'em alone, she could handle 'em. But they would embarrass her and she would cry.*

"My mom was a very proud woman. She brought us up without any help from nobody. She kept the family strong. They say that a family that prays together stays together. I say that a family that works together stays together—because of the suffering. My mom couldn't speak English too good. Or much Spanish, for that matter. She wasn't educated. But she knew some prayers and she used to make us say them. That's another thing: when I see the many things in this world and this country, I could tear the churches apart. I never saw a priest out in the fields trying to help people. Maybe in these later years they're doing it. But it's always the church taking from the people.

"We were once asked by the church to bring vegetables to make it a successful bazaar. After we got the stuff there, the only people havin' a good time were the rich people because they were the only ones that were buyin' the stuff . . ."

---

*"Today, because of our struggles, the pay is up to two dollars an hour. Yet we know that is not enough."

I'd go barefoot to school. The bad thing was they used to laugh at us, the Anglo kids. They would laugh because we'd bring tortillas and frijoles to lunch. They would have their nice little compact lunch boxes with cold milk in their thermos and they'd laugh at us because all we had was dried tortillas. Not only would they laugh at us, but the kids would pick fights. My older brother used to do most of the fighting for us and he'd come home with black eyes all the time.

What really hurt is when we had to go on welfare. Nobody knows the erosion of man's dignity. They used to have a label of canned goods that said, "U.S. Commodities. Not to be sold or exchanged." Nobody knows how proud it is to feel when you bought canned goods with your own money.

45   *"I wanted to be accepted. It must have been in sixth grade. It was just before the Fourth of July. They were trying out students for this patriotic play. I wanted to do Abe Lincoln, so I learned the Gettysburg Address inside and out. I'd be out in the fields pickin' the crops and I'd be memorizin'. I was the only one who didn't have to read the part, 'cause I learned it. The part was given to a girl who was a grower's daughter. She had to read it out of a book, but they said she had better diction. I was very disappointed. I quit about eighth grade.*

"Any time anybody'd talk to me about politics, about civil rights, I would ignore it. It's a very degrading thing because you can't express yourself. They wanted us to speak English in the school classes. We'd put out a real effort, I would get into a lot of fights because I spoke Spanish and they couldn't understand it. I was punished. I was kept after school for not speaking English."

We used to have our own tents on the truck. Most migrants would live in the tents that were already there in the fields, put up by the company. We got one for ourselves, secondhand, but it was ours. Anglos used to laugh at us. "Here comes the carnival," they'd say. We couldn't keep our clothes clean, we couldn't keep nothing clean, because we'd go by the dirt roads and the dust. We'd stay outside the town.

I never did want to go to town because it was a very bad thing for me. We used to go the small stores, even though we got clipped more. If we went to the other stores, they would laugh at us. They would always point at us with a finger. We'd go to town maybe every two weeks to get what we needed. Everybody would walk in a bunch. We were afraid. (Laughs.) We sang to keep our spirits up. We joked about our poverty. This one guy would say, "When I get to be rich, I'm gonna marry an Anglo woman, so I can be accepted into society." The other guy would say, "When I get rich I'm gonna marry a Mexican woman, so I can go to that Anglo society of yours and see them hang you for marrying an Anglo." Our world was around the fields.

I started picking crops when I was eight. I couldn't do much, but every little bit counts. Every time I would get behind on my chores, I would get a carrot thrown at me by my parents. I would daydream: If I were a millionaire, I would buy all these ranches and give them back to the people. I would picture my mom living in one area all the time and being admired by all the people in the community. All of a sudden I'd be rudely awaken by a broken carrot in my back. That would bust your whole dream apart and you'd work for a while and come back to daydreaming.

50   We used to work early, about four o'clock in the morning. We'd pick the harvest until about six. Then we'd run home and get into our supposedly clean clothes and run all the way to school because we'd be late. By the time we got to school, we'd be all tuckered out. Around maybe eleven o'clock, we'd be dozing off. Our teachers would send notes to the house telling Mom that we were inattentive. The only thing I'd make fairly good grades on was spelling. I couldn't do anything else. Many times we never did our homework, because we were out in the fields. The teachers couldn't understand that. I would get whacked there also.

School would end maybe four o'clock. We'd rush home again, change clothes, go back to work until seven, seven thirty at night. That's not counting the weekends. On Saturday and Sunday, we'd be there from four thirty in the morning until about seven thirty in the evening. This is where we made the money, those two days. We all worked.

I would carry boxes for my mom to pack the carrots in. I would pull the carrots out and she would sort them into different sizes. I would get water for her to drink. When you're picking tomatoes, the boxes are heavy. They weigh about thirty pounds. They're dropped very hard on the trucks so they have to be sturdy.

The hardest work would be thinning and hoeing with a short-handled hoe. The fields would be about a half a mile long. You would be bending and stooping all day. Sometimes you would have hard ground and by the time you got home, your hands would be full of calluses. And you'd have a backache. Sometimes I wouldn't have dinner or anything. I'd just go home and fall asleep and wake up just in time to got out to the fields again.

I remember when we just got into California from Arizona to pick up the carrot harvest. It was very cold and very windy out in the fields. We just had a little old blanket for the four of us kids in the tent. We were freezin' our tail off. So I stole two brand-new blankets that belonged to a grower. When we got under those blankets it was nice and comfortable. Somebody saw me. The next morning the grower told my mom he'd turn us in unless we gave him back his blankets—sterilized. So my mom and I and my kid brother went to the river and cut some wood and made a fire and boiled the water and she scrubbed the blankets. She hung them out to dry, ironed them, and sent them back to the grower. We got a spanking for that.

55 　　I remember this labor camp that was run by the city. It was a POW camp for German soldiers. They put families in there and it would have barbed wire all around it. If you were out after ten o'clock at night, you couldn't get back in until the next day at four in the morning. We didn't know the rules. Nobody told us. We went to visit some relatives. We got back at about ten thirty and they wouldn't let us in. So we slept in the pickup outside the gate. In the morning, they let us in, we had a fast breakfast and went back to work in the fields.*

　　The grower would keep the families apart, hoping they'd fight against each other. He'd have three or four camps and he'd have the people over here pitted against the people over there. For jobs. He'd give the best crops to the people he thought were the fastest workers. This way he kept us going harder and harder, competing.

　　When I was sixteen, I had my first taste as a foreman. Handling braceros, aliens, that came from Mexico to work. They'd bring these people to work over here and then send them back to Mexico after the season was over. My job was to make sure they did a good job and pushin' 'em even harder. I was a company man, yes. My parents needed money and I wanted to make sure they were proud of me. A foreman is recognized. I was very naïve. Even though I was pushing the workers, I knew their problems. They didn't know how to write, so I would write letters home for them. I would take 'em to town, buy their clothes, outside of the company stores. They had paid me $1.10 an hour. The farm workers' wages was raised to eighty-two and a half cents. But the braceros were making more money than me, because they were working piecework. I asked for more money. The manager said, "If you don't like it you can quit." I quit and joined the Marine Corps.

"I joined the Marine Corps at seventeen. I was very mixed up. I wanted to become a first-class citizen. I wanted to be accepted and I was very proud of my uniform. My mom didn't want to sign the papers, but she knew I had to better myself and maybe I'd get an education in the services.

　　"I did many jobs. I took a civil service exam and was very proud when I passed. Most of the others were college kids. There were only three Chicanos in the group of sixty. I got a job as a correctional officer in a state prison. I quit after eight months because I couldn't take the misery I saw. They wanted me to use a rubber hose on some of the prisoners—mostly Chicanos and blacks. I couldn't do it. They called me chicken-livered because

---

*"Since we started organizing, this camp has been destroyed. They started building housing on it."

I didn't want to hit nobody. They constantly harassed me after that. I didn't quit because I was afraid of them but because they were trying to make me into a mean man. I couldn't see it. This was Soledad State Prison."

60   I began to see how everything was so wrong. When growers can have an intricate watering system to irrigate their crops but they can't have running water inside the houses of workers. Veterinarians tend to the needs of domestic animals but they can't have medical care for the workers. They can have land subsidies for the growers but they can't have adequate unemployment compensation for the workers. They treat him like a farm implement. In fact, they treat their implements better and their domestic animals better. They have heat and insulated barns for the animals but the workers live in beat-up shacks with no heat at all.

Illness in the fields is 120 percent higher than the average rate for industry. It's mostly back trouble, rheumatism and arthritis, because the damp weather and the cold. Stoop labor is very hard on a person. Tuberculosis is high. And now because of the pesticides, we have many respiratory diseases.

The University of California at Davis has government experiments with pesticides and chemicals. To get a bigger crop each year. They haven't any regard as to what safety precautions are needed. In 1964 or '65, an airplane was spraying these chemicals on the fields. Spraying rigs they're called. Flying low, the wheels got tangled on the fence wire. The pilot got up, dusted himself off, and got a drink of water. He died of convulsions. The ambulance attendants got violently sick because of the pesticides he had on his person. A little girl was playing around a sprayer. She stuck her tongue on it. She died instantly.

These pesticides affect the farm worker through the lungs. He breathes it in. He gets no compensation. All they do is say he's sick. They don't investigate the cause.

There were times when I felt I couldn't take it any more. It was 105 in the shade and I'd see endless rows of lettuce and I felt my back hurting . . . I felt the frustration of not being able to get out of the fields. I was getting ready to jump any foreman who looked at me cross-eyed. But until two years ago, my world was still very small.

65   I would read all these things in the papers about Cesar Chavez and I would denounce him because I still had that thing about becoming a first-class patriotic citizen. In Mexicali they would pass out leaflets and I would throw 'em away. I never participated. The grape boycott didn't affect me much because I was in lettuce. It wasn't until Chavez came to Salinas, where I was working in the fields, that I saw what a beautiful man he was. I went to this rally, I still intended to stay with the company. But something—I don't know—I was

close to the workers. They couldn't speak English and wanted me to be their spokesman in favor of going on strike. I don't know—I just got caught up with it all, the beautiful feeling of solidarity.

You'd see the people on the picket lines at four in the morning, at the camp fires, heating up beans and coffee and tortillas. It gave me a sense of belonging. These were my own people and they wanted change. I knew this is what I was looking for. I just didn't know it before.

My mom had always wanted me to better myself. I wanted to better myself because of her. Now when the strikes started, I told her I was going to join the union and the whole movement. I told her I was going to work without pay. She said she was proud of me. (His eyes glisten. A long, long pause.) See, I told her I wanted to be with my people. If I were a company man, nobody would like me any more. I had to belong to somebody and this was it right here. She said, "I pushed you in your early years to try to better yourself and get a social position. But I see that's not the answer. I know I'll be proud of you."

All kinds of people are farm workers, not just Chicanos. Filipinos started the strike. We have Puerto Ricans and Appalachians too, Arabs, some Japanese, some Chinese. At one time they used us against each other. Buy now they can't and they're scared, the growers. They can organize conglomerates. Yet when we try organization to better our lives, they are afraid. Suffering people never dreamed it could be different. Cesar Chavez tells them this and they grasp the idea—and this is what scares the growers.

Now the machines are coming in. It takes skill to operate them. But anybody can be taught. We feel migrant workers should be given the chance. They got one for grapes. They got one for lettuce. They have cotton machines that took jobs away from thousands of farm workers. The people wind up in the ghettos of the city, their culture, their families, their unity destroyed.

70   We're trying to stipulate it in our contract that the company will not use any machinery without the consent of the farm workers. So we can make sure the people being replaced by the machines will know how to operate the machines.

Working in the fields is not in itself a degrading job. It's hard, but if you're given regular hours, better pay, decent housing, unemployment and medical compensation, pension plans—we have a very relaxed way of living. But the growers don't recognize us as persons. That's the worst thing, the way they treat you. Like we have no brains. Now we see they have no brains. They have only a wallet in their head. The more you squeeze it, the more they cry out.

If we had proper compensation we wouldn't have to be working seventeen hours a day and following the crops. We could stay in one area and it would give us roots. Being a migrant, it tears the family apart. You get in debt. You leave the area penniless. The children are the ones hurt the most. They go to school three months in one place and then go on to another. No sooner do they make friends, they are uprooted again. Right here, your childhood is taken away. So when they grow up, they're looking for this childhood they have lost.

If people could see—in the winter, ice on the fields. We'd be on our knees all day long. We'd build fires and warm up real fast and go back onto the ice. We'd be picking watermelons in 105 degrees all day long. When people have melons or cucumber or carrots or lettuce, they don't know how they got on their table and the consequences to the people who picked it. If I had enough money, I would take busloads of people out to the fields and into the labor camps. Then they'd know how the fine salad got on their table.

Reflective Reading, Informal Writing

REFLECTING ON THE READING:

- What attitudes do Pierce Walker and Roberto Acuna reveal about the work they do? In what do they feel pride? About what do they worry? What values seem to drive them?
- Compare Walker and Acuna's attitudes toward farming methods, including such things as the use of chemicals and machinery.
- Walker and Acuna both show an interest in the generation that preceded them as well as in the generation that will follow. What is the nature of the generational issues on their minds, and to what degree do such issues figure into their respective visions of the future of farming/farm work?

UNDERSTANDING RHETORICAL STRATEGIES:

- In either Walker or Acuna's interview, or both, locate patches of speech that depart from standard English. Why are they here? Why doesn't Terkel simply edit them out? What do they reveal about the speakers or, if your prefer, how do they help to characterize the speakers? Could you argue that their speech patterns reveal a distinct way of thinking, or even, in a sense, a way of life? How would you describe that way of thinking, that lifestyle?
- Terkel describes his method in *Working* as follows:

  I realized quite early in this adventure that interviews, conventionally conducted, were meaningless. Conditioned clichés were certain to come. The question-and-answer technique may be of some value in determining favored detergents, toothpaste and deodorants, but not in the discovery of men and women. There were questions, of course, but they were casual in nature—at the beginning: the kind you would ask while having a drink with someone; the kind he would ask you. The talk was idiomatic rather than academic. In short, it was conversation. In time, the sluice gates of dammed up hurts and dreams were opened.

(Introduction, xx-xxi)

If Terkel did use questions, he seems to have edited them out. As you reread these interviews, can you infer what questions were asked, and where? What patterns or principles of organization seem to prevail in these interviews? Are they organized logically? Chronologically? Psychologically (meaning organization is determined by the patterns of association in the interviewee's mind)? What is the overall effect of this pattern of organization?

- What seems most important to Walker? To Acuna? In writing, we have a number of means at our disposal for achieving emphasis: placement within the essay or the paragraph, sentence structure, diction, and the like. How do interviewees emphasize certain ideas in an oral interview?

INFORMAL WRITING:

- To what extent do the differences between the two men's style of speech, their spoken idioms, reflect deeper differences between them?
- As oral histories are, after all, *histories,* both of these interviews embody a particular view of the past, and of the past's impact on the present. How would you characterize the view of the past in each instance? Is the past a kind of golden age from which we have "fallen," or a kind of brutal, primitive existence above which we have risen, or are now rising? Do Walker and Acuna's views of the past affect the way they think about the future?
- One's private, personal past is also inescapably linked to the public past. Do you find that these two men, in talking about their own lives, reveal at the same time an awareness of larger issues, larger developments within American society?

WALLACE TERRY

After graduating from Brown University in 1959 and earning a Rockefeller Fellowship at the University of Chicago from 1959–1960, Wallace Terry covered the black revolution for *Time* magazine and the *Washington Post*. He spent two years living in Vietnam during the war as a correspondent for *Time*. At the beginning of his stay in Vietnam, he met Black soldiers who supported the war effort and believed in the value of a democratic government. However, he also found that Black soldiers made up 23 percent of the fatalities in the war, proportionately higher than the Black-American population. According to Terry, "Uncle Sam was an equal opportunity employer" in Vietnam.

During his two years in Vietnam, Terry distributed 833 questionnaires to Black and White Americans and interviewed many of the respondents. Terry noticed that by the end of 1967, a new Black soldier had appeared. The war had "used up" the professionals who found military service a "supreme test of their black manhood." Black draftees replaced the "careerists" and brought the rebellious spirit of urban ghetto revolution with them, speaking out against discrimination and racial insults. They unified Black soldiers on the battlefield and called themselves "Bloods." What Terry termed "foxhole brotherhood" disappeared as it became evident that America would not win this war. As the nation grew more divided, American soldiers began to fight against each other. When Black Vietnam veterans returned to America, they expected to come home to more than they had before. Instead, Black unemployment among veterans was higher than the rate for White veterans, and all Vietnam veterans faced the political discontent of America. As Terry describes it, the political right blamed the soldiers for losing the war; the political left blamed them for killing innocent civilians.

Terry chose 20 men to portray their war and postwar experiences in his book, *Bloods* (1984). The experience of the Black veteran is unique because he fought at a time when his "sisters and brothers were fighting and dying at home for equal rights" and for a "color-blind nation promised to him in the Constitution he swore to defend." The Black soldier had much to gain in proving his loyalty and value to a racially divided nation and a lot to lose upon return. As Private Edwards writes, "I had left one war and came back and got into another one."

As you read, pay close attention to the ways Terry's subject talks about loyalty, value, and loss. What do you learn from Private Edwards about war and race?

Private First Class Reginald "Malik" Edwards, Phoenix, Louisiana

Rifleman
9th Regiment
U.S. Marine Corps
Danang
June 1965—March 1966

I'm in the Amtrac with Morley Safer, right? The whole thing is getting ready to go down. At Cam Ne. The whole bit that all America will see on the *CBS Evening News*, right? Marines burning down some huts. Brought to you by Morley Safer. Your man on the scene. August 5, 1965.

When we were getting ready for Cam Ne, the helicopters flew in first and told them to get out of the village 'cause the Marines are looking for VC. If you're left there, you're considered VC.

They told us if you receive one round from the village, you level it. So we was coming into the village, crossing over the hedges. It's like a little ditch, then you go through these bushes and jump across, and start kickin' ass, right?

Not only did we receive one round, three Marines got wounded right off. Not only that, but one of the Marines was our favorite Marine, Sergeant Bradford. This brother that everybody loved got shot in the groin. So you know how we felt.

5   The first thing happened to me, I looked out and here's a bamboo snake. That little short snake, the one that bites you and you're through bookin'. What do you do when a bamboo snake comin' at you? You drop your rifle with one hand, and shoot his head off. You don't think you can do this, but you do it. So I'm so rough with this snake, everybody thinks, well, Edwards is shootin' his ass off today.

So then this old man runs by. The other sergeant says, "Get him, Edwards." But I missed the old man. Now I just shot the head off a snake. You dig what I'm sayin'? Damn near with one hand. M–14. But all of a sudden, I missed this old man. 'Cause I really couldn't shoot him.

So Brooks—he's got the grenade launcher—fired. Caught my man as he was comin' through the door. But what happened was it was a room full of children. Like a schoolroom. And he was runnin' back to warn the kids that the Marines were coming. And that's who got hurt. All those little kids and people.

Everybody wanted to see what had happened, 'cause it was so fucked up. But the officers wouldn't let us go up there and look at what shit they were in. I never got the count, but a lot of people got screwed up. I was telling Morley Safer and his crew what was happening, but they thought I was trippin', this Marine acting crazy, just talking shit. 'Cause they didn't want to know what was going on.

So I'm going on through the village. Like the way you go in, you sweep, right? You fire at the top of the hut in case somebody's hangin' in the rafters. And if they hit the ground, you immediately fire along the ground, waist high, to catch them on the run. That's the way I had it worked out, or the way the Marines taught me. That's the process.

All of a sudden, this Vietnamese came runnin' after me, telling me not to shoot: "Don't shoot. Don't shoot." See, we didn't go in the village to look. We would just shoot first. Like you didn't go into a room and see who was in there first. You fired and go in. So in case there was somebody there, you want to kill them first. And we was just gonna run in, shoot through the walls. 'Cause it was nothin' to shoot through the walls of a bamboo hut. You could actually set them on fire if you had tracers. That used to be a fun thing to do. Set hootches on fire with tracers.

So he ran out in front of me. I mean he's runnin' into my line of fire. I almost killed him. But I'm thinking, what the hell is wrong? So then we went into the hut, and it was all these women and children huddled together. I was gettin' ready to wipe them off the planet. In this one hut. I tell you, man, my knees got weak. I dropped down, and that's when I cried. First time I cried in 'Nam. I realized what I would have done. I almost killed all them people. That was the first time I had actually had the experience of weak knees.

Safer didn't tell them to burn the huts down with the lighters. He just photographed it. He could have got a picture of me burning a hut, too. It was just the way they did it. When you say level a village, you don't use torches. It's not like in the 1800s. You use a Zippo. Now you would use a Bic. That's just the way we did it. You went in there with your Zippos. Everybody. That's why people bought Zippos. Everybody had a Zippo. It was for burnin' shit down.

I was a Hollywood Marine. I went to San Diego, but it was worse in Parris Island. Like you've heard the horror stories of Parris Island—people be marchin' into the swamps. So you were happy to be in San Diego. Of course, you're in a lot of sand, but it was always warm.

At San Diego, they had this way of driving you into this base. It's all dark. Back roads. All of a sudden you come to this little adobe-looking place. All of a sudden, the lights are on, and all you see are these guys with these Smokey the Bear hats and big hands on their hips. The light is behind them, shining through at you. You all happy to be with the Marines. And they say, "Better knock that shit off, boy. I don't want to hear a goddamn word out of your mouth." And everybody starts cursing and yelling and screaming at you.

15   My initial instinct was to laugh. But then they got right up in your face. That's when I started getting scared. When you're 117 pounds, 150 look like a monster. He would just come screaming down your back, "What the hell are you looking at, shit turd?" I remembered the time where you cursed, but you didn't let anybody adult hear it. You were usually doing it just to be funny or trying to be bold. But these people were actually serious about cursing your ass out.

Then here it is. Six o'clock in the morning. People come in bangin' on trash cans, hittin' my bed with night sticks. That's when you get really scared, 'cause you realize I'm not at home anymore. It doesn't look like you're in the Marine Corps either. It looks like you're in jail. It's like you woke up in a prison camp somewhere in the South. And the whole process was not to allow you to be yourself.

I grew up in a family that was fair. I was brought up on the Robin Hood ethic, and John Wayne came to save people. So I could not understand that these guys were supposed to be the good guys, why were they treating each other like this?

I grew up in Plaquemines Parish. My folks were poor, but I was never hungry. My stepfather worked with steel on buildings. My mother worked wherever she could. In the fields, pickin' beans. In the factories, the shrimp factories, oyster factories. And she was a housekeeper.

I was the first person in my family to finish high school. This was 1963. I knew I couldn't go to college because my folks couldn't afford it. I only weighed 117 pounds, and nobody's gonna hire me to work for them. So the only thing left to do was go into the service. I didn't want to go into the Army, 'cause everybody went into the Army. Plus the Army didn't seem like it did anything. The Navy I did not like 'cause of the uniforms. The Air Force, too. But the Marines was bad. The Marine Corps built men. Plus just before I went in, they had all these John Wayne movies on every night. Plus the Marines went to the Orient.

20   Everybody laughed at me. Little, skinny boy can't work in the field going in the Marine Corps. So I passed the test. My mother, she signed for me 'cause I was seventeen.

There was only two black guys in my platoon in boot camp. So I hung with the Mexicans, too, because in them days we never hang with white people. You didn't have white friends. White people was the aliens to me. This was '63. You don't have integration really in the South. You expected them to treat you bad. But somehow in the Marine Corps you hoping all that's gonna change. Of course, I found out this was not true, because the Marine Corps was the last service to integrate. And I had an Indian for a platoon commander who hated Indians. He used to call Indians blanket ass. And then we had a Southerner from Arkansas that liked to call you chocolate bunny and Brillo head. That kind of shit.

I went to jail in boot camp. What happened was I was afraid to jump this ditch on the obstacle course. Every time I would hit my shin. So a white lieutenant called me a nigger. And, of course, I jumped the ditch farther than I'd ever jumped before. Now I can't run. My leg is really messed up. I'm hoppin'. So it's pretty clear I can't do this. So I tell the drill instructor, "Man, I can't fucking go on." He said, "You said what?" I said it again. He said, "Get out." I said, "Fuck you." This to a drill instructor in 1963. I mean you just don't say that. I did seven days for disrespect. When I got out of the brig, they put me in a recon. The toughest unit.

We trained in guerrilla warfare for two years at Camp Pendleton. When I first got there, they was doing Cuban stuff. Cuba was the aggressor. It was easy to do Cuba because you had a lot of Mexicans. You could always let them be Castro. We even had Cuban targets. Targets you shoot at. So then they changed the silhouettes to Vietnamese. Everything to Vietnam. Getting people ready for the little gooks. And, of course, if there were any Hawaiians and Asian-Americans in the unit, they played the roles of aggressors in the war games.

Then we are going over to Okinawa, thinking we're going on a regular cruise. Bu the rumors are that we're probably going to the 'Nam. In Okinawa we was trained as raiders. Serious, intense jungle-warfare training. I'm gonna tell you, it was some good training. The best thing about the Marine Corps, I can say for me, is that they teach you personal endurance, how much of it can you stand.

25   The only thing they told us about the Viet Cong was they were gooks. They were to be killed. Nobody sits around and gives you their historical and cultural background. They're the enemy. Kill, kill, kill. That's what we got in practice. Kill, kill, kill. I remember a survey they did in the mess hall where we had to say how we felt about the war. The thing was, get out of Vietnam or fight. What we were hearing was Vietnamese was killing Americans. I felt that if people were killing Americans, we should fight them. As a black person, there wasn't no problem fightin' the enemy. I knew Americans were prejudiced, were racist and all that, but, basically, I believed in America 'cause I was an American.

I went over with the original 1st Battalion 9th Marines. When we got there, it was nothing like you expect a war to be. We had seen a little footage of the war on TV. But we was on the ship dreaming about landing on this beach like they did in World War II. Then we pulled into this area like a harbor almost and just walked off the ship.

And the first Vietnamese that spoke to me was a little kid up to my knee. He said, "You give me cigarette. You give me cigarette." That really freaked me out. This little bitty kid smokin' cigarettes. That is my first memory of Vietnam. I thought little kids smokin' was the most horrible thing that you could do. So the first Vietnamese words I learned was *Toi khong hut thuoc lo.* "I don't smoke cigarettes." And *Thuoc la co hai cho suc khoe.* "Cigarettes are bad for your health."

Remember, we were in the beginning of the war. We wasn't dealing with the regular army from the North. We was still fightin' the Viet Cong. The NVA was moving in, but they really hadn't made their super move yet. So we were basically runnin' patrols out of Danang. We were basically with the same orders that the Marines went into Lebanon with. I mean we couldn't even put rounds in the chambers at first.

It was weird. The first person that died in each battalion of the 9th Marines that landed was black. And they were killed by our own people. Comin' back into them lines was the most dangerous thing then. It was more fun sneakin' into Ho Chi Minh's house than comin' back into the lines of Danang. Suppose the idiot is sleeping on watch and he wake up. All of a sudden he sees people. That's all he sees. There was a runnin' joke around Vietnam that we was killing more of our people than the Vietnamese were. Like we were told to kill any Vietnamese in black. We didn't know that the ARVN had some black uniforms, too. And you could have a platoon commander calling the air strikes, and he's actually calling on your position. It was easy to get killed by an American.

30   They called me a shitbird, because I would stay in trouble. Minor shit, really. But they put me on point anyway. I spent most of my time in Vietnam runnin'. I ran through Vietnam 'cause I was always on point, and points got to run. They can't walk like everybody else. Specially when you hit them open areas. Nobody walked through an open area. After a while, you develop a way to handle it. You learned that the point usually survived. It was the people behind you who got killed.

And another thing. It's none of that shit, well, if they start shootin' at you, now all of a sudden we gonna run in there and outshoot them. The motherfuckers hit, you call in some air. Bring in some heavy artillery, whatever you need to cool them down. You wipe that area up. You soften it up. Then you lay to see if you receive any fire. An *then* you go on in.

I remember the first night we had went out on patrol. About 50 people shot this old guy. Everybody claimed they shot him. He got shot 'cause he started running. It was an old man running to tell his family. See, it wasn't s'posed to be nobody out at night but the

Marines. Any Vietnamese out at night was the enemy. And we had guys who were frustrated from Korea with us. Guys who were real gung ho, wanted a name for themselves. So a lot of times they ain't tell us shit about who is who. People get out of line, you could basically kill them. So this old man was running like back towards his crib to warn his family. I think people said "Halt," but we didn't know no Vietnamese words.

It was like shootin' water buffaloes. Somebody didn't tell us to do this. We did it anyway. But they had to stop us from doing that. Well, the water buffaloes would actually attack Americans. I guess maybe we smelled different. You would see these little Vietnamese kids carrying around this huge water buffalo. That buffalo would see some Marines and start wantin' to run 'em down. You see the poor little kids tryin' to hold back the water buffalo, because these Marines will kill him. And Marines, man, was like, like we was always lookin' for shit to go wrong. Shit went wrong. That gave us the opportunity.

I remember we had went into this village and got pinned down with a Australian officer. When we finally went on through, we caught these two women. They smelled like they had weapons. These were all the people we found. So the Australian dude told us to take the women in. So me and my partner, we sittin' up in this Amtrac with these women. Then these guys who was driving the Amtrac come in there and start unzippin' their pants as if they gonna screw the women. So we say, "Man, get outta here. You can't do it to our prisoners." So they get mad with us. Like they gonna fight us. And we had to actually lock and load to protect the women. They said, "We do this all the time."

35   One time we had went into this place we had hit. We was takin' prisoners. So this one guy broke and ran. So I chased him. I ran behind him. Everybody say, "Shoot him. Shoot him." 'Cause they was pissed that I was chasin' him. So I hit him. You know I had to do something to him. I knew I couldn't just grab him and bring him back. And his face just crumbled. Then I brought him back, and they said, "You could have got a kill, Edwards."

The first time we thought we saw the enemy in big numbers was one of these operations by Marble Mountain. We had received fire. All of a sudden we could see people in front of us. Instead of waiting for air, we returned the fire, and you could see people fall. I went over to this dude and said, "Hey, man, I saw one fall." Then everyone started yelling, "We can see 'em fall. We can see 'em fall." And they were fallin'. Come to find out it was Bravo Company. What the VC had done was suck Bravo Company in front of us. 'Cause they attacked us and Bravo Company at the same time. They would move back as Bravo Company was in front of us. It was our own people. That's the bodies we saw falling. They figured out what was happening, and then they ceased fire. But the damage is done real fast. I think we shot up maybe 40 guys in Bravo Company. Like I said, it was easy to get killed by an American.

The first time I killed somebody up close was when we was tailing Charlie on a patrol somewhere around Danang. It was night. I was real tired. At that time you had worked so hard during the day, been on so many different details, you were just bombed out.

I thought I saw this dog running. Because that white pajama top they wore at night just blend into that funny-colored night they had over there. All of a sudden, I realized that somebody's runnin'. And before I could say anything to him, he's almost ran up on me. There's nothing I can do but shoot. Somebody get that close, you can't wait to check their ID. He's gonna run into you or stop to shoot you. It's got to be one or the other. I shot him a bunch of times. I had a 20-round clip, and when he hit the ground, I had nothing. I had to reload. That's how many times he was shot.

Then the sergeant came over and took out the flashlight and said, "Goddamn. This is fucking beautiful. This is fucking beautiful."

40   This guy was really out of it. He was like moanin'. I said, "Let me kill him." I couldn't stand the sound he was makin'. So I said, "Back off, man. Let me put this guy out of his misery." So I shot him again. In the head.

He had a grenade in his hand. I guess he was committing suicide. He was just runnin' up to us, pullin' a grenade kind of thing. I caught him just in time.

Everybody was comin' congratulatin' me, saying what a great thing it was. I'm tryin' to be cool, but I'm really freakin' out. So then I start walking away, and they told me I had to carry the body back to base camp. We had a real kill. We had one we could prove. We didn't have to make this one up.

So then I start draggin' this body by the feet. And his arm fell off. So I had to go back and get his arm. I had to stick it down his pants. It was a long haul.

And I started thinkin'. You think about how it feels, the weight. It was rainin'. You think about the mist and the smells the rain brings out. All of a sudden I realize this guy is a person, he got a family. All of a sudden it wasn't like I was carrying a gook. I was actually carrying a human being. I started feeling guilty. I just started feeling really badly.

45   I don't feel like we got beat in Vietnam. We never really fought the war. People saying that America couldn't have won that war is crazy.

The only way we could actually win the war was to fight everyday. You couldn't fight only when you felt like it. Or change officers every month. Troops would learn the language, learn the people, learn the areas. If you're gonna be fighting in an area, you get to know everybody in the area and you stay there. You can't go rotate your troops every 12 months. You always got new people coming in. Plus they may not get to learn anything. They may die the first day. If you take a guy on patrol and he gets killed the first day, what good is he? See, if you have seasoned troops, you can move in and out of the bush at will. You get the smell of the country on you. You start to eat the food. You start to smell like it. You don't have that fresh smell so they can smell you when you're comin'. Then you can fight a war. Then you can just start from one tip of South Vietnam and work your way to the top. To China. Of course, if we had used the full might of the military, we'd be there now. We could never give the country back up. Plus we'd have to kill millions of Vietnamese. Do we want to do that? What had they done to us to deserve all that? So to do it would have been wrong. All we did was give our officers the first combat training they had since Korea. It was more like a big training ground. If it was a real war, you either would have come out in a body bag or you would have come out when the war was over.

Sometimes I think we would have done a lot better by getting them hooked on our lifestyle than by trying to do it with guns. Give them credit cards. Make them dependent on television and sugar. Blue jeans works better than bombs. You can take blue jeans and rock 'n' roll records and win over more countries than you can with soldiers.

When I went home, they put me in supply, probably the lowest job you can have in the Marines. But they saw me drawing one day and they said, "Edwards can draw." They sent me over to the training-aids library, and I became an illustrator. I reenlisted and made sergeant.

When I went to Quantico, my being black, they gave me the black squad, the squad with most of the blacks, especially the militant blacks. And they started hippin' me. I mean I was against racism. I didn't even call it racism. I called it prejudice. They hipped me to terms like "exploitation" and "oppression." And by becoming an illustrator, it gave you more time to think. And I was around people who thought. People who read books. I would read black history where the white guys were going off on novels or playing rock music. So then one day, I just told them I was black. I didn't call them *blanco,* they didn't have to call me Negro. That's what started to get me in trouble. I became a target. Somebody to watch.

50   Well, there was this riot on base, and I got busted. It started over some white guys using a bunch of profanity in front of some sisters. I was found guilty of attack on an unidentified Marine. Five

months in jail, five months without pay. And a suspended BCD. In jail they didn't want us to read our books, draw any pictures, or do anything intellectually stimulating or what they thought is black. They would come in my cell and harass me. So one day I was just tired of them, and I hit the duty warden. I ended up with a BCD in 1970. After six years, eight months, and eight days, I was kicked out of the Corps. I don't feel it was fair. If I had been white, I would never have went to jail for fighting. That would have been impossible.

With a BCD, nothing was happenin'. I took to dressin' like the Black Panthers, so even blacks wouldn't hire me. So I went to the Panther office in D.C. and joined. I felt the party was the only organization that was fighting the system.

I liked their independence. The fact that they had no fear of the police. Talking about self-determination. Trying to make Malcolm's message reality. This was the first time black people had stood up to the state since Nat Turner. I mean armed. It was obvious they wasn't gonna give us anything unless we stood up and were willing to die. They obviously didn't care anything about us, 'cause they had killed King.

For me the thought of being killed in the Black Panther Party by the police and the thought of being killed by Vietnamese was just a qualitative difference. I had left one war and came back and got into another one. Most of the Panthers then were veterans. We figured if we had been over in Vietnam fighting for our country, which at that point wasn't serving us properly, it was only proper that we had to go out and fight for our own cause. We had already fought for the white man in Vietnam. It was clearly his war. If it wasn't, you wouldn't have seen as many Confederate flags as you saw. And the Confederate flags was an insult to any person that's of color on this planet.

I rose up into the ranks. I was an artist immediately for the newspaper. Because of my background in the military, obviously I was able to deal with a lot of things of a security nature. And eventually I took over the D.C. chapter.

55   At this time, Huey Newton and Bobby Seale were in jail and people sort of idealized them. The party didn't actually fall apart until those two were released, and then the real leader, David Hilliard, was locked up. Spiro Agnew had a lot to do with the deterioration when he said take the Panthers out of the newspapers and then they will go away. And the FBI was harassing us, and we started turning on each other because of what they were spreading. And the power structure started to build up the poverty programs. Nobody was going to follow the Panthers if they could go down to the poverty program and get a check and say they are going to school.

We just didn't understand the times. All we wanted to do was kick whitey's ass. We didn't think about buying property or gaining economic independence. We were, in the end, just showing off.

I think the big trip America put us on was to convince us that having money was somehow harmful. That building businesses and securing our economic future, and buying and controlling areas for our group, our family, our friends like everybody else does, was wrong. Doing that doesn't make you antiwhite. I think white people would even like us better if we had more money. They like Richard Pryor. And Sammy Davis. And Jabbar.

Economically, black folks in America have more money than Canada or Mexico. It's obvious that we are doing something wrong. When people say we're illiterate, that doesn't bother me as much. Literacy means I can't read these books. Well neither does a Korean or a Vietnamese. But where they're not illiterate is in the area of economics. Sure, we're great artists, great singers, play great basketball. But we're not great managers yet. It's pretty obvious that you don't have to have guns to get power. People get things out of this country and they don't stick up America to do it. Look at the Vietnamese refugees running stores now in the black community where I live.

Right now, I'm an unemployed artist, drawing unemployment. I spent time at a community center helping kids, encouraging kids to draw.

60   I work for the nuclear-freeze movement, trying to convince people nuclear war is insane. Even when I was in the Marine Corps, I was against nuclear war. When I was a child, I was against nuclear weapons, because I thought what they did to Hiroshima and Nagasaki was totally cold. There's nothing any human being is doing on the planet that I could want to destroy the planet for future generations. I think we should confine war to our century and our times. Not to leave the residue around for future generations. The residue of hate is a horrible thing to leave behind. The residue of nuclear holocaust is far worse.

I went to see *Apocalypse Now*, because a friend paid my way. I don't like movies about Vietnam 'cause I don't think that they are prepared to tell the truth. *Apocalypse Now* didn't tell the truth. It wasn't real. I guess it was a great thing for the country to get off on, but it didn't remind me of anything I saw. I can't understand how you would have a bridge lit up like a Christmas tree. A USO show at night? Guys attacking the women on stage. That made no sense. I never saw us reach the point where nobody is in charge in a unit. That's out of the question. If you don't know anything, you know the chain of command. And the helicopter attack on the village? Fuckin' ridiculous. You couldn't hear music comin' out of a helicopter. And attacking a beach in helicopters was just out of the question. The planes and the napalm would go in first. Then, the helicopters would have eased in after the fact. That was wild.

By making us look insane, the people who made that movie was somehow relieving themselves of what they asked us to do over there. But we were not insane. We were not insane. We were not ignorant. We knew what we were doing.

I mean we were crazy, but it's built into the culture. It's like institutionalized insanity. When you're in combat, you can do basically what you want as long as you don't get caught. You can get away with murder. And the beautiful thing about the military is there's always somebody that can serve up as a scapegoat. Like Calley. I wondered why they didn't get Delta Company I-9 because of Cam Ne. We were real scared. But President Johnson came out and defended us. But like that was before My Lai. When they did My Lai, I got nervous again. I said my God, and they have us on film.

I was in Washington during the National Vietnam Veterans Memorial in 1982. But I didn't participate. I saw all those veterans runnin' around there with all those jungle boots on, all these uniforms. I didn't want to do that. It just gave me a bad feeling. Plus some of them were braggin' about the war. Like it was hip. See, I don't think the war was a good thing. And there's no memorial to Cam Ne, to My Lai. To all those children that was napalmed and villages that were burned unnecessarily.

65   I used to think that I wasn't affected by Vietnam, But I been livin' with Vietnam ever since I left. You just can't get rid of it. It's like that painting of what Dali did of melting clocks. It's a persistent memory.

I remember most how hard it was to just shoot people.

I remember one time when three of our people got killed by a sniper from this village. We went over to burn the village down. I was afraid that there was going to be shootin' people that day, so I just kind of dealt with the animals. You know, shoot the chickens. I mean I just couldn't shoot no people.

I don't know how many chickens I shot. But it was a little pig that freaked me out more than the chickens. You think you gonna be shootin' a little pig, it's just gonna fall over and die. Well, no. His little guts be hangin' out. He just be squiggling around and freakin' you out.

See, you got to shoot animals in the head. If we shoot you in your stomach, you may just fall over and die. But an animal, you got to shoot them in the head. They don't understand that they supposed to fall over and die.

Reflective Reading, Informal Writing

REFLECTING ON THE READING:

- One striking feature that comes through Private Edwards' story of his experiences in Vietnam is the number or absurdities, or paradoxes, he finds himself involved in. Some of these he is aware of, such as being able to shoot the head off a snake, but unable to shoot a potential enemy. Others he seems oblivious to, such as being horrified at the prospect of a child smoking cigarettes, but relatively blasé about children caught in the line of fire. Identify as many paradoxes as you can in Edwards' account. Taken as a whole, what do they suggest about Edwards? About the war?

- What stereotypes about the Marines, the war in Vietnam, and America itself does Edwards begin with? In what ways are these stereotypes modified or destroyed by his experiences? What stereotypes do you bring to your reading of his account? Do you find them changed by his story?

- What experiences seem to stand out in Edwards' memory most clearly? How can you tell? Why do you suppose he remembers these experiences rather than others?

UNDERSTANDING RHETORICAL STRATEGIES:

- If Edwards' story were a movie, it would be given an "R" rating for profanity. Yet Edwards betrays, at least twice, a distaste for "cursing." Discuss his ambivalence toward offensive language. What is there in his personal "code" that causes him to find it shocking? Why, then, does he employ it so heavily himself?

- How does this interview seem to be organized? What pattern or principle of organization seems prevalent? Is the organization logical? Chronological? Psychological (meaning organization is determined by the patterns of association in the interviewee's mind)? Find places where Edwards changes the subject, then determine the nature of the connection between the two subjects. What is the overall effect of this pattern of organization?

- Edwards makes a number of references to popular media: to television (in fact, one of his patrols is actually covered by the *CBS Evening News*), to John Wayne, to the movie, *Apocalypse Now*. How do these references to the media function in Edwards' narrative?

INFORMAL WRITING:

- In Edwards' account, find as many examples of racism or prejudice as you can. Is Edwards strictly a target of the racism of others, or does he sometimes seem racist himself? What does his story seem to reveal about racism?

- Edwards' experience with the military transforms his identity at least twice. The first transformation, in boot camp, was engineered by the Marines. The second, beginning when he was stationed at Quantico, put him at odds with the Marines. Even so, one could argue that both changes were caused by the war. Compare the two transformations Edwards went through. Do you see other important ways in which he was changed by the war?

- Edwards writes, "By making us look insane, the people who made [*Apocalypse Now*] was somehow relieving themselves of what they asked us to do over there. But we were not insane. . . . I mean we were crazy, but it's built into the culture. It's like institutionalized insanity." Explain what Edwards means by "institutionalized insanity."

JOHN TATEISHI

President Franklin D. Roosevelt signed Executive Order 9066 on February 19, 1942, allowing the massive eviction of Japanese-American citizens and aliens from the West Coast during World War II. This resulted in open public racism and racist propaganda. At best, Japanese-Americans were given two weeks to sell everything they owned and relocate; at worst, they were given two days. In either situation, they sold houses, business, and farms at tragically low prices or left them behind altogether.

John Tateishi's work, *And Justice For All* (1984), from which this interview is taken, records the individual experiences of Japanese-Americans imprisoned in internment camps in America during World War II. His work "tries to present for the first time in human and personal terms the experience of the only group of American citizens ever to be confined in concentration camps in the United States." The internment camps, still a silent part of America's history, forced exclusion and detention of more than 120,000 Japanese-Americans who resided on the West Coast during the war. Most of the incarcerated were *Nisei,* American-born citizens, but some were *Issei,* first-generation immigrants. Tateishi explains that the government policy legalizing the internment was based on the notion that Japanese-Americans were "inherently disloyal" to the United States based on their ancestry, even if they had never been to Japan and were American-born citizens.

Proving loyalty to the United States eventually became a point of dissension between Japanese-Americans in the camps when a questionnaire required them to promise to serve in the American armed forces and to "foreswear any form of allegiance or obedience to the Japanese emperor." The latter point proved a problem for the Issei who had been denied citizenship in the United States. Forswearing allegiance to Japan would leave them without a country or home in a time when their future was unknown and threatened. Not agreeing to the order implied an allegiance to Japan even if this was not the case.

Many families stayed in the camps for two or more years. Some left to serve in the Army and left families behind in the camps. When the war ended, families returned to ransacked homes and businesses or found new places to begin again. The humiliation and shame of the experience kept freed families silent. Tateishi's book stands as one of the first to record the lived experience of imprisoned citizens.

In a time of war, at home or abroad, political judgment can be colored by emotion, patriotism, and fear. Nevertheless, Tateishi summarizes the time of internment camps as a time when a "group of American citizens and their alien parents became the innocent victims of a racist policy that ignored all the protections of individual rights which are intrinsic and essential to the very principles of constitutional government." As you read Violet De Cristoforo's story, look for those places that support or deny

5   Tateishi's summary. Are there issues or problems in trying to summarize such experiences? Does oral history as a means of depicting the richness of experience work with or against Tateishi's summary?

Violet De Cristoforo—Tule Lake

Before the war I lived in Fresno, California. When evacuation came I was married and had two children, seven and five years old. I was also pregnant three months. The day of the order was just about two weeks after my operation for a tumor. The doctor tried to have my internment delayed for a while and so asked the provost marshal, but it was not allowed. So I closed the bookshop, closed the home with my two children, carried whatever we were allowed to carry, and left for the camp, which was Fresno Assembly Center.

I couldn't believe that American citizens were being uprooted, especially since my children were so young. I was just unable to answer the question myself as to why such a thing was being done to us. This kept hounding us over and over. Why? What necessity? It just didn't make sense. But to tell the truth, we were brought up to be very law-abiding citizens. We felt that we were compelled to go, and it was not easy: not being able to convince myself, not being able to convince the children. My children and I decided that we would do whatever we had to do in order to survive. It was a matter of survival and nothing else that had made us go to camp and stay there for the next four years. Whether they call this injustice or inhumanity, I don't know, and history must decide. But for me it was an individual tragedy that should never have happened, and I don't think that it could ever be remedied by anyone, or any government.

Because in 1942 I believed in this country wholeheartedly, I wanted to offer something to the United States government at the time Japan bombed Pearl Harbor. But all I had was a Red Cross certificate, my only asset, and I went to Red Cross headquarters and said, "The only thing I have is an advanced certificate in Red Cross training. If at anytime you need my services I will gladly give them to you." And that was the fullest I was able to give, the fullest the United States government could receive from me. I believed in the U.S. government so, so much that I went to the Red Cross and volunteered myself.

In April 1942, my husband and I and our two children left for camp, and my mother-in-law and father-in-law came about a month later. I wasn't afraid, but I kept asking in my mind, how could they? This is impossible. Even today I still think it was a nightmarish thing. I cannot reconcile myself to the fact that I had to go, that I was interned, that I was segregated, that I was taken away, even though it goes back forty years.

5   But we went to the Fresno Assembly Center. And you know what the summer is like in Fresno—110 degrees—and we were living under a low, tar-paper roof. The floors were built right on top of the racetrack. And there was the manure, and there were cracks in the floor, so that every bit of summer heat, every minute of the day when you're in the barracks, pushed the smell up. It was unbearable, the heat and the smell, and being pregnant and very weak, I sheltered myself under the bed and put wet towels on myself as much as I could. Some days we would dig into the ground and get into the ground, but we couldn't do that very well. As the days went on, the alfalfa started growing from under the floor between the cracks. People pinched the alfalfa and started eating it, and I became violently ill because I'm very allergic to hay and to many grasses and seeds.

Then there was the food poisoning. I was the first to succumb. We usually had to wait something like an hour or and hour and a half to be served any food. The line was so long, and things were so disorganized that they didn't have a system that let a sick woman or an older person or a pregnant woman go first. They never did that. So if you wanted to eat something, you stayed in line in that hot sun for an hour, sometimes two hours, and by the time you got your food and took it back to your barracks to eat, the food was spoiled. The first time I got food poisoning I thought I would lose the baby, and I was confined to the hospital, which had no roof, no windows, hardly anything. I was there for about a week and barely sustained the baby's life. When I was released to the barracks, I was under the doctor's care for about a month. But all during the pregnancy, I hemorrhaged, and so the doctor thought that if the baby was to be born, it might not be normal.

Towards the later part of my pregnancy I was in the hospital for about two months, and I had the baby. It wasn't quite a full pregnancy, and she was about five pounds, a very small child. During the stay in Fresno, my mother-in-law was quite ill too, and she wasn't given much medical attention. So with that, and with my two young children not having any schools to go to, not having anything to do, I had my hands full in trying to just look after myself plus my children and the rest of the family.

We stayed there until September. The day my second daughter was born was September 2, and September 18 we were herded off to Arkansas on a dilapidated train which had nothing for babies or sick women. It was a five-day, five-night trip—the most horrible, horrible conditions. The shades were drawn for security reasons, and there was no air. Whenever a troop train came by, we had to sidetrack and let it go first. Even on those little stops, we were not allowed to get off the train. And my two-week-old baby developed double pneumonia the third day out, and there was no formula, no sanitation.

By the time we got to Jerome, Arkansas, the ambulance was waiting for her and she was taken off to a hospital, which had no roof, no windows, no nothing. She stayed there for about two and a half months. After that, in Jerome, she was in the hospital most of the time. But let me tell you, they never let us off the train. There were three or four shipments of internees from the Fresno Center to Jerome. And I guess the husky men for building the camp at Jerome were the first ones to leave, and the sick and the old were the last to leave. And I was on the last trip. But we were not allowed to get off the train. And there was no way babies could sleep in a compartment or a sick woman could stretch out.

10 So I carried the baby for five days, and she lay on the seat for five days. And we were supposed to be on a medical train. There was only one doctor on the train, and he had his hands full, and his wife couldn't even get hot water for the baby's formula. But there were MPs all over, everywhere. And like I said, we were very, very naïve, very trustworthy, very law-abiding. Or maybe stupid, because if they said don't get up, don't do this, don't go to the next coach, we didn't. We absolutely did just as we were told to do. I know they told us not to draw the shade up. We just didn't.

Dr. Miyamoto, who was interned at Jerome with us, took care of my baby. There were many nights we were called, and he would say, tonight is the crisis, would you come and sit. I don't know how many nights we went from the barracks to the hospital, which was from one end of the camp to another. The ambulance would come and get us, and we would stay there many, many nights. I took my children with me, and we would stay there. I couldn't leave the children in the barracks alone, so we sat there all night long, many, many nights in the two and a half months she was there. Then they said we could bring her home, but the weather was very bad in Arkansas. It was just that every little sore would infect, and there was ticks and all kinds of things. So most of the one year that we stayed in Jerome, our youngest daughter was confined in the hospital.

That is when I said that if this child should ever, ever live, she would be dedicated to God. She really owed it to the doctor, or willpower, or our intense prayer for her that she lived through this thing. And do you know, my feelings were, What have I done? That question, What have I done? went away recently. But it was there for the longest time. That was the thing that bothered me. I didn't try to blame it on the government; I didn't try to blame it on anybody— but the self-recrimination: What have I done to deserve this? Why? Why? I love my children dearly, I haven't done anything wrong, and why? That was the only thing that bothered me.

For the longest time, I was a sick woman. It's just in recent years that I have become healthy, and Cris, my husband, knows that.

I was always a sickly woman, and because of that maybe I never spoke about all these things. I kept it to myself. Even my child, the other day when she first learned about it, asked, "Mama, why didn't you tell me these things?" Well, for some reason, I just didn't speak, you know, and I told her she had a very rough childhood.

After I went to live in Japan and sent my two older children back to the States, I told them that Kimi had gone through a very trying time, and the fact that she's living is because God has meant for her to live. And that I owed her more than I owed the other two kids, and that was the reason that if I cannot have the three of them to raise them properly, I felt the younger one, who was always more sickly, should be the one to stay with me. The others should go back to the States where they could be given proper education.

15   At Jerome, my in-laws were in separate barracks, because we were from different parts of Fresno, and certain parts got evacuated at different times. But because my mother-in-law was very sick, I had to go to their place to take care of her, come back and take care of my kids, and then go to the hospital. When the loyalty questionnaire came up, my father-in-law looked at it this way: he was a Japanese; he had been in the Japan-Russia war, and he had quite a bit of property back in Japan. He figured that he was considered an enemy alien, all his assets were frozen, and he had nothing to go back to in California. He was at that time quite elderly too. His wife was very sickly, and he figured that there was no use in even trying to stay in the United States. And he decided to go back to Japan. And naturally, my former husband who was the only child decided that he should go back too. They didn't have anything left in Fresno, and they all decided that if they went to Japan they have so many rentals, they have so much land, they have so much money that they can live off the interest. So they chose to repatriate. I don't believe they answered the questionnaire yes or no; they just said "refuse to answer, seek repatriation." I didn't know what they were saying at the time, but I wrote the same thing. My husband had told me, "Don't answer this because this could be a very involving matter. Don't trust the government, don't trust anybody, just say you're seeking repatriation with my family." And that is the only thing that I wrote. I did not answer yes or no to the questionnaire. "Seek repatriation with the family"—that was the only thing I wrote.

That meant I was segregated to Tule Lake, but before that we were separated again. My father-in-law went first. Then because my mother-in-law was ill and I had a sick child, we were on the last train again. In going to Tule Lake, my mother-in-law became very ill in some little town in Kansas. She became violently ill, and the train's doctor . . . I don't know whether he was a Japanese doctor or whether he was a Caucasian doctor . . . anyway, he decided that the train should stop, that she should be hospitalized right away. They took her off the train, and she stayed behind for about two months in a hospital in Kansas. I had asked to remain with her, and they wouldn't allow it.

She did not speak any English at all. She was an elderly woman, and a very devout Buddhist, very, very devout. And so she was left behind, and when she came back to Tule Lake about two months or so later, oh, she was in a ghastly condition, just absolutely as if death had walked in. She was confined to the hospital right away. When I asked the doctor just what caused her illness, he said she had motion sickness, or wasn't able to withstand long trips like that. Various reasons other than medical reasons were given to me, but I believe at that time she already had cancer.

But our family were all reunited at Tule Lake, and my brother was in Tule Lake too. The camp had already been established two years or so, and a lot of original Tule Lake people were there. But with the segregation movement, those who had decided not to go back to Japan were sent to other camps. And those who were going to Japan remained there. So we were scattered to wherever there was an empty room. So my brother was way on one end, I was someplace else, my in-laws were someplace else, although we did request to have the family together as close as possible. But that wasn't done, and we stayed wherever they had assigned us.

As soon as we got there, we realized certain things were lacking. The mess hall was not quite adequate, we were not given the proportion of food that we were supposed to be given like sugar and milk and butter. We lacked lots of things. Those people who came from other centers decided they would form a Better Living Condition Association to negotiate with the authorities. By then a lot of boys suspected that something must have been going on for them to be getting away with less food for the evacuees, less medical facilities, and such decrepit facilities. That was organized and they started negotiating with the administration. The administration was not very cooperative, and a meeting didn't materialize. And my former husband and brother being young and being community leaders, were naturally in that group to negotiate.

20   Well, one thing led to another, and before you know, they were arrested. Those who were trying to investigate the shortage of food got beaten up and thrown into the stockade, and people like my former husband who were considered leaders—anybody like Buddhist priests, or schoolteachers, or newspaper correspondents—were rounded up and sent to Justice Department camps. That was soon after we went to Tule Lake. Within three months, they were rounded up and sent to different camps.

I was separated from my husband; he went to a Santa Fe, New Mexico, camp. All our letters were censored; all our letters were cut in parts and all that. So we were not too sure what messages was getting through and not getting through, but I do know that I informed him many times of his mother's condition. He should have been allowed to come back to see her, because I thought she wouldn't live too long, but they never did allow him to come back, even for her funeral. They did not allow that. I learned that a lot of the messages didn't get to him; they were crossed out. I now have those letters with me.

In 1944 I was left with his parents and our kids. But I had no time to think of what was going to happen because my child was always sick and I had been quite sick. I didn't realize it until I recently got my camp records from the archives telling that I was hospitalized many times in Tule Lake myself. My mother-in-law was quite sick, my youngest child was sick, and I'd been sick, and my other daughter was in and out of the hospital with nephritis and other things. So in fact, my son was the only one who was healthy. My husband was gone, my brother was by that time in the "bullpen," as some called the torture chamber of the Tule Lake stockade. And I had to care for my mother-in-law who eventually died.

My son knew what was going on, and he too had many times asked me why . . . you know, why? why? Of course, I had no explanation why this was happening to us. He said if other families decided to go out, they were able to go out. When I tried to seek permission to go out, I was denied.

I tried to remain in this country after my husband and father-in-law had gone back to Japan, but I was denied that. So naturally I had no recourse but to go back to Japan. At that time, the Justice Department which conducted the hearing did not give me the reason as to why my leave authorization was not granted. It was on account of that paper, the FBI report against my husband, saying that he was considered an undesirable enemy alien. So that prevented me, but I did everything possible to remain in this country.

Then after my mother-in-law's illness was diagnosed as cancer, there was no way to treat the cancer patient there. Of course, I understand now there were others who died of cancer while they were interned. But at that time I thought she was the only one. I asked the camp authorities, the doctors, and everybody, to send her to a hospital outside where there was a facility to treat cancer patients. And that was denied. I don't know how often I had gone to the hospital, to the administration building, asking for permission to have her sent. It took them so long to answer me, so much red tape and everything. But when she finally did go, it was with two MPs armed with rifles, who came and got her at the hospital. My mother-in-law got up and cried and hugged me and said, "They're going to kill me, they're going to kill me. I've been hospitalized so long since I came into the camp, I'm a nuisance, and they going to kill me. Kazue-san, I don't want to go, don't let them take me." And I said, "Well, I had asked for them to take you to a hospital where you can be treated. Isn't that better?"

She didn't want to go. She wanted to stay with us. And she cried. She cried and she hugged. Sometimes I wish I hadn't let her go. I wish I hadn't let her go. When she went and she came back three weeks later, she looked worse than before. She said the MPs guarded her, sat beside her on the train, and when she went to the bathroom, they went with her and stayed outside the door. Throughout the cancer treatment the MPs stayed outside the door. She said she didn't know what kind of treatment she received. She couldn't understand what the doctor had said to her. But she said to me, "I prayed and I prayed and I prayed," but she said, "Sometimes the *hotokesama* ("Buddha") didn't answer me." And she had been such a devout, devout Buddhist woman. For her to say that must have been very difficult—for her to doubt Buddha for even one minute.

She didn't complain. That's one thing you can ask Dr. Miyamura, who treated her till the last minute. She never complained. All she said was she was in such gross pain—absolutely gross pain—all she said was *namu-amida-butsa* ("oneness with Buddha"), that's all she said and nothing else. She never had any unkind word for the United States government or for anybody. She worried about my brother, she worried about her son, she worried about her husband, and she made me promise her over and over that I would look after her husband, that I would look after her son. She was not quite sixty. And they had guards on her all the time, all the time. At that time, of course, I had no inclination about how advanced she was or anything. They knew that all along.

When she died, my husband was at Santa Fe. My father-in-law was still with me, in a different barracks. My father-in-law lost his mind ever since she died. We had a funeral for her when he found out that his son was not allowed to come back, and my brother was not allowed to come back. He became a different man from that day on. Then he carried his wife's ashes in a little box, and he had me order some material from Montgomery Ward, a white material. I must have ordered five or ten yards for him. He had that box wrapped around, tied to him. When he went to mess hall, he took her with him; when he went to the bathroom, he took her with him; and the day that he left Tule Lake for Japan, he had that thing on him. And he said, "Kameo, we're going to say good-bye to Tule Lake, we're going to say good-bye to Kazue, we're going to say good-bye to Ken." And he got the box and told us to say good-bye to obachan, "Say good-bye to obachan."

And I remember all my children came and cried and cried and cried. They said, "Why do *ojichan* ("grandfather") and obachan have to go back like this to Japan?" And as I understand it, my father-in-law, when he got on the boat, he was like that all the way and went home like that all the way, and so, he was never the same man again.

30   When I went back to Japan this time, I found her grave, but there's no grave for my father-in-law. Nobody did anything for him. You know, he was a very influential Buddhist leader in Fresno, one of the highest contributors. Anytime there was a donation, he was the first one and the biggest contributor. And both of them were very active in the Buddhist church in Fresno. And they had quite a bit of assets in Japan. They had quite a bit of frozen accounts, and as yet, I don't know what became of it all. And to think that he died in poverty. I spoke to my father-in-law's relatives and to the neighbors and found out how he had died, what condition he had died in. I couldn't believe it. This is the only time I have felt any bitterness against the U.S. government; for the way my father-in-law died and the fact that he has no tombstone.

He stayed in the United States forty years. Both of them had worked so hard. They gained three, four rentals in Japan, but when we went to Japan, his tenant farmers were Koreans and lived in the house. Under MacArthur's law, they had squatter's rights. And they wouldn't vacate the house for my father-in-law or later for me. So my children and I had to go and live with his relatives who had ten children. His own home, too—MacArthur's land reform act said you could only keep what you could cultivate yourself. My father-in-law had lost his wife, was not able to farm, and his son was not a farmer type. I didn't know how to farm, and we couldn't keep the land and had to sell at whatever price MacArthur had set.

So that forty years of his fruit, all the land, was sold in pieces like that. We thought we would be able to live with interest alone, but the yen was devalued to a point where there was nothing left. His United States account was frozen by the government, and I read that it's considered enemy assets. Once you repatriate to Japan, you lose it all—$27,000 in 1942 for him. Still, the only bitterness I have is to think of how my father-in-law died in the condition that he did. And there is no tomb for him.

I don't know, this is still my country, I was born here, my children are here, I probably will die here, and this is the place I'd like to be buried in. It's a certain faith I have in this country. I feel that a government such as ours has its good points, its bad points too, and we probably were caught in that. But people shouldn't be too self-centered, too selfish and take advantage of another race or a situation such as ours and make profit out of it. But that's probably an individual act, not a government act.

My life will never be the same. I will take this with me till I die, and I'm sure my children would bear some of the burden too. Three generations of my family has disintegrated as a result of this. I don't know why I'm not bitter. But what good does it do. It would only make me sick. Remember when I told you how I kept on saying, why? why? why?—when I questioned so much—that was when I was getting so sick all the time. I was really sick. I was skin and bone. My husband, Cris, had to nurse me a long time. And when I got that feeling, I was converted to a Catholic after the war. I wasn't a fervent Buddhist but my family was; my in-laws were very, very fervent Buddhist people. I was brought up by an American family, and there was something about their religion even though I wasn't too serious about it. But all during the four years of camp when this was all happening, and having seen my mother-in-law die the way she did, and she being a very, very devout woman, when she said to me, "I must have done something in the other life for hotokesama to ignore me or not listen to me". . . .

35   I got to thinking when I went back to Japan. When I got to Japan we were thrown in the same place where the Japanese soldiers were being returned. We had soldiers from Manchuria, soldiers from China, and Japanese roughnecks all in the same place. There must have been only two hundred or so of us Tule Lake repatriates at that time, and we were thrown in with the soldiers. If you talk about fear, I was afraid that night. We slept there for about a week with the same clothes that we wore when we left Tule Lake. We wouldn't take them off. There was no place to take them off. We were given something like a millet, not even rice *okayu* ("recooked rice"), and some fish and some seaweed. And what I had with me was some crackers and other things that my brother, who was in the U.S. Army, gave me—a few things to take back to Japan, plus some warm clothes and that sort of thing. Having the Japanese soldiers, those who had just come back from the war zone, sleep with us and go to the same bathroom, that was the most horrible experience I ever had. Then we went on a train that was dilapidated—no windows, hardly any seats, no doors. We were shoved in from the window, a broken window; the MP broke the window and shoved us in.

I don't know how many days it took us to go to Hiroshima. When we got off, there was not even a Hiroshima station; it was just a cement block, and we were told to get off there. I knew where my mother's home was. I went there, but there was no bridge to cross to get to my mother's place, because it had been bombed—the atomic bomb. We didn't know how to go anywhere, so we stayed there that night. This was March of 1946. We stayed there that night, huddled up against each other and found some newspaper or something for cover and cried, and just about froze to death that night.

The next day we went to a Japanese policeman, and I said that this is where my mother's home was, how do I get there? He said, "Nobody can go there, everybody's been evacuated, your mother's not there, nobody's living there. She's either dead or she's gone to wherever she can go." I said, "How do I find out?" The police said, "There's no way we can find out."

So then I decided the next best thing was to go to such and such a relative at another place. So I asked how to go there, and the policeman said I'd have to walk. I took my three children, what little luggage I had, and we walked. We walked for about two days and got to our relative's place. And you think they were glad to see us? They were not glad to see us at all. They had no news of my mother. Then I asked this person to take me to my father-in-law's place, which was way out in the country. And there was one train a day or something like that, and we went to my father-in-law's place. And like I said, he had no home to go to; he had been living with his relative who had ten children. Then with my children, we all lived there together for about two months or so.

At that time, my husband was in Nagasaki, and I guess he had already started a family or was living with somebody else. My brother was there too, because they thought that they might find some opportunity for repatriates. There were no jobs in Japan. People who had come back from war and the real Japanese had the priorities if there were any jobs at all. Repatriates had no place to go. Most everything had to be gotten on the barter system, and we had nothing to barter with.

So I stayed with my father-in-law as American forces came in. I pleaded with them to help find my mother who had lived in such and such a place. After a while, with the help of Japanese police they found out my mother was at the place where she was born, which was two mountains away, but there was no transportation to get there. The Counter Intelligence Corps (CIC) officer said, "If you come and work for us, I will take you to the river, by the river where the bridges were blown up, and from there you'll have to walk on your own." I said okay, and I set a date for him when he was to take me to that river. Then he gave me some rations of his own.

Then I walked about a day and a half across two mountains and went to see my mother. I was told that was the house where she was. There were so many women like her. No hair—their hair was just about like a chick's, just a fizzle about half an inch or so—you know, just coming out. And naturally, my mother was burnt on her right side where the ray had hit her, and she looked like a monster with her hair like that. I said, "That's not her, that's not her." Then I started explaining, my name is Kazue Yamane, Kazue. My mother lived at such and such a place; do any of you know where my mother is? And the lady said, "That's her, that's her." So I went up to her, and I said no, that couldn't be her. Then she looked at me and she tried to talk to me. And then, I have a little mole on my back and I showed that to her and then she remembered. She was in such a state of shock or something, she wasn't herself either. And then we got to talking and we got to crying; I think we did more crying than we did talking. Then I found out that she had lost all her hair.

Our house was a very nice house in the city of Hiroshima. But the impact of the bomb had flattened it, and there was only one thing remaining. Just before the war got very bad, my mother had dug a hole and buried those big *kame* ("stoneware vats"), and put the albums in. She had one for me, one for my brother, things we had left behind—whatever she had in those days—and that was the only thing she had. That's the reason that we don't have any pictures of our family or my father or anybody; everything just went with the A-bomb. Anyway, she said that she crawled and crawled and got on somebody else's wagon and then came as far as where she was now. They hardly had anything to eat.

I stayed with my mother and then I learned how to get back, to go over the two mountains, and walk some more, and take the train, and finally get to my father-in-law's place. And that I did twice. Then I got a job in Kure, which was the headquarters for the British Commonwealth and the American forces. But when the Americans found out that I had renounced my citizenship, they couldn't hire me. But they asked the British forces to take care of me. I worked for my uncle's construction company which got me contracts like Fukuoka maintenance, Air Force maintenance, Etajima troop housing, and so forth. In the afternoons I worked for British forces training clerks, interpreters, and translators for the gift shops and the mess halls. I interpreted and taught them how to go about doing things.

I was being paid in the wages of indigenous personnel, Japanese wages, because I did not have United States citizenship and could not be hired as an American citizen. They paid me in terms of indigenous wages, but from them I got American food. But that too had to be bartered because we needed other things. We subsisted on sweet potatoes for two or three weeks and then on leaves of sweet potatoes for two or three weeks. In other words, we had very little to eat for the first two, three, months we were in Japan. I should show you some of the pictures of how my children looked when they were going to Japanese school. In midwinter they were wearing straw sandals, because we had to barter shoes to get rice. My brother had bought them some overcoats, but we had to barter them to buy futon.

45   When I sent my son Ken back to the States, that was the hardest decision ever for me to make. The economy was so bad in Japan

that I could not raise my children, and Japan was no place for them. I wanted them to be brought up as Americans. Why? Because they were born there, and I still thought they had many opportunities there. The war devastated Japan, and we were not accepted in Japan either, first of all because we were different. But I had no one to send him to other than the family that brought me up, Mr. and Mrs. Stewart, who were attorneys. When I wrote to them, I told them all about my condition and that my children had to get back to the States where they must be brought up. Twelve years old was getting too old for Ken to start all over again, so I must send him. I asked Mrs. Stewart—I pleaded with her—if she could find some of her friends who would be willing to take our son. And she inquired many places and finally said there was a family in Marysville who would be glad to have Ken, and he could go to school there.

So I sent Ken over, all by himself, and I had to borrow money to send him back. I borrowed from the CIC officers with the understanding that in five years' time I would pay them back so much a month. And, so, when he was sent back, he stayed with this family in Marysville. Within six months I got a letter saying they did not want him anymore because he had taken some whiskey and things out of their home to the school. What happened was, first he was put in the first grade, then within two months he went up to the third grade and then fourth grade. Well, he wanted to play with the older children, and there was no way he could get in to play with them. He wanted to play football and basketball with them. They wouldn't let him. So he took whiskey out and gave it to the coach so that he would be allowed to play. Well, I didn't know that part of it. All I knew was that he had stolen things and went to school, and school found out, and the school didn't want him. This family didn't want him either.

They told me to come and get him. Well, I went to the American Consulate with the letter, and they said, no, there's no way you can go to the United States because you haven't got U.S. citizenship. We only serve people who have American citizenship. So then I went to a Catholic priest, and I asked him, what do I do now? He said he would plead with the American Consulate. There was no way. I went to CIC and showed them the letter. There was no way.

Then I got another letter. They no longer could care for him and they were going to dump him, because they had found out that I had a distant relative in Los Angeles somewhere, and they were going to dump him there. So with that, I went to the American Consulate again and they said there was no way I could be allowed to go back. Then I heard nothing. I had no way of knowing where he was until one day I got a letter from him about six months later or so, saying that he was with a distant relative of ours, but they were so mean to him. They said that he was a thief, that the people who brought him down said that he was a thief. My distant relatives then said they didn't want a thief around the house and to get out.

He had no place to go. And he said he was going to school and he went to see the counselor, and the counselor said, well, maybe we'll have one of the coaches take you in because he has a mother who is sick, and maybe you can stay there. In the meantime the Catholic priest and I were trying everything possible to see if we could locate him and put him in someplace.

50   Well, since Ken didn't write to us, there was no way that we could get in touch with him. Then, the Catholic priest wrote to many Catholic churches around southern California and northern California. And I tried to find him through *Rafu Shimpo*. I put an ad in the newspaper, and I found him that way.

Finally a family came forth and said, they will take care of him until I was able to come back to the United States. And that was Mrs. Hendry who took care of Ken, and Ken from there went to Santa Clara and to San Jose and got a football scholarship. He then got his M.A., and he taught at Foothill College. Then the Hendrys, being alumni of the University of Southern California, obtained a job for him, and he's been there all these years. He's a very good coach, but as far as Ken is concerned, he has no mother—she died in Japan. He doesn't know anything about the life in Japan; he has nothing to do with that. Ken will not forgive me. I was not given a chance to explain the decision I made to send him back, but I'm glad I did because he is what he is today because I did. Whether he realizes it or not, I don't know, but I don't think I made a mistake. . . . He's doing all right.

I sent my second daughter back two years later, back to the United States for the same reason. I borrowed money again. It took me a long time to pay these debts—and to think my father-in-law had left enough money for them to be educated and all that. We haven't got a cent from that. My daughter Reiko went to Fresno because that's where we lived, and Mrs. Stewart had many lawyers and judges for friends. She said Judge Hoffman would be very glad to take her, somebody whom I had known from the days I was in Fresno too. Judge Hoffman took Reiko in. She, too, I guess tried very hard to be accepted and wanted, but within two or three years, she was let go for the simple reason that while she was bathing a child, she left the child and went to the telephone and the baby almost drowned. And this happened twice.

And then she was taken from home to home, and every time it happened I went to the American Consulate, I went to the Catholic priest, I went to the CIC, the American forces, and everywhere, but I was not able to come back. The Japanese homes in

Fresno soon after the war barely had enough to subsist on, let alone take a stranger's child. So they only took her for one month here, two months there, because they knew my former husband and me. So they would write and write and write and say come and get her, we can't take care of her, she's done this, she's got boyfriends . . . and that tormented me no end. But like I said, I had no way of coming back to the States, so Ken and Reiko had to shift for themselves.

And, because of this trying period they decided that I had let them go because I didn't want them. But Reiko is a registered nurse now, and her daughter is becoming a registered nurse. I met her in Japan this time when I visited. A strange coincidence. I went over to my aunt's house, and who do I see but my daughter? All these years. We didn't have much to say. My aunt had tried awfully hard to establish contact there, but there were very few words spoken between us, and she took off.

55   You can cry about it, but what good does it do me? None. I like to help people. I like to live comfortably. I'd like to live in peace. I know in my own mind now from my last trip to Japan, that what I did for the children, for myself, for others, was the best course that I was able to take. I have no regrets whatsoever. I guess I came through, I had to live, I had to work.

In the days when this was all happening to me I had to take it day by day. But in the last six months since I started reliving this thing it was very hard. I have more peace of mind now. And seeing the children, even though they don't know that I'm up on their activities, that's a big consolation. They've done well. I think only America could have given them that opportunity.

Reflective Reading, Informal Writing

REFLECTING ON THE READING:

- Loss is a predictable by-product of war, but some lose more than others. Make a list of the losses suffered by Violet De Cristoforo.
- Japanese and those of Japanese descent hold special reverence for kinship ties. In how many different ways was the integrity of Violet's extended family challenged by the war?
- Early on, Violet states that "I decided that we would do whatever we had to do in order to survive." Given the enormity of the challenges she faced, from internment, starvation, childbirth, illness, separation from her family, and repatriation, how did she manage to survive? On what inner resources did she draw?

UNDERSTANDING RHETORICAL STRATEGIES:

- Even though sensory deprivation prevailed at each of the camps Violet found herself incarcerated in, from the Fresno Assembly Center to Tule Lake to the repatriation center in Japan, her memory of these places is rich with sensory detail. Of the Fresno Center, for example, she remembers the temperature, the smell of the manure, the alfalfa sprouts protruding though cracks in the floor. What is the rhetorical impact of this sensory detail?
- Even when she is describing bomb-devastated Hiroshima, Violet's characteristic stance is understatement. Is this inclination toward understatement a product of her personality, her religious faith, her culture, or simply the overwhelming tragedy with which she had to deal? What is the effect of this understatement, especially when you consider the alternative?
- How does this interview seem to be organized? What pattern or principle of organization prevails? Is the organization logical? Chronological? Psychological? Why this pattern of organization? How do you account for departures from it?

INFORMAL WRITING:

- Violet writes, "What have I done? That question, What have I done? went away recently. But it was there for the longest time. That was the thing that bothered me. I didn't try to blame it on the government; I didn't try to blame it on anybody—but the self-recrimination: What have I done to deserve this? Why? Why? I love my children dearly, I haven't done anything wrong, and why? That was the only thing that bothered me." Earlier, she wrote "Whether they call this injustice or inhumanity, I don't know, and history must decide. But for me it was an individual tragedy that should never have happened . . . ." There is, of course, no arguing with Violet's feelings, which are what they are, and there is no question but that what happened to her is "an individual tragedy." But why does she place the blame on herself? Where would you place it, and why?
- One leitmotif in this account is the failure of communication. What are some of the various reasons why the people here are unable to communicate with one another? What are some of the effects?
- Despite all that she receives at the hands of the U.S. government, and despite her renunciation of American citizenship, Violet seems to retain an unshakeable faith in the United States. Find evidence of her patriotism. How do you account for it?

VALERIE RALEIGH YOW

The in-depth interview is a research methodology without hard and fast rules but with standards of excellence and guidelines for achieving these standards. Understanding ethics, legalities, and techniques helps build a strong interpersonal relationship during interview situations. Valerie Raleigh Yow writes her book, *Recording Oral History* (1994), as a "user friendly" manual and regards herself as a guide, not as an unquestionable authority. Yow bases her research on her own experience and lays the groundwork for a growing understanding of the methodology behind collecting oral histories.

Yow earned her master's and doctorate degree in history from the University of Wisconsin. She then trained in oral history methodology at the University of North Carolina's Southern Oral History Program. In 1974 her first work focused on women millworkers. As part of the project on the history of women, she also trained and interviewed female clerical workers in Rhode Island. In addition to a variety of publications and research, Yow consults oral history projects, lectures about oral history research, and most recently lived in Chapel Hill, N. C., as an independent scholar researching and writing histories.

In-depth interviews as a resource for research have been used in education, anthropology, folklore, literature, psychology, and sociology. The discussion around interviews and oral history has centered on the issue of making meaning. How do the participants interpret the experience of being interviewed? How do the interviewers interject their own ideas and research process into the interview and the interpretation of that information? Yow looks at the process of the interviewer and the narrator. Previously, the interviewer and narrator relationship was seen as one of subject (the authoritative researcher) to object (the passive resource for information). In the current view, however, even if the power is unequal, both the interviewer and the narrator are seen as having knowledge of the situation as well as deficits in understanding. The interviewer brings particular knowledge about the research and methodology; the narrator has an intimate understanding of her own culture and a specific perspective on that culture. Yow states that the relationship of subject to subject, a collaboration, is the underlying assumption in her book. The interaction of the interviewer and the narrator is important. The project is shared; the interviewer gains new knowledge about a culture, person, and lived experience and the narrator contextualizes her experience, defines it, and comes to understand it by sharing it.

Yow reminds us that oral history is inevitably subjective. It is up to the researcher to reveal the meaning of a lived experience. According to Yow, "Understanding of the multiplicity of experiences in a total life context is the objective." How well do you think oral history works as means for understanding this multiplicity?

Varieties of Oral History Projects: Community Studies

You may choose to interview with the objective of writing an individual's biography or you may choose to interview with the desired outcome being a study of an entire community. Although interviewing techniques will be the same, the overall design of the research project will be different for each kind of project. The special problems that biographies and family studies present are discussed in the next two chapters. In this chapter, you will find discussion on writing studies of communities—a group, a movement, a town, a particular kind of work, a company, or an institution.

When this kind of writing is historical in nature and commissioned, because its targeted audience is the community itself, it is often referred to as *public history*. Definitions of public history vary. Charles Morrissey, an oral historian writing public history, defined it as scholarly history done by professionally trained historians in nonacademic environments.[1] Public history is based on the same research methodology that is used in noncommissioned studies. However, public history's aim is to inform the public rather than the academicians; since about 1950, traditional histories have been written for academicians or at least a highly educated lay public. And yet the lines are not so sharply drawn in reality as on paper. The best academic histories have a wider audience than professors and students, and the best public histories have a wider audience, including academics, than the people written about. Nevertheless, public history's targeted audience differs from that of academic history.

Sociologists and political scientists have long had experience with commissioned research in special communities, and anthropologists are becoming more and more involved in such projects. As in public history, the targeted audience is the commissioner or the commissioner's chosen readers—not necessarily other scholars.

Such commissioned projects are often researched and written under contract in which the commissioner's objectives are spelled out. This situation presents special problems in ethics for researchers and writers in commissioned research. Although ethical problems specific to commissioned studies were examined in the chapter on legalities and ethics, some different kinds of pressure are presented in this chapter.

PREPARATION FOR INTERVIEWING IN COMMUNITY STUDIES

5   Working in the traditional ways, we go into a project with a tentative list of topics we as scholars think are important and begin delving further into the subject by reading similar research. As historians

researching a history of a community in which many members are still living, we would miss an opportunity to learn if we began with a set list of topics. We would tell them what is important in their history instead of learning what they think is important. We, the researchers and writers of contemporary history, can become the instrument through which a community gets its history told. In the same way, the ethnographic researcher can learn at the beginning how people view their lives, what they think is happening, what they see as important, and use this preliminary knowledge in conceptualizing the project.

The researcher is not just a passive recorder of information, however. He or she will pick up on topics informers mention that have relevance beyond the particular project. And the researcher will endeavor to get information on some topics narrators have not given much thought to before the interviewing process.

Historian Kenneth Kann, while engaged in an oral history project on the history of the Jewish community in Petaluma, California, found that he and the narrators differed in what they thought was significant in the history:

> Some called attention to a great community political battle in the 1950's, when the right wing kicked the left wing out of the Jewish Community Center, which left the community split in two. But virtually no one called attention to the social consequences of the displacement of family chicken ranches by corporate poultry production in the 1950's. Everyone recalled the economic trauma of that period, but few had considered how the disintegration of their common economic base had greatly accelerated ongoing changes in family and community life. It required an outside perspective to see.[2]

Thus both researcher and community members brought different interests to the project. Kann recorded information on their interests as well as his own.

10   The strategy for the oral history interviewing project can be more of a shared experience than the traditional approach to historical research where the informants cannot speak beyond the grave. It can be different from early anthropological and sociological research in which the "subject" was fitted into a category. This is a recognition that, in oral history research, members of the community who are experts on their own experience are natural resources for planning the topics to be covered. This can be a collaborative process in which everybody learns something.

The best way to proceed is to become informed as fast as possible by carrying out a literature review and then reading the relevant materials. At the same time, conduct informational interviews (no recording, just taking notes) with individuals who have been directly involved in the community. Questions to ask include:

- If you were writing this history, what events would you include?
- What persons stand out in your mind?
- If you were studying fishing here, what kinds of things would you cover?

Return to the written sources (or your notes from the first perusal) and scan the written work to see what informants have left out. Returning to the informants, mention some of these items to jog their memories and see what significance these have for them. Questions to ask in these informational interviews might include:

- Who knows a lot about this?
- Who would *you* interview?
- What do you think such a history should do?
- What would you like to learn from this study?
- Who has kept a scrapbook or a file on this?
- Where would I find the records I need?

15   At the conclusion of these preliminary talks, compose a list of topics to be covered in the recording process, then the first draft of the interview guide, and a list of possible narrators. You also have a list of possibilities for locating written documents or published records not yet deposited in archives.

After this preliminary period in the research has been completed, write a letter to prospective narrators, stating your goals of the project—the community members' and yours....I have found that such a letter at the beginning of the research gets much better results than an out-of-the-blue telephone call to a narrator. Explain who you are and give any endorsements from members of the community that you have permission to give. State clearly what will happen to the taped histories and your written research. Then request the help of witnesses in the form of taped interviews. Explain why it is important to talk to people who lived through the experience. The letter should end with the notice that you will call.

The exception to this procedure is a situation in which the individuals have reason to distrust anything in print or to feel apprehension about such an invitation. Try to meet a friend of theirs to whom you can explain the project. Ask for help in making your purpose known and for an introduction. Then you can explain the research in person.

It is also important to explain your research project to groups in the community. John Fox, a historian at Salem State College who was conducting interviews for a history of the Parkers' Brothers games, delivered talks to the "brown bag luncheons" employees had. When I began the project on the history of the women's cooperative art gallery, I attended a meeting of the cooperative and explained what I was doing and how I would go about it. When I started working on the hospital history, the editor of the in-house publication wrote a little article about my project. By having this kind of advance publicity, people remembered something about the project and did not regard me as a complete stranger.

Knowing the significance of the project, narrators are more likely to take an interest. Tamara Hareven found when she was seeking narrators who had worked in the Amoskeag Mills in Manchester, New Hampshire, that people were puzzled and asked, "Why ask me? My story is not special." They consented to be interviewed because they wanted to help her. She and her co-workers organized a photographic exhibit of the mill buildings and workers. She commented on the difference this made:

20

> Attitudes changed drastically after the exhibit, "Amoskeag: A Sense of Place, A Way of Life," opened in Manchester. Although this exhibit was primarily architectural and was aimed at professionals and preservationists rather than at the larger public, it evoked an unexpected response from former and current textile workers in the community. It provided the setting for the former workers' public and collective identification with their old work place and it symbolized the historical significance of their work lives. . . . The sudden opportunity to view their own lives as part of a significant historical experience provided a setting for collective identification. Under these circumstances, interviewing ceased to be an isolated individual experience.[3]

The researchers found that the oral histories they recorded were of a different character than those recorded before the exhibit because the narrators were eager to talk to them. The narrators had assumed that everyone looked down on them because they were millworkers. Now they realized that others could be interested and see their work as part of the history of the nation. Hareven concluded, "The exhibit established our credibility as interviewers and laid the foundation for a continuing series of interviews with the same individuals."[4]

Let us say, then, that you are working on this introductory letter, getting to know people in the community, and preparing the advance educational events discussed above; meanwhile, you are searching the written sources and composing the interview guide. As you do this, ask yourself, "Who is being omitted? What is being neglected?"[5]

If you are a historian, the questions in the interview guide will be inspired by the community members you have spoken to, your own knowledge of similar historical events and of the historiography of the general topic, and your own interests. There will also be an awareness of the kind of history you want to write and the kind of history other involved people want. For example, you may want a social history of a craft and the craftspeople may want a history of technological changes in their work. One objective does not necessarily exclude the other, and you can structure the interview guide to reflect the different objectives of the completed history. If you are carrying out ethnographic research, the interview guide will reflect your own interests, the new insights gained from informational interviews, knowledge from your particular discipline, and research purposes—both yours and the people studied. As the interviewing goes on, however, you learn more and evaluate and change the guide.

As you work on the interview guide, do not underestimate the value of informal conversation. True, you should not use specific information of a personal nature or information told to you for your ears only for which you have no release form (unless you send the informant a note and receive permission), but you can use general information and find lines of questioning to pursue. Later you can correct some assumptions you might have made on the basis of guarded recorded testimony. Keep a notebook in which you can, as soon as you get a chance, write down the comments you hear that you suspect will prove valuable (and who said them in case you need to follow up later).

25   The procedure outlined above is the ideal. It is absolutely required for participant-observation research. In practice, it is not always possible for historians to live in the community they are researching or even to stay long enough to do this preparatory work. Paul Buhle, a social and cultural historian, has interviewed radicals from a wide variety of movements, Yiddish cultural activists to labor-movement veterans to Hollywood screenwriters. His objective has been to record their personal histories for the Oral History of the American Left, a national project centered at the archives of the Tamiment Library of New York University.

Buhle's narrators were members of a vibrant community or movement 30 to 60 years ago, but many individuals have moved in old age to different parts of the country. Buhle cannot live in the community—often it has been dispersed—and his interviewing time in a specific place is very limited. He must therefore rely on local people the narrators know and trust to spread the word about his work and his purpose for the interviews. He finds a guide-advisor who will personally introduce him. Before the interview begins, he shows the narrator work that has done, such as his *Encyclopedia of the American Left* and *Oral History of the American Left Guide.* He explains again the project at the Tamiment Library and his reason for coming to record the life story. He gives the narrator leeway to talk about what is important to him or her, at the same time asking the questions he wants answered.[6] Under these conditions, he has the questions on others for advance educational work necessary for productive interviews and on the fact that local people have recommended him as a trustworthy person. His own reputation as a scholar of social and cultural history as well as labor history also comes into play here. All of this illustrates that the ideal situation cannot always exist for the researcher, but it is still necessary within the real limitations to do some educating.

CHOICE OF NARRATORS

The chapter on preparation for the interviewing project presents examples of how to select narrators for a community study. Historians will ask to record the memories of the individuals who held positions of power in the community or company or movement; but they will also need to interview individuals at every level to get a complete view. In researching the history of a Wurlitzer organ factory that was converted during World War II to a plant to manufacture gliders and guided bombs, the research team interviewed men who were the fine craftsmen, unskilled male and female workers who came into the plant to learn crafts, men and women who worked in the office, and floor managers. (We sought higher-up personnel, but they were deceased.) In interviewing for a history of a college, I recorded the testimony of maintenance workers, retired and current college presidents, secretaries, librarians, professors, students, laboratory assistants, public relations people, members of the board of trustees, bookstore employees, the heads of student life, advisors, and so on. I sought information about college life from people with different vantage points, of different levels of power, and with different experiences. I tried to get a variety of witnesses from different time periods. In the same way, ethnographers will search for narrators who offer different experiences and different vantage points.

You must prioritize when you draw up your final list of narrators. For historians, key decision makers are usually at the top (depending on the research topic), but it is also important for a historian to find out who was there the longest, who was in a position to observe developments, and who felt the effects of a decision most directly. Health considerations also play a part in the decision: First interview the oldest or those who have serious health problems.

STRUCTURING THE INTERVIEW GUIDE TO SHOW CONNECTIONS TO THE WIDER WORLD

From the beginning, community studies present some special problems; anticipating this, you can structure the interview guide to help. In his review essay on seven community histories published in *The Oral History Review* in 1989, Michael Gordon discussed the pitfalls of this kind of research. About one project, he wrote that they "dangle brief anecdotes before us and aspire to nothing more than regaling local audiences with stories of bygone days."[7] He explained that "public memories that serve individual, institutional, and community needs do not always contribute to historical understanding."[8] On the other hand, he praised the book by Robert C. Hardy, *Hero: An Oral History of the Oklahoma Health Center,* as a "candid administrative history of the center" that provides "especially important insights about key administrative decisions, internal power struggles, and how people view their pasts and make use of public memory."[9]

30   Linda Shopes, discussing an oral history project in Baltimore neighborhoods in which she was involved, urged historians not to reflect the parochialism and ethnocentrism that characterize some oral testimony. Instead, she advised that "our popular histories ought to convey . . . an understanding of neighborhood not as an isolated collective experience, but as a collective experience that is part of, that has been shaped by, a larger urban process."[10]

In any community study, think in terms of the significance of it to outside researchers as well as to the people living or working there. General questions such as these can be a guide:

- What can be learned from this information about the connections between the community and the wider world?
- How did this community share in experiences common to much of the nation?
- How was this community unique?

In *Nearby History,* David E. Kyvig and Myron Marty presented a bibliographical essay on histories of cities and towns in their chapter titled "Linking the Particular and the Universal." This is a useful place to begin a study of local history, because the discussion of outstanding books will acquaint you with the kinds of questions historians have been asking since the 1960s. These questions include the following general approaches:

- How was modernization brought about?
- To what extent was there economic and social mobility?
- What were the patterns of migration into and out of the community?

- How, and in what ways, was assimilation of immigrants brought about?[11]

35   Also consider such questions as:

- How were gender roles changing?
- What were the effects of changes in technology on working lives?
- How was family structure changing?

SPECIAL RESEARCH SITUATIONS
Studies of Ethnic Communities

If you are an outsider beginning to research the history of an ethnic community, first learn as much as you can about the culture. And even if you know the language and history, you may still have to build trust, as the following two examples illustrate.

As mentioned earlier, Kenneth Kann studied an immigrant community in which three generations still lived in the same place. He commented:

> Nothing happens fast in oral history, especially when the oral historian is not a member of the community he is studying. Communities, and their members, have all kinds of experiences and views that are not for outside ears. The Petaluma Jewish community was particularly interesting to me because it was such an intensely lived collective experience, and because there was unusual continuity over generations, but that also made it less accessible to me as an outsider. Oral history, if nothing else, requires truckloads of patience and perseverance.[12]

40   Antonio T. Diaz-Roys, in collecting ethnobiographies of Puerto Rican migrants to the United States, had to learn again the traditional ways of building trust in that community although he was an insider. He found that, at the beginning, his university affiliation made his respondents cautious lest they say something to devalue themselves in his eyes. He put away his tape recorder. He began to participate in a pattern of visiting: They came to see his family and he visited theirs. Gradually, a relationship of trust developed. He shared his own life story and they began to see why he had become interested in their lives. Only then did he reintroduce the recorder.[13]

In the above examples the interviewer came from the same subculture but not the same community. Can the interviewer who is an outsider carry out productive interviews? In preparing for the Oral History of the American Left project, Paul Buhle learned Yiddish and read the newspapers that had been important to his narrators. These people recognized his deep interest in their lives, his sympathy for their idealism, and his scholarly expertise. The interviews were successful even though there were political and historical differences on specific issues.[14]

The outsider also may profit from reviewing the research on communication styles particular to a subgroup. Some subgroups have ways of communicating that the outsider may not be attuned to such as the excessive politeness shown to strangers in Southern homes. For example, "Y'all come to see us" should not be taken literally until you know the speaker well enough to judge whether she means it literally. In some ethnic groups, an argumentative style is an indication that the narrator wants to establish a friendship on an equal basis with the newcomer. The outsider can be puzzled by behaviors characteristic of a narrator from an ethnic group. For example, in a study of intercultural encounters between Americans and Japanese, the Japanese hearing an American compliment were embarrassed because they were used to keeping personal references out of a conversation. The Americans interpreted this reaction to the compliment as denial.[15]

The insider knows the culture well, and the narrator will probably more readily trust the insider. But as Diaz-Roys learned, there is still work for the insider to do in explaining purpose and in becoming sensitive to nuances in personal relationships in the subculture he or she might have forgotten. The outsider can also carry out productive interviews if he or she is knowledgeable about and appreciative of the culture and is able to communicate the purpose (assuming that the purpose is agreeable to the community).

In addressing the issue of insider versus outsider, Linda Shopes reasoned that "neither is especially better; both have attributes that can both serve the purpose of the inquiry and work against it." She cautioned, "The point is to be aware of one's relationship to the culture being investigated and 'use' whatever strengths of the situation or relationships that there are."[16]

Neighborhood Histories

45   In researching the history of neighborhoods or small towns, make your purposes clear in your own mind from the start. Shopes, surveying common practices in researching neighborhood histories, concluded that there are several possible goals:

> While the specifics of these projects differ widely, most seem to share certain broadly humanistic goals: the encouragement of cooperation between professional historians and lay people in the community; the presentation of aspects of the community's history to the public; the use of history to build community identity and pride; and the development of appreciation and respect for the participation of nonelite groups in the community's history. In addition, some projects consciously adopt progressive social goals by trying to give [a] historical perspective on current issues in the community in the hopes of encouraging activism and change.[17]

She warned that unless these projects are rooted in the community or linked to important centers of community life, these goals will have little meaning. The question is then, How can the researcher involve a community? Or, rather, how can the researcher become the means by which a community gets its story told?

Shopes and her co-researchers received a grant to develop an oral history program at a senior citizens' center in a Baltimore neighborhood that was stable, well kept, multiethnic, and working class. They hoped they could interest the senior citizens in learning oral history methods and becoming interviewers themselves. They also hoped to locate written primary sources within the community. And they envisaged the publication of a popularly written local history. However, they found that at first people saw them as prying, did not share their enthusiasm for a community history, and were not interested in being interviewed or learning to interview. Much time was spent educating people about the project.[18]

Shopes and another project staff member began interviewing. These interviewees, some of their friends, and a few younger people in the community became interested. After months passed, Shopes began teaching a class to community residents in the skills of oral history interviewing. She found that they wanted to talk to each other; trading reminiscences, as much as they wanted to talk about interviewing methods. And although there was an interview guide, as interviewers they generally ignored the guide and let the interviewees talk only about what was important to them. A dominant theme was personal survival; larger social themes were not as prominent. They also wanted to talk about place (what was where and when) and tell stories of their mothers' heroism.[19] The emphasis on personal survival against odds is similar to the dominant theme in Studs Terkel's collection of oral histories in *Hard Times* and may be a familiar experience to many oral historians.

50   Shopes came to this conclusion: "What is at issue here is a tension between the kind of information historians think is important to recover about a community's history and what community residents, however unconsciously, think is important to record about that history."[20] Not trained as historians, the interviewers lacked the background knowledge that would have enabled them to delve deeper into topics of a wider historical significance than the neighborhood. She also saw a tension at the level of method: Neighborhood people interviewing their neighbors are careful not to challenge their interviewee's worldviews; nor are they willing to criticize their interviewee's interpretations of collective experience.[21]

Shopes gave a realistic view of the difficulties likely to be encountered, but she did not mean that neighborhood history projects fully involving the residents at every stage are impossible. She urged that historians first become closely allied with neighborhood groups. The researchers must become sensitive to what interests people in their own history. These interests themselves suggest themes in social history. "They are clues into the mind of a person or group of people," Shopes has written. "This kind of information can then be coordinated with the data gathered from the more traditional sources of the social historian to provide not a simple 'insider's view,' but a more powerful social analysis."[22]

Work Communities

Consider also special problems involved in researching work communities. I base my definition of an occupational community, or work community, on the definitions of theorists such as historian Trevor Lummis and sociologists David Lockwood and Robert Blauner, as well as on my own experience in researching the history of a textile mill, a hospital, a college, and a women's cooperative art gallery. A work community is a group in which members have a strong identification with a specific kind of work, commitment to the same general goal, reliance on a code of behavior specific to the occupation, and a sense of belonging to a special group.[23]

Usually, the researcher steps into these "little worlds" without firsthand information on the occupation and without understanding what it means to the participants to be a part of this work community. As discussed above, the best way to proceed is by asking the group's long-term members what they thought was important in their history and what is important about the present. Often you will have to make a list of technical terms used in that occupation and learn them as quickly as you can.

Find out which individuals who are now active in the occupation as well as those who are retired are considered the most knowledgeable. Charles Morrissey argued that the researcher can best conceptualize a project by interviewing former members of the work community—for example, former members of Congress as distinct from current members.[24] They have gotten some perspective with the passage of time. And their jobs are not at stake. In any case, glean as much information about knowledgeable individuals as you can and keep a file folder with information on each. Also maintain a card file on these potential narrators with addresses and telephone numbers.

55   Locate the places where people in the occupation go to talk—go there and listen. For the hospital history, I found it was the employee cafeteria. For the history of the women's cooperative art gallery, hanging around after gallery meetings and going to shows enabled me to learn a lot. For the college history, I discovered that the faculty dining hall was filled with stilted conversations of people

who were wary of one another and that the "real talk" went on in small intimate groups meeting in private homes. Nevertheless, if I kept the conversation on the past—and far enough back in the past that a frank statement would not threaten their current situation—I could get general ideas about how people regarded a certain event or person. Wherever you go to listen, make sure people know you have an ulterior purpose: to record and write their stories. Let there be no misrepresentation of your role as researcher; you have to be honest with the people you want to be honest with you.

In recording the testimony of people in a work community, be cognizant of the fact that their jobs are at stake. In a small community, what someone says about someone else finds its way back to that person. Working relationships can be affected or company officials may judge a statement as proof of disloyalty and penalize the speaker. As usual, tell the narrator where the tapes will go and who will have access to them. Be aware that when they talk about the near-past and the present, they may have to be guarded.

John Fox, historian at Salem State College, talking about his history of an insurance company, remarked, "I'm certain that in the minds of some employees, I am an agent of the employer."[25] I found in interviewing hospital staff members that they talked frankly and enthusiastically about their research projects or work on the wards but steered clear of comments about the administration. The guardedness of this testimony was revealed by the things they were willing to talk about off-tape.

Historian Carl Ryant chose an industry in which the ownership was moving out of the community and workers felt a desire to tell their story.[26] This situation eliminated the problem of workers' vulnerability.

Most of us, however, are interviewing in ongoing companies or institutions. Respect workers' needs to protect themselves: Do not pressure them to reveal information that is potentially harmful to them. If they freely choose to reveal such information, knowing who will have access to the information, then record, of course. They want the information to be made known. In the case of a nursing home's abuse of patients, for example, employees knowingly risked their jobs to expose the violations. That was their choice. Otherwise, try to get usable on-tape information from people recently retired from the workplace. But even in this situation, people may be afraid that their frank discussions may put their pensions in jeopardy.[27]

60   Robert Byington, who studies workers and organization of work, advised seeking endorsement from the union, not management.[28] Of course, this is not possible if you have been hired by management to write the history; but if you are a free agent, it is

advisable to seek union approval, knowing that you still have to get permission from management to observe in the plant itself.

Commissioned Studies

When you are commissioned to write a history, those who pay the bill have ideas about what kind of history they want. As a scholar, you know what you want, and that is based on your interests and your knowledge of the research history of the topic. Ideally, the two approaches are similar; in reality, they may sometimes by antithetical.

Sociologist Maurice Punch, who was commissioned to write the history of a school in Britain, found that even after several revisions the narrative and analysis could not please the school's administrators. He cautioned:

> Most sponsors, I would suggest, may find it painful to have their protective myths pierced. This should be borne in mind by inexperienced researchers who might learn the subtle art of not treading too irreverently, and too unnecessarily, on institutional corns. Furthermore, research studies might learn that the research process from original aim to successful publication is not always a harmonious progression but can be beset with fieldwork difficulties and with struggles to have the findings accepted.[29]

The public is used to a superficial account. This so-called study delves into no problems and offends no one—for example, a history where, to use David Henige's phrase, "seldom is heard a discouraging word."[30] The truth is that if you are writing with the intention of publishing research on a company or institution for which you work or a town in which you live, then start thinking about how much adverse reaction you can stand. Carol Kammen described the questions she had as she began to write the history of her town:

65

> Was it a history I could tell? The question really is, do we tell the truth? Do we point to reverses in the past when we know that this is not the public's perception of what local history has been and should be? Do we examine unfavorable episodes along with more positive themes when a community generally expects that its local history will be promotional and make the community feel good about itself? Do we expose prejudice, stupidity, bad judgment, errors, or criminal behavior in the past? They are certainly topics dealt with in our newspapers today, yet I have rarely seen a local history that admits these things could have happened or were commonplace.[31]

Sometimes you suspect that the book will never see daylight if you are completely honest and that all your labor will be of no use to anyone. Still, even with these second thoughts, we face the fact that a less than honest account of the research findings profits no one.

Often, however, it is possible to avoid trouble around the issue of the commissioners' desire to protect their image. Educate the commissioners and the lay public about the difference between a public relations document and a serious research study. And the public *needs* to be informed about the way that a professional works. Much information is transmitted through the mass media where careful research is not necessarily valued, so you cannot assume that most people understand the nature of scholarly research.

David Lewis and Wesley Newton, who wrote *Delta: The History of an Airline,* said that no company has gone through a long history without making mistakes. Not to confront and evaluate the effects of the mistakes is to produce a "puff job" that enlightens no one. They advised oral historians to make sure corporate executives understand this "risk of laying bare [the company's] past to objective scholarship."[32]

Carl Ryant, a historian at the University of Louisville, was commissioned to write the history of the L&N Railroad. He was determined to record witnesses at every level in that work community. In an interview for Australian public radio, he explained:

> We wanted to know how the change had taken place from passenger to freight, what had happened when steam engines disappeared and diesel engines came in their place, what it was like if you were a minority on a railroad (and in America most of the people who had what we would have called menial jobs, the porters, the workers in the dining cars, were Blacks). And we wanted to know what happened to women. . . . The railroad, I think, were a little suspicious of this. They never said no but they could not quite understand why we wanted to deal with such specific groups, whereas, they would have preferred us to talk about only nostalgic things, what the station was like.[33]

70 When Ryant asked for pictures, the railroad executives sent him pictures of past presidents. He replied, "This is very nice but I'd like pictures of Blacks and women working in the cars." They said, "We'll send them to you, but why do you want them?" He answered, "This illustrates a theme I want to deal with." He convinced them that that was part of the story, too.[34]

From the beginning, in talking to members of the community, make clear the goals of the professional. Charles Morrissey suggested that historians can state at least three purposes:

> (1)[He or she] can underscore obvious factors in the institution's past performance, but because they are obvious they merit emphasis; (2) [he or she] can remind the institution of forgotten aspects of its history which have passed from collective memory as the institution changed staff or turned in directions away from its earlier experiences; and (3) [he or she] can elucidate the unexamined and often unarticulated premises upon which policy decisions were made.[35]

Ethnographers can stress that they want to help the community they study by providing information useful to its members.[36] Once the commissioners understand that these goals will be helpful to them, they may see that obscuring the truth will defeat this purpose.

To further educate the public at the beginning of the project, Morrissey urged oral historians to conduct a one-day seminar in the company to educate managers on the purpose and methods of history.[37] In the Wheaton College Oral History Project (Norton, Massachusetts), I offered to conduct six two-hour workshops on oral history interviewing for staff and faculty, and a dozen people took me up on it. My purpose was to engage the members of the work community in active participation in the researching of their own history. I soon discovered another benefit: When I recorded the life histories of these participants, they were especially helpful, understanding the questioning process and the importance of the recorded tapes for the college archives and the written history.

75   Another way to structure a project so that you have some help educating the public about the purposes of the research and the nature of ethnographic research is to have an advisory committee or board. Ann Moyall, author of *Clear Across Australia*, the history of Telecom Australia, the national telecommunications company, had a board set up. She insisted that the members include not only Telecom executives but also a professor of political theory who was an expert on communications and a historian respected for his work on technology. She also included an editor employed by an external organization. The board proved to be a great help. When one Telecom executive took chapters and rewrote them according to his view of history, the board was able to persuade Telecom that this would not produce the "scholarly and popular history" the company desired."[38]

I also see an advisory committee as a group of people with expertise who can give other kinds of help. Jeremy Brecher said that his community and labor advisory panel during the research project on brass workers helped locate interviewees and find photographs and documents. They publicized the project and encouraged the research.[39]

Although board members can become valuable resources in educating the public, putting the researcher in contact with narrators, and consulting in the design of the research project, some caution is advised. A board with different kinds of expertise is needed. In his *Oral History Program Manual*, William Moss suggested issues that an advisory council should consider at the onset, such as institutional affiliation and disbursement of funds as well as office space and depository facilities. But the researcher must make it clear that the advisors' role should be to "advise and facilitate, not direct or obstruct."[40] The problem is that a much-involved board can take over the project.

Ultimately, in researching and writing public history our purpose is to help people look at their past again and learn something valuable to them in the present. As ethnographers, we seek an understanding of how individuals participate in, live, and change a community culture. And for us, as researchers and human beings, we learn the answers to some of our questions about our collective past and present.

SUMMARY

Educate the group commissioning the study in purpose and research methods. Make sure these individuals understand that the best research study is an honest one, that it is poor public relations to publish something that omits truths and presents a false picture. This destroys the institution's credibility and the entire project backfires. Furthermore, the community about whom the project will be written needs educating: Advance publicity about the project evokes greater interest and willingness to help.

80   Devising topics for the interview format and a list of narrators can be a shared experience. Begin the project by conducting informational interviews. Find out where community members gather for informal conversation and avail yourself to these informal small-group discussions to ask questions about the topics in which you are interested. Find out what they think is important. Continue to read secondary sources and scan primary sources such as newspapers.

Compose a list of topics for the interviews. For histories of communities, neighborhoods, institutions, and businesses, construct an interview guide that will enable you to write a history that presents not just the unique event but also the ways the local history shares in and differs from the history of the region and the nation.

In researching histories of ethnic communities, reflect on your own relationship to that subculture. Learn about the subculture before you begin the project and become knowledgeable about social expectations, communication styles, and values. In any neighborhood study be sensitive to people's interests and become allied with neighborhood groups so that you can have a network. In researching work communities, be aware that employees' jobs are at stake, and the employers may see the company's interests as being at stake.

Notes

1. Charles Morrissey, communication to author, March 11, 1993.

2. Kenneth Kann, "Reconstructing the History of a Community," *International Journal of Oral History* 2 (February 1981): 4–12; see p. 8.

3. Tamara Hareven, "The Search for Generational Memory," in *Public History Readings*, eds. Phyllis K. Leffler and Joseph Brent (Malabar, Fla: Krieger Publishing, 1992), 270–283; see pp. 277–278.

4. Ibid.

5. Morrissey, manuscript notation, March 11, 1993.

6. Paul Buhle, letter to author, November 14, 1992.

7. Michael Gordon, "Seeing and Fleeing Ourselves: Local Oral Histories of Communities and Institutions," *Oral History Review* 17, no. 1 (Spring 1989): 117–128; see p. 118.

8. Ibid., 119.

9. Ibid., 120. Also Robert C. Hardy, *Hero: An Oral History of the Oklahoma Health Center* (Oklahoma City: Oklahoma Health Sciences Foundation, 1985).

10. Linda Shopes, "Baltimore Neighborhood Heritage Project: Oral History and Community Involvement," *Radical History Review* 25 (1981): 26–44; see p. 38.

11. David E. Kyvig and Myron Marty, *Nearby History: Exploring the Past Around You* (Nashville, Tenn.: American Association for State and Local History, 1982), 223–224.

12. Kann, "Reconstructing the History of a Community," 7.

13. Antonio T. Diaz-Roys, "Maneuvers and Transformations in Ethnobiographies of Puerto Rican Migrants," *International Journal of Oral History* 4, no. 1 (February 1983): 21–31; see p. 21–23.

14. Paul Buhle, letter to author, November 14, 1992.

15. D. Barnlund and S. Araki, "Intercultural Encounters: The Management of Compliments by Japanese and Americans," *Journal of Cross-Cultural Psychology* 16 (1985): 6–26. Quoted in Stephen P. Banks, Gao Ge, and Joyce Baker, "Intercultural Encounters and Miscommunication," In *"Miscommunication" and Problematic Talk*, eds. Nikolas Coupland, Howard Giles, and John M. Wiemann (Newbury Park, Calif.: Sage Publications, 1991), 103–112; see p. 111.

16. Linda Shopes, letter to author, July 20, 1992.

17. Linda Shopes, "Baltimore Neighborhood Heritage Project," 27.

18. Ibid., 30.

19. Ibid., 32.

20. Ibid.

21. Ibid., 33.

22. Ibid., 37.

23. Robert Blauner, "Work Satisfaction and Industrial Trends in Modern Society," in *Labor and Trade Unionism*, eds. Walter Galenson and Seymour Martin Lipset (New Work: John Wiley, 1960), 351; Trevor Lummis, "Occupational Community of East Anglian Fisherman," *British Journal of Sociology* 28, no. 1 (March 1977): 58–61; David Lockwood, "Sources of Variation," in *Working-Class Images of Society*, ed. M. Bulmes (Boston: Routledge & Kegan Paul, 1975), 17.

24. Charles Morrissey, letter to author, March 11, 1993.

25. John Fox, paper delivered at the session "The Historian as Hired Gun," Oral History Association Conference, October 10, 1991, Salt Lake City, Utah.

26. Carl Ryant, interview with Bill Bunbury for Australian Public Radio, Oral History Association Conference, October 10, 1991, Salt Lake City, Utah.

27. *Brass Valley, The Story of Working People's Lives and Struggles in an American Industrial Region*, eds. Jeremy Brecher, Jerry Lombardi, and Jan Stackhouse (Philadelphia: Temple University Press, 1982), 277.

28. Robert H. Byington, "Strategies for Collecting Occupational Folklife in Contemporary Urban/Industrial Contexts," *Western Folklore* 3 (1978): 43–56.

29. Maurice Punch, *The Politics and Ethics of Field Work* (London: Sage Publications, 1986), 75.

30. David Henige, "Where Seldom is Heard a Discouraging Word: Method in Oral History," *Oral History Review* 14 (1986): 35–42.

31. Carol Kammen, *On Doing Local History: Reflections on What Local Historians Do, Why, and What It Means* (Nashville, Tenn.: American Association for State and Local History, 1986), 86.

32. David Lewis and Wesley Newton, "The Writing of Corporate History," *Public Historian* 3, no. 3 (Summer 1981): 68.

33. Carl Ryant, interview with Bill Bunbury for "Talking History," weekly national radio program of the Australian Broadcasting Corporation, recorded at the Oral History Association Conference, October 10, 1991, Salt Lake City, Utah.

34. Ibid.

35. Morrissey, "Public Historians and Oral History," p. 26.

36. R. M. Keesing, "Anthropology in Melanesia: Retrospect and Prospect," in *The Politics of Anthropology: From Colonialism and Sexism Toward a View from Below*, eds. G. Huizer and B. Mannheim (The Hague: Mouton, 1979), 276–277, as quoted in *Ethnographic Research: A Guide to General Conduct*, ed. R. F. Ellen (London: Academic Press, 1984), 137.

37. Morrissey, "Public Historians and Oral History," 27.

38. Ann Moyall, interview with Bill Bunbury in 1991, for "Talking History."

39. *Brass Valley,* 273.

40. William Moss, *Oral History Program Manual* (New York: Praeger, 1974), 20.

Reflective Reading, Informal Writing

REFLECTING ON THE READING:

- Yow observes that oral history projects "can be more of a shared experience than the traditional approach to historical research where the informants cannot speak beyond the grave." Later she refers to oral history as "a collaborative process in which everybody learns something." Shared by whom? Who might be involved in this collaboration, and in what capacity?

- What are some of the pitfalls of conducting oral history projects within a community?

- Would it be fair to say that one should be well prepared to undertake an oral history project, but not too prepared? What are some of the critical preliminary steps? In what respects should one remain flexible and open?

UNDERSTANDING RHETORICAL STRATEGIES:

• Yow includes numerous examples drawn from actual oral history projects done by herself and others. What is the purpose of these examples?

• Sometimes potential interviewees, or "narrators," are reluctant to participate in an oral history project, if only because they don't think they have anything important to say. What are some of the strategies Yow and others have used for educating potential interviewees about their research projects, thereby enhancing their willingness to participate?

• Why is it important to be clear about the goals of an oral history? About the audience for whom it is intended?

INFORMAL WRITING:

• "The researcher is not just a passive recorder of information," Yow writes. In what respects is this claim accurate? But if the researcher is active, rather than passive, how can the result be described as "objective"?

• What are the advantages of being an "insider," a member of the community under study? The disadvantages? How about the advantages/disadvantages of being an outsider? What steps might be taken to reduce the disadvantages of being an outsider?

• Imagine a community within which you might conduct an oral history project. Working either by yourself or with a group of classmates, develop a rough draft of an "interview guide" you might use to conduct this project. You may find some of Yow's recommendations useful.

Oral History Projects: End-of-Section

Sequence One: Community-Based Learning Project

"Working the Land"

"Private First Class Reginald 'Malik' Edwards, Phoenix, Louisiana"

"Violet De Cristoforo—Tule Lake"

"Varieties of Oral History Projects: Community Studies"

Note: It may well be that your instructor has already identified a community or group for you to work with. If this is the case, skip steps 1 and 2 and begin with step 3.

1. As a class, generate a list of communities or subcommunities within which you might conduct an oral history project. These should be communities that are both inherently interesting to you, and accessible. Even if you think of yourself as relatively isolated, you will find a multitude of possibilities: a history of your college or university, or even a department within it; a history of your college town; people who have lived through some traumatic historical event such as the Depression, World War II, or Vietnam; the homeless; ethnic or religious subgroups; individuals living with AIDS; residents of the local rest home, and so on.

2. Having discussed the pros and cons of the possibilities just identified, select the group your class will work with. As a class, develop a written statement of the goals of your project. (See Yow for some guidance on stating goals.)

3. In small groups, or as an entire class, generate a list of everything you know about the community you have chosen. What do you want—or think you need—to know more about? What else will you need to know in order to conduct this project?

4. Based on what you thought you needed to know more about after group exercise 3, divide the class in half with one half doing preliminary research about the community you have identified as your subject, and the other half doing research about how to organize and conduct an oral history project. The former will depend on the community you have chosen and the availability of published materials. For the latter, many good sources are available. Useful sources other than Yow's book include:

    a. Baum, Willa K. *Oral History for the Local Historical Society.*

    b. Dunaway, David K. and Willa K. Baum. *Oral History: An Interdisciplinary Anthology.*

    c. Grele, Ronald J. *Envelopes of Sound: The Art of Oral History.*

    d. Henige, David. *Oral Historiography.*

    e. Ives, Edward D. *The Tape-Recorded Interview: A Manual for Fieldworkers in Folklore and Oral History.*

    f. Martin, Ruth R. *Oral History in Social Work.*

Of these, Baum, Ives, and Martin are more along the lines of "how-to" manuals, while the others are more academic.

In small groups or as individuals, choose a book from this list (or from available sources about your chosen community) and present an oral summary of the book (or other materials) to the class.

5.   Working in small groups, conduct informational interviews and identify potential narrators. These two steps go together. You need informational interviews (note-taking only, no recording at this stage) in order to develop some notion of the background, the issues, and the lay of the land to help you put together an interview guide. Preliminary interviews will also help you generate a list of potential narrators (Who should we talk to? Who knows about X?). On the other hand, you need at least a rough notion of who to talk to in order to conduct an informational interview.

6.   As a class, develop an interview guide, a list of questions you would like each of your interviewees to respond to. The interview guide is mainly to prevent you from forgetting something important; in fact, you will find yourself departing from it regularly as you go with the flow of the interview.

If you have not already thought about the potential audience for this project, this is a good time to do so. What you ask will be, in large part, a matter of what your audience would want to know.

WRITING:

Project #1: Triple-Entry Incident Journal

Begin your triple-entry incident journal and your private journal (optional) for the project. Your private journal will remain private unless you choose to share it or excerpts from it. We recommend that you keep the private journal as a way of creating a safe writing space for yourself since community-based learning can be difficult. You may have feelings or concerns that you are not yet ready to voice in a public forum.

The triple-entry incident journal (see page 350 of the Introduction to this chapter), on the other hand, is both personal and public. Your entries in the triple-entry incident journal will follow this pattern:

Entry 1: This entry takes place prior to meeting or contacting your interviewee. Write one to three pages about your interests, concerns, and fears regarding your project.

Entry 2: Immediately prior to meeting with your interviewee, write one to three pages about your expectations for the interview. What do you expect to happen and why? What do you think his or her expectations of you will be? How do you imagine this meeting starting and taking place—construct an imaginary scenario if you like.

Entry 3: Write one to three pages immediately following your interview. What surprised you and why? Did anything go as you imagined it would? Were any of your preconceived ideas or stereotypes about this interviewee changed in any way? If so, how? Did any of your fears or concerns materialize? Were your expectations met?

The process of writing the triple-entry incident journal should be repeated periodically throughout the term as you conduct other interviews, or at other points in the project as indicated by your instructor.

Project #2: Conduct and Transcribe Interviews

Conduct and tape record interviews. Transcribe them from tape to paper. Your class may first wish to agree on certain basic issues having to do with transcription, such as how to deal with dialect, unintelligible remarks, vocalized pauses, nonverbal gestures, and the like. Will the interviewer's questions remain in the transcription or be edited out? Should any other editing be permitted or encouraged?

Project #3: Headnotes

Write short headnotes to each of your interviews, providing as a minimum whatever basic context your readers will need to make sense of the interviews. You may wish to add a small amount of commentary linking this interview to the aim of the project as a whole.

Project #4: General Introduction (Group Project)

If your class decides to collect these oral histories into a single volume for publication in some form, brainstorm as a group about what might be useful to include in an introduction. You might, for example, wish to include a description of your project, to provide some historical context for it, and to analyze your results. What surprised you about your interviews? What patterns emerge? If you had more time, what additional research would you like to do? Divide the introduction into sections, and have each small group write a section (subject to final editing by one or two individuals).

Project #5: Assessment of the Project

With the help of your instructor, you will need to create a plan to assess the project, your participation, and any desired outcomes from the project. The assessment should include at least the following: a brief summary of the project, what actions were taken, explanation and analysis of what worked and didn't work, suggestions for changes, and finally a conclusion drawing the assessment together. Your instructor may want to modify your assessment and write-up in ways appropriate to your specific project.

Project #6: Reflective and Reflexive Narrative

Write a narrative essay examining your personal experiences with this project. That is, your essay should explore your experience within the frame of your "self," your thoughts, and your reflections as you participated in this project. Equally important is for you to tell the story of any reflexive moments you confronted along the way.

Project #7: Critical/Reflective Introduction to the Term's Work

Compile all six of the previous writing projects into a collection. Write a critical, reflective introduction to your work. This introduction should explain the context for your work, the learning that took place for you as you did this work, where and how you engaged in reflection and reflexivity, and discuss anything transformative for you. Comment on anything else that will help a reader interpret your work and experiences as they appear in this collection of writings.

Sequence Two: How You Say It Is What You Say

"Working The Land"
"Private First Class Reginald 'Malik' Edwards, Phoenix, Louisiana"
"Violet De Cristoforo—Tule Lake"

SMALL GROUP DISCUSSION:

1. If you were going to analyze the style of one of these oral histories, what might you look for? Working together, make a list of stylistic elements you might be able to identify.

2. Using the list you generated, analyze one of the oral histories for style. What does the style of speaking reveal about the interviewee?

3. If you were going to analyze the organization or structure of one of these oral histories, what might you look for? Working together, make a list of organizational patterns you might find. Earlier in this section, we have mentioned chronological, logical, and psychological (or associative) patterns of organization. Do other possibilities suggest themselves? What structural devices permit a speaker (or writer) to emphasize a particular idea? For example, what appears first? And what is the impact of repetition? Are there other structural devices that convey emphasis?

4. Using your list of structural possibilities, analyze one of the oral histories in this section. What do you learn about the speaker, about his or her attitude toward the subject, by looking at structure? Of what significance are departures from the prevailing pattern of organization, such as interruptions, asides, or flashbacks?

WRITING:

1. Compare any two of the oral histories in this section with respect to style. In what ways are they alike? Different? Write an essay explaining what is distinctive about the speakers' respective styles and what the differences reveal about them.

2. Compare any two of the oral histories in this section with respect to organization or structure. Write an essay explaining what is distinctive about the speakers' respective structural patterns and what the differences reveal about them.

3. This sequence is entitled "How You Say It Is What You Say." True, subject matter counts for something. But it is also true that rhetorical strategies, including both style and organization, are critical—even in unpremeditated speech. Write an essay in which you analyze one (or more) of the oral histories in this section, examining both the style and the organizational pattern in relation to the point (or points) the speaker seems to be making. What do the stylistic and structural choices of the speaker suggest about the speaker himself (or herself)?

Sequence Three: History and the Individual

"Working The Land"
"Private First Class Reginald 'Malik' Edwards, Phoenix, Louisiana"
"Violet De Cristoforo—Tule Lake"

SMALL GROUP DISCUSSION:

1. Select one of the oral histories listed, and see how many larger social, political, cultural, or historical forces you find at play in that individual's account. Which details of the story would you label "historical," and which "merely personal"? Do you find situations that you interpret differently than the speaker? For example, Violet De Cristoforo sees her experiences with internment during World War II as an "individual tragedy" as opposed, presumably, to the product of some larger social or historical force. Do you find that certain events are, in some sense, both personal and historical events? Are there "personal" events that are not also historical?

2. Looking briefly at all four of the oral histories here, make a list of the larger social, political, or historical forces operating in them.

3. All of the interviewees here experience, at one time or another, a sense of being "steam-rollered" by social and historical forces seemingly beyond their control. Yet they resist. What moves them to resistance? What form does their resistance take?

WRITING:

1. Select one of the oral histories in this section, and conduct some simple research on historical developments relevant to your choice (that is, developments in agriculture since World War II, the organization of farm workers, the deployment of Black soldiers in Vietnam, the internment of Japanese during World War II, and the like). Write an essay in which you compare the historical generalizations you find to the individual account embodied in the oral history. In what respects do the two accounts differ? Concur? What do you conclude?

2. Drawing on any combination of these oral histories, write an essay about how and why individuals come to resist what they see as oppressive historical developments. (Or, for that matter, why they do not resist.) What developments bring them to the point of resistance, and what strategies do they employ? To what effect? *Note:* You are more likely to avoid sweeping generalizations about racism, social justice, or the invincibility of the human spirit if you stay fairly close to the details of the oral histories you are working with.

3. Write an essay describing the advantages and the limitations of oral history as a form of history.

SAMPLE PROJECT B: AIDS PROJECTS

Whatever else can be argued or said about AIDS (Auto-Immune Deficiency Virus) and HIV (Human Immunodeficiency Virus), they have transformed our world. All of us have been touched by AIDS, some of us directly, but all of us indirectly. It has become a household word. It has brought people together and it has torn people asunder. We hope that the readings in this sequence of Chapter 4 grant you new and varied perspectives on a disease that has had tremendous consequences. As we have learned more about AIDS/HIV over the past decade, we are also beginning to see a wider variety of writings about AIDS. For instance, there are now a number of articles and memoirs about and by women and children. Clearly, there are any number of other readings we could have chosen, and we urge you to find and read others, including some of those by women and children, on your own or as part of your class project. The readings we have included here are not fully representative of the writings on AIDS/HIV, nor are they the most recent. However, they are readings that other students have responded well to, found useful, and in cases where they have been involved with the AIDS/HIV community through courses like the one you are working with now, very helpful in guiding them into this unknown territory.

Often, groups who advocate for persons with AIDS/HIV are chronically underfunded and understaffed. Many are nonprofit agencies, relying on grants, donations, and volunteers. We are not asking you to volunteer. Rather, we are asking you to partner with an agency or group that provides support to the AIDS/HIV community. In this partnership you learn from your experiences with the project, your relationship with your community partner, and from the work you are asked to perform. You also provide your community partner with skills and expertise. Exactly how and what work you will perform is up to your instructor, you, and your AIDS/HIV partner.

Of the many community-based learning projects you could find yourself involved with, one focused on AIDS could be one of the most exciting, but also one of the most difficult. We urge you to trust both yourself and your community partner to create a mutually beneficial experience.

The four readings in this section of Chapter 4 are meant to engage you critically and empathetically with the cultural understanding of AIDS as a disease and with those who live and die with it. Stephen Epstein's chapter, "The Nature of a New Threat," analyzes the ways in which AIDS has been socially constructed and how often research into AIDS has been driven by power and prestige rather than a pure desire to stop a killer virus. Michael O'Brien's journal, published in the *Oregonian* newspaper in 1997, reveals one man's struggle to control his life, and death, in the face of AIDS. A section from Jamaica Kincaid's book, *My Brother*, is a moving and detailed account of her brother's death from AIDS and how his death changed Kincaid and her family. The final reading is from Susan Sontag's *AIDS and Its Metaphors*, an analysis of the metaphors we have used to describe and construct AIDS.

Again, it is possible that you will not engage in a community-based project with this sequence but instead will read, write, and collaborate just as you have in working with the three previous parts of *Writing As Reflective Action*. We believe these readings will open new doors for you as you continue to grow as an active member of our democratic citizenry.

But if you are engaged in a community-based learning project with this sequence, it is impossible for us to know exactly what your project will entail, for that is likely to be a function of your community partner's local needs and contexts. However, by way of example, the following is a list of projects that Portland State University students have been engaged with through their community-based courses on AIDS/HIV:

1. Ecumenical Ministries: Students worked with the HIV Day Center. The day center serves food and offers companionship to an itinerant population of mostly men living with HIV.
2. Women's Inner-city AIDS Resource (WIAR): Students provided help with childcare and housekeeping tasks, staffed "Nurture Night," a monthly gathering of women and children living with AIDS, and conducted in-depth interviews with a volunteer client at the close of her service. WIAR is collecting the interviews for publication.
3. Cascade AIDS Project: Students have staffed the hotline, worked in the office, helped evicted persons move, and created a Housing and Support Services Resource Manual for people living with HIV in Multnomah County.
4. Hopewell House (a hospice for dying HIV patients): Students are trained to work directly with patients and their loved ones.
5. Daily Bread Express: Students deliver food to HIV patients.

As you can see, some of these projects result in direct writing projects and others result in writing about the project. Whatever the case, students have been overwhelmingly positive about these courses and have produced exciting and important writing.

STEVEN EPSTEIN

Steven Epstein is an assistant professor of sociology at University of California, San Diego. His book, *Impure Science* (1996), from which this excerpt is taken, is based on his dissertation that won the American Sociological Association's award for the best dissertation. This unique look at the history of AIDS and how we have come to view this illness considers not only scientific sources of "knowledge," but personal, political, and social sources of knowledge and influence over that knowledge. What makes a researcher or a theory "credible"? Epstein looks at the variety of people and institutions, professionals and laymen involved in the evolution of our understanding of AIDS and offers a multilayered perspective on this complex disease.

Epstein earned his bachelor's degree in social studies from Harvard College and his Ph.D. in sociology from the University of California, Berkeley. *Impure Science* reflects Epstein's interest in the construction of expertise (who we deem as experts), the democratization of science (the role of activists, patients, and "laymen" in the research of AIDS), and the resolution of medical controversies. Epstein's current research expands on these themes by investigating the shifts in U.S. policy designed to improve the health care of women and racial minority groups. These groups have recently been incorporated into medical research populations, and Epstein is looking at how biomedical research responds to and defines identity and difference.

Unrecognized assumptions about "norms" and "differences" influenced the early research into what we know today as AIDS. Epstein illustrates how sexual meanings, values, institutions, and identities are all influenced by society. He explains that it is impossible to understand the moral and political controversy that surround sexuality without considering sexuality as a system of meaning shaped by other social institutions. It is also impossible to understand other institutions without investigating the ways in which sexual meanings intersect with and help shape institutions. This point of view seems particularly relevant to the medical institution and its initial response to the outbreak of AIDS. This excerpt looks at the scientific and political dynamics of a health crisis with immense social impact. Epstein provides a "narrative history" that reveals the unusually wide range of players in the research of AIDS and the current relation between activism and science. Most notably, AIDS research points to the first time a lifestyle was labeled as the cause of a disease. Epstein suggests that this revealed medical science as a "heterosexist and sex-phobic" institution that assumed and reinforced certain "norms" of sexual identity and activity.

If Epstein provides a "narrative history," does it matter that this is an academic, a researcher, telling the history? Would the history differ if it were told, say, by a health care worker in an AIDS clinic?

The Nature of a New Threat

THE DISCOVERY OF A "GAY DISEASE" (1981–1982)

First Reports

When a puzzling new medical syndrome was first reported to be afflicting—and killing—young gay men in certain cities in the United States, there was no particular reason to expect that the cause might be a previously unknown virus. Nor did the deaths immediately take on any great medical significance. Michael Gottlieb, a young immunologist at the teaching hospital of the University of California at Los Angeles, began seeing such cases in late 1980 but found that he couldn't spark the interest of the *New England Journal of Medicine*, the most prestigious medical journal in the country, later to publish hundreds of articles on AIDS. In early 1981 the *New England Journal*'s editor instead referred Gottlieb to the U.S. Centers for Disease Control (CDC), the federal agency in Atlanta, Georgia, responsible for tracking diseases and controlling their spread.[1]

The CDC's first report, published in its *Morbidity and Mortality Weekly Report* in June 1981, noted only that five young men in Los Angeles, "all active homosexuals," had been treated over the course of the past year for *Pneumocystis carinii* pneumonia (PCP).[2] Two of the men had died. The microorganism that causes PCP is ubiquitous but is normally kept easily at bay by the body's immune system; therefore cases of PCP were exceedingly rare, restricted to people who were immunosuppressed because of medical treatment (such as chemotherapy) or who for other reasons had severely malfunctioning immune systems. The CDC report zeroed in on the question of sexuality—"the fact that these patients were all homosexual"—to put forward two tentative hypotheses: that the PCP outbreak was associated with "some aspect of a homosexual lifestyle" or with "disease acquired through sexual contact." However, "the patients did not know each other and had no known common contacts or knowledge of sexual partners who had had similar illnesses."

A few weeks later, the CDC reported twenty-six cases (twenty in New York City and six in California) of young homosexual men suffering from Kaposi's sarcoma, a rare form of cancer normally found in elderly men. At least four of the men also had cases of PCP; eight of them had died.[3] On the basis of this report, Dr. Lawrence Altman, medical reporter for the *New York Times*, wrote a short article about the cases of cancer in homosexuals.[4] Appearing deep inside the newspaper on page A–20, the article sounded what would become one of the most common themes in mainstream media coverage of the epidemic: "The reporting doctors said that most cases had involved homosexual men who have had multiple and frequent sexual encounters with different partners, as many as ten sexual encounters each night up to four times a week." Soon after, Dr. Lawrence Mass, health writer for the *New Work Native*—the most widely read gay newspaper in New York City and one of only a few to have a national readership—also addressed the question of promiscuity. In an article about "Cancer in the Gay Community," Mass wrote: "At this time, many feel that sexual frequency with a multiplicity of partners—what some would call promiscuity—is the single overriding risk factor . . . ."[5]

Mass's article also explored a range of possible explanations for what he called (in quotes) "the gay cancer," including "an infectious or otherwise cancerous agent," but he noted that the "current consensus of informed opinion is that multiple factors are involved in the present outbreak of Kaposi's sarcoma among gay males." He quoted Dr. Donna Mildvan, chief of infectious diseases at Beth Israel Medical Center, who reported a colleague's belief that the outbreak of illnesses "has to do with the bombardment, the clustering of a whole range of infectious diseases among these patients which may be exhausting their immunodefensive capacities." And he cited Dr. Alvin Friedman-Kien, a professor of dermatology and microbiology at New York University Medical Center, who had examined some of the Kaposi's sarcoma patients and who had speculated about the possible role of amyl nitrite or butyl nitrite inhalants. These inhalants, street drugs that were sold legally and were popular in gay male communities at the time, were often called "poppers" because consumers would pop open the packaging to release the fumes, which were then inhaled to produce a "rush" or to intensify orgasm. Nitrites were believed to have immunosuppressive effects. On the other hand, they had been prescribed to cardiac patients for years, and no unusual cases of PCP or Kaposi's sarcoma had ever been reported in that population.

5   By the beginning of 1982, a series of more detailed reports in medical journals such as the *New England Journal*[6] was available as a source of additional information and speculation for researchers and medical practitioners, and for translation into the media, particularly the gay press. Researchers agreed that the telltale marker of these cases of immunosuppression was a deficiency in the numbers of "helper T cells"—or in other accounts, an abnormal ratio of helper T cells to suppressor T cells—types of white blood cells involved in the body's immune response.[7] But questions of etiology and epidemiology were considerably more confusing. For one thing, it was already apparent that the "nationwide epidemic of immunodeficiency among male homosexuals"[8] was in fact not restricted to gay men. According to the CDC's task force on the syndrome, 8 percent

of the 159 cases were among heterosexuals, one of whom was a woman. In the pages of the *New England Journal,* Michael Gottlieb and his coauthors, the Los Angeles clinicians who had first reported the syndrome to the CDC, described finding the same syndrome in two exclusively heterosexual men, while Henry Masur and coauthors reported eleven cases of PCP in the New York area—five injection drug users, four gay men, and two men who were both.

Nonetheless, the focus of attention in all the medical literature remained squarely on the male homosexual sufferers, as evidenced by descriptors such as Brennan and Durack's "Gay Compromise Syndrome"[9] and Masur et al.'s more euphemistic "Community-Acquired *Pneumocystis Carinii* Pneumonia."[10] All speculation about causes proceeded from the premise of the centrality of male homosexuality. In Durack's words: "What clue does the link with homosexuality provide? Homosexual men, especially those who have many partners, are more likely than the general population to contract sexually transmitted diseases. Lesbians are not, and this apparent freedom, whatever its explanation, seems to extend to Kaposi's sarcoma and opportunistic infections." Yet the assumption that the syndrome was somehow linked with homosexuality actually did little to immediately clarify the etiology, as Durack and others realized. Noting that "male homosexuals are at increased risk for the acquisition of common viral infections" such as cytomegalovirus (CMV), hepatitis B, and Epstein-Barr virus, Durack described the "obvious problem" with the hypotheses that CMV, or any of these viruses, might be the cause: "It does not explain why this syndrome is apparently new. Homosexuality is at least as old as history, and cytomegalovirus is presumably not a new pathogen. Were the homosexual contemporaries of Plato, Michelangelo, and Oscar Wilde subject to the risk of dying from opportunistic infections?"[11] Durack's supposition was that "some new factor," such as poppers, "may have distorted the host-parasite relationship." Concluding with some "frank speculation," Durack put forward a model essentially identical to the one Mildvan had proposed to the *Native:* that "the combined effects of persistent viral infection plus an adjuvant drug cause immunosuppression in some genetically predisposed men."

This model, which was sometimes called the "immune overload" or "antigen overload" hypothesis, represented the initial medical frame for understanding the epidemic: the syndrome was essentially linked to gay men, specifically to the "excesses" of the "homosexual lifestyle." The epidemic coincided historically, *Newsweek* suggested in the article "Diseases That Plague Gays," "with the burgeoning of bathhouses, gay bars and bookstores in major cities where homosexual men meet."[12] Urban gay men, enjoying "life in the fast lane," had subjected themselves to so many sexual transmitted diseases, taken so many strong treatments to fight those diseases, and done so many recreational drugs that their immune systems had ultimately given up altogether, leaving their bodies open to the onslaught of a range of opportunistic infections. As one Harvard doctor is reported to have put it informally, "overindulgence in sex and drugs" and "the New York City lifestyle" were the culprits.[13] What distinguished gay men from CMV-infected, sexually adventurous heterosexuals, and from cardiac patients inhaling amyl nitrite, and from the many patients who took strong antibiotic or antiparasitic drugs was, these experts suggested, that only gay men (or those gay men living in the "fast lane") confronted all these risks at once.

The Politics of Lifestyle

The speculative focus on "the gay lifestyle" casts light on the very nature of epidemiological science. When a mysterious illness appears in a specific social group, it makes eminent sense to ask what distinguishes that group from others not affected, or less affected, by the illness. The difficulty is that the isolation of "difference" presupposes a common understanding of what constitutes the "background" against which this difference stands out. In this sense, epidemiology is inevitably a "normalizing" science, employing—and reinforcing—unexamined notions of normality to measure and classify deviations from the norm.[14] Faced with a "gay disease," epidemiologists immediately fastened upon the most sensational markers of homosexual difference, trumpeting the cases of men with histories of thousands of sexual partners, while ignoring the cases, also reported by clinicians from the very beginning, of gay men who were monogamous or who engaged in relatively modest amounts of sexual experimentation.[15]

With the advantage of hindsight, it is easy to recognize that the initial link between gay men and the new syndrome—while certainly the single most consequential aspect of the social construction of the epidemic—in fact reflected the confounding influences of what Irving Zola has called the "pathways" from doctor to patient. As Zola concluded from a more general study, it is often the case that apparent epidemiological differences in the incidence of some medical conditions actually derive from "factors of selectivity and attention which get people and their episodes into medical statistics . . . ."[16] There are important reasons why people do or do not seek medical help, yet, as Eliot Freidson has noted, the doctor tends to "assume that the cases he sees are no different from those he does not. And so he develops conceptions of illness that may have an inaccurate and artificial relationship to the world."[17]

10   To put it simply, some people get better medical attention, which means that medical professionals "attend" to their "unique" conditions. In New York City, if not elsewhere, it appears likely that there were at least as many cases of pneumocystis pneumonia among injection drug users as among gay men at the time of the discovery of the syndrome.[18] But gay men, some of them affluent and relatively privileged, found their way into private doctors' offices and prominent teaching hospitals—and from there into the pages of medical journals—while drug users often sickened and died with little fanfare. Even as cases among injection drug users began to be reported, the "gay disease" frame for understanding the epidemic was already falling into place. Colloquially, the epidemic became known among some medical professionals and researchers in early 1982 as "GRID": Gay-Related Immune Deficiency.[19]

The power of frames as organizers of experience is precisely that they work to exclude alternative ways of interpreting an experience.[20] Because "GRID" was a "gay disease," medical practitioners and researchers sometimes resisted the idea that it might appear elsewhere, and those who proposed that the epidemic could affect other people risked being discredited within the scientific community.[21] Randy Shilts described how, throughout 1981, "there was a reluctance [at the CDC] to believe that intravenous drug users might be wrapped into this epidemic, and the New York physicians also seemed obsessed with the gay angle . . . ." "He says he's not homosexual, but he must be," doctors would confide to one another. One New York pediatrician was ridiculed for his contention as early as 1981 that he was seeing children suffering from the same immune dysfunction as homosexual patients.[22]

But the differences in access to health care and the accident of the initial discovery of the syndrome among gay men are not adequate to account for the potency of this frame or the ease with which it fell into place. If gay men were perceived as *plausible* victims of a medical syndrome, it was in part because in the medical literature their sexualized lifestyle was already depicted as medically problematic. On one hand, epidemiologists and clinicians were genuinely surprised by the appearance of such devastating illness among "previously healthy" homosexual men. On the other hand, they were quick to make use of the existing stock of medical knowledge linking gay men with disease—specifically, the literature on sexually transmitted diseases among gay men that was published in the years just prior to, or coincident with, the onset of the epidemic.[23] This literature, which was often cited by early medical claims-makers discussing the new epidemic of immune dysfunction,[24] described an explosion of venereal diseases among gay men, the apparent aftermath of the "sexual revolution" and gay liberation. Concluding that homosexuality must be considered a risk factor in infectious disease, these articles stressed the need for clinicians to confront what one referred to as "homosexual hazards."[25]

Of course, modern conceptions of gay identity have always been partially medicalized. The very term "homosexual" dates from the nineteenth-century literature of doctors and sexologists. Gay identities have been formed, over the past one hundred years, through the dialectical interplay between an affirmative process of self-definition by homosexuals and the imposition of models by various groups of expert claims-makers.[26] In this sense, what is ironic about the medicalization of gay male sexuality in the years just prior to the beginning of the epidemic is that it presupposed the successes of the gay movement, which were in part directed against an earlier medicalization (or "psychiatrization"). In opposition to a conception of homosexuality as a "mental illness," gay activists had put forward a positive conception of gay identity and the gay community. And in fact, the new medical discourse on gay men took as its starting point a particularly recent conception of the "lifestyle" of the urban gay male; this discourse marked the entry of the modern "gay community" into medical history.

While it cannot be doubted that doctors were genuinely concerned with treating the venereal diseases of gay men, the issue was framed in particular ways that influenced medical perceptions of homosexuality. First, the key phrases that were used—"homosexual hazards," "gay bowel syndrome," "homosexuality as a risk factor"—posed the problem essentially as one of identity and "lifestyle," rather than contraction of specific infections.[27] (It seems far less likely that any medical journal would refer to "heterosexual hazards.") Second, the use of abstract, universalizing terms such as "the gay way of life" masked the considerable diversity of the life experiences and sexual practices of gay men;[28] such stereotypes obscured the fact that researchers had made no attempt even to define, let alone systematically sample, the communities they characterized with rather sweeping generalizations.[29]

15   Yet this was the understanding of gay male sexuality that informed medical speculation in the early days of AIDS. To be sure, the reasoning behind the immune overload hypothesis was not irrational, and the hypothesis was not absurd: after all, the epidemic *was* being observed mainly among gay men; many of these men *did* have many sexual partners; many sexually active gay men *were* known to contract sexually transmitted diseases, as well as use poppers and other drugs. But the strength of the resulting hypothesis depended on a long chain of implicit assumptions—that the syndrome was in essence linked to homosexuals (and the cases among heterosexuals

could be explained away); that the link to gay men meant that the epidemic was related to gay men's *sexuality;* that if gay men (by this view) were "promiscuous," then the illness must be a consequence of their promiscuity; and crucially, that repeated exposure to sexually transmitted pathogens (and to drugs) was actually capable of causing the immune system damage being observed. Furthermore, there was the assumption that the recent reported increases in rates of sexually transmitted disease and of drug use among gay men were indeed of sufficient magnitude to explain why the syndrome was emerging when it was.

As an initial hypothesis, immune overload was probably no more or less reasonable than many in the history of epidemiology or medical science. Nor was it ever hegemonic. For example, the first editorial on the syndrome in *Lancet*, the influential British medical journal, speculated on everything from "new or unrecognised environmental pollutants" to "even another infective agent";[30] and such conjecture continued in the medical and scientific literature throughout 1982 and 1983. Where "immune overload" (or, more generally, what Murray and Payne call the "promiscuity paradigm")[31] exerted its greatest influence was *outside* the world of mainstream scientific practice. Reinforced by the mainstream media and filtering out into diverse arenas, the idea of a linkage between homosexuality, promiscuity, and illness informed an emergent sensibility about the syndrome—a vision, sometimes an unarticulated perception, of the epidemic as somehow the product of "the homosexual lifestyle." At times it has been voiced as a direct accusation: as late as October 1987, North Carolina's Jesse Helms could stand on the U.S. Senate floor and proclaim that "every case of AIDS can be traced back to a homosexual act."[32] The notion that gays brought on the AIDS epidemic—and should be held responsible for having done so—has persisted long after the decline of mainstream biomedical support for etiological arguments focusing on "the gay lifestyle."

The idea that homosexuality "causes" AIDS also indicated the tangle of meanings packed into one short word—"cause"—and the difficulties involved in carrying out a conversation about causation that cuts across a range of lay and specialist communitites.

As Jana Armstrong has observed," the word 'cause' is embedded in the language of public policy, the language of cell biology, the language of epidemiology. But the word does not mean the same thing in every instance of its use."[33] Even a glance at a medical dictionary generates confusion: one such dictionary distinguishes between constitutional causes, exciting causes, immediate or precipitating causes, local causes, predisposing causes, primary causes, proximate causes, remote causes, secondary causes, specific causes, and ultimate causes.[34] ("Etiology" fares little better, since the definition of that term points back to the word "cause.")

Generally speaking, medical doctors were interested in finding a "primary cause"; that is, "the principal factor contributing to the production of a specific result"—in this case, the destruction of cell-mediated immune responses. But epidemiologists, in their focus on identifying risk groups, were in effect concerned significantly with "predisposing causes": "anything that renders a person more liable to a specific condition without actually producing it." Outside of the medical and scientific professions, the various usages of the word "cause" not only blurred these meanings but embedded notions of causation within a more general vocabulary of moral blame. Like cholera epidemics, which in the nineteenth-century United States were blamed on the squalid lifestyle of the poor;[35] like gonorrhea, once regarded even by doctors as arising "from the continual irritation and excitement of the generative organs" of prostitutes;[36] like smallpox and leprosy, which were blamed on the "unclean" practices of the U.S. Chinese population in the late nineteenth century;[37] the genesis of the new epidemic of immune dysfunction was considered all too often with a view to assigning culpability. Partly through the power of the medical definitional process, partly through the ideological work of the opponents of gay liberation, gay men increasingly came to be equated with the emergent epidemic— it came to constitute part of their social identity.

Claiming the Epidemic

20   How did members of the affected communities respond to these formulations? Gay communities in the United States were both contributors to the "gay disease" frame and important critics of it. Initially, rumors of various lifestyle risks—a microbe in the water supply or the ventilation system at the most popular bathhouses, for example—spread rapidly through gay communities.[38] Writers in the gay press showed little tendency, early on, to dispute the homosexual connection, as evidenced by the frequent use of the locution "gay cancer" (though often in quotation marks) to characterize the epidemic in 1981. This phrasing, however imprecise, effectively served as a rallying cry to alert gay men to the presence of a new danger.

Since many of the early reports in medical journals were written by clinicians well connected to gay communities, who were treating the patients in question, many gay people—and particularly health writers such as Lawrence Mass, himself a physician—were inclined toward sympathetic views of the medical and public health authorities. Increasingly, however, many gay writers, especially in the more left-leaning publications, were openly critical of medical researchers' tendency to blame the epidemic on gay promiscuity.[39] Much as an earlier generation of feminists had conceived of medicine as a sexist institution, these writers and activists argued that medical science was a heterosexist and sex-phobic institution that reinforced norms of sexual conformity.

Gay physicians, such as those who were members of Physicians for Human Rights, an organization of gay doctors, found themselves at the fulcrum.[40] On one hand, they were called on to introduce their professional colleagues and epidemiological investigators to many specific aspects of the "gay lifestyle," often running up against a judgmental reception within the biomedical establishment. On the other hand, they felt a sense of responsibility to warn their communities about suspected risk behaviors—but knew they would lose credibility if they were perceived to be "sex-negative" or puritanical, given that gay liberation as a political movement was so closely tied to sexual liberation as a personal ethic.[41]

By early 1982, gay and lesbian activists had created two grassroots organizations that would prove to be pivotal in confronting the epidemic: the Gay Men's Health Crisis in New York City and, across the country, the Kaposi's Sarcoma Research and Education Foundation, later renamed the San Francisco AIDS Foundation. A testament to the high degree of political mobilization and access to resources in gay communities at the time, the appearance of these organizations marked simultaneous attempts to provide services to people suffering from the syndrome, relay relevant information rapidly to gay men at risk, and serve as an organized voice regarding questions of public policy.[42]

In the early period, these organizations took no position on the question of etiology. As the Gay Men's Health Crisis advised gay New Yorkers in an open letter in mid-1982: "Unsettling though it is, *no evidence exists* to incriminate any activity, drug, place of residence, or any other factor, conclusively, in the outbreak facing us."[43] At the same time, simply by organizing gay communities to confront— and, in effect, claim—the epidemic, these organizations helped to solidify the popular connection between the syndrome and homosexuality (as even the name "Gay Men's Health Crisis" implied). AIDS became a "gay disease" primarily because clinicians, epidemiologists, and reporters perceived it through that filter, but secondarily because gay communities were obliged to make it their own.

LIFESTYLE VS. VIRUS (1982–1983)

The Expansion of Risk

25   Sensitive to the fact that gay doctors and activists criticized the informal "GRID" designation, the CDC came up with an official name for the epidemic in May 1982 and first used the term in print in

September of that year.[44] This name was chosen specifically for its neutrality—Acquired Immunodeficiency Syndrome, or AIDS: "acquired" to distinguish it from congenital defects of the immune system; "immunodeficiency" to describe the underlying problem, the deterioration of immune system functioning (and specifically, a decline in the number of helper T cells, causing the body to lose most of its capacity to ward off infection); and "syndrome" to indicate that the condition was not a disease in itself, but rather was marked by the presence of some other, relatively uncommon disease or infection (like PCP or Kaposi's sarcoma), "occurring in a person with no known cause for diminished resistance to that disease." This was strictly a "surveillance" definition, for epidemiological reporting purposes: it did not imply any knowledge about what AIDS "really was." But in the absence of a lab test for a known cause, this definition at least allowed the CDC a crude measure of the scope of the problem.

The newly defined syndrome would, over the course of 1983, achieve the status of a "Worldwide Health Problem," as the headline of one of Lawrence Altman's articles in the *New York Times* labeled it in November. By that time, AIDS cases would be reported "in 33 countries and all inhabited continents."[45] Though most cases were in the United States or Europe, the most striking aspect of the epidemic's spread was the discovery of AIDS in equatorial Africa. In April the *Washington Post* summarized reports appearing in both *Lancet* and the *New England Journal* that described cases of AIDS in European countries, but among patients who had immigrated from or traveled in countries such as Zaire and Chad. Of twenty-nine such cases in France, six patients had become ill before June 1981—that is, before the epidemic was first reported in the United States.[46] Immediately scientists and reporters in the West picked up on the notion that Africa "could have been the breeding place" for the epidemic.[47]

Despite the globalization of the epidemic and the formal change in terminology, the "gay disease" formulation, in various guises, continued to undergird medical investigation of the syndrome through the first half of 1982. For example, an editorial in the *Annals of Internal Medicine* by Dr. Anthony Fauci, a distinguished scientist who would later become the head of the AIDS program at the National Institutes of Health (NIH), laid out a number of etiological possibilities: "Is there a new virus or other infectious agent that has expressed itself first among the male homosexual community because of the unusual exposure potential within this group? Is this an immunosuppressed state due to chronic exposure to a recognized virus or viruses? Is this illness due to a synergy among various factors such as infectious agents, recreational drugs, therapeutic agents administered for diseases that are peculiar to this population such as the 'gay bowel syndrome' . . . ?" But what Fauci never doubted was that the "critical questions" were: "why homosexual men and why occurrence or recognition only as recently as 1979?"[48]

Suddenly, this whole framework for understanding the epidemic was dramatically challenged. On July 9, the CDC reported thirty-four cases of Kaposi's sarcoma or opportunistic infections among Haitians living in five different states in the United States. None of those interviewed reported homosexual activity, and only one gave a history of injection drug use.[49] The following week the agency reported three cases of PCP in people with hemophilia, all of them recipients of a blood product called Factor VIII, "manufactured from plasma pools collected from as many as a thousand or more donors."[50] The CDC refrained from drawing conclusions, but noted that the occurrence of the hemophilia cases "suggests the possible transmission of an agent through blood products." Since bacteria were screened out of Factor VIII in the production process, while smaller particles such as viruses could potentially escape the screen, the "agent" in question would almost certainly have to be a virus.

Mass, writing in the *Native*, quickly noted the significance of these findings: of all the existing etiological hypotheses, "only that of viruses would seem able to provide a unitary hypothesis that could explain the sudden appearance of AID [the *Native*'s term at that time] in a growing number of distinct populations." But he also acknowledged the alternative possibility: Perhaps, he suggested, "we are dealing with a number of superficially similar epidemics, each with its own primary etiology.[51]

Germs and Magic Bullets

30   One syndrome, one cause; many syndromes, many causes: these options suggested not just different etiological hypotheses, but opposing theoretical approaches to the understanding of human illness. Indeed, one of the most intriguing aspects of the early popularity of the immune overload hypothesis was that so many clinicians would readily forsake the approach to disease causation frequently described as the cornerstone of contemporary biomedicine: the principle of "one disease, one cause, one cure." As Allan Brandt has expressed it: "In the paradigm, individuals become infected with a parasite that causes dysfunction of some sort; disease is defined as a deviation from a biological norm. Social conditions, environmental phenomena, and other variables are generally discounted as causes of disease. The physician dispenses 'magic bullets' that restore the patient to health."[52]

Ever since the bacteriological revolution of the late nineteenth century, when germs replaced "miasmas" as the preferred explanation for illness, medical research typically has focused on the discovery of discrete microbial causes for specific diseases. To be more precise, two separate assumptions have been welded together: that most illnesses have a single, fundamental cause, rather than multiple necessary causes; and that the search for the cause of illness should focus primarily on microbes, very secondarily on lifestyle issues, and only incidentally on environmental causes related to the larger organization of the society. Of course, the monocausal/microbial approach has always had its critics. Writing in 1959, René Dubos characterized the "doctrine of specific etiology" as "unquestionably the most constructive force in medical research for almost a century," but noted that "few are the cases in which it has provided a complete account of the causation of disease." Citing the failures, "despite frantic efforts," to find cures for disease such as cancer and mental illnesses, Dubos argued that the "search for *the* cause may be a hopeless pursuit because most disease states are the indirect outcome of a constellation of circumstances . . . ."[53]

Modern-day epidemiologists, more open to multicausal approaches to disease, may speak of a "web of causation" or may endorse "ecological" or "synergistic" models of illness that emphasize the complex interrelationships among environmental and host factors.[54] But in laboratories, examining rooms, and medical school classrooms, the doctrine of specific etiology holds sway.

Many analysts have seen in the monocausal/microbial model of disease the clue to medicine's ideological function within a capitalist society: it encourages people to attribute their illnesses to invisible particles rather than to occupational hazards or defects of social organization."[55] But to understand why clinicians and researchers themselves reach for such explanations, the suggestions of sociologist Andrew Abbott may be more to the point.

First, the germ theory of disease focuses public attention on medicine's greatest triumphs and away from arthritis, heart disease, cancer, and other chronic problems that have proven less amenable to therapeutic success. Second, one of the chief legitimating values of medicine (like other professions) is its perceived efficiency; and as opposed to environmental explanations, monocausal/microbial ones lend themselves to neat and straightforward solutions ("Take two pills every four hours").[56] The search for microbes enhances the power of laboratory researchers, who alone have the tools to conduct it. The search for environmental causes is, by contrast, frequently beyond their ken. In short, the commonly expressed preference of clinicians and biomedical researchers for simple, monocausal, microbial models may in an immediate sense have less to do with medicine's role in legitimating society than with doctors' and scientists' roles in legitimating scientific medicine.

35   In light of the prevailing explanatory preference, early clinical fascination with "the homosexual lifestyle" is all the more noteworthy. Of course, perceptions that illness is linked to lifestyle have become more common in recent years, with increasing attention to the relation between such factors as stress or eating habits and the development of various diseases. But to the extent that doctors endorsed a multicausal lifestyle model, they were going against the prevailing medical currents. It is well worth asking whether they would have been as likely to do so had it not been for the perception that "the gay lifestyle" was peculiarly laden with a potential for medical hazard.

Dissent at the Front Lines

Once put squarely on the table, the notion of a single, unifying cause of AIDS carried with it immediate practical implications. The virus theory, now described by the *Los Angeles Times* as "a potentially much more serious candidate for the cause," was also a scary one, as it "raised the specter" of a communicable disease that might potentially affect anyone.[57] Or as *Newsweek* warned in August, "the 'homosexual plague' has started spilling over into the general population."[58] With the news, toward the end of 1982, of a case of AIDS having developed in a blood transfusion recipient twenty months old (one of whose donors was found to have AIDS)[59] and of other cases in the female sexual partners of intravenous drug users with AIDS,[60] the viral hypothesis gained increasing credibility. It wasn't that the lifestyle theories were immediately abandoned: for example, a news report in the influential *Journal of the American Medical Association* (*JAMA*) surveying the controversy in late September 1982 claimed straightforwardly that "it seems unlikely that a virus alone is inducing AIDS," and devoted significant attention to the poppers theory and others, as well as to two researchers' discovery of a genetic marker in patients with Kaposi's sarcoma.[61] However, the greater the number of risk groups, the less relevant seemed the details of "lifestyle," and the more attractive the notion of a unifying cause that could account plausibly for all manifestations of the syndrome.

    In response to this challenge, advocates of the immune overload hypothesis struggled to fortify their claims. A central player was Dr. Joseph Sonnabend, a South African-born physician and researcher. A specialist in infectious diseases, Sonnabend had also done research in England on the drug interferon, put in a stint at Mt. Sinai School of Medicine as an assistant professor of microbiology, and served as the director of venereal disease control for the New

York City Department of Health. At the time the epidemic emerged, Sonnabend was practicing as a community doctor in New York's Greenwich Village, largely treating the sexually transmitted diseases of his many gay male patients.[62] Sonnabend has little inclination toward simple, monocausal models of illness. As he would later put it, his South African medical education had stressed that "if you want to understand sickness, you have to understand the environment in which sickness occurs."[63]

Writing in the *Native* in September 1982, Sonnabend sought support for his views by warning his readers that endorsement of the viral hypothesis could result in antigay discrimination and prejudice: "To publicly propose that any minority group carried a specific infectious agent capable of causing severe immunodeficiency and cancer is an act of tremendous seriousness. Given the potential repercussions, it verges on the irresponsible that the suggestion is made on the basis of evidence that remains conjectural."[64] The "conjecture" in Sonnabend's view, rested on twin assumptions, both of them debatable: that the same disease was present in "at least four disparate groups" (Haitians, intravenous drug users, hemophiliacs, and gay men) and that the disease was actually new in each group. While Sonnabend was careful to make clear that he was not ruling out these possibilities, his central thrust was to question them by suggesting that there might be various syndromes of immunodeficiency, all with similar symptoms. But rather than attempt to explain the cases of AIDS in the "newer" risk groups, Sonnabend focused attention on immunodeficiency in gay men. He proposed a variant of the original immune overload hypothesis, involving repeated infection with CMV and the reactivation of infection with Epstein-Barr virus. The bottom line, for Sonnabend, was summarized by the title of the *Native* article "Promiscuity is Bad for Your Health." "This is not a moralistic judgment," Sonnabend insisted, "but a clear statement of the devastating effects of repeated infections."

As a neighborhood doctor, Sonnabend had limited resources with which to establish credibility, so his first step was to recruit allies.[65] His advantage, as he later saw it, was his location on the front lines: "I was in the situation, as a physician to many of the men who actually developed this disease, to observe the guys in their setting . . . ."[66] But his problem was that, within the research establishment, he was isolated:[67] "I had this very unique access to information. But it was just myself, a lonely business. There were no takers, because I didn't have an important position in some medical center. . . . However, I did contact David Purtilo, the chairman of pathology at the University of Nebraska. Purtilo was known to me as an expert on Epstein-Barr virus."[68]

With Purtilo and another researcher, Steven Witkin, Sonnabend published an article in *JAMA* in May 1983, presenting his claims to a wide medical audience. (This article was later reprinted in the New York Academy of Science's 1984 volume on AIDS, as well as in *JAMA*'s "official" 1986 anthology of the epidemic, *AIDS: From the Beginning*.)[69] Challenging the "prevailing view" that a novel infectious agent caused AIDS, the authors reminded their readers of "another acquired immunodeficiency syndrome," called Neapolitan disease, which "resulted from malnutrition and various viral infections." Similarly, the authors contended, multiple factors that included "recurrent cytomegalovirus (CMV) infections and immune responses to sperm are likely major causative factors" among promiscuous homosexual men. But on the crucial question of other "risk groups," the authors had little to say: "We cannot, at this time, explain why AIDS is thought to be occurring in Haitians, hemophiliacs, and others. Acquired immunodeficiency has many causes, including malnutrition, hormonal alterations, use of opiates and other intravenous drugs, and acute viral infections."[70]

Also in early 1983, Sonnabend became the editor of a new medical journal, *AIDS Research*, and declared its first issue "an appropriate occasion to review an alternative hypothesis regarding the genesis of AIDS." Here Sonnabend devoted more attention to the other "risk groups," noting that "transfusions are themselves immunosuppressive," since they expose the recipient to a variety of antigens in the donated blood, and that many Haitians are subject to tropical infections, as well as to poverty and malnutrition, both of which are highly correlated with illness. Sonnabend argued that "the risk groups are too broadly defined," and that focused epidemiological research was needed to tease out the specific risk factors (such as exposure to sexually transmitted pathogens in the case of gay men) actually linked to AIDS. Epidemiologists could also assess his model, he suggested, by comparing the prevalence of CMV in populations with and without AIDS.[71]

But Sonnabend had no epidemiologists at the ready, and in the absence of data, his hypothesis was, at best, informed speculation. Much the same could be said about all the "immune overload" theorists. Two years into the epidemic, there was little specific evidence in support of the claim that immune overload caused AIDS in gay men, let alone in other risk groups. Some research had reported on the health effects of poppers, including one study showing that of eight outwardly healthy gay men with signs of T-cell abnormalities, most were consumers of amyl nitrite.[72] But the numbers were too small to warrant strong conclusions. More generally, epidemiologists and statisticians found it "exceeding difficult to disentangle nitrite use from such other risk factors as the frequency of sexual encounters and the multiplicity of sexual partners."[73] While the interwoven nature of these epidemiologically correlated behaviors could be taken as evidence of an overload model, it could just as easily reflect spurious associations. As Mass pointed out in a discussion of the limits of epidemiological thinking, "On the superficial basis of numbers alone . . . wearing handkerchiefed Levi's and having Judy Garland records in one's collection might also seem risky."[74]

Medical Uncertainty and Gay Skepticism

As the number of AIDS cases continued to rise, increasingly fearful gay men struggled to make sense of the shifting and indeterminate medical claims and to sort out the implications for their everyday lives. Toward the end of 1982, *Gay Community News (GCN)*, a left-leaning weekly based in Boston, cited the "growing consensus among experts that AIDS is transmissible . . . and most likely through sexual contact."[75] Expressing the paper's sex-positive philosophy, writers in *GCN* were suspicious of views that blamed gay men for becoming sick, whether voiced by medical authorities or by gay men themselves. One prominent political analyst, Michael Bronski, wrote disapprovingly of the president of Gay Men's Health Crisis, quoting him as saying: "Something we have done to our bodies—and we still don't know what it is—has brought us closer to death."[76] Another writer in the same issue of *GCN* applauded the views of Jim Geary, head of the Shanti Project, a San Francisco organization: "The reason [we] get sexually transmitted diseases is not because we have multiple sexual partners. . . . It's because we don't take the necessary precautions in having sex."[77]

The question of how to translate etiological uncertainty into guidelines for personal safety was deeply troubling to gay communities across the United States. Nowhere did the debate rage more fiercely than in the pages of the *Native* in late 1982. The *Native's* editor and publisher, Chuck Ortleb, introduced side-by-side commentaries by stressing the paper's democratic impulse and the need for the general public to assess scientific and public health debates: "The articles printed on these pages provide good examples of the level of debate prevailing in medical circles. . . . Confusing? Contradictory? Of course. But then, so is much of the discussion surrounding the present crisis. It's a discussion that we feel virtually everyone should be involved in—gay people as well as non-gay, laymen as well as physicians, policy-makers as well as the citizenry . . . ."[78]

One view in the debate was offered by Peter Seitzman, president of New York Physicians for Human Rights, the gay doctors' association.[79] His argument was straightforward, if not altogether reassuring: "The available evidence overwhelmingly suggests that AIDS is caused by some as yet undiscovered transmissible [*sic*] agent," probably a virus. Since the transmission pattern appeared to be similar to that of the hepatitis B virus, prevention guidelines would be "precisely the same as those for avoiding hepatitis B," namely, never use a syringe used by someone else and reduce promiscuity. Eager to avoid any implication of antisex attitudes, Seitzman reassured his readers that he himself had been "no more of an angel than Mae West." But he concluded by affirming the virtues of "monogamy as a survival technique," declaring that promiscuity is not immoral "but simply dangerous."

The "opposing" commentary by Michael Callen and Richard Berkowitz in fact arrived at roughly similar, if far more forceful, conclusions, but began with radically different etiological premises. It was also different quite different in tone. Callen and Berkowitz identified themselves as twenty-seven-year-old men, both "victims of AIDS," each with a history of having been "excessively promiscuous." Although the article didn't say it, they were also both patients of Dr. Sonnabend and they endorsed his immune overload hypothesis. (Callen would go on to become the most prominent "long-term survivor" of AIDS in the United States, a familiar figure at rallies and demonstrations; until his death in 1993, he remained an activist and an ally of Sonnabend's.) Entitled "We Know Who We Are: Two Gay Men Declare War on Promiscuity," the article was nothing short of a manifesto: "Those of us who have lived a life of excessive promiscuity on the urban gay circuit of bathhouses, backrooms, balconies, sex clubs, meat racks, and tearooms know who we are. . . . Those of us who have been promiscuous have sat on the sidelines throughout this epidemic and by our silence have tacitly encouraged wild speculation about a new, mutant, Andromeda-strain virus. We have remained silent because we have been unwilling to accept responsibility for the role that our own excessiveness has played in our present health crisis. But, deep down, we know who we are and we know why we're sick."[80]

Turning to the medical evidence in favor of the different causal hypothesis—which they have evaluated on the basis of "personal experiences," their talks with researchers and doctors, and their "own readings in both the medical and the lay press"—Callen and Berkowitz argued that "AIDS is not 'spreading' the way one would expect a single-virus epidemic to spread." The confinement of AIDS to specific risk groups, they maintained, should lead us to look for the specific explanation for each group's immunosuppression. In practical terms, whatever theory one chose to believe, "the obvious and immediate solution to the present crisis is the end of urban male promiscuity as we know it today," the authors concluded. "The party that was the '70s is over," and anyone who defended promiscuity on political or ideological grounds was simply in denial.

Sharp responses to Callen and Berkowitz were quickly forthcoming, both in the *Native* and in other lesbian and gay publications. Charles Jurrist, writing "In Defense of Promiscuity," argued in his reply that the uncertainty of scientific knowledge about causation had to be factored into any evaluation of personal risk. While granting that the immune overload hypothesis "is the most plausible of the several theories concerning the origins of AIDS," Jurrist reminded readers that the hypothesis was far from proven: "It therefore seems a little premature to be calling for an end to sexual freedom in the name of physical health."[81]

Others, such as Michael Lynch, writing in the pages of the Canadian lesbian and gay newspaper *The Body Politic*, were even more assertive in defending sexual freedom against medical moralism. These writers put the issue in historical and political context: The medical critique of gay promiscuity was simply the latest of many attempts to portray gay sexuality as diseased. At stake in the debate was "gay identity" itself. Gay men had fought to construct an affirmative identity, an essential part of which involved strong defense of sexual freedom and a critique of puritanical attitudes. And many of those they had fought against were doctors and medical researchers. Given this history, it followed that the debate about gay men and their sexual practices were thoroughly intertwined with an older power struggle: who was to say what it meant to be gay—the doctors, or gay men themselves?[82] As Lynch poignantly expressed it: "Like helpless mice we have peremptorily, almost inexplicably, relinquished the one power we so long fought for in constructing our modern gay community: the power to determine our own gay identity. And to whom have we relinquished it? The very authority we wrested it from in a struggle that occupied us for more than a hundred years: the medical profession."[83]

50   In the absence of a cure for AIDS, or even an agreed upon cause—and in the aftermath of an initial scientific framing of AIDS as a "gay disease" linked to promiscuity, a formulation that aroused the wrath of many in gay and lesbian communities—the credibility of doctors, biomedical researchers, and public health authorities suffered greatly in those communities. Increasingly gays were prompted to respond by insisting on their own right to intervene—to weigh the evidence, pass judgment, and remind the medical establishment at every pass whose lives were really on the line. Gay doctors like Mass sought a moderate position; writing in the *Native* in response to Lynch's commentary in *The Body Politic*, he acknowledged: "To an enormous extent, what Lynch is saying is true. Mainstream medicine and psychiatry have in fact been largely responsible for contemporary

stereotypes of homosexuals as 'abnormal,' 'perverse,' and 'sick.' At the same time, however, mainstream medicine and psychiatry continue to serve vital health needs." Maintaining that the problem was not with medical science but with "the political abuse of that science," Mass advised his readers to "be critical but remain open to well-qualified medical advice."[84] But for those on either extreme of the promiscuity debate, from Lynch to Callen and Berkowitz, the watchword was self-reliance. Become your own expert: ultimately, that was the only reasonable hope gay people might have of surviving. "Rely on no single source for your information," exhorted Callen and Berkowitz: "not your doctor, not this newspaper, not the Gay Men's Health Crisis, not the Centers for Disease Control."[85]

Of course, it goes without saying that this strategy of collective empowerment presumed the existence of gay doctors, gay newspapers, and a Gay Men's Health Crisis. To be sure, the spreading disease would decimate the ranks of existing gay leadership. But ironically, the gay response to AIDS both presupposed and furthered the social development of lesbian and gay communities and their political clout—a process that Dennis Altman has called "legitimation through disaster."[86] Gay men and lesbians had long confronted homophobic attitudes, antigay discrimination, and heterosexist presumption on a daily basis in the workplace, in religious settings, in encounters with family members, on television, and in the movies. But in organizing to meet these challenges, lesbians and gay men had developed political and social institutions that were poised to respond to the new threat when it erupted. Moreover, gay communities were dominated by white, middle-class men—people with influence in society and access to an array of social, cultural, and political resources. It's no surprise that gays were hotly debating the details of causation theories while intravenous drug users—often the poorest of the poor—sat on the sidelines: these were the realities of power in the United States in the 1980s. Even people with hemophilia, a diverse group that had the benefit of a preexisting national lobby, did not mobilize forcefully in response to the emergence of the epidemic. In this early period, Haitians were the only other group to challenge medical claims; they objected to the portrayal of Haiti as a possible origin of the epidemic and combated wild epidemiological speculation about the role of voodoo rituals in the transmission of AIDS. And most of the opposition came not from grassroots but from politicians in Haiti and Haitian doctors living in the United States.[87]

The distinctiveness of gay communities' approaches to the emergence of the epidemic is brought out in Cathy Cohen's comparative analysis of gay and African-American responses. Although gay communities were hit harder, both gays and African-Americans came to be disproportionately represented in the statistics of illness and death as the epidemic proceeded. Both of these social groups were marginalized, and historical memory inclined both of them to distrust federal biomedical institutions. Yet "the indigenous norms and structures of these communities" promoted different political outcomes: "In the Gay community AIDS has become associated with the community's struggle for rights and entitlements. In the Black community much of the response to AIDS is based on a framing of the disease that still emphasizes behavior and the individual actions of those who have AIDS, making it much more difficult to transform AIDS into a political issue for the community."[88] As Cohen has described, established African-American organizations eschewed "ownership" of the problem of AIDS. It was often up to black gays and lesbians—those who stood at the intersection of these two social groups—to try to mobilize African-American communities and start up new organizations, while simultaneously confronting racism within gay communities.[89]

THE TRIUMPH OF RETROVIROLOGY (1982–1984)

Gallo's Family of Viruses

Writing in 1988, Robert Gallo, the NIH scientist who would share credit for discovery of what was to become known as the "human immunodeficiency virus," reflected back on the scientific effort to understand AIDS. Gallo concluded that progress had been made possible by "two general earlier developments": "*first,* by major advances that took place in basic sciences, particularly in immunology . . . and molecular biology . . .; and *second,* by the opening of the whole field of human retrovirology that, oddly enough, occurred only a few years before the AIDS epidemic . . . ." To this Gallo added, "There is no doubt in my mind that if AIDS came upon us full force in the 1960s or even in the early 1970s, we would still be wandering in the dark regarding most of what we know today."[90]

Gallo's "odd" fact can be put in different terms: At the moment when people began to suspect that AIDS might be caused by an infectious agent, there existed a small group of prominent scientists working in a very specialized area who were inclined to imagine that a "retrovirus" might be the cause, who were motivated to pursue that speculation, and who were well equipped to do so. Only in the 1960s had researchers discovered that the genetic material of certain viruses consists of RNA (ribonucleic acid) rather than DNA (deoxyribonucleic acid, often called the "blueprint of life"). Normally, viruses infect cells and turn them into virus factories, causing the cells to produce new viruses according to the specifications of the viral DNA. The virus's DNA is copied into RNA, which is then used to manufacture viral proteins; once the new viruses are assembled, they are ejected and go off to infect other cells. When viruses were found that consisted of RNA rather than DNA, they presented a puzzle to scientists, because it was unclear how the viruses could replicate. In 1970, however, in work that would win them the Nobel Prize, researchers David Baltimore at the Massachusetts Institute of Technology and Howard Temin at the University of Wisconsin independently discovered that these RNA viruses contained an enzyme, which they termed "reverse transcriptase," that copied the viral RNA into DNA. This DNA then served as the blueprint for the manufacture of new viruses. So while in normal viruses the sequence was "DNA to RNA to new viruses," in these unusual viruses there was an extra step: "RNA to DNA to RNA to new viruses." To describe the transcription from RNA to DNA and back again, virologists coined the term "retrovirus."[91]

55

During the "War on Cancer" in the 1970s, researchers such as Gallo at the NIH's National Cancer Institute (NCI) investigated links between animal retroviruses and various forms of cancer. However, until the late 1970s, no retroviruses were known to cause disease in humans. At that time, both Gallo and a group of Japanese researchers claimed credit for the discovery of one believed to cause adult T-cell leukemia, a rare form of cancer found mostly in Japanese fishing villages.[92] Gallo named the retrovirus the human T-cell leukemia virus, or HTLV. This work earned him the Lasker Prize, the highest award in biomedicine short of the Nobel Prize. He found another virus in the same family in 1982, which he claimed caused a different type of leukemia; in consequence, the two viruses became known as HTLV-I and HTLV-II.

As Gallo described it in retrospect, when he first heard about the new syndrome in gay men in 1981, he had no reason to think it might be linked to a retrovirus and indeed had little interest in the issue.[93] Or as Joan Fujimura has suggested more generally, scientists construct and pursue "do-able problems": they do not venture off in any direction at random, but rather structure their work by finding effective ways of integrating and coordinating the relationship between the experimental procedures at hand, the organization of the laboratories, and the social worlds through which they move.[94] Given that the initial hypothesis focused on homosexual lifestyle risks, many virologists simply saw no particular reason to be interested.

By Gallo's account, his curiosity was piqued only in 1982, when James Curran of the CDC briefed NIH researchers about the epidemic, expressing to them his own belief that the syndrome was caused by an infectious agent, and stressing that one hallmark of the syndrome was the helper T-cell deficiency.[95] This was enough for Gallo to hypothesize that the epidemic might be caused by HTLV or by a retrovirus of the HTLV family—by a close relative, that is, of the two viruses whose discovery had already brought him considerable acclaim within the world of virology. After all, HTLV specifically infected helper T cells; moreover, HTLV was known to be transmitted in blood and semen, which seemed also to be plausible transmission routes of the putative agent in AIDS. Finally, there was some precedent for a retroviral role in the condition like AIDS, since a feline retrovirus was linked to immune deficiency in cats. Gallo became convinced that AIDS was an HTLV-linked disease. Only some years later would he do an about-face and make an intriguing confession: "That hypothesis, as it turned out, was wrong. Nonetheless, it was fruitful, because it stimulated the search that led to the correct solution."[96]

Gallo had little patience for alternative hypotheses that were common at the time. The medical tendency to, as he put it, "round up the usual suspects"—CMV, Epstein-Barr virus, and the like—seemed to him unlikely to provide an explanation for what was, after all, a *new* epidemic. Nor was he impressed by the popular hypothesis of immune overload. Interestingly, he objected not just on empirical grounds—that immune overload seemed unlikely to account for manifestations in all the risk groups—but also on the basis of his understanding of causality in disease processes: "Whereas some complex diseases . . . are believed to involve different steps and sometimes different factors, most human disease (even some cancers) can be thought of as involving a primary causal factor. Certainly this has been the case for most past epidemic disease for which we in time did learn the cause."[97]

Committed in general to what Dubos called the "doctrine of specific etiology," Gallo dedicated his laboratory to an investigation of his hypothesis: that AIDS was caused by the virus he was already working with and had invested in, HTLV. Within weeks of embarking on this search, Gallo's assistants found the leukemia virus in the T cells of two U.S. gay men, a Haitian woman who died of AIDS in France, and a Frenchman who had received a blood transfusion.[98] Gallo sent two papers describing the findings to *Science* magazine, the preeminent general science publication in the United States. His colleague, Myron ("Max") Essex at the Harvard School of Public Health, sent along a third paper also reporting signs of HTLV infection in AIDS patients.

The French Virus

60   Meanwhile, across the Atlantic, a similar search for a retroviral cause of AIDS was proceeding according to different premises. In Paris, a group of physicians had been meeting informally to discuss the epidemic, and one of them, an immunologist named Jacques Leibowitch, who was familiar with Gallo's work on HTLV, had be-

come convinced that a retrovirus was the cause. Skeptical of arguments about poppers and promiscuity,[99] Leibowitch specifically hoped to demonstrate "that the cause of AIDS was not homosexually related."[100] But neither Leibowitch nor any of his colleagues knew how to look for a retrovirus, so they set out to enlist the support of Luc Montagnier, chief of viral oncology at the famous Pasteur Institute, a private, nonprofit research institution founded by Louis Pasteur in 1887.

The physicians' group had a hunch that if a virus was causing the depletion of T cells, then there might be higher levels of virus present in people who were at an earlier stage of illness, before most of their T cells had been killed off. So they sent Montagnier samples of lymph tissue from a gay male patient with "lymphadenopathy syndrome"—a condition of chronically swollen lymph glands, increasingly prevalent among gay men and believed by many to be a precursor to AIDS. Montagnier's research team extracted T cells from the tissue and put them in an incubator with nutrients, hoping to grow a virus. When tests showed the presence of reverse transcriptase, the enzyme that is the distinctive marker of retroviruses, they knew they had found something. The reverse transcriptase activity rose and then fell—a sign that the virus was killing its host cells—but by adding fresh cells from new sources, the French researchers were able to maintain the culture. With the aid of electron microscopy, the Pasteur group also succeeded in photographing viral particles.

When Montagnier contacted Gallo in early 1982 and informed him of his findings, Gallo encouraged him to submit his paper to *Science,* so that Gallo's, Essex's and Montagnier's papers could all appear together. Since *Science* allows its authors to suggest appropriate peer reviewers, Gallo told Montagnier he would be happy to review the Pasteur Institute's findings for the magazine. In his comments to *Science,* Gallo urged rapid publication, stressing the important of Montagnier's work. But in addition, as reporter John Crewdson has described in a highly critical exposé of Gallo's work, Gallo offered to write the abstract, which Montagnier had neglected to include. Gallo's abstract identified the French virus as a "C-type retrovirus," similar to Gallo's HTLV.[101] Gallo had effectively enlisted the Pasteur researchers behind his own HTLV.

The papers appeared in *Science* in May 1983,[102] where, as Crewdson noted, they "made a considerable splash."[103] But few people paid much attention to Montagnier's paper, which followed the other three in the pages of *Science;* it appeared simply to confirm the findings of the American researchers. As Jay Levy, a virologist at the University of California at San Francisco Medical School (UCSF), who had also embarked on a search for a retroviral causative agent, later recalled, "The write-up in the *Science* papers sounded like the French virus and the Gallo virus were the same."[104]

But Montagnier and his collaborators suspected otherwise. Their photographs didn't especially resemble HTLV. And when they exposed their virus to HTLV antibodies, they didn't observe any "cross-reaction"—as they should have, if the virus were really a close cousin of HTLV. Most crucially, their virus killed T cells in the test tube. HTLV caused its host cells to multiply wildly—the hallmark of cancer. Of course, the French had no actual proof at this point that the virus they had found was indeed the cause of AIDS. But they were increasingly convinced that theirs was a previously undiscovered retrovirus, not HTLV or even a member of the same family; and they set out to demonstrate its causal relationship to the epidemic.

65   By fall 1983, at the virology conference held each September in Cold Springs Harbor, New York, Montagnier could report finding his virus—which he was now calling "LAV," or lymphadenopathy-associated virus—in about 60 percent of patients with lymphadenopathy syndrome and 20 percent of those with AIDS. None of these patients appeared to be infected with HTLV. At the conference, Gallo angrily disputed Montagnier's findings, claiming that the French measurements had to be in error. (Much later, Gallo would write: "I have come increasingly to regret that the tone or spirit of my questioning that day was too aggressive and therefore misunderstood.")[105] What Gallo did not mention to the conference-goers was that, despite his own lab's best efforts, he and his associates had been unsuccessful in finding HTLV in the majority of samples from AIDS patients that they had been studying over the past several months.[106]

An Addition to the Honor Roll?

The events of the subsequent seven months are obscure, and—despite intensive scrutiny by journalists and a half dozen official investigations by various reputable bodies—the facts may never fully be known. What appears beyond dispute is that, shortly after the Cold Springs Harbor conference, Montagnier forwarded to Gallo a sample of LAV for him to study. Then, the following April, reports of Gallo's discovery of a "third variant" of HTLV began to appear in the pages of U.S. newspapers. Just months after insisting that HTLV was the cause of AIDS—while increasingly having trouble finding it in AIDS patients—Gallo presented the world with a new virus, "HTLV-III," which he claimed was a member of the HTLV family. Later, in January 1985, investigators would determine that Gallo's HTLV-III samples had a 99 percent genetic similarity to Montagnier's

LAV—that is, the viruses were much too similar to have come from separate sources. The implications were clear: Whether the consequence of accidental contamination of viral cultures—a common problem in virology labs—or of outright theft and misrepresentation, the Pasteur Institute's LAV had found its way into Gallo's cultures. Almost beyond a doubt, Gallo had in fact "discovered" Montagnier's virus.[107]

Yet none of this was known in 1984. Indeed, there was little said about Montagnier on April 23 that year, when Margaret Heckler, President Ronald Reagan's secretary of health and human services, stood before a roomful of reporters. "The probable cause of AIDS has been found," she announced with some fanfare: "a variant of a known human cancer virus, called HTLV-III." Just a few days earlier, Lawrence Altman, the *New York Times's* medical reporter, had received a scoop from CDC Director James Mason, who told him that a virus discovered in France, called LAV, was the likely culprit; the *Times* had run the story on the front page.[108] "There was so little excitement in the scientific community when the French came up with their announcement last May," noted Mason, claiming he did not understand why it had taken so long for the importance of the Pasteur Institute's work to be recognized. But at the press conference on Tuesday, Mason's boss had a different tune to play.

"Today we add another miracle to the long honor roll of American medicine and science," said Heckler. "Those who have said we weren't doing enough," she added, in response to widespread complaints of inactivity on AIDS by the Reagan administration, "have not understood how sound, solid, significant medical research proceeds." As Randy Shilts described it, the researchers on the podium with Heckler "blanched visibly when she proclaimed that . . . a vaccine would be ready for testing within two years."[109]

Heckler made only brief reference to the Pasteur Institute scientists, describing them as "working in collaboration with the National Cancer Institute"; she indicated her belief that LAV and HTLV-III "will prove to be the same."[110] Nor was mention made of UCSF virologist Jay Levy, who was also close on the heels of a virus linked to AIDS. (He would submit his paper to *Science* the following month.)[111] Pressed by puzzled reporters, Gallo added: "If it [the virus] turns out to be the same I certainly will say so . . . ."[112] Heckler emphasized the crucial role of the U.S. research, noting that only Gallo had succeeded in reproducing large quantities of the virus, which was necessary for the development of a blood test that could detect viral antibodies.[113] Hours earlier, the U.S. government had filed a patent application for just such a test.[114]

70   The *New York Times*, in an editorial printed a few days afterward, was not slow to draw implications from the episode. "In the

world of science, as among primitive societies, to be the namer of an object is to own it," the *Times* noted wryly, pointing to the dispute between "LAV" and "HTLV-III." Since the blood screening test was not yet in commercial operation and no vaccine had yet been produced, "what you are hearing is not yet a public benefit but a private competition—for fame, prizes, new research funds."[115]

"Strong Evidence of a Causative Involvement"

Certainly one of many unusual aspects of the whole affair was that Heckler's press conference was held before Gallo's findings had even been published in a peer-reviewed forum—normally a serious breach of professional scientific etiquette in itself. Those who wanted more substantial information about Gallo's claims had to wait until May 4, when four articles by Gallo's group appeared in the pages of *Science.* This too was extraordinary. As Gallo later commented, "Getting one paper in *Science* is a lot. Getting two is fantastic. Getting three was a record. We had four at one time."[116]

Gallo used these articles to put forward a series of interconnected claims: that he had found a new virus; that he had succeeded in mass-producing it; that the virus was related to HTLV; that antibodies to the virus could be detected in blood; and, most crucially, "that HTLV-III may be the primary cause of AIDS." In the second of the four papers, Gallo and his coauthors focused specifically on the etiological argument. After reviewing the evidence in favor of an infectious agent as the cause of the syndrome, Gallo reminded his readers that "we and others have suggested that specific human T-lymphotropic retroviruses (HTLV) causes AIDS."[117] Gallo's wording was also significant: he had redefined HTLV, from "human T-cell *leukemia* virus" in 1983, to "human T-*lymphotropic* retroviruses" in 1984. While the original name denoted the relation between a single retrovirus and a specific form of cancer, the new name described a family of viruses more vaguely characterized as "T-lymphotropic," that is, having an affinity for T cells. Gallo had reinvented "HTLV" so as to more plausibly encompass new virus as a relative of HTLV-I and HTLV-II.

Moving on to HTLV-III, Gallo described detecting the virus in, and isolating it from, "18 of 21 samples from patients with pre-AIDS [the so-called lymphadenopathy syndrome], three of four clinically normal mothers of juvenile AIDS patients, three of eight juvenile AIDS patients, 13 of 43 . . . adult patients with Kaposi's sarcoma, and 10 of 21 adult AIDS patients with opportunistic infections." Although ideally one would expect to find a primary causative agent in every case of a disease, Gallo noted that "the incidence of virus isolation reported here probably underestimates its true incidence since many tissue specimens were not received or handled under what we now recognize as optimal conditions." In contrast with these findings that associated the virus with the expression of AIDS was the striking absence of HTLV-III in cases where AIDS was also absent. Out of 115 clinically normal heterosexual blood donors, not a single one showed signs of the virus. And out of 22 clinically normal gay male donors, only one tested positive for the virus, and that person developed AIDS within six months. These studies, Gallo and his coauthors concluded, "provide strong evidence of a causative involvement of the virus in AIDS."[118]

What in fact had Gallo established? Four years later, in response to challenges about whether the virus had been proven to cause AIDS, Gallo would maintain: "In my opinion all of the sufficient data was available at the time the cause was first announced in the spring of 1984."[119] But this was a difficult position to sustain, at least on the basis of Gallo's published findings. Gallo had shown that, in specific small samples, laboratory signs indicating the presence of his virus were often correlated with the expression of AIDS at what were believed to be two different stages of disease progression ("pre-AIDS" and AIDS). Moreover, there were no such signs of virus in clinically normal people, suggesting that the virus or viruses had some special relationship to AIDS. But just because HTLV-III and LAV were often *correlated* with the syndrome, did that mean they were causing it? AIDS, after all, was a syndrome whose hallmark was the presence of a range of opportunistic infections; perhaps HTLV-III and LAV were viruses that were contracted by people who *already* had weakened immune systems. Gallo would have been in a better position to respond to this challenge if he had had more cases like that of the clinically healthy but infected gay man who later developed AIDS. But the other 21 of his 22 "clinically normal homosexual donors" all tested negative for the virus, so there was really no evidence that HTLV-III infection was a precursor to immune system damage. (Three out of 4 of the "clinically normal mothers of juvenile AIDS patients" tested positive for the virus, but these numbers were small, and Gallo did not report that any of the women had subsequently developed AIDS symptoms.)[120]

75   When asked ten years afterward whether he had been able, at the time of publication, to rule out the possibility that HTLV-III was an opportunistic infection, Gallo acknowledged that he could not. But "the evidence was overwhelming in my mind," Gallo recalled. "Science is never 100 percent. It's not mathematics. You play not on hunches, but on data that becomes overwhelming in your mind . . . ."[121] To make a credible claim for "strong evidence of a causative involvement," Gallo was in fact relying heavily on the *plausibility* of HTLV-III as a pathogenic agent, given what was known about the virus and about AIDS.

At least in vitro, HTLV-III killed helper T cells. And the central manifestation of immune system damage in people with AIDS was precisely the low numbers of those same helper T cells. Still, at this point, little was known about the effects of HTLV-III in vivo.

Koch's Postulates and the Proof of Causation

Epidemiologists and biomedical researchers rely on a range of principles to establish causation in disease. However, since the acceptance of different versions and interpretations of these principles of causation has itself become one of the stakes in the controversy over the causation of AIDS, these principles cannot be independently invoked as neutral measures. The most well known causation criteria are called "Koch's postulates," named after Robert Koch, the nineteenth-century German microbiologist. The postulates consist of four steps that are easily stated. First, the causal agent must be found in all cases of the disease. Second, the agent must be isolated from a carrier and grown in pure culture. Third, when the culture is injected into a susceptible laboratory animal, the animal must contract the disease. Finally, the casual agent must then be recovered from the diseased animal.

The precise relevance of Koch's postulates in contemporary biomedical research (particularly with regard to viruses, which were unknown at the time of Koch's own work) is in dispute, and this dispute has been magnified as a result of recent debates about the causation of AIDS. Many have proposed that researchers nowadays must work with "modern" or revised versions of the postulates, and have argued that Koch himself did not intend them to be followed rigidly.[122] Nevertheless, Koch's postulates remain a well-known reference point for considering questions of etiology in scientific medicine.

For instance, Richard Krause, the director of the National Institute of Allergy and Infectious Diseases of the NIH, gave a conference talk in the summer of 1983 on "Koch's Postulates and the Search for the AIDS Agent," noting that "technical difficulties" often "impede the fulfillment" of all of Koch's postulates, but concluding: "If we abide by the scientific guidance of Koch's postulates, we are sure to discover the cause of AIDS."[123] Similarly, Lawrence Altman focused squarely on Koch's postulates in an article, published later in 1984, on "How AIDS Researchers Strive for Virus Proof."[124] Altman presented Koch's postulates as an important medical tradition that researchers have looked to for a century, but he noted that doctors are sometimes forced to rely on immunological or other experimental evidence when Koch's postulates cannot fully be satisfied. With less equivocation, James D'Eramo wrote in the *New York Native* soon after the Heckler press conference: "The definitive

classical proof that a virus or bacterium causes disease rests on causing the disease in animals by injecting them with the putative agent.
AIDS has yet to occur in a laboratory animal."[125] Dr. Nathan Fain,
the medical writer for the national, West Coast-based gay news-
magazine the *Advocate,* made roughly the same claim in May when
he explained why "work must continue to prove beyond all doubt
that the candidate virus does cause AIDS."[126]

Clearly, if Koch's postulates are the benchmark, then Gallo's
May 1984 articles in *Science* by no means established HTLV-III as the
cause of AIDS. But since the criteria for proving causation have been
contested, it may be useful to assess the credibility of Gallo's claims-
making by looking at a relatively weak version of the causation criteria presented in a recent epidemiology textbook. According to
Mausner and Kramer, the likelihood that an association is causal can
be evaluated by examining several criteria.[127] First, there is the
strength of the association, which they describe as the "ratio of disease
rates for those with and without the hypothesized causal factor": here
Gallo's evidence is compelling but far from perfect, since he was able
to isolate the virus only in fewer than half of the samples from people
actually diagnosed with AIDS. Second, the "dose-response relationship": does a higher dose of the causal factor result in higher rates of
disease expression? Gallo had no data on this point. Third, the consis-
tency of the association across different studies: clearly this was yet to
be determined. Finally, is the association a "temporally correct" one,
meaning that the cause precedes the expression with a sufficient "induction period" or "latency period"? With the exception of the one
virus-positive, clinically health gay man who developed AIDS within
six months, Gallo had no relevant data to report.

80

Given the state of the evidence in early 1984, perhaps a more
plausible claim was that of Jay Levy, whose results in isolating what
he called "ARV," or AIDS-associated retrovirus, were published in
August.[128] Levy found signs of ARV in about half his AIDS patients
and in about 20 percent of clinically health homosexual men, but in
only 4 percent of clinically healthy heterosexuals. Levy recalled agonizing over how to phrase the conclusion: "I called a good friend of
mine . . . who's an editor, and I said, 'How do I do this? I don't want
to say it *isn't,* but I don't want to say it *is.*'"[129] In the end, Levy's
wording was cautious: "Although no conclusion can yet be made
concerning their etiologic role in AIDS, their biologic properties and
prevalence in AIDS patients suggest that these retroviruses could
cause this disease."[130]

But for Gallo, the notion that he had proven the virus to be the
cause became something crucial to defend, particularly as his credibility on other claims was challenged. In 1985, the Pasteur Institute sued
the U.S. government in a patent dispute over the discovery of the

virus, and in 1987 the heads of the two governments, Jacques Chirac and Ronald Reagan, signed an agreement splitting the royalties for the commercial antibody test. Especially after it became apparent that Montagnier's LAV had found its way into Gallo's viral cultures—a point that Gallo would formally concede in 1991—Gallo gradually backed off from claiming any primacy. And although Gallo continued to present the discovery of HTLV-III as a natural outgrowth of HTLV research,[131] he was eventually forced to accept the prevailing view that, from a genetic standpoint, the new virus was not reasonably classifiable as an HTLV virus. In response to the confusing array of acronyms then in use—HTLV-III, LAV, ARV, HTLV-III/LAV, and others—the Human Retrovirus Subcommittee of the International Committee of the Taxonomy of Viruses rebuffed Gallo and agreed on a new, compromise, name in 1986: HIV, human immunodeficiency virus. (Levy and Montagnier signed the agreement, Gallo and his close associate, Max Essex, dissented.)[132]

The Framing of Aids

The naming of the virus by the Human Retrovirus Subcommittee marked the initial stabilization of "HIV" as a unitary object of medical knowledge.[133] But even before this point, the illness AIDS had become a relatively stable cultural entity whose social meanings, however fluid and multiple, had at least begun to congeal. Over the course of a few years, AIDS had come to be "framed," or constructed, within the context of strong beliefs and attitudes about sexuality, promiscuity, and homosexuality and through recourse to a wide range of analogies: Was AIDS like cancer? Was it like herpes? Was it like hepatitis B? Was it an HTLV-like illness? AIDS itself had also come to serve as a frame for understanding other events and social behaviors. Perhaps most notably, as sociologist Steven Seidman has argued, "AIDS . . . provided a pretext to reinsert homosexuality within a symbolic drama of pollution and purity."[134]

These framings, and the associated stigma, had also provided possibilities for gay men to assert claims for "ownership" of the epidemic (however ambivalently), or at least some of the public responses to it.[135] Indeed, the same social networks and institutional linkages that had permitted rapid amplification of a virus also gave rise to the organization of a concerted grassroots response. Lesbians, subject to what Erving Goffman has called a "courtesy stigma," or stigma by association, acted as collaborators with gay men in these efforts, often playing leadership roles.[136] This extraordinary success of gay and lesbian communities in establishing their right to speak about the epidemic would fuel a willingness and capacity to challenge the knowledge-making practices of biomedicine in the coming years.

Biomedical researchers, and in particular virologists, had also staked out claims to "ownership" of AIDS, and had done so through powerful findings concerning a probable causal agent. The credibility of AIDS research would rapidly become linked to the credibility of this particular causal claim: between 1984 and 1986, the retroviral hypothesis would achieve near-hegemonic status among scientists. It would also, by and large, be taken for granted in the communities affected by the epidemic, in the mass media, and among the lay public. . . . .

Notes

1. Dominique Lapierre, *Beyond Love*, trans. Kathryn Spink (New York: Warner Books, 1991), 51–54; Randy Shilts, *And the Band Played On: Politics, People, and the AIDS Epidemic* (New York: St. Martin's, 1987), 42–67.

2. "*Pneumocystis* Pneumonia—Los Angeles," *Morbidity and Mortality Weekly Report* 30 (5 June 1981): 250–252.

3. "Kaposi's Sarcoma and *Pneumocystis* Pneumonia among Homosexual Men—New York City and California," *Morbidity and Mortality Weekly Report* 30 (3 July 1981): 305–308.

4. Lawrence K. Altman, "Rare Cancer Seen in 41 Homosexuals," *New York Times*, 3 July 1981, A–20.

5. Lawrence Mass, "Cancer in the Gay Community," *New York Native*, 27 July 1981, 1, 21, 30.

6. Michael S. Gottlieb et al., "*Pneumocystis Carinii* Pneumonia and Mucosal Candidiasis Found in Previously Healthy Homosexual Men," *New England Journal of Medicine* 305 (10 December 1981): 1425–1431; Henry Masur et al., "An Outbreak of Community-Acquired *Pneumocystis Carinii* Pneumonia," *New England Journal of Medicine* 305 (10 December 1981): 1431–1438; Frederick P. Siegal et al., "Sevre Acquired Immunodeficiency in Male Homosexuals, Manifested by Chronic Perianal Ulcerative Herpes Simplex Lesions,' *New England Journal of Medicine* 305 (10 December 1981): 1439–1444; David T. Durack, "Opportunisitc Infections and Kaposi's Sarcoma in Homosexual Men," *New England Journal of Medicine* 305 (10 December 1981): 1465–1467; Centers for Disease Control Task Force on Kaposi's Sarcoma and Opportunistic Infections, "Special Report: Epidemiologic Aspects of the Current Outbreak of Kaposi's Sarcoma and Opportunistic Infections," *New England Journal of Medicine* 306 (28 January 1982): 248–252.

7. Helper T cells go by various names, including T_4 cells and CD4 cells, the latter term referring to the CD4 molecule that serves as the receptor site by which other entities bind to the cell. Colloquially, in discussions of AIDS, these cells are often simply called T cells, and I shall do the same except when it is important to distinguish the helper T cells from other varieties of T cells. Increasingly, however, laypeople who are "in the know" use the term "CD4" to demonstrate their linguistic competence. In the later chapters of the book, I adopt that term as well.

8. Siegal et al., "Severe Acquired Immonodeficiency in Male Homosexuals," 1441.

9. Robert O. Brennan and David T. Durack, "Gay Compromise Syndrome," *Lancet* 2 (December 1981): 1338–1339 (letter to the editor).

10. Masur et al., "Outbreak of Community-Acquired *Pneumocystis Carinii* Pneumonia."

11. Durack, "Opportunistic Infections and Kaposi's Sarcoma in Homosexual Men," 1466.

12. Matt Clark and Mariana Gosnell, "Diseases That Plague Gays," *Newsweek*, 21 December 1981, 51–52.

13. Dennis Altman, *AIDS in the Mind of America* (Garden City: Anchor Press/Doubleday, 1986), 33–36, esp. 35; see also Cindy Patton, *Sex and Germs: The Politics of AIDS* (Boston: South End Press, 1985), 6–7.

14. On "normalization," see Michel Foucault, *Discipline and Punish: The Birth of the Prison* (New York: Vintage Books, 1979).

15. Gottlieb et al., for instance, reported in December 1981 that, of four patients, one had been monogamous for four years, two had several regular partners, and only one "was highly sexually active and frequented homosexual bars and bathhouses" (*"Pneumocystis Carinii* Pneumonia and Mucosal Candidiasis," 1429).

16. Irving Kenneth Zola, "Pathways to the Doctor: From Person to Patient," in *Perspectives in Medical Sociology,* ed. Phil Brown (Belmont, Calif.: Wadsworth, 1989), 223–238, quote from 234.

17. Eliot Freidson, *Profession of Medicine: A Study of the Sociology of Applied Knowledge* (Chicago: Univ. of Chicago Press, 1988), 270.

18. David Perlman, "Drug Users Started AIDS Epidemic, Doctor Says," *San Francisco Chronicle*, 18 October 1985, 28; Cindy Patton, *Inventing AIDS* (New York: Routledge, 1990), 27–28.

19. The currency of this term has been reported by Shilts, among others, and it was used in the *New York Times* (Shilts, *And the Band Played On*, 121; Lawrence K. Altman, "New Homosexual Disorder Worries Health Officials," *New York Times*, 11 May 1982, C1). However, as Murray and Payne have noted, few instances can be found in the published medical literature, suggesting that "GRID" never became institutionalized as a legitimate designation for the syndrome (Stephen O. Murray and Kenneth W. Payne, "Medical Policy without Scientific Evidence: The Promiscuity Paradigm and AIDS," *California Sociologist* 11 [winter-summer 1988]: 13–54, esp. 44, note 5). But see Michael S. Gottlieb et al., "Gay-Related Immunodeficiency (GRID) Syndrome: Clinical and Autopsy Observations" (abstract submitted to the Thirty-Ninth Annual National Meeting of the American Federation for Clinical Research, Washington, D.C., 7–10 May 1982), *Clinical Research 30* (April 1982): 349A; M. Vogt et al., "GRID-Syndrome," *Deutsche Medizinische Wochenschrift* 107 (15 October 1982): 1539–1542.

20. On "framing," see Erving Goffman, *Frame Analysis: An Essay on the Organization of Experience* (New York: Harper & Row, 1974). On the framing of illnesses, see Charles E. Rosenberg, "Introduction: Framing Disease: Illness, Society, and History," in *Framing Disease: Studies in Cultural History,* ed. Charles E. Rosenberg and Janet Golden (New Brunswick, N.J.: Rutgers Univ. Press, 1992), xiii–xxvi.

21. See Gerald M. Oppenheimer, "In the Eye of the Storm: The Epidemiological Construction of AIDS," in *AIDS: The Burdens of History,* ed. Elizabeth Fee and Daniel M. Fox (Berkeley: Univ. of California Press, 1988), 279–280.

22. Shilts, *And the Band Played On*, 83, 104, 171.

23. Henry L. Kazal et al., "The Gay Bowel Syndrome: Clinico-Pathologic Correlation in 260 Cases," *Annals of Clinical and Laboratory Science* 6 (March-April 1976): 184–192; Yehudi M. Felman, "Examining the Homosexual Male for Sexually Transmitted Diseases," *Journal of the American Medical Association* 238 (7 November 1977): 2046–2047; Samuel Vaisrub, "Homosexuality—A Risk Factor in Infectious Disease," *Journal of the American Medical Association* 238 (26 September 1977): 14 (editorial); Alexander McMillan, "Gonorrhea in Homosexual Men: Frequency of Infection by Culture Site," *Sexually Transmitted Diseases* 5 (October-December 1978): 146–150; Richard R. Babb, "Sexually Transmitted Infections in Homosexual Men," *Postgraduate Medicine* 65 (March 1979): 215–218; Yehudi M. Felman, "Homosexual Hazards," *The Practitioner* 224 (November 1980): 1151–1156; Franklyn N. Judson, "Comparative Prevalence Rates of Sexually Transmitted Diseases in Heterosexual and Homosexual

Men," *American Journal of Epidemiology* 112 (December 1980): 836–843; William M. Owen Jr., "Sexually Transmitted Diseases and Traumatic Problems in Homosexual Men," *Annals of Internal Medicine* 92 (June 1980): 805–808; H. Hunter Handsfield, "Sexually Transmitted Diseases in Homosexual Men," *American Journal of Public Health* 71 (September 1981): 989–990 (editorial); R. R. Willcox, "Sexual Behaviour and Sexually Transmitted Disease Patterns in Male Homosexuals," *British Journal of Venereal Diseases* 57 (June 1981): 167–169.

24. See Steven Epstein, "Moral Contagion and the Medicalizing of Gay Identity: AIDS in Historical Perspective," *Research in Law, Deviance and Social Control* 9 (1988):3–36.

25. Felman, "Homosexual Hazards."

26. Michel Foucault, *The History of Sexuality*, vol. 1 (New York: Vintage, 1980), 43; Jeffrey Escoffier, "The Politics of Gay Identity," *Socialist Review*, July-October 1985, 119–153; Jeffrey Weeks, *Sexuality and Its Discontents: Meanings, Myths and Modern Sexualities* (London: Routledge & Kegan Paul, 1985); Peter Conrad and Joseph W. Schneider, *Deviance and Medicalization: From Badness to Sickness* (St. Louis: C. V. Mosby, 1980).

27. For a history of "gay bowel syndrome" and its relation to essentialist conceptions of the gay male body, see Michael Scarce, "Urban Bums and Rough Rides: A Bad Case of Gay Bowel Syndrome" (master's thesis, Ohio State University, 1995). Clearly, there are important parallels here to the medical portrayal of gender and racial differences; see Deborah Lupton, *Medicine as Culture: Illness, Disease and the Body in Western Societies* (London: Sage, 1994).

28. Alan P. Bell and Martin S. Weinberg, *Homosexualities: A Study of Diversity among Men and Women* (New York: Simon and Schuster, 1978).

29. In fact, most of these blanket characterizations of gay male sexuality were based on studies of patients at clinics for treatment of sexually transmitted diseases. One study did attempt to recruit a large sample of homosexual men from the "gay community" at large by distributing questionnaires in a gay magazine and through gay organizations (William Darrow et al., "The Gay Report on Sexually Transmitted Diseases," *American Journal of Public Health* 71 [September 1981]: 1004–1011); but it is doubtful that the 1.5 percent response rate generated a representative sample of readers of the magazine or members of the organizations, let alone members of "the gay community," whatever its supposed locus and boundaries.

30. "Immunocompromised Homosexuals," *Lancet* 2 (12 December 1981): 1326 (editorial).

31. Murray and Payne, "Medical Policy without Scientific Evidence"; Stephen O. Murray and Kenneth W. Payne, "The Social Classification of AIDS in American Epidemiology," *Medical Anthropology* 10 (March 1989): 115–128.

32. Quoted in "Safe-Sex Comic Book for Gays Riles Senate," *San Francisco Chronicle*, 15 October 1987, A–7.

33. Jana L. Armstrong, "Causal Explanations of AIDS," in *The Meaning of AIDS: Implications for Medical Science, Clinical Practice, and Public Health Policy*, ed. Eric T. Juengst and Barbara A. Koenig (New York: Praeger, 1989), 12.

34. *Dorland's Illustrated Medical Dictionary*, 27th ed. (Philadelphia: W. B. Saunders Company, 1988), 285.

35. Charles Rosenberg, *The Cholera Years* (Chicago: Univ. of Chicago Press, 1962), 133–150.

36. Judith Walkowitz, *Prostitution and Victorian Society: Women, Class, and the State* (Cambridge, England: Cambridge Univ. Press, 1980), 56.

37. Joan Trauner, "The Chinese as Medical Scapegoats in San Franscisco, 1870–1905," *California History*, spring 1978, 70–87.

38. Shilts, *And the Band Played On*, 149.

39. See Michael Bronski, "AIDing Our Guilt and Fear," *Gay Community News*, 9 October 1982, 8.

40. A publication called *BAPHRON*, the newsletter for the Bay Area chapter, is a useful source of information about the activities and concerns of this group.

41. See Dennis Altman, *The Homosexualization of America* (Boston: Beacon Press, 1982).

42. See D. Altman, *AIDS in the Mind of America*; Patton, *Sex and Germs*; Steven Petrow, Pat Franks, and Timothy R. Wolfred, eds., *Ending the HIV Epidemic: Community Strategies in Disease Prevention and Health Promotion* (Santa Cruz, Calif.: Network Publications, 1990).

43. Quoted in Lawrence Mass, "An Epidemic Q&A," *New York Native*, 21 June 1982, 11 (emphasis in the original).

44. "Update on Acquired Immune Deficiency Syndrome (AIDS)—United States," *Morbidity and Mortality Weekly Report* 31 (24 September 1982): 508.

45. Lawrence K. Altman, "AIDS Now Seen as a Worldwide Health Problem," *New York Times*, 29 November 1983, C–1.

46. Christine Russell, "Body's Immune System Disease Seen Occurring Also in Equatorial Africa," *Washington Post,* 2 April 1983, A–7.

47. Victor Cohn, "Africa May Be the Origin of AIDS Disease," *Washington Post*, 27 November 1983, A–4.

48. Anthony S. Fauci, "The Syndrome of Kaposi's Sarcoma and Opportunistic Infections: An Epidemiologically Restricted Disorder of Immunoregulation," *Annals of Internal Medicine* 96 (June 1982): 777–779 (editorial).

49. "Opportunistic Infections and Kaposi's Sarcoma among Haitians in the United States," *Morbidity and Mortality Weekly Report* 31 (9 July 1982): 353–361.

50. *"Pneumocystis Carinii* Pneumonia among Persons with Hemophilia A," *Morbidity and Mortality Weekly Report* 31 (16 July 1982): 366.

51. Lawrence Mass, "A Major Meeting on the Epidemic," *New York Native*, 2 August 1982, 11, 12.

52. Allan M. Brandt, *No Magic Bullet: A Social History of Venereal Diseases in the United States Since 1880* (New York: Oxford Univ. Press, 1985), 4.

53. René Dubos, *Mirage of Health: Utopias, Progress, and Biological Change* (New York: Harper & Brothers, 1959), 86.

54. Judith S. Mausner and Shira Kramer, *Epidemiology—An Introductory Text*, 2d ed. (Philadelphia: W. Saunders, 1985), 27–34. For a critique of such approaches, see Sylvia Noble Tesh, *Hidden Arguments: Political Ideology and Disease Prevention Policy* (New Brunswick, N.J.: Rutgers Univ. Press, 1990).

55. See, for example, Barbara Ellen Smith, "Black Lung: The Social Production of Disease," in *Perspectives in Medical Sociology*, ed. Phil Brown (Prospect Heights, Ill: Waveland Press, 1992), 122–141.

56. Andrew Abbott, *The System of Professions: An Essay on the Division of Expert Labor* (Chicago: Univ. of Chicago Press, 1988), 136, 193.

57. Harry Nelson, "Mysterious Fever Now an Epidemic," *Los Angeles Times*, 31 May 1982, 1, 3, 20.

58. "'Homosexual Plague' Strikes New Victims," *Newsweek*, 23 August 1982, 10.

59. "Possible Transfusion-Associated Acquired Immune Deficiency Syndrome (AIDS)—California," *Morbidity and Mortality Weekly Report* 31 (10 December 1982): 652–654.

60. "Immunodeficiency among Female Sexual Partners of Males with Acquired Immune Deficiency Syndrome (AIDS)—New York," *Morbidity and Mortality Weekly Report* 31 (7 January 1983): 697–698.

61. Catherine Macek, "Acquired Immunodeficiency Syndrome Cause(s) Still Elusive," *Journal of the American Medical Association* 248 (24 September 1982): 1423–1431.

62. For biographical information on Sonnabend, see Bruce Nussbaum, *Good Intentions: How Big Business and the Medical Establishment Are Corrupting the Fight Against AIDS* (New York: Atlantic Monthly Press, 1990), chapter 4.

63. Anne-Christine d'Adesky, "The Man Who Invented Safer Sex Returns," *Out*, summer 1992, 29.

64. J. A. Sonnabend, "Promiscuity Is Bad for Your Health: AIDS and the Question of an Infectious Agent," *New York Native*, 13 September 1982, 39.

65. On the importance of recruiting allies in scientific controversies, see Bruno Latour, *Science in Action* (Cambridge, Mass.: Harvard Univ. Press, 1987), chapter 4.

66. Barry Adkins, "Looking at AIDS in Totality: A Conversation with Joseph Sonnabend," *New York Native*, 7 October 1985, 22.

67. Latour has stressed that the effect of powerful scientific rhetoric is precisely to "isolate" opponents and make them feel "lonely"; see *Science in Action*, 33, 44.

68. Adkins, "Looking at AIDS in Totality," 24.

69. Joseph Sonnabend, Steven S. Witkin, and David T. Purilo, "Acquired Immunodeficiency Syndrome, Opportunistic Infections, and Malignancies in Male Homosexuals: A Hypothesis of Etiologic Factors in Pathogenesis," *Journal of the American Medical Association* 249 (6 May 1983): 2370–2374. Reprinted in Irving J. Selikoff, Alvin S. Teirstein, and Shalon Z. Hirschman, eds., *Acquired Immune Deficiency Syndrome*, vol. 437 of *Annals of the New York Academy of Sciences* (New York: 1984); and in Helene M. Cole and George D. Lundberg, eds., *AIDS: From the Beginning* (Chicago: American Medical Association, 1986).

70. Sonnabend, Witkin, and Purilo, "Acquired Immunodeficiency Syndrome."

71. J. A. Sonnabend, "The Etiology of AIDS," *AIDS Research* 1 (1983): 1–12.

72. James J. Goedert et al., "Amyl Nitrite May Alter T Lymphocytes in Homosexual Men," *Lancet* 1 (20 February 1982): 412–415.

73. Mass, "Major Meeting on the Epidemic," 11.

74. Lawrence Mass, "The Epidemic Continues: Facing a New Case Every Day, Researchers Are Still Bewildered," *New York Native*, 29 March 1982, 1, 12–15.

75. Gordon Murray, "The 'Gay Disease' Epidemic," *Gay Community News*, 9 October 1982, 8.

76. Bronski, "AIDing Our Guilt," 9.

77. G. Murray, "'Gay Disease' Epidemic," 11.

78. Editors' note, *New York Native*, 8–21 November 1982, 22.

79. Peter Seitzman, "Good Luck, Bad Luck: The Role of Chance in Contracting AIDS," *New York Native*, 8–21 November 1982, 22.

80. Michael Callen and Richard Berkowitz, "We Know Who We Are: Two Gay Men Declare War on Promiscuity," *New York Native*, 8 November 1982, 23–29, quote from 23.

81. Charles Jurrist, "In Defense of Promiscuity: Hard Questions about Real Life," *New York Native*, 6 December 1982, 27, 29.

82. D. Altman, *AIDS in the Mind of America*, 40–47; Patton, *Sex and Germs*, 119–158.

83. Michael Lynch, quoted in D. Altman, *AIDS in the Mind of America*, 137.

84. Lawrence Mass, "The Case against Medical Panic," *New York Native*, 17 January, 1983, 25.

85. Callen and Berkowitz, "We Know Who We Are," 29.

86. Dennis Altman, "Legitimation through Disaster: AIDS and the Gay Movement," in *AIDS: The Burdens of History*, ed. Elizabeth Fee and Daniel M. Fox (Berkeley: Univ. of California Press, 1988), 301–315. On the role of community in social movement mobilization, see Clarence Y. H. Lo, "Communities of Challengers in Social Movement Theory," in *Frontiers in Social Movement Theory*, ed. Aldon D. Morris and Carol McClurg Mueller (New Haven: Yale Univ. Press, 1992), 224–247.

87. See, for example, Jean-Robert Leonidas and Nicole Hyppolite, "Haiti and the Acquired Immunodeficiency Syndrome," *Annals of Internal Medicine* 98 (June 1982): 1020–1021. More generally, see Paul Farmer, *AIDS and Accusation: Haiti and the Geography of Blame* (Berkeley: Univ. of California Press, 1992).

88. Cathy Jean Cohen, "Power, Resistance and the Construction of Crisis: Marginalized Communities Respond to AIDS" (Ph.D. diss., University of Michigan, 1993), 472, 484.

89. Ibid., 450–451.

90. Robert C. Gallo, "HIV—The Cause of AIDS: An Overview on Its Biology, Mechanisms of Disease Induction, and Our Attempts to Control It," *Journal of Acquired Immune Deficiency Syndromes* 1 (December 1988): 521.

91. John M. Coffin, "Introduction to Retroviruses," in *AIDS and Other Manifestations of HIV Infection*, 2d ed., ed. Gary P. Wormser (New York: Raven Press, 1992), 37–56; Steve Connor and Sharon Kingman, *The Search for the Virus*, 2d ed. (London: Penguin Books, 1989), 29.

92. Connor and Kingman, *Search for the Virus*, 29.

93. Robert Gallo, *Virus Hunting* (New York: Basic Books, 1991), 133.

94. Joan Fujimura, "Constructing 'Do-Able' Problems in Cancer Research: Articulating Alignments," *Social Studies of Science* 17 (May 1987): 257–293.

95. Gallo, *Virus Hunting*, 134.

96. Robert C. Gallo and Luc Montangier, "AIDS in 1988," *Scientific American* 259 (October 1988): 40ff.

97. Gallo, *Virus Hunting*, 148–149.

98. John Crewdson, "The Great AIDS Quest (Part 1: Science under the Microscope)," *Chicago Tribune,* 19 November 1989, C–1.

99. Jacques Leibowitch, *A Strange Virus of Unknown Origin* (New York: Ballantine Books, 1985), esp. chapter 1.

100. Quoted in Crewdson, "The Great AIDS Quest (Part 1)."

101. Ibid.; Connor and Kingman," *Search for the Virus*, 33.

102. Robert C. Gallo et al., "Isolation of Human T-Cell Leukemia Virus in Acquired Immune Deficiency Syndrome (AIDS)," *Science* 220 (20 May 1983): 865–867; F. Barré-Sinoussi et al., "Isolation of a T-Lymphotropic Retrovirus from a Patient at Risk for Acquired Immune Deficiency Syndrome (AIDS)," *Science* 220 (20 May 1983): 868–870.

103. Crewdson, "The Great AIDS Quest (Part 1)."

104. Jay Levy, interview by author, tape recording, San Francisco, 16 December 1993.

105. Gallo, *Virus Hunting*, 170.

106. Crewdson, "The Great AIDS Quest (Part 1)."

107. In November 1993, the Office of Research Integrity of the Department of Health and Human Services concluded a four-year investigation by dropping all accusations of scientific misconduct against Gallo. Gallo declared himself "completely vindicated," but the office said it was "acting reluctantly" in response to the adoption of a new, more stringent definition of what constitutes misconduct in science. See Philip J. Hilts, "Misconduct Charges Dropped against AIDS Virus Scientist," *New York Times*, 13 November 1993, A–1.

108. Lawrence K. Altman, "Federal Official Says He Believes Cause of AIDS Has Been Found," *New York Times*, 22 April 1984, 1.

109. Shilts, *And the Band Played On*, 451.

110. Lawrence K. Altman, "New U.S. Report Names Virus That May Cause AIDS," *New York Times*, 24 April 1984, C–1.

111. Levy, interview.

112. Connor and Kingman, *Search for the Virus*, 41.

113. Shilts, *And the Band Played On*, 451.

114. John Crewdson, "The Great AIDS Quest (Part 4: 'Could You Patent the Sun?')," *Chicago Tribune*, 19 November 1989, C–7.

115. "A Viral Competition over AIDS," *New York Times*, 26 April 1984, 22 (editorial).

116. Crewdson, "The Great AIDS Quest (Part 4)."

117. Robert C. Gallo et al., "Frequent Detection and Isolation of Cytopathic Retroviruses (HTLV-III) from Patients with AIDS and at Risk for AIDS," *Science* 224 (4 May 1984): 500–502.

118. Ibid., 502.

119. Gallo, "HIV—The Cause of AIDS," 523.

120. In one of the other papers, Gallo and his colleagues reported finding *antibodies* to the virus in three of five asymptomatic IV drug users and six of seventeen asymptomatic homosexual men. Again, there was no knowledge at that point about whether these individuals would develop AIDS. Moreover, the presence of antibodies to the virus was somewhat weaker evidence than the presence of the virus itself (M. G. Sarngadharan et al., "Antibodies Reactive with Human T-Lymphotropic Retroviruses [HTLV-III] in the Serum of Patients with AIDS," *Science* 224, 4 May 1984, 506–508).

121. Robert Gallo, interview by author, tape recording, Bethesda, Md., 3 November 1994.

122. Gallo, *Virus Hunting*, 227–280; Alfred S. Evans, "Does HIV Cause AIDS? An Historical Perspective," *Journal of Acquired Immune Deficiency Syndromes* 2 (April 1989): 107–113.

123. Richard M. Krause, "Koch's Postulates and the Search for the AIDS Agent," *Reviews of infectious Diseases* 6 (March-April 1984): 272, 278. The original talk was presented at the International Congress for Infectious Diseases, Vienna, Austria, August 24–27, 1983.

124. Lawrence K. Altman, "How AIDS Researchers Strive for Virus Proof," *New York Times*, 23 October 1984, C–3.

125. James E. D'Eramo, "Federal Health Officials Announce Cause of AIDS," *New York Native*, 7 May 1984, 8.

126. Nathan Fain, "Researchers Track Down Virus They Believe Is AIDS' Cause," *Advocate*, 29 May 1984, 8–9.

127. Mausner and Kramer, *Epidemiology—An Introductory Text*, 185.

128. Jay A. Levy et al., "Isolation of Lymphocytopathic Retroviruses from San Francisco Patients with AIDS," *Science* 225, 24 August 1984; 840–842.

129. Levy, interview.

130. Levy et al., "Isolation of Lymphocytophathic Retroviruses," 225.

131. See, for example, Flossie Wong-Staal and Robert C. Gallo, "The Family of Human T-Lymphotropic Leukemia viruses: HTLV-I as the Cause of Adult T Cell Leukemia and HTLV-III as the Cause of Acquired Immunodeficiency Syndrome," *Blood* 65 (February 1985), 253–263.

132. John Coffin et al., "Human Immunodeficiency Viruses," *Science* 232 (9 May 1986): 697 (letter to the editor).

133. On the stabilization of HIV, see also Paula A. Treichler, "AIDS: An Epidemic of Signification," in *AIDS: Cultural Analysis, Cultural Activism*, ed. Douglas Crimp (Cambridge, Mass.: Massachusetts Institute of Technology Press, 1988), 31–70, esp. 57.

134. Steven Seidman, "Transfiguring Sexual Identity: AIDS and the Contemporary Construction of Homosexuality," *Social Text* 19/20 (fall 1988): 187–205.

135. On struggles over the ownership of social problems, see Joseph R. Gusfield, *The Culture of Public Problems* (Chicago: Univ. of Chicago Press, 1981).

136. On courtesy stigmas in AIDS, see Peter Conrad, "The Social Meaning of AIDS," *Social Policy* (summer 1986), 53. On the role of lesbians, see Amber Hollibaugh, "Lesbian Denial and Lesbian Leadership in the AIDS Epidemic: Bravery and Fear in the Construction of a Lesbian Geography of Risk," in *Women Resisting AIDS: Feminist Strategies of Empowerment,* ed. Beth E. Schneider and Nancy E. Stoller (Philadelphia: Temple Univ. Press, 1995), 219–230; Nancy Stoller, "Lesbian Involvement in the AIDS Epidemic: Changing Roles and Generational Differences," in *Women Resisting AIDS*, 270–285.

Reflective Reading, Informal Writing

REFLECTING ON THE READING:

- Epstein's chapter, "The Nature of a New Threat," is in a section of his book entitled "The Politics of Causation." Having read this chapter, what do you think Epstein means by the politics of causation and how does it relate to this chapter?
- Epstein seems to suggest that AIDS was socially constructed. What does he mean by this? How could it be? After all, real people are dying of a real disease.
- Epstein implies that horrific injustices may have been done to gay men in the public construction of AIDS. Yet, he also points to positive aspects of this constructed causation. Does Epstein think the injustices outweigh the benefits? Is he neutral? Do you think the injustices of this constructed causation hurt anyone?
- Epstein writes that "AIDS became a 'gay disease' primarily because clinicians, epidemiologists, and reporters perceived through that filter, but secondarily because gay communities were obliged to make it their own." How and why were gays "obliged" to make it their own? What meaning does the word "obliged" give to this sentence?
- Identify at least two cases or situations in the history of the "nature of a new theory" as Epstein calls it, where the nature of AIDS was misunderstood, or a possible understanding for the disease was missed because of "scientific blindness," a desire to perpetuate a particular view of the disease, or a desire for self-serving gain such as fame or recognition.

UNDERSTANDING RHETORICAL STRATEGIES:

- Epstein claims that the Center for Disease Control intentionally came up with the name AIDS (Acquired Immune Deficiency Syndrome) specifically for its neutrality. Are the words themselves neutral? When you hear someone has AIDS, do you respond neutrally? What are the first thoughts and reactions you have? If you think that the words themselves (acquired, immune, deficiency, syndrome) are neutral, but you have reactions to them, what do you think is happening with the interplay of language and culture?
- Epstein explains a very complex and scientific situation in this selection. How difficult do you know or imagine scientific writing to be? How readable is Epstein's version against your understanding of scientific writing? What accounts for this—his audience? His purpose? His ethos?

- One could argue that Epstein's work bridges various academic disciplines as well as activist and public concerns. What specifically does he do rhetorically to create this bridge?
- What does Epstein use for evidence? Is it appropriate and sound evidence? How and where is this evidence placed in the essay? How does Epstein set you up, or prepare you, for this evidence? Does he analyze this evidence for us?

INFORMAL WRITING:

- What do you think Epstein's thesis or point is?
- How does it make you feel that politics and social, scientific, and personal blindness may account for grave injustices against certain groups of people—in this case, gays? Would any circumstance you can think of make such a thing okay? Why or why not?
- Do you trust Epstein's version of the "story"? Why or why not?

MICHAEL O'BRIEN

According to his good friend, Dan Hortsch, Michael O'Brien had more friends and a broader range of friends than anyone Dan has ever known. Shortly after his death, one of Michael's sisters discovered his journal on his computer. Whether O'Brien had an audience in mind or not, it is hard to tell. He left no instructions about the journal, but must have been aware that it would be discovered.

Michael O'Brien committed suicide at the age of 50 on March 11, 1992, rather than suffer the trials of AIDS. The journal detailing his decision and plan to kill himself, published as "Dying has Turned out to be Complicated" (1997), resonates clearly with honesty, determination, confidence, some fear, and an amazing amount of humor. For instance, at the wake O'Brien planned and asked two close friends to carry out, friends of O'Brien's met for the first time and shared common stories about him. At his request, throughout the entire wake, a videotape of O'Brien swimming the swift and cold Columbia River in Oregon on Independence Day played continuously in the background as a testament to his pride at such an accomplishment and as a humorous farewell to his friends.

As his journal attests, O'Brien stayed aware of the ironies and complexities in planning his own death, his own funeral and wake, and the issue around the method of dying. Dan marveled at a memory of him and his wife meeting O'Brien for lunch shortly before O'Brien died. O'Brien told a story about a mistake he'd made in trying to fill a prescription that would be part of his suicide plan. Dan recalls the three of them laughing hysterically at this tale, marveling that even though the irony did not escape them, they could still make light of such a serious and emotional situation.

Although O'Brien took part in support groups and counseling available to AIDS patients, his private and independent ways seem to have been what sustained him throughout his decision. A bothersome rash is one of the common symptoms of this disease, and when a counselor in an AIDS support group suggested that the patients think of the rash as their friend, O'Brien could not accept such a concept and quit the group. Although he appreciated support, he did not want pity or sympathy, and befriending a symptom of such a violent and inevitably deadly disease was something he refused to do.

Michael O'Brien, an average man with an advanced journalism degree and a range of creative careers including owning a bookstore, wrestled remarkably with a disease we still know little about and a moral and political issue we still hotly debate—the right to end one's own life. O'Brien's journal is about his death. Do you think, though, that there is also a way in which it is a "composing" of his life?

Dying Has Turned Out To Be Complicated

It's a curious thing. Although I am mortally ill, people who don't know any better keep telling me how good I look.

On the one hand, that's funny, in a wry sort of way. Although I feel a touch hypocritical accepting their praise and thanking them for their comments, on the other hand, imagine if I told them what was really going on. As payback for a polite comment, usually in passing, they would get my impending death dumped on them. No, not the best of all possible ideas.

There's also the fact that most, if not all, of the people saying this are referring to the first part of this year when I was so sick—two different kinds of pneumonia and a blood clot, all within about a month and a half of each other. (The blood clot had nothing to do with AIDS. That was merely a free-lance piece of misery that happened by.) I lost 27 pounds and didn't work a full day for something like 2 1/2 months. Terrible, terrible time.

More terrible than is generally understood, too, since that was when I learned that I had a year left, give or take. Until then, I had thought it was about twice that much time.

I've known for 2 1/2 years that I was going to die of AIDS—to be precise, since Feb. 4, 1989, at 3:01 p.m., when my doctor told me I tested HIV positive—but I calculated then that I had four years or more. When I learned this past January that I had pneumocystis pneumonia, however, I also learned that I had only about a year left.

That was a strange time. In keeping with my usual pattern, I fall apart over little things, but handle the big ones—and I think we can all agree that impending death is a big one—like a champ.

So, for a couple of months, I just dealt with it. Made out my will. Talked to my sister Kathy about the whole thing, and about her being my executor. Told Ed at work about it, both because he's a good man and a friend, and also so he would understand what was happening when I start getting tired a lot.

Did other death-related things as well. Straightened up my place; put some things in file boxes; got rid of a lot of trash and extraneous stuff that wasn't worth keeping, or leaving behind for others to deal with; organized the stuff I kept; and wrote my obit and gave it to Dan to place in the paper.

Writing my own obit was passing strange. It also was somewhat otherworldly talking to the attorney about what I was doing and why I was doing it.

But without question, the most surpassingly strange moment of all was having to make the arrangements for my cremation. I just don't think things will get any weirder or more macabre than that.

Turned out the guy with whom I made the arrangements gets a significant percentage of his business that way. (He told me that because I asked him.) People who are about to undergo serious surgery, for example, often make arrangements with him. Rarely, however, do they tell him that they are going to kill themselves. I had to do that because I had to know if that was going to negate or complicate things for the guy, and for Kathy. With luck, it won't.

As for this matter of ending things myself, it seems to me to be not only a sensible approach, but also a responsible one. Consider:

15   AIDS is 100 percent fatal. It has no cure, and to pretend that there is one or might be one is a fool's game and a desperately stupid form of denial. Furthermore, Dylan Thomas' twaddle about "Do not go gentle into that good night/Rage, rage against the dying of the light" has always struck me as being stupefyingly vainglorious. I'm going to die, like the 150,000 or so people who already have died of this, I'm going to die fairly soon, and that's the name of that tune.

There is the very real misery and pain and sometimes outright agony of the patient, and of course, there is also the complete loss of his dignity during the disease's final stage. Wasting away, probably blind, likely mindless—I can say with as much certainty as I have about anything in this world that that is not how I will be remembered.

There is the matter of the unnecessarily prolonged pain that staying alive through the final stages brings to family and friends. Surely the only thing worse about this disease than having it is watching its ravages in somebody else.

Finally, reflecting my straight-arrow, Protestant work ethic kind of life, there is the matter of the obscene medical bills racked up and left for someone else to deal with.

So, yes, my intention is to kill myself, ideally with a drug overdose. This however, raises the problem of finding the means to my end. (Nice phrase, that.)

20   I have approached three people about getting the Seconal for me, two of whom turned me down, and one who said he would help and then didn't. Nor can I blame him. It's an awesome thing to have asked of you. I have to say immediately that I have been approaching others for help with this, not because I want to get other people

involved—Lord, no—and certainly not to shift the responsibility for my decision to somebody else.

I have gone to other people because I am so utterly innocent of knowledge about drugs, and so abysmally street dumb, that I simply don't know how to go about getting them myself. Whoever would have thought that would end up being a problem? Life just gets curiouser and curiouser.

Nonetheless, although I don't want to, it's beginning to look as though I am going to have to go to the street for the Seconal. This makes me exceedingly nervous because, first, I have never had dealings with a drug dealer in my life, and I'm sure that will be so obvious and could very well lead to some kind of rip-off. Second, the idea of dealing with a dealer goes counter to everything I know, and frankly it scares the hell out of me. (The irony of being more afraid of the means than of the end they are to lead to does not escape me.) Third, I don't even know how to begin to do such a thing. However, at this point at least, it's looking as though I have no choice.

One of the things that looms larger than usual in my particular universe is my job. On the one hand, at times it drives me crazy, and because I am supposed to avoid stress, that's not good. On the other, I am absolutely tied to the job and cannot possibly leave it.

One reason is that it provides me with a good salary so that I can continue to live at the level I find comfortable. but that's only about 10 percent of the reason I have to keep the job.

25   The other 90 percent is, in four words, Blue Cross/ Blue Shield. I simply could not afford to live without that. It's phenomenal how much of my medical bills the insurance covers—well more than 90 percent, I think—and it also pays for all of my medicine. One hundred percent.

Another reason I have to keep my job, a reason that ties me to it even more tightly than the medical insurance: If I were to get another job, I would have to get a physical. Obviously I can't do that.

Although the people at work don't realize it, I have become a kind of indentured servant. No matter what happens there, no matter what they might dump on me or demand of me, I have to put up with it. I have no choice.

Less melodramatically, the job also gives some structure to my life and allows me to get my mind off my illness as much as anything does.

Another, somewhat curious thing about my relationship with my job is that although the long-range plans and programs of the place are utterly without consequence for me and should play little or no part in my thinking, I find that they do. I continue to originate and promote new ideas, I continue to agitate for programs I think would do us and our members some good, and I continue to be upset with some we have in place. It makes no sense, but I guess it's like the patella tendon, just a reflexive action that can't be stopped.

30   This whole matter of knowing that I am dying has turned out to be complicated. Much more so than I had anticipated.

For one thing, I have had to involve far more people than I had thought would be the case. Just the mechanics of it have involved my doctor, my sister who will be my executor, her friend, the man who will cremate me, my lawyer and the people whom I've asked to get me the Seconal.

There also are the friends and colleagues whom I have felt obliged to tell, the ones close enough that it would be an insult if I didn't tell them and help prepare them for what is to come.

And even in that I see a complicating ethical problem.

How pure is my motive in telling these people? Am I really doing it because I don't want it to come as a shock to them when it happens? Or am I doing it to be sensational and to get an absolute lock on their attention? Unquestionably, the former plays a large part. And unfortunately, I think some of the latter is mixed in as well. And I hate that. Along with getting the drugs, this has become one of my biggest dilemmas.

35   But in most cases I just plunge in anyway and tell them I'm dying, tell them what the disease is, how long I've known, and the fact that I don't intend to go through the final phase.

By now I've worked out how to do this while expending a minimum of emotion. On either side. I couldn't get through it otherwise.

For example, I almost always use a public place—restaurants, usually, although I once used the Red Carpet Lounge at La Guardia in New York. I also almost never look at the person I'm telling and, most important, I use an absolutely flat, unemotional tone of voice. Even with those precautions, though, a few times I have found that I can't talk about one or another aspect of it without the strong possibility of breaking down. When that happens, I shut it off and move to another topic within the same area.

In only three or four cases have the people I've told actually cried, and a couple of those instances deeply surprised me. And touched me. And if I'd focused on it, I wouldn't have been able to continue. The ones who have cried also have made me worry all over again about my motives for telling them.

Lord, Lord, they ain't nothin' easy.

40   I'm still not entirely certain how I feel about this whole business of dying fairly soon.

The only thing I am certain about, in fact, is that it makes absolutely no difference how I feel about it. I am going to die, and I am going to do it soon, and no matter how I feel about it, that's not going to change. How I feel about it just flat doesn't signify.

Still and all, it's hard not to think about it, even though it's going to happen to everybody sooner or later. It's just happening to me sooner than I had expected.

For one thing, I'm not terribly frightened about it. In fact, I don't think I ever have been. As far as I can tell, it's always seemed to me to be something that's going to happen, and so it's kind of pointless and a waste of time to worry about it or be scared of it. When you're born, you begin to die. That sort of thing. I'll be joining The Great Majority after all. Also, just try rereading "After Many a Summer Dies the Swan" (Aldous Huxley novel written in 1939) to see what ludicrous lengths can be gone to when you're afraid of it. And, perhaps as much as anything else, I don't want to be ludicrous.

No, I think I view it as essentially a huge annoyance, a major inconvenience. It's going to prevent me from doing some things and accomplishing some things. I'll never see Machu Picchu. I'll never swim the Great Barrier Reef. I'll never have a book published. And so on.

45   I have some apprehension—not a whole lot—about what happens or doesn't happen afterward, but even that is pointless because I can't do anything about it.

I probably will cry the weekend I kill myself. That seems almost a certainty. But, like everything else, that's not going to make any difference about anything.

I will of course miss some things. One of them, dumb as it sounds, is the introduction of new car models. Ever since Chrysler bumped its model up a year back when I was a kid, I've been a sucker for new car introductions, and I'll miss those.

I also will miss the first few weeks of spring, really good rainstorms, the sound of a breeze as it goes through a tree, laughing and feeling warm with good friends, and my Wednesday night poker game. I'm not being trivial. That has been important to me from the first time I joined the group, and now it's one of the stabilizing factors in my life. If this is Wednesday, it must be poker night.

And now for a few words about the wonderful people who brought us my support group.

50   When I tested HIV positive, my doctor told me about HIV support groups. I signed up immediately, although with some misgivings. I wanted to see how other men in the same position were dealing with this on a day-to-day basis. Of course, I would have worked that out for myself eventually, but I figured that actually seeing them and watching them would accelerate the process. I was right, too.

     About half the guys in the group were really good guys. I am in touch with a few of them now, a couple of years later. Having said that, I've said about everything positive I know to say.

     Just on the annoyance level there were the awful phrases such as "Thank you for sharing that with us," and the programmed hugging. Not just once, but twice. I have never done well with hugging as an agenda item.

     The main thing that truly got to me was the institutionalized whining that the group fostered. I tend in that direction anyway (and, truth to tell, I did more than a bit of it in the group myself), but to have it formalized, institutionalized and, in fact, encouraged, as it was there, eventually made me want to throw up.

     The second major objection was the group dynamic that almost of necessity fostered the feeling that we were all special and somehow deserving of special treatment. Just as with acting like an invalid, I reject that utterly. For Pete's sake, I know people with real problems, people who are going to die and leave families behind, for example. Only one of us in the group had that problem. And we all were acting as though we were the only ones who had ever faced death. More than that, because we're afflicted with the AIDS virus, we also were pretending, or at the least I read it so, that we were just a little bit better than people facing death through other causes. Come on. Death is death. How you arrive there is ultimately meaningless.

55   Unexpectedly, I find some advantages to knowing my time is limited.

     For one thing, I don't have to worry about a lot of the silly things that worry people. For example, I can smoke with impunity now. It simply doesn't make any difference. In addition, although it never was high on my list of worries, my cholesterol count now means less than nothing, and I can have bacon and eggs and milk three times a day if I wish. And since I very much like all three, that's actually a small relief.

     A bigger thing is that I am truly lousy with money. All I've ever wanted is enough. Enough to do the reasonable things I want to do, enough to cover my bills and still have a little left over. And one of the ramifications is that I have—had—absolutely nothing set aside for retirement. And because I worry about a lot of dumb things, I used to worry about that, or at least think of it, probably daily. Now it is no longer a matter of concern.

It also is important to me to make a tidy exit, and this has certainly provided the impetus to do that. Not just things like the will and cremation arrangements, but even down to going through everything I own and getting rid of the junk. Amazing how good that felt.

Finally it gives me the chance to appreciate my friends more than I might otherwise, and to let them know the extent to which I have been honored by their kind regard.

Reflective Reading, Informal Writing

REFLECTING ON THE READING:

- O'Brien's journal suggests that there were several "pivotal points" at which he was forced to come to terms with the fact that "Dying has turned out to be complicated." List as many of these pivotal points as you can. What forced him to come to this knowledge? Some internal force? An external force?
- Implicit in O'Brien's journal entries is the theme of control. Clearly, he understands that he can't control the fact that he is going to die, but nonetheless he wants to be in control. What are those things he can control? What do you notice about how he writes about these issues?
- O'Brien's journal was printed in a metropolitan newspaper with a large public readership. Should it have been? Why or why not?
- How do you think O'Brien would have wanted readers to react to his writing about his dying (anger? sadness? neutrality?)? What clues are in his text that convince you of this?

UNDERSTANDING RHETORICAL STRATEGIES:

- Make a list of all the information we are given about O'Brien's journal (when it was written, where he kept it, how people know about it, etc.). Do you think he meant for this journal to be read? What in his journal makes you think it was or was not?
- Following up on the last question: Carefully examine the language of O'Brien's journal. Does he seem to be speaking solely to himself? Do you feel included as a reader? How would you characterize the tone and voice in his journal? Would you place this journal in the category of private writing or public writing? Why?

INFORMAL WRITING:

- Write about how comfortable (or uncomfortable) you were reading O'Brien's thoughts about his own death by AIDS. How do we tend to deal with death (and those dying) by AIDS in our culture? Do we deal with it differently from other kinds of death? Do you agree with O'Brien that "Death is death. How you arrive there is ultimately meaningless"? Think about how some would argue that those with AIDS deserve to die. Would they agree or disagree with O'Brien? With you?
- Imagine that you were in Mike O'Brien's shoes. In your own voice and way of seeing the world, write a two-page journal entry about having this fatal illness.
- Write a letter to Mike O'Brien, asking him anything you would like to about what it is like to be dying of AIDS or the way in which he chose to die.

JAMAICA KINCAID

Jamaica Kincaid was born in Antigua in the British West Indies as Elaine Potter Richardson. Her mother sent her to school at the age of three because she could not contain her energy at home. Kincaid eventually earned a scholarship to the Princess Margaret School after coming in second out of all the children tested on the island of Antigua to attend this school. Her "very Empire" education included listening to Shakespeare, Milton, Keats, the Brontës, and Hardy being read to the children outside under a tree. It may sound idyllic, but to Kincaid, "my whole upbringing was something I was not: it was English."

As a result, Kincaid left Antigua at age 17 to become an au pair in New York. She studied photography at the New York School for Social Research and attended Franconia College in New Hampshire. When she began working for *The New Yorker*, her writing career began. Kincaid did not feel like a part of her family in Antigua, nor a part of her new home in New York, so she changed her name from Elaine Potter Richardson when she started writing professionally and felt no connection to her given name. She chose Jamaica because she wouldn't go home to revisit that part of the world, so she re-created it in the form of her name.

She said Kincaid simply seemed to go with Jamaica. This comfortable choosing of a name without attaching any deeper meaning to it than a location and the sound of it suggests something of Kincaid's writing style. As in this excerpt from *My Brother* (1997), Kincaid comfortably dwells in ambiguities, honestly stating that an experience was neither good nor bad but accepting the moment for what it was. She defines the tone of her writing when she discusses her father-in-law, to whom she told things even though he didn't want to know them. His curiosity made him listen anyway. Kincaid does not tell her readers how to feel about any particular incident, but her detailed and honest report of what she sees, feels, and remembers creates a whole picture, leaving it up to the reader to feel good or bad or unsure. Even though readers may not share the experience of Kincaid's childhood in Antigua or her professional writing career in the United States, her writing has been labeled as universal, transcending geographical locations, cultures, and experiences and getting to the heart of something essential to many lives. In this excerpt from *My Brother* where she tells part of the story of her brother's death by AIDS, what seems universal or transcending?

My Brother

When I saw my brother again after a long while, he was lying in a bed in the Holberton Hospital, in the Gweneth O'Reilly ward, and he was said to be dying of AIDS. He was not born in this hospital.

Of my mother's four children, he was the one born at home. I remember him being born. I was thirteen years of age then. We had just finished eating our supper, a supper of boiled fish and bread and butter, and my mother sent me to fetch the midwife, a woman named Nurse Stevens, who lived on the corner of Nevis and Church Streets. She was a large woman; the two halves of her bottom rolled up and down with each step she took , and she walked very slowly. When I went to give her the message that my mother wanted her to come and assist with my brother's birth, she was just finishing her own supper and said that she would come when she was through. My brother was born in the middle of the night on the fifth of May in 1962. The color of his skin when he was born was a reddish-yellow. I do not know how much he weighed, for he was not weighed at the time he was born. That night, of course, the routine of our life was upset: the routine of my two other brothers and I going to sleep, our father taking a walk to a bridge near the recreation grounds—a walk recommended by his doctor as good for his bad digestive tract and for his bad heart—the heavy black of the streetlampless night falling, our father returning from his walk, a dog barking at the sound of his steps, the door opening and being locked behind him, the click of his false teeth as they were placed in a glass of water, his snoring, and then the arrival of early morning. We were sent to neighbors' houses. I do not remember exactly to whose house my other brothers were sent. I went to the house of a friend of my mother's, a woman whose six-year-old daughter took sick not so very long after this night of my brother's birth and died in my mother's arms on the way to the doctor, exhaling her last breath as they crossed the same bridge that my father walked to on his nightly outing. This was the first person to die in my mother's arms; not long after that, a woman who lived across the street from us, Miss Charlotte was her name, died in my mother's arms as my mother tried to give her some comfort from the pain of a heart attack she was having.

I heard my brother cry his first cry and then there was some discussion of what to do with his afterbirth, but I don't know now what was decided to do with all of it; only that a small piece of it was dried and pinned to the inside of his clothes as a talisman to protect him from evil spirits. He was placed in a chemise my mother had made, but because she had two other small children, my other brothers, one of them almost four years old, the other almost two years old, she could not give his chemise the customary elaborate attention involving embroidery stitching and special washings of the cotton fabric; the chemises he wore were plain. He was wrapped in a blanket and placed close to her, and they both fell asleep. That very next day, while they were both asleep, he snuggled in the warmth of his mother's body, an army of red ants came in through the window and attacked him. My mother heard her child crying, and when she awoke, she found him covered with red ants. If he had been alone, it is believed they would have killed him. This was an incident no one ever told my brother, an incident that everyone else in my family has forgotten, except me. One day during his illness, when my mother and I were standing over him, looking at him—he was asleep and so didn't know we were doing so—I reminded my mother of the ants almost devouring him and she looked at me, her eyes narrowing in suspicion, and she said, "What a memory you have!"—perhaps the thing she most dislikes about me. But I was only wondering if it had any meaning that some small red things had almost killed him from the outside shortly after he was born and that now some small things were killing him from the inside; I don't believe it has any meaning, this is only something a mind like mine would think about.

That Thursday night when I heard about my brother through the telephone, from a friend of my mother's because at that moment my mother and I were in a period of not speaking to each other (and this not speaking to each other has a life of its own, it is like a strange organism, the rules by which it survives no one can yet decipher; my mother and I never know when we will stop speaking to each other and we never know when we will begin again), I was in my house in Vermont, absorbed with the well-being of my children, absorbed with the well-being of my husband, absorbed with the well-being of myself. When I spoke to this friend of my mother's, she said that there was something wrong with my brother and that I should call my mother to find out what it was. I said, What is wrong? She said, Call your mother. I asked her, using those exact words, three times, and three times she replied the same way. And then I said, He has AIDS, and she said, Yes.

If she had said he had been in a terrible car accident, or if she had said he was suddenly stricken with a fatal cancer, I would have been surprised, for he did not drive a car—I knew that. What causes a fatal cancer? I do not know that. But he lived a life that is said to be typical in contracting the virus that causes AIDS: he used drugs (I was only sure of marijuana and cocaine) and he had many sexual partners (I only knew of women). He was careless; I cannot image him taking the time to buy or use a condom. This is a quick judgment, because I don't know my brothers very well, but I am pretty sure that a condom would not be something he would have troubled himself to use. Once, a few years ago when I was visiting my family—that is, the family I grew up in—I sat on his bed in the house he lived in alone, a house which was two arm's lengths from our mother's house, where she lived with another son, a grown man, I told him to use condoms when having sex with anyone; I told him to protect himself from the HIV virus and he laughed at me and said that he would never get such a stupid thing ("Me no get dat chupidness, man"). But I might have seemed like a ridiculous person to him. I had lived away from my home for so long that I no longer understood readily the kind of English he spoke and always had to have him repeat himself to me; and I no longer spoke the kind of English he spoke, and when I said anything to him, he would look at me and sometimes just laugh at me outright. You talk funny, he said. And then again, I was not fat, he had expected after not seeing me for twenty years that I would be fat. Most women where we are from become fat after a while; it is fashionable to be a fat woman.

5   When I saw my brother lying in the hospital bed, dying of this disease, his eyes were closed, he was asleep (or in a state of something like sleep, because sleep, a perfectly healthy and normal state to be in, could not be what he was experiencing as he lay there dying); his hands were resting on his chest, one on top of the other, just under his chin in that pious pose of the dead, but he was not dead then. His skin was a deep black color, I noticed that, and I thought perhaps I noticed that because I live in a place where no one is of his complexion, except for me, and I am not really of his complexion. I am only of his complexion in the way of race. But many days later my mother said to me, He has gotten so black, the disease has made him so black (she said this to me in this kind of English, she makes an effort to speak to me in de kind of English that I now immediately understand). His lips were scarlet and covered with small sores that had a golden crust. When he opened his eyes and saw me, he made a *truups* sound (this is done by placing the teeth together while pushing out both lips and sucking in air with force all at once). He said he did not think I would come to see him ("Me hear you a come but me no tink you a come fo' true").

At the time the phone call came telling me of my brother's illness, among the many comforts, luxuries, that I enjoyed was reading a book, *The Education of a Gardener,* written by a man named Russell Page. I was in the process of deciding that as a gardener who designed gardens for other people he had the personality of the servant, not the personality of the artist, that his prose was fussy, tidy, timid; though the book bored me I would continue to read it because it offered such an interesting contrast to some other gardeners whose writing I loved. (I only thought all that before the phone rang. I now love *The Education of a Gardener* and look forward to reading it again.) And so when the phone rang I put this book down and answered it and I was told about my brother.

The next time I opened this book I was sitting on the lawn in front of the Gweneth O'Reilly ward and my brother was sitting in a chair next to me. It was many days later. He could barely walk, he could barely sit up, he was like an old man. The walk from his bed to the lawn had exhausted him. We looked out on the ordinary Antiguan landscape. There was a deliberate planting of willow trees, planted, I suspect, a long time ago, when Antigua was still a colony and the colonial government would have been responsible for the running of the hospital. It was never a great hospital, but it is a terrible hospital now, and only people who cannot afford anything else make use of it. Near the willow trees was an old half-dead flamboyant tree; it needed pruning and food. There was an old lopsided building in the near distance; and the rest of the landscape was taken up with cassi (cassia) trees. And when I picked up that book again, *The Education of a Gardener,* I looked at my brother, for he was a gardener also, and I wondered, if his life had taken a certain turn, if he had caused his life to take a different turn, might he have written a book with such a title? Behind the small house in which he lived in our mother's yard, he had planted a banana plant, a lemon tree, various vegetables, various non-flowering shrubs. When I first saw his little garden in the back of his little house, I was amazed at it and I asked him if he had done it all himself and he said, Of course, ("How you mean, man!"). I know now that it is from our mother that we, he and I, get this love of plants. Even at that moment when he and I were sitting on the lawn, our mother had growing on a trellis she had fashioned out of an old iron bedstead and old pieces of corrugated galvanize a passion-fruit vine, and its voluptuous growth was impressive, because it isn't easy to grow passion fruit in Antigua. It produced fruit in such abundance that she had to give some of it away, there was more than she could use. Her way with plants is something I am very familiar with; when I was a child, in the very place where my brother's house is now, she grew all sorts of vegetables and herbs. The red ants that attacked him when he was less than a day old had crawled up some okra trees that she had planted too near the house and the red ants went from okra trees through a window onto the bed in which he and my mother lay. After she killed all the red ants that had attacked her child, she went outside and in a great fit of anger tore up the okra trees, roots and all, and threw them away.

I only now understand why it is that people lie about their past, why they say they are one thing other than the thing they really are, why they invent a self that bears no resemblance to who they really are, why anyone would want to feel as if he or she belongs to nothing, comes from no one, just fell out of the sky, whole.

For one day when my mother and I were outside in the back yard and she was complaining, though she did not know it, of how dependent on her one or the other of her children was, and did not notice that she did this all the time, said bad things to each of us about the others behind their back, I noticed that the lemon tree my sick brother had planted was no longer there and I asked about it, and she said quite casually, Oh, we cut it down to make room for the addition. And this made me look at my feet immediately, involuntarily; it pained me to hear her say this, it pained me the way she said it, I felt ashamed. That lemon tree would have been one of the things left of his life. Nothing came from him; not work, not children, not love for someone else. He once had a job doing something in the public works department, but he talked back too much—he had a nasty tongue when crossed, my mother said—and one day in an argument with his supervisor he said something rude ("He cuss dem out") and was fired. Someone told me he had made a lot of money then. He gave my mother a lot of it to save for him, but after he was out of work he would often ask her for some of it, until eventually there was nothing left, and when he became sick he was destitute, without any financial support at all. This did not seem to worry him; I could not tell if it had any meaning. When his father, my mother's husband, died, he left my mother a pauper and she had to borrow money to bury him. My brother did not have a steady girlfriend, a woman, someone other than his own mother, to take care of him; he had no children, as he lay dying, his friends had abandoned him. No one, other than the people in his family and his mother's friends from her church, came to visit him.

10   But this too is a true picture of my mother: When he was ill, each morning she would get up very early and make for her sick son a bowl of porridge and a drink of a fortified liquid food supplement and pack them in a little bag and go to the hospital, which is about a mile away and involves climbing up a rather steep hill. When she set out at about half past six, the sun was not yet in the middle of the sky so it was not very hot. Sometimes someone would give her a lift in a car, but most often no one did. When she got to the hospital, she would give my brother a bath, and when she was doing that she wouldn't let him know that she saw that the sore on his penis was still there and that she was worried about it. She first saw this sore by accident when he was in the hospital the first time, and when she asked him how he got such a thing, he said that from sitting on a toilet seat he had picked up something. She did not believe or disbelieve him when he told her that. After she bathed him, she dressed him in the clean pajamas she brought for him, and if his sheets had not been changed, she changed them and then while he sat in bed, she helped him to eat his food, the food she had prepared and brought to him.

When I first saw him, his entire mouth and tongue, all the way to the back of the inside of his mouth, down his gullet, was paved with a white coat of thrush. He had a small sore near his tonsil, I could see it when he opened his mouth wide, something he did with great effort. This made it difficult for him to swallow anything, but especially solid food. When he ate the porridge and drank the fortified liquid food supplement that my mother had brought for him, he had to make such an effort, it was as if he were lifting tons upon tons of cargo. A look of agony would come into his eyes. He would eat and drink slowly. Our mother, who loves to cook and see people eat the food she has cooked, especially since she knows she is an extremely good cook, would urge him to eat whenever she saw him pause ("Come on, man, yam up you food") and he would look at her helplessly. Ordinarily he would have made his own sharp reply, but at those moments I do not think one crossed his mind. After she saw him eat his breakfast, she would tidy up his room, put his dirty clothes and bath towel in a bag to be taken home and washed; she would empty the pan that contained his urine, she would rub cream into the parched skin on his arms and legs, she would comb his hair as best she could. My mother loves her children, I want to say, in her way! And that is very true, she loves us in her way. It is *her way.* It never has occurred to her that her way of loving us might not be the best thing for us. It has never occurred to her that her way of loving us might have served her better than it served us. And why should it? Perhaps all love is self-serving. I do not know, I do not know. She loves and understands us when we are weak and helpless and need her. My own powerful memories of her revolve around her bathing and feeding me. When I was a very small child and my nose would become clogged up with mucus, the result of a cold, she would place her mouth over my nose and draw the mucus into her own mouth and then spit it out; when I was a small child and did not like to eat food, complaining that chewing was tiring, she would chew my food in her own mouth and, after it was properly softened, place it in mine. Her love for her children when they are children is spectacular, unequaled I am sure in the history of a mother's love. It is when her children are trying to be grown-up people—adults—that her mechanism for loving them falls apart.; it is when they are living in a cold apartment in New York, hungry and penniless because they have decided to be a writer, writing to her, seeking sympathy, a word of encouragement, love, that her mechanism for loving falls apart. Her reply to one of her children who found herself in such a predicament was "It serves you right, you are always trying to do things you know you can't do." Those were her words exactly. All the same, her love, if we are dying, or if we are in jail, is so wonderful, a great fortune, and we are lucky to have it. My brother was dying; he needed her just then.

In this overbearingly charming reminiscence of how he became a gardener, Russell Page writes:

> When I was a child there was a market each Friday in the old Palladian butter market near the Stonebow in Lincoln. The farmers' wives would drive in early in the morning, dressed in their best, with baskets of fresh butter, chickens, ducks and bunches of freshly picked mint and sage. I used often to be taken there by my grandfather's housekeeper while she made her purchases, and I remember that always, in the spring, there would be bunches of double mauve primroses and of the heavenly scented *Daphne mezereum.* Later when my passion for gardening developed I wanted these plants but could

never find them in our friends' gardens. They seemed to grow only in cottage gardens in hamlets lost among the fields and woods. I gradually came to know the cottagers and their gardens for miles around, for these country folk had a knack with plants. Kitchen windows were full of pots with cascades of *Campanula isophylla,* geraniums, fuchsias and begonias all grown from slips. I would be given cuttings from old-fashioned pinks and roses which were not to be found in any catalogue, and seedlings from plants brought home perhaps by a sailor cousin—here was a whole world of modest flower addicts.

What would my brother say were he to be asked how he became interested in growing things? He saw our mother doing it. What else? This is what my family, the people I grew up with, hate about me. I always say, Do you remember? There are twelve banana plants in the back of his little house now, but years ago, when I first noticed his interest in growing things, there was only one. I asked my mother how there came to be twelve, because I am not familiar with the habits of this plant. She said, "Well . . ." and then something else happened, a dog she had adopted was about to do something she did not like a dog to do, she called to the dog sharply, and when the dog did not respond, she threw some stones at him. We turned our attention to something else. But a banana plant bears one bunch of fruit, and after that, it dies; before it dies it will send up small shoots. Some of my brother's plants had borne fruit and were dying and were sending up new shoots. The plantsman in my brother will never be, and all the other things that he might have been in his life have died; but inside his body a death lives, flowering upon flowering, with a voraciousness that nothing seems able to satisfy and stop.

15   I am so vulnerable to my family's needs and influence that from time to time I remove myself from them. I do not write to them. I do not pay visits to them. I do not lie, I do not deny, I only remove myself. When I heard that my brother was sick and dying, the usual deliberation I allow myself whenever my family's needs come up—should I let this affect me or not?—vanished. I felt I was falling into a deep hole, but I did not try to stop myself from falling. I felt myself being swallowed up in a large vapor of sadness, but I did not try to escape it. I became afraid that he would die before I saw him again; then I became obsessed with the fear that he would die before I saw him again. It surprised me that I loved him; I could see that was what I was feeling, love for him, and it surprised me because I did not know him at all. I was thirteen years old when he was born. When I left our home at sixteen years of age, he was three years of age. I do not remember having particular feelings of affection or special feelings of dislike for him. Our mother tells me that I liked my middle brother best of the three of them, but that seems an invention on her part. I think of my brothers as my mother's children.

When he was a baby, I used to change his diapers, I would give him a bath. I am sure I fed him his food. At the end of one day, when he was in the hospital and I had been sitting with him for most of the time, watching his body adjust to the AZT, medicine I had brought to him because I had been told that it was not available in Antigua, I said to him that nothing good could ever come of his being so ill, but all the same I wanted to thank him for making me realize that I loved him, and he asked if I meant that ("But fo' true?") and I said yes, I did mean that. And then when I was leaving for the day and I said good night to him and closed the door behind me, my figure passed the louvered window of his room and from his bed, lying on his back, he could see me, and he called out, "I love you." That is something only my husband and my children say to me, and the reply I always make to them is the reply I made to him: "I love you, too."

He was lying in a small room with a very high ceiling, all by himself. In the hospital they place patients suffering from this disease in rooms by themselves. The room had two windows, but they both opened onto hallways so there was proper ventilation. There was a long fluorescent light hanging from the high ceiling. There was no table lamp, but why should there be, I only noticed because I have become used to such a thing, a table lamp; he did not complain about that. There was a broken television set in a corner, and when there were more than two visitors in the room it was useful as something on which to sit. It was dirty room. The linoleum floor was stained with rust marks; it needed scrubbing; once he spilled the pan that contained his urine and so the floor had to be mopped up and it was done with undiluted Clorox. He had two metal tables and a chair made of metal and plastic. The metal was rusty and the underside of this furniture was thick with dirt. The walls of the room were dirty, the slats of the louvered windows were dirty, the blades of the ceiling fan were dirty, and when it was turned on, sometimes pieces of dust would become dislodged. This was not a good thing for someone who had trouble breathing. He had trouble breathing.

Sometimes when I was sitting with him, in the first few days of my seeing him for the first time after such a long time, seeing him just lying there, dying faster than most people, I wanted to run away, I would scream inside my head, What am I doing here, I want to go home. I missed my children and my husband. I missed the life that I had come to know. When I was sitting with my brother, the life I had come to know was my past, a past that does not make me feel I am falling into a hole, a vapor of sadness swallowing me up. In that dirty room, other people before him had died of that same disease. It is where they put people who are suffering from the virus that causes AIDS. When he first told me that he had tested positive for the virus, he did not tell our mother the truth, he told her he had lung cancer, he told someone else he had bronchial asthma, but he knew and my mother knew and anyone else who was interested would know that only people who tested positive for the AIDS virus were placed in that room for isolation.

I left him that first night and got into a car. I left him lying on his back, his eyes closed, the fluorescent light on. I rode in a hired car and it took me past the Magdalene maternity ward, where I was born, past the place where the Dead House used to be (a small cottage-like structure where the bodies of the dead were stored until their families came to claim them), but it is not there anymore; it was torn down when it grew rotten and could no longer contain the smells of the dead. And then I came to a major crossing where there was a stoplight, but it was broken and had been broken for a long time; it could not be fixed because parts for it are no longer made anywhere in the world—and that did not surprise me, because Antigua is a place like that: parts for everything are no longer being made anywhere in the world; in Antigua itself nothing is made. I passed the prison, and right next to it the school my brother attended when he was a small boy and where he took an exam to go to the Princess Margaret School, and in the exam, which was an islandwide exam, he took third place of all the children taking this exam. I passed the Princess Margaret School. It was when he got to this school that he started to get into trouble. My mother says, about the friends he made there, that he fell into bad company, and I am sure the mothers of the other boys, his friends, thought of him in the same way— as bad company. It was while attending this school that he became involved in a crime, something to do with robbing a gas station, in which someone was killed. It was agreed that he did not pull the trigger; it is not clear that he did not witness the actual murder. At some point, years ago, my mother told me that he had spent a short time in jail for this crime and she got him out through political connections she then had but does not have any longer. Now she will not mention the murder or his time in jail. If I should bring it up, she says it is an old story ("e' a' ole time 'tory; you lub ole-time 'tory, me a warn you"), and for my mother an old story in a bad story, a story with an ending she does not like.

20   The car then turned onto Fort Road and passed Straffee's funeral establishment. I did not know then whether Mr. Straffee was dead or alive; when I was small child and saw him, I thought he looked like the dead, even though at the time I thought that, I had never seen a dead person. I passed a house where my godmother used to live; she was a seamstress, she had been very nice to me. I do not know what has become of her. And I passed the road where Englishman, Mr. Moore, who used to sell my mother beefsteak tomatoes, lived. This man also had cows, and one day when I was

going to visit my godmother, they were returning from pasture and I saw them coming toward me, and I was so afraid of those cows that I threw myself into a ditch facedown and waited until I knew they had gone by. The road has been widened and the ditch is no more. I passed the place where the Happy Acres Motel used to be. It, too, is no more. On a road that led from this hotel a friend of our family used to live, a friend whom my brothers would not have known because by the time they were born my mother no longer spoke to this person. The friend reared pigs and guinea hens and chickens and also cultivated an acre or so of cotton. At the height of their friendship my mother had bought shares in a sow this friend of hers owned, and also, since it was at the height of their friendship, I was sent one year to spend August holidays with her. This part of Antigua was considered the country then, and I was terrified of the darkness, it was so unrelieved by light even from other houses; also from the house where I lived I could see the St. John's city grave-yard, and it seemed to me that almost every day I could see people attending a funeral. It was then I decided that only people in Antigua died, that people living in other places did not die and as soon as I could, I would move somewhere else, to those places where the people living there did not die. After another minute or so of driving, the car arrived at the inn where I was staying and I went into my room alone, my own isolation.

My mother and I almost quarreled over this, that I would not stay in her house with her. She told a friend of hers, a woman my age, this, knowing that her friend would repeat it to me. I could have said to my mother, You and I do not get along, I am too well, I am not a sick child, you cannot be a mother to a well child, you are a great person but you are a very bad mother to a child who is not dying or in jail; but I did not say that. A few years ago, when she was visiting me in Vermont, we had an enormous quarrel and I then asked her if she could at all say that she was sorry for some of the pain I believe she caused me, whether she meant to or not. And she said then, I am never wrong, I have nothing to apologize for, every-thing I did at the time, I did for a good reason. Even now, years later, I am still surprised by this, because I spend a good part of my day on my knees in apology to my own children. That time when my mother was visiting me and we had the enormous quarrel, she told a friend of mine, a woman who she knew was very devoted to me, that the reason I did not like her was that when I was a girl she had been very strict with me and if she had not been I would have ended up with ten children by ten different men. It is a mystery to me still why my mother would think I would not be grateful to someone who saved me from such a fate. As an illustration of how strict she had been with me, she told my friend that I loved books and loved reading and there was a boy who used to come around looking for me, and to hide his true intentions, when he saw her he would say that he had come to me to borrow books; she grew sick of listening to this excuse for his coming around to see me and one day she told him not to come to her house anymore because it was not a library. My friend only told me all this because she wanted to say to me that my mother feels that she loves me very much. But after my mother left, I was sick for three months. I had something near to a nervous breakdown, I suffered from anxiety and had to take medicine to treat it; I got the chicken pox, which is a disease of childhood and a disease I had already had when I was a child. Not long after she left, I had to see a psychiatrist.

My brother who was lying in the hospital dying, suffering from the virus that causes AIDS, told the brother who is two years older than he is, the brother I am eleven years older than, that he had made worthlessness of his life ("Me mek wutlessness ah me life, man"). He told my mother that he was sorry he had not listened to her when all the time she told him not to behave in the way he had been, not to conduct his life so heedlessly, not to live so much without caution, that he had been to too careless. He was sorry now that he lay dying that he had not listened to her and used to think all the things she said she had said only because she was an old lady. He said to me that he couldn't believe he had AIDS ("Me carn belieb me had dis chupidness"). Only he could not say the words AIDS or HIV, he referred to his illness as stupidness ("de chupidness").

After I saw my brother that first time and returned to the place I was staying, the place that was not my mother's house, I went to the manageress and said, "I need a drink." I have heard people say just that before, "I need a drink," but I thought it was a figure of speech, I had never needed a drink or any other kind of mood alterer before; I have taken mood-altering substances many times, but I never felt I needed them. I drank five rum-and-Cokes. I do not like the taste of rum, really, and I do not like the taste of Coke, really, but I drank five of these drinks all the same and could have drunk more than five but did not. The manageress, a very nice woman, sat next to me and we struck up a conversation; I told her my brother was sick and in the hospital, and when she asked me the cause of his illness I told her he had AIDS. This disease, in Antigua, produces all the prejudices in people that it produces elsewhere, and so like many other places, the people afflicted with it and their families are ashamed to make their suffering known. It was for my own peace of mind that I said it; I wanted it to be real to me, that my brother was suffering and dying from AIDS; hearing that he was sick and dying was new to me and so every opportunity I got I would say it out loud: "My brother is sick from and dying of AIDS." But my announcing it to this woman led to something. She told me of a doctor in Antigua who she said was always on the radio or television talking about the danger of AIDS, how it could be contracted and how to avoid contracting it. He was considered the leading authority in Antigua in regard to this disease (though in fact he was the only doctor in Antigua who was publicly involved with this disease). She said his name was Dr. Ramsey. The next day I looked him up in the telephone book and I called him.

The reason my brother was dying of AIDS at the time I saw him is that in Antigua if you are diagnosed with the HIV virus you are considered to be dying; the drugs used for slowing the progress of the virus are not available there; public concern, obsession with the treatment and care of members of the AIDS-suffering community by groups in the larger non-AIDS-suffering community, does not exist. There are only the people suffering from AIDS, and then the people who are not suffering from AIDS. It is felt in general, so I am told, that since there is no cure for AIDS it is useless to spend money on a medicine that will only slow the progress of the disease; the afflicted will die no matter what; there are limited resources to be spent on health care and these should be spent where they will do some good, not where it is known that the outcome is death. This was the reason why there was no AZT in the hospital; but even if a doctor had wanted to write a prescription for AZT for a patient, that prescription could not be filled at a chemist's; there was no AZT on the island, it was too expensive to be stocked, most people suffering from the disease could not afford to buy this medicine; most people suffering from the disease are poor or young, not too far away from being children; in a society like the one I am from, being a child is one of the definitions of vulnerability and powerlessness.

25   When I called Dr. Ramsey I asked him if he would meet me at the hospital and examine my brother and give us, his family, medical advice, as to what we could do, what we could not do, what we could expect and, perhaps, when to expect it. He agreed to meet me and at the time he said he would arrive, he arrived. I only mention this because in Antigua people never arrive when they say they will; they never do what they say they will do. He was something I had long ago thought impossible to find in an Antiguan with authority: he was kind, he was loving toward people who needed him, people who were less powerful than he; he was respectful. He greeted my brother as if they were old friends; he spoke to him of cricket, of calypso, and of a trip he had taken to Trinidad to celebrate the carnival there. He examined my brother with his bare hands, he felt his neck, he listened to his breathing through an stethoscope, he looked in my brother's mouth, at his throat, and he made me look at the large ulcer

that was near his tonsils. After he was done, he sat and talked to my brother some more; he spoke to him in broken English; I could not understand what they were saying, they spoke very fast, it was the most animated I had seen my brother since I first say him lying there dying. He even laughed out loud at something Dr. Ramsey said, something I did not understand.

Afterward Dr. Ramsey told me that since my brother did not yet have diarrhea, one of the symptoms common to AIDS suffers in the Caribbean, there was a chance that AZT could slow the progress of the disease and allow my brother to live longer than we thought; certainly it would alleviate some of his immediate suffering. When I had heard about my brother, I asked my mother with what medicines he has been treated and she said they were giving him something for pneumonia and something else for thrush, medicines a doctor at the hospital had given her a prescription for and she had gone to a pharmacy in town and purchased. These medicines common in the treatment of AIDS-related illnesses are not kept in the hospital; people who are not infected with the virus that causes AIDS do not get an extreme case of thrush, do not get a terrible kind of pneumonia, and so the medicines that would treat these afflictions are not on hand at the hospital. But then this: one night my brother had a terrible headache and needed something to ease the pain; there was no aspirin on the ward where he was staying and no aspirin in the dispensary. A nurse on duty had some in her purse for her own personal use and she gave my brother two of them. There are people who complain that a hospital in the United States will charge six dollars for a dose of Tylenol; they might wish to look at this way of running a hospital: bring your own medicines.

When my mother told me AZT could not be obtained in Antigua, I called someone I know, a friend who is a doctor, and I asked her if she would write a prescription for a month's worth. She said yes immediately, and said she would give me more if it was necessary. I was used to this sort of kindness. I did not know then if even a month's worth would be of any use to him. She gave me a prescription for a more powerful drug than the one he was taking to treat the pneumonia he had and a more powerful drug that the one he was taking to treat his thrush; when I first saw him, the thrush had made it so difficult for him to swallow anything that the pills had to be crushed before he could swallow them.

After he saw my brother, Dr. Ramsey told me that, with one exception, he had not seen anyone over the age of thirty-two suffering from AIDS. The exception was a man sixty-six years of age. He said that in August one year, in a two-week period, seven people, young people, all under thirty-two, had died of the disease. As far as he could tell, the people who died did not know each other. He said that people who are not HIV-positive give up too soon on the people who are, but that he tries to keep everybody alive, because you never know when a cure might come along. He said that—you never knew when a cure might come along—and I could not tell if, in that, he was asserting native Antiguan foolishness or faith in science. Antigua is a place in which faith undermines the concrete. He said my brother did not look too bad, he had seen people who looked worse; what he meant of course is he had seen people who were on the verge of dying, and by the time he saw them, it was too late to do anything. But what he could do, I wanted to ask him, if there was no medicine available, if the people suffering did not have a sister who lived in the United States and this sister could call up a doctor who would write a prescription for some medication that might be of help, what would happen then? He is a very loving man and the other reason I have for saying this is I saw that wherever he went, people, ordinary people, would go out of their way to greet him and ask him how he was, but not because they really wanted to know: it was just to hear his voice.

I went to hear Dr. Ramsey give a lecture about AIDS and other sexually transmitted diseases to a group of twelve people who were attending a workshop on counseling the HIV-afflicted. I had never seen any of their faces before. Among them were a man and a woman, Antiguans, whose thirty-year-old daughter had died of AIDS. She was their only child. They carried with them pictures of her which they showed to the other people in the workshop. They were attending this workshop because they hoped to be able, if need be, to give solace to other parents who might also find themselves losing a child to this disease. This was something very new to me: ordinary people in Antigua expressing sympathy and love for one another at a time of personal tragedy and pain, not scorn or rejection or some other form of cruelty. Dr. Ramsey explained to us what the HIV virus is, how it behaves in the body, how a virus behaves and how the HIV virus, a retrovirus, differs from a normal virus, but I cannot really remember any of it because he showed extraordinary slides of people in various stages of affliction from sexually transmitted diseases. The pictures were amazing. There were penises that looked like ladyfingers left in the oven too long and with a bite taken out of them that revealed a jam-filled center. There were labias covered with thick blue crusts, or black crusts, or crusts that were iridescent. There were breasts with large parts missing, eaten away, not from a large bite taken at once but nibbled, as if by an animal in a state of high enjoyment, each morsel savored for maximum pleasure. There were pictures of people emaciated by disease, who looked very different from people emaciated from starvation; they did not have that parched look of flesh and blood evaporated, leaving a wreck of skin and bones; they looked like the remains of a black hole, something that had once burned brightly and then collapsed in on itself. These images of suffering and death were the result of sexual activity, and at the end of Dr. Ramsey's talk, I felt I would never have sex again, not even with myself. This feeling I had of pleasure being overwhelmed by fear and death was not new; I remembered how as a child when I was living in Dominica with my mother's family I would look up at a black sky with a big moon full of light in it and the large mountains in the distance silhouetted against the mysterious (to me, a small girl) horizon, and I would find this the most beautiful, the most wonderful thing in the world, but then I would see a light moving about in the mountains and knew that it was a jablessé and would run inside to bed and pull the sheets over my head. And lying in bed with the sheets over my head, I would become afraid to fall asleep with the sheets over my head because I might suffocate and die. . . .

30   And that night he was dying in the dark of that small room, thirty-three years of age, with none of the traditional attachments ordinary to a man his age—thirty-three—a wife, a companion of some kind, children, his own house, even a house he rented, his own bed (I had gone to a furniture store one day and purchased the one which he lay dying on, and even as I did that, I could remember his father, Mr. Drew, repairing the crib that he lay in when he was a baby just born, but that crib was first made for Joe and then refurbished for Dalma and then refurbished again for his birth; I don't remember that too much attention was lavished on the crib by the time he arrived, because his arrival pushed the family to a brink over which we all fell, our family was never the same after his birth).

He had read in a novel written by me about a mother who had tried and tried and failed and failed to abort the third and last of her three male children. And when he was dying he asked me it that mother was his mother and if that child was himself ("Ah me de trow'way pickney"); in reply, I laughed a great big Ha! Ha! and then said no, the book he read is a novel, a novel is a work of fiction; he did not tell me that he did not believe my reply and I did not tell him that he should not believe my reply.

That night as he lay dying and calling the names of his brothers and sisters and his mother, he did not call my name, and I was neither glad nor sad about this. For why should he call my name? I knew him for the first three years of his life, I came to know him again in the last three years of his life, and in the time between I had changed my name, I did not have the name our mother had given to me, and though he always called me by the new name I had given myself, he did not know the self I had become (which isn't to say that I know this, the self I have become), he did not know who I was, and I can see that in the effort of dying, to make sense of me and all that had happened to me between the years he was three and thirty was not only beyond him but also of no particular interest to him. And that feeling of his lack of interest in me, his sister, not being included in the roll call of his family, seemingly forgotten by him in the long hours before he left the world, seems so natural, so perfect; he was so right! I had never been a part of the tapestry, so to speak, of Patches, Styles, and Muds; I had only heard about the time he was involved in murdering a gas-station attendant and our mother used her substantial political connections to get him out of jail, his sentence reduced because he became a witness against the others, his friends, who along with him were involved in this murder, and then his emerging to live a life made up of strong feelings (positive feelings) for a man who was king of a small country in a landlocked part of Africa (Haile Selassie of Ethiopia), smoking the leaves of a plant which would cause him to have hallucinations. I shall never forget him, my brother, but this was not because of his smile, or the way he crossed a swelling river and saved a dog, or his sense of humor, or his love of John Milton (he loved not so much John Milton as all the people who came after and were influenced by John Milton; but all the people he met who came after John Milton and were influenced by John Milton were servants in the British colonial enterprise); I shall never forget him because his life is the one I did not have, the life that, for reasons I hope shall never be too clear to me, I avoided or escaped. Not his fate, for I, too, shall die, only his life, with its shadows dominating the brightness, its shadows eventually overtaking its brightness, so that in the end anyone wanting to know him would have to rely on that, shadows; and in the shadows of his life is a woman emerging from an audience in a bookstore in Chicago and telling me the secrets in his life, his life as he lived it in the shadows.

And at the time he was dying, all through that night, all through the night I was a continent away, seated in an airplane as it flew through the dark atmosphere, then sitting in the falsely lighted rooms in the airport, waiting for planes to transport me home to my family, traveling through these spaces in a natural dark and then a false light, carrying plants (those rhododendrons, native to a part of the world, New Guinea, that was foreign to me but has shaped my memory all the same: plants that would make prosper a population of annoying small flies in my house and then die, and nothing I could do, no remedy in any of many plant encyclopedias I have, could save them. They bloomed beautifully and then died, dying, as always, being so irreversible).

My mother's house after he was dead was empty of his smell, but I did not know that his dying had a smell until he was dead and no longer in the house, he was at the undertaker's, and I never asked my mother about the smells in the house. I wanted to see what he looked like when he was dead and so I had asked the undertaker not to do anything to his body before I arrived. Only now, a little more than a year later, I wonder how I knew to say such a thing, for I am grateful (only because I would have wondered, been haunted about it, and so now my interest is satisfied, even as it raises another kind of interest, another haunting) that I did, but at the time it happened—he was dead, I had been told so—I felt removed from events, I wished something else was happening, I wished I was complaining about some luxury that was momentarily causing me disappointment: the lawn mower wouldn't work, my delicious meal in a restaurant was not at an ideal temperature, a meadow I loved to walk past never achieved a certain beauty that I wanted it to achieve.

35   He was in a plastic bag with a zipper running the length of its front and middle, a plastic bag of good quality, a plastic bag like the ones given to customers when they buy an expensive suit at a store that carries expensive clothing. The zipper coming undone sounded just like a zipper coming undone, like a dangerous reptile warning you of its presence; oh, but then again, it was so much like the sound of a zipper, just any zipper, or this particular zipper, the zipper of the bag which held my brother's body (for he was that, my brother's body). He looked as if he had been deliberately drained of all fluids, as if his flesh had been liquefied and that, too, drained out. He did not look like my brother, he did not look like the body of my brother, but that was what he was all the same, my brother who had died, and all that remained of him was lying in a plastic bag of good quality. His hair was uncombed, his face was unshaven, his eyes were wide-open, and his mouth was wide-open, too, and the open eyes and the open mouth made it seem as if he was looking at something in the far distance, something horrifying coming toward him, and that he was screaming, the sound of the scream silent now (but it had never been heard, I would have been told so, it had never been heard, this scream), and this scream seemed to have no break in it, no pause for an intake of breath; this scream only came out in one exhalation, trailing off into eternity, or just trailing off to somewhere I do not know, or just trailing off into nothing.

My husband's father had died four years before, and when I had seen him dead, I had a strong desire to tell him what it was like when he died, all the things that happened, what people said, what they did, how they behaved, how his death made them feel; he would not have liked hearing about it at all, I knew that, but I also know how curious he was about experiences he did not like or want to have, and that one of the ways I became a writer was by telling my husband's father things he didn't want me to tell him but was so curious about that he would listen to them anyway.

My brother would not have wanted to hear how he looked when he died, he would not have wanted to know how everyone be-

haved, what they said and what they did. He would not have
wanted to know anything about it, except if someone had a mishap;
an embarrassing mishap would have made him laugh, he loved to
laugh at other people's mishaps, I cannot remember him showing
sympathy, and yet I do not remember him being cruel, his own
mother was cruel. He would have found his death—his lying in the
plastic bag of good quality, his mouth open, his eyes staring into
something, a void that might hold all of meaning, or staring into
nothing in particular—funny, but only if it was happening to someone else. I do not know, I do not know. And when next I saw him
again, lying in the coffin made of pitch pine, the wood which Mr.
Drew, his father, my mother's husband, a carpenter, used mainly to
make all sorts of furniture, his hair was nicely combed and dyed
black—for how else could it have gotten to such a color—his lips
were clamped tightly together and they made a shape that did not
amount to his mouth as I had known it; and his eyes had been sewn
shut, sewn shut, and I have to say it again, sewn shut. And so he
looked like an advertisement for the dead, not like the dead at all;
for to be dead young cannot be so still, so calm, only the still alive
know death to be still and calm; I only say this after having seen my
brother just dead, before the people still in life arranged him. My
mother said that the body in the coffin did not look like her son at all
("E no look like 'e, 'e no look like Devon"), and that was true, but it
was only that he did not look like the Devon we had gotten used to
looking at as he got sick and then declined amazingly into death, living while being dead. She forgot that for a long time he did not look
like Devon, the Rastafarian, the reggae singer, the seducer of women
(we did not and cannot now know what he looked like as the seducer of men), that the body in the coffin was of someone we did not
know, the body lying there would never become familiar to us, it
would have no likes and dislikes, it would never say anything mem-
orable, we would never quarrel with it, he was dead. The undertaker went among the mourners asking if we wanted one last look
before the coffin lid was put in place, and after that all views of him
on this earth would be no more.

Such a moment, a final goodbye, must be complicated. I put it
this way, "must be," because this was something happening in my
life, a real thing, something so important that I wanted my own children to witness it. I had taken them with me to visit him, I had taken
them with me when he died, and they, too, viewed his body before
the undertaker had transformed him from someone just dead to
someone ready to be seen just before his burial. And so, goodbye. My
mother looked at him for the last time, his brothers looked at him for
the last time, I looked at him for the last time, my children looked at
him for the last time, my mother's friends from her church looked at

him for the last time, some men his age who knew him from school, who had not seen him when he was sick but now attended his funeral, looked at him for the last time. Oh, the indignity to be found in death; just as well that the dead seem unable to notice it.

It was in the funeral home in which he lay that I first encountered the dead. The dead then was a girl with a hunchback and I did not know her, I only saw her on the street in her school uniform, but her deformity had made her well known to other schoolchildren who were not deformed at all, and so when she died I wanted to see what she looked like. Seeing her lying in her coffin created a sense of wonder in me; seeing my brother did not, but that might have been because by the time my brother died I was so old that the idea of death seemed possible, but still only possible, something other people might decide to do. When I had seen the girl with the hunchback lying dead in her coffin, my brother was not yet born, and even my own life, the life that I now live, was not yet born, and so I could not imagine, would not have been capable of wondering, if this place, Straffee's funeral parlor (the funeral parlor where the girl lay, the funeral parlor where my brother lay), would resonate in me, would come up in any way in my life again. My brother's body lay not in the same room as hers, he lay in the room next to the one in which her body had been; the funeral parlor had expanded, and in any case, the room in which she had lain held another body, another funeral, a man thirty-five years old who also had died of AIDS, or the virus that causes AIDS, or something like that; whatever is the right way to say it, he had died of the same thing as my brother. Mr. Straffee, the owner of the funeral parlor, died in the same year as my brother; Mr. Straffee was very old then, and I cannot tell if he got involved in such, the business of burying people, to accustom himself to the idea of his own death, or if he hoped such an intimacy with death would protect him from its actual occurrence, or lessen his fear of its actual occurrence.

40   My brother's coffin was most plain, it was in the category of the ones that cost less, pitch pine stained with a very dark varnish. I had known how much it would cost, and so before I returned for his funeral I went to the bank in the small town in which I lived and purchased traveler's checks. The undertaker took payment in traveler's checks.

His funeral procession was not large, and there might have been many reasons for this. He had died of a disease that carried a powerful social stigma. People in the place that I am from are quite comfortable with the shame of sex, the inexplicable need for it, an enjoyment of it that seems beyond the ordinary, the actual peculiarity of it; only then when you die from it, sex, does the shame become, well, shame. Then he was not a well-known person, a famous person, and this would have disappointed him, he so longed to be well known and well thought of. Funerals in Antigua have always been social events, especially the funerals of young people, but he was not so young, he was not well known, he died of a disease that had a great shame attached to it.

His death, and so his funeral, was not like that of the little boy, only four years old, who died while taking a swimming lesson with his schoolmates in the seawater at Fort James, just died suddenly, fainting, losing consciousness and then dying, and that is what was said of his death; he just died suddenly, while learning to swim; he fainted and lost consciousness and then died. He lay in a refrigerator in a funeral home, the same funeral home that took care of my brother's burial, while his mother's and father's relatives who were living in various parts of the world, all far away from Antigua, in climates different from the one in Antigua, returned to Antigua. His mother and some close female relatives of both his parents all wore brand-new dresses made from the same material, though not in the same style, and also, they did not show their feelings of sorrow at the same time. The church service part of this little boy's funeral was held in the same church in which my brother (and I) had been christened and confirmed (the Methodist church, though in that tradition you are received not confirmed), and I had no real feelings when I saw that his coffin was in the same place, in front of the altar where I had taken my first communion and just plain communion many times after that. I was, at that moment I was seeing his coffin, trying to find my brother's doctor, Dr. Prince Ramsey. The church was filled with the dead four-year-old boy's relatives and their friends, people were standing on the steps of the church trying to see the little coffin and of course the family, because the sorrow expressed by the family, the sorrow shown by the family excites observers, evoking pity for the mourner and, ultimately, superiority, for to see someone suffer in a moment when you are not suffering can inspire such a feeling, superiority, in a place like Antigua, with its history of subjugation, leaving in its wake humiliation and inferiority; to see someone in straits worse than your own is to feel at first pity for them and soon better than them. And so it was that a large number of people who did not know this little boy or any member of his family but had heard of his death though hearsay had come to see his little coffin, something made out of cheap wood and then covered with white velvet, and had come to see his family suffer over their loss. His little classmates stood not far from the coffin, and later they sang a song about Jesus and his particular love for children. The children were not at the graveyard, and so they did not see his mother as she wept over his coffin being lowered into the ground and his mother weeping and throwing up nothing but mucus, the only thing left in her stomach. The children did not see this, but many onlookers did, they saw the mother vomiting nothing but mucus at the sight of her son's coffin being lowered into the ground, and the father, her husband, holding her up after she had slumped to the ground, and then leading her away from the grave to sit on a grave nearby, a grave of someone I do not believe they knew, yet it was a good place to sit all the same. I was at the graveyard still looking for Dr. Ramsey, but he was not there, and when next I saw him in the graveyard, it was at my brother's funeral, and between that boy's burial and my brother's death I saw and spoke to Dr. Ramsey many times, but on that day I did not see him.

And so my brother's funeral; the undertaker (and it was not at that moment that I first made the observation that an undertaker often looks like a corpse in one way or another: bloated like a dead body that has been neglected, or thin and emaciated like a dead body properly preserved so that it decays slowly, dryly, or like a dead body that has been carefully manicured and tended to make the relatives doubt slightly the sight they are witnessing: I am looking at the dead)—the undertaker called us, his family, to take a last look at him, and this call for a last look only reminded me of scenes in other narrative forms in which there is a bartender and just before the bar closes there is a last call for drinks. We all looked at him, I and his and my mother, my brother who no longer speaks to my mother even though they continue to live in the same house, and my other brother, who broke my mother's neck by throwing her onto the ground in the process of trying to stop her from throwing stones at him because she disapproved of him bringing a girlfriend, or any woman with whom he had a sexual relationship, into the structure where he—they all—lived; this structure was so near to my mother's own house that she could hear all their conversations and all their sounds, and the conversations and sounds were an abomination to her (and that is the word for the feelings that roiled in her heart toward his actions, his wanting to live: abomination!), and when he would not cease this behavior of which she disapproved she first quarreled with him and then threw stones at him, and while trying to stop her from stoning him (and this was not exactly a defense of himself, for I say a defense of himself would have been to throw stones back at her), he threw her to the ground and broke her neck; it was a break so serious that she should have died or become a quadriplegic, yet she recovered so completely that she has buried one of her own children. When once she was complaining to me about her health, I jokingly said, "Oh, Mother, you will bury us all"; she said in reply, "You think so," and she laughed, but I did not laugh, I could not laugh, I was—am—one of the "us." There were her two sons still alive, and then there was me, her only daughter, but not Devon's only sister in the world, for his father, Mr. Drew, had had other girl children with other mothers, but I was his only sister at his funeral, and I, too, went to take a last look at him, but it was unreal the way he looked: his hair styled in a way I had never seen it styled when I knew him alive; his eyes closed, shut, sealed, like an envelope, not a vault; his body was delicate, fragile-seeming, all bones, finally stilled, not ever so slightly moving up and down; his farawayness so complete, so final, he shall never speak again; he shall never speak again in the everyday that I speak of speech.

The coffin lid was put in place and the sounds of the screws securing it did not cause us to cry or vomit or pass out. My mother said it did not look like Devon at all, and that was true, but I did not know which Devon she meant: Was it the baby a day old almost eaten alive by red ants, or was it the two-year-old boy who was left in my charge and whose diaper I neglected to change as it became filled with his still-baby feces because I had become absorbed in a book; or was it the Devon who was involved in the homicide of a gas-station attendant; or the one who played cricket so well and learned to swim at Country Pond; or the one who smoked the Weed, the way she referred to his marijuana addiction; or the one who changed from a vibrant young man who had come down with a very bad case of pneumonia and then was told in an open hospital ward by a doctor accompanied to two nurses that he had the HIV virus and that shortly he would be dead; or the one who was well enough shortly after that to begin having unprotected sex with women and sex with other people who were not women but who we—that is, his family—did not know about? Which Devon was he? All of them, I suppose; and which did he like best, and which one of his selves made him happiest? I cannot tell this, and perhaps neither could he.

45   And that day that he was buried was not at all unlike the day on which I first saw him lying almost dead in a bed in the Gweneth O'Reilly ward of the Holberton Hospital. All days in Antigua must be the same, people count on it, it is for this reason they go there, it is for this reason they leave there; the days are the same, the sun shines, no rain will fall, the sun rises at around six in the morning, the sun sets at around six in the evening; if this does not remain so, it is a catastrophe; a hurricane can change this, or the coming-awake of a volcano, but Antigua does not have such a thing as a volcano. He died on a sunny day, he was buried on a sunny day. At the funeral parlor there were people milling around outside and I did not know them, but that made sense when I realized that there was another young man being buried, a young man with a family and not many friends; he too, had died of AIDS. His grave was not more than twenty yards away from my brother's, and their graveside ceremonies coincided; the families and friends of the two dead men did not speak to one

another; the two men were buried at the margins of the cemetery, far away from the entrance, and this was so not because of the thing that had caused their death but because of something that long ago perhaps had the same social stigma as AIDS: they or their families were not members of respectable churches. The other man was buried in the place reserved for Seventh-Day Adventists, my brother was buried in the place reserved for the Church of the Nazarene. Nothing about their death ceremonies made communication between their families occur; not sharing the same funeral parlor, not sharing the margin of the burial ground. The other dead man's family did not say a sympathetic word to us and we did not say a sympathetic word to them. The Church of the Nazarene was our mother's church, she attended services there regularly, her fellow church members came often to pray with my brother, though he did not believe in anything himself, except if he thought, just at that moment he needed to, that faith in the thing in front of him might serve him well. But he died, and on the way to the church part of the service, we passed some men who were in a yard, sitting under a tree making coffins, and they looked up as we passed by, perhaps to see their handiwork, for his coffin had been made by them, they worked for Mr. Straffee, and also out of curiosity, for it must be true for them, too, even as they make these houses for the dead that are in constant demand, the wondering if it is something real, will it happen to them; if it is so certain, death, why is it such a surprise, why is everybody who is left behind, who is not dead, in a state of such shock, as if this thing, death, this losing forever of someone who means something to you, has never happened before. Why is it so new, why is this worn-out thing, death, someone dying, so new, so new?

And yet when the minister preached a sermon about us all being reunited at some later date, I did not like that at all, I wanted to tell him that I did not want to see these people with whom I had shared so much—a womb in the case of my brother, blood and breath in the case of my mother—I did not want to be with any of these people again in another world. I had had enough of them in this one; they mean everything to me and they mean nothing, and even so, I do not really know what I mean when I say this. My brother, the one who lives in the same house as my mother but who does not speak to her and will not make a reply to her no matter what she says to him, and says he would not make a reply to her even if she asked him to save her life, especially if she asked him to save her life (and he is not the one who threw her down and broke her neck, a break that should have left her dead of crippled from the waist down and instead she made a complete recovery and has buried one of her children so far), this brother said a few words about the dead sibling, the one he had named "Patches," but he did not mention that, the part about the name Patches, he only recalled that Devon loved to play cricket, how close they had been when they were schoolboys together; he did not say how afraid they were when their father (Mr. Drew) died and they did not want to attend his funeral and hid from our mother, who had to beat them (in one case) or threaten to beat them (in another case) to attend; he did not say how his dead brother's carelessness with his own life might have led to such an early death and was a contrast to his own caution and industriousness (he held three jobs: an accountant, a peddler of imported foods in the market, and a bass-steel-drum player in the most prominent steel band in Antigua). His voice broke as he spoke of his brother; I cried when I heard him speak of his brother, but why did he and I do that, for so many times we used to say that if by some miracle Devon could be cured of his disease he would not change his ways; he would not become industrious, holding three jobs at once to make ends meet; he would not become faithful to one woman or one man. But this was the end and he was lying in the coffin, the least expensive coffin in Mr. Straffee's display of coffins for adults; he was thin, so diminished that his bedclothes and bed linen, freshly cleaned by his mother, had to be packed inside the coffin to keep his body from rattling around (though really he would not have been able to hear it and he certainly would not have been able to feel it).

I became a writer out of desperation, so when I first heard my brother was dying I was familiar with the act of saving myself: I would write about him. I would write about his dying. When I was young, younger than I am now, I started to write about my own life and I came to see that this act saved my life. When I heard about my brother's illness and his dying, I knew, instinctively, that to understand it, or to make an attempt at understanding his dying, and not to die with him, I would write about it.

For many years I wrote for a man named William Shawn. Whenever I thought of something to write, I immediately thought of him reading it, and the thought of this man, William Shawn, reading something I had written only made me want to write it more; I could see him sitting (not in any particular place) and reading what I had written and telling me if he liked it, or never mentioning it again if he didn't, and the point wasn't to hear him say that he liked it (though that was better than anything in the whole world) but only to know that he had read it, and why that should have been so is beyond words to me right now, or just to put it into words now (and it was only through words that I knew him) would make it either not true, incomplete, like love, I suppose: why do I love you, why do you love me? Almost all of my life as a writer, everything I wrote I expected Mr. Shawn to read, and so when I first heard of my brother dying and immediately knew I would write about him, I thought of

Mr. Shawn, but Mr. Shawn had just died, too, and I had seen Mr. Shawn when he was dead, and even then I wanted to tell him what it was like when he had died, and he would not have liked to hear that in any way, but I was used to telling him things I knew he didn't like, I couldn't help telling him everything whether he liked it or not. And so I wrote about the dead for the dead, and all along as I was writing I thought, When I am done with this I shall never write for Mr. Shawn again, this will be the end of anything I shall write for Mr. Shawn; but now I don't suppose that will be so. It was because I had neglected my brother when he was two years old and instead read a book that my mother gathered up all the books I owned and put them on a pile on her stone heap, sprinkling them with kerosene and then sitting them alight; I cannot remember the titles of these books, I cannot remember what they were about (they would have been novels, at fifteen I read only novels), but it would not be so strange if I spent the rest of my life trying to bring those books back to my life by writing them again and again until they were perfect, unscathed by fire of any kind. For a very long time I had the perfect reader for what I would write and place in the unscathed books; the source of the books has not died, it only comes alive again and again in different forms and other segments. The perfect reader has died, but I cannot see any reason not to write for him anyway, for I can sooner get used to never hearing from him—the perfect reader— than to not being able to write for him at all.

Reflective Reading, Informal Writing

REFLECTING ON THE READING:

- Kincaid's book is entitled *My Brother*, and is, of course, about her brother's death by AIDS. In what ways is the excerpt about Kincaid herself and her relationship both to her brother and to AIDS? What happens to and for Kincaid as she comes to terms with her brother's dying and ultimately his death?
- As Kincaid writes about her brother's death, she also writes about life (his birth, her own family back in Vermont, memories from her childhood). In fact, she spends a great deal of time talking about the book *The Education of a Gardener* and various plants, flowers, and trees. Why does she use all of this plant imagery? How does it relate to her brother's AIDS?
- On page 491, Kincaid goes to great lengths to describe the filth of the room her brother is dying in. In part, Kincaid wants her description to bring us into the present just as she is, so that we too can ex-

perience it. What other motives might she have for such a concrete, painful description?

UNDERSTANDING RHETORICAL STRATEGIES:

- Even though Kincaid is greatly moved by her brother's condition and feels that things might have turned out differently if he had more money or lived someplace besides Antigua, she never directly points a finger of blame. How does she let us know she is not just telling a story about AIDS but also making a commentary on society's response to AIDS, or at least certain people with AIDS? Look for specific passages and examine how they work to achieve Kincaid's purpose.
- Why does Kincaid, in the last few pages, bring Mr. Shawn into her narrative? What purpose does he serve? What does she want us to understand?
- Kincaid writes:

  I became a writer out of desperation, so when I first heard my brother was dying I was familiar with the act of saving myself: I would write about him. I would write about his dying. When I was young, younger than I am now, I started to write about my own life and I came to see that this act saved my life. When I heard about my brother's illness and his dying, I knew, instinctively, that to understand it, or to make an attempt at understanding his dying, and not to die with him, I would write about it.

  What does she mean by this? Why would she die with him? How could writing keep her from dying with him? Do you think there is any way in which this writing keeps both of them alive?

INFORMAL WRITING:

- Write about the differences and/or similarities in tone, style, genre, and purpose in "Dying Has Turned Out to br Complicated" and the selection from *My Brother*.
- What have you learned about AIDS from these "unscientific," more personal accounts of what it means to die of AIDS?

SUSAN SONTAG

Susan Sontag is most known as a critic, essayist, and scholar of modernism. Her multigenre and multimedia work in writing, film, philosophy, and art attest to her diverse ways of interpreting the world. Sontag graduated from high school at the age of 15 and enrolled in University of California, Berkeley, that same year. She graduated from the University of Chicago with a bachelor's degree in 1951, earned her master's degree in English at Harvard University in 1954, her master's degree in philosophy in 1955, and was a Ph.D. candidate in 1955–1957. The multitude of degrees and publications confirms Sontag's reputation as an American intellectual and part of the foundation of works on modernist writing and Western culture.

Sontag sparked reactions from intellectuals and readers when she began publishing her writing. Her ability to offend and ignite discussion formed part of her popularity. She was admired for her often shocking work and made criticism a "medium of intellectual scandal" that earned her celebrity status. Although Sontag has been criticized for overwhelming readers with intimidating language and pretentious writing, her work remains remarkably accessible on a first read and invites a second and third read to garner the deeper, underlying messages and ideas presented in her work.

In 1976, Sontag was diagnosed with breast cancer and given six months to live if she did not immediately undergo surgery. She told a reporter in 1978 that facing death "added a fierce intensity to my life" an intensity she turned toward her writing. By looking at the assumptions underneath the metaphors we use to talk about illnesses, Sontag unearths our desire to blame, victimize, and hide from illness. She looks at the cultural myths that have developed around disease and the meaning we invest in illness beyond its physical debilitation. In looking at our metaphors for illness, Sontag helps us move beyond them and unmask our fears so we face illness for what it is, not what we imagine it to mean or be.

Sontag fights against using sickness as a way of interpreting a person's character or looking for causes of an illness in a person's actions, thoughts, behavior, or personality. For instance, tuberculosis sufferers were once thought to have caused the disease or been susceptible to the disease because of their excess of feeling; their passion and expression of emotion brought on the deadly disease. Conversely, cancer was thought to be brought on by a repression of emotion and desire; those repressed feelings fermented inside and became cancer. She questions our use of military metaphors to talk about illness and of disease as an "invasion," which makes a patient a victim, and invites questions about persons contracting this disease—whether it was somehow deserved, and whether they are guilty or innocent. Such questions have nothing to do with the actual illness.

Particularly in this excerpt from *AIDS and Its Metaphors* (1988), Sontag shows us the power of language and the power of interpretation. Much of the pain and suffering surrounding illnesses like cancer and AIDS stem from our language defining these illnesses and our fears about them. In changing our language, we can change our perceptions about illness and perhaps find a better way of dealing with and "curing" the diseases contemporary cultures face. As you read, consider carefully what Sontag's argument might mean for how we respond to AIDS as an illness and to those who are ill with it.

from *AIDS and Its Metaphors*

1

By metaphor I meant nothing more or less than the earliest and most succinct definition I know, which is Aristotle's, in his *Poetics* (1457b). "Metaphor," Aristotle wrote, "consists in giving the thing a name that belongs to something else." Saying a thing is or is like something-it-is-not is a mental operation as old as philosophy and poetry, and the spawning ground of most kinds of understanding, including scientific understanding, and expressiveness. (To acknowledge which I prefaced the polemic against metaphors of illness I wrote ten years ago with a brief, hectic flourish of metaphor, in mock exorcism of the seductiveness of metaphorical thinking.) Of course, one cannot think without metaphors. But that does not mean there aren't some metaphors we might well abstain from or try to retire. As, of course, all thinking is interpretation. But that does not mean it isn't sometimes correct to be "against" interpretation.

Take, for instance, a tenacious metaphor that has shaped (and obscured the understanding of) so much of the political life of this century, the one that distributes, and polarizes, attitudes and social movements according to their relation to a "left" and a "right." The terms are usually traced back to the French Revolution, to the seating arrangements of the National Assembly in 1789, when republicans and radicals sat to the presiding officer's left and monarchists and conservatives sat to the right. But historical memory alone can't account for the startling longevity of this metaphor. It seems more likely that its persistence in discourse about politics to this day comes from a felt aptness to the modern, secular imagination of metaphors drawn from the body's orientation in space—left and right, top and bottom, forward and backward—for describing social conflict, a metaphoric practice that did add something new to the perennial description of society as a kind of body, a well-disciplined body ruled by a "head." This has been the dominant metaphor for

the polity since Plato and Aristotle, perhaps because of its usefulness in justifying repression. Even more than comparing society to a
family, comparing it to a body makes an authoritarian ordering of
society seem inevitable, immutable.

Rudolf Virchow, the founder of cellular pathology, furnishes
one of the rare scientifically significant examples of the reverse
procedure, using political metaphors to talk about the body. In the
biological controversies of the 1850s, it was the metaphor of the
liberal state that Virchow found useful in advancing his theory of
the cell as the fundamental unit of life. However complex their
structure, organisms are, first of all, simply "multicellular"—mul-
ticitizened, as it were; the body is a "republic" or "unified commonwealth." Among scientist-rhetoricians Virchow was a maverick,
not least because of the politics of his metaphors, which by mid-
nineteenth-century standards, are antiauthoritarian. But likening
the body to a society, liberal or not, is less common than compar-
isons to other complex, integrated systems, such as a machine or
an economic enterprise.

At the beginning of Western medicine, in Greece, important
metaphors for the unity of the body were adapted from the arts.
One such metaphor, harmony, was singled out for scorn several
centuries later by Lucretius, who argued that it could not do justice
to the fact that the body consists of essential and unessential organs, or even to the body's materiality: that is, to death. Here are
the closing lines of Lucretius' dismissal of the musical metaphor—
the earliest attack I know on metaphoric thinking about illness and
health:

5

> Not all organs, you must realize,
> Are equally important nor does health
> Depend on all alike, but there are some—
> The seeds of breathing, warm vitality—
> Whereby we are kept alive, when these are gone
> Life leaves our dying members. So, since mind
> And spirit are by nature part of man,
> Let the musicians keep that term brought down
> To them from lofty Helicon—or maybe
> They found it somewhere else, made it apply
> To something hitherto nameless in their craft—
> I speak of *harmony*. Whatever it is,
> Give it back to the musicians.

—*De Rerum Natura*, III, 124–35
trans. Rolfe Humphries

A history of metaphoric thinking about the body on this potent
level of generality would include many images drawn from other
arts and technology, notably architecture. Some metaphors are
anti-explanatory, like the sermonizing, and poetic, notion enunci-

ated by Saint Paul of the body as a temple. Some have considerable scientific resonance, such as the notion of the body as a factory, an image of the body's functioning under the sign of health,
and of the body as a fortress, an image of the body that features
catastrophe.

The fortress image has a long prescientific genealogy, with illness itself a metaphor for mortality, for human frailty and vulnerability. John Donne in his great cycle of prose arias on illness,
Devotions upon Emergent Occasions (1627), written when he thought
he was dying, describes illness as an enemy that invades, that lays
siege to the body-fortress:

> We study Health, and we deliberate upon our meats, and drink, and
> ayre, and exercises, and we hew and wee polish every stone, that goes
> to that building; and so our Health is a long and a regular work; But in
> a minute a Canon batters all, overthrows all, and demolishes all; a
> Sicknes unprevented for all our diligence, unsuspected for all our cu-
> riositie . . . .

Some parts are more fragile than others: Donne speaks of the brain
and the liver being able to endure the siege of an "unnatural" or "rebellious" fever that "will blow up the heart, like a mine, in a
minute." In Donne's images, it is the illness that invades. Modern
medical thinking could be said to begin when the gross military
metaphor becomes specific, which can only happen with the advent
of a new kind of scrutiny, represented in Virchow's cellular pathology, and a more precise understanding that illnesses were caused by
specific, identifiable, visible (with the aid of a microscope) organisms. It was when the invader was seen not as the illness but as the
microorganism that causes the illness that medicine really began to
be effective, and the military metaphors took on new credibility and
precision. Since then, military metaphors have more and more come
to infuse all aspects of the description of the medical situation.
Disease is seen as an invasion of alien organisms, to which the body
responds by its own military operations, such as the mobilizing of
immunological "defenses," and medicine is "aggressive," as in the
language of most chemotherapies.

10   The grosser metaphor survives in public health education,
where disease is regularly described as invading the society, and efforts to reduce mortality from a given disease are called a fight, a
struggle, a war. Military metaphors became prominent early in the
century, in campaigns mounted during World War I to educate people about syphilis, and after the war about tuberculosis. One example, from the campaign against tuberculosis conducted in Italy in the
1920s, is a poster called *"Guerra alle Mosche"* (War against Flies),
which illustrates the lethal effects of fly-borne diseases. The flies
themselves are shown as enemy aircraft dropping bombs of death on

an innocent population. The bombs have inscriptions. One says *"Microbi,"* microbes. Another says *"Germi della tisi,"* the germs of tuberculosis. Another simply says *"Malattia,"* illness. A skeleton clad in a hooded black cloak rides the foremost fly as passenger or pilot. In another poster, "With These Weapons We Will Conquer Tuberculosis," the figure of death is shown pinned to the wall by drawn swords, each of which bears an inscription that names a measure for combating tuberculosis. "Cleanliness," is written on one blade. "Sun" on another. "Air." "Rest." "Proper food." "Hygiene." (Of course, none of these weapons was of any significance. What conquers—that is, cures—tuberculosis is antibiotics, which were not discovered until some twenty years later, in the 1940s.)

Where once it was the physician who waged *bellum contra morbum,* the war against disease, now it's the whole society. Indeed, the transformation of war-making into an occasion for mass ideological mobilization has made the notion of war useful as a metaphor for all sorts of ameliorative campaigns whose goals are cast as the defeat of an "enemy." We have had wars against poverty, now replaced by "the war on drugs," as well as wars against specific diseases, such as cancer. Abuse of the military metaphor may be inevitable in a capitalist society, a society that increasingly restricts the scope and credibility of appeals to ethical principle, in which it is thought foolish not to subject one's actions to the calculus of self-interest and profitability. War-making is one of the few activities that people are not supposed to view "realistically"; that is, with an eye to expense and practical outcome. In all-out war, expenditure is all-out, unprudent—war being defined as an emergency in which no sacrifice is excessive. But the wars against diseases are not just calls for more zeal, and more money to be spent on research. The metaphor implements the way particularly dreaded diseases are envisaged as an alien "other," as enemies are in modern war; and the move from the demonization of the illness to the attribution of fault to the patient is an inevitable one, no matter if patients are thought of as victims. Victims suggest innocence. And innocence, by the inexorable logic that governs all relational terms, suggests guilt.

Military metaphors contribute to the stigmatizing of certain illnesses and, by extension, of those who are ill. It was the discovery of the stigmatization of people who have cancer that led me to write *Illness as Metaphor.*

Twelve years ago, when I became a cancer patient, what particularly enraged me—and distracted me from my own terror and despair at my doctors' gloomy prognosis—was seeing how much the very reputation of this illness added to the suffering of those who have it. Many fellow patients with whom I talked during my initial hospitalizations, like others I was to meet during the subsequent two and a half years that I received chemotherapy as an outpatient in several hospitals here and in France, evinced disgust at their disease and a kind of shame. They seemed to be in the grip of fantasies about their illness by which I was quite unseduced. And it occurred to me that some of these notions were the converse of now thoroughly discredited beliefs about tuberculosis. As tuberculosis had been often regarded sentimentally, as an enhancement of identity, cancer was regarded with irrational revulsion, as a diminution of the self. There were also similar fictions of responsibility and of a characterological predisposition to the illness: cancer is regarded as a disease to which the psychically defeated, the inexpressive, the repressed—especially those who have repressed anger or sexual feelings—are particularly prone, as tuberculosis was regarded throughout the nineteenth and the early twentieth centuries (indeed, until it was discovered how to cure it) as a disease apt to strike the hypersensitive, the talented, the passionate.

These parallels—between myths about tuberculosis to which we can all feel superior now, and superstitions about cancer still given credence by many cancer patients and their families—gave me the main strategy of a little book I decided to write about the mystifications surrounding cancer. I didn't think it would be useful—and I wanted to be useful—to tell yet one more story in the first person of how someone learned that she or he had cancer, wept, struggled, was comforted, suffered, took courage . . . though mine was also that story. A narrative, it seemed to me, would be less useful than an idea. For narrative pleasure I would appeal to other writers; and although more examples from literature immediately came to mind for the glamorous disease, tuberculosis, I found the diagnosis of cancer as a disease of those who have not really lived in such books as Tolstoy's "The Death of Ivan Ilyich," Arnold Bennett's *Riceyman Steps,* and Bernanos's *The Diary of a Country Priest.*

15   And so I wrote my book, wrote it very quickly, spurred by evangelical zeal as well as anxiety about how much time I had left to do any living or writing in. My aim was to alleviate unnecessary suffering—exactly as Nietzsche formulated it, in a passage in *Daybreak* that I came across recently:

> *Thinking about illness!*—To calm the imagination of the invalid, so that at least he should not, as hitherto, have to suffer more from thinking about his illness than from the illness itself—that, I think, would be something! It would be a great deal!

The purpose of my book was to calm the imagination, not to incite it. Not to confer meaning, which is the traditional purpose of literary endeavor, but to deprive something of meaning: to apply that quixotic, highly polemical strategy, "against interpretation," to the real world this time. To the body. My purpose was, above all, practical. For it was my doleful observation, repeated again and again, that the metaphoric trappings that deform the experience of having cancer have very real consequences: they inhibit people from seeking treatment early enough, or from making a greater effort to get competent treatment. The metaphors and myths, I was convinced, kill. (For instance, they make people irrationally fearful of effective measures such as chemotherapy, and foster credence in thoroughly useless remedies such as diets and psychotherapy.) I wanted to offer other people who were ill and those who care for them an instrument to dissolve these metaphors, these inhibitions. I hoped to persuade terrified people who were ill to consult doctors, or to change their incompetent doctors for competent ones, who would give them proper care. To regard cancer as if it were just a disease—a very serious one, but just a disease. Not a curse, not a punishment, not an embarrassment. Without "meaning." And not necessarily a death sentence (one of the mystifications is that cancer = death). *Illness as Metaphor* is not just a polemic, it is an exhortation. I was saying: Get the doctors to tell you the truth; be an informed, active patient; find yourself good treatment, because good treatment does exist (amid the widespread ineptitude). Although *the* remedy does not exist, more than half of all cases can be cured by existing methods of treatment.

In the decade since I wrote *Illness as Metaphor*—and was cured of my own cancer, confounding my doctors' pessimism—attitudes about cancer have evolved. Getting cancer is not quite as much of a stigma, a creator of "spoiled identity" (to use Erving Goffman's expression.) The word cancer is uttered more freely, and people are not often described anymore in obituaries as dying of a "very long illness." Although European and Japanese doctors still regularly impart a cancer diagnosis first to the family, and often counsel concealing it from the patient, American doctors have virtually abandoned this policy; indeed, a brutal announcement to the patient is now common. The new candor about cancer is part of the same obligatory candor (or lack of decorum) that brings us diagrams of the rectal-colon or genito-urinary tract ailments of our national leaders on television and on the front pages of newspapers—more and more it is precisely a virtue in our society to speak of what is supposed *not* to be named. The change can also be explained by the doctors' fear of lawsuits in a litigious society. And not least among the reasons that cancer is now treated less phobically, certainly with less secrecy, than a decade ago is that it is no longer the most feared disease. In recent years some of the onus of cancer has been lifted by the emergence of a disease whose charge of stigmatization, whose capacity to create spoiled identity, is far greater. It seems that societies need to have one illness which becomes identified with evil, and attached blame to its "victims," but it is hard to be obsessed with more than one.

2

Just as one might predict for a disease that is not yet fully understood as well as extremely recalcitrant to treatment, the advent of this terrifying new disease, new at least in its epidemic form, has provided a large-scale occasion for the metaphorizing of illness.

20 Strictly speaking, AIDS—acquired immune deficiency syndrome—is not the name of an illness at all. It is the name of a medical condition, whose consequences are a spectrum of illnesses. In contrast to syphilis and cancer, which provide prototypes for most of the images and metaphors attached to AIDS, the very definition of AIDS requires the presence of other illnesses, so-called opportunistic infections and malignancies. But though not in *that* sense a single disease, AIDS lends itself to being regarded as one—in part because, unlike cancer and like syphilis, it is thought to have a single cause.

AIDS has a dual metaphoric genealogy. As a micro-process, it is described as cancer is: an invasion. When the focus is transmission of the disease, an older metaphor, reminiscent of syphilis, is invoked: pollution. (One gets it from the blood or sexual fluids of infected people or from contaminated blood products.) But the military metaphors used to describe AIDS have a somewhat different focus from those used in describing cancer. With cancer, the metaphor scants the issue of causality (still a murky topic in cancer research) and picks up at the point at which rogue cells inside the body mutate, eventually moving out from an original site or organ to overrun other organs or systems—a domestic subversion. In the description of AIDS the enemy is what causes the disease, an infectious agent that comes from the outside:

> The invader is tiny, about one sixteen-thousandth the size of the head of a pin. . . . Scouts of the body's immune system, large cells called macrophages, sense the presence of the diminutive foreigner and promptly alert the immune system. It begins to mobilize an array of cells that, among other things, produce antibodies to deal with the threat. Single-mindedly, the AIDS virus ignores many of the blood cells in its path, evades the rapidly advancing defenders and homes in on the master coordinator of the immune system, a helper T cell . . . .

This is the language of political paranoia, with its characteristic distrust of a pluralistic world. A defense system consisting of cells "that, among other things, produce antibodies to deal with the threat" is, predictably, no match for an invader who advances "single-mindedly." And the science-fiction flavor, already present in cancer talk, is even more pungent in accounts of AIDS—this one comes from *Time* magazine in late 1986—with infection described like the high-tech warfare for which we are being prepared (and inured) by the fantasies of our leaders and by video entertainments. In the era of Star Wars and Space Invaders, AIDS has proved an ideally comprehensible illness:

> On the surface of that cell, it finds a receptor into which one of its envelope proteins fits perfectly, like a key into a lock. Docking with the cell, the virus penetrates the cell membrane and is stripped of its protective shell in the process . . . .

25   Next the invader takes up permanent residence, by a form of alien takeover familiar to science-fiction narratives. The body's own cells *become* the invader. With the help of an enzyme the virus carries with it,

> the naked AIDS virus converts its RNA into . . . DNA, the master molecule of life. The molecule then penetrates the cell nucleus, inserts itself into a chromosome and takes over part of the cellular machinery, directing it to produce more AIDS viruses. Eventually, overcome by its alien product, the cell swells and dies, releasing a flood of new viruses to attack other cells . . . .

As viruses attack other cells, runs the metaphor, so "a host of opportunistic diseases, normally warded off by a healthy immune system, attacks the body," whose integrity and vigor have been sapped by the sheer replication of "alien product" that follows the collapse of its immunological defenses. "Gradually weakened by the onslaught, the AIDS victim dies, sometimes in months, but almost always within a few years of the first symptoms:" Those who have not already succumbed are described as "under assault, showing the telltale symptoms of the disease," while millions of others "harbor the virus, vulnerable at any time to a final, all-out attack."

Cancer makes cells proliferate; in AIDS, cells die. Even as this original model of AIDS (the mirror image of leukemia) has been altered, descriptions of how the virus does its work continue to echo the way the illness is perceived as infiltrating the society. "AIDS Virus Found to Hide in Cells, Eluding Detection by Normal Tests" was the headline of a recent front-page story in *The New York Times* announcing the discovery that the virus can "lurk" for years in the macrophages—disrupting their disease-fighting function without killing them, "even when the macrophages are filled almost to bursting with virus," and without producing antibodies, the chemicals the body makes in response to "invading agents" and whose presence has been regarded as an infallible marker of the syndrome.* That the virus isn't lethal for *all* the cells where it takes up residence, as is now thought, only increases the illness-foe's reputation for wiliness and invincibility.

What makes the viral assault so terrifying is that contamination, and therefore vulnerability, is understood as permanent. Even if someone infected were never to develop any symptoms—that is, the infection remained, or could by medical intervention be rendered, inactive—the viral enemy would be forever within. In fact, so it is believed, it is just a matter of time before something awakens ("triggers") it, before the appearance of "the telltale symptoms." Like syphilis, known to generations of doctors as "the great masquerader," AIDS is a clinical construction, an inference. It takes its identity from the presence of *some* among a long, and lengthening, roster of symptoms (no one has everything that AIDS could be), symptoms which "mean" that what the patient has is this illness. The construction of the illness rests on the invention not only of AIDS as a clinical entity but of a kind of junior AIDS, called AIDS-related complex (ARC), to which people are assigned if they show "early" and often intermittent symptoms of immunological deficit such as fevers, weight loss, fungal infections, and swollen lymph glands. AIDS is progressive, a disease of time. Once a certain density of symptoms is attained, the course of the illness can be swift, and brings atrocious suffering. Besides the commonest "presenting" illnesses (some hitherto unusual, at least in a fatal form, such as a rare skin cancer and a rare form of pneumonia), a plethora of disabling, disfiguring, and humiliating symptoms make the AIDS patient steadily more infirm, helpless, and unable to control or take care of basic functions and needs.

30   The sense in which AIDS is a slow disease makes it more like syphilis, which is characterized in terms of "stages," than like cancer. Thinking in terms of "stages" is essential to discourse about AIDS. Syphilis in its most dreaded form is "tertiary syphilis," syphilis in its third stage. What is called AIDS is generally understood as the last of three stages—the first of which is infection with a human immunodeficiency virus (HIV) and early evidence of inroads on the immune

---

*The larger role assigned to the macrophages—"to serve as a reservoir for the AIDS virus because the virus multiplies in them but does not kill them, as it kills T–4 cells"—is said to explain the not uncommon difficulty of finding infected T–4 lymphocytes in patients who have antibodies to the virus and symptoms of AIDS. (It is still assumed that antibodies will develop once the virus spreads to these "key target" cells.) Evidence of presently infected populations of cells has been as puzzlingly limited or uneven as the evidence of infection in the populations of human societies—puzzling, because of the conviction that the disease is everywhere, and must spread. "Doctors have estimated that as few as one in a million T–4 cells are infected, which led some to ask where the virus hides . . ." Another resonant speculation, reported in the same article (*The New York Times,* June 7, 1988): "Infected macrophages can transmit the virus to other cells, possibly by touching the cells."

system—with a long latency period between infection and the on-set of the "telltale" symptoms. (Apparently not as long as syphilis, in which the latency period between secondary and tertiary illness might be decades. But it is worth noting that when syphilis first appeared in epidemic form in Europe at the end of the fifteenth century, it was a rapid disease, of an unexplained virulence that is unknown today, in which death often occurred in the second stage, sometimes within months or a few years.) Cancer *grows* slowly: it is not thought to be, for a long time, latent. (A convinc-ing account of a process in terms of "stages" seems invariably to include the notion of a normative delay or halt in the process, such as is supplied by the notion of latency.) True, a cancer is "staged." This is a principal tool of diagnosis, which means classi-fying it according to its gravity, determining how "advanced" it is. But it is mostly a spatial notion: that the cancer advances through the body, traveling or migrating along predictable routes. Cancer is first of all a disease of the body's geography, in contrast to syphilis and AIDS, whose definition depends on constructing a temporal sequence of stages.

Syphilis is an affliction that didn't have to run its ghastly full course, to paresis (as it did for Baudelaire and Maupassant and Jules de Goncourt), and could and often did remain at the stages of nui-sance, indignity (as it did for Flaubert.) The scourge was also a cliché, as Flaubert himself observed. "SYPHILIS. Everybody has it, more or less" reads one entry in the *Dictionary of Accepted Opinions*, his treasury of mid-nineteenth-century platitudes. And syphilis did manage to acquire a darkly positive association in late-nineteenth- and early-twentieth-century Europe, when a link was made between syphilis and heightened ("feverish") mental activity that parallels the connection made since the era of the Romantic writers between pulmonary tuberculosis and heightened emotional activity. As if in honor of all the notable writers and artists who ended their lives in syphilitic witlessness, it came to be believed that the brain lesions of neurosyphilis might actually inspire original thought or art. Thomas Mann, whose fiction is a storehouse of early-twentieth-century dis-ease myths, makes this notion of syphilis as muse central to his *Doctor Faustus*, with its protagonist a great composer whose volun-tarily contracted syphilis—the Devil guarantees that the infection will be limited to the central nervous system—confers on him twenty-four years of incandescent creativity. E. M. Cioran recalls how, in Romania in the late 1920s, syphilis-envy figured in his ado-lescent expectations of literary glory: he would discover that he had contracted syphilis, be rewarded with several hyperproductive years of genius, then collapse into madness. This romanticizing of the dementia characteristic of neurosyphilis was the forerunner of

the much more persistent fantasy in this century about mental illness as a source of artistic creativity or spiritual originality. But with
AIDS—though dementia is also a common, late symptom—no com-
pensatory mythology has arisen, or seems likely to arise. AIDS, like
cancer, does not allow romanticizing or sentimentalizing, perhaps
because its association with death is too powerful. In Krzysztof
Zanussi's film *Spiral* (1978), the most truthful account I know of
anger at dying, the protagonist's illness is never specified; therefore,
it *has* to be cancer. For several generations now, the generic idea of
death has been a death from cancer, and a cancer death is experienced as a generic defeat. Now the generic rebuke to life and to hope
is AIDS.

3

Because of countless metaphoric flourishes that have made cancer
synonymous with evil, having cancer has been experienced by
many as shameful, therefore something to conceal, and also unjust, a
betrayal by one's body. Why me? the cancer patient exclaims bitterly. With AIDS, the shame is linked to an imputation of guilt; and
the scandal is not at all obscure. Few wonder, Why me? Most people
outside of sub-Saharan Africa who have AIDS know (or think they
know) how they got it. It is not a mysterious affliction that seems to
strike at random. Indeed, to get AIDS is precisely to be revealed, in
the majority of cases so far, as a member of a certain "risk group," a
community of pariahs. The illness flushes out an identity that might
have remained hidden from neighbors, jobmates, family, friends. It
also confirms an identity and, among the risk group in the United
States most severely affected in the beginning, homosexual men, has
been a creator of community as well as an experience that isolates
the ill and exposes them to harassment and persecution.

Getting cancer, too, is sometimes understood as the fault of
someone who has indulged in "unsafe" behavior—the alcoholic
with cancer of the esophagus, the smoker with lung cancer: punishment for living unhealthy lives. (In contrast to those obliged to perform unsafe occupations, like the worker in a petrochemical factory
who gets bladder cancer.) More and more linkages are sought between primary organs or systems and specific practices that people
are invited to repudiate, as in recent speculation associating colon
cancer and breast cancer with diets rich in animal fats. But the unsafe habits associated with cancer, among other illnesses—even
heart disease, hitherto little culpabilized, is now largely viewed as
the price one pays of excesses of diet and "life-style"—are the result
of a weakness of the will or a lack of prudence, or of addiction to legal (albeit very dangerous) chemicals. The unsafe behavior that

produces AIDS is judged to be more than just weakness. It is indulgence, delinquency—addictions to chemicals that are illegal and to sex regarded as deviant.

The sexual transmission of this illness, considered by most people as a calamity one brings on oneself, is judged more harshly than other means—especially since AIDS is understood as a disease not only of sexual excess but of perversity. (I am thinking, of course, of the United States, where people are currently being told that heterosexual transmission is extremely rare, and unlikely—as if Africa did not exist.) An infectious disease whose principal means of transmission is sexual necessarily puts at greater risk those who are sexually more active—and is easy to view as a punishment for that activity. True of syphilis, this is even truer of AIDS, since not just promiscuity but a specific sexual "practice" regarded as unnatural is named as more endangering. Getting the disease through a sexual practice is thought to be more willful, therefore deserves more blame. Addicts who get the illness by sharing contaminated needles are seen as committing (or completing) a kind of inadvertent suicide. Promiscuous homosexual men practicing their vehement sexual customs under the illusory conviction, fostered by medical ideology with its cure-all antibiotics, of the relative innocuousness of all sexually transmitted diseases, could be viewed as dedicated hedonists—thought it's now clear that their behavior was no less suicidal. Those like hemophiliacs and blood-transfusion recipients, who cannot by any stretch of the blaming faculty be considered responsible for their illness, may be as ruthlessly ostracized by frightened people, and potentially represent a greater threat because, unlike the already stigmatized, they are not as easy to identify.

35   Infectious diseases to which sexual fault is attached always inspire fears of easy contagion and bizarre fantasies of transmission by nonvenereal means in pubic places. The removal of doorknobs and the installation of swinging doors on U.S. Navy ships and the disappearance of the metal drinking cups affixed to public water fountains in the United States in the first decades of the century were early consequences of the "discovery" of syphilis's "innocently transmitted infection"; and the warning to generations of middle-class children always to interpose paper between bare bottom and the public toilet seat is another trace of the horror stories about the germs of syphilis being passed to the innocent by the dirty that were rife once and are still widely believed. Every feared epidemic disease, but especially those associated with sexual license, generates a preoccupying distinction between the disease's putative carriers (which usually means just the poor and, in this part of the world, people with darker skins) and those defined—health professionals and other bureaucrats do the defining—as "the general population." AIDS has revived similar phobias and fears of contamination among

this disease's version of "the general population": white heterosexuals who do not inject themselves with drugs or have sexual relations with those who do. Like syphilis a disease of, or contracted from, dangerous others, AIDS is perceived as afflicting, in greater proportions than syphilis ever did, the already stigmatized. But syphilis was not identified with certain death, death that follows a protracted agony, as cancer was once imagined and AIDS is now held to be.

That AIDS is not a single illness but a syndrome, consisting of a seemingly open-ended list of contributing or "presenting" illnesses which constitute (that is, qualify the patient as having) the disease, makes it more a product of definition or construction than even a very complex, multiform illness like cancer. Indeed, the contention that AIDS is invariably fatal depends partly on what doctors decided to define as AIDS—and keep in reserve as distinct earlier stages of the disease. And this decision rests on a notion no less primitively metaphorical than that of a "full-blown" (or "full-fledged") disease.* "Full-blown" is the form in which the disease is inevitably fatal. As what is immature is destined to become mature, what buds to become full-blown (fledglings to become full-fledged)—the doctors' botanical or zoological metaphor makes the development or evolution into AIDS the norm, the rule. I am not saying that the metaphor creates the clinical conception, but I am arguing that it does much more than just ratify it. It lends support to an interpretation of the clinical evidence which is far from proved or, yet, provable. It is simply too early to conclude, of a disease identified only seven years ago, that infection will always produce something to die from, or even that everybody who has what is defined as AIDS will die of it. (As some medical writers have speculated, the appalling mortality rates could be registering the early, mostly rapid deaths of those most vulnerable to the virus—

---

*The standard definition distinguishes between people with the disease or syndrome "fulfilling the criteria for the surveillance definition of AIDS" from a larger number infected with HIV and symptomatic "who do not fulfill the empiric criteria for the full-blown disease. This constellation of signs and symptoms in the context of HIV infection has been termed the AIDS-related complex (ARC)." Then follows the obligatory percentage. "It is estimated that approximately 25 percent of patients with ARC will develop full-blown disease within 3 years." Harrison's *Principles of Internal Medicine*, 11th edition (1987), p. 1394.

The first major illness known by an acronym, the condition called AIDS does not have, as it were, natural borders. It is an illness whose identity is designed for purposes of investigation and with tabulation and surveillance by medical and other bureaucracies in view. Hence, the unselfconscious equating in the medical textbook of what is empirical with what pertains to surveillance, two notions deriving from quite different models of understanding. (AIDS is what fulfills that which is referred to as either the "criteria for the surveillance definition" or the "empiric criteria": HIV infection plus the presence of one or more diseases included on the roster drawn up by the disease's principal administrator of definition in the United States, the federal Centers for Disease Control in Atlanta.) This completely stipulative definition with its metaphor of maturing disease decisively influences how the illness is understood.

because of diminished immune competence, because of genetic pre-disposition, among other possible co-factors—not the ravages of a uniformly fatal infection.) Construing the disease as divided into distinct stages was the necessary way of implementing the metaphor of "full-blown disease." But it also slightly weakened the notion of inevitability suggested by the metaphor. Those sensibly interested in hedging their bets about how uniformly lethal infection would prove could use the standard three-tier classification—HIV infection, AIDS-related complex (ARC), and AIDS—to entertain either of two possibilities or both: the less catastrophic one, that *not* everybody infected would "advance" or "graduate" from HIV infection, and the more catastrophic one, that everybody would.

It is the more catastrophic reading of the evidence that for some time has dominated debate about the disease, which means that a change in nomenclature is under way. Influential administrators of the way the disease is understood have decided that there should be no more of the false reassurance that might be had from the use of different acronyms for different stages of the disease. (It could never have been more than minimally reassuring.) Recent proposals for redoing terminology—for instance, to phase out the category of ARC—do not challenge the construction of the disease in stages, but do place additional stress on the *continuity* of the disease process. "Full-blown disease" is viewed as more inevitable now, and that strengthens the fatalism already in place.*

From the beginning the construction of the illness had depended on notions that separated one group of people from another—the sick from the well, people with ARC from people with AIDS, them and us—while implying the imminent dissolution of these distinctions. However hedged, the predictions always sounded fatalistic. Thus, the frequent pronouncements by AIDS specialists and public health officials on the chances of those infected with the virus coming down with "full-blown" disease have seemed mostly an exercise in the management of public opinion, dosing out the harrowing news in several steps. Estimates of the percentage expected to show symptoms

---

*The 1988 Presidential Commission on the epidemic recommended "de-emphasizing" the use of the term ARC because it "tends to obscure the life-threatening aspects of this stage of illness." There is some pressure to drop the term AIDS, too. The report by the Presidential Commission pointedly used the acronym HIV for the epidemic itself, as part of a recommended shift from "monitoring disease" to "monitoring infection." Again, one of the reasons given is that the present terminology masks the true gravity of the menace. ("This longstanding concentration on the clinical manifestations of AIDS rather than on all stages of HIV infection [i.e., from initial infection to seroconversion, to an antibody-positive asymptomatic stage, to full-blown AIDS] has had the unintended effect of misleading the public as to the extent of infection in the population. . . .") It does seem likely that the disease will, eventually, be renamed. *This* change in nomenclature would justify officially the policy of including the infected but asymptomatic among the ill.

classifying them as having AIDS within five years, which may be too low—at the time of this writing, the figure is 30 to 35 percent—are invariably followed by the assertion that "most," after which comes "probably all," those infected will eventually become ill. The critical number, then, is not the percentage of people likely to develop AIDS within a relatively short time but the *maximum* interval that could elapse between infection with HIV (described as lifelong and irreversible) and appearance of the first symptoms. As the years add up in which the illness has been tracked, so does the possible number of years between infection and becoming ill, now estimated, seven years into the epidemic, at between ten and fifteen years. This figure, which will presumably continue to be revised upward, does much to maintain the definition of AIDS as an inexorable, invariably fatal disease.

The obvious consequence of believing that all those who "harbor" the virus will eventually come down with the illness is that those who test positive for it are regarded as people-with-AIDS, who just don't have it . . . yet. It is only a matter of time, like any death sentence. Less obviously, such people are often regarded as if they *do* have it. Testing positive for HIV (which usually means having been tested for the presence not of the virus but of antibodies to the virus) is increasingly equated with being ill. Infected *means* ill, from that point forward. "Infected but not ill," that invaluable notion of clinical medicine (the body "harbors" many infections), is being superseded by biomedical concepts which, whatever their scientific justification, amount to reviving the antiscientific logic of defilement, and make infected-but-healthy a contradiction in terms. Being ill in this new sense can have many practical consequences. People are losing their jobs when it is learned that they are HIV-positive (though it is not legal in the United States to fire someone for that reason) and the temptation to conceal a positive finding must be immense. The consequences of testing HIV-positive are even more punitive for those selected populations—there will be more—upon which the government has already made testing mandatory. The U.S. Department of Defense has announced that military personnel discovered to be HIV-positive are being removed "from sensitive, stressful jobs," because of evidence indicating that mere infection with the virus, in the absence of any other symptoms, produces subtle changes in mental abilities in a significant minority of virus carriers. (The evidence cited: lower scores on certain neurological tests given to some who had tested positive, which could reflect mental impairment caused by exposure to the virus, though most doctors think this extremely improbable, or could be caused—as officially acknowledged under questioning—by "the anger, depression, fear, and panic" of people who have just learned that they are HIV-positive.) And, of course, testing positive now makes one ineligible to immigrate everywhere.

40   In every previous epidemic of an infectious nature, the epidemic is equivalent to the number of tabulated cases. This epidemic is regarded as consisting *now* of that figure plus a calculation about a much larger number of people apparently in good health (seemingly healthy, but doomed) who are infected. The calculations are being made and remade all the time, and pressure is building to identify these people, and to tag them. With the most up-to-date biomedical testing, it is possible to create a new class of lifetime pariahs, the future ill. But the result of this radical expansion of the notion of illness created by the triumph of modern medical scrutiny also seems a throwback to the past, before the era of medical triumphalism, when illnesses were innumerable, mysterious, and the progression from being seriously ill to dying was something normal (not, as now, medicine's lapse or failure, destined to be corrected). AIDS, in which people are understood as ill before they are ill; which produces a seemingly innumerable array of symptom-illnesses; for which there are only palliatives; and which brings to many a social death that precedes the physical one—AIDS reinstates something like a premodern experience of illness, as described in Donne's *Devotions*, in which "every thing that disorders a faculty and the function of that is a sicknnesse," which starts when we

> are preafflicted, super-afflicted with these jealousies and suspitions, and apprehensions of Sicknes, before we can cal it a sicknes; we are not sure we are ill; one hand askes the other by the pulse, and our eye askes our own urine, how we do. . . . we are tormented with sicknes, and cannot stay till the torment come . . . .

whose agonizing outreach to every part of the body makes a real cure chimerical, since what "is but an accident, but a symptom of the main disease, is so violent, that the Phisician must attend the cure of that" rather than "the cure of the disease it self," and whose consequence is abondonment:

> As Sicknesse is the greatest misery, so the greatest misery of sicknes is solitude; when the infectiousnes of the disease deterrs them who should assist, from comming; even the Phisician dares scarse come. . . . it is an Outlawry, an Excommunication upon the patient . . . .

In premodern medicine, illness is described as it is experienced intuitively, as a relation of outside and inside: an interior sensation or something to be discerned on the body's surface, by sight (or just below, the listening, palpating),which is confirmed when the interior is opened to viewing (in surgery, in autopsy). Modern—that is, effective—medicine is characterized by far more complex notions of what is to be observed inside the body: not just the disease's results (damaged organs) but its cause (microorganisms), and by a far more intricate typology of illness.

45   In the older era of artisanal diagnoses, being examined produced an immediate verdict, immediate as the physician's willingness to speak. Now an examination means tests. And being tested introduces a time lapse that, given the unavoidably industrial character of competent medical testing, can stretch out for weeks; an agonizing delay for those who think they are awaiting a death sentence or an acquittal. Many are reluctant to be tested out of dread of the verdict, out of fear of being put on a list that could bring future discrimination or worse, and out of fatalism (what good would it do?). The usefulness of self-examination for the early detection of certain common cancers, much less likely to be fatal if treated before they are very advanced, is now widely understood. Early detection of an illness thought to be inexorable and incurable cannot seem to bring any advantage.

Like other diseases that arouse feelings of shame, AIDS is often a secret, but not from the patient. A cancer diagnosis was frequently concealed from patients by their families; an AIDS diagnosis is at least as often concealed from their families by patients. And as with other grave illnesses regarded as more than just illnesses, many people with AIDS are drawn to whole-body rather than illness-specific treatments, which are thought to be either ineffectual or too dangerous. (The disparagement of effective, scientific medicine for offering treatments that are *merely* illness-specific, and likely to be toxic, is a recurrent misconjecture of opinion that regards itself as enlightened.) This disastrous choice is still being made by some people with cancer, an illness that surgery and drugs can often cure. And a predictable mix of superstition and resignation is leading some people with AIDS to refuse antiviral chemotherapy, which, even in the absence of a cure, has proved of some effectiveness (in slowing down the syndrome's progress and is staving off some common presenting illnesses), and instead to seek to heal themselves, often under the auspices of some "alternative medicine" guru. But subjecting an emaciated body to the purification of a macrobiotic diet is about as helpful in treating AIDS as having oneself bled, the "holistic" medical treatment of choice in the era of Donne. . . .

8

Epidemics of particularly dreaded illnesses always provoke an outcry against leniency or tolerance—now identified as laxity, weakness, disorder, corruption: unhealthiness. Demands are made to subject people to "tests," to isolate the ill and those suspected of being ill or of transmitting illness, and to erect barriers against the real or imaginary contamination of foreigners. Societies already administered as garrisons, like China (with a tiny number of detected cases) and Cuba (with a significant number of the already ill), are responding more rapidly and peremptorily. AIDS is everyone's Trojan horse: six months before the 1988 Olympics the South Korean government announced that it would be distributing free condoms to all foreign participants. "This is a totally foreign disease, and the only way to stop its spread is to stop sexual contacts between Indians and foreigners," declared the director general of the Indian government's Council for Medical Research, thereby avowing the total defenselessness of a population nearing a billion for which there are presently *no* trained hospital staff members or treatment centers anywhere specializing in the disease. His proposal for a sexual ban, to be enforced by fines and prison terms, is no less impractical as a means of curbing sexually transmitted diseases than the more commonly made proposals for quarantine—that is, for detention. The incarceration in detention camps surrounded by barbed wire during World War I of some thirty thousand American women, prostitutes and women suspected of being prostitutes, for the avowed purpose of controlling syphilis among army recruits, caused no drop in the military's rate of infection—just as incarceration during World War II of tens of thousands of Americans of Japanese ancestry as potential traitors and spies probably did not foil a single act of espionage or sabotage. That does not mean that comparable proposals for AIDS will not be made, or will not find support, and not only by the predictable people. If the medical establishment has been on the whole a bulwark of sanity and rationality so far, refusing even to envisage programs of quarantine and detention, it may be in part because the dimensions of the crisis still seem limited and the evolution of the disease unclear.

Uncertainty about how much the disease will spread—how soon and to whom—remains at the center of public discourse about AIDS. Will it, as it spreads around the world, remain restricted, largely, to marginal populations: to the so-called risk groups and then to large sections of the urban poor? Or will it eventually become the classic pandemic affecting entire regions? Both views are in fact being held simultaneously. A wave of statements and articles affirming that AIDS threatens everybody is followed by another wave of articles asserting that it is a disease of "them," not "us." At the beginning of 1987, the U.S. Secretary of Health and Human Services predicted that the worldwide AIDS epidemic would eventually make the Black Death—the greatest epidemic ever recorded, which wiped out between a third and a half of the population of Europe—seem "pale by comparison." At the end of the year he said: "This is not a massive, widely spreading epidemic among heterosexuals as so many people fear." Even more striking than the cyclical character of public discourse about AIDS is the readiness of so many to envisage the most far-reaching of catastrophes.

Reassurances are multiplying in the United States and Western Europe that "the general population" is safe. But "the general population" may be as much a code phrase for whites as it is for heterosexuals. Everyone knows that a disproportionate number of blacks are getting AIDS, as there is a disproportionate number of blacks in the armed forces and a vastly disproportionate number in prisons. "The AIDS virus is an equal-opportunity destroyer" was the slogan of a recent fund-raising campaign by the American Foundation for AIDS Research. Punning on "equal-opportunity employer," the phrase subliminally reaffirms what it means to deny: that AIDS is an illness that in this part of the world afflicts minorities, racial and sexual. And about the staggering prediction made recently by the World Health Organization that, barring improbably rapid progress in the development of a vaccine, there will be ten to twenty times more AIDS cases in the next five years than there were in the last five, it is assumed that most of these millions will be Africans.

50   AIDS quickly became a global event—discussed not only in New York, Paris, Rio, Kinshasa but also in Helsinki, Buenos Aires, Bejing, and Singapore—when it was far from the leading cause of death in Africa, much less in the world. There are famous diseases, as there are famous countries, and these are not necessarily the ones with the biggest populations. AIDS did not become so famous just because it afflicts whites too, as some Africans bitterly assert. But it is certainly true that were AIDS only an African disease, however many millions were dying, few outside of Africa would be concerned with it. It would be one of those "natural" events, like famines, which periodically ravage poor, overpopulated countries and about which people in rich countries feel quite helpless. Because it is a world event—that is, because it affects the West—it is regarded as not just a natural disaster. It is filled with historical meaning. (Part of the self-definition of Europe and the neo-European countries is that it, the First World, is where major calamities are history-making, transformative, while in poor, African or Asian countries they are part of a cycle, and therefore something like an aspect of nature.) Nor has AIDS become so publicized because, as some have suggested, in rich countries the illness first afflicted a group of people who were all men, almost all white, many of them educated, articulate, and knowledgeable about how to lobby and organize for public attention and resources devoted to the disease. AIDS occupies such a large part in our awareness because of what it has been taken to represent. It seems the very model of all the categories privileged populations feel await them.

What biologists and public health officials predict is something far worse than can be imagined or than society (and the economy) can tolerate. No responsible official holds out the slightest hope that the African economies and health services can cope with the spread of the disease predicted for the near future, while every day one can read the direst estimates of the cost of AIDS to the country that has reported the largest number of cases, the United States. Astonishingly large sums of money are cited as the cost of providing minimum care to people who will be ill in the next few years. (This is assuming that the reassurances to "the general population" are justified, an assumption much disputed within the medical community.) Talk in the United States, and not only in the United States, is of a national emergency, "possibly our nation's survival." An editorialist at *The New York Times* intoned last year: "We all know the truth, every one of us. We live in a time of plague such as has never been visited on our nation. We can pretend it does not exist, or exists for those others, and carry on as if we do not know. . . ." And one French poster shows a giant UFO-like black mass hovering over and darkening with spidery rays most of the familiar hexagon shape of the country lying below. Above the image is written: "It depends on each of us to erase that shadow" (*IL depend de chacun de nous d'effacer cette ombre.*) And underneath: "France doesn't want to die of AIDS" (*La France ne veut pas mourir du sida*). Such token appeals for mass mobilization to confront an unprecedented menace appear, at frequent intervals, in every mass society. It is also typical of a modern society that the demand for mobilization be kept very general and the reality of the response fall well short of what seems to be demanded to meet the challenge of the nation-endangering menace. This sort of rhetoric has a life of its own: it serves some purpose if it simply keeps in circulation an ideal of unifying communal practice that is precisely contradicted by the pursuit of accumulation and isolating entertainments enjoined on the citizens of a modern mass society.

The survival of the nation, of civilized society, of the world itself is said to be at stake—claims that are a familiar part of building a case for repression. (An emergency requires "drastic measures," et cetera.) The end-of-the-world rhetoric that AIDS has evoked does inevitably build such a case. But it also does something else. It offers a stoic, finally numbing contemplation of catastrophe. The eminent Harvard historian of science Stephen Jay Gould has declared that the AIDS pandemic may rank with nuclear weaponry "as the greatest danger of our era." But even if it kills as much as a quarter of the human race—a prospect Gould considers possible—"there will still be plenty of us left and we can start again." Scornful of the jeremiads of the moralists, a rational and humane scientist proposes the minimum consolation: an apocalypse that doesn't have any meaning. AIDS is a "natural phenomenon," not an event "with a moral meaning," Gould points out; "there is no message in its spread." Of course, it is monstrous to attribute meaning, in the sense of moral judgment, to the spread of an infectious disease. But perhaps it is only a little less monstrous to be invited to contemplate death on this horrendous scale with equanimity.

Much of the well-intentioned public discourse in our time expresses a desire to be candid about one or another of the various dangers which might be leading to all-out catastrophe. And now there is one more. To the death of oceans and lakes and forests, the unchecked growth of populations in the poor parts of the world, nuclear accidents like Chernobyl, the puncturing and depletion of the ozone layer, the perennial threat of nuclear confrontation between the superpowers or nuclear attack by one of the rogue states not under superpower control—to all these, now add AIDS. In the countdown to a millennium, a rise in apocalyptic thinking may be inevitable. Still, the amplitude of the fantasies of doom that AIDS has inspired can't be explained by the calendar alone, or even by the very real danger the illness represents. There is also the need for an apocalyptic scenario that is specific to "Western" society, and perhaps even more so to the United States. (America, as someone has said, is a nation with the soul of a church—an evangelical church prone to announcing radical endings and brand-new beginnings.) The taste for worst-case scenarios reflects the need to master fear of what is felt to be uncontrollable. It also expresses an imaginative complicity with disaster. The sense of cultural distress or failure gives rise to the desire for a clean sweep, a tabula rasa. No one wants a plague, of course. But, yes, it would be a chance to begin again. And beginning again—that is very modern, very American, too.

AIDS may be extending the propensity for becoming inured to vistas of global annihilation which the stocking and brandishing of nuclear arms has already promoted. With the inflation of apocalyptic rhetoric has come the increasing unreality of the apocalypse. A permanent modern scenario: apocalypse looms . . . and it doesn't occur. And it still looms. We seem to be in the throes of one of the modern kinds of apocalypse. There is the one that's not happening, whose outcome remains in suspense: the missiles circling the earth above our heads, with a nuclear payload that could destroy all life many times over, that haven't (so far) gone off. And there are ones that are happening, and yet seem not to have (so far) the most feared consequences—like the astronomical Third World debt, like overpopulation, like ecological blight; or that happen and then (we are told) didn't happen—like the October 1987 stock market collapse, which was a "crash," like the one in October 1929, and was not. Apocalypse is now a long-running serial: not "Apocalypse Now" but "Apocalypse From Now On." Apocalypse has become an event that is happening and not happening. It may be that some of the most feared events, like those involving the irreparable ruin of the environment, have already happened. But we don't know it yet, because the standards have changed. Or because we do not have the right indices for measuring the catastrophe. Or simply because this is a catastrophe in slow motion. (Or *feels* as if it is in slow motion, because we know about it, can anticipate it; and now have to wait for it to happen, to catch up with what we think we know.)

55   Modern life accustoms us to live with the intermittent awareness of monstrous, unthinkable—but, we are told, quite probable—disasters. Every major event is haunted, and not only by its representation as an image (an old doubling of reality now, which began in 1839, with the invention of the camera). Besides the photographic or electronic simulation of events, there is also the calculation of their eventual outcome. Reality has bifurcated, into the real thing and an alternative version of it, twice over. There is the event and its image. And there is the event and its projection. But as real events often seem to have no more reality for people than images, and to need the confirmation of their images, so our reaction to events in the present seeks confirmation in a mental outline, with appropriate computations, of the event in its projected, ultimate form.

Future-mindedness is as much the distinctive mental habit, and intellectual corruption, of this century as the history-mindedness that, as Nietzsche pointed out, transformed thinking in the nineteenth century. Being able to estimate how matters will evolve into the future to is an inevitable byproduct of a more sophisticated (quantifiable, testable) understanding of process, social as well as scientific. The ability to project events with some accuracy into the future enlarged what power consisted of, because it was a vast new source of instructions about how to deal with the present. But in fact the look into the future, which was once tied to a vision of linear progress, has, with more knowledge at our disposal than anyone could have dreamed, turned into a vision of disaster. Every process is a prospect, and invites a prediction bolstered by statistics. Say: the number now . . . in three years, in five years, in ten years; and, of course, at the end of the century. Anything in history or nature that can be described as changing steadily can be seen as heading toward catastrophe. (Either the too little and becoming less: waning, decline, entropy. Or the too much, ever more than we can handle or absorb: uncontrollable growth.) Most of what experts pronounce about the future contributes to this new double sense of reality—beyond the doubleness to which we are already accustomed by the comprehensive duplication of everything in images. There is what is happening now. And there is what it portends: the imminent, but not yet actual, and not really graspable, disaster.

Two kinds of disaster, actually. And a gap between them, in which the imagination flounders. The difference between the epidemic we have and the pandemic that we are promised (by current statistical extrapolations) feels like the difference between the wars we have, so-called limited wars, and the unimaginable more terrible ones we could have, the latter (with all the appurtenances of science fiction) being the sort of activity people are addicted to staging for fun, as electronic games. For beyond the real epidemic with its inexorably mounting death toll (statistics are issued by national and international health organizations every week, every month) is a qualitatively different, much greater disaster which we think both will and will not take place. Nothing is changed when the most appalling estimates are revised downward, temporarily, which is an occasional feature of the display of speculative statistics disseminated by health bureaucrats and journalists. Like the demographic predictions, which are probably just as accurate, the big news is usually bad.

A proliferation of reports or projections of unreal (that is, ungraspable) doomsday eventualities tend to produce a variety of reality-dragging responses. Thus, in most discussions of nuclear warfare, being rational (the self-description of experts) means not acknowledging the human reality, while taking in emotionally even a small part of what is at stake for human beings (the province of those who regard themselves as the menaced) means insisting on unrealistic demands for the rapid dismantling of the peril. This split of public attitude, into the inhuman and the all-too-human, is much less stark with AIDS. Experts denounce the stereotypes attached to people with AIDS and to the continent where it is presumed to have originated, emphasizing that the disease belongs to much wider populations than the groups initially at risk, and to the whole world, not just to Africa.* For while AIDS has turned out, not surprisingly, to be one of the most meaning-laden of diseases, along with leprosy and syphilis, clearly there are checks on the impulse to stigmatize people with the disease. The way in which the illness is such a perfect repository for people's most general fears about the future of some extent renders irrelevant the predictable efforts to pin the disease on a deviant group or a dark continent.

---

*"AIDS cannot be stopped in any country unless it is stopped in all countries," declared the retiring head of the World Health Organization in Geneva, Dr. Halfdan Mahler, at the Fourth International Conference on AIDS (Stockholm, June 1988), where the global character of the AIDS crisis was a leading theme. "This epidemic is worldwide and is sparing no continent," said Dr. Willy Rozenbaum, a French AIDS specialist. "It cannot be mastered in the West unless it is overcome everywhere." In contrast to the rhetoric of global responsibility, a specialty of the international conferences, is the view, increasingly heard, in which AIDS is regarded as a kind of Darwinian test of a society's aptitude for survival, which may require writing off those countries that can't defend themselves. A German AIDS specialist, Dr. Eike Brigitte Helm, has declared that it "can already be seen that in a number of parts of the world AIDS will drastically change the population structure. Particularly in Africa and Latin America. A society that is not able, somehow or other, to prevent the spread of AIDS has very poor prospects for the future."

Like the effects of industrial pollution and the new system of global financial markets, the AIDS crisis is evidence of a world in which nothing important is regional, local, limited; in which everything than can circulate does, and every problem is, or is destined to become, worldwide. Goods circulate (including images and sounds and documents, which circulate fastest of all, electronically). Garbage circulates: the poisonous industrial wastes of St. Etienne, Hannover, Mestre, and Bristol are being dumped in the coastal towns of West Africa. People circulate, in greater numbers than ever. And diseases. From the untrammeled intercontinental air travel for pleasure and business of the privileged to the unprecedented migrations of the underprivileged from villages to cities and, legally and illegally, from country to country—all this physical mobility and interconnectedness (with its consequent dissolving of old taboos, social and sexual) is as vital to the maximum functioning of the advanced, or world, capitalist economy as is the easy transmissibility of goods and images and financial instruments. But now that heightened, modern interconnectedness in space, which is not only personal but social, structural, is the bearer of a health menace sometimes described as a threat to the species itself; and the fear of AIDS is of a piece with attention to other unfolding diasters that are the byproduct of advanced society, particularly those illustrating the degradation of the environment on a world scale. AIDS is one of the dystopian harbingers of the global village, that future which is already here and always before us, which no one knows how to refuse.

60   That even an apocalypse can be made to seem part of the ordinary horizon of expectation constitutes an unparalleled violence that is being done to our sense of reality, to our humanity. But it is highly desirable for a specific dreaded illness to come to seem ordinary. Even the disease most fraught with meaning can become just an illness. It has happened with leprosy, though some ten million people in the world, easy to ignore since almost all live in Africa and the Indian subcontinent, have what is now called, as part of its wholesome de-dramatization, Hansen's disease (after the Norwegian physician who, over a century ago, discovered the bacillus). It is bound to happen with AIDS, when the illness is much better understood and, above all, treatable. For the time being, much in the way of individual experience and social policy depends on the struggle for rhetorical ownership of the illness: how it is possessed, assimilated in argument and in cliché. The age-old, seemingly inexorable process whereby disease acquire meanings (by coming to stand for the deepest fears) and inflict stigma is always worth challenging, and it does seem to have more limited credibility in the modern world, among people willing to be modern—the process is under surveillance now. With this illness, one

that elicits so much guilt and shame, the effort to detach it from these meanings, these metaphors, seems particularly liberating, even consoling. But the metaphors cannot be distanced just by abstaining from them. They have to be exposed, criticized, belabored, used up.

Not all metaphors applied to illnesses and their treatment are equally unsavory and distorting. The one I am most eager to see retired—more than ever since the emergence of AIDS—is the military metaphor. Its converse, the medical model of the public weal, is probably more dangerous and far-reaching in its consequences, since it now only provides a persuasive justification for authoritarian rule but implicitly suggests the necessity of state-sponsored repression and violence (the equivalent of surgical removal or chemical control of the offending or "unhealthy" parts of the body politic). But the effect of the military imagery on thinking about sickness and health is far from inconsequential. It overmobilizes, it overdescribes, and it powerfully contributes to the excommunicating and stigmatizing of the ill.

No, it is not desirable for medicine, any more than for war, to be "total." Neither is the crisis created by AIDS a "total" anything. We are not being invaded. The body is not a battlefield. The ill are neither unavoidable casualties nor the enemy. We—medicine, society—are not authorized to fight back by any means whatever. . . . About that metaphor, the military one, I would say, if I may paraphrase Lucretius: Give it back to the war-makers.

Reflective Reading, Informal Writing

REFLECTING ON THE READING:

- On page 511, Sontag writes: "Of course, one cannot think without metaphors. But that does not mean there aren't some metaphors we might well abstain from or retire. As, of course, all thinking is interpretation. But that does not mean it isn't sometimes correct to be 'against' interpretation." What does Sontag mean when she says we can't think without metaphors? Do you agree? How can one be "against" interpretation?
- Sontag claims that military metaphors now permeate all descriptions of the medical situation. Why would military metaphors be so prevalent? Do you see any problem with the military metaphor as the governing metaphor? What are Sontag's issues with military metaphors?
- Sontag argues that the military metaphor ultimately leads to the demonization of victims, to the suggestion of guilt. What does she

mean by this? Do you agree or disagree? Why? What does it matter, say, in the case of AIDS?

- What does Sontag mean when she writes and quotes Stephen J. Gould: "AIDS is a 'natural phenomenon,' not an event 'with a moral meaning'" (530)?
- Sontag implies that AIDS may not be the all-around killer that we have come to believe it is. What are her reasons for implying this?

UNDERSTANDING RHETORICAL STRATEGIES:

- Sontag writes: "Modern medical thinking could be said to begin when the gross military metaphor becomes specific. . . . It was when the invader was seen not as the illness but as the microorganism that causes the illness that medicine really began to be effective, and the military metaphors took on new credibility and precision" (513). What does Sontag use for evidence to support this claim? Does she give you enough evidence? Why or why not?
- Sontag reveals that she became interested in the metaphors around illness when she was diagnosed with cancer (514). Why do you think she interjects this personal story? Does it jibe with her ethical appeal? Or does it take away from the credibility of her analysis? Why or why not?
- On page 514, Sontag speaks of being "enraged." How does her rage work rhetorically within this piece? Does it differ from bell hooks' and Jane Tompkins' use of rage as a rhetorical strategy? Does using rage as a rhetorical strategy make the rage any less real or important to Sontag?
- Why does Sontag spend so much time on disease in general and cancer in particular? Why doesn't she just start and stick with AIDS?

INFORMAL WRITING:

- Make a list of the metaphors Sontag says describe AIDS. Can you add any to that list?
- Write about your understanding of how metaphors and AIDS relate to one another.

AIDS Projects: End-of-Section

Sequence One: Community-Based Learning Project

"The Nature of a New Threat"
"Dying Has Turned Out To Be Complicated"
My Brother
AIDS and Its Metaphors

SMALL GROUP DISCUSSION:

1. In small groups, or as an entire class, generate a list of everything you know about AIDS/HIV. What do you notice about this list? Do particular categories arise? What do you notice about the language of your list? What do you think you need to know more about?

2. Publications on AIDS/HIV are numerous. The following is a very limited list of books that other students have found interesting or helpful:

    a. Bergman, Susan. *Anonymity: The Secret Life of an American Family.*

    b. Brodkey, Harold. *This Wild Darkness: The Story of My Death.*

    c. Burns, Janice A. *Sarah's Song.*

    d. Duesberg, Peter. *Inventing the AIDS Virus.*

    e. Joseph, Stephen, C., M.D. *Dragon Within the Gates: The Once Future AIDS Epidemic.*

    f. Mackenzie, Nancy F., ed. *The AIDS Reader: Social, Political, Ethical Issues.*

    g. McCarroll, Tolbert. *Morning Glory Babies: A Community Effort to Care for Children With AIDS.*

    h. Monette, Paul. *Becoming a Man: Half a Life Story.*

    i. Rudd, Andrea and Darien Taylor, eds. *Positive Women.*

    j. San Francisco AIDS Foundation. *Ending the AIDS Epidemic: Community Strategies.*

    k. The Act UP/New York Women and AIDS Book Group. *Women, AIDS, and Activism.*

    l. Verghese, Abraham. *My Own Country: A Doctor's Story.*

    m. White, Ryan. *Ryan White: My Own Story.*

    n. Winik, Marion. *First Comes Love.*

    o. Zuger, Abigail. *Strong Shadows: Scenes from an Inner-City AIDS Clinic.*

    Determine, in collaboration with your teacher and community partner, what other readings on AIDS/HIV you should read to be prepared for your community-based learning project. With the guidance of your teacher, choose as many of these readings as you can. In small groups or as individuals, select a reading and present an oral summary of the reading back to the class.

3.   In small groups, or as an entire class, create a "code of conduct" for your interactions with your community partner(s).

Writing:

As explained in the introduction to Chapter 4, your community-based project will have several writing components to it. Please note that some or all of these projects will probably overlap.

Project #1: Triple-Entry Incident Journal

Begin your triple-entry incident journal and your private journal (optional) for the project. Your private journal will remain private unless you choose to share it or excerpts from it. We recommend that you keep the private journal as a way of creating a safe writing space for yourself since community-based learning, especially in an area as volatile and painful as AIDS work, can be difficult. You may have feelings or concerns that you are not yet ready to voice in a public forum.

The triple-entry incident journal (see page 350 of the Introduction to this chapter), on the other hand, is both personal and public. Your entries in the triple-entry incident journal will follow this pattern:

Entry 1: This entry takes place prior to meeting or contacting your community partner. Write one to three pages about your interests, concerns, and fears regarding your project.

Entry 2: Immediately prior to meeting with your community partner, write one to three pages about your expectations for your encounter with your community partner. What do you expect to happen and why? What do you think his or her expectations of you will be? How do you imagine this meeting starting and taking place? Construct an imaginary scenario if you like.

Entry 3: Write one to three pages immediately following your meeting with your community partner. What surprised you and why? Did anything go as you imagined it would? Were any of your preconceived ideas or stereotypes about this community partner changed in any way? If so, how? Did any of your fears or concerns materialize? Were your expectations met?

The process of writing the triple-entry incident journal should be repeated periodically throughout the term as you meet with your partner or attend to the work you have been asked to undertake.

Project #2: The Writing Project for Your Partner

It is impossible for us to tell you what this writing project might be. It will arise out of your community partner's needs in negotiation with you and your instructor. It may also be that your community partner does not need you to work on a writing project but instead has other needs you will be meeting. If this is the case, your instructor may want to assign another writing project for you to work on.

Project #3: Social Analysis and Commentary

In what ways does culture shape AIDS/HIV and our responses to it? Write a critical, analytical essay encompassing both your personal and academic experiences with the project, locating both within a larger cultural context. Think about the effect of cultural forces on your personal response to AIDS/HIV. On your community partner's response to the disease. Does culture shape, support, or limit the work of your community partner? Finally, based on this analysis, can you imagine strategies or ways of understanding AIDS that might transform our society at large, and/or those living and dying with AIDS, your community partner, or you?

Project #4: Assessment of the Project

Create a plan to assess the project, your participation, your partner's participation, and any desired outcomes from the project. Create this plan with the guidance of your instructor and your community partner. The assessment will include at least the following: a brief summary of the project, what actions were taken, explanation and analysis of what worked and didn't work, suggestions for changes, and finally a conclusion drawing the assessment together. Your instructor and/or community partner may want to modify your assessment and write-up in appropriate ways for your specific project.

Project #5: Reflective and Reflexive Narrative

Write a narrative essay examining your personal experiences with your community project. That is, your essay should explore your experience within the frame of your "self," your thoughts, and your reflections as you participated in this project. Equally important is for you to tell the story of any reflexive moments you and/or your community partner(s) confronted along the way.

Project #6: Critical/Reflective Introduction to the Term's Work

Compile all five of the previous writing projects into a collection. Write a critical, reflective introduction to your work. This introduction should explain the context for your work, the learning that took place for you as you did this work, where and how you engaged in reflection and reflexivity, and discuss anything transformative for you or your community partner. Comment on anything else that will help a reader interpret your work and experiences as they appear in this collection of writings.

Sequence Two: AIDS As Historical and Social Construct

"The Nature of a New Threat"

My Brother

AIDS and Its Metaphors

SMALL GROUP DISCUSSION:

1. Discuss the ways in which all three of these authors suggest that AIDS is, at least in some ways, socially and historically constructed. Kincaid's piece might be more difficult to pin down for this analysis,

but we believe that if you look you will find such suggestions at least implied.

2. Make a list of as many metaphors as you can that you have heard or seen describing AIDS. Do different kinds of metaphors come from the medical field than from lay persons? Are there any other kinds of differences or similarities that you notice?

WRITING:

1. Go to your school or local library and search popular magazines for at least two articles on AIDS/HIV. Examine, alongside Epstein, Kincaid, and Sontag, the language used to talk about and describe AIDS. Write an essay in which you examine the language, metaphors, etc. you find. Do these metaphors matter? How do they construct AIDS in certain ways?

2. Write an essay in which you apply the arguments that Sontag and Epstein make to Jamaica Kincaid's personal account of her brother's death. In other words, how do the historical and linguistic construction of AIDS reveal themselves in Kincaid's narrative?

Sequence Three: AIDS and Bodies

"The Nature of a New Threat"
"Dying Has Turned Out To Be Complicated"
My Brother
AIDS and Its Metaphors

SMALL GROUP DISCUSSION:

1. Discuss, through the ways in which all these writers discuss AIDS, what you take to be the difference between personal bodies and the body politic. How do personal bodies and the body politic intersect?

2. Each of these writers suggest, some more overtly than others, how either individuals or groups of people might take control of their own bodies in the face of AIDS. What are those ways of taking control?

WRITING:

1. Write an essay in which you examine how private a person's body is or is not once that person has been diagnosed with AIDS. You might consider what role laws, the medical world, families, and friends play in the public and private roles of persons living with and dying of AIDS. O'Brien, Kincaid, and Sontag should prove to be very useful for your analysis.

2. Write an essay in which you express your understanding of how AIDS plays itself out in the body politic at large (not just on individuals). Refer back to your discussions in your group work for this sequence. What is the body politic? How does or can AIDS affect an entire culture? Please be specific, and incorporate the readings into your essay.

Sequence Four: The Changing Face of AIDS/HIV

"The Nature of a New Threat"

"Dying Has Turned Out To Be Complicated"

My Brother

AIDS and Its Metaphors

SMALL GROUP DISCUSSION:

1. Individually, go to the library and find a recent (published within the last two years) essay or book on AIDS/HIV that seems interesting and/or important to you. Read your essay or as much of your book as you can, and write a summary of it. Then, bring a summary of your reading to your group. Share your summaries and what you found important and interesting in your reading.

2. With your group members, list out the essays collected here in *Writing As Reflective Action* and those that each of you contributed, noting the date of publication for each of them. Paying specific attention to the publication dates of each, discuss what differences you see in the readings that might be related to the time in which it was written, to the genre in which it was written, and to whether or not it was written for an academic audience, a medical audience, or a lay audience.

WRITING:

1. Choose one of the readings from *Writing As Reflective Action* and one of the more current readings discussed in your group. Write an essay in which you analyze the differences in the ways in which the two articles approach the subject matter. Your analysis could focus on differences in genre, differences in purpose and audience, differences of race, class, or gender, differences of historical circumstances, any other differences you might notice, or some combination of these differences. You might also want to note similarities if and when appropriate.

2. Choose several articles or readings on AIDS/HIV that span at least 10 years. Write an essay in which you examine what changes these readings reflect in our understanding of AIDS, medical breakthroughs, or any other changes you find important.

SAMPLE PROJECT C:
OTHER COMMUNITY-BASED PROJECTS

We suggest that one reasonable approach to Chapter 4 might be to identify and pursue a community-based project of your own design, one not covered in this book. This would allow you to select a project better suited to the needs and opportunities presented by your own local context, and perhaps better suited to the interests of your class.

We hope you have already noticed how many different types of projects fall under the general headings of oral histories and AIDS projects, the sample projects outlined here. Each of these examples includes readings selected to stimulate reflective, reflexive, and analytical thought and writing. The sample experiences we provide might ultimately lead to community service writing such as gathering and writing the stories of elderly persons or assembling the history of one's own family or university. The possibilities for oral history projects are endless. Other writing projects might include writing grants for AIDS support services, collecting and writing the stories of workers and clients in AIDS hospices, working with AIDS victims to complete reading and writing needs they might have, and so on. Perhaps the types of projects we represent here may suggest still others more suited to your local setting. (Note the list of projects undertaken by Portland State University students in their classes on AIDS/HIV—page 433.)

It should be clear, however, that the number of possible projects is almost infinite. Among the possibilities:

- Tutoring
- The school, especially elementary or middle schools; serving as teachers' aides, etc.
- Music education; collecting, repairing, redistributing second-hand instruments
- Prisons, jails
- Agencies providing food for the needy and/or elderly, such as Meals on Wheels, Loaves and Fishes, the Food Bank, etc.
- Hospices
- Assisted living facilities, other homes for the aged
- Adult literacy projects
- Environmental projects or agencies: air pollution studies, watershed restoration, recycling projects, environmental stewardship
- City, state, or local government agencies
- Small businesses
- Labor unions

This list is intended to be suggestive rather than exhaustive. Almost certainly, the unique needs and possibilities of your college/university or community will suggest other opportunities for community-based work. If you have trouble identifying a suitable project, consider consulting the business, education and/or social work departments in your college or university. Or talk to representatives of the clergy, the local school district, or small businesses in the area.

Once you have identified a community partner you will need to negotiate your role. What is it your community partner wants or needs? How will you be able to fulfill these needs within the constraints of your schedule? We recommend that you review our discussion of the tensions inherent in such negotiations (in the Introduction to Chapter 4).

Quite aside from the kinds of writing you may be doing for your community partner, we strongly recommend that you maintain a triple-entry incident journal (see Introduction to Chapter 4). Such a journal will provide a place for reflective and reflexive writing about your experiences.

Your instructor will doubtless specify the kinds of writing he or she will expect of you in conjunction with this project. So we will settle for pointing out that the assignment sequences at the ends of Sections A and B may serve as models for the writing sequences accompanying any such project. This is particularly true of the first sequence of each section. These sequences suggest a similar process, from small group discussion of what is already known about the project, to generating a bibliography of relevant readings, to establishing a code of conduct for your interactions with community partners. Writing projects include a triple-entry incident journal, the writing you do for your partner, social analysis and commentary, assessment of the project, reflective and reflexive narrative, and finally a critical/reflective introduction to the term's work.

Whatever project you find yourself involved in, we urge you to become consciously reflexive within your experiences, being open to transformation and to taking action.

Meta Sequences

Sequence One: The Identity Landscape

"On Being a Self Forever"
"Excerpts from My Life"
"Sexual Identity and Bisexual Identities"

SMALL GROUP DISCUSSION:

1. All three essays suggest and illustrate ways in which a definition of self comes into being. In small groups, discuss how Updike and Iserhoff form a definition of self. Examine the kinds of experiences that lead them to these definitions. Find and be prepared to share specific, relevant passages with the entire class. Do you see conflicts or differences in their definitions of self? What accounts for these differences (or similarities)?

2. Individually, write out a definition of "sexual landscape" as discussed by Rust. Share your definitions, negotiating until you reach some agreement about the best definition for what she means. Once you have a working definition of Rust's term, broaden the idea of landscape to *identity* landscape. What kinds of events, places, obstacles, and objects would you find in an identity landscape? Be specific and explain as best you can how what you choose would function in this identity landscape.

WRITING:

1. Describe some of the encounters or relationships with others you have had in your life. How have they affected who you are? How has your "self" been influenced by these encounters?

2. Review Rust's essay, this time attempting to isolate the process by which, according to Rust, individuals identify themselves with a particular sexual identity, and locate themselves among the various identities they see as potentially available to them. How different is this process from the process by which individuals identify or locate themselves with respect to political beliefs, religion, social class, even academic disciplines? Write an essay in which you examine the process of sexual identification in relation to, in contrast to, or in likeness to these other processes of identification.

3. Imagine that the process Rust describes could be used to describe the process by which individuals come to label themselves politically, academically, or in terms of religion or social class. Using Rust's description

of this process, write about yourself coming to awareness, "coming out," as a Republican, an anthropology major, a Unitarian, or the like. Does Rust's conceptual strategy help you in this project of self-definition? Why or why not? (Alternatively, apply this same strategy to Updike or Iserhoff rather than to yourself.)

Sequence Two: Entitlement

"Entitlement"

"Ruth's Song (Because She Could Not Sing It)"

"The Brass Ring and the Deep Blue Sea"

My Brother

INFORMAL WRITING:

1. Define for yourself what Coles means by "entitlement."

2. Write about any connections you see among these essays.

SMALL GROUP DISCUSSION:

1. In groups, "read" Ruth's situation in life ("Ruth's Song") and/or Patricia Williams' ("The Brass Ring and the Deep Blue Sea") and/or Kincaid's brother's (from *My Brother*) as you think Coles might. In other words, using Coles as a lens, interpret Ruth's and Williams' stories. As you talk this through together, help each other begin to solidify a thesis or focused "reading" for an essay on this topic.

WRITING:

1. Write an essay in which you describe and explain Coles' theories of entitlement while applying his theories to the "life situation" of Ruth, Patricia Williams (and those she writes about), or Kincaid's brother. What does this extended application of Coles' theories reveal about the life situations to which you have applied them? About Coles' theories?

2. Where does one's sense of entitlement come from? What are its sources? Drawing upon all four of these essays, write an essay that attempts to identify the different kinds of sources leading to the development of a sense of entitlement. To which of these sources would you attribute your own sense of entitlement?

3. The lives of Ruth, Patricia Williams, and Kincaid's brother might be seen as a challenge to Coles' conception of entitlement. Drawing upon all three of these essays, talk back to Coles, explaining what he has missed, misrepresented, oversimplified, or otherwise misunderstood.

Sequence Three: What Have Race, Class, and Gender Got To Do With It?

"Tlilli, Tlapalli/The Path of the Red and Black Ink"

"Paintball as Combat Sport"

"Excerpts from My Life"

"Boys Will Be Men: Boys' Superhero Comics"

"The Hurt, Betrayed Son"

"Ruth's Song (Because She Could Not Sing It)"

"Working the Land"

"An American of Color"

SMALL GROUP DISCUSSION:

1. Each of these writers seems to be making a comment about how culture shapes a sense of racial identity, manhood, womanhood, or class identity. Choose four of these essays, doing your best to arrive at a balance of the readings by men and women and that may represent differing class or cultural understandings. Have a recorder write up a brief rationale for your choice of essays. Then, talking carefully about each essay, pinpoint what you think each writer is saying about culture, race, class, and/or gender. Be prepared to report back to the rest of your class what your determinations are for all four essays.

2. While we could argue that all these writers are examining and exploring the ways culture impacts our understandings and definitions of selfhood, some are written from a more "objective," distanced stance, and others from a more intentionally "personal" stance. Make two lists, one headed "objective" and the other, "personal." Decide which of each of these eight essays belongs under which heading. Then, find at least two passages from each text that support (or challenge) your placement of that essay under the "personal" or "objective" heading. Finally, discuss whether one (the objective or personal stance) is more effective than another. Why or why not?

WRITING:

1. Write an essay in which you tell a personal story that illustrates something about your self and identity as it relates to race, class, and/or gender. Reexamine Anzaldua, Iserhoff, Steinem, Terkel, and Villanueva, thinking of them as potential models for your own essay. As you work on your essay, consider how these writers use the personal to amplify a point about race, class, and/or gender.

2. Considering three of the four essays, write an analytic essay in which you consider the importance of the writer's gender, race, and or class to their subject matter, the ways in which they make arguments, the conclusions they draw, the ways in which they choose to tell the stories and so on. You will, of course, need to pay close attention to what

each writer explicitly says about this connection, but you will also need to add your own interpretation by looking critically at what the authors don't say, as well. In other words, what, as an engaged and critical reader, do you see or interpret as the relationship between the writers and their gender, race, or class?

3. Middleton argues that superhero comics have something to do with the way men are socialized. Robinson argues that the original Rambo story is positive and healing for men. Gibson argues that paintball isn't just a harmless game but part of a larger warrior culture. All three, Rambo, paintball, and comic book superheroes shaped men in one sense, according to these writers. Write an essay in which you examine what Iserhoff, Steinem, and Anzaldua say shape women. Beyond the subject matter, are these essays different from the male writers' essays? If so, how so? Be as specific as you can and use passages from the various texts to support your interpretations.

Sequence Four: Private Experience As Public Argument

"Killing Rage"
"Ruth's Song (Because She Could Not Sing It)"
"The Brass Ring and the Deep Blue Sea"
"On Being a Self Forever"
My Brother
"Violet De Cristoforo—Tule Lake"
"Private First Class Reginald 'Malik' Edwards, Phoenix, Louisiana"

SMALL GROUP DISCUSSION:

1. Each of these essays tells a very personal story and yet they all make public arguments as well. Together, summarize what you believe to be the argument put forth in each (or those that you have read). Be sure to take notes on your summaries and write down specific passages from the texts that support your summaries.

2. Discuss with your group members how each of the writers uses his or her experiences to make a public point or argument. What specifically are they doing to turn their experiences from "just a story" or private diary entry into a story for public consumption?

3. Find a passage from "Killing Rage," "Ruth's Song," "On Being a Self Forever," and from *My Brother* (or any other combination of the readings) that appears to you and your group members to be an example of reflexivity. Discuss what part you think these passages play in turning the private stories into public argument. In other words, is there something about reflexivity that makes personal and private experience important to more than just the person who has had the experience? If so, why would this be so? Be prepared to share with your classmates your passages and your analysis both of how they are reflexive and of how they might work as private experiences in the public realm.

4. "Private First Class Reginald 'Malik' Edwards, Phoenix, Louisiana" and "Violet De Cristoforo—Tule Lake" are somewhat different from the other pieces in that the experiences of Private Edwards and Ms. Cristoforo are filtered through the oral historians who interviewed them and edited their stories. Discuss whether you think it is the oral historians or the subjects themselves who are making public arguments. What is your reasoning for this? What clues do you find in the texts themselves? Choose at least two passages from each text that support your reasoning.

WRITING:

1. Choose two to four readings from the list provided. Write an analysis of the argument being made in each essay. In other words, what is the argument? How and what evidence is the writer using? How does this argument work? And so on. Include clear discussions about the part that private experience is playing within the arguments.

2. Write an essay about an important private experience of your own. Be sure to make use of both reflection and reflexivity. Beyond that, make sure that your essay is more than just a story. In other words, make sure that you are fashioning a public argument from your own experiences. For help and ideas, return to your notes and ideas generated in your groups regarding how these writers have made arguments based on their private experiences.

3. Do a fairly extensive interview with someone you know about an important or life-changing experience they have had. Taking Wallace Terry's example of Private Edwards and John Tateishi's example of Violet De Cristoforo as your models, shape the information your interviewee gives you into a story with an interesting public point or argument.

Sequence Five: The Rhetorical Appeals: Ethos (Ethical), Logos (Logical), Pathos (Emotional)

"The Domestication of Motherhood"

"Sexual Identities and Bisexual Identities"

"Killing Rage"

"Tlilli, Tlapalli/The Path of the Red and Black Ink"

"Dying Has Turned Out To Be Complicated"

"Entitlement"

"The Nature of a New Threat"

Note: The ancient rhetor, Aristotle, suggests that arguments rely on three "appeals" to the audience: that of ethos or ethical appeal, that of logos or logical appeal, and that of pathos or emotional appeal. Someone's ethical appeal, or ethos, might be said to be their believability or credibility. Ethos applies to how they present themselves to and construct themselves for an audience. Logos applies to whether the argument or story being told is logical, or at least to how it comes across as making sense. How something in writing appears logically may have to do with organization, use of evidence, believability, and so on. Pathos, or emotional appeal, is fairly easy to understand. It has to do with how the speaker or writer is able to "move" the listener or reader through emotions.

SMALL GROUP DISCUSSION

1. Each of these essays and O'Brien's journal make arguments that could be seen by some readers as controversial. If a topic is controversial, the use of the three rhetorical appeals discussed become very crucial no matter what genre we might place the writing in (e.g. academic, personal, journal or diary, etc.). Together, examine the ways in which each of these writers creates his or her own ethical appeal. For instance, in the Rich essay, "The Domestication of Motherhood," what role does the extensive literature survey she provides play in the construction of her ethos?

2. Similarly, examine and discuss each reading for how it works or appeals logically to an audience. You might pay special attention to how the essays differ from one another—especially the ways in which Anzaldua's "Tlilli, Tlapalli/The Path of the Red and Black Ink" and O'Brien's "Death Has Turned Out to Be Complicated" differ from others.

3. Examine and discuss how each essay illustrates emotional appeals. Consider why some writers seem to rely more heavily than other writers on pathos. Also, consider whether some writers don't use enough pathos, or conversely, too much pathos.

4. Finally, discuss how you see these rhetorical appeals connected in the readings. That is, do you see any ways in which someone's ethos is supported by emotional appeals? Or do you see how ethos and logos might be connected? Or logos and pathos? In the end, if you had to claim that one of the rhetorical appeals were more important than the others which would it be? Why?

WRITING:

1. Choose two or three of the readings that you find most controversial. Write an essay in which you examine and analyze them for the ways in which ethos, logos, and pathos are at work. Feel free to make assessments about how well the authors employ these appeals as well as how well (or not so well) these appeals work to convince a reader to understand, if not agree, with the position the author has taken.

2. Write your own essay on something you consider a controversial topic. Make sure your opinion on this topic is clear, but make sure it is not merely a rant by consciously employing all three appeals (ethos, logos, and pathos) and by crafting a thoughtful position or argument. You will also need to pay special attention to what you use as evidence. After completing your essay, write a brief analysis of your use of these appeals. Explain how you established your ethos, what, how, and why you chose what you chose for emotional appeals, and what you have done to establish logos.

Sequence Six: Constructing Bodies in Print and Film

"The Hurt, Betrayed Son"

"Paintball as Combat"

"Private First Class Reginald 'Malik' Edwards, Phoenix, Louisiana"

"The Domestication of Motherhood"

My Brother

"Ruth's Song (Because She Could Not Sing It)"

"Killing Rage"

"Entitlement"

"Excerpts from My Life"

SMALL GROUP DISCUSSION

1. With your group members, brainstorm a list of causes for violence in our culture. Then discuss the ways in which Robinson, Terry, and Gibson seem either to construct, or to suggest that culture constructs, violence in men. If you think they are suggesting other things about war and men (perhaps something about the psychology of men, or a healing catharsis that takes place for men in such games as paintball, etc.), discuss those things too. How does your initial list compare to the list you constructed from the readings? What do you think is important about what you discovered in your examination and discussion?

2. As a group, brainstorm a list of everything that comes to mind when you think of motherhood. Then, examine and talk about the ways in which motherhood and mothers are discussed or depicted in "Ruth's Song," "The Domestication of Motherhood," and the selection from *My Brother*. What do you notice? Are there differences among the essays? Between the essays and your list? Similarities? What do these depictions or discussions of mother or motherhood matter?

3. Think again about the essays "Killing Rage," "Entitlement," and "Excerpts from My Life." Two of these writers are minorities writing about their lives as outside the majority (White) culture. One is a White man writing, in part, about what race and class have to do with feelings of entitlement. What tensions arise among different ethnicities in these writings? Why might those tensions be there? How does our culture create them? Or, do we create them as individuals?

4. As a group decide on one of three sets of readings to reread and make the focus of your next essay: a) "The Hurt, Betrayed Son," "Private First Class Reginald 'Malik' Edwards, Phoenix, Louisiana," and "Paintball as Combat"; b) "The Domestication of Motherhood," the selection from *My Brother*, and "Ruth's Song"; or c) "Killing Rage," "Entitlement," and "Excerpts from My Life." If you chose selections from a), rent, and watch as a group, the movies *First Blood* and *Full Metal Jacket*. If you chose selections from b), rent, and watch as a group, *The Good Mother* and *Rosemary's Baby*. If you chose the selections from c), rent, and watch as a group, *Dances With Wolves, Do*

the Right Thing, and *Hair Spray.* After watching these movies and rereading the essays, discuss how each deals with men and war, motherhood and mothers, or race and class. Do you notice differences among the readings and films in your section that might be accounted for by historical circumstances? By social or economic conditions? Do you notice anything about the way each of the readings or films in your section tells a story or narrative? Are there certain codes, expectations, or ways of constructing men, motherhood, or race and class? Do these differ among the print and visual texts?

WRITING:

1. As a group, write a collaborative paper in which you take up and analyze the questions you discussed in your group work under question 4. Include any other points you would like to include.

2. Based on the readings and films you have studied from the previous list, write an essay in which you analyze the differences between how the print texts and the films construct or work with the narratives surrounding men, women, war, motherhood, race, or class.

3. Write an essay in which you analyze the narrative structures of both the films and texts in the section you chose. What do those narrative structures tell us about the subject matter and about how we view the subject matter (men, women, war, race, class, or motherhood) in our culture?

Sequence Seven: Methodology

"Varieties of Oral History Projects: Community Studies"
"Ruth's Song (Because She Could Not Sing It)" and from My Brother
"Boys Will Be Men: Boys' Superhero Comics" and "Paintball as Combat"
"The Domestication of Motherhood" and from AIDS and Its Metaphors
"Me and My Shadow" and "The Brass Ring and the Deep Blue Sea"
"Entitlement" and "From the Native's Point of View"

SMALL GROUP DISCUSSION:

1. Prior to meeting in your group, reread Valerie Raleigh Yow's "Varieties of Oral History Projects." Note how she talks about and defines methodology. In your small group, share your notes on how Yow defines methodology. What does she think is important and why? Can you draw any conclusions about methodology in general based on Yow's discussion?

2. Examine any one of the articles listed with an eye toward identifying and describing the author's methodology. Note that this is not the same as the author's organization. It would include, for example, assumptions about what kinds of questions matter, about what counts as evidence that would answer those questions, and even about appropriate strategies for analyzing that evidence. In short, it includes assumptions about what is "true" and how the truth might best be established.

(What we are calling "methodology" here might also be called "epistemology.") Collaborate to make a list of things that will help you explain to your classmates the methodology used by your author.

Then, think about why the author of the selection you have chosen elected to use this particular methodology rather than another. What are its advantages? Disadvantages? Again, make a list of these advantages and disadvantages to present to the larger group. How is the methodology related to the questions the author is asking here? To the audience for which the piece is intended? To the author's academic discipline (where relevant)?

3. Compare your answers to group exercises 1 and 2 with those of other small groups in your class. Account for your differences.

INFORMAL WRITING:

Write about what you have learned about the concept of "methodology" from this comparison.

WRITING:

1. Working with any one of the articles listed, perhaps even the one you worked with in group exercise 1, write an essay identifying and describing the author's methodology. Remember that this is not the same as the author's organization. What kinds of questions are being asked? What kind of evidence counts as an answer? How does the author go about analyzing that evidence? Speculate on why the author might have chosen this methodology rather than some other. How does the methodology relate to the questions being asked? To the audience? To the author's academic discipline?

2. Write an essay in which you identify and describe the methodology of one of the articles listed, comparing it to the methodology of the article with which it is paired (e.g. Steinem with Kincaid, Middleton with Gibson, and so on). In what respects is the methodology of the paired articles similar? Why? Account for their differences.

3. Write an essay in which you compare the methodology of articles in one pair with those in another pair.

Sequence Eight: Reflexivity

"On Being a Self Forever"

"Entitlement"

"Ruth's Song (Because She Could Not Sing It)"

"An American of Color"

"Me and My Shadow"

"The Brass Ring and the Deep Blue Sea"

"From the Native's Point of View"

"Violet De Cristoforo"

My Brother

SMALL GROUP DISCUSSION:

1. Individually, write out a definition of reflexivity. In your group, draw on all of your definitions to create the single best definition you can. As part of this definition explain how reflexivity differs from "reflection." Then make two lists in which you identify the two or three least reflexive and the two or three most reflexive articles from those listed here. Be prepared to explain your selections.

2. In those articles you identified as "most reflexive," do you see any patterns? Do these articles have anything in common?

3. Discuss whether or not you think there might be different kinds or versions of reflexivity. Try to identify and describe at least two or more versions of reflexivity from your readings of these four essays. Be prepared to explain your findings to your classmates.

WRITING:

1. Write an essay in which you argue for or against different kinds or versions of reflexivity in these essays. Do different versions even exist? If not, why not? If so, what different purposes might these different versions serve? Let your discussions from your group work support your writing of this essay. Also, make sure that readers have a clear understanding of how you are interpreting the term "reflexivity."

2. Is reflexivity desirable? Drawing from any three or four of the essays listed, write an essay in which you argue that reflexivity is (or is not) desirable. What is its function? Be sure to support your claims with examples from the essays you have chosen.

3. Would you assume that personal writing is generally more reflexive than academic writing, or vice versa? Why? Write an essay in which you argue that more "personal" essays are more or less reflexive than more "academic" essays. Consider: Does an academic essay have to have some personal connection to or for the writer before there can be either reflection or reflexivity? Would you consider any of these essays sustained moments of reflexivity?

Credits

Anzaldua, Gloria. "Tlilli Tlapalli/The Path of the Red and Black Ink" from *Borderland/La Frontier: The New Mestiza*. Copyright © 1987. Reprinted by permission of Aunt Lute Books.

Coles, Robert. "Community Service Work" from *Liberal Education*. Reprinted by permission of Robert Coles.

Coles, Robert. "Entitlement" from *Children of Crisis: A Study of Courage and Fear*. Reprinted by permission of Robert Coles.

Epstein, Steven. "The New Nature of a Threat" from *Impure Science: AIDS, Activism, and the Politics of Knowledge*. Reprinted by permission of The University of California Press.

Geertz, Clifford. "'From the Native's Point of View': On the Nature of Anthropological Understanding" from *Local Knowledge: Further Essays in Interpretive Anthropology*. Reprinted by permission of the American Academy of Arts and Sciences.

Gibson, James William. "Paintball as Combat Sport" from *Warrior: Violence and Manhood in Post-Vietnam America*. Copyright © 1994 by James William Gibson. Reprinted by permission of Hill and Wang, a division of Farrar, Straus and Giroux, LLC.

hooks, bell. From *Killing Rage: Ending Racism*. Copyright © 1995 by Gloria Watkins. Reprinted by permission of Henry Holt and Company, LLC.

Iserhoff, Annie Neeposh. "Excerpts from My Life" from *Our Agendas: Autobiographical Essays*. ed. Ann Beer and Margaret Gillett. Reprinted by permission McGill-Queen's University Press.

Kincaid, Jamaica. Excerpt from *My Brother*. Reprinted by permission of Farrar, Straus, and Giroux LLC.

Middleton, Peter. "Boys Will Be Men: Boys' Superhero Comics" from *Inward Gaze: Masculinity and Subjectivity in Modern Subject*. Reprinted by permission of Taylor & Francis Books, Ltd.

O'Brien, Michael. "Death Has Turned Out To Be Complicated" from *The Oregonian* November 30, 1997. Copyright © 1997, Oregonian Publishing Co. All rights reserved. Reprinted with permission.

Rich, Adrienne. "The Domestication of Motherhood" from *Of Woman Born: Motherhood as Experience and Institution*. Copyright © 1986, 1976 by W.W. Norton & Company, Inc. Used by permission of W.W. Norton & Company, Inc.

Robinson, Douglas. "The Hurt, Betrayed Son" from *No Less a Man*. Reprinted by permission of Bowling Green University Popular Press.

Rust, Paula C. "Sexual Identity and Bisexual Identities: The Struggle for Self-Description in a Changing Sexual Landscape" from *A Lesbian, Gay, Bisexual & Transgender Anthology*. ed. Eliason, Mickey, and Brett Reemyn. Reprinted by permission New York University Press.

Sontag, Susan. Excerpt from *Illness as Metaphor and AIDS and its Metaphors*. Reprinted by permission of Farrar, Straus, Giroux LLC.

Steinem, Gloria. Adapted from "Ruth's Song" from *Outrageous Acts and Everyday Rebellions*. Copyright © 1983 by Gloria Steinem, 1984 by East Toledo Productions, Inc. Reprinted by permission of Henry Holt and Company, LLC.

Tateshi, John. "Violet De Cristoforo – Tule Lake" from *And Justice for All: An Oral History of the Japanese American Detention Camps*. Reprinted by permission of Tateshi/Shinoda Associates.

Terkel, Studs. "Working the Land" from *Working: People Talk About What They Do All Day and How They Feel About What They Do*. Reprinted by permission of Donadio and Ashworth Literary Inc.

Terry, Wallace. "Private First Class Reginald 'Malik' Edwards, Phoenix, Louisiana" From *Bloods: An Oral History of the Vietnam War by Black Veterans*. Copyright © 1984 by Wallace Terry. Reprinted by permission of Random House Inc.

Tompkins, Jane. "Me and My Shadow." *New Literary History* 19:1 (1987), 169–178. © The University of Virginia. Reprinted by permission of the Johns Hopkins University Press.

Updike, John. From *Self-Consciousness*. Copyright © 1989 by John Updike. Reprinted by permission of Alfred A. Knopf, a division of Random House Inc.

Villanueva, Victor. "An American of Color" from *Bootstraps: From an American Academic of Color*. Reprinted by permission of the National Council of Teachers of English.

Williams, Patricia. "The Brass Ring and the Deep Blue Sea" from *Alchemy of Race and Rights*. Reprinted by permission of Harvard University Press.

Yow, Valerie Raleigh. "Varieties of Oral History Projects: Community Studies" from *Recording Oral History: A Practical Guide for Social Scientists*. Reprinted by permission of Sage Publications, Inc.

Index